Exceptional Students in Regular Classrooms

Challenges, Services, and Methods

Ted Gloeckler
The University of Akron

Carol Simpson
Learning Disabilities Teacher

MAYFIELD PUBLISHING COMPANY
MOUNTAIN VIEW, CALIFORNIA

To our students

Copyright © 1988 by Mayfield Publishing Company

All rights reserved. No portion of this book may be reproduced in any form or by any means without written permission of the publisher.

Library of Congress Cataloging-in-Publication Data

Gloeckler, Ted.
    Exceptional students in regular classrooms: challenges, services, methods / by Ted Gloeckler, Carol Simpson.
       p.   cm.
    Bibliography: p.
    Includes index.
    ISBN 0-87484-793-1
    1. Handicapped children—Education—United States.
    2. Mainstreaming in education—United States. 3. Special education—United States. I. Simpson, Carol. II. Title.
LC4031.G55   1988
371.9′046′0973—dc19   87-26863
                                                                                                                  CIP

International Standard Book Number: 0-87484-793-1
Manufactured in the United States of America
10 9 8 7 6 5 4 3 2 1

Mayfield Publishing Company
1240 Villa St.
Mountain View, California 94041

Sponsoring editor, Franklin C. Graham; production services coordinator, Cathy Willkie; production editor, Richard Mason; manuscript editor, Betty Duncan-Todd; cover and text designer, Hal Lockwood; illustrator, Elizabeth Morales. The text was set in 10/12 Sabon by Carlisle Graphics and printed on 50 lb. Roosevelt Matte by R. R. Donnelley & Sons.

Photo Credits: The Image Works and Alan Carey (chapter 1); Stock, Boston, and Lionel J-M Delevingne (chapter 2); The Image Works and Mark Antman (chapter 3); Stock, Boston, and George Bellerose (chapter 4); Stock, Boston, and Christopher Morrow (chapter 5); Stock, Boston, and Peter Vandermark (chapter 6); The Image Works and Alan Carey (chapter 7); The Image Works and Harriet Gans (chapter 8); Tim Davis (chapter 9); Stock, Boston, and Michael Grecco (chapter 10); Stock, Boston, and Jim Harrison (chapter 11); Stock, Boston, and Elizabeth Crews (chapter 12); Stock, Boston, and Elizabeth Crews (chapter 13); Stock, Boston, and Elizabeth Crews (chapter 14); Stock, Boston, and Elizabeth Hamlin (chapter 15); Stock, Boston, and Jean-Claude Lejeune (chapter 16); Stock, Boston, and Hazel Hankin (chapter 17).

Contents

PART I	THE STUDENTS	
1	**Perspectives and Challenges**	1

Who Are the Students? 1
What Do Teachers Need to Know? 2
What Do Teachers Need to Know About the Law? 5
Challenges in Teaching 8
Summary 10
References 11
Suggested Readings 12

2	**Characteristics of Exceptional Students**	15

Defining Exceptionality 15
Categories of Exceptional Individuals 16
From Categories to Individuals 24
Behavior Characteristics 26
Characteristics Unique to Disability Areas 34
Characteristics as a Basis for Planning 35
Summary 39
References 40
Suggested Readings 41

PART II	PLANNING AND COORDINATING FOR EXCEPTIONAL STUDENTS	
3	**Planning and Coordinating Educational Services**	43

Determining the Need for Services 43
The Individual Educational Plan 50
Placement in a Regular and a Special Setting 53
Coordinating Services 57
Returning Students to the Regular Class 62
Maintaining Professional Competence 65
Summary 65
References 66
Suggested Readings 67

4 Resource Services and Personnel — 69

Resource Services   69
Indirect Services   70
Direct Services   74
Other Resource Personnel   75
Educator Expectations of Each Other: Professionalism   81
Community Resources   82
Team Approach   84
Summary   84
References   85
Suggested Readings   85

5 Understanding and Working With Parents — 89

The Parents' Role in Developing Services for Exceptional Students   89
The Child With a Handicap in the Family   90
Parents of Exceptional Students in School   92
Degrees of Home-School Cooperation   96
Parent-Teacher Conferences   104
Additional Services to Parents   106
Referral Outside the School   109
Summary   110
References   111
Suggested Readings   113

PART III THE FOUNDATIONS FOR LEARNING

6 Learning Environments — 115

The Physical Environment   115
The Social Environment   118
The Psychological Environment   123
Summary   125
References   126
Suggested Readings   128

7 Managing Behavior — 131

Goals, Definitions, and Some Postulates   132
Factors Influencing Methods Selection   133
Causes of Behavior Problems   135
Strategies for Management   136
Management Programs   143
Transfer of Behavior From One Setting to Another   146
Behavior Management and the Home   147
Support Services   148
Summary   149
References   149
Suggested Readings   150

8   Learning How to Learn   153

Learning, Motivation, and Readiness   153
Becoming Better Learners   157
Teaching Activities Affecting Learning   158
Classroom Behaviors   159
Support Skills   160
Learning Skills   166
Summary   173
References   174
Suggested Readings   175

PART IV   CURRICULUM AND METHODS FOR TEACHING EXCEPTIONAL STUDENTS

9   Organizing Curriculum and Methods   177

Aspects of Instruction   177
Curriculum   178
Methods   184
Summary   205
References   206
Suggested Readings   207

10   Methods for Teaching Oral Language   209

Language Processing   209
Language Development   212
Language Differences and Language Disorders   214
Language Development and Exceptional Students   214
Planning for Instruction   217
Role of Teachers in Facilitating Language Development   218
Language Programs   221
Oral Language Problems in Adolescence   221
Summary   222
References   223
Suggested Readings   225

11   Methods for Teaching Reading   227

An Organization of Language and Reading Skills   227
Specific Techniques   231
Oral and Silent Reading   243
Reading to Students   244
Free Reading   244
Assessment   244
Reading Approaches   251
Reading and the Exceptional Learner   254
Reading Approaches and Handicapped Learners   256
Exceptional Learners and Selected Reading Skills   258

High-Interest/Easy-Reading Materials   261
Summary   263
References   264
Suggested Readings   266

12 Methods for Teaching Written Language: Spelling, Handwriting, and Written Expression   269

Spelling   269
Summary   280
Handwriting   280
Summary   287
Written Expression   287
Summary   292
References   292
Suggested Readings   294

13 Methods for Teaching Mathematics and Science   297

Arithmetic and Mathematics   297
Levels of Mathematics   297
Language and Mathematics   298
Readiness   299
Motivation   299
Assessment   301
Methods   304
Specific Instructional Techniques   304
Mathematics and Exceptional Learners   319
Scope and Sequence Charts, Programs, and Materials   321
Summary   323
Science   323
Science and Exceptional Learners   326
Summary   329
References   330
Suggested Readings   331

14 Methods for Teaching Art, Music, and Physical Education   335

Scheduling and Preparation   335
General Considerations   336
Art   337
Summary   341
Music   341
Summary   345
Physical Education   345
Summary   351
References   352
Suggested Readings   353

15 Methods for Teaching Affective Concepts 355

Rationale 355
Classroom Objectives for Affective Education 356
Relationship to Behavior 356
Teachers and Affective Education 357
Discussion and Activities in the Seven Areas of Affective Education 358
Summary 370
References 371
Suggested Readings 371

PART V   TRANSITIONS FOR EXCEPTIONAL INDIVIDUALS

16 Educating Exceptional Adolescents 373

Causes of Increase in Secondary Enrollment 373
Secondary Education and PL 94–142 374
Goals of Secondary Education 374
Characteristics 376
Educational Planning 379
Support Services 386
Summary 386
References 387
Suggested Readings 388

17 Career and Vocational Education and Transition to Adulthood 391

Definitions 391
Career Education 392
Vocational Education 397
The Transition to Adulthood 406
A Continuing Challenge 410
Summary 410
References 411
Suggested Readings 413

Appendix A Publishers and Producers of Special Education Learning Materials 415
Appendix B Selected Organizations and Agencies 421
Glossary 423
Index 429

Preface

Teachers today are challenged to find ways of responding to the needs of the increasing numbers of exceptional students who participate in their classes. After being identified as exceptional, many of these students remain in regular classes on a full-time basis. Some exceptional students have returned from special education classes, while others continue to attend special classes on a part-time basis. Many students receive additional services, such as tutoring or speech therapy.

The concept of this book evolved from our recognition of the needs of classroom teachers in meeting these challenges. Our experience, both at the university level and in public schools, demonstrates that teachers can profit from assistance in developing the requisite competence for instructing students with special needs. This competence includes becoming knowledgeable about their characteristics and functioning, developing the confidence to work effectively with them, learning new teaching techniques, and becoming aware of the supportive services available. Teachers can be provided with specific information and guidance to enable them to accomplish these objectives.

This text is designed for college students and professionals in the field, that is regular elementary and secondary teachers, and special education teachers; administrators; school psychologists; and resource personnel. These professionals interact in meeting the challenges of all students, including those who are exceptional. The book is unique in that it provides procedures for facilitating these interdisciplinary relationships. It addresses directly the continuing challenges of coordinating services and communication among the several professionals who may be working concurrently with the students.

Both teachers and the majority of college students in regular and special education classes are familiar with the concept of mainstreaming, and teachers are familiar with the history, theory, and etiology of handicapping conditions. Therefore, rather than presenting theory and etiology, we focus on practical aspects—namely, the *what* and the *how* of working with exceptional students.

We take a cross-categorical view of exceptionality, asserting that the behavior and functioning of students that teachers need to address occur across disability categories. Our book aids classroom teachers in understanding *these* characteristics rather than expecting them to teach students on the basis of a disability label. We further suggest that there is a continuum of functioning and abilities among all students and that a continuum of programs and services be developed to meet their needs. We also address the needs of individual learners, namely those students who have not been labeled as exceptional but who have unique learning styles and who experience difficulties in the classroom. These students can profit from the individual attention, planning, and careful group instruction that characterize the teaching techniques used with exceptional students.

Our expectation is that this book will be a practical text and a resource guide, and that it will ultimately profit both professionals and regular and exceptional students.

Acknowledgments

We would like to express appreciation to the many individuals who have assisted in the preparation of this book. We especially thank Dr. Gil Guerin, San José State University, and Dr. Michael Ross, University of Akron, both of whom made significant contributions to the text. We thank the manuscript reviewers for their helpful comments and constructive suggestions: Al Marshall and Patricia Phipps, California State University, Chico; Paul Retish, University of Iowa; and Jeri Traub, San José State University. We are grateful to Patricia Edwards for her computer assistance, Jo Brooks and Jeanne Post for typing, and Kimberly Madigan, Shelley Nemec, Ed Roshong, and Mary Sanders for their aid in proofreading references and appendices. We appreciate the support of our colleagues, and the encouragement and helpful suggestions of Sandra Delafield, Connie Miley, and Ann Louise Robbins. The staff at Mayfield Publishing Company provided invaluable guidance and assistance.

We are especially grateful to our children—Laura, Emily, and Andy Gloeckler, and Peggy McGinley, Mike, and Joe Simpson—for their patience and support during the lengthy preparation of this work.

Ted Gloeckler
Carol Simpson

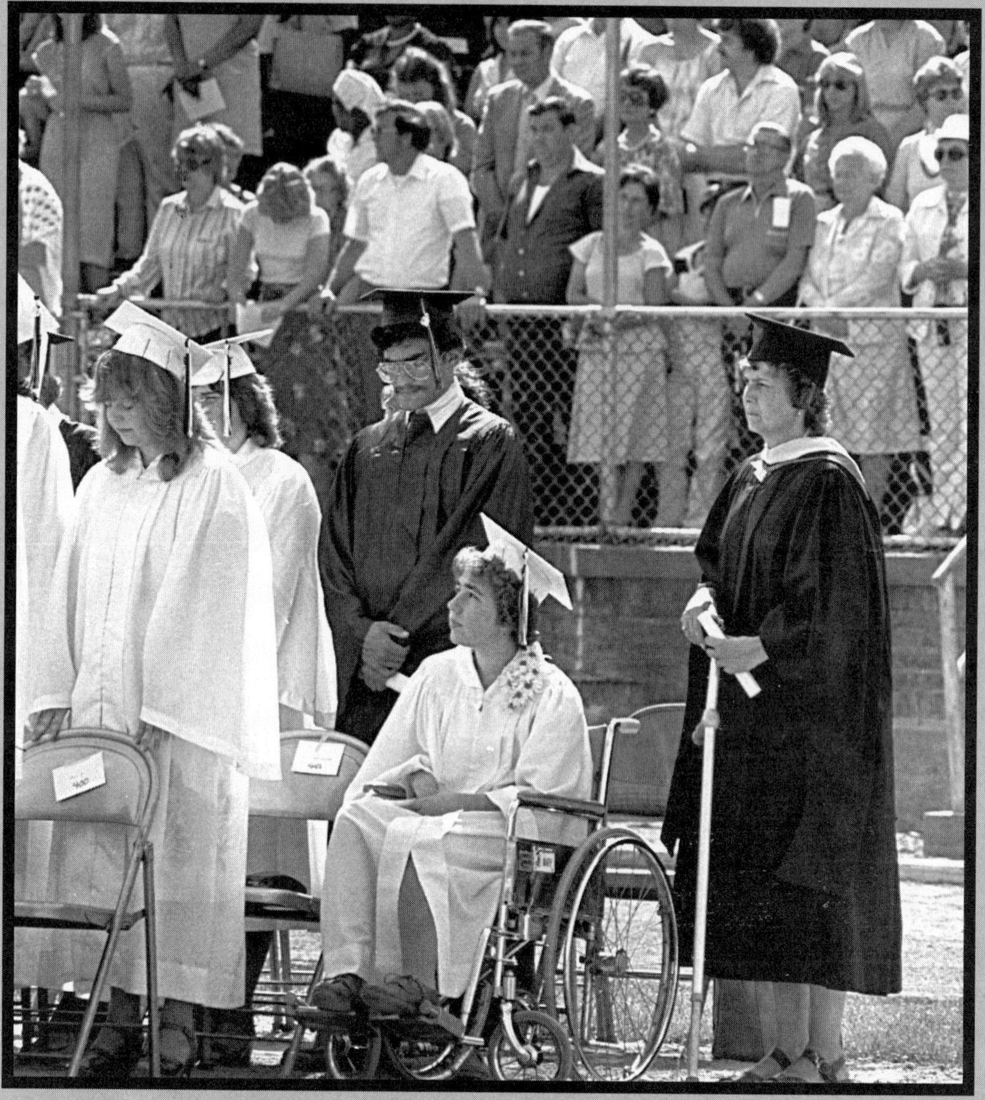

1

Perspectives and Challenges

Teachers entering the classroom each year discover that although students are alike in many ways each is unique. The individual differences of *all* students affect their learning. Most differences fall within a range that teachers, using ordinary techniques, can accommodate. Many students learn successfully. Others learn moderately well, while some survive in the classroom with difficulty. Still others have pronounced intraindividual differences that severely compromise their ability to learn. Increased understanding of these differences becomes the basis for improved, sensitive teaching and effective management procedures and facilitates student academic, social, and personal development.

Who Are the Students?

It has been common practice within schools to recognize students as belonging to one of two major groups—normal or exceptional. That determination is usually made on the basis of general school behavior, quality of academic achievement, and the presence or absence of conditions that are identified with exceptionality. However, educators are now realizing that dividing students into two classifications is neither realistic nor productive.

Individual abilities and characteristics of students exist on a continuum. The range may include gifted students, high achievers, individual learners, low achievers, and those with some degree of impairment ranging from mild to moderate to severe (Figure 1.1).

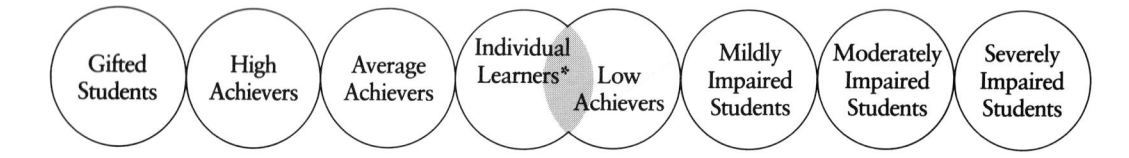

FIGURE 1.1

Continuum of students

*Individual learners are students with unique learning characteristics that interfere with their achievement.

[Gifted Students — High Achievers — Average Achievers — Individual Learners* — Low Achievers — Mildly Impaired Students — Moderately Impaired Students — Severely Impaired Students]

Students identified as exceptional do not possess traits different from those of other humans as was once believed. All persons share the same basic qualities and have the potential for intellectual, physical, social, and personal/psychological development. These attributes are found in all students from the well-adjusted, intellectually superior to the most seriously impaired, intellectually limited (Figure 1.2). Exceptional students and individual learners demonstrate differences in the quantity of each of these traits (Bogdan & Taylor, 1976). Ultimately, each student functions as a whole person, possessing a unique personality with individual abilities, and exhibits various behaviors in specific classroom situations.

The premise of this book is that teaching and management are more effective when planned and implemented on the basis of the characteristics of individual students rather than on the basis of the groups to which they are assigned.

What Do Teachers Need to Know?

How do teachers begin to address this classroom filled with students of diverse capabilities and skill levels? Surveys indicate that teachers' concerns include, among many others, behavior management, curriculum and methods, materials, resource services available to teachers and students, the roles of teachers, support personnel and parents, and understanding and implementing the legal mandates that now influence educational practices (Boyle & Sleeter, 1981; Rude, 1978; Voeltz, Bailey, Nakamura & Axama, 1979). A few concerns are considered.

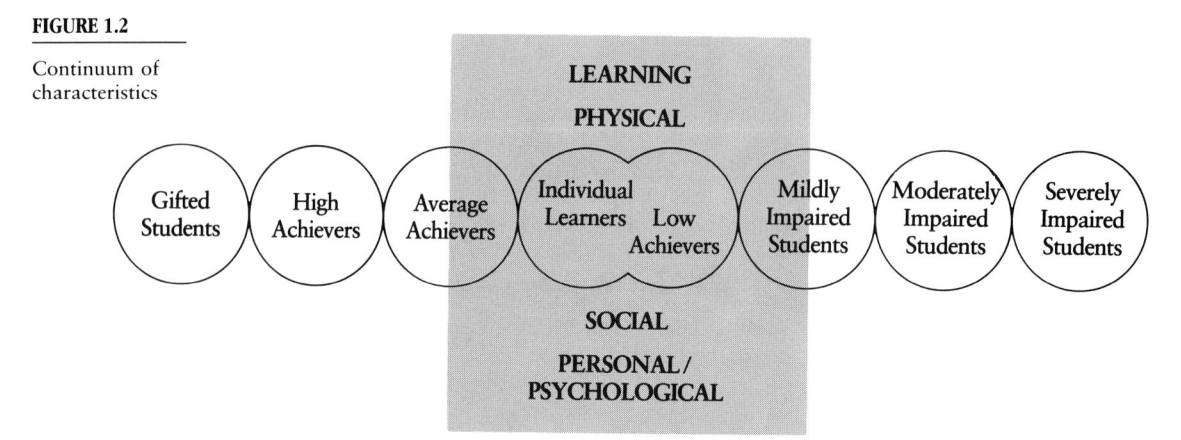

FIGURE 1.2

Continuum of characteristics

LEARNING
PHYSICAL

[Gifted Students — High Achievers — Average Achievers — Individual Learners — Low Achievers — Mildly Impaired Students — Moderately Impaired Students — Severely Impaired Students]

SOCIAL

PERSONAL/
PSYCHOLOGICAL

Behavior Management

An essential aspect of successful teaching and learning is effective behavior management of all students—those who respond as expected and those who demonstrate disruptive or unacceptable behavior. Teachers develop expertise through knowledge of behavioral principles, specific methods, and management programs; knowledge and understanding of students; consistency; fairness; and especially love and respect for students. These skills and attributes become refined with experience.

Regular teachers who work with exceptional students who have behavior problems rely not only on their knowledge and experience but also on the expertise of special education personnel and school psychologists. The role of these professionals is to provide support and assistance in sharing ideas and techniques in specific situations, in solving daily problems, and in providing encouragement. (Behavior management is discussed in more detail in Chapter 7.)

Curriculum and Methods

A firm foundation in curriculum and methods at the grade level or in the content area to be taught is the starting point for individual teachers. Directors of special education, consultants, and support teachers serve as resource persons, assisting regular teachers to determine what accommodations and adaptations are needed for exceptional students and individual learners. Curriculum may be adapted by omitting or adding content or by altering the sequence of presentation. The methods used to teach exceptional students are adaptations of those used with nonhandicapped members of the class. The use of specific techniques is determined by the subject content and student characteristics, which includes level of intellectual functioning, achievement, and learning style. Provision of special materials and equipment may be required. (Curriculum and methods are addressed more fully in Chapter 9.)

Resource Services

Services to teachers include consultation, administrative support, and in service training. Also, services are available in most schools for regular class students who need additional support. Resource services include Chapter I programs, remedial reading and mathematics, and peer and volunteer tutoring. Other services for students identified as exceptional are professional tutoring, speech and language therapy, physical and/or occupational therapy, vision or hearing training, and counseling (Figure 1.3).

Students with moderate or severe impairments may need to attend classes in a separate setting before being integrated in a public school. For example, students with considerable physical involvement are assisted in an orthopedic unit separate from the regular class until they are able to function adequately in a regular school environment. Students with severe hearing or visual impairment may need special training in a separate setting so that they will be able to participate in regular class.

Many students identified as exceptional require services that cannot be provided in regular classes. They need to be placed in a separate setting, either part-time or

FIGURE 1.3

Continuum of resource services within the school

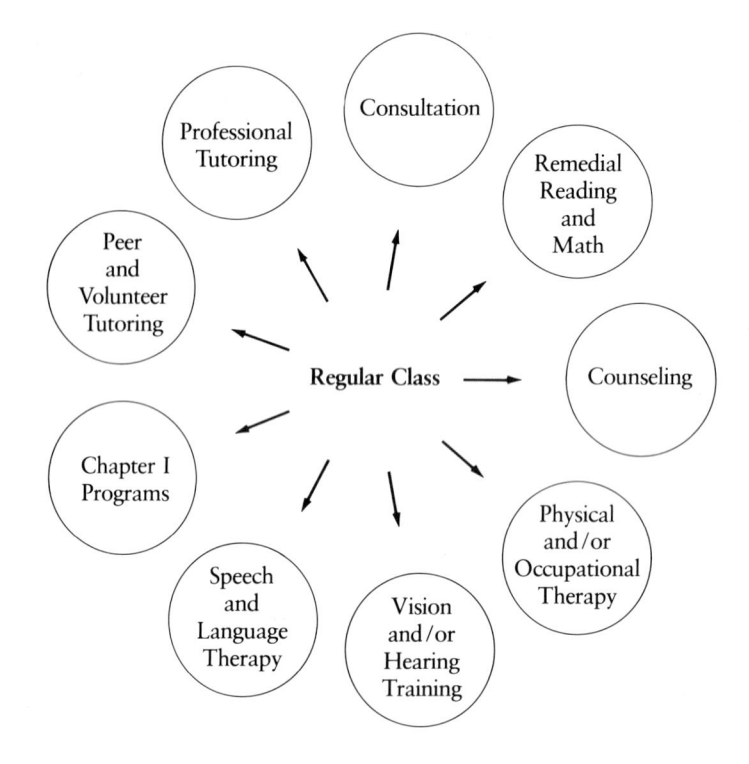

Figure shows "Regular Class" at center, surrounded by: Consultation, Professional Tutoring, Peer and Volunteer Tutoring, Chapter I Programs, Speech and Language Therapy, Vision and/or Hearing Training, Physical and/or Occupational Therapy, Counseling, Remedial Reading and Math.

full-time, receiving services from special education teachers. These students are listed in Figure 1.4.

Some students with severe impairments will continue to need the services of special class teachers. These include students with moderate, severe, and profound retardation; with emotional handicaps; and a few with severe physical handicaps and visual or hearing impairments.

The breadth of support offered by these services has the potential for providing optimal educational opportunity. There is, however, also the potential for fragmen-

FIGURE 1.4

Students served by special education teachers

Chart under "Resource Rooms": Students With Learning Disabilities, Students With Mild Retardation, Students With Severe Behavior Problems, Students With Physical Impairments, Students With Visual Impairments, Students With Hearing Impairments.

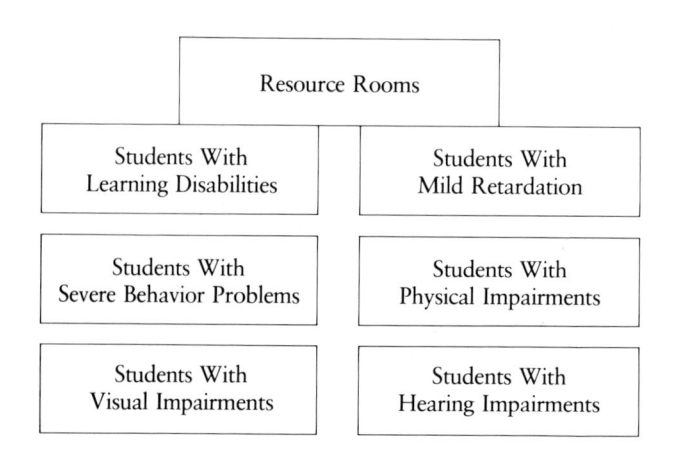

tation of such services with students caught between the expectations of two teachers and differences in methods and management. If the advantages of these services are to be realized in the educational and personal growth of students, it requires coordination and communication among the professionals involved. Administrators must appreciate the complexity of the task and make provisions to facilitate planning and implementation. A range of services to meet the identified needs of all exceptional class members is to be provided as specified in federal and state laws. (Resource services are discussed in detail in Chapter 3.)

What Do Teachers Need to Know About the Law?

It is important for teachers who work with exceptional students to have a knowledge and understanding of the law.

At one time all students identified as exceptional were excluded from formal education. The movement to include some students began early, and gradually larger numbers were taught in special schools or in separate classes in regular schools. Since the 1960s significant changes have resulted because of the belief that exceptional students were more successful in regular classes than in separate settings.

Public Law 94–142

The movement accelerated in 1975 when Congress enacted Public Law (PL) 94–142, *The Education for All Handicapped Children Act*. The major provisions of the law are summarized as follows:

- All handicapped children without regard to severity of impairment are to receive a free, appropriate public education.
- Exceptional students are to be assigned to the "least restrictive environment" and "to the maximum extent appropriate, handicapped children . . . are to be educated with children who are not handicapped."
- No area of school participation is to be closed to handicapped students.
- The school must demonstrate cause if the student is placed in any environment other than the regular classroom.
- An individual educational program should be developed for each student so identified. Specifications are given as to the nature of the program and the participants in its development, including parents.
- The student will receive a multifactoral, multidisciplinary, and nondiscriminatory assessment.
- Parents have the right to obtain a separate, independent assessment at their expense and to have the results considered in planning.
- Parents will receive notice of any change in program or placement.
- If the parents disagree with the decisions made by the school, they have recourse through due process procedures.
- Parents have the right to examine all school records.
- Such school records and information are further restricted from access by others.

The individual states were given the responsibility to adjust their laws and school guidelines to conform with these and other specifications of PL 94–142 and were to monitor compliance with the law. Although the "quiet revolution," as it was termed by Dimond (1973), culminated with the passage of PL 94–142, many specific issues regarding the parameters of responsibility and the extent of services remain unanswered.

The two provisions of the law that have had the most immediate and profound impact on local schools are those for *due process* and for placement in the *least restrictive environment*.

Due Process

The law guarantees the right of parents to participate in decision making about their children and the kinds of services that will be provided. Due process provides a structured procedure for the resolution of disagreements that may arise between school personnel and parents. State guidelines and local policy across the country differ in regard to implementation of this section of PL 94–142, but the following steps are typical of the procedure.

1. *Resolution* results from informal discussion among the individuals concerned.
2. *Case conferences* or *mediation* allow for a review of the information and a statement of positions with resolution as the goal.
3. *Administrative review* is conducted by the district superintendent.
4. *Impartial due process hearing*, which is a formal proceeding, is conducted by an impartial hearing officer. Parents and the school may be represented by attorneys. The impartial hearing officer weighs the merits of the arguments and renders a decision about the student's status and subsequent placement and instruction.
5. *State-level review* is the next step in the appeals process. Written data are presented to the State Board of Education who render a decision.
6. *Referral to the courts* may be necessary if the decision of the State Board of Education is disputed. Although infrequent, appeals have reached the United States Supreme Court.

Either the parents or the school system has recourse to this system for the resolution of disputes.

Least Restrictive Environment

Nix (1977, p. 288) describes least restrictive environment as follows:

> The concept of least restrictive environment can ... be interpreted to mean that children have concurrent rights to live their lives in as near normal a manner as possible and to have access to any and all educational services and settings necessary for their optimal development both educationally and socially. Restrictions, if necessary, in educational placement stem from the child's needs rather than an arbitrary denial of access to the normal educational milieu.

As implied by this description, the law does not specify that all exceptional students must be placed in regular classrooms for even brief periods of time. It means that they should be placed in as normal a situation as possible with their needs being met in a manner that provides successful educational experiences.

The concept of least restrictive environment emerged from the diversification of services first proposed by Reynolds (1962) and later from *service delivery systems* such as those recommended by Chaffin (1975), Deno (1970), and Dunn (1973). These arrangements prescribe levels of placement based upon the severity of students' handicapping conditions and the extent of their educational needs. Not all school systems have identical organizations of services (Box 1.1).

Because national and state mandates require conformance to the principle of least restrictive environment, many students identified as exceptional are no longer placed in a special setting. They remain in the regular classroom and receive additional services as described in Figure 1.3. Other students, once in a self-contained special class, have been returned to the regular class on a full-time or part-time basis. This practice has been termed *mainstreaming*.

In various school systems most exceptional students remain in regular classes. Regular teachers collaborate with resource persons who work in the classroom directly with teachers and students or they suggest curriculum, methods, and materials. Depending on the organizational structure of the school, support personnel may be special education consultants, support teachers, or teacher assistance teams. Reynolds, Wang, and Walberg (1987) advocate restructuring regular education and categorical programs for mildly handicapped students. They state, "We propose a new wave of innovation in which special educators would join with others to advance a broad program of adaptive education for all students, including intensive efforts on behalf of children who have not progressed well under current programs" (p. 396).

The authors contend that it is time for regular and special educators and administrators to look at local programs. Determination of placement remains a decision based upon individual needs and eligibility. Administrators are challenged to provide materials and in-depth, in-service training to regular teachers. With adequate teaching tools and sufficient, direct assistance from support personnel, regular teachers can meet the needs of many more exceptional learners in regular classrooms.

BOX 1.1

Placement Options

- Regular classroom
- Regular classroom with supplementary services
- Regular classroom with tutoring
- Resource room
- Part-time special class
- Self-contained special class
- Homebound instruction
- Special school or nonschool setting

Challenges in Teaching

Numerous challenges face educators as exceptional students become an integral part of the student body. The complexity of instructing students with a wide range of abilities and limitations as well as providing for individual needs must be recognized by administrators, support personnel, parents, and related professionals. Several of these challenges are addressed.

To improve the quality of education. Teachers are challenged to realize that they have a responsibility to every member of the class. Each student has abilities and skills which need to be developed; many require intensive instruction. The entire class benefits from competent teaching, good discipline, and up-to-date materials in an environment that is conducive to learning. All students must be prepared to take their places in a changing society, to cope, to get along, and to have a satisfying and productive livelihood.

To meet individual needs. Meeting the individual needs of all students while attending to the specific needs of exceptional students requires skill, planning, and organization.

Individual needs are identified as those areas of academic, social, and personal functioning that must be improved through intervention to enable the individual to meet the expectancies of the environment. Some students learn primarily through hearing, others visually. Some process a thought rapidly, others slowly. Some grasp a concept the first time it is presented; others require repetition and alternative methods of instruction. Some need a highly structured environment; others learn in a more flexible setting. Students with physical handicaps and those with hearing or visual impairments may need special accommodations to allow them to benefit fully from classroom instruction.

Socialization objectives must deal with acceptance by peers, decision-making skills, problem solving, and accepting age-appropriate responsibilities. Some students must be taught *how* to learn.

To determine accurately the least restrictive environment for each exceptional student. Service delivery systems typically describe a range of resource services and the settings in which exceptional students might be placed when eligibility requirements are met. Determination of the least restrictive environment requires early and accurate evaluation based upon a multifactoral assessment in which all facets of functioning, not just test scores, are examined. To be considered are curricular, emotional, and social needs. How do students best learn? Where will they receive optimal challenges? Where can they be relatively successful? It is not a once-in-a-lifetime occurrence, but periodic evaluations are made to ascertain the continuing appropriateness of the setting. If a student is ineligible for special services, a resource support system in the regular classroom must be maintained.

To provide adequate resource services. School systems are mandated to develop and make available resource services based on identified needs. They may consist of a continuum of alternative placements, supplementary interventions, or therapy provided by professionals other than regular classroom teachers. Administrators are challenged to encourage teachers' use of these services and personnel and to create an atmosphere of team effort.

To establish optimal learning environments. Students learn best when the environment is physically, psychologically, and socially supportive.

Physical accommodations may need to be made for exceptional students, but all deserve an attractive, comfortable, and safe classroom in which to learn.

Psychologically, the environment should be one that is conducive to growth. A warm and secure atmosphere with well-planned lessons and activities, characterized by fairness, knowledge of expectations, and consistency in rules and discipline are desirable goals. Attention is paid to the development of a positive self-concept and feelings of capability resulting from responsibilities accepted and met.

Socially, the environment is friendly, accepting, and helpful. Nonhandicapped students are prepared for their interaction with exceptional students. Ridicule and rejection are not tolerated, and every effort is made to encourage cooperative attitudes. Solicitousness or a patronizing attitude is avoided.

To determine the parameters of intervention for exceptional students and individual learners in regular classrooms. In regular classrooms there is a continuum of characteristics among students. The complexity of instructing such a range of abilities as well as providing for individual needs may not be recognized by administrators, support personnel, parents, or professionals in other fields. Advocates of mainstreaming may overestimate what is possible for regular teachers to do with limited time and training. They may recommend highly specialized methods of instruction, behavior management, and psychological procedures to meet the needs of particular exceptional students.

Teachers are teachers first. That is, their role is to provide instruction in academic subjects. They establish a supportive environment, determine appropriate curriculum, choose optimal methods and materials, and manage behavior. Although they attempt to meet the challenge of providing for individual differences, they cannot "spoon-feed" individual students. Nor are they special education teachers, therapists, counselors, psychologists, social workers, or administrators. Cooperating with other professionals, teachers identify the realistic parameters of intervention that can be incorporated with the ongoing procedures in the classroom.

To identify the knowledges, methods, and attitudes that constitute the competencies of excellence in teaching and to establish procedures for imparting and encouraging them in teachers' professional lives. Experience and research suggest that excellence in teaching is the most sound prevention of academic difficulties as well as a prerequisite to remediation. It is incumbent upon the teaching profession to identify the knowledges, methods, and attitudes that constitute effective practice. The groundwork for the establishment of these competencies is laid during preservice training and developed throughout the teacher's career. They are strengthened by experience; administrative expectations and rewards; continuing education; in-service training; and high standards of self-expectancy, caring, and commitment.

To support developing positive attitudes among regular educators and other school personnel toward exceptional students. In some places remarkable attitudes have occurred in which schools have welcomed, supported, and encouraged students with handicaps. Individual teachers have performed beyond expectations in providing an education for them, and many have reported that they have profited in return. Administrators have expressed gratitude for the example given by students with a handicap and for the attitude of caring and concern among staff and students.

Resistance has occurred, however, at all levels from the elementary school to the university. Researchers have suggested that such attitudes constitute one of the major impediments in educating handicapped students in regular classrooms. In some schools fear and reticence exist.

Combinations of procedures appear to be required to change these attitudes. Teachers need to be helped to see beyond the categorical labels and to gain knowledge about individuals with handicapping conditions. They must recognize that exceptional students, regardless of their handicaps, are individuals first—not blind or deaf or retarded individuals. While there may be distinct differences, there are also many similarities to other students. Through continued education, encouragement from administrators, and experience, regular teachers supported by resource personnel may come to know the rewards of teaching students with handicaps.

To improve relationships with parents. Teachers are challenged to become partners with parents by working together to develop each student's full potential. Respect and communication are necessary to develop positive relationships. Teachers assume and maintain professional viewpoints, providing for the student's welfare while being nonjudgmental. The level of parental ability to deal with the handicapping condition, to manage the child, to cooperate with school personnel, and to participate in the program must be considered. Teachers must be aware of the fears and apprehensions parents may have about their child's placement in special classes or about a student's return to regular classes. Because parents know their child, they can make a valuable contribution regarding placement and success in the appropriate setting.

Challenges are always present in education. While some are short-lived, others continue, and new challenges emerge. Although those listed are addressed in subsequent chapters, no book can provide professionals with easy means to achieve difficult goals. Rather, teachers are challenged to examine each one thoughtfully, to accept situations that cannot be changed, and to work toward the improvement or achievement of others.

SUMMARY

Traditionally, students have been classified into one of two groups—normal or exceptional. However, it is increasingly recognized that this dichotomy is neither realistic nor practical. Students in the two groups do not possess different sets of traits. Rather they share the same basic learning, social, physical, and personal/psychological characteristics. Abilities and characteristics exist on a continuum; students differ in the quantity of each attribute possessed.

Teachers recognize the diversity of individual differences, which is the basis for educational planning. Teachers need to be aware of procedures for managing behavior, organizing curriculum, and selecting methods and for using available resource services. Teachers also need to be cognizant of legislation that affects education, especially PL 94–142, *The Education for All Handicapped Children Act.*

Of the various provisions of the law, due process and least restrictive environment are of particular importance. The former provides procedures to resolve differences between parents and the school. The latter assures that, to the extent possible, students with handicaps are educated with their nonhandicapped peers. This practice has become known as mainstreaming.

In addressing the needs of regular and exceptional students, teachers, principals, and other school personnel face a number of challenges. These include:

- To improve the quality of education
- To meet individual needs
- To determine accurately the least restrictive environment for each exceptional student
- To provide adequate resource services
- To establish optimal learning environments
- To determine the parameters of intervention for exceptional students and individual learners in regular classrooms
- To identify the knowledges, methods, and attitudes that constitute the competencies of excellence in teaching and to establish procedures for imparting and encouraging them in teachers' professional lives
- To support developing positive attitudes among regular educators and other school personnel toward exceptional students
- To improve relationships with parents

The premise of this book is that teaching and management are more effective when planned and implemented on the basis of the characteristics of individual students rather than on the basis of the groups to which they are assigned.

REFERENCES

Bodgan, R., & Taylor, S. (1976). The judged, not the judges: The insider's view of mental retardation. *American Psychologist, 31,* 47–52.
Boyle, M., & Sleeter, C. E. (1981). Inservice for a federally mandated educational change: A study of PL 94–142. *Journal of Research and Development in Education, 14*(2), 79–91.
Chaffin, J. D. (1975). Will the real "Mainstreaming" program please stand up! (or . . . should Dunn have done it?) In E. L. Meyen, G. A. Vergason, & R. J. Whelan (Eds.). *Alternatives for teaching exceptional children* (pp. 173–204). Denver: Love.
Deno, E. (1970). Special education as developmental capital. *Exceptional Children, 37,* 229–237.
Dimond, P. (1973). The constitutional right to education: The quiet revolution. *The Hastings Law Journal, 24,* 1087–1127.
Dunn, L. M. (Ed.) (1973). *Exceptional children in the schools: Special education in transition* (2nd ed.). New York: Holt, Rinehart & Winston.
Nix, G. W. (Ed.) (1977). *The rights of hearing-impaired children.* Washington, DC: Alexander Graham Bell Association for the Deaf.
Reynolds, M. C. (1962). A framework for considering some issues in special education. *Exceptional Children, 28,* 367–370.
Reynolds, M. C., Wang, M. C., & Walberg, H. J. (1987). The necessary restructuring of special and regular education. *Exceptional Children, 53,* 391–398.
Rude, C. R. (1978). Trends and priorities in inservice training. *Exceptional Children, 45,* 172–176.
Voeltz, L., Bailey, E., Nakamura, A., & Azama, M. (1979). A needs assessment of special education inservice training priorities for teachers. *Educational Perspectives, 18*(4), 12–17.

SUGGESTED READINGS

Bloom, B. S. (1981). All our children learning: A primer for teachers, and other educators. New York: McGraw-Hill.

Budoff, M., Orenstein, A., & Kervick, C. (1982). *Due process in special education: On going to a hearing.* Cambridge, MA: Ware.

Buscaglia, L. F., & Williams, E. H. (Eds.) (1979). *Human advocacy and PL 94–142: The educator's roles.* Thorofare, NJ: Slack.

Hardman, M. L., Drew, C. J., & Egan, M. W. (1987). *Human exceptionality: Society, schools and family.* Boston: Allyn & Bacon.

Morris, R. J., & Blatt, B. (1986). *Special education: Research and trends.* Elmsford, NY: Pergamon.

Reynolds, M. C. (Ed.) (1982). *The future of mainstreaming: Next steps in teacher education.* Reston, VA: Council for Exceptional Children.

Ysseldyke, J. E., & Algozzine, B. (1982). *Critical issues in special and remedial education.* Boston: Houghton Mifflin.

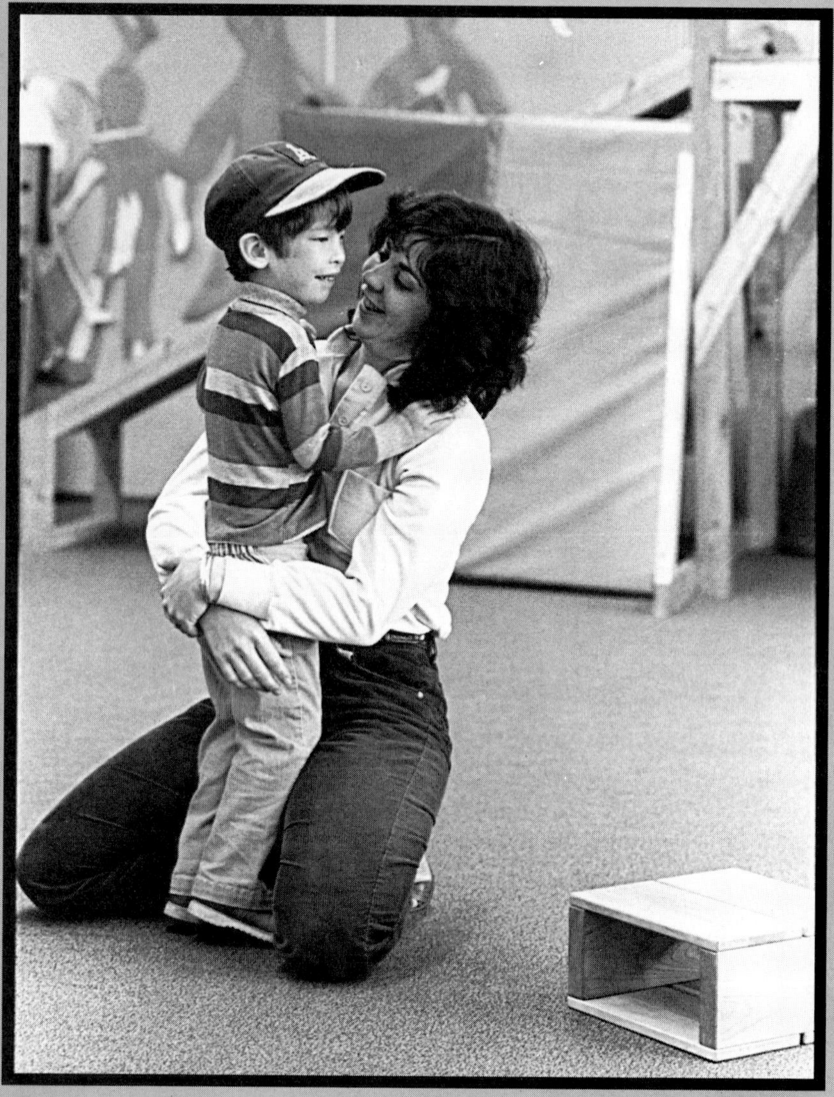

2

Characteristics of Exceptional Students

EXCEPTIONAL INDIVIDUALS have existed throughout history. Changes in their treatment and education have paralleled scientific and medical progress and society's changing attitudes on what it means to be different. Treatment has progressed from persecution in ancient civilizations to today's humanitarianism. Education for exceptional students was not begun until 200 years ago. Excluded from schooling earlier, handicapped individuals have more recently been given opportunities for full participation in educational programs.

Defining Exceptionality

Many authors have proposed definitions of exceptional individuals. Kirk and Gallagher (1986, p. 5) identify the exceptional child as

> ... the child who differs from the average or normal child in (1) mental characteristics, (2) sensory abilities, (3) communication abilities, (4) social behavior, or (5) physical characteristics. These differences must be to such an extent that the child requires a modification of school practices, or special education services, to develop to maximum capacity.

The definition is not designed for direct application to individual students but rather describes the broad parameters of the complex field of special education. It should be noted that Kirk and Gallagher refer to "educational exceptionality." Neither the existence of a physical condition (for example, visual or hearing impairment) nor deviation from the norm on a standardized test (for example, IQ scores) is sufficient for the designation of exceptionality. Only when these (or other) conditions result in the need for special services can students be considered exceptional.

Clarification of Terms

Many people have preconceptions about how individuals with handicaps can be expected to act. It is often believed that certain kinds of social behaviors are an inevitable consequence of the handicapping condition. To clarify this misconception, the terms *impairment, disability, behavior,* and *handicap* are distinguished. An impairment is the fact or condition of a physical or psychological anomaly inherent to the individual. Disability represents the precise behavioral limitations imposed by the impairment. It is what the individual cannot do (*dis*-ability) as a direct result of the impairment. The man who is blind cannot see; the youth who has cerebral palsy may be unable to use thumb and forefinger to pick up a small object. Behavior is that activity that results from the individual with the impairment and disability interacting with the environment. Social behaviors evolve from learning and experience; they are not a direct consequence of the impairment. A handicap is a condition imposed by society or self. Individuals are prevented from functioning to the extent of their capabilities because others restrict opportunities or because of self-imposed limitations. What this means to teachers is that, although academic ability and social perception may be compromised by disability limitations, neither learning performance nor classroom behavior is outside teacher influence. Misbehavior is not a direct result of mildly handicapping conditions. Learning and social behaviors can be modified using specific techniques determined by needs.

Categories of Exceptional Individuals

Persons identified as belonging to a category of exceptionality share a particular characteristic or group of characteristics. The nomenclature used to designate these categories and the criteria for inclusion change over time and across professional and regional boundaries. These changes occur in response to new research, new theories, and social and professional preference. State departments of education provide funding consistent with their own categorical specifications. As a result, there are few universally accepted terms, definitions, or descriptions. The category names and definitions used here are the more prevalent. They are purposefully chosen to provide for maximum consistency, understanding, and clarity. The categories are described and followed by a discussion of characteristics.

Students With Mental Retardation

Many definitions of mental retardation have been proposed. The most widely accepted definition and criteria are those which have been offered by the American Association on Mental Deficiency (AAMD). The *Classification in Mental Retardation* (Grossman, 1983, p. 1) presents the following: "Mental retardation refers to significantly subaverage general intellectual functioning existing concurrently with deficits in adaptive behavior and manifested during the development period."

Further clarification is provided by defining subaverage intellectual functioning as "approximately IQ 70 or below" (Grossman, 1983, p. 1). In terms of incidence, 2 to 3 percent of the population would be considered retarded. By adaptive behavior, Grossman indicates "the effectiveness or degree with which individuals meet the standards of personal independence and social responsibility expected for age and cultural group" (p. 1). Developmental period is defined as that span of time between birth and the individual's eighteenth birthday. The AAMD classification system specifies four subgroups of retardation: mild, moderate, severe, and profound.

Substantial criticism has been lodged against the use of the IQ score as the sole criterion for diagnosing mental retardation as was the practice in the past in many localities. It has been argued that intellectual subnormality as indicated on norm-referenced intelligence tests is a necessary but not sufficient criterion. Although they correlate highly with school grades, IQ scores do not measure the relative competence of the individual in interacting with the larger social environment. To meet the criteria for retardation, individuals must also demonstrate problems in adjusting to their environment. Adaptive behavior is difficult to measure with the preciseness that characterizes IQ testing. Four instruments used for such measurement are the *AAMD Adaptive Behavior Scale, School Version* (Lambert & Windmiller, 1981), the *Adaptive Behavior Inventory for Children* (ABIC) (Mercer & Lewis, 1977), the *Vineland Adaptive Behavior Scale* (Sparrow, Balla, & Cicchetti, 1984), and the *Scales of Independent Behavior* (Bruininks, Woodcock, Weatherman, & Hill, 1984).

School Classification System

Many state departments of education and school systems have adopted classification systems that vary from the AAMD standards (Huberty, Koller, & Ten Brink, 1980). They often identify a three-tiered organization that includes the Educable Mentally Retarded (EMR), the Trainable Mentally Retarded (TMR), and the Severely and Profoundly Retarded. These levels may vary from the AAMD specifications in IQ ranges, but they are essentially parallel to the mild, moderate, severe, and profound classifications.

Students With Mild Retardation Students in this classification are familiar to most public school personnel. They are limited in conceptual abilities to the extent that the rate of academic learning is slowed and ultimate achievement is compromised. The traditional placement had been the self-contained classroom with curriculum and instruction adapted to their individual abilities and progress rates. Elementary school classes centered around the acquisition of basic academic skills and social competencies. As the students moved into secondary classes, they were subjected to a curriculum that became increasingly vocationally oriented. With the implementation of "least restrictive environment" many students have been successfully placed part-time in regular classes and part-time in resource rooms.

Students With Moderate Retardation Students in this classification are largely restricted to learning self-help and social skills. Although some have been taught minimal skills in reading, spelling, and writing, more commonly they receive instruction in the survival skills of living and vocational tasks, which can be performed in closely supervised settings such as group homes or sheltered workshops.

At one time nearly all programs for moderately retarded individuals were housed in settings outside the public schools, because they were not considered educable. Increasing numbers of these classes have moved into public schools. The students receive their instruction in the special education class and can benefit from the normal school environment. (Berdine & Cegelka, 1980).

Students With Severe and Profound Retardation Individuals in this category are at the lowest ranges of intellectual ability and often demonstrate physical anomalies. Some children and adults are institutionalized. Little concern was expressed in the past for their enrollment in educational programs but current laws mandating universal education have resulted in increased activities. Schools and classes with professionally trained teachers have been established within residential institutions. Others live at home and are taught in community centers.

Students With Learning Disabilities

The definition of learning disabilities used in federal legislation is a revision of one originally formulated by the National Advisory Committee on Handicapped Children. It reads:

> "Specific learning disability" means a disorder in one or more of the basic psychological processes involved in understanding or in using language, spoken or written, which may manifest itself in an imperfect ability to listen, think, speak, read, write, spell or do mathematical calculations. The term includes such conditions as perceptual handicaps, brain injury, minimal brain dysfunction, dyslexia, and developmental aphasia. The term does not include children who have learning problems which are primarily the result of visual, hearing, or motor handicaps, of mental retardation, of emotional disturbance, or of environmental, cultural, or economic disadvantage.
> — (U.S. Office of Education, 1977)

Neither this definition nor any other has been unanimously accepted by professionals in the various disciplines associated with the field. This lack of acceptance of a definition continues to spark debate and pose serious problems (Ames, 1983; Cruickshank, 1983; Kirk & Kirk, 1983; Keogh, 1983; National Joint Committee on Learning Disabilities, 1987; Sabatino, 1983).

Practitioners in the public schools responded to this lack of professional consensus and to local social pressure by identifying large numbers of students with disparate characteristics as learning disabled. In an attempt to curb the growing numbers, as well as the spiraling costs and services, a more restrictive set of guidelines was created. The *Federal Register* (December 29, 1977) further specified that those students should be considered learning disabled who demonstrated

> ... a severe discrepancy between achievement and intellectual ability in one or more of the following areas: (i) Oral expression; (ii) Listening comprehension; (iii) Written expression; (iv) Basic reading skill; (v) Reading comprehension; (vi) Mathematics calculation; or (vii) Mathematics reasoning.
> — (U.S. Office of Education, 1977)

Intellectual ability is determined by the student's score on an individual IQ test. Achievement is determined by the administration of standardized tests in the seven academic areas. For example, if a fourth-grade student's IQ score is within the average range, he or she can be expected to achieve at the fourth grade level. If, however, the score on the achievement test indicates that a "severe discrepancy" exists between expectations and actual achievement, he or she may be considered learning disabled. The *Federal Register* does not specify what constitutes a "severe discrepancy" but leaves this determination to the local planning committee. Many state departments of education and local school administrations have prepared formulas and charts as guidelines in determining how much of a discrepancy is "severe."

What is evident in this change of definitions is a shifting of emphasis by professionals in the field. From an earlier stance of identifying presumed dysfunctioning of internal processes of learning, the focus is now on a behavioral orientation that identifies deficits in specific academic skills and tasks.

In any case, the population remains heterogeneous. Students with learning disabilities are likely to be served by itinerant tutors or to be placed part-time in the regular class and part-time in a resource room. Whereas small group instruction is not unwarranted, individualization is the main ingredient of successful intervention programs in learning disabilities.

Gifted Students

The classic concepts of giftedness evolved largely from the monumental work of Lewis Terman and his thirty-five-year longitudinal research, *Genetic Studies of Genius*. While recognizing the validity and importance of Terman's work with a very narrowly defined population, some authors have questioned the applicability of the resulting data to a present-day, less rigidly identified group (Whitmore, 1980). Following nomination by public school teachers in California, students were tested with the (then) new revision of the Binet–Simor scales, and those with scores of 140 or above were selected for the study. Since that time both these procedures have been the principal methods of identifying the gifted (Alvino, McDonnel, & Richert, 1981), although other "cutoff" scores have been used. The Marland (1972) report, the first national survey in the area of giftedness noted the limitations of both methods. Based on an extensive review of the data, Fox (1981, p. 1108) recommends using "a variety of psychometric and nonpsychometric measures for initial screening."

Over time, concepts of giftedness have changed in response to cultural and social influences (Gallagher, 1985). Aspects of individual functioning other than those demonstrated on IQ tests were incorporated into definitions. The addition of the term "talented" further expanded the concept. In 1978 *The Gifted and Talented Children's Act* (PL 95–561) was signed by President Carter. The legislation contains the following definition:

> The term "gifted and talented children" means children, and whenever applicable, youth who are identified at the preschool, elementary, or secondary level as possessing demonstrated or potential abilities, that give evidence of high performance responsibility in areas such as intellectual, creative, specific academic, or leadership ability, or in the performing and visual arts and who by reason thereof require services or activities not ordinarily provided by the school.

The gifted may not be receiving the educational support they deserve. Thomason (1981, p. 102) states that "using either the more conservative 3% incidence figure for this population or the more liberal 5%, between 39% and 63% of the potentially gifted and talented children of our country are still not identified or not receiving specialized instruction."

Another even less recognized population that may suffer from neglect is that of gifted children who are also handicapped—those with physical, social, or emotional disabilities and those who have learning disabilities. Gearheart and Weishahn (1976) suggest there may be between 120,000 and 180,000 gifted/handicapped students in the public schools.

Students With Visual Impairments

The category of visual impairment encompasses both those who are blind and those who have low vision. In actual numbers, there are far more students in the latter category. The National Society to Prevent Blindness (1966) defines legal blindness as "visual acuity for distance vision of 20/200 or less in the better eye with the best possible correction or field vision no greater than 20 degrees."

Although there have been advantages for having a "legal" definition of blindness, acuity levels of individuals with low vision have not served as the best indicators of the use of vision. Other scales that are comprised of descriptions of functional vision—the use individuals make of vision—better determine the degree to which they can function independently and, conversely, the need for supportive services (Barraga, 1983).

In the past, various alternative placements were made available to students with visual impairments. Each state still maintains residential schools for the blind and visually impaired. These schools provide the kinds of specialized training that students need to survive in a sighted society—various self-help skills, mobility training, and typewriting. Braille is frequently but not universally taught. Often students equipped with these skills can return to their own community and enroll in the public school. The less severely impaired may be able to attend public school classes without specialized training.

Within the public school students with visual handicaps, for the most part, can be included fully in the regular program. The provision of large print books, braille books and periodicals, magnification devices, and talking books have reduced many of the problems students once encountered in public education. However, as Martin and Hoben (1977) reported, there are other areas in which some supportive services may be needed. These include social, communication, and daily-living skills, which may have been restricted in development by the limitations imposed by the visual impairment.

Students With Hearing Impairments

The term *hearing impaired* refers to two groups of individuals: the hard-of-hearing and the deaf. As with a visual handicap, there are fewer individuals who have a total sensory loss (deafness) than there are who have a partial loss. Hearing loss is measured in decibels (dB), which represent intensity or loudness. Various authors have presented scales that describe the degree of hearing loss in terms of decibel levels. Level of acuity, however, is not the only factor that determines the quality of the functioning of hard-of-hearing students. Their use of residual hearing affects communication ability and often social adjustment. For the severely impaired and those who have become deaf, the age of onset is a critical factor. Those whose loss occurred prior to the development of language are usually more seriously handicapped in receptive and expressive language and in some aspects of cognitive functioning than those whose adventitious loss occurred after oral language had been acquired.

Extensive educational programming is often needed for students with hearing impairments. Preschool intervention may begin as early as two-and-a-half or three years of age although parents often receive assistance in working with their children earlier. Preschool programs are highly structured toward the development of auditory and visual communication, speech therapy, language development, social interaction, and cognitive growth. Continued support may be needed throughout the school years for most students.

Students with hearing impairments have a potential for normal cognitive development, but achievement in school subjects is frequently below that of hearing students (Lowenbraun & Thompson, 1986). Hearing impairment, particularly deafness, is frequently accompanied by social and psychological problems. A major, but by no means the only, source of these problems is the severe limitation in communicating with others and feelings of isolation. In this regard, auditory impairment is more debilitating than visual impairment.

Students With Physical Impairments

Students with physical handicaps include those who are orthopedically impaired, those who are neurologically impaired, and those with special health problems.

Students With Orthopedic Handicaps Students in this group have been afflicted with muscular dystrophy, missing limbs, poliomyelitis, spina bifida, or other conditions of the skeletomuscular structure. If students with orthopedic handicaps are not concomitantly handicapped by other impairments (for example, mental retardation), the major school interventions are related to mobility and physical accommodations. As the current pressure for barrier-free public facilities continues and as public schools respond, increasing numbers of students with orthopedic handicaps enjoy a wider variety of educational opportunities.

Students With Neurological Handicaps Students in this group suffer from damage to, or dysfunction of, the central nervous system or the peripheral nervous system. The two most common impairments found in the schools are convulsive disorders and cerebral palsy. Most children who have convulsive disorders and who have no other disabilities attend regular classes. Children with mild cerebral palsy may also attend regular classes although those with more severe complications are educated in special classes or by community agencies.

Students With Special Health Problems Closely related to the orthopedically and neurologically handicapped are students with special health problems. Those with diabetes, respiratory ailments, cardiac problems, and allergies are included in this classification. As with the orthopedically and neurologically impaired, those who do not demonstrate mental or learning problems can frequently be integrated into regular programs. A major factor in their success seems to be the degree of acceptance by nonhandicapped students and teachers. Students with severe health problems requiring hospitalization for prolonged periods receive educational services in that setting.

Students With Communication Disorders

The area of communication disorders encompasses both students with defective speech and those with language dysfunctions. Van Riper (1978, p. 43) provides the following definition of a speech disorder: "Speech is abnormal when it deviates so far from the speech of other people that it calls attention to itself, interferes with communication, or causes the speaker or his listener to be distressed."

Speech handicaps may be evident in faulty articulation, dysfluent production (stuttering), or voice disorders. For most students who have a speech problem, it is their only disability although others with different handicapping conditions may also exhibit speech difficulties.

Language disorders are more difficult to define. Bloom and Lahey (1978, pp. 290–291) provide the following elaboration:

> Children with a language disorder may have a problem in formulating *ideas* or conceptualizing information about the world; they may have difficulty in learning a *code* for representing what they know about the world; they may be able to learn a code that does not match the conventional system used in the linguistic community; they may have learned something about the world and something about the conventional code, but are unable to *use* the code in speaking or understanding in certain contexts or for certain purposes; or they may develop ideas, the conventional code, and the use of the code, but later than their peers, or with dysfunctions in the interactions among components.

Proper diagnosis and determining the need for intervention is properly the work of the professional speech/language pathologist. For most speech disorders and mild language problems, remediation is conducted by a pathologist operating on an itinerant basis. The student remains in the regular classroom except for periods of training. For severe language problems or language disorders associated with a hearing impairment, students may be placed in a resource room or in self-contained special classes.

Students With Behavior Disorders and Emotional Handicaps

Probably more than any other category, the behavior disordered/emotionally handicapped grouping has suffered from the abrasions of the interface between two professions—the educational and the mental health. Earlier the term *emotionally disturbed* prevailed. Learning problems and misbehaviors in school were seen as manifestations of pathology within the student. For the most part, diagnosis and treatment were in the hands of practitioners in private practice or in child guidance clinics, which were dominated by psychoanalysts. The complexity of the classification system and the treatment process were alien to school personnel. Recommendations made to the school were sometimes unrealistic in terms of what was possible within a public school classroom.

In more recent years, interest in the operant conditioning theories of B. F. Skinner (1968) has increased. The term *behavior disorders* has become popular because it focuses on presently observed behaviors rather than upon inferred etiology. Further, it is recognized that some of the behavior problems of students result from, rather than being the cause of, their inability to achieve academically and/or socially. Teacher training in behavior modification and other management techniques provide school personnel with methods for controlling undesirable behavior.

This is not to suggest that school management procedures are effective substitutes for mental health treatment. There are students who need skilled professional mental health services which are beyond the purview of the school.

There has been an improvement, however, in the ability of professional educators to observe behaviors and delineate those that are environmentally specific from those that represent more serious personality problems.

Various provisions have been made for students with such problems. The majority are enrolled in regular classes with behavior managed by teachers on their own or in consultation with other professionals. In one survey Peterson, Zabel, Smith, and White (1983) found mildly emotionally disabled students were placed within resource programs while the more severely impaired—those considered "truly" emotionally disturbed—were placed in self-contained or residential programs.

Students With Multiple Handicaps

Multiply handicapped students are those who manifest two or more disabilities such as cerebral palsy/blind or orthopedic/retarded/blind. Students with severe impairments are treated by professionals from several disciplines in settings outside the schools. Less severely impaired students may be in special classes or resource programs.

Categorization, which facilitates research and professional communication, has remained the organizational structure of special education since its inception in the early 1900s. In most states it constitutes the basis for funding and teacher preparation. Conversely, some have argued that categorization highlights deficiencies and leads to stereotyping and self-fulfilling prophecy. A major criticism has been that categorical descriptions do not provide sufficient information about individual differences necessary to plan specific educational intervention, remediation, and habilitation.

Although the authors do not suggest that categories can be abandoned, they do recommend that special education placement and programs be based primarily upon behavioral functioning rather than on categorical labels. Information that focuses on characteristics of behavior and on individual educational and management needs provides a better base for planning than descriptions of categories.

From Categories to Individuals

An alternative to the traditional classification system is the noncategorical or cross-categorical approach. These terms, often used interchangeably, shift the focus of assessment and intervention to individual functioning and needs.

Identifying Variables and Behavioral Functioning

Understanding the noncategorical approach requires a distinction between identifying variables and behavioral functioning. *Identifying variables* are those factors upon which the designation of a category of exceptionality and eligibility for special services are made. They are usually of an intellectual, emotional, physiological, or neurological nature that affect all interactions and can be thought of as underlying or causative agents. *Behavioral functioning* refers to overt activities of individuals and their relationship with the environment. They are learned behaviors and may be situationally specific, occurring in response to the demands of different environmental settings. Students' scores on individual intelligence tests represent their levels of mental functioning and are identifying variables. The same students' skills in reading represent their behavioral functioning. Although not all characteristics can be easily divided into two groups, a theoretical distinction between them is of critical importance in making decisions in regard to the education of students (Figure 2.1).

Identifying Variables, Behavior Functioning, and Instructional Decisions

Education in the categorical approach was based on the assumption that students within a category would have similar behavioral functioning and needs and therefore could profit from similar instructional experiences. Conversely, the noncategorical approach challenges the uniqueness of the separate categories, suggesting that the behaviors exhibited by students with mild handicapping conditions occur *across* rather than *within* categorical boundaries (Brady, Conroy, & Langford, 1984; Hallahan & Kauffman, 1976; Lilly, 1982). But the frequency of occurrence of any specific behavior may differ from one category to another. For example, many mildly handicapped students, regardless of disability designation, may exhibit hyperactive behavior although hyperactivity is commonly associated with learning disabilities. Many mildly handicapped students may show difficulties in conceptualization although this problem occurs almost universally among individuals with retardation.

In addition, the noncategorical approach recognizes that this same behavioral functioning can occur among students who have not been identified as exceptional nor associated with a disability category.

Individual Learners

Individual learners are not exceptional students in the usual sense of the word. They are not marked by physical or functional differences that make them eligible for special educational services. Yet they share with mildly handicapped students learning difficulties in the regular classroom. They also demonstrate behaviors that are

2 Characteristics of Exceptional Students   25

IDENTIFYING VARIABLES	BEHAVIORAL FUNCTIONING
Intellectual	**Learning**
Scores on tests of intelligence and history of low school achievement or academic failure	Demonstrated behaviors and abilities that interfere with or support academic achievement
Classification: Retardation	*Classification:* None
Emotional	**Physical**
Maladaptive behaviors and attitudes presumed to be caused by internal states, drives, or needs	Demonstrated behaviors that inhibit effective interaction with classroom learning activities
Classification: Emotionally Handicapped / Behavior Disordered	*Classification:* None
Physiological	**Social**
Sensory impairments or other physical condition limiting access to information or participation in learning activities	Demonstrated behaviors that interfere with or support positive interaction with peers and adults
Classification: Visual Impairment, Hearing Impairment, Orthopedic Handicaps, or Special Health Problems	*Classification:* None
Neurological	**Personal / Psychological**
Scores on tests of motor, perceptual, and/or linguistic processing	Demonstrated behaviors that interfere with or support progressive development and effective interaction with the environment
Classification: Learning Disabilities	*Classification:* None

Implication for Action

1. Determination of eligibility for special services
2. Placement in remedial, special, or mainstreamed setting

Implication for Action

1. Identification of learning styles, interactive patterns, and specific learning competencies
2. Development of programs responsive to student, teacher, curriculum, methods, and environmental variables

FIGURE 2.1

Comparison of identifying variables and behavioral functioning similar to those of exceptional students but that result from their inability to cope with the demands of the classroom environment rather than from an innate impairment.

Individual learners may be "casualties" of the school system who may not have learned as well as expected in the first grade. Promoted to second grade without the entry skills needed for success, they progressed more slowly than their peers and by the end of the year had fallen further behind. Individual learners may not have the necessary learning skills. Attention is variable, memory may be poor, study skills are weak, and learning itself is inefficient. In any case, demoralizing failure compromises striving, and the cycle continues. They do not start out in school with retardation, learning disabilities, or behavior disorders but may be identified as having these exceptionalities before their education is complete.

All teachers are familiar with individual learners. Often these students are relegated to the status of slow learner or underachiever. They need the same attention given to students identified as exceptional so that they do not become exceptional. Individual learners *can* learn. The skills and attitudes that teachers employ to promote growth and learning in all students can be instrumental in successfully teaching individual learners.

AN INDIVIDUAL LEARNER

Terry, a quiet sixth grader, works slowly, does not complete his work on time, and usually does not finish tests. He pays attention inconsistently and does not ask questions when directions are not understood. Because he has a poor memory, answers to math problems are frequently incorrect, and spelling test grades are low. The support system at home is inadequate.

The resource teacher made the following suggestions at the beginning of the year:

1. *Give him shortened assignments.*
2. *Call on him frequently to help assist in focusing attention.*
3. *Ask him to repeat directions.*
4. *Give direct instruction for listening and remembering with the entire class.*
5. *Set up a reward system for finishing work on time.*
6. *Allow extra time to complete tests.*
7. *Use a peer teacher or volunteer to practice spelling words.*
8. *Assign group projects to enhance social interaction.*

Behavioral Characteristics

Many characteristics are common among exceptional students and individual learners. It is recognized, however, that no one will manifest all of them. Each student has a unique pattern of behavioral traits and functioning. The following discussion includes many of the common traits. Descriptions of behavioral characteristics are presented in four groups: Learning, Physical, Social, and Personal/Psychological

(Figure 2.2). These traits are interactive, and the delineation is made only to facilitate their presentation.

Learning Characteristics

Reasoning Students with difficulties in thinking and reasoning may learn satisfactorily at the concrete level but not at the symbolic or abstract levels. Students with mild handicaps may learn facts and lists and do well in spelling through intensive memorization. In the middle grades and above, as reading comprehension demands go beyond literal meaning to inference and association, students with reasoning difficulties fall further behind their peers. In mathematics, story problems, numerical reasoning, or application of time, money, and measurement concepts are difficult.

Learning Skills Often overlooked in concern for descriptions of academic functioning are learning skills. There is evidence that many exceptional students do not

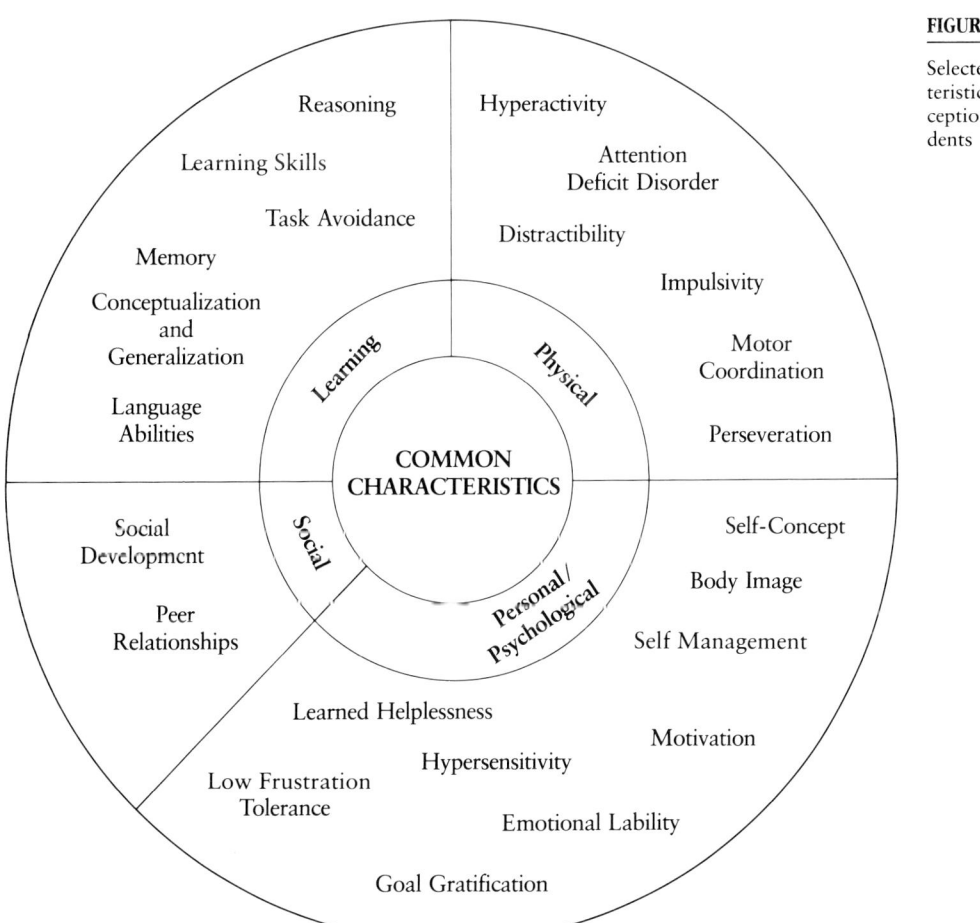

FIGURE 2.2

Selected characteristics of exceptional students

grasp what others assimilate without direct instruction. They do not know the skills of study, notetaking, and outlining and the efficient use of textbook and reference materials, maps, graphs, and charts. Teaching these skills may be as beneficial to the students as instruction in content areas.

Task Avoidance By the time they are identified as exceptional, most students have experienced failure. If parents and teachers have reacted with negativism, blame, and recrimination, the problem is compounded. The students may avoid assigned tasks in various passive or aggressive ways. Daydreaming, giving attention to other students' activities, doodling and drawing, active resistance, misbehavior, and, in the upper grades and secondary school, high absenteeism are only a few of the resulting behaviors.

To keep from doing an assignment students may ask unnecessary questions, engage in manipulative conversation to get the teacher "off the track," purposely disturb another student, daydream, feign illness, ask to use the restroom, or ask to sharpen pencils.

Several of these behaviors can be avoided. Discuss rules the first week of school to establish expectations. Provide consistent positive consequences and carry out negative consequences when students choose to break the rules. Give specific directions and have the students repeat the directions. Check individually in a few minutes to determine that directions are being followed. Give short assignments. Use stations and learning-center activities as seatwork alternatives. In group instruction, move around the room; call on students to respond; use objects to teach. Do not permit manipulations. Arrange the physical environment to minimize opportunities to avoid tasks.

Memory Memory problems characterize many exceptional students. A common teacher complaint is "He knew it yesterday but doesn't know it today!" Students may remember only one or two items on a list or may forget steps within an orally given sequence of directions. Often exceptional students and individual learners have not learned to "chunk" materials such as grouping small sequences of digits within a telephone number. Others do not automatically engage in verbal rehearsal or do not associate new information with past learning. Some have not learned to use mnemonic devices to assist in remembering. Memory problems also occur when students try to remember specific facts without understanding the overall concept, or when they do not practice newly learned skills.

Conceptualization and Generalization Nonhandicapped students often gain insights into concepts almost automatically as a result of meaningful, specific practice. As students work with a series of multiplication problems, for example, they not only practice the skill but also learn to recognize number relationships and principles, which are the basis for multiplication. On the other hand, learning for students with handicaps may be restricted to the skill level. They may learn to solve a page of problems but not perceive the concepts involved. Then presented with the problem to find the area of a rectangle, they may be unable to use those skills to multiply height and width. They are unable to make generalizations—that is, to transfer the skill to other problems in different contexts.

Language Ability A central difficulty of many students with handicaps is language impairment, which severely limits academic achievement. It may be due to early language experience deprivation, hearing loss, auditory perceptual problems, or bilingualism. Some students may not have mastered the grammar system, and others may have a receptive vocabulary that far surpasses their expressive vocabulary. Students having language difficulties may demonstrate average or superior abilities in perceptual-motor activities but are unable to influence others verbally, to decode or to understand at an inferential level in reading, or to express knowledge they may understand. Because language becomes increasingly related to reasoning ability, students become further handicapped.

Physical Characteristics

Hyperactivity Hyperactivity refers to excessive bodily movements with little or no purpose. Some students may be "fidgity," tapping fingers or feet. Others may show expansive movements including continuous arm flexing, pacing, or wandering about the room. Hyperactive students are more noticeable in classrooms in which quiet, conforming behavior is expected rather than in open classrooms. Hyperactivity cannot be considered a unitary phenomenon. There are different kinds of hyperactivity and different causative factors. An additional difficulty is identification. Subjective descriptive rating scales and checklists exist, but there are no valid tests for use in the classroom. It is difficult to distinguish between hyperactivity and the normal activity of highly motivated, inquisitive students who seek out "new worlds" to discover in the classroom and neighborhood.

Dale, a fourth grader, continuously moves his arms, scratches his head frequently, taps his foot, drops his pencil, and gets out of his seat. Constant reminders from his teacher are ineffective. He blurts out at frequent intervals, making loud noises or hitting the desk when he is ignored.

To address the problem, Mrs. Miller uses a number of techniques. A seatwork assignment is given that can be completed in ten minutes. Direct instruction is used that includes student response and writing answers as the lesson progresses. Dale is allowed to recline on a rug during reading group. He can move without disturbing others. Lessons on tape with a headset and practice on a computer hold his attention. Dale moves to stations at regular times. Alternatives to seatwork are given and physical activity is encouraged during recess.

Attention Deficit Disorders Deficits in attentional behavior are among the most common characteristics of exceptional students. Learning requires students to be alert to the visual and auditory stimulation in the environment, to scan the perceptual field, to select relevant aspects, and to maintain focus on them for analysis and retention. Exceptional students may have difficulties in any one or more of these processes. They may omit steps in oral or written directions or perform them in incorrect sequence. Often students will remember examples the teacher used in a previous lesson rather than the concept being illustrated. By failing to focus on visual stimuli for a sufficient period of time, they may not note fine details that distinguish similar letters, words, or pictures. In oral reading, they may give incorrect words based on one or a few initial letters or may fail to attend to the content long enough to integrate the information with past knowledge.

Distractibility   Distractibility is a disorder in which students frequently change focus of attention. They are often referred to as having a "short attention span" because they can concentrate on one activity for only a short time. Visually distractible students appear to notice everything in the environment, constantly looking from one thing to another. Students who are auditorily distractible do not seem to be able to screen out extraneous sounds in the environment but hear and respond to various noises that occur in routine classroom activity. Recent research has suggested that stimuli that are in close proximity to the students' work area are more distracting than those that occur at some distance.

Impulsivity   Impulsivity describes students who react spontaneously to the slightest provocation. They may raise their hands at every question without waiting for the question to be finished. When called upon in class or when taking tests, they give the first answer that occurs to them without evaluating alternative possibilities. These students react instantaneously, not considering the consequences of their behavior.

Motor Coordination   Students who are developmentally delayed demonstrate poor motor coordination in comparison to peers and to expectations based on chronological age. Some students with severe retardation or neurological impairments may show difficulties in gross motor (large muscle) functioning. Students with mild handicaps, such as those who would be assigned to the regular classroom, frequently perform satisfactorily in locomotion or ambulation but often show difficulties in fine motor activities and coordination. This is manifested in using scissors, coloring within the lines, forming letters and numbers, and tying shoes. The most common evidence of fine motor incoordination is poor handwriting, shown by illegibility and messy work. Teachers can encourage effort, legibility, and neatness although they cannot demand a level of performance beyond students' physical capabilities.

Perseveration   Perseverative students continue to perform a behavior beyond its usefulness or are unable to change from one activity to another without experiencing distress. Perseveration can be seen in drawing and coloring as students overwork lines or continue to color in a section that is already solidly colored. Another form of perseveration occurs when students continuously repeat an answer or a behavior because the teacher praised them for being correct the first time. Although perseveration has been associated with neurological impairment, many students continue in an activity in which they are secure, fearful of changing to a new activity with which they might not be successful.

Social Characteristics

Social Development Exceptional individuals are sometimes "loners," unable to establish and maintain interpersonal relationships to the level of emotional involvement implied in the concept of friendship. Because of parental overprotection or the lack of experience, exceptional students often have not learned to be sensitive to a social environment or to "read" the subtle signs of facial expressions and body language to alert them to modify their own behavior. Frequently, they have not learned the appropriate behaviors and conventions of social interaction and dialogue. Sometimes the need for status, attention, belonging, and approval makes students assertive in ways that are perceived by others to be self-centered, and further rejection follows. For handicapped youth and adults, inappropriate social behavior is one of the major reasons for failure to hold jobs.

Conversely, it is not uncommon to find exceptional students who demonstrate an unusual degree of social competence. They are sometimes astute observers of behavior. Often good social adaptation can be traced to a good self-image, understanding parents, and a supportive and nurturing home environment.

Peer Relationships An aspect of social development of exceptional students is poor peer relationships. Students with mental retardation, learning disabilities, physical impairments, and emotional handicaps are often rejected by nonhandicapped students. In the early grades such students are sometimes harrassed on the way home from school or on the bus and are called such names as "Retard" and "Dummy." Occasionally, one finds exceptional students allowing themselves to become scapegoats or to be physically abused to obtain some status in the group.

Peer relationship problems can be particularly acute for exceptional students in a regular classroom. Whereas they may function at a level that makes assignment to the special class unnecessary, their achievements remain below that of others. Exceptional students tend to be isolated in regular classrooms; they are *in* the class, but not a member *of* the class.

Often exceptional students have not learned the give and take of play. Popular myth suggests that students who cannot be successful in academics may achieve well on the playground. In reality, however, many students with mild handicaps have poor motor coordination and visual-spacial relationship perceptions that result in their doing poorly in games requiring throwing, catching, or hitting a ball. Usually they are chosen last for team membership.

Nonhandicapped students are often better able to appreciate students who are blind, deaf, or obviously physically handicapped. Such conditions are apparent and understandable. Students with mild handicapping conditions, on the other hand, often do not look different from others. They may be accepted as friends only to be dropped abruptly and cruelly because the partners feel deceived. The students who appeared to be normal turned out not to be normal. Their behavior and interests are those of younger children.

Some exceptional students sit by themselves on the bus and in the cafeteria. They are never included in group activities on the playground. Others may fight when they are teased or called a name. Still others do the name calling, initiate fights, or vandalize. In games they may interrupt with selfish demands, attempt to change the rules to fit themselves, and complain about unfairness by other players.

To facilitate acceptable peer interaction and to develop friendships, assign a class "buddy" when students are new to the class. Have them sit near students who are friendly and well-liked. Arrange a cooperative learning experience. Have frequent group discussions. Alert the gym teacher, home economics or shop teachers, and playground aides to encourage group activities and to watch for possible misbehavior. Enlist the principal's support in administering positive and negative consequences consistently. Teach specific social skills to small groups. Role play situations that are likely to occur.

Personal/Psychological Characteristics

Self-Concept Although not shared by all exceptional students, a poor self-concept is a pervasive characteristic across disability areas. Students see themselves as being different from others. They have experienced failure, possible ridicule, and devaluation as persons. Rappaport (1966) compared the development of a handicapped and a normal child. The latter achieves developmental milestones as anticipated by parents and perceives their pleasure and pride, rejoices in his or her own accomplishments, and develops the attitude that "I am one who can." In marked contrast, a child with a handicap is delayed in development and perceives the tension, fear, and possible rejection by anxious parents. Knowing failure, he or she thinks "I am one who cannot." Later, teachers become the "significant others" who either enhance or limit the students' feelings. Self-concept, positive or negative, affects all areas of functioning—academic, social, and psychological.

Body Image Closely related to self-concept are individuals' perceptions of their own physical beings. Students with perceptual handicaps are often slow in developing body awareness, do not know the names of body parts, and have correlated physical problems such as clumsiness and awkwardness. Students who are blind may not know what they look like and have no basis for comparison with others. If the handicapping condition is accompanied by physical stigma, the effect can be as psychologically debilitating as physically limiting. Students with deformed or missing limbs, unusual facial features, and uncontrolled movement frequently become overly self-conscious. They are convinced that others are staring at them or talking about their looks, and they avoid associating with peers.

Self-Management Management of one's property and control of one's self are difficult tasks for many exceptional students. They are characterized by disorganization, losing belongings and school papers, and having desks and lockers constantly cluttered. They may take work home and return it late or not at all. Similarly, they have difficulty controlling themselves. Time and work schedules are made but not kept; they may put off studying for tests, preparing for field trips, or beginning projects until the last minute. Their behavior is often a reaction to environmental events rather than self-directed, planned, and purposeful activity. Frequently, they fail to accept responsibility for the consequences of their own behavior or expect others to assume responsibility for them.

Motivation Motivation is a complex construct occasionally misconstrued as a simple drive within students. It is related to many factors including personality, learning style, health, intelligence, and home and school expectations. Orientation toward achievement is strengthened or weakened by students' past history of successes and failures in school. Exceptional students, particularly those assigned to regular classrooms, often demonstrate limited motivation toward academic achievement.

Learned Helplessness Learned helplessness is a learned behavior in which students with poor self-concepts become unnecessarily dependent. They create the situation by manipulating others to "help" them to do what they are either capable of doing or can learn to do themselves. As a result, academic and social growth is prevented, and dependency is reinforced. It becomes progressively worse. "I can't" or "I don't know" is heard more often. Students find numerous ways to avoid tasks; they criticize themselves and others; or they "brag." Most often mistakes are blamed on others or the situation. They may be aggressive or withdrawn.

The term indicates that teachers and parents need to be aware of their part in fostering independence by allowing students to solve problems, to make decisions, to take responsibility, and to learn to risk gradually.

These students are frequently heard to say, "I don't know how" ... "This is too hard" ... "I can't do it" ... "I can't decide." Students are convinced that they cannot learn how to outline or understand a new concept in algebra. They continually ask for help when they do not need it. They blame others for their mistakes. They use "put-downs" on themselves and others. They may be withdrawn because they are fearful and unable to take risks.

To overcome learned helplessness, insist that students do for themselves. When students say, "I can't," ask them to do the first step. When it is completed, ask what they are to do next. Give choices. Do not lecture or threaten. Discuss the situation not the student When students come to class without supplies, lend or rent them. If students have not done the assignment, they must do it. Use contracts in which the student chooses the conditions.

Teach problem solving skills by discussing good and bad alternatives. Ask "What are the consequences of each alternative?" and "What should we do?" Do not rescue students. Allow them to take responsibility for their own behavior. Use natural consequences. Encourage risk taking one small step at a time. Give opportunity to develop abilities.

Emotional Lability Some students react with a level of emotional response out of proportion to the circumstances. They become unduly upset when things do not go right the first time. They often react to the emotionality of others. Teachers who habitually shout to gain class control will find emotionally labile students becoming upset or reacting with outbursts of anger. Unexpected changes in classroom routine result in similar responses. Students who are emotionally labile may overreact to punitive discipline, and yet such punishment may have little effect on changing their behavior.

Hypersensitivity Hypersensitivity is related to poor self-concept. Students who think little of themselves are alert to negative reactions of others and sometimes interpret innocent remarks or actions of others as injurious to themselves. Their feelings are easily hurt, and they are suspicious of others.

Goal Gratification Some exceptional students have not learned to engage in behavior when its rewards are not immediate. The delay in gratification embodied in long-term goals make such goals unacceptable. Teaching and management procedures that use frequent rewards for continuing successes result in improved learning and behavior. Long-term goals culminate from the series of short-term rewarded activities. However, because such remedies have the effect of reinforcing students' need for immediate satisfaction, behavior management techniques, which gradually increase the delay between behavior and reinforcement, may need to be a part of the intervention program.

Low Frustration Tolerance Students with learning disabilities, emotional handicaps, or orthopedic or physical impairments sometimes show bursts of anger or temper tantrums during school or playground activities. These students, intellectually capable of recognizing how the task should be done, cannot achieve at the expected level of performance due to the handicapping condition. Sometimes such students expect perfection on their first attempt. When an art project does not compare well with the teacher's completed model or the answers on a worksheet are incorrect, these students blame the impairment, failing to appreciate that errors are a part of everyone's learning and that perfection is not necessary.

Characteristics Unique to Disability Areas

The authors believe that most behaviors manifested by students with mild handicaps that teachers must address occur *across* categorical divisions. There are, however, some characteristics that are clearly associated with specific disability areas (Table 2.1). Knowledge of these characteristics will provide teachers with a more comprehensive view of students' functioning and can provide data that are useful in both educational planning and referral decisions.

Positive Characteristics

The characteristics presented above have tended to provide a negative view of exceptional students. This may be unavoidable because it is of primary importance that teachers be aware of the factors that interfere with learning and that need to be addressed in classroom instruction. However, all exceptional children are, first

TABLE 2.1
Characteristics Unique to Disability Areas

		ACADEMIC			
Visual Impairment	Hearing Impairment	Physical and Special Health Problems	Retardation	Learning Disabilities	Behavioral Disorders/ Emotional Handicaps
Loses place while reading Handwriting deficits	Discrepancy between ability and achievement Failure to respond when called on Failure to follow oral directions Does not volunteer answers	Lack of experiential base	Slow in intellectual development Poor achievement in all academic areas Weak comprehension skills Below average ability to generalize and conceptualize Visual memory and discrimination Sequencing Limited short-term memory skills	Discrepancy between ability and achievement Consistent success in one subject while failing in another Inability in written and verbal expression while understanding concepts Perceptual disorders Language-processing interferences Visual discrimination and visual memory Sequencing	Inability to learn Discrepancy between ability and achievement

(continued)

of all, children. As with all persons there are many positive characteristics as well; the breadth of these is the same for those with handicaps and those who are nonhandicapped. Given favorable environmental circumstances, exceptional students can display the whole gamut of desirable characteristics. They may be cooperative, thoughtful, insightful, appreciative, friendly, and affectionate. They may also show a sense of humor, be dependable, try to please others, and have special talents. There are those exceptional students who are highly motivated and a joy to teach.

Characteristics as a Basis for Planning

Educational planning for exceptional students must be based upon a breadth of valid information about individual students, their learning, physical, social, and personal/psychological characteristics; strengths and weaknesses in academic performance; and the environment in which they learn.

TABLE 2.1
(continued)

PHYSICAL

Visual Impairment	Hearing Impairment	Physical and Special Health Problems	Retardation	Learning Disabilities*	Behavioral Disorders/ Emotional Handicaps
Lack of visual stimulation resulting in failure to learn by imitation	Head turning	Range of motor difficulties from awkwardness to inability to control muscles	May be smaller or weigh less	May have large and small motor difficulties	Complains of physical ailments
Eye rubbing and/or watery eyes	Distorts face		May have large and small motor coordination difficulties		
	Leans forward				
	Differences in volume or voice quality	May fatigue easily			
Poking the eyes	Articulation problems	May have physical discomfort or pain			
Squinting	Frequent earaches and colds				
Holding objects too close to the eyes	May have watery drainage from ear	May have reaction to medication			
Headaches		Speech problems			
Dizziness					
Rocking					
Delayed development					
Large and small motor coordination difficulties					
Erratic handwriting, especially in spacing and letter size					
Difficulty in controlling environment					
Mobility and spatial orientation					

*Characteristics common to children with learning disabilities and behavior disorders as listed in the earlier section include: hyperactivity, perseveration, distractibility, and impulsivity.

TABLE 2.1
(continued)

SOCIAL

Visual Impairment	Hearing Impairment	Physical and Special Health Problems	Retardation	Learning Disabilities	Behavioral Disorders/ Emotional Handicaps†
Problems with establishing relationships	Problems with establishing relationships	May have limited social opportunities	Play interests of younger children	Poor social perceptions	Poor interpersonal relationships
Lack of social experience	Lack of social experience	Shyness	Unaware of rules in social situations	Poor interpersonal relationships	Disruptive
Concern about appearances in adolescence	Prefer solitary activities	Immaturity	Easily manipulated or taken advantage of	Disruptive	Immaturity
Lack of eye contact		Often display temper tantrums	Immaturity	Immaturity	Aggressiveness
				Aggressiveness	Hostility
				Hostility	Negativism
				Negativism	Manipulation
				Manipulation	Unacceptable language
				Unacceptable language	Disrespectful
					Defies authority
					Unwillingness to participate
					Little or no sensitivity for feelings of others
					Bullies other children
					Frequent absence without good reason

†More frequent and severe than in Retardation and Learning Disabilities

(continued)

All students, handicapped or not, function as whole persons. No one is simply the sum of these or any other set of characteristics that can be listed. They do not occur as isolated behaviors but are manifested within specific classroom situations. They are addressed within the context of the total personality and the classroom environment.

Alert teachers are sensitive to the interaction of student response and classroom environment. They do not observe textbook descriptions of "impaired reasoning" but see the particular limitations in comprehension in the reading of a passage. They do not simply observe the movements of a hyperactive student; they note the variance in activity level as the student reacts to the complexity or difficulty of the response demanded by the lesson. Individual differences are considered, and instruction and

TABLE 2.1
(continued)

PERSONAL/PSYCHOLOGICAL

Visual Impairment	Hearing Impairment	Physical and Special Health Problems	Retardation	Learning Disabilities	Behavioral Disorders/ Emotional Handicaps
Tension and anxiety facing unknown	Inattention	May be independent	Generally slow	Inadequate impulse control	Inadequate impulse control
Seems uninterested in environment	Seems disinterested in environment	May be dependent	Sometimes apathetic	May fail to show common sense	Unable to handle stress
No nonverbal communication	May be stubborn, shy, withdrawn	May show physical fears or have over concern with health	Inadequate impulse control	May become confused easily	May fail to show common sense
Delayed development	Tend to avoid group activities	Possible separation problems in young children	Delayed speech and language development	Overattention to detail	May become confused easily
Delayed development in speech and language	Lack of sense of humor		May fail to show common sense		Frequent crying and temper tantrums
	Delayed development in speech and language		May become confused easily		Depression
	Behavior and personality problems				Withdrawal into fantasy
					Exaggerated fears and phobias
					Perfectionism

expectations are adapted. In learning to teach and manage students with mild handicaps in the regular classroom, teachers increase sensitivity and understanding. They become knowledgeable of teaching and management techniques that can be incorporated in the classroom and expand their ability to address a wider range of individual differences.

Goals for Exceptional Students and Individual Learners

As teachers gain knowledge of the students, they are better able to put individual differences in perspective and identify goals. The long-term goals of education are the same for both handicapped and nonhandicapped students but the short-term goals may vary.

Goals are based upon knowledge of students, realistic expectations, and the belief that they can learn and function. They may include the following:

Learning
- To teach content area concepts and skills
- To modify curriculum to meet special needs
- To guide students to achieve in subject areas within the limits of their abilities
- To teach students to learn how to learn

Physical
- To develop the ability to attend and maintain task orientation
- To teach acceptable behavior
- To improve motor skills and coordination

Social
- To develop interpersonal relationships among peers and adults
- To teach prevocational skills and to assist students in making vocational decisions
- To increase the ability of students to communicate effectively

Personal/Psychological
- To provide for the development of self-management skills
- To develop a positive self-concept
- To teach skills in decision making, problem solving, self-discipline, self-control, and coping
- To motivate students to achieve and develop self-motivation
- To encourage students to formulate their own goals

Hopefully, knowledge and understanding of students with special needs will give teachers confidence in working to fulfill these needs. Students must also be taught to accept responsibility and to cooperate with teachers in the realization of these goals. The following chapters address these goals by dealing with the behaviors and characteristics listed, within the context of environmental preparation, behavior management, curriculum planning, and academic instruction.

SUMMARY

Exceptional students differ from others in mental, sensory, or communication abilities; in behavior; or in physical characteristics. They have traditionally been grouped into disability categories. Although there is considerable variation across the country, the categories typically are: mental retardation, learning disabilities, giftedness, visual impairments, hearing impairments, physical handicaps, communication disorders, behavior disorders or emotional handicaps, and multiply handicapping conditions.

Although categorization has been the organizational structure of special education, there has been considerable criticism of its negative aspects: emphasis on the individual's limitations, labeling, stereotyping, and the possibility of self-fulfilling prophecy. Further, categorization does not provide sufficient information for individual planning and intervention.

The alternative is the noncategorical approach that recognizes that all students, including the nonhandicapped, share the same basic characteristics. Individual learners are students who have not been identified as exceptional but who demonstrate learning and behavior problems that can be addressed by the same methods as those used with exceptional students. The noncategorical approach also posits that behaviors exhibited by exceptional students occur *across* rather than *within* categories.

The following characteristics were discussed. Learning characteristics include reasoning, learning skills, task avoidance, memory, conceptualization and generalization, and language ability. Physical characteristics are hyperactivity, attentional deficit disorders, distractibility, impulsivity, motor coordination, and perseveration. Social characteristics include social development and peer relationships. Personal/psychological characteristics are self-concept, body image, self-management, motivation, learned helplessness, emotional lability, hypersensitivity, goal gratification, and low frustration tolerance. Positive characteristics of exceptional students are included. These characteristics are the basis for individual educational planning and the establishment of goals.

REFERENCES

Alvino, J.; McDonnel, R. C.; & Richert, S. (1981). National survey of identification practices in gifted and talented education. *Exceptional Children, 48,* 124–132.

Ames, L. B. (1983). Learning disability: truth or trap? *Journal of Learning Disabilities, 16,* 19–20.

Barraga, N. C. (1983). *Visual handicaps and learning.* Austin, TX: Exceptional Resources.

Berdine, W. H., & Cegelka, P. T. (1980). *Teaching the trainable retarded.* Columbus, OH: Merrill.

Bloom, L., & Lahey, M. (1978). *Language development and language disorders.* New York: Wiley.

Brady, M.; Conroy, M.; & Langford, C. (1984). Current issues and practices affecting the development of noncategorical programs for students and teachers. *Teacher Education and Special Education, 7,* 20–26.

Bruininks, R. H.; Woodcock, R. W.; Weatherman, R. F.; & Hill, B. K. (1984). *Scales of independent behavior: Woodcock–Johnson psycho-educational battery, Part four.* Allen, TX: Teaching Resources.

Cruickshank, W. M. (1983). Learning disabilities: A neuropsychological dysfunction. *Journal of Learning Disabilities, 16,* 27–29.

Fox, L. (1981). Identification of the academically gifted. *American Psychologist, 36,* 1103–1111.

Gallagher, J. J. (1985). *Teaching the gifted child* (3rd ed.). Boston: Allyn and Bacon.

Gearheart, B. R., & Weishahn, M. W. (1976). *The handicapped child in the regular classroom.* St. Louis: Mosby.

Grossman, H. J. (Ed.) (1983). *Classification in mental retardation* (1983 revision). Washington, DC: American Association on Mental Deficiency.

Hallahan, D. P., & Kauffman, J. M. (1976). *Introduction to learning disabilities: A psychobehavioral approach.* Englewood Cliffs, NJ: Prentice-Hall.

Huberty, T. J.; Koller, J. R.; & Ten Brink, T. D. (1980). Adaptive behavior in the definition of mental retardation. *Exceptional Children, 46,* 256–261.

Keogh, B. K. (1983). Classification, compliance, and confusion. *Journal of Learning Disabilities, 16,* 25.

Kirk, S. A., & Gallagher, J. J. (1986). *Educating exceptional children* (5th ed.). Boston: Houghton Mifflin.

Kirk, S. A., & Kirk, W. D. (1983). On defining learning disabilities. *Journal of Learning Disabilities, 16,* 20–21.

Lambert, N., & Windmiller, M. (1981). *AAMD adaptive behavior scale, School edition.* Monterey, CA: American Association on Mental Deficiency.

Lilly, S. (1982). The education of mildly handicapped children and implications for teacher education. In M. Reynolds (Ed.). *The future of mainstreaming: Next steps in teacher education.* Minneapolis: University of Minnesota.

Lowenbraun, S., & Thompson, M. D. (1986). Hearing impairments. In N. G. Haring, & L. McCormick (Eds.). *Exceptional children and youth: An introduction to special education* (4th ed.) (pp. 359–395). Columbus, OH: Merrill.

Marland, S. P. (1972). *Education of the gifted and talented: Report to the Congress of the United States by the United States Commissioner of Education.* Washington, DC: Government Printing Office.

Martin, G. J., & Hoben, M. (1977). *Supporting visually impaired students in the mainstream.* Reston, VA: Council for Exceptional Children.

Mercer, J. R., & Lewis, J. F. (1977). *Adaptive behavior scale for children: Parent interview manual.* New York: Psychological Corporation.

National Joint Committee on Learning Disabilities, (1987). 1. Learning disabilities: Issues on definition. *Journal of Learning Disabilities, 20,* 107–108. Author.

National Society to Prevent Blindness. (1966). *Manual on use of the NSPB standard classification of causes of severe vision impairment and blindness: Index of diagnostic terms pertaining to severe vision impairment and blindness.* New York: Author.

Peterson, R. L.; Zabel, R. H.; Smith, C. R.; & White, M. A. (1983). Cascade of services model and emotionally disabled students. *Exceptional Children, 49,* 404–408.

Rappaport, S. R. (1966). Personality factors teachers need for relationship structure. In W. M. Cruickshank (Ed.). *The teacher of brain-injured children: A discussion of the bases for competency* (pp. 49–55). Syracuse, NY: Syracuse University Press.

Sabatino, D. A. (1983). "The house that Jack built." *Journal of Learning Disabilities, 16,* 26–27.

Skinner, B. F. (1968). *The technology of teaching.* New York: Appleton-Century-Crofts.

Sparrow, S. A.; Balla, D. A.; & Cicchetti, D. V. (1984). *Vineland adaptive behavior scale.* Circle Pines, MN: American Guidance Service.

Thomason, J. (1981). Education of the gifted: A challenge and a promise. *Exceptional Children, 48,* 101–103.

U.S. Office of Education. (1977, August 23). Education of handicapped children: Implementation of Part B of the Education for Handicapped Act. *Federal Register, Part II, 42*(163). Washington, DC: U.S. Department of Health, Education, and Welfare.

U.S. Office of Education. (1977, December 29). Assistance to states for education of handicapped children: Procedures for evaluating specific learning disabilities. *Federal Register, Part III, 42*(250). Washington, DC: U.S. Department of Health, Education, and Welfare.

Van Riper, C. (1978). *Speech correction: Principles and methods* (6th ed.). Englewood Cliffs, NJ: Prentice-Hall.

Whitmore, J. R. (1980). *Giftedness, conflict, and underachievement.* Boston: Allyn and Bacon.

SUGGESTED READINGS

Hardman, M. L.; Drew, C. J.; & Egan, M. W. (1987). *Human exceptionality: Society, school and family.* Boston: Allyn and Bacon.

Hewett, F. M., & Forness, S. R. (1984). *Education of exceptional learners* (3rd ed.). Boston: Allyn and Bacon.

Kauffman, J. M., & Hallahan, D. P. (Eds.). (1981). *Handbook of special education.* Englewood Cliffs, NJ: Prentice-Hall.

Miller, T. L., & Davis, E. E. (Eds.). (1982). *The mildly handicapped student.* New York: Grune & Stratton.

Orlansky, M. D., & Heward, W. L. (1981). *Voices: Interviews with handicapped people.* Columbus, OH: Merrill.

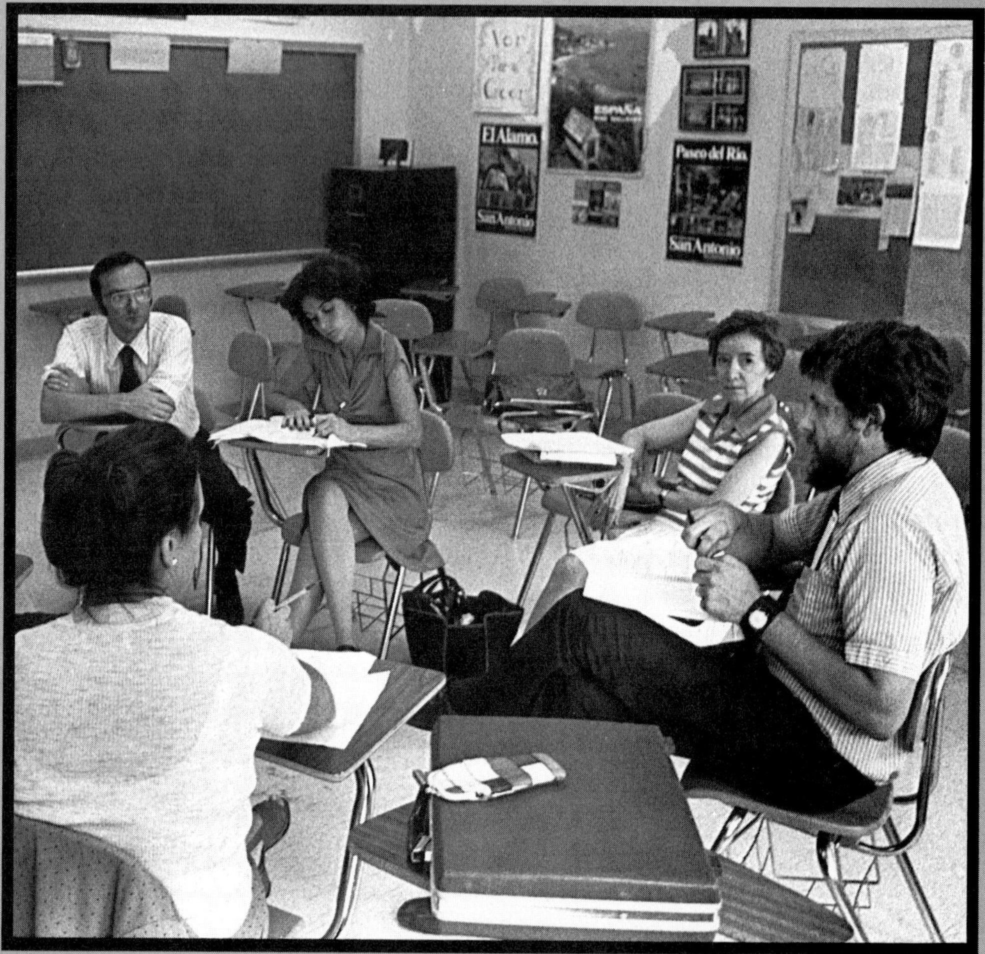
El Alamo.
San Antonio
ESPAÑA
Paseo del Rio.
San Antonio

3

Planning and Coordinating Educational Services

WHETHER STUDENTS ARE assigned to a special class or receive supplementary services, they have particular needs that cannot be met in the regular class alone. The goal of providing optimal educational opportunity and the special methods and techniques employed in instruction are applicable to all students with various needs. If these objectives are to be reached, it is of paramount importance that educational experiences are planned and coordinated by the professionals involved, working and communicating together.

Determining the Need for Services

At the outset of the school year, some students will already have been scheduled for supplementary services or will be placed in a special setting. Teachers and other professionals (tutors, special teachers, therapists) need to establish a procedure for communicating and working together.

As the year progresses, other students will require special attention. Usually, attempts will be made to aid these students within the classroom structure by providing corrective or individualized instruction or additional materials. Environmental changes such as preferential seating may be made. For students whose problems are behavioral, a management program is established.

Should these interventions be unsuccessful, teachers may examine office records and reports for clues on solving the problem. Other professional personnel—the principal, counselor, nurse, other teachers in departmentalized schools, or former teachers—may be consulted. Additional options are to provide volunteer or peer tutoring or to assign a remedial reading or mathematics teacher.

At times, students demonstrate such severe behaviors or react to family crises in such harmful ways that immediate action must be taken. Professionals may need to forgo data gathering and committee meetings to facilitate a prompt solution. For most students the usual procedures for referral to special services are followed.

The Decision to Refer

Referring a student for extensive testing and consideration for placement is a serious step and one which should be undertaken only after other options have been exhausted. In some schools the decision to refer is the responsibility of the teacher in consultation with the building principal and pupil personnel coordinator. This decision must be made with care. Referral is to be made if the student continues to be unable to perform academically, exhibits behaviors significantly different from those of others, and/or has not responded to individual attention and intervention.

Teachers are sometimes concerned that school administrators or other teachers will question their ability if they make a referral. It is impossible to handle some individual situations in the regular classroom regardless of competence and experience. One teacher cannot solve the difficulties of all students, and the welfare of the student is the first priority. If teachers know that they have tried to examine and understand the student's individual differences and have made a sincere effort to assist the student within the limitations imposed by class size and resources available, they should not hesitate to make the referral.

Prereferral Activities

The tasks to be completed as part of the prereferral consist of data gathering, parent contact, and completion of the referral form.

Data Gathering   Teachers provide information about students and the steps taken to this point to address the problem. The assessment team is assisted when the activities on the checklist in Figure 3.1 are completed.

Informing Parents About the Referral   Whether the referral continues depends upon the informed consent of the parents. A conference, at which the following information as required by PL 94–142, is held:

1. The reason for referral is presented.
2. A description of the diagnostic procedures, including an enumeration of the areas to be assessed, is reviewed.
3. All resulting data will be confidential, and release of information to others will be controlled solely by the parents.
4. Parents have the right to refuse referral and testing.
5. A placement committee is to be convened to review all test data, and parents will be expected to participate in decisions.
6. The range of recommendations, including the possibility of placement in a special education class, that may result from the testing and placement committee conference is stated.

FIGURE 3.1

Checklist of Prereferral Activities

Examine Data in the Cumulative Folder
 1. Birthdate and age at school entrance _____
 2. Kindergarten attendance _____
 3. Grade levels repeated _____
 4. School achievement _____
 5. Test results _____
 6. Anecdotal information _____
 7. Attendance patterns _____

Examine School Screening Results
 1. Vision _____
 2. Hearing _____
 3. Speech _____

Examine Other Medical Records
 1. Reports from physicians _____
 2. Notifications from parents _____
 3. Medication history _____
 4. Allergies; special health conditions _____

Consultation
 1. Former teachers _____
 2. Resource personnel _____
 3. Principal _____
 4. Parents _____

Maintenance of Logs, Anecdotal Records, and Other Information
 1. Daily behaviors _____
 2. Academic performance _____
 3. Academic skills checklist _____
 4. Folder of work samples _____
 5. Remedial techniques attempted _____
 6. Individual procedures used _____

7. Parents have the right to seek an alternative evaluation after learning of the school's findings and recommendations and have the right to submit these data for consideration along with those generated by the school.
8. Parents have the right to reject recommendations made by the placement committee.
9. Parents have recourse through due process proceedings should they and school personnel reach an impasse regarding placement.
10. Parents must be notified for approval if any changes are subsequently made in the placement or program.

Parents then are requested to sign an informed consent to indicate permission for the referral to proceed.

Completion of the Referral Form Each special services unit has a preferred form and routing procedure. Commonly, the form requests the kinds of information given in Figure 3.1 in the checklist of prereferral data. Conscientious completion of the form usually expedites the referral process. Resource personnel can assist regular teachers in completing this form.

When the referral is received, the four major phases of activity are assessment, planning, accuracy, and intervention. The first three are discussed in this chapter. Intervention is addressed in subsequent chapters.

Assessment Procedures

Assessment is conducted by a multidisciplinary team consisting of the school psychologist and others, who may include the teacher, speech/language pathologist, school nurse, and a teacher or administrator knowledgeable about special education. The assessment is multifactoral, examining all areas of functioning.

The areas of testing include:

- Intellectual functioning
- Academic achievement
    General achievement survey
    Spelling
    Reading: basic skills and comprehension
    Mathematics: calculation and reasoning
- Language
    Receptive language
        Vocabulary
        Grammatic understanding
        Listening comprehension
    Expressive language
        Vocabulary
        Grammatic expression
        Oral communication
        Written expression
- Speech
- Affective and emotional development
- Perceptual-motor functioning
- Behavior
    Adaptive behavior
    Classroom behavior
    Social behavior
- Health
    General health
    Vision
    Hearing

The assessment data then are organized into a written report.

Planning

The Planning Committee A representative of the assessment team, usually the school psychologist, must be a member of the planning committee. Other members include a school administrator, the referring teacher, a teacher knowledgeable about special students (preferably the receiving teacher if the student is likely to be placed in a special class), the parents, and when feasible, the student.

The committee reviews all data—the material on the referral form, the written report of the assessment team, and information from the referring teacher. Next, they ascertain the eligibility for special services. Considerations are given to federal and state legal requirements, state department guidelines, and local practices. The decision affects the student and his or her family not only for the present but also in the future.

Ineligibility for Special Services Students who are ineligible for special services remain in the regular classroom. Some students who have been referred for special services may have needs that can be met in the regular classroom by environmental modification and individualization through curriculum adaptations, careful selection of methods, and adjustments in assignments and testing.

Eligibility for Special Services If the committee decides to place the student in a special educational program, they must determine the nature of the intervention to be initiated. They specify the type of education and/or therapeutic activities that have the potential for meeting the demonstrated needs. They formulate goals and objectives. At the same time they determine placement.

Sandra, a third grader, has above average mental ability and is in the top reading group. However, she has difficulty with simple arithmetic problems and sometimes cries in frustration about the arithmetic assignment. Diagnostic testing reveals an erratic pattern of mathematics skills and concepts extending back to readiness abilities. Her deficits are significant enough to qualify her for a learning disabilities program.

The following intervention was proposed:

1. *Goal: Learn identified math skills and concepts from the readiness level to present grade placement.*
2. *Plan: Complete reteaching of math skills and concepts through the use of a commercial, structured program.*
3. *Placement: Place in a regular class and resource room. Sandra will remain in the regular class for all subjects except math. During that period she will go to a resource room for instruction.*

Placement

Placement is the setting(s) in which the educational program is activated. Many more students are remaining in regular classes and frequently are receiving supplementary services. Students with more serious learning problems and disabilities are placed in a resource room or part-time special class. Infrequently, a full-time special class is recommended. A few students may temporarily receive homebound or hospital instruction. Also, a special school or nonschool setting is provided.

Regular Class With Consultive Services Students are assigned to the regular classroom and receive no direct special services. A consulting or support teacher, however, provides indirect services by working with the classroom teacher, interpreting the assessment data and the committee's decisions. Teachers are helped in becoming knowledgeable about the limitations imposed by the handicapping condition and about specific learning behaviors that might realistically be expected. Further assistance is provided in integrating the Individual Educational Plan (IEP) objectives within the classroom curriculum. Support is given in the complex job of planning and monitoring an educational program for a large class. Through discussions of alternative instructional techniques, classroom teachers can expand their repertoire of methods, which benefit other students. Finally, the consulting or support teacher is responsible for researching possible procedures, locating and providing new materials, and guiding the continuing evaluation of exceptional students.

Regular Class With Supplementary Services Students remain in the regular class but receive additional services such as speech therapy, counseling, remediation for visual or hearing disabilities, or physical or occupational therapy.

In addition, teachers may use classroom activities that augment the work being done by the specialist. They complement the other professional's program, for example, by proper response to a speech handicapped student using a language master to give a multisensory approach to language development or by adoption of particular management procedures for students in counseling.

Regular Class With Tutoring In some situations tutors trained in special education techniques assume the responsibility to provide a total program in one or more academic areas or to provide supportive instruction in subjects that the student is studying in the regular class. In both cases, but particularly in the latter, coordination of curriculum objectives and approaches is imperative.

Resource Room A resource room is a special educational setting in which identified exceptional students receive direct instruction in content areas needing remediation. They are members of the regular class who move to the resource room at scheduled times.

Scope and Operation Instruction, depending on state requirements, is given individually, in small groups, or in a large group of varying numbers. Students are grouped according to ability and functional level. Subjects to be taught are designated in the IEP. Students receive instruction in all skills appropriate to their grade level (developmental aspect). Goals and objectives of the IEP must be taught as well as skills that are deficient (remedial aspect).

In some models, only reading and mathematics are taught; in others, all subjects are included. Many teachers include affective education as a part of the curriculum. They also address behavior, motivation, and study and organizational skills. In some instances, instruction involves only reinforcement of materials taught in the regular class.

The amount of individual versus group instruction depends upon the number of students in the program and scheduling. There is no one "correct" way to implement a resource room program. The plan is determined by the needs of the individual students.

Time in the Resource Room   For some students the least restrictive environment means being in the resource room for all subjects other than music, art, and gym. Others receive instruction in one or two subjects. The important consideration is that sufficient time is allowed for concentrated, in-depth instruction and practice.

Part-Time Special Class   A less common placement occurs when students leave the regular class to receive instruction at a designated time in a self-contained special class. This may be needed if the handicapping conditions make students more compatible with the special class group or if the special class curriculum is consistent with students' needs.

Self-Contained Special Class   Students spend the entire day in the classroom with a special teacher. The teacher is responsible for all subjects, and the students attend music, art, gym, lunch, and other activities as a group. In some areas of exceptionality (such as mental retardation), a special curriculum may be followed. In classes for students with severe behavior disorders, the regular curriculum is used but emphasis is placed on behavior management, social skills, and interpersonal relationships.

Although self-contained classes are a necessary part of the continuum of services for exceptional students, they are presently used only for severely impaired students or in settings other than the public school.

Homebound Instruction   Some students receive homebound instruction from an itinerant tutor during the period of convalescence after an injury, surgery, or serious illness. Some students who are severely impaired may not attend school and must be educated in their homes. To keep students in touch with the school program, closed circuit television may be used. In addition, telephone communication using special equipment in the classroom allows participation with the entire class.

Hospital Instruction   Some students with orthopedic or special health problems may spend extended periods of time in a hospital. Continuity of educational experiences may be difficult to maintain not only because of intermittent attendance but also because of limitations imposed by physical conditions and medical treatment. The school system may need to provide tutors who give basic instruction. Some school systems employ teachers who work in the hospital. The classroom teacher can cooperate with the hospital teacher in providing curriculum and methods information, materials, and, in some cases, worksheets. Students cannot be expected to maintain the amount or pace of class work and may need further consideration when they return to the classroom.

Special School or Nonschool Setting   Students who are not enrolled in public schools may receive training full-time in a separate setting. This setting may be either a day school or a residential facility.

Students with severe and/or multiple handicaps may live at home while attending a day school. Self-help and social skills, a modified academic program, and prevocational competencies are included in the curriculum. When students are older, they may attend a vocational training school, become employed in a sheltered workshop or receive appropriate services through a rehabilitation agency.

The most severely impaired or students with emotional problems may live in a residential institution. Classrooms are maintained by certified teachers trained to work with this population.

It may be necessary for some students to be removed from the public school and placed in one of these settings. Such arrangements take considerable time. During this period, teachers continue to include students in classroom activities and to expect them to meet limited educational and behavioral demands. Responsibility terminates only when students are officially removed from the class. Later, teachers may be asked to provide information concerning achievement, learning characteristics, and behaviors to professionals in the new setting.

When a suitable placement is determined, the committee incorporates their decisions into the IEP.

The Individual Educational Plan

One of the requirements of PL 94–142 is that an IEP be developed and written for each identified exceptional student for whom special educational or other support services are to be provided. Students who may be recognized as handicapped (for example, students with visual impairments) but who have no modifications of program or instruction need not have an IEP.

The content of the IEP is based on individual goals and objectives. The law specifies that the document should include the following:

1. The student's present level of academic performance
2. Annual goals of the program
3. Short-term objectives that constitute the basis for the special instruction or other interventions
4. Identification of special services that are needed
5. Time references for initiation of the program and anticipated length of time needed to achieve the stated goals
6. Expected portion of the student's time that will be spent with nonhandicapped students
7. Evaluation procedures

EXAMPLES OF IEP GOALS AND OBJECTIVES

Sally, an eleventh grader with cerebral palsy, cannot write reports in American history and English. She has not learned how to write paragraphs, to express her thoughts in written form, or to use periods, commas, and quotation marks correctly.

The following IEP goals and objectives were planned:

1. Goal I: *To improve paragraph structure*
   Objectives

1. *Given a topic, Sally will select details to support the topic.*
2. *Given a topic sentence, Sally will write supporting sentences.*
3. *On the computer, Sally will write a paragraph with a topic sentence and three to ten detail sentences using indentation.*

2. Goal II: *To improve written expression skills*
   Objectives
   1. *In a twenty-minute period, Sally will write sentences about a particular experience.*
   2. *Given five simple sentences, Sally will use descriptive words to enhance the ideas.*
   3. *Given the theme, Sally will write eight sentences about a favorite animal.*

3. Goal III: *To use correct punctuation*
   Objectives
   1. *On the computer and in written assignments, Sally will use periods at the end of sentences, with initials and abbreviations with 90 percent accuracy.*
   2. *In every sentence, Sally will write commas in a series—between city and state, between month and year, after years and months, after the greeting and closing in a letter, and in direct quotations.*
   3. *Given a worksheet, Sally will use quotation marks before and after direct quotations and in titles of songs, poems, and articles.*

Annual Goals

In developing goals, priorities are established based on test results and information from the teacher. The main concepts that the student needs to learn are listed, for example, in reading, to improve decoding or comprehension skills, or to increase word-recognition or word-analysis skills. In math, goals may be listed such as computation, multiplication, division, fractions, decimals, and measurement skills. Goals for study and organizational skills, affective development, and behavior may also be included.

Short-Term Objectives

There is probably no other single requirement of the IEP over which there is so much divergence in practice than the formation of short term objectives. Some school systems contain their IEPs in one or two pages, thus limiting the number of short-term objectives that might be included. Others have documents that are several pages in length and may even include lesson plans (Odle & Galtelli, 1980). Such decisions remain the prerogative of state and local administrations. However, the task of writing the IEP can become so burdensome as to be counterproductive. If too many objectives are listed, it may not be possible to accomplish all of them. If they are too detailed, the program becomes rigid; teachers are unable to present other concepts not mentioned in the IEP that may need to be taught. Hayes (1977) recommends that a few short-term objectives, which are important steps toward the realization of the annual goals, are sufficient. The planning committee should not usurp the educational expertise of teachers. Teachers must retain the professional responsibility to determine the best procedures for each individual student in reaching goals.

Other concerns are related to the specificity of the goals and objectives in describing expected instructional outcomes. Some are stated in general terms whereas others are highly detailed, conforming to Mager's (1975) criteria for behavioral objectives. It is the authors' opinion that a compromise must be made to create objectives that are neither too general nor too specific. Short-term objectives as listed in the IEP must be stated in behavioral terms to specify expectations and to give teachers and other personnel curriculum directives. If the goals and objectives are not reached, evaluation procedures can then pinpoint difficulties so that revisions of the program can be made.

Additional Special Services

All services such as speech therapy or special transportation needed by the student are listed.

Time References

Dates for the beginning of services and time estimates expected for goal achievement are given.

Time Spent in the Regular Class Setting

A major aspect of the law is the requirement that students with handicaps be educated in the least restrictive environment. Thus, the estimated time that the student will spend with nonhandicapped peers is prescribed.

Evaluation

The achievement of short-term objectives and annual goals is to be objectively measured. The IEP identifies the evaluation procedures and the times at which they will be employed.

Parent Approval

The parents or guardians are requested to provide approval of the program and informed consent to its implementation by signing the document. The IEP is to be reviewed and/or revised annually, and the parents are requested to provide approval.

Accountability and the Individual Educational Plan

Concern has been expressed that the IEP might become a "contract" and that the school or teachers might be held legally accountable for achievement of the specified goals and objectives. However, comments of clarification, which are included in the law, do protect both agency and teachers from liability. The section states that both the school and teachers must make "good faith" efforts to assist the student in achieving the goals and objectives listed in the IEP [PL 94–142; Final Regulations, Section 127a, 349; 1977 (Comments)]. This same section, however, supports the parents' right to question revisions and resort to due process procedures if they feel such "good faith" efforts are not being made.

To educators the document has advantages. As a curriculum specification, it provides a consensus of direction for parents and professionals for the educational program. The IEP provides for individualization of the curriculum. Once it has been written, it can become a viable working document indicating a unity of purpose and providing direction and organization for teachers in curriculum and instructional procedures.

Role of the Teacher in the IEP

As members of IEP committees, classroom teachers provide input in writing the plan. They can describe present functioning and advise on needed intervention in conjunction with testing results. Teachers implement objectives as they apply to regular class subjects. For example, if students are expected to maintain assignment logs, teachers require them in regular class subjects.

Prior to the annual review, special education teachers consult with regular teachers. Together they assess progress and the necessity for improvement in organizational or study skills and social or behavioral functioning. They determine the extent of services in regular class subjects and accommodations to be made in the regular class.

Placement in a Regular and a Special Setting

Planning and Preparation

Placement into a special setting in addition to the regular class is facilitated with careful planning and preparation. It includes determining responsibility for instruction, curriculum planning, scheduling, the role of regular classroom teachers, preparation of exceptional students, preparation of students in the regular class, and defining reasonable expectations.

Responsibility for Instruction The responsibility for instruction of any student—gifted, nonhandicapped, exceptional—belongs to the classroom teacher to whom the student is assigned. For students who receive full-time instruction in a special class, the special teacher plans curriculum and implements IEP objectives. When an exceptional learner is placed in a regular class and a resource room, the subjects to be taught in each setting must be specified and assigned to the respective teachers. If tutors teach a subject, they manage that subject. If tutors and regular teachers share the instruction for the same subject, they also share the responsibility for planning and the IEP. If consultive services are provided in a regular classroom in which students are enrolled full-time, the regular teacher plans and implements the program. Each teacher must carefully determine who keeps records and who does the necessary paperwork.

Although the responsibility for instruction belongs to the teacher of the classroom in which students are assigned, other personnel may provide direct or indirect services from consulting or counseling to a friendly word from the cafeteria workers. The entire school system has the responsibility to work together for the education of all students in the community. Therefore *all* students belong to *all* professionals.

Curriculum Planning Special teachers plan the curriculum for subjects taught in the special class based on the IEP and the functional level of students. Regular curriculum may be adapted, or special programs may be used. Instruction—developmental and remedial—is planned sequentially, emphasizing learning modality and adapting to physical limitations. Emphasis is on learning how to learn and affective education. The goal is to return students to the regular class if possible. Regular teachers plan curriculum for subjects taught in the regular class.

Scheduling Scheduling ranks second in a list of regular classroom teacher concerns in planning for special education students (Treblas, McCormick, & Cooper, 1982). Often the master schedule limits teachers in arranging schedules for exceptional students. They must be in the resource room for instruction in subjects needing remediation during the time period when these subjects are taught in the regular class. They must also participate with the regular class in nonacademic and academic subjects in which they are on grade level. Arranging for each student to receive instruction in all academic and nonacademic subjects is a major challenge to special education teachers. When a student is placed in a special program, teachers cooperate with the special teacher who is usually responsible for scheduling. Regular teachers need to be aware of the factors, be it speech therapy or classes in a resource room, that are involved in determining satisfactory schedules for each student. Usually they are asked to give the special teacher a copy of their schedule.

Nonacademic Subjects The master schedule for music, art, and gym classes is predetermined by the teaching assignments of those teachers. Each regular and special teacher plans around these classes.

Regular Class Subjects When students are in the regular class for a subject such as mathematics, they must be in the room when this subject is taught. If they are to receive remediation in a particular subject, they should be out of the room when that subject is taught. Schedules of teachers, tutors, and resource teachers are planned accordingly. Students with learning deficits cannot be expected to maintain work in two settings because of different expectations, assignment demands, and teaching styles.

A scheduling disadvantage is that it locks regular teachers into a schedule. For example, a science class must end at 1:40 PM so that students can return to the resource room for remedial instruction. Inconvenience can be reduced and occasional adjustments made when both teachers are flexible and when they communicate regularly.

A copy of the schedule should be provided to both classroom teachers and students. It is students' responsibility to be in the right place at the appropriate time.

This arrangement not only eliminates the need for teachers to remind students but also improves their self management skills.

Scheduling Objectives   Scheduling will be affected by the length of time needed in the special setting to address the IEP objectives. Because instruction is both developmental and remedial, sufficient time must be allowed to present all necessary concepts. Further, students with similar ability levels and IEP objectives must meet at the same time.

Travel Time   Individual students go to the resource room at different time periods because of regular class schedules. If possible, schedules should be arranged to minimize numerous trips. Such an arrangement reduces the need to monitor students whose hall behavior may be disruptive or those who prefer to take the "long way" to the other class.

Socialization   When classes are departmentalized, it is advantageous for exceptional students to remain with one group. They can "belong" to the class and make friends more easily. It is important for those in special programs to participate in class activities, parties, assemblies, and field trips.

Additional Planning Considerations

Paperwork   Special education teachers accept that they will do much paperwork—IEPs, written records of individual pupil progress, accurate test data on permanent records, written communication to parents and regular teachers—in addition to routine records, planning, and grading. Usually no additional planning time is given special teachers, and it becomes a challenge to organize and complete these tasks.

Considering the paperwork and the large number of students in regular classes, special teachers should avoid asking regular teachers to do substantial amounts of additional paperwork.

Time   Having sufficient time is a continuing problem for teachers. For special education teachers the preponderance of work with exceptional students is on an individual, rather than group, basis and involves separate lesson plans for individuals in diverse subjects each day. In addition, time for paperwork, communication with teachers and support personnel, and planning becomes a challenge. Regular teachers spend additional time talking with special teachers, writing notes, adjusting assignments, and providing individual attention to exceptional students. Administrators must also spend a proportionately large amount of time in serving the needs of special education students.

Role of Regular Classroom Teachers

Specific expectations are to

- Become apprised of students' academic and social/emotional needs.
- Become familiar with the IEP and determine with special teachers how goals and objectives can be reinforced in the regular class.

- Make students a part of all class activities.
- Work with special education teachers or the consultant in solving problems occurring in class, on the playground, on the bus, and in similar places.
- Accommodate individual differences in teaching strategies, in activities, and when grouping.
- Communicate regularly with special teachers and, when appropriate, with the special education consultant or director.
- Set an example of acceptance for regular students.

Preparation of Exceptional Students Before students enter the special class, the resource teacher has the responsibility to become acquainted with them; to show them the resource room; and to explain the rules, consequences, expectations, and routine. Adjustment is easier when students come informally into the room to meet other class members. They must be aware of the purpose of the class. If they verbalize why they are there and if goals are discussed, students can resolve questions about placement and be ready to participate productively. Students must know that it is alright to make mistakes, that they will be taught in a way that they can learn.

In this orientation, students learn that the teacher understands their point of view. They will have two teachers, two or more classrooms, two sets of expectations, and possibly different rules. They have experienced failure, frustration, and, too often, ridicule. Teachers need to verbalize understanding of their difficulty. It can be pointed out that many students leave the regular class at different times of the day for band, chorus, remedial reading or math, tutoring, speech, or to help in the cafeteria. They must be reassured that they do not have to do the whole job alone; that teachers and they both have responsibilities; and that the teachers, parents, and they will work together. These comments, stated sincerely, often serve as motivation.

Defining Reasonable Expectations Every student, not just exceptional students, must know what is expected of them. In the regular class some adjustments can be made for physical or sensory limitations, but generally exceptional students must be able to perform, with accommodations, as their peers do.

In the resource room, expectations are based on current levels of functioning. At first, work might be oral until students can follow directions, write adequately, and/or complete a task. If assignments are adjusted, they know that as they improve, they will be expected to do more. In *all* instances, they are to do their best.

Preparation of Regular Class Students When students with retardation, physical handicaps, visual or hearing impairments, or learning disabilities attend public schools, nonhandicapped students must be aware of the importance of an accepting attitude. Prior to the time students with handicaps enter the class, regular students should discuss differences in all people as well as facts about the handicapping condition. They can determine when to assist their new classmates and when they should let them do things for themselves. They can consider that many exceptional students need little, if any, assistance; that they are more like them than different; and that they are capable of being in a regular class and are to be welcomed like any new student.

Time must be provided to answer questions, to prevent misunderstanding, and to build positive attitudes. In a few situations, the special teacher may address the regular class to discuss special handicapping conditions.

Coordinating Services

When students are placed in two educational settings such as a regular class and a resource room, it is imperative that services be coordinated. Because school systems do not usually employ case managers, the director of special education or the principal are responsible for leadership roles. It is incumbent on the professionals in the two settings to coordinate educational activities by effective, continuing communication and by cooperating in such areas as students' organization and study skills, written work and tests, monitoring behavior, and grading.

Communication

Productivity in each setting and in overall child development is facilitated by communication among all professionals. Speece and Mandell (1980, p. 55) state that a major role of each resource room program is "intensive communication." In the context of resource services, communication involves possessing interpersonal communication skills and working effectively with teachers, other professionals, administrators, parents, and students Box 3.1.

BOX 3.1

Interpersonal Communication Skills

Teachers can develop interpersonal communication skills by

- Accepting each student as he or she is.
- Establishing empathy and rapport.
- Understanding individual differences in professionals and students
- Concentrating on what is being said and not said.
- Having a positive, supportive attitude.
- Looking at all points of view.
- Encouraging students and adults to clarify what they mean to prevent assumptions and misunderstandings.
- Working to change attitudes when necessary.
- Emphasizing personal contact.
- Having a good self-image.

Communication With Teachers

Staff Preparation In service training is essential to the success of any type of program. It is necessary to accept that difficulties and frustrations exist and that many problems can be solved through dialogue.

If students are to be in regular classes, special teachers have the responsibility to talk to their teachers at the beginning of the year, familiarizing them with their strengths and weaknesses, and to discuss the IEP, expectations, and consistent management.

It is also important for special teachers to get to know regular teachers, to express appreciation for cooperation, to use their professional expertise and to inform them of test results and placement changes.

Ongoing Communication Verbal and written communication between resource and regular teachers continues at regular intervals throughout the school year. It must be open and honest with both teachers feeling free to ask questions. Contacts must necessarily be brief and should be at the convenience of regular teachers. Frequency is determined by individual need. Usually a weekly discussion or report is sufficient, although in some cases daily contact may be necessary. A form to maintain a weekly written check on performance and assignments saves time. (Figure 3.2). Special teachers work to accommodate regular teachers although flexibility by all teachers is desirable. Interrupting either class must be avoided. Ideally, time should be provided by the administration.

Communication With Administrators The amount of communication with administrators depends upon the individual. Some principals want to be thoroughly informed about each student, and others do not. It is a courtesy to give them copies of parent communiques and to inform them about important decisions and occurrences. Telling them about positive feedback from parents, happenings, and behaviors and inviting them to visit the classroom indicates how the program is successful.

Communication With Parents The teachers' role with parents is to communicate about the students—goals, testing, academic ability, behavior, and social performance—and about school policies, the IEP, and the overall plan for students. Discussion about attitudes and behavior at home, as it is different from or similar to that at school, gives insight into students' problems. Talking about parents' personal lives is best left to other professionals, although referral to agencies is needed at times. Some special teachers prefer to write notes on a weekly basis in addition to report cards, parent conferences, phone calls, homework notes, and positive notes such as "happigrams."

Communication With Students Establishing good communication with students involves using language that they can understand without talking down to them. Many exceptional students do not listen to everything that is said or are overly stimulated by too much talk. It is important to speak clearly in few words. The use of cue words and giving reasons also facilitate understanding. A smile, a pat on the shoulder, stickers, words, or stars written on papers are other forms of communication.

FIGURE 3.2

Weekly Checklist

Weekly Checklist

Teacher: Date:
Subject:
Students:

Topics covered:

Test ☐   Mon. ☐   Tue. ☐   Wed. ☐   Thus. ☐   Fri. ☐
Assignment for next week or long range:

Current assignments completed ☐ Yes ☐ No
Assignments or homework not completed:

Having difficulty with:

Comments:

Need conference   Best time _____

Older students relate to honesty, a straightforward approach, and humor. Listening to their dilemmas, interests, and hobbies is another form of communication.

Additional Ways to Communicate   Other ways to communicate are to

- Define roles.
- Observe students in the regular classroom.
- Have both regular and special teachers present at parent conferences.
- Hand out agendas for meetings.
- Send notices about professional workshops and conferences.
- Appreciate each professional's capabilities.

Organization and Study Skills

A major part of intervention involves teaching students how to learn. To function adequately in a regular class, they must be responsible for bringing materials to class, following a schedule, being prompt, keeping track of books and assignments, beginning and completing work, and handing it in on time.

In resource rooms there is an emphasis on teaching students how to follow directions, outline, take notes, study for and take tests, use the library, use reference books, and find information quickly. Techniques for listening, attentional behavior, remembering, and planning time are also stressed.

Written Work and Tests

Resource room teachers assist exceptional students with written assignments in the regular class by checking reference materials, determining that the content is accurate, and proofreading the paper for grammar and punctuation. Students may need help with outlining, notetaking, and following written directions.

When they are preparing for a regular class test, students are aided by resource teachers who quiz them by reviewing definitions, notes, and study sheets. If necessary, they can administer the test in the resource room.

Monitoring Behavior

Strategies in behavior management are a part of intervention. Techniques used in the resource room behavior program can be discussed with regular teachers to determine how they might be applied. Perhaps a system to monitor behavior in various settings will be necessary, with rewards and reinforcement in the resource room for acceptable behavior in other places. Similarly, consequences for inappropriate behavior must be agreed on. Consistency is the key to success.

Grading

Grading is an issue that needs to be resolved when students are placed in another setting, a special class, or a regular class. It is necessary that grading policies be established for daily work and projects and separately for report cards. To be determined are the criteria on which grades are based and the identification of personnel responsible for the grades. The school administrator, the teachers involved, the parents, and the students themselves must have a clear understanding of the policy.

Grading on Daily Work and Projects

The Special Class   Grades in the special class are often based on achievement in programs in which both curriculum and methods are adapted. Students are taught at a level at which they can succeed. For example, to reteach spelling skills to sixth graders, they may be instructed individually at the third grade level. They will progress quickly and achieve acceptable grades. However, the grades are different from those they would earn were they in regular sixth grade classes. They must receive earned grades but know that the work is assigned at their ability level. They must also realize that they represent individual achievement and cannot be compared to those of peers.

During instruction, concepts are thoroughly presented. Students practice at the board and with selected worksheets or other activities. They receive corrective feedback as a basis for improvement. Then other assignments are completed for a grade. As an alternative to evaluating extensive written work, grades can be given for oral work and for tasks performed at learning centers and stations.

The Regular Class   Teachers are responsible for awarding grades in regular class work. The criteria are the same for all students. However accommodation for individual differences can be made. For example:

- Students who are slow workers but not slow learners may need to be given additional time to complete worksheets and other assignments. Reduction in the number of math problems or written sentences in language arts may also be made. Thus, the grade is based on knowledge of the material rather than on the time it takes to complete the task.
- Students with written language difficulties may be graded on oral responses.
- For students who have conceptual difficulties, a choice of topics may be given for oral or written reports.
- A teacher may use more than one text in a class. By using supplementary books, students may be given texts appropriate to their reading level. When a topic is assigned, the text is read, and preparation is made for class discussion.
- For students who are not accurate in arithmetic problems but who are working diligently to learn the processes, separate grades—one for process and one for product—can be given.

Administration and Grading of Tests   To assist students in taking tests, the following is recommended:

- Directions, although written, should be read aloud with students given the opportunity to ask questions.
- Students who work slowly may be given extra time.
- Tests may be given in the resource room where students with visual-perception difficulties can receive individual assistance with matching or filling in all the blanks.
- Resource room teachers or tutors may read the test questions and write the responses if the students cannot.
- Teachers may prerecord the questions on a cassette. Students work at a listening center with earphones, stopping the tape after each question as they write their answers.

In grading tests, it is necessary to distinguish between the students' knowledge of the subject content and their ability to produce answers in the format of the test. They may have difficulty in understanding the questions, following directions on items such as matching or filling in the blanks, in reading test questions, or in writing the answers. Exceptional students may also do poorly due to test anxiety. They should not be penalized for difficulties in these areas if the grade is to represent what they have learned.

Grading for Report Cards

In the Regular Class and Other Settings Regular classroom teachers are responsible for subjects taught in the regular classroom whereas special teachers determine grades for subjects taught in the resource room. If students are receiving instruction from a tutor in addition to participating in the regular classroom, both teachers decide on report card grades. Citizenship, behavior, and work–habit grades may be either an individual or a mutual decision. Often it is important for the parents to be aware of differences in the regular class and the resource setting.

Alternatives for Grading in Special Class Subjects Several alternatives exist:

- It should be noted if grades are based on functional levels rather than grade placement.
- Separate report cards may be used.
- Short paragraphs about the performance in special subjects can be inserted or attached to the regular report card in place of letter grades.
- Checklists may be used instead of grades.
- Use of S (Satisfactory) or U (Unsatisfactory) can be used instead of letter grades.
- No report card is given. Instead, a written report, which includes comments on the performance in academic and nonacademic areas and on behavior, may be sent to the parents; or parent conferences may be held.

If grades are based on individual ability, a note should be made on the permanent record. Then if a sixth grader on a fourth grade level is given a B, the junior high school teacher will not expect B work on a seventh grade level the following year.

Returning Students to the Regular Class

One of the areas requiring continuing attention is the return of students from the special setting to the regular class, or "phasing in." The decision to initiate this process is made by special teachers based on their knowledge of academic, behavioral, and social progress. There are distinct advantages to exceptional students and their classmates. Daily contact with students with varying personalities and abilities serves as a model for exceptional students. Nonhandicapped students learn about handicaps and become accustomed to students with special needs.

Guidelines must be available to teachers in planning the transition. In formulating these guidelines, the following points are considered: criteria and procedures, additional considerations for students with low-incidence handicaps, and selection and preparation of the receiving teachers.

Criteria and Procedures

When students return from a special class, ideally they will have met most of the criteria that permit them to succeed in the regular class:

- *They will be near grade level in a group situation*. Often students are on grade level only when taught individually or in a small group. To determine whether they can maintain this level of achievement, special teachers gradually withdraw continuous support, structure, and monitoring. If students do not continue to achieve, they may not be ready for the transition.
- *They are able to meet modified curriculum demands*. Exceptional students are often taught with a specialized program. Before returning to the regular class, they are phased into the curriculum and texts used there.
- *They will be able to handle adjusted volume and maintain the pace of the work*. Included in these criteria are skills such as following written and oral directions, working independently, and completing work in a reasonable length of time.
- *They have acceptable behavior in a group situation*. Ordinary behavior management techniques are used. Behavior is within acceptable limits and does not interfere with the learning of other students.
- *They have satisfactory study habits*. They understand and apply direct instruction in written assignments. They can perform the following tasks as well as most of their peers: reading, taking notes, preparing for tests, and completing assignments and homework.

Additional Considerations For exceptional students to function adequately, several factors must be considered. Where applicable, the following accommodations and assistance are made:

- *Extent or type of impairment*. What physical accommodations are necessary in the school building? Is there a need for a signer for students with hearing impairments or braille materials for students with visual impairments?
- *Self-image*. Do they like themselves well enough to be able to relate to others? Do they set attainable goals? Do they have the self-confidence to attempt new academic challenges?
- *Speech and language development*. Can they express themselves adequately, and will they participate orally? Will they be understood by their peers and teachers?
- *Mobility*. Are students able to move about unassisted, or will others need to be assigned to them? Can they get to classes on time and move easily on the stairs?

It is not necessary to wait until the end of the semester or the school year. It is recommended that each student be phased one subject at a time.

Special teachers prepare students psychologically, being careful to indicate the desirability of attendance in the regular class and emphasizing that academic achievement is related to regular attendance. Fears of making the change may be lessened if teachers assure them of their continued interest.

The Receiving Teachers

Selection and preparation of teachers with whom students will be placed are crucial to the success of the transition. The major criterion is their willingness to accept the students. They should have a knowledge of the students' impairments as well as complete information about their learning characteristics. A structured classroom with behavioral expectations will provide a sense of security during the phasing in. They must be conscious of the amount of teacher attention given to exceptional students, treating them the same as others. They must not cater to excessive need for attention or to attempts at manipulation.

It also may be advantageous to match teachers' and students' personalities, if possible. One quiet student may need an outgoing personality whereas another might be threatened by such a teacher.

A problem that arises is that the same teachers are selected repeatedly. Thus, having still another exceptional student in the class has the aspect of a punishment for their cooperation and competence. Guetzloe and Cline (1983, pp. 363–364) suggest teachers could be compensated by "(a) additional pay, (b) compensatory or released time . . . , (c) lowering the pupil–teacher ratio, and (d) lowering the pupil–adult ratio by assigning other support personnel to the regular classroom."

Mrs. Singleton will have Dave in her seventh grade social studies class. He will also be assigned to the learning disabilities resource room. Before school starts, Mrs. Singleton meets with Miss Rollins, the resource teacher, who informs her that Dave is on a fourth grade reading level, has inadequate memory skills, and a short attention span. His visual-perception difficulties hinder him in taking multiple choice and answer fill-in tests. He has the ability to draw well.

The teachers discuss strategies that can be carried out in a large class. The plan includes the following accommodations:

1. *Miss Rollins will arrange to obtain the history textbook on tape from the Recording for the Blind.*
2. *She will borrow the special tape recorder necessary to slow the voice on the tape.*
3. *Dave is instructed to follow in the text as he listens to the tape during study hall in the resource room. He is to listen to important parts several times. Listening to tapes is an effective technique to increase attention span.*
4. *In class, group grades will be given when students work together.*
5. *There will be a choice of assignments to permit Dave to choose one with less reading.*
6. *He can use his artistic ability to describe Civil War battles and other assignments.*
7. *He will be permitted to use a marker when taking tests to assure that he fills in each answer.*
8. *He will be instructed to cross out each multiple choice answer as it is used.*
9. *If necessary, Miss Rollins or an aide, will read the test to him in the resource room.*

Class Size

A reduced class size allows more opportunity for individual attention. One solution is the "weighting" of handicapping conditions in terms of class load. One exceptional student may be counted as 1.5 students while another may be counted as 2.5. Thus, the weighted count could be over 30 while the actual class size would be less.

Follow-up

Students do not become "regular kids" when they return to a regular class full-time. Additional support is needed. Students can make voluntary visits to the special education teacher or tutor. The teachers can show continued interest and can give encouragement.

Regular teachers receive assistance when consultation services are made available by the special teacher or supervisor. Adjustment difficulties or lack of academic progress are discussed and suggestions for improvement can be made.

Maintaining Professional Competence

Because the field of education is continually changing, teachers must become informed not only with new laws and state guidelines but also about teaching techniques and behavior strategies. They need encouragement in meeting the challenges and demands of everyday teaching.

School districts provide professional days, grade level meetings, and opportunities to participate on committees. Teachers can take courses, read books and articles, and attend meetings with speakers who are experts in various aspects of education.

Three prominent ways for teachers to "keep up" are in service training, workshops, and conventions.

SUMMARY

Teachers find some students in their classes already receiving support services, and some are assigned to a special setting at the start of the year. They identify other students who need help in learning. Teachers attempt to provide assistance by gathering additional information and by providing direct instructional intervention.

Information about individual students can be gained from records and reports or from former teachers or other teachers who may presently work with the students in departmentalized programs. Consultation for information or for recommendations can be obtained from other building personnel—principal, counselor, school nurse, or special education teachers—or with special services personnel. Consultation and cooperation of the parents may be sought. Tutoring or assignment to a remedial teacher can be employed.

If students do not improve with these interventions, referral to special services may be considered. The process requires that teachers gather information to describe students and their needs and complete a referral form. Parents are also contacted by the principal to obtain their informed consent for the referral and testing. The data are then forwarded to special services.

Four major phases of activity occur after referral: assessment, planning, placement, and intervention.

Students are examined in all areas of functioning by a multidisciplinary team. They describe them as learners and determine eligibility to receive services. A written report is sent to a planning committee of parents and school personnel, who use the data to plan educational programs if students are eligible for services. The committee determines the type of intervention—that is, the program and placement. The placements from which they can choose include the regular classroom with consultive services; support services; the regular classroom with supplementary services; the regular classroom with additional tutoring; a resource room; a special, part-time or full-time classroom; and, occasionally, homebound or hospital instruction. Some students are removed from school entirely and placed in a separate educational setting.

The decisions are incorporated into the IEP, which must state the student's present level of academic functioning, annual goals, short-term objectives, additional special services, time references, and evaluation procedures.

Intervention occurs when students are placed in the setting and the educational program is put into effect. Of concern to both special and regular teachers is the student who is placed in a regular class and a special setting. To be resolved among professional personnel are responsibility for instruction, curriculum planning, methods, expectations, and monitoring behavior. Scheduling students into the regular class at the appropriate time, arranging for them to participate in nonacademic subjects, and being in the resource room for subjects needing remediation is a challenge to special teachers. Exceptional students, regular teachers, and regular class students are prepared prior to placement.

Effective communication among parents and professionals is essential in successfully implementing intervention. It is achieved mainly by developing interpersonal communication skills and by regular communication with teachers, administrators, parents, and students.

Grading procedures must be established because different criteria may exist in special and regular classes. A distinction is made between grades on daily work and projects and tests. Several alternatives may be considered for grading report cards.

Careful consideration is necessary when students are returned to the regular class. Guidelines must be available to teachers when planning the transition.

REFERENCES

Guetzloe, E., & Cline, R. (1983). Compensation for regular classroom teachers: State and territorial provisions. *Exceptional Children, 49,* 363–366.

Hayes, J. (1977). Annual goals and short term objectives. In S. Torres (Ed.). *A primer on individualized educational programs for handicapped children* (pp. 14–20). Reston, VA: Foundation for Exceptional Children.

Mager, R. F. (1975). *Preparing instructional objectives* (2nd ed.). Belmont, CA: Fearon.

Odle, S. J.; & Galtelli, B. (1980). The individualized educational program (IEP). Foundation for appropriate and effective instruction. In J. W. Schifani, R. M. Anderson, & S. J. Odle (Eds.). *Implementing learning in the least restrictive environment: Handicapped children in the mainstream* (pp. 245–257). Baltimore: University Park Press.

Speece, D. L., & Mandell, C. J. (1980). Interpersonal communication between resource and regular teachers. *Teacher Education and Special Education, 3,* 55–60.

Treblas, P. V.; McCormick, S. H.; & Cooper, J. O. (1982). Problems in mainstreaming at the grassroots. *The Directive Teacher, 4*(2), 14–17.

SUGGESTED READINGS

Biklen, D. (1985). *Achieving the complete school: Strategies for effective mainstreaming.* New York: Teachers College Press.

Cohen, J. H. (Ed.). (1982). *Handbook of resource room teaching.* Rockville, MD: Aspen.

Gearheart, B. R., & Weishahn, M. W. (1984). *The exceptional student in the regular classroom* (3rd ed.). Columbus, OH: Merrill.

Golin, A. K., & Ducanis, A. J. (1981). *The interdisciplinary team: A handbook for the education of exceptional children.* Rockville, MD: Aspen.

Harris, W. J., Jr., & Schutz, P. N. B. (1986). *The special education resource program: Rationale and implementation.* Columbus, OH: Merrill.

Hawisher, M. F., & Calhoun, M. L. (1978). *The resource room: An educational asset for children with special needs.* Columbus, OH: Merrill.

Heron, T. E., & Harris, K. C. (1987). *The educational consultant: Helping professionals, parents, and mainstreamed students.* Boston: Allyn & Bacon.

Idol-Maestas, L. (1983). *Special educators' consultation handbook.* Rockville, MD: Aspen.

Pasanella, A. L., & Volkmor, C. B. (1977). *Coming back . . . Or never leaving: Instructional programming for handicapped students in the mainstream.* Columbus, OH: Merrill.

Reynolds, M. C., & Birch, J. W. (1982). *Teaching exceptional children in all America's schools* (Revised edition). Reston, VA: Council for Exceptional Children.

Wehman, P., & McLaughlin, P. J. (1981). *Program development in special education: Designing individualized programs.* New York: McGraw-Hill.

Weiner, B. (Ed.). (1978). *Periscope: Views of the individualized education program.* Reston, VA: Council for Exceptional Children.

Wiederholt, J.; Hammill, D. D.; & Brown, V. (1983). *The resource teacher: A guide to effective practices* (2nd ed.). Austin, TX: Pro-Ed.

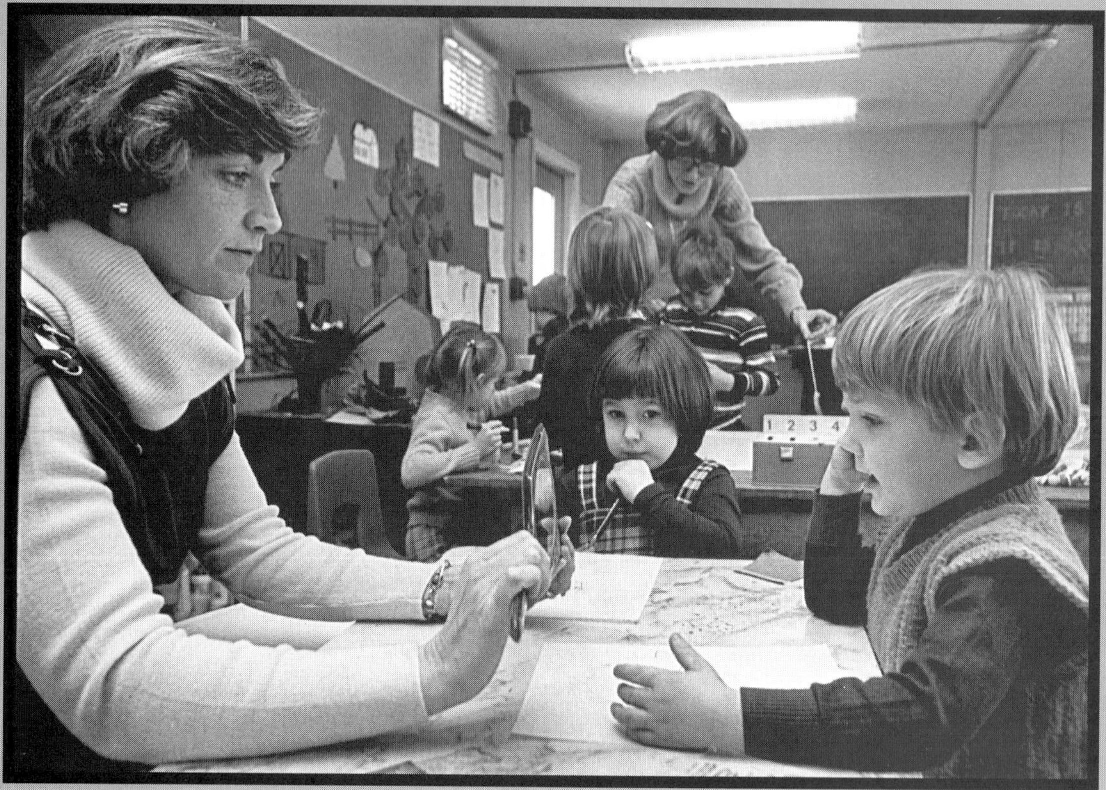
1 2 3 4

4

Resource Services and Personnel

AT EACH GRADE LEVEL teachers find students with individual academic and behavioral characteristics and various learning styles as well as those with identified special needs. The challenge to teachers is formidable. Successful instruction and management of these diverse populations depends on many professionals and appropriate services. In addition to relying on their own competence and resourcefulness, teachers can expect a range of support services and the expertise of resource personnel within the school system and the community.

Resource Services

Resources consist of any personnel, activities, systems, or data sources outside the classroom that serve the purpose of assisting teachers in meeting group or individual needs, be it academic, behavioral, or social. All teachers use common resources such as texts, teachers' manuals, and instructional materials. Special methods or activities include data about students and information gained from college texts, professional journals, in service training, or other individuals. Support personnel can provide special resources for the regular class. Speech/language pathologists can work with classroom teachers to coordinate and reinforce articulation, memory, vocabulary, or language processing skills. Counselors can suggest techniques to improve self-image or assist in developing ways to instruct in problem solving and coping. Special education consultants and resource room teachers can share various techniques or programs in any content area or in behavior management.

Students Who Are Served

Resource services are often perceived to be special help for special students. Federal legislation and state guidelines, both of which are influenced by financial considerations, may limit who receives particular services and specify eligibility requirements. In the broader view espoused here, a range of resource services should be available to *all* teachers for *all* students. Assistance should be provided for those with potential problems and for individual learners who do not qualify for special services. Although difficult to document on a cost-effective basis, this assistance may prevent or reduce the need for more costly services.

Cantrell and Cantrell (1976) found that teachers receiving support services were able to effect gains in academic achievement at all IQ levels. Follow-up revealed significantly fewer referrals to special services from these teachers than from those in a control group who did not receive such support.

Resource services are categorized as indirect or direct. Indirect services are data gathered from records and reports and consultation. Direct services include tutoring, counseling, and testing in which there is contact with students. Other professionals may be involved but they work indirectly through classroom teachers.

Indirect Services

Indirect services, with the goal of supporting teachers in their work with individual students, take the forms of information found in records and reports and consultation with other professionals.

Information From Written Sources

The cumulative folder may contain data which can give insights about students and a perspective on classroom problems. Is the pattern of grades earned earlier consistent with present achievement? Is there a point at which grades changed suddenly? Do scores on routinely administered, standardized tests correspond with grades? Do test scores indicate a marked difference between verbal and nonverbal performance? Was a grade repeated? Is there a pattern of excessive absences? Did students change schools often? Are there anecdotal notes from former teachers with observations of behavior or methods used in dealing with unacceptable behavior?

Occasionally there are progress logs, checklists, or competency record forms from an academic program. Teachers can then learn what skills were reported to have been mastered and which are yet to be learned. Work samples indicate how students function as compared to grade level expectations. Psychological reports may be available for those identified as exceptional. Medical records often give valuable information about vision, hearing, or other health factors that may influence attentiveness or energy level. Have students been or are they on medication? When was the last time the school was asked for a report on behavior with the medication?

While data in past records and written reports may provide answers to many questions and on occasion give valuable clues to treatment, they should be approached with caution. Historical data are difficult to validate, and teachers may not know the conditions under which they were gathered. The management of the classroom in which the reported behaviors occurred may have been different from the present setting. Earlier behaviors may not have been predictive of, nor characteristics of, present behavior. The older the test scores, the less representative they are likely to be of present performance. Caution must be taken when interpreting any score from tests on which poor readers were required to read.

Consultation with Building Personnel

Principals Before proceeding beyond the examination of written data, arrange a tactful consultation with the school principal. Principals are also responsible for exceptional students. They can provide information and recommendations for other sources of assistance, give insight about family situations, and comment on the advisability for home contact. They can indicate legal and placement procedures and suggest approaches that could be instrumental in securing parental support and cooperation. They are involved in the referral and placement process, in integrating students into regular classes, and in working with parents.

Principals support the education of individual learners and exceptional students through the routine activities of their offices, making room assignments, overseeing scheduling, approving curriculum changes, and encouraging staff development through continuing in service training. They confer with individual teachers in their work with students who have academic and behavior problems.

School Psychologists School psychologists consult with teachers to recommend prereferral and preventative strategies. They organize the assessment team, test students, conduct the planning and IEP meetings, and meet with parents. They can provide in service training programs and can supervise preschool screening and intervention strategies, which may include monitoring student behavior. They also counsel students and parents.

Former Teachers Those who have worked with students in the past can be of invaluable assistance by describing behavior and academic performance as they experienced them. They may also relate which methods of instruction and behavior management worked and which were unsuccessful.

Although former teachers may be competent professionals, their personalities and classroom procedures may be different from those of the present teacher. Behavior was and is respondent to those factors. How students performed in one classroom for one teacher at an earlier stage in development can be different from their performance in another situation. Whether a technique worked for a former teacher is not a guarantee as to how it will work when used by another teacher.

Teachers in Departmentalized Programs and Nonacademic Subjects A perspective on behavior and achievement can be gained by consultation with other teachers. For example, where there is departmentalization, there is a natural communication among teachers. Because nonacademic subjects are often taught in less structured environments, homeroom teachers can gain a knowledge of students' self-control, interaction with teachers and peers, and activity and attention levels. In addition, insight can be provided about attitude and motivation toward subjects that make different demands from those of the academic curriculum.

Counselors Traditionally, counselors have been employed at the secondary level to provide guidance services. Fewer are found in elementary schools, and their roles at this level have been diverse. As resource persons to teachers, counselors can interpret test scores and other information, including family data. If students have been referred earlier, relevant information that does not violate students' rights to privacy or the confidentiality of the counseling relationship can be shared. This information and its implications for room assignments, curriculum adaptions, behavior management, and instructional procedures can be discussed with teachers and the principal.

Counselors may be a liaison between school and home, contacting parents for initial and continuing conferences and providing explanations and interpretations of school policy and referral procedures. At the secondary level where students' have different teachers for each subject, counselors can become coordinators of information as well as identified professionals with whom parents can make contact.

Social Workers Some school districts employ social workers who facilitate communication between the school and the home and consult with teachers and the school staff. They may serve as members of the assessment and placement teams when students are referred to special services. Social workers often provide liaison and coordination of services among home, school, and other community agencies when referrals are necessary. They may work in a counseling role at the school, at home in the family setting, or in emergency situations.

School Nurses School nurses usually provide services in several buildings. They maintain a health record, separate from that in the cumulative folder, for each student. Nurses provide teachers with information about students whose sensory, physical, or other health problems could affect classroom performance. They can give instructions on handling seizure activity and managing students with orthopedic involvement. With the consent of the parents, they are the logical contacts with the family physician or other medical professionals.

Special Education Teachers Potential sources of assistance are special education teachers who have experience in managing students with unacceptable behavior and various learning difficulties. They can discuss their concerns with classroom teachers. Together they may design a management program or adapt an instructional sequence.

Consultation With Special Personnel

Depending on the size and administrative organization of the local districts, a number of professionals may be available to consult with teachers. Titles may include county supervisor, consultant, and coordinator or director of special education. From their perspective in working with exceptional students, these professionals may comment on the severity of the presenting problem and the appropriateness of subsequent referral.

BOX 4.1

Specific Techniques for Working With Seizure Disorders

Seizure activity is the primary characteristic of epilepsy but may accompany other impairments. Seizures are classified as *generalized* or *partial* with the latter subdivided into a number of types. Teachers are more commonly instructed that there are *grand mal, petit mal,* and *psychmotor seizures.* In working with students with seizure disorders, teachers may be guided by the following procedures:

1. Do not be fearful about seizure activity. The seizures of most students are controlled through medication.
2. Learning disabilities are common among students with epilepsy and may be of more concern to school personnel than the seizure activity.
3. The primary role of teachers is to educate all students, including those with seizure activity. Curriculum and methods are the same as with all students.
4. Academic expectations are based on a variety of factors—for example, IQ score, past educational experiences, and the presence of other disabilities. For most students the seizure activity is not a significant factor in educational planning.
5. Do not be reluctant to manage behavior. Routine classroom discipline will not precipitate a seizure episode.
6. Teachers should be aware of the petit mal seizures in which students may lose consciousness for short periods of time but without losing general motor control. These may occur frequently during the day, and they interfere with students' acquisition of consistent patterns of complete information and their verbal and/or written responses.
7. The school nurse may provide direct instruction to teachers on their response to generalized (grand mal) seizures. The Epilepsy Foundation of America (1974) recommends the following:
    a. Keep calm. Ease the child to the floor and loosen his collar. You cannot stop the seizure. Let it run its course and do not try to revive the child.
    b. Remove hard, sharp, or hot objects which may injure the child but do not interfere with his movements.
    c. Do not force anything between his teeth.
    d. Turn the head to one side for release of saliva. Place something soft under his head.
    e. When the child regains consciousness, let him rest if he wishes.
    f. If the seizures last beyond a few minutes, or if the child seems to pass from one seizure to another without gaining consciousness, call the school nurse or doctor for instructions and notify his parents. This rarely happens but it should be treated immediately.

Brochures available from the Epilepsy Foundation instruct teachers and students about the disease. Kits are presented with posters and lessons to teach the rest of the class about epilepsy and how they should react when a student has a seizure.

Although speech and hearing screening is routinely conducted, classroom teachers should not hesitate to consult with a speech/language pathologist or audiologist whenever a problem is indicated.

Consultation Committee/Building Assistance Teams Initiated by teachers concerned about students and motivated by waiting lists for special services, some faculties have developed in-school staffing procedures. The purpose is to screen referrals to special services and to provide assistance in solving learning and behavior problems. A panel of teachers, often on a rotating basis, meets at a regularly scheduled time. A member of special services is sometimes invited to participate in an advisory capacity. Only teachers who wish to do so participate and present data. The panel has two roles: to determine the advisability of referral to special services and to directly help teachers in solving problems at the school level if referral is not made.

Direct Services

Among the direct services are academic testing, supportive or supplemental academic instruction, curriculum adaptations, counseling, use of special materials, and referral to medical professionals for community services. (Medical resources are discussed under "Community Resources" later in the chapter.)

Academic Testing

Classroom teachers or resource persons administer individual diagnostic tests within the subject areas. Such assessment may be criterion-referenced and formative, which reveal competencies and deficiencies. They provide a basis to determine the need for modification of the instructional program or for special services.

Supportive or Supplemental Academic Instruction

Depending on the extensiveness of need, additional academic instruction can be provided in several ways. Classroom teachers give individualized instruction. For intermittent difficulties with academic content, regular tutors, itinerant teachers, paraprofessionals, peers, or volunteers can provide short-term tutoring. More serious problems may require the services of remedial reading or math teachers.

Curriculum Adaptation

Adapting the curriculum is another procedure for addressing individual differences in the regular classroom. Modifications in the amount of material given, the sequence of presentation, or the omission of content need not interfere with curriculum objectives.

Counseling

Academic difficulties are often accompanied by a poor self-image and unsatisfactory social relationships. Students may feel markedly different from their peers and may develop a negative attitude about school. The major role of counselors is to meet on a one-to-one basis with the student or in small groups and to counsel families. When counselors are available in elementary schools, they can interrupt the cyclical pattern of failure, frustration, and behavior problems. In meeting with students, they can discuss self-concept and self-understanding, academic progress, classroom behavior, peer or teacher relationships, crisis situations, home problems, values and feelings, goal setting, and identification of steps toward goal achievement.

Counselors can assist with adjustment to placement in special programs. Students may need to verbalize feelings about placement, other students in the program, and being different.

Use of Special Materials

Historically, materials developed for exceptional students have been subsequently adopted by regular educators. These materials offer alternative procedures for instruction and concrete experiences in learning. They can be borrowed from instructional materials centers or university libraries. Materials purchased as part of grants can be another source. All class members benefit from these learning aids.

Other Resource Personnel

Other individuals, professionals and paraprofessionals, may be able to provide indirect or direct services. Their titles, job descriptions, and availability may vary depending on the organization and practices within the local system. Such personnel include remedial teachers, regular short-term tutors, special education tutors, consulting teachers, speech/language pathologists, audiologists, physical therapists, occupational therapists, parents, paraprofessionals, volunteers, and peer tutors.

Remedial Teachers

Some schools employ remedial reading and remedial mathematics teachers. These teachers are experts in their respective subject areas and can share their knowledge with others in the building. In some schools the class is federally funded as part of a "title," or more recently, "chapter" program. Remedial teachers consult with regular teachers, discussing learning characteristics, examining work samples, and making recommendations about instruction, materials, and sources of additional information. They conduct classes for students not identified as exceptional. Eligibility and referral procedures are locally determined. Students are removed from the classroom for the specific subject (for example, reading) and attend that class with the remedial teacher.

Regular Short-Term Tutors

Some school districts provide itinerant tutors who meet with students from regular classes on a one-to-one or small-group basis to provide short-term academic support. They work under the supervision of the classroom teacher on topics being currently covered in the regular class. Service consists of direct instruction on topics that students may have missed during an absence or on difficult concepts. Another function is to provide feedback about students and their progress in tutoring sessions.

Special Education Tutors

Some states provide categorical or noncategorical tutors. In addition to reinforcing the curriculum of the regular class, tutors are responsible for the specialized part of the program as prescribed in the IEP. They plan curriculum, work closely with regular teachers, and provide feedback on academic progress. They teach individuals or small groups identified and placed in special education. Developmental and remedial instruction is given in specific content areas. They can also reinforce concepts taught in the regular class and help students prepare for tests.

Consulting Teachers

Consulting teachers usually have masters' degrees and successful teaching experience with exceptional students. They do not have the responsibility for direct instruction, nor are they supervisors. They work with regular teachers who have exceptional students in their classes. This necessitates having a knowledge of regular classroom techniques as well as special education procedures. The primary role of consulting teachers is, as the title suggests, indirect. After observing students, they examine the presenting problems and relevant data. With regular teachers they identify educational goals, determine academic instructional procedures, and behavior management strategies. Consulting teachers then make recommendations about instruction, locate materials, find special equipment for visually impaired students, instruct teachers in their use, and assist in developing a plan for continuing evaluation. Their role may also include being a listener and giving support and reinforcement to regular teachers.

Consulting teachers may be members of the planning and placement committees for students referred to special services. They may also be assigned the responsibility for in service training. Some school programs allow consulting teachers to do individual diagnostic testing in specific academic subjects, to work with teachers in demonstrating methods, and to interact with students.

Speech/Language Pathologists

Speech therapists have long practiced in schools, primarily providing screening and speech assessment and subsequent remediation of articulation, voice disorders, or stuttering. Their areas of interest have been expanded to include hearing problems and, more recently, language development.

Pathologists may be available to regular and special education teachers to discuss apparent potential problems observed in the classroom and to provide direct assessment of either speech or language. Recommendations can be made for general environmental enrichment and specific activities to foster language development for the entire class and to aid with specific students.

In addition to these indirect services, Dublinske and Healey (1978, p. 191) list direct services:

- Identification of children with speech and language disorders
- Diagnosis and appraisal of specific speech or language disorders
- Referral for medical or other professional attention necessary for the habilitation of speech or language disorders
- Provision of speech and language services for the habilitation or prevention of communicative disorders
- Counseling and guidance of parents, children, and teachers regarding speech and language disorders

Speech and language clinicians have traditionally provided therapy on a one-to-one or small-group basis at regularly scheduled times. They consult with teachers of students in therapy. In some school systems speech and language clinicians may also serve as audiologists.

Audiologists

Audiologists identify students who exhibit hearing loss and indicate the range and degree of impairment. They determine need for an amplification device and/or special class placement. They consult with teachers regarding individual students suspected of hearing loss whether such was indicated by routine screening. Following screening and assessment they provide data to teachers, speech and language clinicians, and/or the assessment team. Descriptions of students' hearing, recommendations for classroom provisions and activities, and information on the use and limitations of hearing aids can be given.

Audiologists also work closely with special teachers who maintain separate classes for students with hearing impairments.

Physical Therapists and Occupational Therapists

Both the physical therapist (PT) and the occupational therapist (OT) work in the school setting. The American Physical Therapy Association (cited in Kalish & Presseller, 1980) describes the role of physical therapists in educational settings:

> Physical therapy is a health profession concerned with providing services to individuals that prevent or minimize the disability, relieve pain, develop and improve motor function, control posture deviations and establish and maintain maximum performance within the individual's capabilities. Physical therapy services within the educational environment are directed toward the development and maintenance of the handicapped child's physical potential for independence in all education related activities.

The role of the occupational therapist in the educational setting is described in PL 94–142.

Occupational therapy includes (1) improving and developing or restoring functions impaired or lost through illness, injury or deprivation; (2) improving ability to perform when functions are impaired or lost; (3) preventing through early intervention, initial or further impairment or loss of function.

Several differences between the two professions have been suggested: The PT works with large muscles, and the OT works with small muscles; The PT works with the lower extremities, and the OT works with the upper extremities; and the PT is concerned with facilitating general motor functioning, and the OT is concerned with the use of muscles for the accomplishment of adaptive tasks and self-help skills. The distinction is often blurred, and in some programs the term *developmental therapist* is applied to a single individual who integrates the practices of both professions (Tyler & Chandler, 1978).

In school settings the PT and the OT work with students with physical handicaps, developmental delays, and special health problems. They inform teachers about adaptive devices used in handwriting and typewriting as well as mobility arrangements.

Parents

Parents can assume the role of resource personnel. They provide indirect services by explaining learning and behavior problems. They give teachers insight about home situations and possible outside contributions to academic and social behaviors. Developmental history—not included in the cumulative folder—students' interests and out-of-school activities, reports of parenting practices and parent–child relationships may be revealed in parent conferences.

In providing direct services, parents can carry out behavior management programs at home, following through with teacher suggestions. They can present an attitude supportive of the school and teachers. They can supervise homework and set up a schedule that requires sufficient time for study. They can provide positive feedback for home and school accomplishments and attend school functions.

Paraprofessionals

Paraprofessionals are employees who often receive initial and/or continuing training from the school system. Greer (1978) distinguishes between teacher assistants and teacher aides. Assistants provide direct support and have limited decision making authority. Aides do not work independently but only under the supervision of teachers. Greer also lists the following direct and indirect activities, which may be performed by teacher assistants:

- Reinforcing positive behavior
- Assisting in large-group instruction
- Tutoring individuals and small groups of children
- Correcting home and seat work activities
- Checking standardized and informal tests
- Observing and recording behavior
- Collecting materials and preparing displays, teaching centers, and similar instructional activities

- Assisting children with make-up work as a result of absence from school or class
- Assisting students with oral and written communication
- Participating in reading and story-telling activities
- Assisting with hands-on activities
- Assisting with fine and gross motor activities, physical development, and lifetime physical and recreational activities
- Providing a model with whom the children can identify
- Recording written materials for children who have visual or other learning disabilities
- Assisting children with extended day activities
- Helping children solve personal conflicts with other children
- Assisting on instructional field trip activities
- Assisting children with self-care activities
- Assisting with feeding and toileting activities
- Working with audio-visual equipment
- Assisting the teachers with noninstructional tasks
- Assisting in classroom organization and management

— (Reprinted from J. V. Greer, *Focus on Exceptional Children*, Vol. 10, No. 6, p. 4. Copyright 1978 by Love Publishing Company.)

In some school districts aides perform the same duties as those listed for teacher assistants. In other locations they are restricted to secretarial duties, correcting papers, filing, organizing materials, setting up audiovisual equipment, and monitoring students as they move between classes.

Volunteers and Peer Tutors

Parents, grandparents, college students, and others in the community or peer tutors assist classroom teachers. Their role is the same as paraprofessionals or aides. Following a class presentation, each volunteer or peer tutor works with a small group reexplaining, answering questions, using concrete materials or workbooks, and helping them master difficult concepts. The most common duties also include drilling for math facts and spelling words, listening to oral reading, preparing students for tests, and helping them in the use of reference materials.

Careful planning and training are essential. Persons working individually with exceptional students not only must accept and be patient with them but also tolerate mistakes. Often, individual attention is the most beneficial service.

Teacher Expectations of Resource Personnel

If classroom teachers are expected to learn to manage and teach classes in which there are broad ranges of individual differences, they must have a support system of personnel and services.

Administrative Support Regular and special teachers need administrative support in three areas—for special programs, for students, and for their efforts on behalf of the students. Administrators must facilitate the operation of each special program with the same level of enthusiasm as for any other program in the school. Assistance should be expected in solving problems whether they are disagreements among staff members, resolution of schedule conflicts, discipline of students, or relationships with parents. Maintaining a positive attitude toward students with special needs and giving them recognition for their accomplishments advance the goals of the program.

Availability   A roster of resource personnel is not enough. The individuals on the list should be available without extensive delay.

Answers to Questions About Receiving Special Services

- What approaches can be used to teach this student?
- What management techniques can be tried?
- How long should one technique be used before trying something else?
- Is the problem serious enough to warrant referral?
- Are there materials available?
- How can parents be dealt with effectively?
- How is stress handled and "burn out" prevented?
- What is the exact nature of the student's handicap?
- Specifically, how will it affect the classroom? Learning? Socialization? Behavior?
- What about grading?
- What adaptations in instruction, curriculum, management, and environment will need to be made?
- What is the relationship with parents?
- Who, specifically, is available to listen to teacher concerns?

Feedback   Teachers should expect regular reports about the services being provided.

Information   Relevant information including specifics about the handicapping condition, test scores and their interpretations, psychological records, and placement plans must be available for students receiving services.

Consultation Services   Consultation may be provided by either a supervisor, director of special education, or a consultant depending on their role in a particular school system. Consultants are not expected to have all the answers nor solve all academic or behavior problems. They should avoid reiteration of their own experiences and textbook generalizations; teachers will need practical help with immediate problems. Consultants are to be nonjudgmental. They work constructively through the strengths and potentials of teachers. Alternative approaches may be examined; new procedures may be learned. Assistance may also be needed in dealing with administrators, with other teachers, with parents, or in developing skills in classroom management and teacher self-confidence. Teachers thus grow in professional competence and are able to apply new skills for the benefit of all students.

Materials   Teachers ought to have access to supplemental materials if they are prescribed and recommended.

Resource Personnel Expectations of Teachers

Attitude Teachers are expected to have an attitude of acceptance and respect for both exceptional and nonhandicapped students. They must display honesty, openness, and willingness to cooperate in implementing academic and social goals and objectives.

Knowledge Teachers are expected to know about the growth and development of children in general and of students in the grade levels they teach in particular. They must be willing to become knowledgeable about the characteristics of exceptional students and how they are alike and different from others.

Competency Teachers are expected to be skilled in the basic methods, applying them in individualized instruction, adapting curriculum and methods, and employing positive support procedures in evaluating classroom performance. They are expected to communicate on a regular basis with resource personnel. They can anticipate increased planning and paperwork, which necessitate teacher organizational skills.

ATTITUDE CHANGE ON THE PART OF TEACHERS

The Middletown school system reorganized their special services unit into a diagnostic center. Referred students were provided with case managers who were experienced classroom teachers, recruited from the system's respected teachers. Each case manager participated in the multidisciplinary assessment and worked with the team and the classroom teacher in developing interventions. Further, each one worked on an itinerant basis with the classroom teachers of the mainstreamed students. They assisted in the classroom, demonstrated methods, identified and found training materials, or consulted about problems. Gradually they reduced their participation, allowing the classroom teacher to take over the job completely. They did not work on attitudes directly but allowed the teachers to discover that they could be successful with mainstreamed, exceptional students. In a follow-up survey, nearly every teacher so aided reported improvement in their teaching competencies and improved attitudes toward exceptional students. Further, nearly all declared their willingness to receive additional students with handicaps.

Educator Expectations of Each Other: Professionalism

Regular and special personnel expect each other to be professionals. Educators respect themselves, adhering to the ethical standards and practices that characterize their chosen occupations. They are primarily concerned with the welfare of students. They demonstrate integrity in the development of attitudes, knowledge, and skills in teaching and in guiding each student. Professionalism involves mutual respect, accepting others, and considering their opinions. Professionals refrain from discussing difficulties with students, family, or staff who are not concerned with solving the problem.

Community Resources

For some students, the inability to achieve is the central fact of their problem. School failure may be related to environmental, instructional, or curriculum variables and/or innate intellectual limitations. For other students school problems are only one manifestation of more pervasive difficulties in their lives. Medical, emotional, social, and family problems are of additional or even primary concern.

Assistance to such students cannot be managed by the school alone; optimal educational conditions are necessary but insufficient. Community resources such as medical, psychological, and welfare agencies may become involved. For these students school personnel interact with a variety of professionals and agencies in the community.

Medical Resources

Teachers may have concerns about students' fine or gross motor coordination, energy and activity level, short attention span, neurological signs, frequent absences, reoccurring illnesses, enuresis, general appearance, or symptoms of convulsive activity. Consultation should be made with the school nurse and the parents to recommend a medical examination by the family physician. Similarly, if teachers note indications that visual or hearing problems exist, referral should be made.

Family Physician or Pediatrician For most families the physician is the more constant and respected professional. He or she provides primary health care and advises the family of the need for other medical specialties. The physician may assist families in becoming aware of or accepting handicapping conditions.

Neurologist The neurologist specializes in the development and functioning of the central nervous system. School personnel may be more familiar with the neurologist's concern with children identified as hyperactive. It is the prerogative of the neurologist and the pediatrician to determine the need for and to prescribe medication for hyperactive behavior.

Ophthalmologist and Optometrist The ophthalmologist is a medical professional whose concern is the care of the eyes—that is, the organic aspects, disease, and fitting for glasses. The optometrist is not a medical doctor but specializes in testing and correcting vision and providing vision training.

Otologist The otologist is a medical professional specializing in the health of the hearing mechanisms and the testing, diagnosing, and treatment of auditory disorders.

It is the primary role of each of these medical professionals to offer direct services to students in the form of diagnosis and treatment of problems within their respective areas of expertise. They may provide indirect service through written reports to the school. Less common are direct contacts between teacher and physician.

The Role of School Personnel for Students Receiving Medication Some students receive medication for hyperactivity, convulsive disorders, or other health problems.

In cases of suspected hyperactivity, teachers confer with parents, describing classroom behavior. They may recommend consultation with the family physician. Teachers or other school personnel must never recommend medication; it is the physician's prerogative to determine treatment. If medication is subsequently prescribed, teachers cooperate in the program. A major aspect of this cooperation is monitoring behavior. Sprague and Gadow (1976) identify three phases. First, behavior is observed before treatment is initiated because the behavior is likely to be different in school than in the physician's office. Teachers may also list behavior management strategies being used to reduce or eliminate unacceptable behavior. Second, as treatment is initiated, teachers note changes in behavior or the occurrence of side effects. Often a physician will have a prepared checklist. Finally, the behavior is observed and recorded as the student continues in the treatment program.

Because some students take medication during school hours, it is imperative that the school have a standard policy for procedures. Courtnage, Stainback, and Stainback (1982) recommend that this policy requires an authorization statement with both physician and parent signatures, specification of school personnel and their responsibilities, proper labeling and storage of medication, and record keeping (including a drug administration log and anecdotal records of behavior). Copies of recommended procedures entitled *Development and Use of Policies Regarding Administration of Prescribed Medication to Children* are available from The Council for Exceptional Children, 1920 Association Drive, Reston, Virginia 22091.

Although relatively large numbers of students receive medication for hyperactivity and other behaviors (Safer & Krager, 1984), this treatment should not be considered as the only recourse for intervention. Simms (1985) warns that medication is not a substitute for classroom management or teaching academic or social skills. Teaching students to control their own behavior is better for them than treating symptoms that can have adverse side effects.

Child Guidance Clinics

Child guidance clinics operate on a team approach, which frequently includes psychiatrists or psychologists, social workers, counselors, and educators. Many communicate with medical professionals. Services are to children with various problems, although traditionally such agencies have been concerned with emotional and behavior disorders. Frequently, a family therapy approach is used in which all members participate and the therapist attempts to clarify thinking and to modify patterns of interaction.

Guidance clinics usually function autonomously although, with the consent of the parents, reports may be available to the school. There may be, however, little functional or consultive cooperation between school and clinic. Sometimes teachers are asked to cooperate in carrying out recommendations to enhance self-image or socialization.

Welfare Services

County welfare agencies provide a wide range of services. Their relationship with the school centers around counseling for troubled families and placement in foster homes when necessary, thus removing the child from an unsuitable environment.

A major cooperative effort is the protection of children from neglect and physical or sexual abuse. Teachers and administrators have the obligation to report suspected cases by calling the county department of welfare, children's services intake department, or the police department. Following the verbal referral, teachers complete a written school report form. In some instances, they participate in a case conference. Any person who makes a report may do so anonymously and is immune from liability. An investigation is to be made within twenty-four hours.

Teachers have the responsibility to become aware of symptoms of neglect and abuse. Information is available from the Office of Public Information of the State Department of Public Welfare or the county welfare agency. Information and a list of materials on Child Protective Services can be obtained from The American Humane Association, Child Protection, 5351 S. Roslyn Street, Englewood, Colorado 80111.

Team Approach

The team approach is widely advocated in the professional literature. Consideration of the "whole child" and the complexity of problems that can comprise handicapping conditions demand contributions from several disciplines. No one professional has all the answers nor the breadth of expertise to solve all problems. Further, teachers cannot be expected to be psychologists, social workers, nurses, and counselors. However, gathering together a number of people from representative disciplines only for the sake of using a team approach can be counterproductive. Some professionals identify particular activities or skills as their exclusive domain. Occasionally, they are unwilling to share knowledge with those in other disciplines. Differing theoretical orientations and vocabulary may interfere with communication.

Determination must be made on the basis of individual needs. Regular teachers, the principal, and appropriate resource personnel work together to solve problems.

SUMMARY

Resource services include any activity, personnel, or data sources outside the classroom that support teachers in meeting individual and group classroom goals. Such resources, often restricted to exceptional students, should be available to all teachers for all students. Services may be either direct or indirect. Indirect services include information found in records and reports and from consultation with other personnel. Teachers may consult with principals, school psychologists, former teachers, other teachers in nonacademic or departmentalized programs, counselors, social workers, school nurses, special education teachers, or a consultation committee. Direct services include academic testing, supportive or supplemental academic instruction, curriculum adaptations, counseling, and the use of special materials. Other resource personnel who may provide direct services include remedial teachers, regular short-term tutors, special education tutors, consulting teachers, speech/language pathologists, audiologists, physical therapists, and occupational therapists. Parents, paraprofessionals, volunteers, and peer tutors also support teachers with direct and indirect services.

Teachers should expect administrative support, availability of resource personnel, and answers to questions as well as feedback from people who work with students in another setting. Resource personnel should expect classroom teachers to maintain a positive attitude toward students, gain knowledge about them and their exceptionality, and develop skills in working with them in the classroom. Educators can expect professionalism from each other. Working as a team they cooperate to serve students effectively.

Community resources is another area of resource services. Medical personnel, the child guidance clinic, and welfare services cooperate with the school.

REFERENCES

Cantrell, R. P., & Cantrell, M. L. (1976). Preventive mainstreaming: Impact of a supportive services program on pupils. *Exceptional Children, 42,* 381–386.

Courtnage, L., Stainback, W., & Stainback, S. (1982). Managing prescription drugs in school. *Teaching Exceptional Children, 15,* 5–9.

Dublinske, S., & Healey, W. C. (1978). PL 94–142: Questions and answers for the speech–language pathologist and audiologist. *ASHA, 20,* 188–205.

The Epilepsy Foundation of America (1974). *Epilepsy school alert.* Washington, DC: Author.

Greer, J. V. (1978). Utilizing paraprofessionals and volunteers in special education. *Focus on Exceptional Children, 10*(6), 1–15.

Kalish, R. A., & Presseller, S. (1980). Physical and occupational therapy. *Journal of School Health, 50,* 264–267.

Safer, D. J., & Krager, J. M. (1984). Trends in medication therapy for hyperactivity: National and international perspectives. In K. D. Gadow (Ed.). *Advances in learning and behavioral disabilities, Vol. 3* (pp. 125–149). Greenwich, CT: JAI Press.

Simms, R. B. (1985). Hyperactivity and drug therapy: What the educator should know. *Journal of Research and Development in Education, 18,* (3) 1–7.

Sprague, R. L., & Gadow, K. D. (1976). The role of the teacher in drug treatment. *School Review, 85,* 109–140.

Tyler, N. B., & Chandler, L. S. (1978). The developmental therapists: The occupational therapist and the physical therapist. In K. E. Allen, V. A. Holm, & R. L. Schiefelbusch (Eds.), *Early intervention—A team approach.* Baltimore: University Park Press.

SUGGESTED READINGS

Ehly, S. W., & Larsen, S. C. (1980). *Peer tutoring for individualized instruction.* Boston: Allyn and Bacon.

Frith, G. H. (1982). *The role of the special education paraprofessional: An introductory text.* Springfield, IL: Thomas.

Gadow, K. D. (1986). *Children on medication, Vol. I: Hyperactivity, learning disabilities, and mental retardation.* San Diego, CA: College-Hill Press.

Harris, W. J., Jr., & Schutz, P. N. B. (1986). *The special education resource program: Rationale and implementation.* Columbus, OH: Merrill.

Haslam, R. H. A., & Valletutti, P. J. (Eds.). (1985). *Medical problems in the classroom: The teacher's role in diagnosis and management* (2nd ed.). Austin, TX: Pro-Ed.

Heron, T. E., and Harris, K. C. (1982). *The educational consultant: Helping professionals, parents, and mainstreamed students.* Boston: Allyn and Bacon.

Idol-Maestas, L. (1983). *Special educator's consultation handbook.* Rockville, MD: Aspen.

Lombana, J. H. (1982). *Guidance for handicapped students.* Springfield, IL: Thomas.

Neal, W. R. (1986). *Speech–language pathology services in secondary schools.* Austin, TX: Pro-Ed.

Reynolds, C. R., and Gutkin, T. B. (Eds.). (1982). *The handbook of school psychology.* New York: Wiley.

Ross, D. M., & Ross, S. A. (1982). *Hyperactivity: Current issues, research, and theory* (2nd ed.). New York: Wiley.

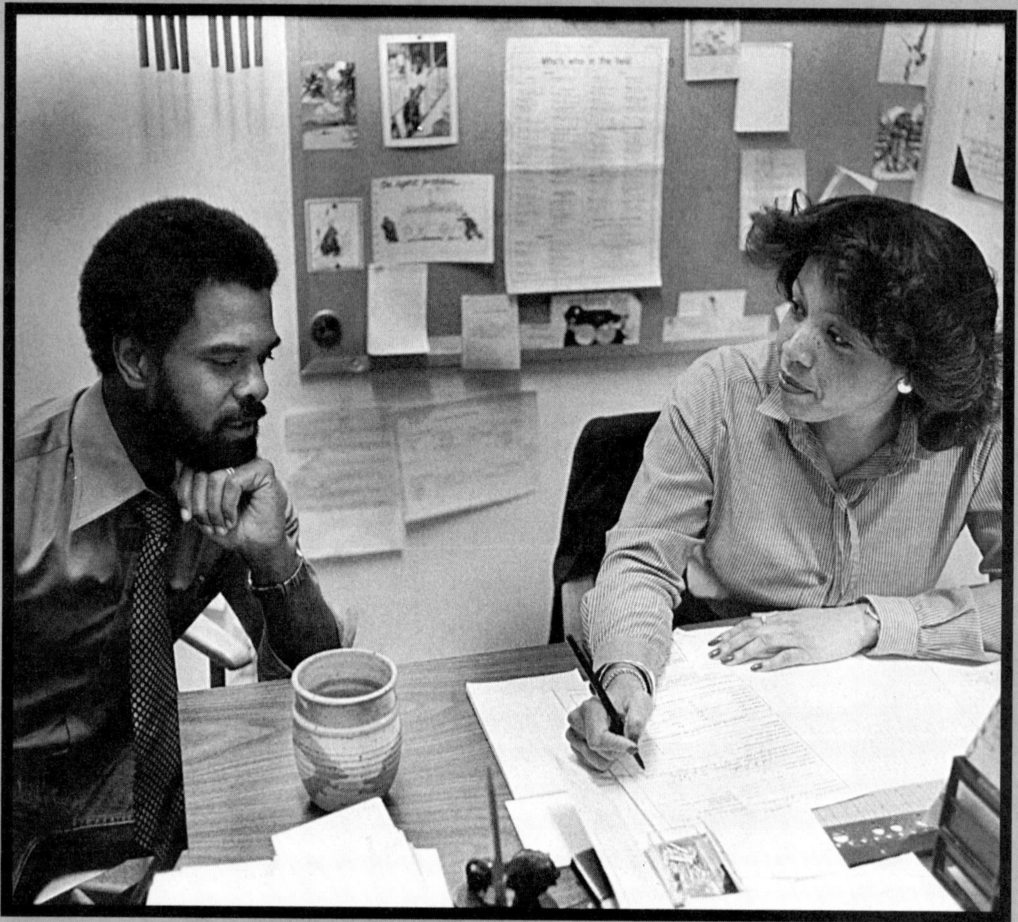

5

Understanding and Working With Parents

PARENTS OF EXCEPTIONAL students play an important role in working with school personnel to achieve educational goals. They, too, can be considered as resource persons, contributing according to their abilities to assist in developing their children's potential. Teachers and administrators have the responsibility to cooperate with parents and include them in planning and implementing educational objectives, to share information, and to support them.

The Parents' Role in Developing Services for Exceptional Students

The first parent organizations were formed in the 1920s (Cain, 1976), but they became open and vocal in the 1940s. Cruickshank (1975) cites the influences of World War II, from which many men returned physically and mentally handicapped, as augmenting a general societal change in attitudes toward the disabled. This in turn fostered parental activity. New parent groups were formed and gained in membership. The Civil Rights Movement of the 1960s also influenced parents toward increased militancy. The dramatic expansion of services in recent decades has resulted largely from the untiring work of parent groups and handicapped adults supported by a cadre of professionals. Within the sphere of social reform, they used litigation and pressed for legislation. Barrier-free access to public buildings, increased employment opportunities, public awareness and information programs, public funding for rehabilitative and educational services, and universal education for exceptional children are among the results of their endeavors.

In the schools parents demanded equal educational opportunities. Their role changed from mostly passive acceptance and nonparticipation to that as described by Wolf (1982) as parent advocacy, parents as teachers of their own children, parents as aides, and parents as team members.

The Child With a Handicap in the Family

A Traditional Psychological/Sociological View

The professional literature of several disciplines—psychology, sociology, and education—provides variations of a common paradigm that describes the sequence of parental reactions to the birth and growth of a child with a handicap. A typical sequence includes shock, denial, depression and grief, guilt, anger, and working through toward acceptance (Cansler & Martin, 1974; Emde & Brown, 1978; Solnit & Stark, 1961). Wolfensberger and Menaloscino (1970) report that many professionals viewed these reactions as evidence of pathology within the parents. Because the condition of the child was thought immutable, emphasis was given to psychiatric treatment of parents to help them adjust to their situation and lead them to a nebulously defined state of acceptance.

Criticisms have been made of the paradigm (Blacher, 1984; Featherstone, 1980; Seligman, 1979). It has been argued that the sequence of reactions cannot be simply attributed to all families who have exceptional children and that mitigating factors—family size, socioeconomic status, religious beliefs, and parent education—are ignored. There has been a growing reaction against the view of parents as pathologic and attributing to them the blame for their child's condition (Gallagher & Gallagher, 1978; Roos, 1978; Schleifer, 1981).

It has been recognized that parents of children with handicaps are subject to increased stress and that they will respond differently according to their psychological and environmental resources (Crnic, Friedrich, and Greenberg, 1983). Emotional states can be viewed as emerging in response to the nature of particularly stressful situations at critical periods within the life of the child. They diminish when the child is adjusting to a special school or program and intensify at times of critical decisions. Hammer (cited in Marion, 1981, p. 17) identifies such critical periods:

- At birth or upon suspicion of the handicap
- At the time of diagnosis and treatment of the handicapping condition
- As the child nears age for school placement
- As the child nears puberty
- As the child nears the age of vocational planning
- As parents age and the child may outlive them

Parents must adjust to the fact that they cannot have the same expectations for their child as parents of nonhandicapped children. When this realization occurs depends on the nature and degree of involvement of the handicapping condition, sociocultural variables of the family, and personal characteristics of its members.

Parental Reactions to the Child With a Mild Handicap

The shock–acceptance model evolved from clinical practice with parents of children with physical impairments and/or severe retardation evidenced at birth. The generalization of findings to the parents of children with mild-handicapping conditions, those diagnosed after entry to school, is questionable. Several factors mitigate parental reactions. These include evidence of the handicapping condition, the severity of the handicap, the role of the child in the family, and the status of the diagnosing individual or agency.

Evidence of the Handicapping Condition   The child with a severe handicap may have been marked by genetic or chromosomal factors or by insult early in pregnancy, which result in physical abnormalities. These present irrefutable evidence of the child's disability. Exceptionality of the child with a mild handicap is usually not evident at birth and often does not manifest itself visibly. Some children may demonstrate delays in achieving developmental milestones, but without sibling comparison such delays may go unnoticed or be of vague concern to the parents. They commonly report that pediatricians give little information and suggest that the child "will grow out of it." Given the wide variability of infant and early childhood development, the limited opportunities for observation by physicians, and their awareness of the parents' propensity toward overconcern, this conservatism is understandable. The mental limitations that often characterize the child with a mild handicap are unseen, less easily understood, and more easily denied.

Severity of the Handicapping Condition   One cannot disregard or minimize the emotional impact of any exceptionality of any child. Nevertheless, there may be a difference in the kinds of problems and emotional reactions of parents relative to the severity of the handicapping condition. Although one cannot predict what children with severe handicaps will ultimately accomplish, there is the inevitability of their not achieving an independent place in society. This is a factor with which the parents must come to terms. On the other hand, the parents of children with mildly handicapping conditions (and the children themselves) may face the continuing frustration and disappointment in their role of being almost but never quite like others.

Role of the Child in the Family   Parents may react differently to the diagnosis when children are older and have accommodated to family life. Their personalities are developed, family relationships have been established, and emotional bonds have grown. If there were earlier suspicions that problems might exist, the diagnosis can be a confirmation rather than a surprise. If there were no earlier indications, denial might be vigorous.

Status of the Diagnosing Individual or Agency   Pediatricians are usually the most important professionals in the life of the family. They have cared for the children since birth and are trusted and believed. Although a confirming second opinion might be sought, there is a finality about a medical diagnosis. Some parents who later find a physiological explanation for earlier problem behavior are relieved as it vindicates them, giving evidence that the cause is not found in their child-rearing practices. In school situations, parents rarely meet the psychologist until the diagnosis is presented. Sometimes they blame teachers or believe the data are exaggerated for placement for the school's convenience rather than for the welfare of the children.

Parents of Exceptional Students in School

An agreeable and productive relationship can exist between parents and school personnel. Many situations exist in which students with handicaps are assimilated into the life of the school and managed so capably that they, their nonhandicapped peers, and the professional staff of the school all profit from the experience. The literature, however, suggests that these occurrences are the exception rather than the rule (deBoor, 1975; Gorham, 1975; Gorham, Des Jardins, Page, Pettis, & Scheiber, 1975; Turnbull & Turnbull, 1978). The proportions of satisfactory versus unsatisfactory relationships with school systems and administrators are difficult to determine because dissatisfaction is more likely to be reported. However, cumulative evidence seems to identify this situation as a major area of concern.

Barriers to Effective Communication

With Parents Historically, a consistent level of satisfactory relationships has not been maintained between parents and professionals in the helping professions, including school personnel. Parents comment that:

- Although they are ultimately responsible for decisions about their children, clinical information that affects those decisions are often restricted from them.
- Professionals make diagnoses without fully explaining implications or being sensitive to parents' feelings.
- Professional jargon and technical terminology often interfere with communication and understanding.
- Professionals do not listen to parents and often discount observations about their children's behavior.
- Professionals do not fully describe options in placement or treatment and do not fully consider parents' opinions in these decisions.
- Professionals may assume condescending attitudes implying that parents are less capable or less intelligent or that they are responsible for their children's conditions.

With School Personnel Another barrier to effective cooperation may be the lack of knowledge of some professionals about exceptional children and their families. Often the training of regular teachers, administrators, and other personnel does not include information about students with handicaps. These factors can seriously compromise their receptiveness in working with them and their parents. Sometimes when resolving difficulties or interpreting the law regarding special education placement, teachers and administrators cannot agree. Parents are put in an awkward position in which they must take sides or make the decision and demand appropriate services.

Changes in parent–professional interaction have occurred as a result of the increase in militancy and parents' rejection of a subservient role. The two, however, have not generally achieved a continuing level of mutual respect and understanding but rather maintain, in the words of Sonnenschein (1981), "an easy relationship."

Perspectives in Understanding Parents of Exceptional Students

Professionals, no matter how well they have mastered the skills of their disciplines, cannot be fully effective if they are not sensitive to the attitudes and feelings of parents. It is not the intent here to dictate others' values but to present some information that has been found to improve relationships in working with the parents of exceptional students.

Parents of exceptional children are more like the parents of nonhandicapped children than they are different. Parents of all children have similar hopes, fears, joys, and concerns. Attitudes, child-rearing practices, and values vary regardless whether there is a handicapped child in the family.

Parents of exceptional children do not constitute a pathological group. All families encounter stress and employ coping mechanisms in response. The advent of a child with a handicap creates stress that continues throughout family life. The attitudes and behaviors of most parents can be viewed as expected coping strategies rather than abnormal reactions.

Parents of children with handicaps, in general, are not the cause of their children's disabilities. Child-rearing theories fashionable in past decades viewed child behavior as the result of parental influence alone without considering the child's natural propensity for generating behavior. Wender (1971, p. 152) notes that "psychological deviance in the parents may be a *response to* deviance in the child." Teachers may encounter some parents, as Wender recognizes, who were "seriously inadequate, immature, or impulsive individuals long before they had to contend with their children" (p. 153).

Obviously, parents cannot cause physical conditions, blindness, deafness, neurological handicaps or retardation. However, they can influence the child's condition psychologically. Their reactions, coping abilities, and intellectual and emotional resources either deter or help children to accept their limitations and develop their potential.

Parents of children with handicaps are interested in their welfare and will react positively to those whom they believe to be sincerely interested in their children. Most parents have had sufficient interaction with professionals to have become sensitive to their attitudes and sincerity. They are aware when attempts are made to manipulate them into accepting what intervention is convenient and available rather than providing what is needed. Parents are won over, not by raised hopes, sympathy, and unrealistic promises, but by individuals who are receptive to needs and who will take steps *with the parents* toward solving problems.

The family is a social unit and all members must be considered. Various authors have emphasized the need to observe the family as an ongoing, social unit in which members assume roles that have unique functional interrelationships. Satir (1967) popularized a therapeutic approach, which recognizes this structure. One tenet of this approach is that nothing ever happens to *one* member of a family. Changes in the status or role of any member affects everyone and causes stress for all family members.

Fathers are important. Although the historical view is that of the mother being the central family figure and the prime nurturer of the children, there is increased attention to the role of the father (Meyer, 1986). Sexual stereotypes have changed markedly in the past few years. Most fathers are interested in and affected by the status of their children. Cummings (1976) found fathers of children with retardation to exhibit feelings of depression and lowered evaluations of their own, and their wives, competencies as parents. It is obvious that such attitudes can affect the emotional climate of the home as well as specific child-rearing practices. Further, fathers may be affected when the son, in whom they see themselves reflected, is diagnosed as exceptional. The fact that 75 percent of the students identified as learning disabled are males suggests that fathers need to be included, especially in initial conferences that report the results of assessment.

Parents have the right to know as much about their child's diagnosis, behavioral functioning, and prognosis as the professional. Buscaglia (1975) has described parents as the "continuum" in the life of their children. They bear the ultimate responsibility for decisions about them. They can make them wisely only with full and accurate knowledge about their conditions and consequent functioning. Rather than assuming the professional prerogative to withhold information on the basis that parents may not understand it, school personnel are responsible for explaining data and discussing their implications.

Parents are specialists in regard to their own children. Webster (1977, p. 27) writes "each parent is a specialist in certain matters concerning his own child; . . . The parent knows and interacts with a child at home and within a family. The parents' experience predates and exceeds the experience others have with the child."

Parents cannot view their own children with complete objectivity; perceptions are always biased by the relationship. Yet, parents do know their children at home, and they are often more informed about the handicapping condition than school personnel. When parents' and teachers' descriptions of behavior are markedly divergent, it does not necessarily mean that one or the other is misperceiving or reporting inaccurately. A deeper exploration of the environmental conditions that foster the differing behaviors may bring new insights, which facilitate treatment.

Improving Home–School Relationships

The attitudes of both parents and school personnel and the action they take regarding one another or the students influence the quality of home–school relationships. Rutherford and Edgar (1979, p. viii) suggest that prerequisite to effective relationships between teachers and parents are that "first, teachers must believe that parents have a role in the education process" and that "second, before parents and teachers can cooperate, they must trust each other." These criteria are particularly applicable to parents and teachers of exceptional students.

Parent Attitudes If parents carry over from other experiences any suspicions about professionals' commitment and ability to help and if these perceptions are reinforced in initial contacts with the school, the opportunity for effective cooperation is diminished. Historically, parents have been called to the school to receive "bad news"—their children's poor academic progress or unacceptable behavior. Sometimes accompanying this information is the implicit message that the parents are to blame and that they are responsible for changing the child. Parents of exceptional students and individual learners have learned to anticipate the negative nature of school contacts.

Parents are not always able to be open or to communicate easily. They sometimes direct blame for their child's handicap on teachers. Teachers and principals should be aware that parents may need to vent feelings and express concerns. The reaction of school personnel is crucial. If parents' views are met with hostility and rejection, relationships can deteriorate. If these views are perceived as first steps in communication, other steps including explanation, clarification, and discussion can follow. If parents perceive the genuine interest of school personnel and if they receive concrete evidence in responsible action, a foundation for continued cooperation will be established. Some parents who have emotional resources and who have reached a level of acceptance work well with school personnel and may volunteer or serve in the class in other capacities.

School Personnel The attitudes of personnel toward having students with a handicap in the school or class and toward parents and their participation are major factors affecting the tone and quality of cooperation between home and school. If these attitudes are rejecting, little improvement can be expected. If they are open, a basis for the development of positive relationships is established. Whereas the parents may *react*, sometimes emotionally, to immediate problems, school personnel should be expected to *act* (rather than react) professionally, focusing on the long-term objectives of the student's education.

HOME–SCHOOL COOPERATION

Mrs. Thompson, Eric's mother, consulted Miss Blair, his teacher, about a problem at home. Eric, who is mildly retarded, is inconsistent in taking the trash to the curb, his once a week chore. Tom, Eric's older brother, is asked to do the job when Eric forgets. But Tom resents this and has resorted to physical fighting with Eric. Mrs. Thompson wants help in explaining to Tom that Eric's forgetfulness is a part of his handicapping condition and that Tom should be tolerant of his brother.

Miss Blair explained that it is sometimes difficult to determine which behaviors are related to the handicapping condition and which are not, but that Eric's forgetfulness should not be excused by his handicap. She agrees with Tom that he should not be requested to do his brother's work. Miss Blair advises Mrs. Thompson to assign a daily chore rather than a weekly one to establish a regular routine. She also agrees to work with Mrs. Thompson in determining a behavior-management plan to cue and reinforce Eric's performance of the assigned task.

A few surveys have been conducted that indicate what parents expect from professionals (Dembinski & Mauser, 1977; Gloeckler, Matavich, & Myers, 1985). They wish to be told fully and accurately about their children's conditions and with information being communicated clearly and in understandable terms. They believe that they are entitled to copies of reports and would like recommendations of readings as a source of additional information and guidance.

Although they are interested in causative factors, parents are more concerned with immediate, practical, relevant advice. What do we do now? Where do we go for help? How can we handle this particular situation? How can we manage behavior at home?

One area of interest to parents that professionals may not be able to predict is long-term expectations. Parents want to know the prognosis for the condition and the outlook for continuing education and subsequent occupational possibilities. The professional may comment on the permanence of the condition but needs to be cautious about making predictions about the student's future. Too many variables exist, including growth and development, motivation, and the intervention of professionals.

Initial steps toward making the parents feel more comfortable include the establishment of an accepting attitude toward parents and the provisions of a basis for productive interaction. There must be mutual respect, openness, and honesty. Parents need to be told about the positive characteristics and abilities of their child and what they have done "right." They do not need to be viewed as inadequate or pathological but as worthwhile individuals working to cope with the demands of raising a child with a handicap, deserving of the professional's support.

Another technique is to involve parents *before* problems occur. Activities such as assisting with class parties, being a room parent, or accompanying the class on field trips may prevent difficulties and allow parents to see their child in relation to other students.

Degrees of Home–School Cooperation

Home–school cooperation can be conceptualized at five levels representing the degree of interaction. These are information, participation, communication, involvement with instruction, and involvement in planning.

Information

The school provides parents with information about the school system in general, specific school and classroom expectations, and how the student is to meet these expectations. Parents supply identifying and ontological data to the school upon initial enrollment. Later they notify the school of changes in health or family status. However, this degree of cooperation is predominantly one-way, with the school providing information to parents through newsletters, report cards, work samples, and notes.

Newsletters Newsletters describing the school system, operating procedures, attendance and grading policies, and the yearly calendar are distributed to all families in the district in some systems. Others provide this information and other pertinent data on a school-by-school basis. Notices are sent home with students at the beginning and throughout the school year.

Report Cards Report cards are virtually universal as the procedure for informing parents about the academic progress and behavioral performance of their children. A discussion of report cards and grades for exceptional students in special settings is included in Chapter 3.

Work Samples Student papers or completed tests are sent home to be signed and returned. Equal in importance but far less practiced is sending home good papers as indicators of progress. Teachers assume that satisfactory work returned to students will arrive at home anyway; but they may not—especially papers of exceptional students who may not have learned to take pride in their good work. Teachers might occasionally request that such papers be signed and returned. An additional advantage of this procedure is that it relates to parents that teachers are aware of and value students and their accomplishments.

Notes and Happigrams Informal notes sent home with students or through the mail can reassure parents of teachers' continuing interest and provide information about behavior and academic work. They should not only be restricted to negative reports but also should be used to praise success and effort. Such notes are called happigrams. Examples are illustrated in Figure 5.1. They should not be marred with judgmental comments as "This proves he can do it if he would only put his mind to it." This kind of statement abbrogates the positive reinforcement aspects of the note and can be perceived by parents as a rejection of the student's general performance.

When providing parents with either negative or positive comments about behavior or work, teachers must do it judiciously. Some parents may use negative comments as a stimulus to become overly critical or rejecting of the student. A few may use physical abuse upon notification of misbehavior or poor grades. For the welfare of students, teachers should refrain from any comments to parents who might be provoked to such action.

Similar caution should be used with positive feedback. It is important to encourage students and parents with information about accomplishments and effort. However, teachers should take care that notes, telephone calls, and happigrams do not bring about unrealistic expectations on the part of the parents. Both must be aware that praise is given for the accomplishment of a specific task (not necessarily representing overall achievement) or for achievement within the context of the *adjusted* goals of the special program.

Several publishing companies have printed forms or ditto masters that can be used to report a good day, a successful activity, or an academic accomplishment by students. Taking only a few minutes to complete, they become tangible rewards for students who then receive positive attention from most parents.

Parents' Access to Records In general, parents have the right to know whatever the school knows about their children. This right is guaranteed in The Family

FIGURE 5.1

Happigrams

Educational Rights and Privacy Act (PL 93–380) of 1974 and commonly is known as the Buckley Amendment. Parents must be informed of the nature and location of all files and documents pertaining to their children and can examine all records. They may request school personnel to provide explanations of the information they do not understand and an interpretation of test scores. Limitations on this right include personal notes made by counselors or teachers for their own use in working with students and where these notes are not available to other school personnel. With few exceptions, records must also be made available to students over the age of eighteen.

Parents have the right to challenge the accuracy of the content of the reports and to request an alteration or amendment or removal of information. Should the school not comply, they can request a due process hearing. If the decision of the hearing officer is that the records shall remain intact, the parents have the right to insert a statement of objection and rebuttal.

The Buckley–Pell Amendment further protects the privacy of the content of school records by giving parents (and students over eighteen) control over their use. Parents may request in writing the release of records to specifically identified individuals and must do so for each request. The school must notify parents each time a request is made for records by an outside individual or agency. The school may release "directory information"—general identifying data such as those commonly used in newspaper articles or school publications.

Participation

Participation means that parents occasionally or routinely attend parent–teacher organizations and other school meetings. They may assist teachers in a number of ways—as room parents; to recruit other parents to plan and supervise class parties; to work on PTA activities; to provide transportation or to chaperone field trips; to work in the library, cafeteria, or office; or to assist the school nurse. Parent–teacher groups offer another opportunity to meet other parents, to participate in school activities, and to provide the means to raise needed funds for equipment and materials.

Parent Information Groups Parent information groups form the bridge between the information level and the communication level of home–school cooperation. Frequently special class teachers will organize a meeting of parents of students in special education. Because of the expanded agenda, a meeting during the school's regularly scheduled open house night might not be feasible. Teachers may present their philosophy of education, views on classroom expectations, rules, grading practices, schedules, goals, and mainstreaming procedures. They encourage participation and specify areas of needed assistance. Further, the overall school system plan for educating students should be reviewed because parents will have questions not only in regard to present planning but also about the long-term educational prospects. Opportunity is given for questions and expressions of concern, although discussions of individual problems are avoided. Another use of parent information groups is for contact with parents of nonhandicapped students in which they learn about special education and, hopefully, will understand and accept the presence of exceptional students in their child's classes.

Communication

Communication is defined as an interchange between parents and the school. It allows school personnel to keep parents informed but also provides opportunity for parents to express opinions and concerns, to discuss progress, and to receive answers to their questions.

Telephone Calls Telephone conferences can be advantageous for addressing minor problems or for clarification of information misinterpreted to parents by students. To save time needed to compose and write notes to parents, teachers can use the telephone for brief messages of concern or praise or to inquire about a prolonged absence. Telephones are more useful after rapport has been established in face-to-face meetings. Major problems might be better handled through a home visit or a school conference.

Home Visits Home visits are recommended in texts and teacher-preparation courses. They are probably recommended more than they are carried out. Occasionally, a particularly good rapport between teacher and parents sharing a mutual concern for a chronically ill student may result in the teacher's visiting the home. The lack of transportation, a new infant in the family, or a handicapping condition of the parent may make attendance at a parent conference difficult for the otherwise cooperative family. Home visits in these circumstances can be both pleasant and profitable as well as being appreciated by the parents.

Unfortunately, other home visits are necessitated by parents who will not come to school for routine or special conferences. For example, the parents of a student receiving special services must sign a new IEP each year. Lack of cooperation and possible resentment and hostility on the parents' part can result in the teacher's discomfort in the home visit and a further lack of parental cooperation. Often, the teacher's telephoned persistence, offering to make a home visit, results in the parents' decision to come to the school instead.

Involvement With Instruction

A broad spectrum of activities can be included. Parents can be volunteers in the classroom. At home they can monitor homework or provide supplemental instructional assistance. Some parents conduct extensive tutoring on a regular basis at home with or without the knowledge and/or cooperation of the school. Some parents may serve as resource persons.

Volunteers in the Classroom Parents can volunteer to be paraprofessionals or tutors for students other than their own children.

Homework Some teachers encourage parents to monitor homework although they expect the students to do the work themselves. Parents can provide a place and a time for study—away from the television set and other distractions—and be available for occasional assistance. A common problem is that a student may persistently not remember or reveal the extent of assignments. A chart can be provided for assignments, which can be checked by the parents. For some students an arrangement is made for teachers to initial the assignment block, including the notation "No homework." A smaller daily sheet may be necessary for students who lose papers routinely. They are illustrated in Figures 5.2 and 5.3.

Home Instruction   Many parents of exceptional children with visual, hearing, or physical impairments have routinely provided supplemental therapy at home and have been expected to do so by professionals. Educators, on the other hand, have not been in agreement as to the extent to which parents should teach their children at home or whether they should provide any assistance.

School personnel who object to home instruction cite several reasons:

- Parents usually have not had training in teaching methods, particularly those used with exceptional students.
- If students are in a highly structured, special program, parents are unaware of the sequence and content.
- Material that seems relevant to parents may be beyond students' present capabilities.
- Home should not be made an extension of the school; parents should not be placed in the role of teachers.
- Students are placed in a position of showing their poorest work to the people from whom approval is most needed.
- Students may be compared with siblings who are successful in school and who do not receive home tutoring.
- Home teaching sessions sometimes put too much pressure on students and break down into emotional confrontation.
- Students may perceive that they will not be loved if they cannot achieve in academic work. This can be frightening to students who do not believe they can be successful.

Others believe that parents can and should assist at home. They reason that:

- Exceptional students need more practice at each skill than do nonhandicapped students.
- Teachers, no matter how capable, cannot give sufficient time to each member of the class.
- Parents can learn to work with their children without emotional confrontation and upset.
- Exceptional students in the mainstream no longer receive needed instructional support and require home instruction.
- Over the years parents of exceptional students have, of necessity, learned to instruct their children in social and self-help skills. Therefore, academics can be taught as well.

A number of authors have not only advocated that parents teach their children at home but also have provided instruction for doing so (Berger, 1971; Bricker, 1978; Lillie & Trohanis, 1976; Weiss & Weiss, 1976). Some parents work well with exceptional learners, and others cannot. Still other parents do the work for children who may need to be prodded to do their own work. Teachers are usually able to determine which parents should be encouraged to help.

FIGURE 5.2

Homework Chart

Date	Monday ___		Tuesday ___		Wednesday ___		Thursday ___		Friday ___	
	No Hmwk		No Hmwk		No Hmwk		No Hmwk		No Hmwk	
Reading										
Math										
English										
Spelling										
Social Studies										
Science										
Health										
Parent signature										

FIGURE 5.3

Daily Homework Chart

```
Name  Rickie                    Date  October 14

                  Homework

1.  Memorize New England and Middle Atlantic states
    and capitols.
2.  Read Health chapter 3, pp. 62-67.
3.  Practice math facts X and ÷ 2.
4.
5.



Parent signature _____
```

Parents as Resource Contributors Parents can serve as resource persons in many classroom situations. Parents may be requested to share information about their occupation and arrange a tour of the place of business (for example, a bank, or a computer center). Parents may share information about a hobby or specialized interest. Slides of a foreign country in which parents may have visited or lived may be shown. A musician could demonstrate folk instruments. Such presentations can easily be worked into the curriculum content, can enrich the program, and can be a source of pride for those students whose parents perform.

Involvement in Planning

Involvement in planning may find the parent in an advisory role on a curriculum or other planning committee. Simpson and Poplin (1981) suggest that school personnel assist parents in learning how to become effective partners with the school in planning for their children's education. As discussed in Chapter 3, parents of exceptional students are required to be members of the placement and planning committee that examines assessment data and writes the IEP.

Research data show a disparity between the professed importance of parents in planning and their actual contribution during IEP meetings (Gilliam, 1979; Gilliam & Coleman, 1981; Knoff, 1983; Yoshida, Fenton, Kaufman, & Maxwell, 1978). Some meetings tend to be dominated by selected professionals with parents often making little input. Several authors have recommended procedures for improving parent involvement. Goldstein and Turnbull (1982) suggest sending lists of questions to parents prior to the conference and providing a school counselor to act as a parent advocate during the conference. Their research data suggest that parents provided with questions did not participate significantly more but when the counselor initiated questions on behalf of parents, they followed that lead. Gilliam and Coleman (1981) recommend that parents be included in the assessment and data-gathering phase in order to contribute in the conference.

It is important to establish positive home–school cooperation far earlier, keeping in mind the sequence of activities and attitude development previously discussed. Parents might be more comfortable in the team meeting and be willing to participate to a greater extent.

Not all parents will or should achieve these final degrees of cooperation with the school. The importance of this list lies in its specification of a sequence of participation. It is unrealistic to expect parents who have not cooperated with the school at earlier levels to be able to interact effectively with school personnel at the educational planning stage. Teachers must recognize various feelings and differing needs of parents in dealing with them in any given situation. Karnes and Zehrbach (1972, p. 8) state that "parents of handicapped children have needs, hopes, desires, wants, and frustrations like any other parents." They further indicate that successful parental involvement depends on:

- A positive professional attitude
- Recognition that parents can be involved in a variety of ways
- Belief that parents are capable of growth

Parent–Teacher Conferences

Parent conference days are commonly held at the elementary school level. Conferences are scheduled at regular intervals throughout the day. Evening sessions allow visits by working parents. Opportunity is provided for teachers to report about students' academic performance and social behavior and for some limited discussion. Structure is dictated by these purposes and time limits. At the secondary level, individual conferences are not usually scheduled for each family but may be held as required situationally.

Special and/or additional parent conferences may be necessitated to allow more comprehensive and in-depth discussions in regard to academic progress and social behaviors of some students.

Preparation

Preparing the Parents The school sends written notification of routine conferences to parents. An outline may be sent to them explaining why the conference is being conducted and giving information that can be discussed from the parents' and the teachers' points of view. Thus, the parents may be better able to participate and to remain on the topic.

The ninth grade counselor and the homeroom teacher met with Jeff's mother to discuss what adjustments will be needed as he enters high school. They assure her that accommodations are made for blind students. He will be assigned a "buddy" in each class for as long as is necessary to learn how to get to each class and other areas of the school. They explained that some texts will be available from the Recording for the Blind on tape and others will be in braille. A typewriter will be used for tests and written assignments for most subjects. The Director of Special Education will consult with other teachers, such as the gym teacher, to ensure his maximum participation in all subjects.

Physical Arrangements When all teachers in the building are conducting conferences, classrooms are used. For special conferences teachers may use a borrowed office to ensure privacy. They have limited control over environmental conditions but sensitive materials, guidance folders, class lists, and schedules should be removed from the desk. The chairs may be arranged away from the desk because, classically, the desk has been viewed as a barrier to communication.

Time and Length of the Conference Special conferences should be scheduled to allow both parents to attend. Organization and structure are necessary to prevent aimless discussion and time wasting, although sufficient time should be scheduled to allow achievement of the goals of the meeting.

Review of Data Teachers can be best prepared for a parent conference by a review of all related data. Foremost is the current information in regard to daily classroom achievement and behavioral performance. Reexamination of the gradebook and work samples will allow for accurate recall of specific information during the conference.

Personal Reflection A few moments of personal reflection is important. Teachers need to examine their attitudes toward students and families and resolve to be objective in their dialogue. They may have a checklist with points to be discussed, noting those which apply to individual students.

Conducting the Conference The following suggestions will hopefully lead to successful conferences:

- Be punctual. Start the conference on time so that other parents do not have lengthy waits.
- Establish rapport. Attend to the social amenities in greeting parents but do not "socialize." A professional but friendly and courteous demeanor is preferred.
- State the objectives of the conference at the outset. This is especially important for meetings not regularly scheduled but held in response to teacher concerns about the student. Do not keep the parents in suspense when giving background information leading to what they may anticipate as "the bad news."
- Demonstrate respect for parents. Do not use a manner that might appear to be condescending. Treat parents as persons who are capable of managing their responsibilities in this endeavor to solve problems together.
- Set an atmosphere of sharing concerns.
- Describe academic behaviors in terms of classroom and personal expectations.
- Describe social behaviors in terms of classroom expectations without recriminating judgments about personalities.

- Answer all questions. Be honest and truthful. When it is necessary to discuss negative points, present information factually, mentioning positive aspects, if possible.
- Do not mention other students by name or compare them to others.
- Avoid educational jargon. Describe the student's behaviors and abilities; do not use words such as hyperactive or immature.
- Use notes if necessary when referring to test scores or other specific data.
- Display student work samples to demonstrate academic growth or to illustrate specific problem areas. Do not use red-marked papers as a virtual accusation of student incompetence. Parents can become defensive or sense this practice as hostility.
- Do not criticize former teachers or the school administration. If parents criticize or complain about others, remain noncommittal and steer the discussion to other topics.
- Encourage parents to contribute to the conversation and make suggestions and comments from their perspective.
- Listen to their contributions and concerns.
- Take notes of parents' suggestions as a reminder to seek out additional information or to take some action on behalf of students and parents.
- Be aware of your own body language. Avoid facial expressions of shock, disapproval, disbelief, or rejection. Maintain eye contact, attentive posture, and a warm tone of voice.
- Terminate tactfully but firmly when objectives of the conference have been reached or when there are no more prospects for productivity.
- Summarize major points of the conference, particularly reviewing action that is to be taken by teachers or parents.

Postconference Activities

It is important to make a record of the conference as soon as possible after its termination. This should include the general content of the discussion, decisions reached, and specific agreements or action to be taken. Other activities depend on agreements made that include providing parents with additional information (book references, referral addresses, materials sources), regularly scheduled contacts through notes or telephone, or additional meetings. Cooperative attitudes and rapport are maintained between the school and the home not only for the present school term but also for subsequent years if teachers follow through with the planned activities, promises, and contacts with parents.

Additional Services to Parents

Parent Groups

Interested school personnel are often instrumental in starting parent groups. McDowell (1976) organizes work with parents into three categories: informational, parent training, and psychotherapeutic.

Information Groups As discussed earlier in the chapter, one kind of parent information group can be conducted by special class teachers. The meeting consists of one or two sessions to allow teachers and parents to become acquainted and to provide the parents with information about the class and the school.

Parents whose children were identified as exceptional in infancy or during the preschool years often have been aided by professionals from community agencies. They have received information about the handicapping condition, the development of and expectancies for their children, and direction in child management. Parents of children identified by the school may not have had the advantages of such resources. Thus, a second kind of parent information group may be organized for these parents.

The group may be conducted by one or two professionals: school psychologist, social worker, counselor, special education supervisor, and/or special education teacher. The group meets for a specified number of sessions with preplanned programs and time provided for discussion. By belonging to an information group, parents may receive emotional support from professionals and other parents.

Some parents will need to receive information regarding the disability area into which their child was designated. The group leader may accept the responsibility for answering questions or invite a resource person from the professional staff to meet with the group. Parents may also be aided by reading material about their child's handicapping condition and about parenting of exceptional children. A number of books on these topics can be found in the "Suggested Readings" at the end of the chapter.

In addition, parents may be provided with information about local, state, and national parent organizations. (A list of these is in Appendix A.) Groups such as the National Association for Retarded Citizens, Association for Children and Adults with Learning Disabilities, and the Epilepsy Foundation of America can provide short-term assistance or continuous support. Activities include meetings, discussion groups, and fund-raising and social functions.

Training Groups A topic of central concern to parents is behavior management at home and in the community. They may ask themselves several questions: Can behavior be attributed to the handicapping condition or to normal growth and development? If the behavior is "caused by" the condition, can I do anything about it, or is that behavior inevitable? Can I discipline my child? If so, how? How much freedom can I give him in the neighborhood? Can I expect her to be responsible for chores? What kind of punishment shall I use? Will I damage him emotionally by being too strict?

Parents who are interested may be invited to attend a parent training group. They are usually organized for the purpose of helping parents manage behavior at home. Henry (1979) identifies three approaches commonly used by leaders in parent-training groups. These are behavioral, Adlerian, and interpersonal communication.

Behavioral Approach Behavior modification techniques apply B. F. Skinner's operant conditioning theories. Groups are formed in which the parents are instructed in how to specify and record behaviors and in the principles of reinforcement that are discussed within the context of practical examples. They are asked to begin a modification program at home by selecting a behavior and planning, with the aid of the leader and the group, a sequence of procedures for management or change. Progress of the program is reported during the continuing sessions with recommendations for modifications being made as needed. Through their participation in the program, each parent can gain a perspective for the use of the principles in many situations.

The group leader may select a book upon which to base discussion or elect to use a published management program for parents. The "Suggested Readings" include a list of books and programs. Some of these contain filmstrips, cassettes, and other audiovisual and supplementary material.

Adlerian Approach   The principles of this approach come from the work of Alfred Adler, a disciple of Sigmund Freud and psychoanalytic theories. Adlerian counselors perceive misbehaviors as the child's maladaption to the family organization. Counseling has the goal of reorganizing the family structure toward growth-facilitating interaction rather than the hardening of positions that lead to confrontation and conflict. *Children, the Challenge* (Dreikurs & Soltz, 1964), *Family Council* (Dreikurs, Gould, & Corsini, 1974), and *STEP, Systematic Training for Effective Parenting* (Dinkmeyer & McKay, 1976) are examples of programs employing this approach.

Interpersonal Communication Approach   The focus of attention in this approach is that parents develop and understand family relationships and the child's behavior, resolve conflicts, and improve the nature and quality of parent–child communication. The theoretical basis for this approach can be traced to the work of Carl Rogers (1951). He hypothesizes that individuals behave on the basis of their perceptions of their environments, and thus to change behavior one must first provide conditions that allow the individuals to change their perceptions. The objectives of the interactional approach are to provide parents with the opportunity to alter their own perceptions as a result of information, discussion, and insight, and to enable them to appreciate and understand the perceptions and behaviors of their children.

Parent Counseling   School systems usually do not extend their services into the area of clinical counseling of parents, either individually or in groups. Some systems have comprehensive diagnostic-service units, funded experimental programs, or liasion with a nearby university, which allows them to offer counseling services. In other situations the interest of a licensed or certificated psychologist, counselor, or social worker in the system facilitates group meetings.

Definition   Counseling and psychotherapy have been given a number of definitions. Ivey (1980, p. 12) proposed that a common underlying base of several helping therapies is a "reasoned search for individual–society or person–environment connectiveness leading to the growth of both individual persons and their significant others (family, group, organization, institution)." This definition is appropriate to parent counseling as presented here.

Goals   Specific goals emerge out of the counselor's thorough understanding of and sensitivity to the needs of parents in their response to their child's handicap. The goals for counseling parents of children with handicaps are as diverse as for any other client or group. Counseling may offer emotional support, development of self-understanding, improved interpersonal relationships, and insights into problems. The counselor will address the multidimensional nature and range of problems.

Group or Individual Counseling   Whether the counselor meets with individuals or groups depends on the preference of the therapist, the needs of the parents, the nature of the problems, and agency policy. Parents who are experiencing serious adjustment difficulties either in relation to their handicapped child or with family dynamics and who cannot yet expand their perspectives beyond their own immediate situation may need individual counseling before being introduced to the group. For many others, those with continuing but less severe problems and stress, a group may be more beneficial. Parents can see that they are not alone in the kinds of problems they face, can gain perspective, and can learn from others.

Methods   A wide range of theories, methods, and approaches are used by counselors and psychotherapists. Research has consistently failed to support any one procedure in comparison to others. Using a meta-analysis procedure, Smith and Glass (1977) examined 400 research reports regarding the success of various types of therapy. They found no one to be superior nor a difference between behavioral and non-behavioral strategies. Carkhuff (1972, p. 10) suggests that the differences in counseling effectiveness can be traced to "the skills with which the helpers relate to other people (interpersonal skills) and the skills which they have in their special areas (program skills)."

Referral Outside the School

Services beyond those available in schools may be necessary for some parents and students. Special services personnel should maintain a directory or file of outside services and be cognizant of the scope of each agency and the clientele that they are prepared to serve. When appropriate, referrals may include:

- Mental health centers
- Child guidance clinics
- Social services
- Parent organizations
- Community day schools
- Day care services
- Family service agencies
- University diagnostic centers
- Welfare services
- Recreational facilities
- Summer camps for handicapped children
- Special community agencies (Easter Seals, Cancer Society)
- Hospitals and medical centers (especially those that specialize in particular health/disability areas)

- Physicians, pediatricians, neurologists, and other health care specialists
- Psychologists, psychiatrists, and other mental health professionals

School personnel should avoid the implication that the recommended agency will be successful with the child/family problems or become involved directly in making the contact. Rather, the parents are invited to ascertain on their own whether the service might fit their needs. They have the right to decide whether to follow through with the referral recommendation. If they do, the agency may request information from the school.

SUMMARY

Parents of exceptional students play an important role in developing their children to their fullest potential. Changes came about as the result of parent groups, attitudes of school personnel, litigation, and legislation.

The reaction of parents to their child's handicap depends on the severity of the condition, the role of the child in the family, and their perceptions of the diagnosing individual or agency.

It is the school's responsibility to establish a positive working relationship with parents by eliminating barriers to communication, by understanding parents' perspectives, and by developing a relationship based on mutual respect, trust, and openness.

Parent cooperation begins at the information level and proceeds through participation, communication, involvement with instruction, and involvement in educational planning. At the information level, parents and school exchange necessary data about students and school progress. As parents become more comfortable, they may participate in school activities and groups. A more open exchange of attitudes and ideas characterizes the communication level. Some parents become further involved by monitoring homework, by serving as resource persons, by volunteering or becoming aides in the classroom, or by instructing their children at home. Parents of exceptional students participate in planning the IEP.

Parent conferences are an important vehicle for exchanging information with parents and providing them with an accounting of the progress of their children. Preparation includes contacting parents, arranging the physical environment, and reviewing data to be covered. Teachers establish rapport with the parent(s) and state the objectives of the conference at the outset. During the conference they describe students' academic and social behaviors accurately, respond to questions honestly, and solicit and listen to parents' contributions. Afterwards they implement decisions made during the conference.

Schools may offer additional services to parents, including information groups, parent training, and counseling. They may also direct them to outside agencies that may be of temporary or continuing support to students with handicaps and their families.

REFERENCES

Berger, E. H. (1981). *Parents as partners in education: The school and home working together.* St. Louis: Mosby.

Blacher, J. (1984). Sequential stages of parental adjustment to the birth of a child with handicaps: Fact or artifact? *Mental Retardation, 22*(2), 55–68.

Bricker, D. B. (1978). A rationale for the integration of handicapped and nonhandicapped preschool children. In M. Guralnick (Ed.). *Early intervention and the integration of handicapped and nonhandicapped children* (pp. 3–26). Baltimore: University Park Press.

Buscaglia, L. F. (Ed.). (1975). *The disabled and their parents: A counseling challenge.* Thorofare, NJ: Slack.

Cain, L. F. (1976). Parent groups: Their role in a better life for the handicapped. *Exceptional Children, 42,* 432–437.

Cansler, D. P., & Martin, G. H. (1974). *Working with families: A manual for developmental centers.* Reston, VA: The Council for Exceptional Children.

Carkhuff, R. R. (1972). The development of systematic human resource development models. *Counseling Psychologist, 3*(3), 4–11.

Crnic, K. A.; Friedrich, W. N.; & Greenberg, M. T. (1983). Adaptation of families with mentally retarded children: A model of stress, coping, and family ecology. *American Journal of Mental Deficiency, 88,* 125–138.

Cruickshank, W. M. (1975). The development of education for exceptional children. In W. M. Cruickshank, & G. O. Johnson, (Eds.). *Education of exceptional children and youth* (3rd ed.) (pp. 3–41). Englewood Cliffs, NJ: Prentice-Hall.

Cummings, S. T. (1976). The impact of the child's deficiency on the father: A study of fathers of mentally retarded and of chronically ill children. *American Journal of Orthopsychiatry, 46,* 246–255.

de Boor, M. F. (1975). What is to become of Katherine? *Exceptional Children, 41,* 517–518.

Dembinski, R. J., & Mauser, A. J. (1977). What parents of the learning disabled really want from professionals. *Journal of Learning Disabilities, 10,* 578–584.

Dinkmeyer, D., & McKay, G. (1976). *STEP: Systematic training for effective parenting.* Circle Pines, MN: American Guidance Service.

Dreikurs, R.; Gould, S.; & Corsini, R. J. (1974). *Family council.* Chicago: Henry Regnery.

Dreikurs, R., & Soltz, V. (1964). *Children: The challenge.* New York: Hawthorn.

Emde, R. N., & Brown, C. (1978). Adaptation to the birth of a Down's syndrome infant: Grieving and maternal attachment. *Journal of the American Academy of Child Psychiatry, 17,* 299–323.

Featherstone, H. (1980). *A difference in the family: Life with a disabled child.* New York: Basic Books.

Gallagher, J. J., & Gallagher, C. G. (1978). Family adaptation to a handicapped child and assorted professionals. In A. P. Turnbull, & H. R. Turnbull, III (Eds.). *Parents speak out: Views from the other side of the two-way mirror* (pp. 198–210). Columbus, OH: Merrill.

Gilliam, J. E. (1979). Contributions and status rankings of educational planning committee participants. *Exceptional Children, 45,* 466–468.

Gilliam, J. E., & Coleman, M. C. (1981). Who influences IEP committee decisions? *Exceptional Children, 47,* 642–644.

Gloeckler, T.; Matavich, M.; & Myers, R. (1985). *An evaluation of the Child Learning Center: Results of the second parent survey.* Unpublished Report: Department of Counseling and Special Education, The University of Akron, Akron, OH.

Goldstein, S., & Turnbull, A. P. (1982). Strategies to increase parent participation in IEP conferences. *Exceptional Children, 48,* 360–361.

Gorham, K. A. (1975). A lost generation of parents. *Exceptional Children, 41,* 521–525.

Gorham, K. A.; Des Jardins, C.; Page, R.; Pettis, E.; & Scheiber, B. (1975). Effect on parents. In N. Hobbs (Ed.). *Issues in the classification of children, Vol. II* (pp. 154–188). San Francisco: Jossey-Bass.

Henry, S. A. (1981). Current dimensions of parent training. *School Psychology Review, 10,* 4–14.

Ivey, A. (1980). Counseling 2000: Time to take charge. *The Counseling Psychologist, 8*(4), 12–16.

Karnes, M. B., & Zehrbach, R. R. (1972). Flexibility in getting parents involved in the school. *Teaching Exceptional Children, 5,* 6–19.

Knoff, H. M. (1983). Effect of diagnostic information on special education placement decisions. *Exceptional Children, 49,* 440–444.

Lillie, D. L., & Trohanis, P. L. (Eds.). (1976). *Teaching parents to teach: A guide for working with the special child.* New York: Walker.

Marion, R. L. (1981). *Educators, parents, and exceptional children: A handbook for counselors, teachers, and special educators.* Rockville, MD: Aspen.

McDowell, R. L. (1976). Parent counseling: The state of the art. *Journal of Learning Disabilities, 9,* 614–619.

Meyer, D. J. (1986). Fathers of handicapped children. In R. R. Fewell, & P. F. Vadasy (Eds.). *Families of handicapped children: Needs and supports across the life span* (pp. 35–73). Austin, TX: Pro-Ed.

Rogers, C. R. (1951). *Client centered therapy.* Boston: Houghton Mifflin.

Roos, P. (1978). Parents of mentally retarded children—Misunderstood and mistreated. In A. P. Turnbull, & H. R. Turnbull, III (Eds.). *Parents speak out: Views from the other side of the two-way mirror* (pp. 12–27). Columbus, OH: Merrill.

Rutherford, R. B., & Edgar, E. (1979). *Teachers and parents: A guide to interaction and cooperation.* Boston: Allyn and Bacon.

Satir, V. M. (1967). *Conjoint family therapy: A guide to theory and technique.* Palo Alto, CA: Science and Behavior Books.

Schleifer, M.J. (1981). Let's all stop blaming the parents. *The Exceptional Parent, 11*(3), 16–19.

Seligman, M. (1979). *Strategies for helping parents of exceptional children: A guide for teachers.* New York: The Free Press.

Simpson, R. L., & Poplin, M. (1981). Parents as agents of change. *School Psychology Review, 10,* 15–25.

Smith, M. L., & Glass, G. V. (1977). Meta-analysis of psychotherapy outcome studies. *American Psychologist, 32,* 752–760.

Solnit, A. J., & Stark, M. H. (1961). Mourning and the birth of a defective child. *Psychoanalytic Study of the Child, 16,* 523–537.

Sonnenschein, P. (1981). Parents and professionals: An uneasy relationship. *Teaching Exceptional Children, 14,* 62–65.

Turnbull, A. P., & Turnbull, H. R., III (Eds.) (1978). *Parents speak out: Views from the other side of the two-way mirror.* Columbus, OH: Merrill.

Webster, E. J. (1977). *Counseling with parents of handicapped children: Guidelines for improving communication.* New York: Grune & Stratton.

Weiss, H. G., & Weiss, M. S. (1976). *Home is a learning place: A parents' guide to learning disabilities.* Boston: Little, Brown.

Wender, P. H. (1971). *Minimal brain dysfunction in children.* New York: Wiley.

Wolf, J. S. (1982). Parents as partners in exceptional education. *Theory into Practice, 21,* 77–81.

Wolfensberger, W., & Menolascino, F. J. (1970). A theoretical framework for the management of parents of the mentally retarded. In F. J. Menolascino (Ed.). *Psychiatric approaches to mental retardation* (pp. 475–492). New York: Basic Books.

Yoshida, R. K.; Fenton, K. S.; Kaufman, M. J.; & Maxwell, J. P. (1978). Parental involvement in the special education pupil planning process: The school's perspective. *Exceptional Children, 44,* 531–534.

SUGGESTED READINGS

Chinn, P.; Winn, J.; & Walters, R. (1978). *Two-way talking with parents of special children: A process of positive communication.* St. Louis: Mosby.

Ehly, S. W.; Conoley, J. C.; & Rosenthal, D. (1985). *Working with parents of exceptional children.* St. Louis: Times Mirror/Mosby.

Gallagher, J. J., & Vietze, P. M. (Eds.) (1986). *Families of handicapped persons: Current research, programs, and policy issues.* Baltimore: Brookes.

Gargiulo, R. M. (1985). *Working with parents of exceptional children: A guide for professionals.* Boston: Houghton Mifflin.

Kroth, R. L. (1975). *Communicating with parents of exceptional children: Improving parent–teacher relationships.* Denver: Love.

Losen, S. M., & Diament, B. (1978). *Parent conferences in the schools: Procedures for developing effective partnership.* Boston: Allyn and Bacon.

Michaelis, C. T. (1980). *Home and school partnerships in exceptional education.* Rockville, MD: Aspen.

Mori, A. A. (1983). *Families of children with special needs: Early intervention techniques for the practitioner.* Rockville, MD: Aspen.

Schulz, J. B. (1987). *Parents and professionals in special education.* Boston: Allyn and Bacon.

Seligman, M. (Ed.) (1983). *The family with a handicapped child: Understanding and treatment.* New York: Grune & Stratton.

Simpson, R. L. (1982). *Conferencing parents of exceptional children.* Rockville, MD: Aspen.

Stewart, J. C. (1986). *Counseling parents of exceptional children* (2nd ed.). Columbus, OH: Merrill.

Turnbull, A. P., and Turnbull, H. R., III (1986). *Families, professionals, and exceptionality: A special partnership.* Columbus, OH: Merrill.

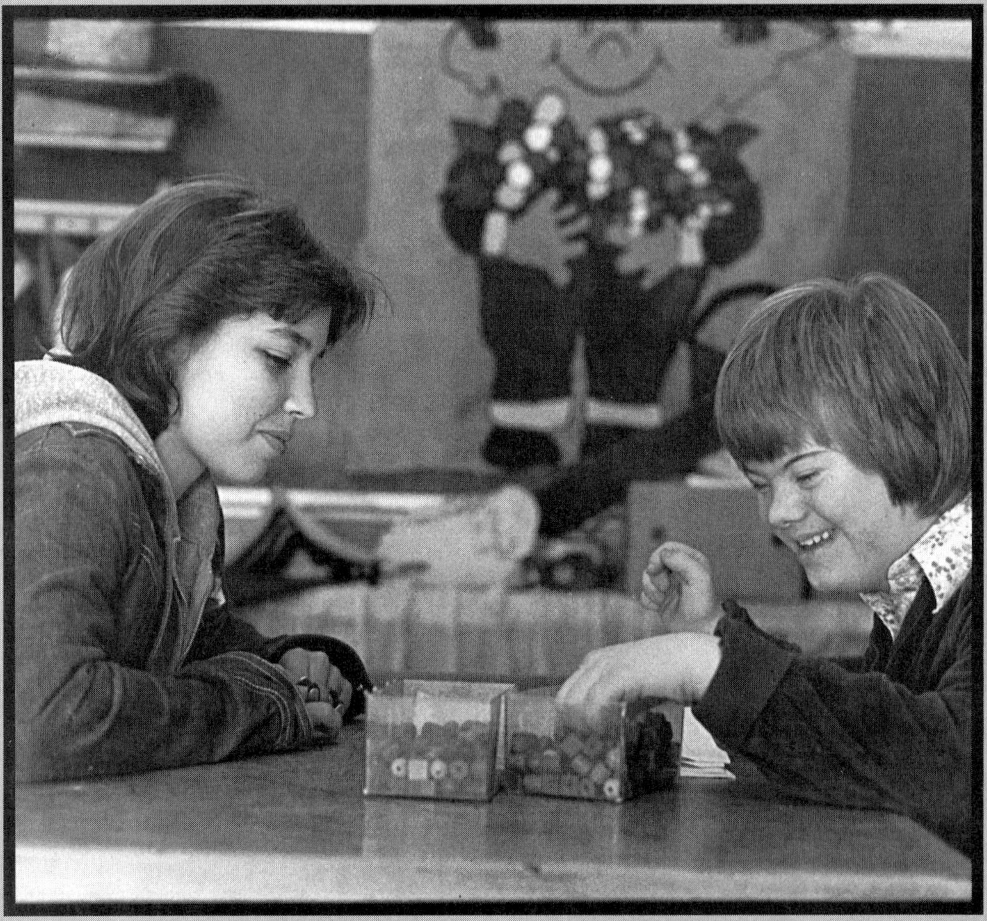

6

Learning Environments

TEACHERS ARE the central effectors of change of behavior not only through instruction but also by establishing the classroom conditions in which learning takes place. As a young teacher, Haim Ginott (1972) came to this realization and wrote:

> I have come to a frightening conclusion. I am the decisive element in the classroom. It is my personal approach that creates the climate. It is my daily mood that makes the weather. As a teacher I possess tremendous power to make a child's life miserable or joyous. I can be a tool of torture or an instrument of inspiration. I can humiliate or humor, hurt or heal. In all situations it is my response that decides whether a crisis will be escalated or de-escalated, and a child humanized or de-humanized.
> — (Reprinted from Haim G. Ginott, *Teacher And Child: A Book for Parents and Teachers*, p. 13. Copyright 1972 by Dr. Alice Ginott.)

Teachers must be aware of the three interactive environments—physical, social, and psychological—that they must manage to achieve the goals of academic learning and personal growth for their students.

The Physical Environment

The physical environment consists of the school building and classrooms, the furniture and equipment, and climatic conditions—heat, ventilation, light, and sound. Although often overlooked during planning for instruction, the physical facilities do influence behavior and learning. Maintenance of optimal conditions regarding size, arrangement, decor, and order is important. Additional concerns are adaptations that need to be made for students with physical and sensory impairments.

Adaptations

With the increased participation of students with physical and sensory impairments, it has become apparent that architectural modifications needed to be made in public buildings to allow free access by those in wheelchairs or on crutches. Schools are subject to PL 93–111, Section 904, which mandates such provisions for all public facilities supported by federal funds.

The School Building Schools that serve students with physical handicaps often have a separate entrance—a door near a stopping place for vans and buses equipped with wheelchair lifts. A roof extension over the area is desirable. A ramp to the doorway is a necessity. The entrance and doors throughout the building must be sufficiently wide to permit wheelchair passage. Ramps with nonskid surfaces and handrails should be provided at every change of level. An elevator will need to be available in multilevel buildings. Provision should be made for wheelchairs in restrooms, and handles on water fountains may need to be adjusted.

The Classroom Few modifications of the physical structure of the regular classroom are needed. Of more importance is the arrangement—seating, aisles, access to materials, and visibility and audibility. Such accommodations are made not only for students with orthopedic handicaps but also for those with sensory impairments.

Impact of the Physical Environment on Learning and Behavior

Barker (1968) noted that the nature of the environment establishes behavioral expectations. The traditional classroom arrangement with students' desks in rows and the teacher's desk in front sets the stage for teacher dominance and student conformity. More recently, teachers have become sensitive to the fact that learning and behavior are affected by the environment. By using a more flexible arrangement, they have initiated student interaction and discussions, quiet seatwork, or independent activity at learning centers.

Modifying the Physical Environment

Seating Arrangements Preferential seating is given to students with sensory impairments. Students with visual impairments are placed near the teacher, the chalkboard, and in a location with reduced glare on desks and the board. Students with hearing impairments must be seated to allow maximum aural receptivity, which means placing them with the bet   ear toward the center of the room rather than toward a wall. They also need optimal visibility of both the chalkboard and teachers' faces to allow speechreading. Those in wheelchairs or with crutches are seated near the door with ample room to move.

For students with mild retardation or learning disabilities, reduction of distractibility is a major goal. They can focus attention more easily and are less distracted by others when desks are placed near teachers, facing the board, and away from windows and doors. Separating desks reduces student interaction and increases attention to learning tasks. Teachers need to be cautious when determining which students can have desks grouped successfully.

Organization of Learning Areas Some teachers organize the classroom into areas based on principles of behavior reinforcement. The Premack Principle (Premack, 1959) proposes that activities with high reinforcement value can be used as a reward for performing less desirable activities. In practice the classroom is divided into instructional areas and reinforcement areas. If students perform as expected in group lessons, study, and written assignments, they are rewarded with time in a reinforcement area. It is a place with attractive enrichment activities, games, craft materials, animals, or audiovisual materials. Some teachers provide a study/reading reward area with a rug and pillows or a rocking chair.

Provision for a Quiet Corner A quiet corner can be made with carrels or behind a bookcase or file cabinet. Some students, both exceptional and individual learners, can monitor their own levels of anxiety. They know when they need a respite from classroom pressure and stimulation. They know that they can go for a brief time of relaxation to regain control or to work without distraction. They also know they cannot use the corner as an escape from classroom expectations but must return to complete the assignment they left even if others in the class have moved on to other activities. The quiet corner can also be used as a reward for students who complete assignments ahead of others. They may have time for free reading or other activities until the start of the next group lesson.

Use of Carrels A set of carrels for general use can be beneficial in the regular classroom. They provide a reduced stimuli environment for concentrated study or for students working on individual projects, assignments, or make-up work. Carrels may be used to form a time-out corner or for punishment.

Other Environmental Conditions

Lighting and Climate What little research exists on lighting, temperature, and ventilation indicates that moderate variations in these conditions do not have a strong influence on behavior or achievement (Weinstein, 1979). Experience suggests, however, that prolonged or marked variations in any of them can have a detrimental effect on performance.

Noise Level The day of the totally quiet classroom is past. It is recognized that noise can be indicative of productive work. Most students apparently adjust to variations in noise level without decline in achievement (Weinstein & Weinstein, 1979). However, some nonhandicapped as well as exceptional students may be auditorily distractible with concentration and attention to task being reduced by high-noise levels. For these students accommodations are possible by monitoring and controlling noise level, by providing a carrel separated from the noise source, or with the use of a headset during individual study and work.

Classroom Neatness The attention of students with mild impairments can be diverted by general classroom clutter—bright scraps not cleared away after an art project, piles of papers or unshelved books, or fading construction-paper displays. To encourage attention, desktops can be cleared, and pencils put away while the teacher is making a formal presentation, giving instructions, or assigning homework. Books and worksheets are not distributed until after preliminary instructions have been given and students are ready to attend to them.

Teachers' awareness of student response to these factors in the physical environment will enable them to make modifications that result in improvement in both learning and behavior.

The Social Environment

How students interact with teachers, classmates, and the larger population of the school comprises the social environment. It is important to create an atmosphere that will facilitate the learning of social skills and provide opportunities for non-handicapped students to know and accept exceptional students and individual learners.

Social Status of Exceptional Individuals

Research on the social status of students with handicaps in the classroom finds them largely rejected and isolated. These findings accrue from data concerning students with mental retardation (Gottlieb, Semmel, & Veldman, 1978; MacMillan & Morrison, 1980), students with learning disabilities (Bryan & Bryan, 1978; Garrett & Crump, 1980; Siperstein, Bopp, & Bak, 1978), and for students with emotional handicaps and/or behavior disorders.

Although research has been consistent in presenting evidence of isolation and rejection of exceptional students, the causes have been more elusive. Among those hypothesized are that

- Students have not learned acceptable social skills.
- In a learning environment that places a premium on academic achievement, students with handicaps are often at the bottom of the class.
- The disability label (for example, mental retardation or learning disability) sets negative expectations and an initial barrier to acceptance.
- Hyperactive, acting out, or disruptive behavior draws unfavorable attention.
- Language deficits limit social communication.
- Students in the class detect a rejecting attitude on the part of teachers and model their behavior.
- Students with perceptual deficits "misread" subtle verbal and behavioral messages of others and therefore do not adjust their own behaviors to conform to group expectations.
- Exceptional students are less mature than their same-age peers.

Some of these factors are more valid explanations than others. In any one situation several of the variables may contribute to the social limitations. Thus, remediation cannot be unilateral but must address students, the group, and the nature of the interactions. Administrators and teachers can reverse the conditions that result in these research findings. In service sessions provide information to enable teachers to learn about various types of handicapping conditions and specific techniques to accommodate physical or mental limitations. Administrators provide support for teachers and students. Some students with handicaps relate well to peers and adults and are accepted. They contribute to the group and make friends even though some activities are limited due to their disability.

Improving the Social Environment A number of potentially effective procedures have been recommended to teach socially acceptable behavior and the acceptance of exceptional students. They are attitude change among nonhandicapped peers, modifications of teachers' attitudes and behavior, peer-mediated procedures, other classroom procedures, social skills training, preparing for the social environment in the regular classroom, and self-image.

SOCIAL SKILLS TRAINING

Paul had been diagnosed as learning disabled in the third grade. With the help of a tutor and the support of his teachers, he was able to overcome the disability and is now, in seventh grade, achieving reasonably well in all academic subjects. However, he was concerned that he was not popular and was picked last for teams and classroom activity groups. When he made a new friend, the relationship would last for only a few days before he was "dropped." Paul's former tutor referred him to the guidance counselor, Miss Taggert. She obtained a series of interactive video social skills training tapes from the local resource materials center. Actors in the video presented common social situations. At crucial points the action stopped, and Paul was asked to select from several options, indicating the behavior he believed the character should perform next. The video demonstrated what the social consequence would be. If Paul selected an inappropriate behavior, he could see the negative reactions of others to it. Then he would discuss other options with Miss Taggert. Through the interactive video, Paul learned appropriate social behavior and by the end of the year was having success in establishing and maintaining friendships with several students.

Attitude Change Among Nonhandicapped Peers Most people receive no formal training about handicapping conditions. Much of what is believed by adults and students is derived from hearsay evidence and popular media presentations, both of which can provide distorted data. It has been suggested that providing accurate information about the conditions and by describing exceptional individuals as "more like others than different" may alter perceptions and establish a basis for acceptance. Research supports the improvement of peer attitudes through instruction about handicapping conditions and individuals with handicaps (Fiedler & Simpson, 1987). A number of curricula for this purpose have been developed (Barnes, Berrigan, & Biklen, 1978; Bookbinder, 1978; Cohen, 1977).

Experience with individuals with handicaps has resulted in both positive and negative attitudes on the part of nonhandicapped students (Horne, 1982). Simple exposure to exceptional persons will not necessarily result in improved attitudes. A combination of information and experience is more likely to be successful.

Nonhandicapped students need to learn about various exceptionalities. This is often accomplished through puppet shows in which the character portrayed has a limitation and answers questions for the class. Students take turns being a buddy for the student with a handicap by carrying books or equipment for blind students or by accompanying students in wheelchairs, on elevators, and to the bus.

Modification of Teachers' Attitudes and Behavior Although many teachers welcome exceptional students in their classes, others harbor negative feelings toward them. These feelings may have roots in misperceptions of the disabilities and resentment of the presence of the students. Some may fear that they will not be able to manage or teach exceptional students, which would result in lowered expectations and different treatment from other students. Further, nonhandicapped peers might perceive this attitude and adopt similar rejecting behaviors.

If this situation occurs, amelioration would need to be directed toward teachers' attitudes and to reinforcement of teaching capabilities. These objectives can be accomplished indirectly through courses, in service training, and recommended readings. Directly, a resource teacher, a consultant, or a principal can provide support and assistance in individual situations.

Research on this topic has been published by Forness and Esveldt (1975); Gickling and Theobald (1975); Graham, Burdg, Hudson, and Carpenter (1980); Larrivee and Cook (1979); and others.

Peer-Mediated Procedures Several procedures enlist the aid of individual students or an entire class to improve the social behavior of target students. Group-oriented contingencies result in class members being rewarded for reinforcing suitable behavior and ignoring antisocial behavior of a class member. A variation of this method is to train selected, nonhandicapped peers in operant conditioning principles that they employ in initiating and maintaining social communication with a withdrawn class member. Greenwood and Hops (1981) report research in which positive side effects include spontaneous tutoring, social reinforcement, and increased social interaction.

Another form of peer-mediated intervention is the use of models either on film, videotape, or live. Because it has been indicated that students cannot be expected to imitate modeled behavior spontaneously (Bandura, 1977), the teacher (or film narrator) directs attention of the exceptional student to the desired behaviors. This procedure is easy to adapt to special or regular classroom instruction for social skills training. Research includes that of Gresham and Nagel (1980) and LaGreca and Santogrossi (1980).

Peer tutoring can also be used to improve social acceptance through mutual reinforcement. Teacher praise of both students can provide incentive for continued cooperation. Peer tutoring arrangements have been successful with students with mental retardation, learning disabilities and behavior disorders. Reviewing the research on peer tutoring are Allen and Feldman (1977) and Barry and Overman

(1977). Brown (1986) noted that improved social status was one of the additional benefits when the student with a handicap was the tutor.

Other Classroom Procedures

Changing Unacceptable Behaviors Teachers use behavior management techniques to reduce excessive activity, talking out, antisocial acts and communication, and undesirable mannerisms. When behavior conforms to peer expectations, students are in a better position to be accepted.

Grouping Grouping exceptional and nonhandicapped students for projects may foster interaction and encourage acceptance. Groups should be small enough to require participation of all members and allow sufficient teacher guidance. Exceptional students can be assigned a task they are capable of accomplishing although it may be necessary to adapt activities. They must be an essential part of the group. Because it has been found that short-term associations are not likely to generalize beyond the termination of the project, the activity should be of substantial length to require continuing interaction.

Cooperative Learning Cooperative learning (Johnson and Johnson, 1980) is a method that requires learning academic content in small groups that include both nonhandicapped and exceptional students. Johnson and Johnson (1986) and Madden and Slavin (1983) found that members of cooperative learning groups improve significantly more than control groups in both academic learning and social acceptance of the handicapped members. Cooperative learning as a teaching method is discussed more fully in Chapter 9.

Social Skills Training for Students With Handicaps Social skills training involves the identification, assessment, and instruction of specific behaviors that students need to initiate and maintain positive social relationships. Gresham and Elliott (1984, pp. 294–297) identify the following procedures commonly employed in assessment: "sociometric techniques, ratings by others, behavior role play, self-reporting measures, behavioral interviews, and naturalistic observation."

Morrison and Borthwick (1983) found that the pattern of personality characteristics unique to each student were determining factors in peer social interaction. They recommend these be considered in aiding individual students to increase social competencies.

Some of the specific skills to be taught include those listed in Figure 6.1. Although these skills can be taught by regular teachers, they are often part of the special education classroom curriculum.

Instruction can take several forms including modeling, role playing, sociodrama, and direct instruction. Stephens (1978) provides an extensive program which identifies 136 skills grouped into four categories: behaviors related to environment, interpersonal behaviors, self-related behaviors, and task-related behaviors. Each skill is keyed to other commercial materials including stories from basal readers which relate to or are designed to teach the skill.

FIGURE 6.1

Selected Social Skills

Introductions	Manners
Initiating a conversation	Following directions
Praising others	Understanding others' feelings
Responding to praise	Sensitivity to nonverbal behavior of others
Giving compliments	
Thanking another	Cooperative behavior
Requesting help	Sharing
Apologizing	Taking turns
Appropriate emotional responses	Helping others
Listening to others—not interrupting	Sportsmanship
	Eating habits

Specific behaviors in social situations: eating out, public transportation, attending sporting events

Other programs for building social skills and facilitating the development of interpersonal relationships include *Basic Skills Enrichment* (Opportunities for Learning), *Social Responsibility* (Ohio Department of Education), Developing Social Acceptability (Walker), *People Need Each Other* (Opportunities for Learning), and *Developing Understanding of Self and Others* (DUSO Kits 1 and 2, American Guidance Service).

As exceptional students reach adolescence, the range of social relationships expands and expectations increase. For many, social skills training will continue to be important. (Argyle, 1985). Methods are similar to those already discussed, although specific skills vary with age and social environment demands. Others will need counseling or assistance from special teachers or psychologists to develop acceptable social skills. Programs for teaching social skills are also available for adolescents.

Preparing for the Social Environment in the Regular Classroom In the environment of the special education classroom, failure has been largely eliminated. Competition among students may be reduced; positive reinforcement has been increased, and some students may be dependent on teachers. They are not contrasted to their peers. They may feel more secure there and be apprehensive when returning to the regular class. Before students move to the regular classroom, special teachers will need to prepare them for the different social environment. This is accomplished by reducing reinforcement, by increasing behavioral expectations, and by creating an environment similar to that of the regular class.

Self-Image

When exceptional students have learned these skills and have been successful in social situations, they will usually accept and like themselves with their abilities and limitations. When they like themselves, they learn to communicate and to reveal themselves, which enable them to relate to and then to love others. Through success experiences they develop confidence in their abilities. They can develop their potential and reach beyond to achieve. It is the role of teachers to inspire students just as parents, spouses, and friends endeavor to do with those they love.

The Psychological Environment

The psychological environment, or classroom climate, refers to the kinds of relationships established between teachers and students and among peers; the nature of classroom communication, structure, management techniques; and academic expectations. The quality of these characteristics can have a significant impact on learning and behavior.

Impact of the Psychological Environment on Learning and Behavior

Teachers' personalities, styles of teaching, and philosophies are major factors in establishing a healthy psychological environment in which there is an atmosphere of acceptance, warmth, and enthusiasm. Rules, expectations, and consequences are clearly defined and consistently enforced. When structure and organization are added, teachers can be confident that rapport will be established, good relationships will be maintained, learning will be promoted, and self-image will improve.

However, the psychological environment of some classrooms may have an adverse effect. When students are treated unfairly, belittled, or yelled at regularly, they may become fearful and resentful. They may "give up" on themselves and learning.

In summarizing the research, Medley (1979, p. 22) suggests that the productive classroom "tends to be orderly and psychologically supportive." Soar and Soar (1979, p. 105) suggest that while an "effectively neutral classroom can be functional," it is of crucial importance that the climate not be negative. Students can survive without constant praise but they can be damaged by constant criticism. Studies show that many regular teachers spend more time interacting negatively with students with mild retardation and learning disabilities than with nonhandicapped students. A survey of college freshman indicated that they remembered and resented specific incidents of criticism and negative feedback from former teachers over a period of several years (Vaughan, 1984)

Characteristics of the Psychological Environment

Most research on classroom environments has been done at the secondary level because reliable student responses and perceptions can be investigated. In the absence of conclusive research at the elementary level, teachers follow the recommendations and learn from the experiences of the many professionals who have worked with students with handicaps. Over 100 adjectives and descriptive phrases of recommended attributes were found in the professional writing. Six major focuses are identified: flexibility, a student-centered classroom, a climate conducive to learning, an organized classroom, psychological support, and communication.

Flexibility Curriculum and methods are selected and adjusted to meet individual needs. Teachers are receptive to a change of approach if one is more successful than another. Various learning experiences are provided. Adaptation to scheduling, grouping, and students entering and leaving the room are accepted as routine. Teachers are open to new ideas and suggestions.

Student-Centered Classroom Students are accepted, which enable them to accept themselves. Teachers encourage them to become self-reliant and to accept responsibility for themselves and their actions. Efforts, perseverance, and achievement are rewarded. The focus is on strengths, assets, and the interests of students. There is recognition of individual differences, needs, and learning styles. Students are given acceptable choices in academic situations and when learning suitable behavior. Success experiences are planned and expected.

An accepting and understanding environment is described as one that is safe and secure. It is relaxed and enjoyable yet structured. There is open and honest communication. Students are trusted and trusting and know that they will be treated fairly. They are appreciated. They are able to share and express feelings appropriately. They are free to make mistakes without reproach.

Climate Is Conducive to Learning Realistic academic expectations are established in a climate in which success and stimulating lessons are the rule rather than the exception. Individual instruction and purposeful, task-oriented activities are organized that students are capable of performing. Immediate feedback is given. Library and study skills, problem solving techniques, and similar learning-how-to-learn skills are taught early in the year to improve skills in all content areas. Various materials are provided. When the climate is conducive to learning, students are more likely to be motivated to learn.

Organized Classroom Exceptional students need a structured classroom with routine and predictability of what will happen and when it will happen. Policies and rules must be established and enforced consistently. Teachers must also be consistent with procedures and management techniques. They conduct classroom activities objectively and in a businesslike way, giving evidence of classroom control and indicating that sufficient time has been spent in preparation. The key to a well-organized classroom is consistency.

Psychological Support A sound psychological environment is established with students by purposeful, planned interactions that are based upon positive and genuine personality characteristics of teachers. They have a positive self-image: They know, accept, and like themselves. They value and encourage the students, keeping in mind their strengths and limitations. They are kind but firm, are calm yet enthusiastic, and empathize with their concerns. They convey to students their belief that they can succeed and learn. They provide positive feedback whenever possible.

Communication Several aspects of communication affect the psychological environment. Teachers set the tone by how and what they say to students, other professionals, and parents. Affective dialogue influences learning, self-image, and how colleagues work together.

Teachers establish rapport with students primarily by talking to them. They maintain a good relationship by being honest, respectful, and by displaying a sense of humor. Time must be provided to listen to students so that trust can be established and to let them express their ideas, concerns, and ask questions. Conversations must remain nonjudgmental and supportive.

Students need to develop the ability to communicate with their peers. If the environment is comfortable, they can learn to discuss, make decisions, solve problems, and develop self-confidence by sharing with their classmates. During language development classes, students are encouraged to share experiences and feelings and to respond readily.

Communication among regular and special teachers is the key to a successful special education program. Special education teachers have the responsibility to make regular teachers comfortable and to be available to discuss referrals, progress, and problems pertaining to students with special needs.

GENERALIZING GOOD BEHAVIOR

The intermediate level resource room teacher, Mrs. McMahon, (aware that behaviors are often specific to the environments in which they are taught) received comments that social behaviors taught in her room were not carrying over into other areas of the school. She developed a program of generalization that involved the entire staff. Each day she provided a three-by-five-inch card to each student to be carried throughout the day. When another teacher or staff person observed appropriate behaviors, they took time to write the comment on the student's card. At the end of the day, each student had the opportunity to share these comments with the students in the resource room. This allowed additional reinforcement for the behavior and served as an incentive for others.

A suitable classroom environment is enhanced when parents are aware of and supportive of the program. Teachers encourage this by maintaining regular communication with parents, especially in regard to their children's successes in academic work and behavior. Parents need to feel at ease when talking to teachers about their children. As discussed in Chapter 5, teachers must be sensitive to parents' feelings, must be willing to listen to them, and must discuss issues in language that all parents can understand.

SUMMARY

The physical, social, and psychological environments of the school and the classroom have a direct influence on student learning and behavior. The physical facilities are adapted to allow access by students with orthopedic impairments. Those with vision and hearing impairments are given preferential seating to allow maximum receptivity and participation. In addition, teachers organize the classroom using instructional and reinforcement areas, a quiet corner, and carrels to foster productive learning. They are aware of the effect of climatic conditions on learning, although some of them are beyond teacher control.

The quality of the social environment involves acceptable interaction with teachers and students in special and regular classes. Regular teachers facilitate good relationships among students through their own positive attitudes toward and acceptance of students with handicaps. They encourage similar attitudes among the nonhandicapped students and also enlist their aid with peer-mediated procedures including behavior management techniques, modeling, and peer tutoring. Teachers also use carefully planned grouping and cooperative learning situations to foster successful interaction. Regular and special teachers cooperate to reduce undesirable behaviors and to improve the self-image of exceptional students by direct instruction of social skills.

The psychological environment refers to the kinds of relationships established between teachers and students and among peers and the nature of classroom communication, structure, management techniques, and academic expectations. Teachers are responsible for establishing a healthy classroom climate and support system that promotes growth in behavior, academic achievement, and self-concept. This is accomplished through avoidance of destructive criticism and unfair treatment and the use of encouragement and positive management procedures. Six major focuses of a good psychological environment include flexibility, a student-centered classroom, a climate conducive to learning, an organized classroom, psychological support, and communication.

Together the physical, social, and psychological environments influence the nature of learning and behavior in both regular and special classrooms.

REFERENCES

Allen, V. L., & Feldman, R. J. (1977). Learning through tutoring: Low-achieving children as tutors. *Journal of Experimental Education, 42*(1), 1–5.

Argyle, M. (1985). Social behavior problems and social skill training in adolescence. In B. H. Schneider, K. H. Rubin, & J. E. Ledingham (Eds.), *Children's peer relations: Issues in assessment and intervention* (pp. 209–224). New York: Springer-Verlag.

Bandura, A. (1977). *Social learning theory.* Englewood Cliffs, NJ: Prentice-Hall.

Barker, R. G. (1968). *Ecological psychology: Concepts and methods for studying the environment of human behavior.* Stanford, CA: Stanford University Press.

Barnes, E.; Berrigan, C.; & Biklen, D. (1978). *What's the difference?: Teaching positive attitudes toward people with disabilities.* Syracuse, NY: Human Policy Press.

Barry, N. J., Jr., & Overman, P. B. (1977). Comparisons of the effectiveness of adult and peer models with EMR children. *American Journal of Mental Deficiency, 82,* 33–36.

Bookbinder, S. R. (1978). *Meeting street school curriculum.* Boston: Exceptional Parent Press.

Brown, W. (1986). Handicapped students as peer tutors. *Academic Therapy, 22,* 77–79.

Bryan, T. H., & Bryan, J. H. (1978). Social interaction of learning disabled children. *Learning Disabilities Quarterly, 1*(1), 33–38.

Cohen, S. (1977). *Accepting individual differences.* Niles, IL: Developmental Learning Materials.

Fiedler, C. R., & Simpson, R. L. (1987). Modifying the attitudes of nonhandicapped high school students toward handicapped peers. *Exceptional Children, 53,* 342–349.

Forness, S. R., & Esveldt, K. C. (1975). Classroom observation of children with learning and behavior problems. *Journal of Learning Disabilities, 8,* 382–385.

Garrett, M. K., & Crump, W. D. (1980). Peer acceptance, teacher preference, and self-appraisal of social status of learning disabled students. *Learning Disabilities Quarterly, 3*(3), 42–46.

Gickling, E. E., & Theobald, J. T. (1975). Mainstreaming: Affect or effect. *Journal of Special Education, 9,* 317–328.

Ginott, H. G. (1972). *Teacher and child; A book for parents and teachers.* New York: Avon Books.

Gottlieb, J.; Semmel, M. I.; & Veldman, D. J. (1978). Correlates of social status among mainstreamed mentally retarded children. *Journal of Educational Psychology, 70,* 396–405.

Graham, S.; Burdg, N. B.; Hudson, F.; & Carpenter, D. (1980). Educational personnel's perceptions of mainstreaming and resource room effectiveness. *Psychology in the Schools, 17,* 128–134.

Greenwood, C. R., & Hops, H. (1981). Group-oriented contingencies and peer behavior change. In P. Strain (Ed.). *The utilization of classroom peers as behavior change agents* (pp. 189–259). New York: Plenum.

Gresham, F. M., & Elliott, S. N. (1984). Assessment and classification of children's social skills: A review of methods and issues. *School Psychology Review, 13,* 292–301.

Gresham, F. M., & Nagel, R. S. (1980). Social skills training with children: Responsiveness to modeling and coaching as a function of peer orientation. *Journal of Consulting and Clinical Psychology, 48,* 718–729.

Horne, M. D. (1982). Facilitating positive peer interactions among handicapped and non-handicapped students. *The Exceptional Child, 29,* 79–86.

Johnson, D. W., & Johnson, R. T. (1980). Integration of handicapped students into the mainstream. *Exceptional Children, 47,* 90–98.

Johnson, D. W., & Johnson, R. T. (1986). Mainstreaming and cooperative learning strategies. *Exceptional Children, 52,* 553–561.

LaGreca, A. M., & Santogrossi, D. A. (1980). Social skills training with elementary school students: A behavioral group approach. *Journal of Consulting and Clinical Psychology, 48,* 220–227.

Larrivee, B., & Cook, L. (1979). Mainstreaming: A study of the variables affecting teacher attitude. *Journal of Special Education, 13,* 315–324.

MacMillan, D. L., & Morrison, G. M. (1980). Correlates of social status among mildly handicapped learners in self contained special classes. *Journal of Educational Psychology, 72,* 437–444.

Madden, N. A., & Slavin, R. E. (1983). Effects of cooperative learning on the social acceptance of mainstreamed academically handicapped students. *Journal of Special Education, 17,* 171–182.

Medley, D. M. (1979). The effectiveness of teachers. In P. L. Peterson, & H. J. Walberg (Eds.). *Research on teaching: Concepts, findings, and implications* (pp. 11–27). Berkeley, CA. McCutchan.

Morrison, G. M., & Borthwick, S. (1983). Patterns of behavior, cognitive competence, and social status for educable mentally retarded children. *Journal of Special Education, 17,* 441–452.

Premack, P. (1959). Toward empirical behavior laws. I. Positive reinforcement. *Psychological Review, 66,* 219–233.

Siperstein, G. N.; Bopp, M. J.; & Bak, J. J. (1978). Social status of learning disabled children. *Journal of Learning Disabilities, 11,* 98–102.

Soar, R. S., & Soar, R. M. (1979). Emotional climate and management. In P. L. Peterson, & H. J. Walberg (Eds.). *Research on teaching: Concepts, findings, and implications* (pp. 97–119). Berkeley, CA: McCutchan.

Stephens, T. M. (1978). *Social skills in the classroom*. Columbus, OH: Merrill.
Vaughan, L. R. (1984). *Psychological abuses of children in the public schools*. Unpublished master's thesis. The University of Akron, Akron, OH.
Weinstein, C. S. (1979). The physical environment of the school: A review of the research. *Review of Educational Research, 49*, 577–610.
Weinstein, C. S., & Weinstein, N. D. (1979). Noise and reading performance in an open space school. *Journal of Educational Research, 72*, 210–213.

SUGGESTED READINGS

Anderson, K., & Milliren, A. (1983). *Structured experiences for integration of handicapped children*. Rockville, MD: Aspen.
Birch, J. W., & Johnstone, B. K. (1975). *Designing schools and schooling for the handicapped*. Springfield, IL: Thomas.
Bormaster, S. J., & Treat, C. L. (1982). *Talking, listening, communicating*. Austin, TX: Pro-Ed.
Cartledge, G., & Milburn, J. F. (1986). *Teaching social skills to children: Innovative approaches* (2nd ed.). New York: Pergamon.
Ehly, S. W., & Larsen, S. C. (1980). *Peer tutoring for individualized instruction*. Boston: Allyn and Bacon.
Loughlin, C. E., & Sunia, J. H. (1982). *The learning environment: An instructional strategy*. New York: Teacher's College Press.
Moos, R. H. (1979). *Evaluating educational environments*. San Francisco: Jossey-Bass.
Smith, R. M.; Neisworth, J. T.; & Greer, J. G. (1978). *Evaluating educational environments*. Columbus, OH: Merrill.
Strain, P. S. (Ed.) (1981). *The utilization of classroom peers as behavior change agents*. New York: Plenum.
Strain, P. S. (Ed.) (1982). *Social development of exceptional children*. Rockville, MD: Aspen.

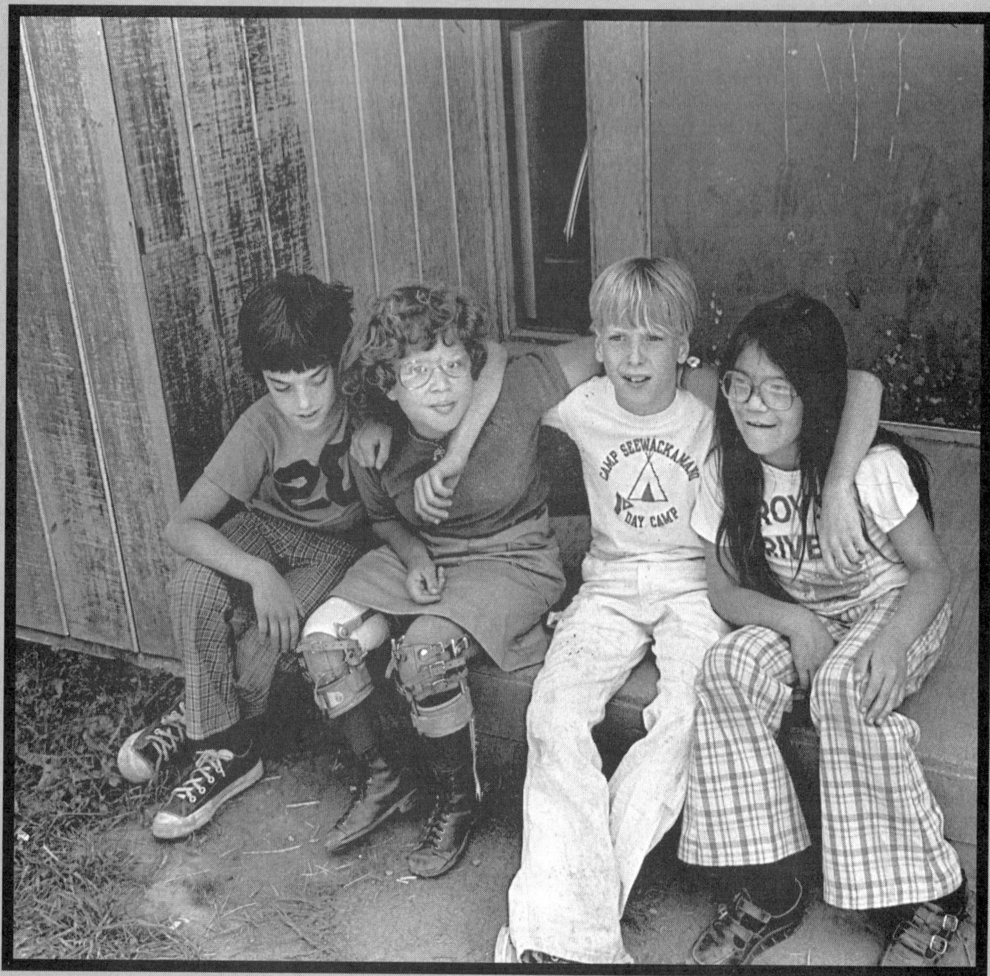
DAY CAMP

7

Managing Behavior

STUDENT BEHAVIOR is a major concern to regular and special classroom teachers, tutors, administrators, and auxiliary personnel. Parents and community leaders also express alarm about the severity of the problem. Gallup polls have consistently found that discipline is the major concern the American public has about its schools.

By and large, teachers have learned effective behavior management techniques and conduct organized and productive classes. Most are empathetic with students, interested in their welfare, and supportive in their continued growth toward learning, maturity, and self-control. They may become apprehensive, however, about the behaviors of exceptional students who are assigned to their classes. They may share with the beginning teacher the continuing concern: What do I do with the student who is a behavior problem? How do I control the class?

Teachers need to develop personal philosophies about the entire issue of classroom behavior. They need to define behavior, to develop conceptualizations about the origins of behavior patterns, and to develop a set of tenets relative to the purposes and goals of a management program. They need to learn and develop skills in incorporating various management strategies within the ongoing educational program. Finally, they need an administrative and auxiliary personnel support system to assist in the entire behavior management endeavor.

What follows is a response to these stated needs. Beginning with definitions and a philosophy of behavior control, this chapter will outline procedures, methods, and techniques for the classroom, combining various approaches. These presentations do not constitute a cookbook, nor are they conceived as being either the only way or a panacea for all behavior problems. They represent the authors' personal convictions and practices evolved from both educational research and classroom experience.

Goals, Definitions, and Some Postulates

Goals

There are two major goals of behavior management procedures in the classroom. One is the establishment of an orderly environment in which all students can engage in the business of learning. The other is to provide activities by which individual students are progressively taught to manage their own behavior. Both goals involve establishment of discipline. To understand the intent of the statement as it is used here requires an examination of definitions and postulates that represent assumptions about behavior and its management.

Definitions

Behavior   A psychological definition of behavior is that it is any activity performed by the individual. Teachers and parents sometimes use the term to refer to a restricted kind of behavior. The psychological definition is accepted here and applies to each instance in which the word *behavior* is used.

Behavior Management   This term refers to *any* procedure or practice that has the purpose of influencing, changing, or controlling behavior. It is applicable to all practices of any approach that has the management of behavior as the goal. Further, it refers both to practices in which one individual (usually the parent or teacher) attempts to influence the behavior of another (usually the child) as well as to those practices that are self-management procedures. The term *behavior management* is *not* synonymous with the term *behavior modification* although some writers may use them interchangeably. Behavior management is a generic term that encompasses not only behavior modification but other procedures as well.

Behavior Modification   This term refers to a specific kind of management procedure that is based on the operant conditioning principles of B. F. Skinner. There is substantial misunderstanding about these procedures by many teachers and parents, evolving partly from an overemphasis with only one technique—that of a token economy. In addition, the term sometimes instills revulsion that such procedures are akin to "brainwashing" and that the professional exercises a degree of "control" over the client. Teachers sometimes forget that the term *learning* itself is most simply defined as a change in behavior and that it is their job to change behavior. Behavior modification techniques can be employed for this purpose and are no more menacing than is the primary goal of promoting learning in the classroom. A careful reading of the literature also helps one understand that such procedures can be used in a humane manner and can help students to learn to manage their own social and learning behavior.

Discipline   Despite dictionary definitions and the widespread use of this word as a euphemism for physical or other punishment, the word is used here as the consistent and continued organization of behavior for the purposes of teaching acceptable ways of behaving in a group situation, for academic achievement, or for personal productive living.

Some Postulates

Understanding student behavior increases the probability that behavior can be effectively managed. Several premises follow.

1. *Behavior is a learned activity.* Behavior is learned over time within the environment in which the person functions. It is the product of all the individual brings to the situation—the physiological, cognitive, and psychological characteristics—and past learnings interacting with the characteristics of the environment.
2. *Behavior is developmental.* Individuals develop characteristic behavior patterns and control over their own behavior longitudinally throughout their lives, particularly during the school years.
3. *Discipline, as an organization of behavior, is concomitantly developmental.* One of the tasks of the school is to help students organize behavior for productive social and academic achievements.
4. *Behavior is not a static characteristic that "dwells" within the student ready to be expressed, intact, in any circumstance.* The behavior of one individual can vary from environment to environment.
5. *Teachers have the responsibility for the class.* Teachers employ behavior management procedures that are ultimately beneficial to students and not simply for their convenience. This involves identifying goals and expectations; defining the sequences of learning tasks; securing the physical and psychological environments; selecting methods and techniques for both instruction and control; setting and reinforcing limits on behavior; and providing encouragement, support, and opportunities for individual growth.

Factors Influencing Methods Selection

In the light of the awesome charge given teachers, it becomes obvious that no one method nor any single approach will be sufficient in meeting the needs of both teachers and students. Teachers need to be armed with a variety of techniques from several approaches. Selected methods from more than one approach can be used together in the classroom. Further, competence in a wide variety of techniques provides teachers with a flexible repertoire for meeting the myriad and challenging behaviors that are often exhibited in the classroom by regular and special students. Which methods and techniques are chosen will depend on a number of factors including teacher personality, knowledge of students, and academic considerations.

Teacher Factors

Teachers are probably the most influential persons in the lives of the students outside the home. They are representatives of "the real world," that world that is apart from the usually supportive and protective unit of the family, and they may be the first contact with a member of another culture, socioeconomic, or ethnic group. Teachers' personalities and behaviors affect students' social attitudes, self-concept, perceptions of the world, and value systems in ways that are not immediately discernible or measurable. Students' perceptions of their own ability in coping with "the real world" and in being accepted by others begin with interactions with classroom teachers.

Teacher Personality Behavior management methods are neither effective nor ineffective in and of themselves. They are dynamic when they become integrated with teachers' professional personalities, which become a factor in the selection and effective use of techniques.

Comfort With the Methods Teachers need to feel comfortable about the methods they use. One teacher may find it difficult to ignore irritating behaviors; another may have reservations about using a recommended reward system. Before threatening a student with corporal punishment, teachers must come to terms with their own ability to follow through should the need arise.

In managing behavior, a plan must be adopted and followed consistently if it is to be effective. Therefore, teachers should examine each of the methods incorporated in the plan prior to its initiation to make sure they feel comfortable about its use.

Teacher Learning Although teacher personality is important, most teachers cannot control classes on the strength of personality alone. Further, the methods and techniques that may be needed are not acquired through general experience prior to entering the teaching profession. Techniques specific to classroom management must be identified and purposefully learned. As in any learning, the initial steps may be neither comfortable nor easy. Often, initial attempts are ineffective. It is common for teachers using behavior-modification programs for the first time to give up when a technique does not bring about behavior change in a short time or when the behavior appears to get worse (as it may during initial steps). However, persistence is needed for the ultimate benefit of both teacher and student.

Knowledge of Students

A paramount criterion for the selection of methods is knowledge of the individual student with whom the techniques are to be used. As methods must be appropriate to the personality of the teacher, they also must be appropriate to the personalities of the students. As teachers must learn new management skills, students must learn to respond to new classroom organizations and management procedures. Students have developed learning and behavior styles and ways of responding to various situations. Students who welcome changes in activity and who are curious to learn new things differ from students who are threatened by the insecurity of change. With the former students, teachers can use the promise of a new activity as motivation or a reward. For others, they will need to use tact in introducing change lest anxiety erupt in recalcitrance, crying, or other acting-out behaviors.

Development of Self-Control Student's control over their behavior is learned and developed gradually. Teachers sense how much can be expected at any one point and set reasonable expectations for behavior conformity. Few rules must be stated as students cannot follow several at once. This is especially true as they learn to meet divergent expectations between home and school or between teacher and teacher. If they realize that teachers are willing to work with them on troublesome behaviors, they can relax, anxiety diminishes, behavior is improved, and control is developed at an increasing rate.

Out-of-School Environments The choice of behavior techniques is influenced by out-of-school and home environments. Some students live in neighborhoods where violence is a daily routine. Young children may be literally afraid of their violent world. Their misbehaviors in school are not so much extentions of their environment but a defense against it. Not having other models for better ways of coping, their defenses take the form of the violence around them. This is an important distinction. Teachers who use or threaten to use physical means to manage behavior merely reinforce the perception that the world is a violent place. With no alternative model for dealing with the problem, students continue to react maladaptively. Those who are abused at home do not need physical punishment in school. Spoiled children need help in learning gratification delay. The welfare of students and classroom behavior control are enhanced when they are taught to interact with others and to solve problems acceptably.

Academic Considerations

Unquestionably, there is a link between the academic program and classroom behavior. Disruptive activities and poor academic performance occur together with high frequency. It is sometimes assumed that classroom troublemakers are also the failing students. School personnel also note that these students are often from poor home environments and are members of a socially unacceptable peer group. They are therefore perceived as being resistant to authority and antagonistic toward academic pursuits.

Although this pattern may exist, it does not in and of itself constitute a sufficient explanation for students' behavior problems. Glasser (1969) suggests that students' inability to maintain pace with a lockstep academic program results in their falling further behind until a pattern of failure is established. Students' reaction to this failure eventually leads to social, emotional, and behavior problems and a cyclical sequence of lack of trying, failure, and acting out.

Causes of Behavior Problems

The extent to which the causes of behavior problems need to be considered in the selection of control methods is a subject for debate among the proponents of the various theoretical approaches. A number of causes are frequently cited in the literature (for example, Erickson, 1987; Hewett & Taylor, 1980; Kauffman, 1981; Reinert, 1980). Knowledge of these factors increases teacher sensitivity to the complexity of the etiologies of behavior problems.

Influences Outside the School

Factors that are included in this group include the sociocultural milieu, the quality of the home environment, parent–child relationships, economic status, and stability of family patterns in regard to membership, values, and emotional response. The influence of peers, particularly during the adolescent years, and the existence of alcohol and drug use are frequently designated influences.

Teachers report that students who demonstrate poor behavior in school also have negative attitudes that result in their withdrawal from participation in learning or in belligerence to authority. They are also described as having little motivation and may appear to have negative self-concepts. They are often noted to be preoccupied with peer and home problems. Others may find school irrelevant to their own value systems and those of the street culture in which they live. There is an obvious interaction among such variables and factors outside the school.

Physical variables including fatigue, hunger, and health problems may also influence behavior. The possibility of neurological predeterminers of behavior exist in some students, and others are limited in intelligence or have other exceptionalities.

Influences Within the School

Various factors within the school directly affect behavior. Among these are instructional variables including the quality of teaching, pace, length, difficulty of class presentations and assignments, and the nature of behavior management. Teachers' expectations in the areas of discipline and academic accomplishment do have a direct effect on behavior. Certainly involved are teacher and administrator personality characteristics, teacher–student relationships, and teachers' competence in management strategies. The general school environmental climate, supportive or punitive, affects behavior as well. Staff morale—including that which results from the various social, administrative, and financial crises in the school—can affect the behaviors of both teachers and students.

It is important that teachers and administrators avoid "explaining" behavior in terms of these causative factors as substitutes for action. School personnel cannot use them as excuses for continued inappropriate behavior nor for ineptitude in classroom instruction and management. The stance of professional educators must be that of positive constructive manipulation of these variables within their control to the end of affecting immediate and long-term growth in behavior and learning.

Strategies for Management

A Word About Theory

Many behavior management techniques are related to the principles of behavior modification. There is substantial evidence that the application of such principles constitutes effective strategies for management of academic instruction and behavior control. Within the literature on behavior modification is a wealth of information and effective techniques such as shaping, modeling, time-out, response cost, and reinforcement of competing behaviors.

Teachers have expressed reservations about the use of behavior modification. Some texts and instructors present highly sophisticated and technically accurate information and how-to-do-it instruction. Some of this information has to do with the recording of behavior occurrences, especially in the establishment of baseline data. These procedures are extremely important for controlled scientific experiments and are necessary in special situations for students with severe behavior interferences who are receiving a highly structured one-to-one program. Such collection of data is helpful in all situations; it assists in the identification of the specific behavior to be observed, keeps teachers at the task, and provides evidence of change. However, the complications of the recording process and the adamancy with which instructors insist it be done causes some teachers to reject the whole concept of behavior modification. The effectiveness of the various principles of reinforcement do not depend on the prior counting of behaviors. Routine daily demands on classroom teachers may be far too complex to allow them to attend to such counting procedures. They need not be discouraged from using the powerful tools of operant conditioning simply because there is no time to count behaviors.

The principles of behavior modification are compatible with other approaches, particularly the humanistic. Some teachers reject behaviorism because it appears to be mechanistic. However, the proper use of behavioral principles in praising, encouraging, and in reinforcing good behavior is far more characteristic of positive human interaction than the alternative of screaming, devaluing, and punishing misbehavior.

The following discussion incorporates various techniques and methods that are effective in behavior management of exceptional students and their nonhandicapped peers.

Classroom Organization

Students' behavior is affected by the organization of the classroom, which includes structure, planning and sequencing learning activities, and ensuring success.

Structure   Structure is the degree of organization and control that characterizes the classroom. The physical arrangement promotes orderly activities. Listening centers and seatwork areas are away from direct instruction and activity areas. Structure is characterized by predictability, routine, and a logical sequence of activities. Curriculum and instruction are planned according to the needs of the students. Rules, consequences, and expectations are explained. Students know what they are to do each day. Posters or bulletin boards with assignments explain assignments; numbers correspond to numbers at stations (Figure 7.1).

The structured classroom enables teachers to limit choices, thus directing students toward successful accomplishment of predetermined tasks. The kind and degree of structure is based on the academic needs of students rather than to a prearranged, formal, and inflexible plan. The degree of restrictiveness must be modified in response to developing abilities in self-direction and self-management.

Planning for Learning Activities   Management in any classroom, regular or special, will be facilitated by careful planning in all aspects of the endeavor: sequence of

FIGURE 7.1

A Poster Explaining Assignments

> **To Do**
> 1. Check assignment sheet and do
> 2. Worksheets in folder
> 3. Practice math facts
> 4. Read Social Studies chapter on tape
> 5. Vowel sounds station
> 6. Count the cash station
> 7. Find the verbs
> 8. All about me center
> 9. Update assignment sheet
> 10. Hand in folder
> 11. Do classroom job

events, learning tasks, success experiences, and environmental control. Teachers who are well-organized and prepared for the day's activities can move comfortably through the sequence of planned events and still be free to attend to students both individually and as a group. Teachers who are preoccupied with improvising something for them to do next will easily lose them to chaos.

Sequence of Activities It is common in special classrooms for the morning to be devoted to the more demanding academic tasks such as reading and arithmetic. As the day moves on, many exceptional students deteriorate in their ability to concentrate. The less rigorous and more enjoyable activities planned for later in the day can be used as encouragement to complete earlier work.

A daily sequence of activities is necessary to provide the security of routine needed by many students. Often they are concerned about what will occur next. They may be fearful that later tasks will be more difficult and unpleasant. Therefore, they interrupt present activities with queries about subsequent plans. Teachers may reduce anxiety and increase on-task behavior by writing the planned sequence of activities on the chalkboard and reviewing it at the start of the school day. Individual learners may be given three-by-five-inch cards with the list of activities along with approximate times of occurrence. Students may carry the card in their pockets or post it on their desks. This is particularly helpful for students who leave the room individually to work with the speech pathologist or other support personnel or who move between the regular classroom and a resource room on a regularly scheduled basis. Students whose daily routine includes such an individual activity may also create a small poster with a clockface showing the time of the event (Figure 7.2).

Although routine is important in the structure of the classroom, teachers must not allow it to lead to repetitive and uninteresting tasks that will decrease learning. Reading should be taught at the same time each day but within each reading lesson variations of topic, content, and method will keep interest. In addition, teachers must plan for at least one success experience within that subject each day. Learning

FIGURE 7.2

A Poster Showing Time

stations, interest centers, and a variety of materials may be helpful in maintaining motivation. However, too many materials, as attractively as they are now made, can become "gimmicky" and may literally interfere with the lesson because students attend to these rather than the objective they are intended to teach.

Ensuring Success Ensuring that students are successful learners within the parameters of their capabilities goes a long way toward reducing the potential for class disruption. Successful school experiences lay the foundation for continued positive growth and personality development. Glasser (1969), in his concern for the effects of school failure, wrote that the individual *"will not succeed in general until he can in some way first experience success in one important part of his life"* (p. 5). The school is viewed by Glasser as a major social institution that can provide or deny success to the individual. Glasser further states that *"unless we can provide schools where children, through reasonable use of their capabilities can succeed, we will do little to solve the major problems of our country"* (p. 6).

There are many ways in which teachers can guarantee successful learning, including individualization, criterion-referenced instruction and evaluation, diagnostic or clinical teaching, and task-analytic techniques. Further, planning for academic success is synonymous with planning for behavior management. Learning and behavior are related in both cause and effect. As students are successful academically, they are less inclined to become behavior problems; as they are managed behaviorally, they are also prepared to become more efficient learners and hence more successful. It has been found that working with students with problems that neither academics nor behavior must be remedied first. Academic and behavior problems can be addressed concurrently, and improvement is made in both areas.

Teacher Behaviors

Teachers must be in charge at all times. Students must be aware that teachers provide directions and limitations for all class activities. They must be able to distinguish between the important and the unimportant incidental behaviors and between intentional and unintentional behaviors. More importantly, they must know when to overlook the unimportant and the unintentional. Students may continuously use offensive language, and teachers will need to intervene. However, if an offensive word slips out, they might be wise not to overreact. Similarly, teachers must be able to control their own emotions and to avoid appearing shocked at bad language or with the reporting of events at home that are best not aired in the classroom. These incidents can be used as opportunities for teaching more socially appropriate language.

MODIFYING LANGUAGE BEHAVIOR

Leigh was mildly retarded and had spent two years in a kindergarten program during which time she remained electively mute. She was placed in Mrs. Zigler's first grade class. It was hoped that her peers wold be role models encouraging her to speak. The strategy worked but with unexpected results.

When Mrs. Zigler distributed worksheets, Leigh stood up and shouted, using profanity, that the work was too difficult for her. Even though Mrs. Zigler quickly assured her she could do the work and promised to help, the problem persisted.

After consultation with the school psychologist, Mrs. Zigler tried a different technique. As soon as Leigh began shouting, she assisted another student whether that student needed help or not. As soon as Leigh stopped shouting, she went to her immediately. For the first week Mrs. Zigler described herself as a yo-yo moving from and toward Leigh. However, by the end of the second week the standing, shouting, and profanity were nearly eliminated. The continuing attention to Leigh was decreased but she continued to be rewarded for appropriate language interaction.

Teachers must know when to be assertive and when to make demands and be prepared to see them through. Beginning teachers sometimes hesitate to exercise the necessary degree of firmness. They are often afraid that the teacher–student relationship will be impaired and that the students will no longer like them. Students need the security of limits and will not resent firmness on the part of teachers as long as it is expressed in a nonjudgmental manner.

There is a difference between discussion and argument. Discussion is an important learning method, whereas argument is destructive. Students will sometimes attempt to lead teachers into arguments over the interpretation of class rules or behavior. They can avoid it by not responding to the baiting, procrastination, or demands for justification. Once the decision is made, it is too late to revert to discussion and attempts at manipulation. Students do not always have to be convinced of the merits of the activity or why it should be performed. There are times when they should comply simply because a request has been made.

If a routine has become established, students may become upset when it is violated. Exceptional students, in particular, must be prepared for changes in the routine, such as an assembly or a visitor. It would be well to reassure them by reviewing the schedule ahead of time and how they will return to the expected routine later. Many teachers have discovered, much to their dismay, the consequences of introducing sudden or exciting events without adequate preparation. Often students revert to earlier developmental behavior, increased activity, uninhibited behavior, or uncontrolled noise.

Teachers as Models Whether teachers' behavior is exemplary or poor or whether they attempt to withdraw from the model role and be noncommittal, their behavior remains a model. Students learn poor behavior in the same way they learn acceptable behavior, in part by identification with and emulation of adults. Therefore, teachers must be aware of their own behavior and its effects.

To maintain respect teachers must also follow rules that are intended to teach social conventions, courtesy, and consideration of others. Teachers who assume a "do-as-I-say-not-as-I-do" attitude may find students, particularly older students, resentful and uncooperative. But more important is the fact that by assuming such an attitude, they denigrate the moral value of expected behaviors. Students are reduced to conforming to rules and expectations not because of "rightness" but because of coercion. Teachers set the stage for students to move away from and reject the demanded behaviors to identify with adult status. Teachers who wish to establish an environment of positive interpersonal relationships and to encourage the growth of honesty and integrity can do so by demonstrating, not talking about, those values in their own behavior.

Reinforcement and Consequences

Planning the classroom environment will reduce the likelihood of the occurrence of misbehavior in the first place. Using appropriate reinforcement is one aspect of this preparation.

It is a basic premise of behaviorism that consequences that are perceived to be favorable or rewarding by the student will tend to elicit a repetition of the behavior that preceded those consequences. Behaviors that are followed by consequences that are perceived to be unfavorable or unpleasant will tend not to be repeated. It is difficult to convince many teachers that continued attention to inappropriate behavior increases the incidence of that behavior and that withholding attention from a behavior that is being maintained by that attention will reduce the incidence of that behavior.

Teachers must know what students perceive to be favorable or unfavorable. They may believe that their highly vocal reprimands are perceived as unfavorable and thus have the effect of reducing the unwanted behavior. This, however, may be the only attention students receive. In addition, it may be rewarding to be able to manipulate teachers into a display of temper.

Threatening the class with consequences that cannot be carried out must be avoided. Feeling sorry for students and refusing to administer the punishment or refusing to provide an earned reward will destroy discipline. Just as rules are stated, so must consequences be shared. Then as infractions occur, consequences can be administered calmly and matter of factly. What is to be avoided are spur-of-the-moment and "just-for-that" consequences. They are made in a moment of frustration or anger and may be ineffective if they cannot be carried out or if their administration becomes too costly in terms of time, energy, fairness, or teacher–student relationships.

Differential Reinforcement Whereas behavior management techniques are more easily applied to an entire class, teachers are often concerned with applying them individually. Is it fair to reward John for progressively increasing the length of time he can sit and work on assigned tasks while Mary who sits diligently working throughout the entire period is not rewarded?

Differential reinforcement can be successful if all students realize that each is growing and developing in an area in which he or she needs to improve. The difficulty that may occur in a differential treatment program is not jealousy or a feeling of unfairness. Even young elementary students, particularly those with older siblings, accept differences in treatment if they also get their share of attention. Each student needs teacher attention and rewards for good behavior. Quiet comments, complimentary remarks on papers, "happigrams" sent home, and other kinds of approval may be given. A major error is the acceptance of good or conforming behavior as the norm, the expected, as though it will automatically occur with most "good" students and that such behavior needs no attention. If teachers do not attend to acceptable behavior it can easily deteriorate while misbehavior flourishes in the limelight of teachers' attention.

Occasionally, a student's maladaptive behavior is so unique, pervasive, or counterproductive that special attention is required. For students identified as having behavior disorders, management procedures may be included in the IEP. They are discussed with and approved by the parents. With other students, unproductive behavior patterns may occur during the year. The teacher, individually or with consultation, plans an individual behavior modification, assertive discipline, or other specific management program. The planned program is discussed with the principal and the parents. It may be that the parents are also observing inappropriate behavior at home and a consistent and coordinated management strategy can be developed.

Physical Punishment A substantial controversy arises over the use of physical punishment. Surveys of teachers, adminstrators, and parents have supported its use, and legal decisions have upheld the right of school personnel to administer corporal punishment. It is used because it works—that is, there is an immediate cessation of the undesired behavior. However, physical punishment is not beneficial for the overall development of students. In several states laws are being enacted to ban corporal punishment. Teachers need alternative forms of discipline. The authors reject the use of routine physical punishment especially with exceptional students who already may have defeated self-concepts and feelings of worthlessness and with those who may be abused at home. Teachers must be willing to use alternative methods. If the school accepts its role of leading students to socially acceptable ways of behaving, then it must do so through socially appropriate means.

Consistency The single most important aspect of any management program is consistency. Studies of child-rearing practices over the years have suggested that the important element in success is not the nature of the program, authoritarian or lenient, but the consistency with which it was followed. The same is true in the classroom. Teachers must follow through with a consistent program as planned. Students must know without question, that consequences follow rules, that the promised threat will be carried out, and that the promised reward will be given. If teachers do not take time to follow up *each* request or demand, they teach students that they do not mean what is said. One of the auxiliary advantages of following through is that they soon modify their own behavior and reduce the number of orders given in the classroom.

Teacher–Student Relationships

The teacher–student relationship is one of the most critical factors in the management of behavior. Morse (1980, p. 267) states that "the empathetic relationship which the teacher generates underlies any 'technique' and is more imposing in its impact than is any method per se." Mutual feelings of trust, respect, and affection will often develop in the classroom and will be strong motivators in both learning and social behavior. For many students praise from a respected adult is far stronger than tangible rewards. It is unfortunate that some teachers do not realize this power of personal relationship; not so they can exploit it, but so they can nurture it. Unfairness, sarcasm, rejection, and group punishment for individual infractions when practiced on a daily basis will negate positive relationships, which may have developed. Teachers have then lost the power to manage behavior by any means other than coercion, and the situation is unpleasant for teachers and students.

An extremely important aspect of management is the separation of students from the behavior. *The behavior may be rejected as undesirable, but students must still be valued as individuals worthy of respect.* Students who misbehave and then are rejected as persons have little motivation to conform to the expectations of teachers who devalued them. Students who misbehave but are still valued as individuals have the motivation to become even more worthy of that respect.

Management Programs

Teachers have available all the elements of a good behavior management program. These elements are essentially the skills of teaching. An industrious study of some of the books recommended at the end of the chapter, along with the support of a helpful psychologist or resource teacher, can enable teachers to get started on an effective management program.

One alternative to this procedure would be to adopt a prescribed or preorganized program. They are published independently or appear in professional periodicals. Teachers will want to thoroughly examine available programs to determine their appropriateness for the classroom situation, for their usefulness, and if they are realistic. Two programs that appear to meet these criteria are summarized. Teachers who wish to explore either approach are advised to study the original sources.

Assertive Discipline Model

To apply the principles of Assertive Discipline (Canter and Canter, 1976), teachers establish a plan that consists of rules, rewards, and consequences. It is a systematic program effective with elementary and secondary students when used consistently. Administrative support and calm firm behavior are at the core of the program. Nonassertive and hostile responses are not used.

Components emphasized are:

- Teachers have educational rights to a satisfactory learning environment, to appropriate behavior, and to support from administrators and parents.

- In the classroom, students' rights are to have teachers limit negative behavior and reinforce positive behavior. Students have the right to choose behavior and accept the consequence.
- Students must understand expectations and consequences of behavior before it occurs.
- Effective communication means being genuinely positive, saying "No" without feeling guilt, expressing and standing up for beliefs and feelings, and being firm without threats or yelling.

The following are ways to be assertive in the classroom:

- State expectations and consequences before behavior occurs.
- Repeat positive expectations often, if necessary, and eliminate negative expectations.
- Set limits.
- Follow through with consequences consistently.
- Deal with behavior without making negative value judgments about students.

Consequences are listed in a hierarchy. When students choose to break a rule, their name is put on the chalkboard as a warning. The next four offenses result in minutes of lost recess, minutes after school, or detention. The fourth offense also requires a telephone call to parents. On the fifth offense minutes are lost, parents are called, and the principal is notified. When a serious violation (a "severe") occurs, the hierarchy is not used. The consequence, in which the student is sent to the

---

BOX 7.1

Guides for Establishing Class Rules

Rules must be:

- Stated clearly and positively when possible.
- Observable.
- Enforced consistently.
- Posted in the classroom, with a maximum of five.
- Discussed with students the first day of class.
- Sent to parents in written form.
- Presented to the principal with a request for support.
- Reviewed periodically to determine if they need to be changed.

Examples are:

- Follow directions the first time they are given.
- Raise hand and wait to be recognized before speaking.
- Keep hands, feet, and objects to yourself.
- No put-downs or inappropriate language.
- Bring books, materials, and assignments.

principal, is administered immediately. Severe behaviors include fighting, vandalism, defying a teacher, and stopping the class from functioning. Contacting parents and sending students to the principal are near the end of the hierarchy.

The key to successful discipline is positive reinforcement, individually and as a class. A schoolwide discipline plan is also provided. Examples of rules, positive reinforcement, and negative consequences are thoroughly explained in the Canter materials.

RAID Technique

The RAID technique was developed by Madsen, Madsen, Saudargas, Hammond, Smith, and Edgar (1970). Rules, Approval, Ignoring, and Disapproval are the major elements in the program. Table 7.1 summarizes this technique.

Rules Rules should be few in number, positively and behaviorally stated, and displayed in the classroom. They may be developed with the class so that each student knows and understands the rules and the context to which they apply. Rules should be enforceable and temporary.

Approval Teachers show approval by rewarding students for on-task behavior and for other acceptable activity. What constitutes a reward in RAID depends on the student and the situation. Rewards need not be tangible and should include social reinforcement.

TABLE 7.1
The RAID Technique

ELEMENT	DESCRIPTION	OPERATION
Rules	Few in number Positive and behaviorally stated Enforceable Temporary	Each student knows and understands rules and context to which they apply; remove from list when mastered
Approval	Praise Support Tangible rewards Intangible rewards	Reward students for on-task behavior and acceptable behavior; reward depends on student and situation
Ignoring	Students not on-task Mistakes Failures	Attend to those who are on task; consistency
Disapproval	Behaviors that cannot be ignored, cause harm to persons or property, disrupt others' work or class activities, or violate class rules	Sufficiently strong to reduce unwanted behaviors

Ignoring   Ignoring inappropriate behavior is another major element of the program. Teachers ignore students not working on task and attend to those who are. Mistakes and failures are ignored. By ensuring success, teachers will have opportunity to respond positively.

Disapproval   Disapproval should be used for behaviors that cannot be ignored or when ignoring has no apparent effect. Behavior that causes harm to persons or property, disrupts others' work or class activities, or violates class rules cannot be ignored. Disapproval that is sufficiently strong to have the effect of reducing unwanted behavior can be used instead of ignoring.

The focus of this chapter has been on the responsibility of teachers to develop strategies for managing behavior. Whether they originate their own procedures or whether they adopt a program such as RAID, there remain other considerations. One is the question of whether behavior trained in one class or tutorial setting will transfer to another classroom. There is also the issue of home–school relationships when there are behavior problems at school. Finally, there is the inevitable realization that teachers alone cannot be responsible for total behavior management.

Transfer of Behavior From One Setting to Another

Behavior improvement in special settings takes place as a result of group size, teacher attention, adapted academic demands, and a specific management program. In some cases behavioral change is the major focus of intervention. However, it is frequently not maintained in a regular class setting or in less structured situations. The literature indicates that immediate transfer of newly acquired behavior patterns from one setting to another cannot be expected (Glavin, 1973; Glavin, Quay, Annesley, & Werry, 1971; Walker, Hops, & Johnson 1975).

The arithmetic skill learned in a tutorial setting might well be directly usable when students return to the regular class. This skill is a highly specific behavior, and the context in which it is employed (the arithmetic problem) is nearly identical in the two settings. On the other hand, attending, cooperating, responding, and contributing constitute a far more complex constellation of behaviors. The setting into which these behaviors are expected to transfer—the regular classroom, the lunch room, and the playground—are sufficiently different from the setting in which they were learned and practiced. Further, newly acquired behavior patterns are less easily and less rapidly integrated with students' present behavior repertoire, and behavior patterns are particularly dependent upon the stimulus situation. Thus, when students return to the regular class, that environment gives rise to the habitual ways of behaving, which were earlier learned and reinforced in that setting.

Gardner (1977, pp. 320–323) lists and discusses four procedures for increasing the transfer of behaviors learned in one setting to another. These are to "1. Increase similarity between training and other situations. 2. Practice new behavior in numerous settings. 3. Train people in the natural environment. 4. Teach the child to manage his own behavior."

Before each student is phased into regular classes, the special teacher must provide specific training in social skills required in the new setting. Students rehearse how to walk in line to the cafeteria, how to sit quietly in the auditorium, how to ignore others on the playground who try to influence them to break rules, or how to remain on-task despite contrived distractions. The special teacher helps regular teachers monitor the maintenance of these behaviors. Regular teachers must use the same management procedures as those used in the special setting. When professionals work together and a consistent management program is used, general behavior improvement and increased social adaptability can result.

Behavior Management and the Home

Ideal home-school relationships are envisioned as parents and teachers working together and using similar behavior techniques consistently. This situation is not always possible because some parents do not have the intellectual or emotional resources or because of a poor home environment. Such an environment often creates a set of attitudes and traits that can result in behavior inconsistent with school expectations. In addition, if exceptional students are allowed to remain dependent or overly protected, they may not become independent or develop self-control.

Difficult situations can occur when there are marked differences between the home and school in attitudes, values, and methods of control. However, none of these circumstances can be used as excuses for teachers' failure to initiate and continue behavior management strategies in the classroom because many behaviors can be controlled in the school environment. Neither should parents be blamed for all behavior problems.

Teachers maintain communication independent of the occurrence of behavior or academic problems. Contacting parents to initiate a positive relationship in a cooperative, constructive project may curb the potential behavior problem or set the stage for a more favorable rapport when a parent conference is needed. Some parents will be resistive and no amount of encouragement will seem to work. Efforts must be continued, however, to establish improved relationships even though it appears to be a one-way street.

When there are serious behavior problems in the classroom, parents are informed but not expected to deal with the situation. Often, they can provide insight into the cause of the problem. They cannot be expected to effect changes in the classroom.

When behavior problems exist at home, parents can receive guidance from teachers and support personnel such as the school psychologist, director of special education, or a school counselor. Parents are directed to give exceptional students as much responsibility as is age-appropriate, taking into account any physical or mental limitations. They are encouraged to treat their child the same as his or her siblings with reasonable behavior expectations, using rules and consequences, rewards and punishments, and an abundance of TLC.

COORDINATING A BEHAVIOR-MANAGEMENT PROGRAM AT SCHOOL AND AT HOME

Bob, a sixth-grade boy, who has been identified as behavior disordered, has frequent verbal outbursts when he does not want to perform tasks. He defies his mother, uses inappropriate language, and does not take responsibility at home.

Mrs. Freeman expresses her concern about similar behaviors in school and asks for support. If the same techniques are used consistently at school and at home, Bob's behaviors are likely to change. Assertive discipline responses such as remaining calm but firm, maintaining eye contact, and replying to the request rather than responding to excuses and manipulative comments are discussed. Other techniques that are suggested are: Do not argue; "catch" him doing good things and respond positively; show affection and other nonverbal responses when Bob acts appropriately; set limits before behaviors can occur.

Other important aspects discussed were:

1. *Negative consequences must be something that Bob does not like but that are not harmful.*
2. *He should have a choice of consequences.*
3. *The consequences must be carried out every time the misbehavior occurs.*
4. *One must stay calm, speaking in a matter-of-fact tone in a nonhostile way.*
5. *The consequence takes place as soon as possible after the behavior.*

Support Services

In-school support services are established to assist classroom teachers in the development of a management program and to provide support in dealing with severe behavior problems. A sensitive observer in the classroom may be able to provide feedback, interpret present classroom interactional patterns, and recommend management techniques to improve teacher effectiveness and student behavior.

Teachers need the active support of school personnel. In the area of behavior, the principal has primary responsibility. Special education supervisors, school psychologists, and counselors can also assist. School administrative personnel can mediate conflicts and establish a cooperative relationship. Teachers alone must not bear the brunt of parental dissatisfaction.

In some cases, conditions and treatment of children in the home are actually counterproductive not only to the school's effort but also to the growth and welfare of the student. Teachers cannot accept the responsibility of dealing with problems of parents in addition to working with students. In some cases, there are students whose behaviors go beyond those that can be managed in the classroom and who may have significant emotional or social problems. In these situations the school administration and other school personnel recommend that parents seek professional counseling or other community services. In some extreme cases, the school may need to assume the role of child–advocate in initiating legal proceedings.

SUMMARY

Behavior problems are a concern to teachers and parents. The wealth of theory and recommended practices are often contradictory and confusing and leave them with no real understanding and little in the way of uncontested direction or intervention. It is left to teachers to develop a working theory of the causes of behavior and some rationale for the selection of behavior management methods. Teachers need opportunities to learn and practice a set of skills that are effective in the classroom. Aspects of various theoretical approaches can be combined in such a program. Exceptional students and individual learners, however, respond to behavior modification with its emphasis on the reinforcement of appropriate behavior. The Assertive Discipline model and the RAID technique are two approaches that apply behavior management principles effectively.

In initiating a behavior management program, teachers give considerable attention to the establishment of goals for the class and for individual students. Comprehensive planning of activities and methods toward goal attainment can result in a classroom atmosphere that facilitates learning, diminishes the possibility of disruptive behavior, and is productive to students and teachers.

Teachers need to be aware of their own behavior. By exhibiting self-control in difficult situations, they can set an example for students who are growing in self-control. A valuable tool is teachers' ability to separate the students and their behavior, rejecting and modifying unacceptable behavior while continuing to value students as worthwhile persons. Continued positive support for appropriate behavior and individual achievement, no matter how small, and guaranteeing success experiences are means to encourage individual students in their growth toward the establishment of the skills of self-management, which are vital in productive living.

REFERENCES

Canter, L., & Canter, M. (1976). *Assertive discipline: A take-charge approach for today's educator*. Los Angeles: Canter and Associates.

Erickson, M. T. (1987). *Behavior disorders of children and adolescents*. Englewood Cliffs, NJ: Prentice-Hall.

Gardner, W. I. (1977). *Learning and behavior characteristics of exceptional children and youth: A humanistic behavioral approach*. Boston: Allyn and Bacon.

Glasser, W. (1969). *Schools without failure*. New York: Harper & Row.

Glavin, J. P. (1973). Followup behavioral research in resource rooms. *Exceptional Children, 40*, 211–213.

Glavin, J. P.; Quay, H. C.; Annesley, F. R.; & Werry, J. S. (1971). An experimental resource room for behavior problem children. *Exceptional Children, 38*, 131–137.

Hewett, F. M., & Taylor, F. D. (1980). *The emotionally disturbed child in the classroom: The orchestration of success* (2nd ed.). Boston: Allyn and Bacon.

Kauffman, J. M. (1981). *Characteristics of children's behavior disorders* (2nd ed.). Columbus, OH: Merrill.

Madsen, C. H.; Madsen, C. K.; Saudargas, R. A.; Hammond, W. R.; Smith, J. B.; & Edgar, D. E. (1970). Classroom RAID (rules, approval, ignore, disapproval): A cooperative approach for professionals and volunteers. *Journal of School Psychology, 8,* 180–185.

Morse, W. C. (1980). Worksheet on life space interviewing for teachers. In N. J. Long, W. C. Morse, & R. G. Newman (Eds.). *Conflict in the classroom: The education of emotionally disturbed children* (4th ed.) (pp. 267–271). Belmont, CA: Wadsworth.

Reinert, H. R. (1980). *Children in conflict: Educational strategies for the emotionally disturbed and behaviorally disordered* (2nd ed.). St. Louis: Mosby.

Walker, H. M.; Hops, H.; & Johnson, S. M. (1975). Generalization and maintenance of classroom treatment effects. *Behavior Therapy, 6,* 188–200.

SUGGESTED READINGS

Alberto, P. A., & Troutman, A. C. (1986). *Applied behavior analysis for teachers* (2nd ed.). Columbus, OH: Merrill.

Charles, C. M. (1983). *Elementary classroom management: A handbook of excellence in teaching.* New York: Longman.

Charles, C. M. (1985). *Building classroom discipline: From models to practice.* New York: Longman.

Craighead, W. E.; Kazdin, A. E.; & Mahoney, M. J. (1981). *Behavior modification: Principles, issues, and applications* (2nd ed.). Boston: Houghton Mifflin.

Cullinan, D.; Epstein, M. H.; & Lloyd, J. W. (1983). *Behavior disorders of children and adolescents.* Englewood Cliffs, NJ: Prentice-Hall.

Epstein, C. (1979). *Classroom management and teaching: Persistent problems and rational solutions.* Reston, VA: Reston.

Long, J. D., & Frye, V. H. (1981). *Making it till Friday: A guide to successful classroom management* (2nd ed.). Princeton, NJ: Princeton Book Co.

Martin, G., & Pear, J. (1983). *Behavior management: What it is and how to do it* (2nd ed.). Englewood Cliffs, NJ: Prentice-Hall.

Millman, H. L.; Schaefer, C. E.; & Cohen, J. J. (1980). *Therapies for school behavior problems.* San Francisco: Jossey-Bass.

Wolfgang, C. H., & Glickman, C. D. (1986). *Solving discipline problems: Strategies for classroom teachers.* Boston: Allyn and Bacon.

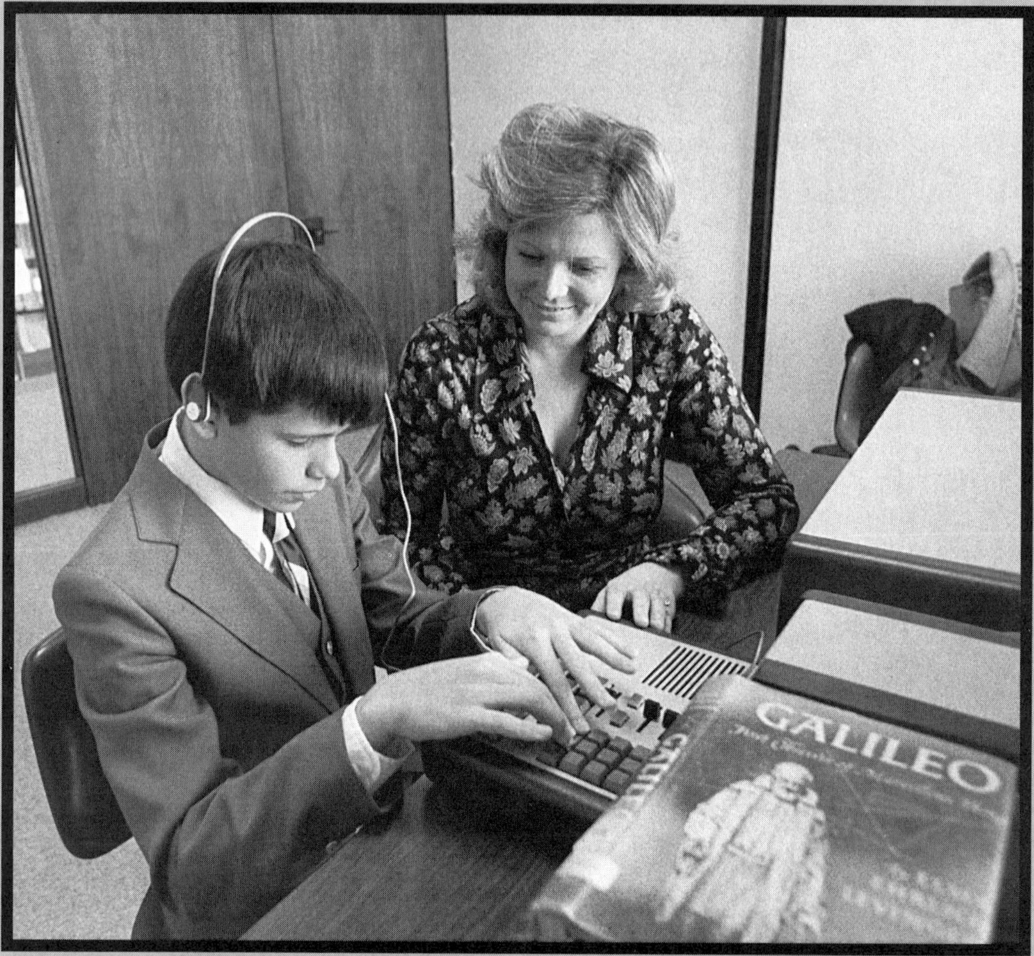
GALILEO

8

Learning How to Learn

TEACHING AND LEARNING are separate but interactive processes. Instructional approaches, curriculum, and methods—all managed by teachers—constitute the major topics in preservice education classes. Less attention has been given to the identification and development of the skills students need to become efficient learners. This chapter discusses the role of teachers and procedures to help students learn how to learn.

Learning, Motivation, and Readiness

Learning

Learning is the relatively permanent alteration of internal structures that is evidenced by changes in overt behavior that is attributable to environmental influences and that cannot be accounted for solely on the basis of growth and maturation. Gagne (1977) has postulated an information-processing model of learning that consists of the following sequential elements:

- Attending
- Short-term memory
- Encoding
- Storage
- Retrieval
- Response generalization

- Performance
- Feedback

Sensations in the environment impinge upon the sensory mechanisms and are briefly stored in the short-term memory system. Some of these sensations are selected and encoded into the long-term memory system. This is the important step in which meaning is acquired and encoded data are integrated with previously stored information. This information can be retrieved from storage and used in the generalization of a response (a motor act) in the environment. Feedback consists of data returned to the system that affects learning by reinforcement, by making it permanent, and by providing opportunity for alteration.

Motivation

Motivation is concerned with the "arousal, strength, and direction of behavior" (Arkes & Garske, 1977, p. 3). Individual behavior is influenced by positive or negative reinforcement from the environment, or *extrinsic motivation*. Behavior is also influenced by internal psychological make-up, or *intrinsic motivation*. Individuals demonstrate goal-directed behavior in the absence of apparent external reinforcement.

Teachers can easily interpret frequent handraising, sustained attention to task, and alert facial expressions as evidences of motivation. It is also easy to interpret the lack of participation and the presence of negative behaviors as the absence of positive, school-directed motivation. Students may vary, however, in their overt expressions of inner feelings and drives. These variations are often due to response patterns developed in the home and from past school experiences. Some students may not appear to be enthusiastically involved in either group or individual work but may, in fact, be profiting from the class. Teachers would do well to evaluate each student's response patterns before drawing conclusions about the quality of his or her motivation.

Motivational Techniques   There are three general groups of techniques that may be used: reward systems, content-specific techniques, and general environmental conditions.

Reward Systems   The first group of techniques includes the various rewards teachers provide systematically in the classroom. Both tangible and intangible, they are not inherently related to the learning tasks but are applicable to many learning and behavioral situations. At the elementary level they include such devices as stars, checks, tokens, trinkets, awards, happigrams, play and activity time, grades, and prizes. However, such rewards tend to be highly individualistic, and they often require a rigidly demanding system of administration to be successful. In addition, most rewards have short temporal and cumulative value; after the student has garnered so many stars, are they meaningful anymore?

Content-Specific Techniques   The second group of motivational techniques differs from the first in that they are more directly related to particular tasks. They include various means of enhancing the value of the subject matter itself. Such techniques include:

- Making the task relevant
- Demonstrating the utility of the task
- Associating and integrating the new task with those that students have already mastered
- Making the task itself interesting by various strategies that may include acting out parts of stories or plays, skits, debates, writing mock newspaper articles about historical events, illustrating events, student-created puzzles and math stumpers, the use of a popular quiz-show format for review and evaluation of factual material, recreating an historical event, or creating a courtroom format for debatable issues
- Using contemporary materials, events, and illustrations
- Guest speakers
- Field trips in the community
- Group discussions in which students are allowed to freely express their opinions
- Three-dimensional and practical experiments in which students must apply learned principles and skills
- Various creative projects by students such as scrapbooks, posters, mockups, models, or interviews with selected adults in the community

Such techniques are excellent devices, but they, too, have drawbacks. The motivational "gimmick" must not be allowed to be so unique or exciting that it diverts attention to itself and away from the material that is to be learned. Similarly, overemployment of such methods could detract from the continuity or the overall perspective of the academic lesson. Everything in the lesson need not be relevant to the lives and interests of students. There is much in nearly every discipline that must be learned simply as a basis for subsequent learnings, for the attainment of long-term rather than short-term goals, or as ends in themselves. However, despite these potential hazards, the use of techniques that integrate motivation with the topic to be mastered is an invaluable procedure and an important step toward the development of intrinsic motivation.

QUIZ SHOW REVIEW

Mr. Matthews, an eighth grade Social Studies teacher, devised a version of the television game show "Jeopardy" for fact review. He painted a piece of plywood to resemble the game board with spaces for categories of questions along the top. Below each category were columns of squares. Each one had a point designation and pockets into which answers could be placed.

Before class on review day, Mr. Matthews thumbtacked the tagboard with categories across the top and prepared answers on individual slips of paper for the pockets. Enough questions were prepared to give a thorough review and allow total class participation. Teams of students selected categories and points for which they wished to try. Mr. Matthews picked an answer from the pocket, and the students had to give the correct question.

General Environmental Conditions The third kind of motivational strategy does not depend on techniques that are associated with particular learning tasks. It centers around the relationship of students to the entire classroom environment, including their personal interaction with teachers. The creation of a supportive milieu revolves around the personality and attitudes of teachers and includes their enthusiasm for the subject and their respect for and confidence in the students. It is manifested in student enthusiasm and participation in the direction of their own learning. It is within such a context that students receive sufficient impetus to move on to the next step in intrinsic motivation, the enjoyment of discovery and the love of learning.

Motivation and Exceptional Learners Although the existence of a disability may interfere with learning, there is nothing inherent in most handicapping conditions that predetermines the level or kind of motivation. As described above, these result from students, with their exceptionalities, interacting with the environment.

Many students identified as exceptional have failed in past academic endeavors. Often teachers and parents have lowered expectations. Students' noncompliance in class participation and homework assignments are behaviors characteristic of avoidance of failure. New curriculum tasks hold the threat of failure rather than success and promise no extrinsic rewards.

For these students there is little incentive to try again. If they are to continue to learn, they must begin by rebuilding their self-concepts and desire to learn. Teachers begin by building the extrinsic motivational structure through organizing learning activities that ensure success and instituting a reinforcement system. Then as students realize that they can achieve, fears of failure are reduced, and their willingness to participate in learning experiences is heightened.

In the beginning stages of remediation, teachers focus on and reinforce success in learning. They respond to both correct and incorrect answers. Statements such as "That shows you are thinking" and "You are on the right track" give positive feedback without insincerity for answers that are less than optimal. Positive comments and marks are placed on students' written work, but this does not suggest that inaccuracies are overlooked. Some responses will be incorrect, and students must learn to recognize that these concepts are yet to be learned. The emphasis is on learning from mistakes rather than being devastated by failure.

Students begin to take responsibility for learning by cooperating in class, when they respond in a group situation, and when they try individual activities. They accept responsibility for both success and failure. As they are able to internalize these, a substantial part of the intrinsic motivational structure is restored.

As students move into regular classrooms, both regular and special teachers cooperate in the transfer of behaviors, attitudes, and motivation. Although regular teachers cannot restructure curriculum and instructional patterns, they can develop a positive attitude, an emphasis on achievement, and a reinforcement system that rewards success.

Readiness

Readiness is the preparedness of students to be receptive to and be able to profit from formal and informal aspects of the environment that should result in learning.

There is an interaction of maturation and learned skills. Students must achieve a level of physiological and psychological development before they can master certain skills and understandings. However, failure to demonstrate these does not necessarily mean students are immature. Other factors including the opportunity to learn, appropriate sensory stimulation, as well as early experiences and encouragement are necessary prerequisites for learning.

In practice, this means that school personnel should not employ the ambiguous word *immaturity* to explain away students' failure to learn. Nor should repetition of an early grade be the automatic or sole remedy. It should be recommended only after an evaluation of all factors that contribute to students' lack of success. In addition, the specific competencies that appear to be deficient should be identified and incorporated within students' instructional programs as they repeat the grade (Gloeckler, 1986).

Two other concepts are important. First, readiness is not a unitary phenomenon that develops evenly. Instead, there are many kinds of readiness, each related to the separate traits of personal growth and factors of academic learning. Students may have progressed normally in some aspects of physical or cognitive development or in prerequisite skills but may be delayed in the development of others. Second, readiness is not confined to preschool and first grade. The concept of readiness is applicable to the entire and continuous progression of skills, abilities, and maturation at all grade levels and at all ages. As such, these varying levels of preparedness constitute an important aspect of individual differences that school personnel must consider in both placement and teaching.

Readiness and Exceptional Students All students vary in both maturational rates and the development of skills and attitudes necessary for learning and successful school experience. Exceptional students and individual learners may vary significantly from their normal peers in both aspects. Unless these individual differences can be reduced by intensive supplementary instruction early in formal learning, they may become increasingly exaggerated during successive years. The failure cycle is initiated and perpetuated, and factors within students are blamed. Maturation, learning, and their interactions must be considered in planning for school entry, for individual programming, and as a basis for continued learning. This planning needs to embrace both curricular and methodological interventions for exceptional students.

Becoming Better Learners

Most students are prepared to learn when they first enroll in school. They soon demonstrate the ability to interact with the environment in ways that will allow them to learn efficiently. Others, including exceptional students and individual learners, may need help to become better learners; they need to learn how to learn. In the early grades, this may mean the encouragement of classroom behaviors that enable them to be receptive to and profit from instruction. In the later grades, it encompasses direct instruction in specific classroom and study skills. Figure 8.1 describes several factors that enable students to become better learners.

FIGURE 8.1

Organization of Learning Skills

A. Teaching Activities Affecting Learning
    Effective Teaching
    Learning Centers and Stations

B. Classroom Behaviors

C. Support Skills
    Study Skills
    Library Skills
    Notetaking and Outlining
    Vocabulary
    Following Directions
    Tables, Maps, Charts, Graphs
    Use of the Textbook
    Work Habits
    Test-Taking Skills
    Use of Crutches
    Listening Skills

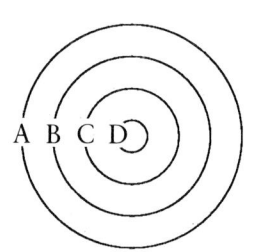

D. Learning Skills
    Attentional Skills
    Cognitive Skills
    Retention Skills

The circles illustrate the proximity to the individual of the elements that can influence learning. The outermost circle A represents teaching activities of the instructor, which impinge upon the quality of learning. Circle B consists of behaviors of the individual that can enhance the acquisition of knowledge or, if absent, may interfere with the process. Circle C includes a group of specific teachable tasks such as study and research skills that, if mastered, can improve the central learning abilities. Circle D is the individual and the internal cognitive processes by which the student knows, thinks, and learns.

Teaching Activities Affecting Learning

Effective Teaching

One often overlooked but nonetheless effective way of teaching students how to learn is to teach well in the first place. Excellent teaching has a number of components. Lessons are well-planned and presented in a logical sequence in both the development of skills and conceptualizations. By following the step-by-step sequence, students gain clarity of subject and organization. Good teaching includes an awareness of students and a consideration of pace, modality preference, and amount of practice that affect individual learning. It involves student participation in the process through constant interaction with the subject material. It is also concerned with the evaluation of learning, feedback to both students and teachers, options for correction and relearning, and reinforcement for effort and success.

Learning Centers and Stations

The term *learning centers* refers to a physical and instructional organization of the classroom into areas in which students interact with a variety of learning activities and materials. Learning centers are not simply free time or supplementary activities but are a central vehicle for instruction in the classroom. Thomas (1975) describes many kinds of centers including Inquiry, Discovery, Problem-Solving, Interest, Skills, Construction, Invention, Enrichment, Diagnostics, Motivational, and others.

Among the advantages are individualization of instruction (Marshall, 1975). Noar (1972) suggests learning centers as an alternative to traditional seatwork activity and emphasizes that they provide practice at students' own pace, motivation, and immediate feedback. In providing for direct interaction with the learning tasks, they may acquire sequences of reasoning, problem-solving abilities, and knowledge of the developmental organization of subject content.

Some difficulties may be encountered with the use of learning centers for exceptional students. They may not be able to organize their own behavior to perform productively. Students with mental retardation may need considerable direction. Learning stations may be more appropriate. They are activity centers in which the tasks are limited in number and complexity and instruction is directed rather than unstructured.

Classroom Behaviors

Special and regular teachers have long worked with management techniques that reduce interfering behaviors and increase the occurrence of more desirable activity. Teachers can expand their purposes and target behaviors to include those that contribute to classroom control and to those that promote the development of good work habits and learning skills.

A list that most elementary teachers could develop might include the ability to:

- Accept directions
- Organize materials for learning
- Conform to routine classroom procedures
- Sustain attention to tasks
- Interact effectively with peers
- Follow directions
- Move from one activity to another without undue stress or confusion
- Direct work toward short-term goals
- Inhibit impulsive behavior

Support Skills

Study Skills

Students do not know instinctively how to study. It is a learned skill that requires direct instruction. Many study techniques have been developed. Many are based on the classic SQ3R method developed by Robinson (1970). The tasks that comprise the procedure are Survey, Question, Read, Recite, and Review.

In the first step, Survey, students read quickly through the assigned pages or chapter. They note section headings, topic sentences, and other highlights. They carefully examine the questions at the beginning or end of the chapter before reading it page by page.

In the second step, Question, students formulate questions based on the material just skimmed. These may be either general in nature, referring to the overall content, or specific, referring to facts and definitions.

The third step, Read, consists of careful reading of the passage either as a whole unit or section by section. One purpose is to answer the questions posed in step two. The intensive reading also provides a more comprehensive view of the material than that provided by simply answering the questions.

For the fourth step, Recite, students turn away from the printed text and recite the answers to the questions. For some questions, verbatim responses might be required. More commonly, the answers will be in students' own words, thus increasing the meaningfulness of the material and reinforcing retention.

The final step, Review, indicates the need for review of the material, questions, and answers. Review takes place after the initial reading and prior to a test.

If students are to learn the method and benefit from it, the teaching, complete with practice sessions, must be carefully planned, presented, and evaluated. For some students, step two will be the most difficult. Teachers may find that considerable attention must be given to enable students to create appropriate questions based on a preliminary screening of the text material.

Library Skills

Teaching library skills is frequently included in reading curricula in the intermediate grades. It is essential for exceptional students to be taught each skill and practice doing each activity in the library. They include:

1. Using the card catalog: finding books listed by subject, by title, and by author.
2. Locating fiction and nonfiction sections.
3. Finding material in encyclopedias or other reference materials.
4. Using a thesaurus, atlas, and almanacs.
5. Learning procedures for finding, checking out, and returning books.

Notetaking and Outlining

Neither notetaking nor outlining is an easily learned skill. Both demand sophisticated conceptual processing. Not only exceptional students report difficulties with these tasks. What should be included in notes? How do we determine what is important? When taking notes from printed material, how does one get the essential ideas without plagiarism? Taking notes on lecture material is even more difficult because of the fleeting nature of the communication.

Two kinds of outlining are commonly required. They appear to be similar in final product but actually make different conceptual demands. Outlining material from the textbook is easier and is similar to notetaking from printed matter. The sequence of material provided by the professional author is a distinct advantage. Students may need assistance in reading skills that permit them to identify key and subordinate points.

More difficult is the creation of an outline as a preparatory step in creative or expository writing. Teachers can assist by directing instruction toward and emphasizing the relationship between the outline and the final product. They need to teach outlining as a procedure for organizing divergent thinking. Also stressed is the need for additional drafts that refine the outline as the writing progresses.

Vocabulary

Often, young students have difficulty because of the vocabulary and language demands of teachers and the printed material. That "circle" in the first grade means the same thing as "put a ring around" did in kindergarten may come as a surprise. For students with learning disabilities and for others who have body-orientation difficulties, direction words are sometimes confusing. It is necessary to reteach words such as *around, under, in front of, beside, behind, between, in, on,* and *in back of* and other terms such as *more, less, fewer, some,* and *many*. Older students are taught word meaning as part of the regular curriculum. Some exceptional students need additional questioning to determine understanding. They must also be taught how to choose the correct meaning to fit the context.

BOX 8.1

Guides for Outlining

1. Teach mechanics and content separately.
2. Have a sample.
3. Emphasize format:
    - Show placement of Roman numerals, letters, numbers.
    - The first word in each line begins with a capital letter.
    - Sentences are not used.
4. Explain and demonstrate terms such as headings and subheadings.
5. Skim content for important parts and list headings first.
6. Make sure subheadings are related to headings.
7. Do an outline with the class, step by step.

Following Directions

Students need specific instruction in following oral and written directions. When giving oral directions, teachers must get students' attention and then speak slowly, clearly, and briefly. Students may need to repeat the directions aloud. For some, one part of the direction may be given and the task completed before the next part is given. When learning how to follow written directions, students must focus on them. Perhaps they will need to read, discuss, and think them through with the teacher. They can practice by reading directions for making something or putting it together, such as a kite, and then doing it.

Teachers can alert students to signal words and phrases such as "Put an X on," "Draw a circle around," "Underline," "Circle," and "Make a check in front of." Skills can be reinforced by purposeful reinstruction and reminders as part of regular class directions.

Tables, Maps, Charts, and Graphs

Tables, maps, charts, and graphs of various types are all visual symbol systems, which commonly appear in textbooks and newspapers. They are complex in that they demand an association between visual-spatial presentation and verbal-conceptual understanding. Students, especially those with learning problems, may have difficulty in using such data presentations. Practice in these skills is necessary. Color coding lines to be emphasized and using markers improve accuracy when reading maps, charts, tables, and graphs.

Use of the Textbook

It cannot be presumed that students know how to make the best use of textbooks. Tables of content, indexes, appendices, glossaries, footnotes, visual material, and references are all aids to learning. Teachers ensure students' knowledge of these "built-in" resources by discussing and practicing using the table of contents to find page numbers on which chapters begin, telling on what page a particular concept is found in the index, writing definitions from the glossary, and discussing pictures and captions.

Work Habits

Young students need direct instruction and monitoring to develop satisfactory work habits and organizational skills. Verbal reminders are used daily. Some teachers in the primary grades or in special classes may use posters for initial teaching in work habits. Suggested posters appear in Figures 8.2.

Discussions with intermediate level students center around the following:

1. Assignment sheets to note when tests will take place and when assignments and homework are due are used.
2. Schedules are taped to notebooks.
3. Attendance and punctuality are followed.

FIGURE 8.2

Sample Posters for Teaching Good Work Habits

We Work Better When

1. We have necessary supplies.
2. Our desks are orderly.
3. We use folders to separate unfinished work from finished work.

We Follow Directions Better When We

1. Think about one thing at a time.
2. Repeat directions.
3. Ask questions.
4. Block out distractions.
5. Ask ourselves what we should be thinking or doing now.

We Remember Better When We

1. Want to remember.
2. Are quiet.
3. Think about one thing at a time.
4. Listen.
5. Use clues such as key words and ideas.
6. Study out loud.

---

4. Books are brought home, homework assignments are completed daily, all assignments are turned in on time, and a distraction-free place is available to do homework.

Many exceptional students may need assistance to begin and complete a task before beginning another. They need training in learning how to work independently. Teachers must be careful not to give help when it is not needed. Talking through the task and rehearsing how to do it develop the skill.

Test-Taking Skills

Exceptional students and individual learners need instruction in how to take tests. Teachers find that scores improve when these recommendations are followed:

- Determine how much time can be spent on each part of the test. Stress the importance of finishing.
- Read the entire test, answering the easiest questions and those students are sure are correct.
- Some questions may answer other questions.
- In matching statements, determine if an answer can be used more than once.
- Match people with people, places with places, events with dates.
- Cross off each answer as it is completed.
- For multiple choice statements, usually two are not probable. Of the others, decide which is the *best* choice. The longest answer is frequently correct.
- Do not read too much into true or false statements. *Never* and *always* are usually false. Do not change answers; the first choice is usually correct.
- If the answer is not known, guess.
- Students or teachers check answers to avoid leaving blanks.
- In an essay test, think about the topics and make an outline if time permits. If little is known about the topic, write anything. The topic sentence must be understood, and terms explained.
- Make own test while studying.
- On standardized tests, practice on test booklets, grids, or answer sheets. Use a marker if needed.
- Studying daily, keeping up with assignments, and asking questions as lessons progress are better test preparations than "cramming."

Students in special classes or in tutoring may be granted permission to use alternative procedures. Responding orally instead of in writing may be one such adaptation. Some students may need additional time to complete the test or may need to take the test in another setting. Often, resource teachers can provide such a place. On teacher-made tests, allow sufficient space between statements. Too much information on a page is confusing. Students may also need help in reading skills to determine what the questions ask.

Use of Crutches

Devices and activities used as aids to initial learning and later recall are sometimes referred to as "crutches." Examples of crutches are counting on fingers, color cues, the use of perpendicular lines to keep numerals in columns in arithmetic, mnemonic devices, and the use of a finger, card, or other marker to keep one's place in reading.

There is no universal agreement as to what constitutes a crutch. Many teachers believe a number line taped across the top of a desk to be a valuable aid in arithmetic. Others would classify this as a crutch that fosters dependence on the visual aid rather than requiring students to use abstract thinking to solve the problem.

Initial learning of new material may be by rote or on a "mechanical" level, meaning that students practice the mechanics of multiplication, for example, before its meaning can be integrated with their conceptualization of arithmetic functions. It may be necessary for them to use crutches when they have not reached the necessary stage of conceptual development or when learning isolated new facts or processes. Lehtinen (Strauss & Lehtinen, 1947) recognized this in her descriptions of working with students with handicaps. She stressed that rather than attending to the task of eliminating crutches, teachers should accept responsibility for the more difficult task of ensuring conceptualization. Punishing students for using a needed crutch may not only handicap them further in their learning of a vital step in the process but also can create negative attitudes for the present classroom, teachers, and learning itself.

Most students will give up a crutch when they have learned the concept. For some, however, the crutch may remain. It is better for them to succeed with the aid of a crutch than not to be able to learn to perform the task at all.

Listening Skills

Related to attending and impulse control, listening skills are particularly important for exceptional students and individual learners. When students fail to listen, learning is fragmented, and abilities are correspondingly compromised. One estimate of the use of time in kindergarten through third grade suggests that students spend 9 percent in writing, 16 percent in reading, 30 percent in talking, and 45 percent is listening (Anderson & Lapp, 1979). Despite the obvious importance of listening ability, the topic is often neglected as a curriculum entry.

Otto and Smith (1980, p. 307) identify four factors which contribute to poor listening: "(1) poor motivation to hear the speaker's message, (2) too much teacher talk, (3) excessive noise and other distractions, and (4) lack of mental set for anticipating the speaker's message." Like specific listening skills, each of these factors is amenable to control by both special and regular teachers.

Lists of specific listening skills frequently include the following:

- Perception of nonverbal sounds
- Attention to environmental stimuli
- Sound localization
- Recognition of whole words and sentences
- Sequential memory of auditory sounds
- Auditory discrimination
- Auditory closure
- Perception of language and speech patterns
- Listening comprehension, which includes understanding and following directions, remembering sequences of events, noting details, getting the main idea, making inferences, and critical listening

Most exceptional students have not received sufficient training to be able to become effective listeners. Therefore, teachers need to evaluate each student's ability in this area and develop intervention procedures. Teaching these skills takes time and continuous practice in the special setting or a regular class. The following activities provide reinforcement:

- Practice in following directions
- Adding new elements to incomplete stories
- Scrambled sentences given orally
- Interpretation of orally read messages
- Identification of objects in the room from verbal descriptions
- Identification of near and far sounds
- Identification of soft and loud sounds
- Determination of likenesses and differences in paired words
- Discrimination of nonsense words
- Sounds, sequences, or sentences
- Writing from dictation
- Auditory memory games

A simple unit or set of exercises alone is not sufficient. Listening skills need to be continually practiced and reinforced by special teachers, tutors, and regular classroom teachers. Although regular teachers may not have time to conduct specific listening training for individual students, they need to attend to listening in other ways. They can assist students by presenting a unit that emphasizes good listening. Teachers can also remind students during their academic work and can use a cue poster (Figure 8.3).

The quality of achievement in content areas can be influenced directly by students' abilities in these support skills. Because many exceptional students and individual learners—and those in the regular class—often demonstrate difficulties in one or more of these skills, remedial or minicourses are warranted. Teaching them to become better self-learners through the effective use of research, study, and listening skills may be fully as important as content subjects. Further, such training in both special and regular classrooms must be taught not as separate units but as practical skills integrated into the rest of the curriculum.

Learning Skills

As previously discussed, learning is a process internal to the learner as represented by the innermost of the concentric rings in Figure 8.1. If the goal of helping students

FIGURE 8.3

A Cue Poster

We Listen Better When We

1. Are aware.
2. Are quiet.
3. Ignore others.
4. Do not touch anything.
5. Think only about what we are doing.
6. Do not think about other places, recess, or when to go to another class.
7. Do not daydream.

to become better learners is to be realized, procedures need to be employed that more directly affect these internal processes. In addition, control needs to shift from teachers to students. Three areas are discussed: attentional skills, cognitive skills, and retention skills.

Attentional Skills

Attention is a complex process or series of interdependent processes that change (that is, become more refined) during the developmental period (Hagan & Kail, 1975). This development is likely to be the result of a combination of maturation and learning. There are three main attentional tasks: orienting behavior, selective attention, and sustained attention. Students first develop the ability to orient their receptors to the source of stimulation. Selective attention is developed as they focus on the centrally important stimuli within the environment and screen out those stimuli that are not immediately relevant. Sustained attention requires individuals to focus on the important stimuli long enough to permit storage in the short-term memory system and ultimately for encoding into the long-term memory system.

Because attending behavior is developmental and learned, it follows that inter-individual differences will be evidenced. Exceptional students and other individual learners may be impaired or delayed in the acquisition of these skills with the resulting occurrence of problems in learning.

Orienting Behavior Virtually all students have the ability to orient themselves to the source of stimulation within the environment. Difficulties occur with hyperactive and distractible students who change orientation indiscriminantly and with rapidity over a wide range of environmental stimuli. They are described by teachers as having a short attention span. Students with more severe problems will need considerable individual attention and reduced stimulus environments. Operant conditioning techniques (Gardner, 1977) have been recommended and found to be successful.

Selective Attention Students with difficulties in selective attention may not be able to determine which of the many facts presented by teachers or in the textbook constitute the central elements to be learned and which are supportive or illustrative data. Most teachers have experienced having students respond on tests or in question-and-answer sessions with information that was incorporated in the presented material but that was not the main point.

The problem can be addressed by pointing out those aspects of each lesson that students are expected to learn. The array of irrelevant stimuli within the lesson to which they might respond can be reduced. In practice both procedures can be complementary strategies. Teachers can use verbal instructions to direct attention to major points of the lesson. Simple statements such as "Pay attention to this" or "This is important" highlight significant elements. Teachers can use the chalkboard or other visual aids for presentation of the central aspects of the lesson while elaborations are not similarly emphasized in a multisensory manner. For young students and those with learning or language problems, repetition or reteaching is presented in a similar context so that it does not appear to be a new concept. Rate of presentation, pauses, and voice emphasis assist in identifying major elements in the lesson.

Sustained Attention The concept of sustained attention is closely related to impulsivity/reflectivity (Kagan, Rossman, Day, Albert, & Phillips, 1964). This is not to suggest that the two are synonymous but that one of the manifestations of students characterized as impulsive is inattentive behavior. Impulsive students can react in several ways. They may attend to the first stimulus group presented in a lesson and then quickly shift attention elsewhere. They may attend to the central factors of the lesson but so fleetingly that there is little time for the stimuli to be recorded in the short-term memory system or organized by the perceptual processes. In response to problem-solving situations, impulsive students characteristically select the first apparent procedure or choice without scanning the alternatives for comparison. Research has suggested that such responses are more likely to be incorrect than those of students who take time to think through the problem or question (Finch & Spirito, 1980).

Two general approaches can be used to increase attention time. The first consists of manipulation of subject and instructional variables. Chalfant and Foster (1976) suggest that the subject content be arranged in a sequence from easy to difficult. Students, having mastered the easier material, will more likely continue to attend to the task than if the earlier material had resulted in a failure experience. They further recommend that initial material be overlearned, which will facilitate transfer of attention to successive tasks. Lively instruction through the use of surprise, humor, and novelty can also increase attention. Chalfant and Foster further recommend the continued use of reinforcement of attending behavior with "verbal praise, confirmation, and visual or auditory feedback" (p. 93).

The second general approach toward increasing attention span involves various methods of working with students directly on the problem. Behavior management techniques can be effective with students being reinforced for successively longer periods of attending behavior. They like to work with a portable timer in their carrels in the special class. They learn to monitor their own improvement in sustaining attention. Digate, Epstein, Cullinan, and Switzky (1978) summarize the research findings regarding six instructional strategies for managing impulsive behavior: required delay, direct instruction, self-verbalization, differentiation training, modeling, and response consequence. As these authors indicate, such procedures have been found to be successful in controlled, experimental research. Far less data have been accumulated regarding their use in classroom situations.

Cognitive Skills

Cognition refers to those most complex of mental processes that have to do with the acquisition of knowledge and the use of that knowledge in mediating behavior. Mussen, Conger, and Kagan (1979, p. 271) state that "cognitive activity consists . . . of the active processes of perception, memory, generalization of ideas, evaluation, and reasoning." Much of the research has remained at a theoretical level. A few investigators have identified specific cognitive skills. Most notably among them are Bloom and his associates (1956) with the *Taxonomy of Educational Objectives: Handbook I. Cognitive Domain*. Classroom teachers may find a taxonomy organized by Thomas (1972) to be of more immediate use. Rather than beginning with a theoretical base, Thomas analyzed the elements of sixty-three elementary school programs for cognitive training. He arranged them in levels from kindergarten through sixth grade and in six activity groupings. The areas of Thomas' taxonomy are listed below:

Higher Order Cognitive Skills Taxonomy
  I. Learning to learn skills
     - Attending and orienting
     - Decoding
     - Memorizing
     - Studying
  II. Communication skills
     - Observing
     - Describing
     - Explaining
     - Discussing
  III. Classifying and comprehension skills
     - Differentiating and grouping
     - Ordering
     - Comparing
     - Using numbers
  IV. Synthesizing and producing skills
     - Inventing
     - Associating
     - Elaborating
     - General implications
     - Planning
     - Solving problems using strategies
  V. Skills of judging and inferencing
     - Coding
     - Judging
     - Inferring
     - Testing
  VI. Skills of value analysis and decision making
     - Valuing
     - Evaluating
     - Deciding
     — (Reprinted from J. W. Thomas (1972). *Varieties of Cognitive Skills: Taxonomies and Models of Intellect*, p. 21. Copyright, 1972. Research for Better Schools, Inc.)

Cognitive Training With Exceptional Learners   Most exceptional students need and can profit from cognitive training. For the sensory impaired, aid in this direction is imperative. Limitations in the breadth and quality of experience compromise the development of accurate concepts for both hearing and visually impaired students. The inability of students with orthopedic handicaps to move freely and independently results in limitations on their interactions with a variety of environments, and they may become experientially deprived. There is nothing inherent in any of these conditions that directly affects mental ability. Rather, these conditions present barriers between individuals and their environments that, if not overcome, result in less than optimal growth in mental ability and conceptualization.

Virtually by definition, students with learning disabilities have difficulties in those processes by which learning takes place and therefore have problems in conceptual areas. One characteristic is their inability to generalize among percepts to form concepts. Further, attentional problems inhibit learning sequences and strategies for problem solving. They do not learn incidentally or induce from teachers' presentations as others do.

Popular conceptions about students with mental retardation suggest that they are lacking in the basic abilities that are needed to enable them to profit from cognitive training. Therefore, the preponderance of training given is within a behavioral, competency-based framework. This approach has resulted in dramatic improvements in specific functional competencies. However, higher-functioning students may fail to learn some cognitive skills because of the emphasis on behavioral techniques.

Teaching Cognitive Skills Individual patterns of achievement, abilities, and learning styles need to be considered in the selection of methods for teaching cognitive skills. Teachers should not automatically rule out learn-by-discovery methods simply because one or more students have been identified as handicapped. Depending on the nature of the handicapping condition and other individual characteristics, some exceptional students may be able to learn by this method. Most will need direct instruction with emphasis on specific skills.

It is important to note that the experiences provided in published materials and in many teacher-made exercises may not be sufficient as instruction. It may be easy for young children to classify things that are red or that are round, but the task becomes more difficult when they are expected to differentiate between living and nonliving things. Exercises are augmented with instruction in discrimination and generalization.

Students need to recognize the parallel nature of the elements in an analogy and in learning accurate responses.

    Lemons are sour;
    Candy is _____.

Students may respond "good." From their vantage point the statement is correct. Candy *is* good. Many nonhandicapped students will abstract the concept or method required by a task after some practice. Such insightful learning may not occur for many exceptional students. It necessarily becomes a part of individual or group instruction that they be taught the concepts that others seem to learn automatically.

Teachers must not simply "cover" or present this instruction but should assure student mastery at each level through repetition. At first, such practice should be restricted to specific problems similar to the original examples. When each step has been learned, they can be applied to new situations.

The education of exceptional learners can be enhanced by instruction within a cognitive approach. Incidental lessons and strategies taught as supplementary activities

BOX 8.2

Ways to Teach Cognitive Skills

Classification

- Objects in the classroom
- Jobs and occupations
- Kinds of sports and other activities
- Fish or animals
- Words
- Cities from states
- Real versus imaginary things

Sequencing

- Birth order in the family
- Holidays
- School activities
- Historical events and eras
- Steps in solving a problem

Changing factual presentation into challenging questions

- Why did towns grow up along the new railroad in the West rather than in other locations?
- What are some of the reasons the culture in America developed to be so much like the cultures of Europe and not like the cultures of the Orient?

BOX 8.3

Steps in Teaching Problem Solving

Direct instruction in problem solving can be taught within a framework of content instruction.

- Specify particular academic task to be learned.
- Identify sequence of steps leading to objective.
- Teach procedures for each step.

are not likely to have a significant impact on either individual learners or groups of students. Cognitive skills must be taught in a systematic manner by adjusting the curriculum and adapting instruction.

Teachers can use prepackaged programs, parts of programs, or other published materials. The *Peabody Language Development Kits* (American Guidance Service), for example, contain a wealth of materials and instruction for teaching such skills as listening, classifying, thinking, and describing. *MiroSoc Thinking Games* (AGS) provides computer activities for elementary students in several cognitive skills. Two programs are Feuerstein's (1980) *Instrumental Enrichment* and de Bono's (1983) *Cort Thinking Program*.

Retention Skills

The third learning skill in Figure 8.1, retention skills, enables students to remember and store information. They recall the information at a later time.

The importance of memorization as an aspect of learning is obvious. Psychology literature is rich with theory and research in this area since the beginning of the science. Several kinds of memory have been identified.

Rote memory is the acquisition of data and their subsequent rehearsal to the point at which they can be retrieved and reproduced verbatim on demand. There is no implication that the data need be understood.

Short-term memory is the temporary retention of data that allows them to be reproduced or used seconds or minutes after initial acquisition. After a period time, however, they can no longer be produced at will.

Long-term memory means that data, which have been learned and stored for retrieval, can be used over long periods of time. Such storage is relatively permanent and includes those knowledges that constitute the individual's cognitive structures.

Sequential memory is the acquisition and subsequent retrieval of data, the elements of which occur in an invariant order (for example, alphabetical, numerical, or categorical). This does not imply that there is necessarily an inherent relationship among the elements but only that they are retained and recalled in the same sequence in which they were learned.

Although there are interindividual differences in memory abilities, few of these appear to be related to the separate disability categories. Students with mild retardation do poorly in short-term memory tasks but once they have learned the material, their long-term memory and recall are as adequate as that of nonhandicapped students. Memory problems are characteristic of students with learning disabilities, especially in sequential skills. Johnson and Myklebust (1967) relate memory deficits to attention problems during initial learning. Further, students with learning disabilities may demonstrate differences in regard to modality preferences and memory. For most other handicapping conditions, there appears to be little substantiation for any assumption that retention difficulties are related to the inherent nature of the disability.

Instruction must be geared to maximum understanding that integrates new knowledge with those already mastered by:

- Carefully planning lessons
- Step-by-step sequential subject development

- Using a whole-part-whole approach
- Relating content to present and potential needs
- Providing immediate and spaced review

Overlearning is another method for building memory skills. Students intensely review and practice material beyond the degree that would be necessary for immediate recall. Vergason (1964) demonstrated that following routine teaching procedures to two groups, students with mild retardation forgot significantly more than normal students. Under conditions of overlearning, the former subjects retained as much as their normal peers for a substantial period of time.

Drill is a common procedure for overlearning. Undoubtedly, drill is effective in learning mathematics facts and spelling words. However, it needs to be used discriminately. Practice may make perfect, but perfect in reproduction not necessarily correctness. Teachers of individual learners in particular must monitor what is being practiced lest they make perfect in memory facts that are incorrect. Nor does drill guarantee understanding. Some students, as a result of attentive practice, are able to see relationships with past learning, and conceptualization is enhanced. Many other students do not integrate what is being memorized with past learning. Understanding should precede drill. It is the teachers' responsibility to teach for conceptualization and not assume it will occur with practice or drill. Once information has been learned and mastered, teachers can provide for application. Facts must be used to be remembered. Adults remember multiplication facts and combinations not because they drilled in elementary school but because they applied those facts in practical situations ever since.

Other techniques such as mnemonic devices, contextual learning, chunking, and multisensory approaches can be used. There is evidence that some students with neurological handicaps learn better with a multisensory approach (Adams, 1978).

As with other skills in this chapter, the ability to retain and retrieve information efficiently can be taught. Further, they are applicable beyond both the immediate classroom situation and the limits of school experience.

SUMMARY

Teaching is only part of education. The complementary system within the individual is the learning process. It follows that not only the quality of teaching but also the quality of learning affects the outcome of instruction. Motivation and readiness are essential beginnings. Teachers can affect learning with the quality of instruction, in particular by organized, sequential, and clear presentations. They can also promote classroom behaviors that facilitate learning.

Students can be aided in learning sets of skills that are needed in becoming effective learners—in effect, learning how to learn. Necessary are study skills; library skills; notetaking and outlining; use of the textbook, maps, graphs, and other resource materials; vocabulary development; and test-taking skills. Although more difficult to teach, the central processes of attention, cognition, and retention are crucial to effective learning.

Of prime importance is the attitude of teachers. They cannot simply accept that "this is the way the student is" but must appreciate that part of teaching is aiding students to learn how to learn. These skills are needed not only to allow them to achieve but also to enable them to be effective learners throughout their lifetimes.

REFERENCES

Adams, J. (1978). Visual and tactile integration and cerebral function in children with learning disabilities. *Journal of Learning Disabilities, 11*, 197–204.

Anderson, P. S., & Lapp, D. (1979). *Language skills in elementary education.* New York: Macmillan.

Arkes, H. R., & Garske, J. P. (1977). *Psychological theories of motivation.* Monterey, CA: Brooks/Cole.

Bloom, B. S. (Ed.) (1956). *Taxonomy of educational objectives: The classification of educational goals. Handbook 1. Cognitive domain.* New York: McKay.

Chalfant, J. C., & Foster, G. E. (1976). Learner's needs: Specific learning disabilities. In F. B. Withrow, & C. J. Nygren (Eds.). *Language, materials, and curriculum management for the handicapped learner* (pp. 86–109). Columbus, OH: Merrill.

de Bono, E. (1983). *The Cort thinking program.* Elmsford, NY: Pergamon Press.

Digate, G.; Epstein, M. H.; Cullinan, D.; & Switzky, H. N. (1978) Modification of impulsivity: Implications for improved efficiency in learning for exceptional children. *The Journal of Special Education, 12*, 459–468.

Feuerstein, R. (1980). *Instrumental enrichment: An intervention program for cognitive modifiability.* Baltimore: University Park Press.

Finch, A. J., Jr., & Spirito, A. (1980). Use of cognitive training to change cognitive processes. *Exceptional Education Quarterly, 1*, 31–39.

Gagne, R. M. (1977). *The conditions of learning* (3rd ed.). New York: Holt, Rinehart & Winston.

Gardner, W. I. (1977). *Learning and behavior characteristics of exceptional children and youth: A humanistic behavioral approach.* Boston: Allyn and Bacon.

Gloeckler, T. (1986). Data-based decision-making procedures for in-grade retention. *Education, 107*, 182–186.

Hagan, J. W., & Kail, R. V., Jr. (1975). The role of attention in perceptual and cognitive development. In W. M. Cruickshank, & D. P. Hallahan (Eds.). *Perceptual and learning disabilities in children, Vol. II: Research and theory* (pp. 165–192). Syracuse, NY: Syracuse University Press.

Johnson, D. J., & Myklebust, H. R. (1967). *Learning disabilities: Educational principles and practices.* New York: Grune & Stratton.

Kagan, J.; Rossman, B. L.; Day, D.; Albert, J.; & Phillips, W. (1964). Information processing in the child: Significance of analytic and reflective attitudes. *Psychological Monographs, 78* (1, Whole No. 578).

Marshall, K. (1975). *Opening your class with learning stations.* Palo Alto, CA: Learning Handbooks.

Mussen, P. H.; Conger, J. J.; & Kagan, J. (1979). *Child development and personality* (5th ed.). New York: Harper & Row.

Noar, G. (1972). *Individualized instruction: Every child a winner.* New York: Wiley.

Otto, W., & Smith, R. J. (1980). *Corrective and remedial teaching* (3rd ed.). Boston: Houghton Mifflin.

Robinson, F. P. (1970). *Effective study* (4th ed.). New York: Harper & Row.

Strauss, A., & Lehtinen, L. (1947). *Psychopathology and education of the brain-injured child.* New York: Grune & Stratton.

Thomas, J. I. (1975). *Learning centers: Opening up the classroom.* Boston: Holbrook.

Thomas, J. W. (1972). *Varieties of cognitive skills; Taxonomies and models of the intellect.* Philadelphia: Research for Better Schools.

Vergason, G. (1964). Retention in retarded and normal subjects as a function of amount of original training. *American Journal of Mental Deficiency, 68,* 623–629.

SUGGESTED READINGS

Avery, M. L., & Higgins, A. (1962). *Help your child learn how to learn.* Englewood Cliffs, NJ: Prentice-Hall.

Bragstad, B. J., & Stumpf, S. M. (1987). *A guidebook for teaching study skills and motivation* (2nd ed.). Boston: Allyn and Bacon.

Cochran, E. V. (1973). *Teach and reach that child.* Palo Alto, CA: Peek Publications.

Russell, D. H., & Karp, E. E. (1981). *Reading aids through the grades* (4th ed.). New York: Teachers College Press.

Russell, D. H., & Russell, E. F. (1959). *Listening aids through the grades.* New York: Teachers College Press.

Shulman, L. S., & Keislar, E. R. (Eds.). (1966). *Learning by discovery: A critical appraisal.* Chicago: Rand McNally.

Stauffer, R. G. (1969). *Directing reading maturity as a cognitive process.* New York: Harper & Row.

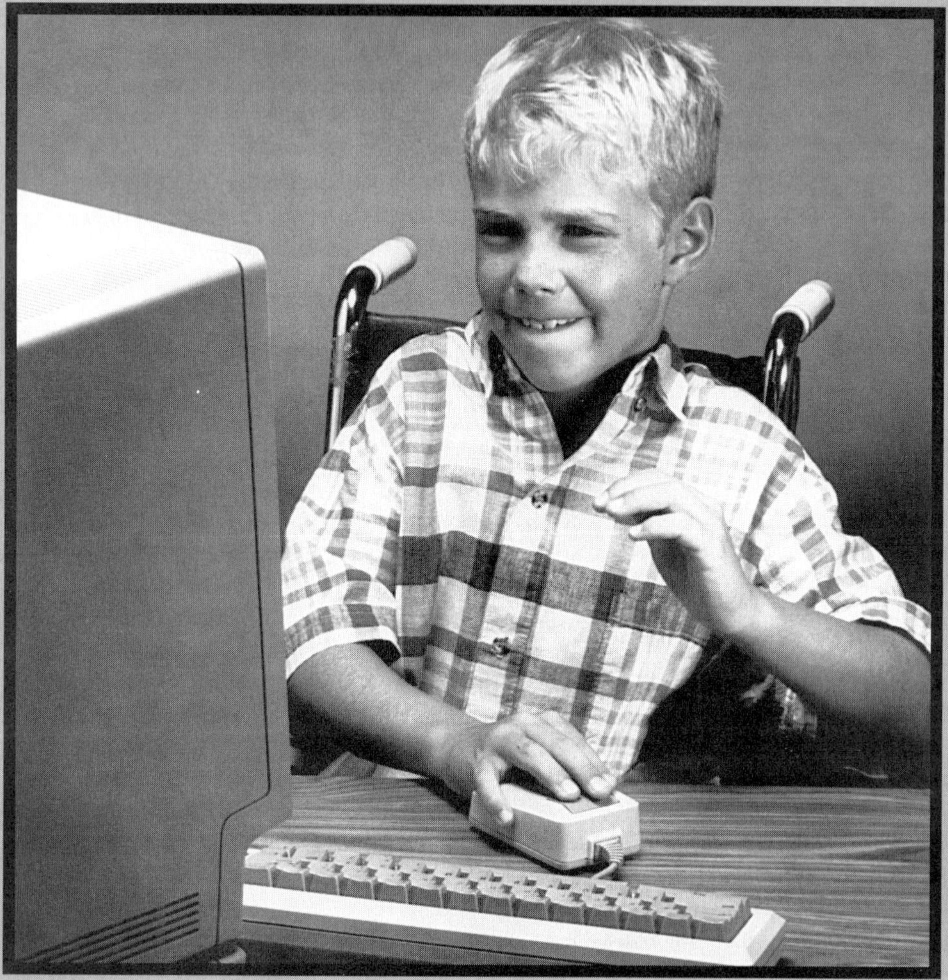

9

Organizing Curriculum and Methods

Curriculum and methods constitute the *what* and the *how* of teaching. Curriculum is the overall plan in which subject content is specified and organized sequentially. It must be specific in providing sufficient structure and direction to permit individual teachers to plan experiences, which may be diverse yet consistent, with the goals of the curriculum.

Curriculum is different from methods. Methods constitute the techniques whereby the elements of the curriculum are transmitted to the learner. Methods, combined with materials, are the vehicles of instruction.

Aspects of Instruction

Instruction is a generic term that encompasses curriculum and methods. It may be developmental, remedial, or compensatory. *Developmental instruction* considers academic content and students. It is organized in a logical, sequential presentation of the subject content, geared to normal student growth and development and learning capabilities. *Remedial instruction* is provided for students who have not progressed or achieved at appropriate age and grade placement expectations. It follows individual assessment and includes adaptations of curriculum and teaching methods to provide skills and knowledges missed earlier and to promote continued learning toward expected competencies. *Compensatory instruction* has two thrusts. The first presumes that, because of socioeconomic or cultural disadvantage, some students have not developed an experiential base upon which to develop new knowledges and skills. Compensatory instruction provides these experiences. This thrust is most associated with such programs as Headstart and Follow-Through. The second thrust of compensatory instruction is with students who have sensory or orthopedic impairments and who may be limited in obtaining information from the usual oral and written sources. It provides access to these knowledges and instructs students in techniques for achieving learning on their own.

Curriculum

Organization of Curricula

Traditionally, organization has been influenced by subject content, by the development and needs of students, and by the goals and objectives of education as defined by society. Emphasis has shifted from one to another in response to changing social and political philosophies. However, because most curricula ultimately must be stated in terms of what should be taught, subject-centered orientation has remained dominant.

Curriculum content can be divided into regular and special curricula.

Regular Curriculum Regular curriculum is developmental, presenting the scope, sequence, and content of the academic and nonacademic program. It is highly structured, assigning particular content to each grade level, both elementary and secondary.

Special Curricula Curricula were developed in special education for students who were unable to meet the demands of and profit from the regular curriculum. They may be developmental with content, scope, and sequence adapted to correspond to students whose individual growth and development are divergent from those of nonhandicapped students. They may be remedial, providing opportunities for students to gain academic competencies not achieved in previous educational experiences. The goals and objectives of the IEP must be addressed when determining what is to be taught. Special education curricula are addressed in separate disability categories to give regular teachers an understanding of and a perspective about the development of special curricula.

Curricula in Mental Retardation Moderately and severely retarded individuals were once confined to residential institutions where they received training in self-help skills. More recently, classes have been established in institutions, and many individuals have been returned to community living. Curricula activated through behavioral techniques of instruction have been implemented. For the severely retarded, these continue to include self-help skills—eating, bathing, and dressing as well as social and family living skills. Those returned to group homes in the community learn various daily living tasks, including basic functional reading and arithmetic skills to which they would never have been exposed to in institutions.

Early curricula in the public schools concentrated on academic and social competencies. They were developmental but based on the concept of mental age rather than chronological age or grade level. Mental age was considered a better indicator of the growth and development of students with retardation. Academic expectations were reduced (resulting in the term "watered-down curriculum") and presented within a functional format—survival skills in reading and arithmetic. Particular emphasis was given to social skills development and, at the secondary level, to vocational preparation through work–study programs.

Goldstein (1975, p. 3) developed a comprehensive *Social Learning Curriculum* designed to "produce mature individuals who can think critically and act independently to such an extent that they are socially and occupationally competent." Kolstoe (1976) presented another curriculum that consists of a developmental hierarchy of instructional outcomes.

CURRICULUM MODIFICATION FOR STUDENTS WITH RETARDATION

In Miss Johnson's fifth grade Social Studies class, there are three slow learning students who are unable to read the text with understanding. Two have difficulty retaining facts. They cannot read tests or complete them in the allotted time.

Curriculum modifications include rewriting the tests to include fewer questions and rewording other questions. Each chapter is outlined by the resource room teacher to be used as a study guide. In class the chapters are read aloud and discussed. A choice of projects is given, one being suitable for the three students. They are included in small groups to review for tests, which are administered in the resource room. Extra time is given to complete them, when necessary.

Curricula in Learning Disabilities Similar changes have occurred in the area of learning disabilities since its meteoric rise in the 1960s. Early curricula were centered around the training of visual and auditory perception, and perceptual-motor processes presumed to underlie and interfere with the ability to learn. More recently, learning disabilities have been redefined to reflect discrepancies between ability and academic achievement. Because of this trend and the fact that students with learning disabilities are not a homogeneous population, no specific curricula have been widely accepted. Published programs are used to remediate specific kinds of problems in content areas. However, curriculum must be both developmental and remedial so that capable students can be returned to regular classes. The regular curriculum may be adapted for students on an individual basis, using diagnostic teaching, task analytic approaches, and individualization of instruction.

Curricula in Other Disability Categories Depending on the severity of their handicapping conditions, students with vision, hearing, or orthopedic impairments were fully integrated into regular classes or taught entirely in separate settings. Because these handicapping conditions are presumably unrelated to mental ability, academic content expectancies are the same as in the regular curriculum and thus are developmental. They are also remedial, providing for achievement in those skills and knowledges not learned earlier. The curriculum for these populations is primarily compensatory. They aid in circumventing the limitations imposed by their handicapping conditions in achieving optimal educational and personal functioning.

Trends in Newer Curricula Examination of these developments in curriculum reveals several major trends.

- There is a movement away from earlier busy-work curricula and toward a content designed to prepare students for maximum social and vocational adjustment in the community.
- There has been a recognition that, for students with moderate or severe handicaps, a "watered-down" regular curriculum is insufficient, and more realistic goals and objectives have guided modification of curriculum content.
- Curricula for students with mild handicaps have become increasingly similar to regular curricula. Modifications are more commonly made in instructional procedures toward the realization of regular curriculum goals rather than the creation of extensive separate curricula.
- Curriculum and curriculum adaptations are based on individual assessment that identifies specific deficit areas.
- Curricula are no longer based solely on theoretical positions and expectations related to the disability areas but rather are based directly on the abilities and needs of students.

Curriculum Goals

Presently, long-term curriculum goals have changed from self-realization, human relationships, economic efficiency, and civic responsibility to emphasis on academic, vocational, and social goals. Voelker (1975) states that the long-term goals of education are the same for handicapped and nonhandicapped students. Responsible provisions need to be made *within* a flexible curriculum structure to support the endeavors of individual students in achieving short-term goals, which are consistent with the long-term goals of education.

Four Focuses of the Curriculum

A model of curriculum organization is presented here with four focuses. The word *focuses* is used to indicate that what is proposed is not a new curriculum but a way of looking at (or focusing on) four elements of the curriculum. The four focuses are regular curriculum, cognitive support curricula, supplementary curricula, and special curricula.

Regular Curriculum Regular curriculum is that organization of instructional goals and objectives developed within the school system for regular classes. It specifies the content of the academic and nonacademic programs as well as their scope and sequence. It results from the influences of chronological age expectations and the development of students, the nature of publishers' textbooks and materials, university teacher education programs, and the expectations of parents and the community.

The regular curriculum is the beginning point for identifying goals, objectives, and content for both handicapped and nonhandicapped students. Teachers attempt through manipulation of environmental factors and instructional methods to help each one achieve the expectations of the regular curriculum. If these are not successful for some students, curriculum adaptations such as those listed below may be necessary.

Cognitive Support Curricula The cognitive support focus is a modification of the regular academic curriculum. Its purpose is to allow for individual differences and to permit students to achieve the short-term goals of the regular curriculum. Adaptations made in this focus include the following:

- Providing additional supplementary experiences
- Using specialized programs
- Alerting the sequence of presentation of the topic
- Breaking topic content down into smaller steps for better assimilation by students (task analysis)
- Allowing additional time for the accomplishment of goals
- Using textbooks other than those prescribed for most students—easier reading texts that cover the same materials
- Varying assignments
- Varying the amount of work to be accomplished within identified time limits
- Using programmed learning materials
- Assigning independent projects (with a classroom contract)
- Using high-interest/low-vocabulary materials

Supplementary Curricula Supplementary curricula have goals that are compatible with those of the regular curriculum. The content, however, is designed to meet other individual needs. They include an array of skills, knowledges, and tasks that are not usually found in the regular curriculum or that are generally given minimal attention.

LISTENING TRAINING FOR BLIND STUDENTS

Albert is a seventh grade, blind student with no residual vision. He depends upon braille textbooks in most classes and taped novels and stories in English class. He also tape records each teacher's presentations. However, visually impaired students do not automatically develop good listening skills, and the kinds of errors Albert makes on tests and quizzes indicates difficulties in identifying the main ideas within the continuing flow of the teachers' presentations. A supplementary curriculum was developed for Albert and taught in a resource room. This curriculum consists of instruction in the skills of listening and in vocabulary development. Coordinated with the curriculum of Albert's regular classes, this instruction resulted in improved efficiency in listening and in better learning and grades.

Some possible curriculum entries are given next.

Learning How to Learn Exceptional learners may be just that—deficient in the skills necessary to be good learners. Chapter 8 discussed study habits, listening, questioning, outlining techniques, research, and other skills that are necessary for successful learning. The supplementary curriculum focus may well serve as a vehicle for teaching these abilities.

Affective Education A curriculum entry of particular importance to the development of exceptional students is affective education. Goals and programs for affective education are discussed in Chapter 15. They center around the development of self-concept and self-image, values and decision making, communication abilities, self-discipline and self-control, problem-solving strategies, and capabilities for the establishment of human relationships.

Social Skills Exceptional students often do not learn the social skills of everyday interaction automatically as others do, and they do not profit from experience in social situations. Often individuals with mild retardation lose jobs because they lack the required social skills, which include promptness, cleanliness, and attention to expected detail such as signing forms, punching the time clock, and getting along with their co-workers. Efficacy studies, which have been used to justify the education of students with retardation in regular classes, consistently report that they achieve better academically in regular classes but learn more social skills in separate classes. If they are removed from this social instruction, they may be further lacking in skills needed for successful interaction with others. It may be incumbent on the school system to give direct instruction in these skills.

Perceptual-Motor Training Less emphasis has been placed on perceptual-motor training since a series of efficacy studies questioned their success in influencing academic learning. However, perceptual-motor training has a place in special education, especially for students with physical handicaps, students whose learning disabilities are based in a neurological handicapping condition, and others who show gross and fine motor deficiencies. Modified perceptual-motor training activities improve gross and fine motor skills, including handwriting, start-and-stop activities, motor coordination, and left-right progression. In addition, perceptual-motor training can be integrated with academic learning. Programs such as Distar Reading incorporate movement with cognitive learning.

Curriculum Adaptations for Students With Physical and Sensory Impairments Students with physical problems or orthopedic handicaps may not be able to conform to all curriculum demands in the regular classes and may need additional instructional support or modifications in curriculum. Most obvious is the need for an adapted physical education program. Unless there are medical restrictions from the physician, all students should participate in gym class. However, the extent and kind of participation may need to be altered on the basis of individual limitations (see Chapter 14).

Ordinarily, there are no adaptations of curriculum for students with visual impairments. For blind students, it is usually possible to obtain textbooks in braille although the current edition may not be immediately available. Teachers would need to adapt expectations and assignments to conform to the available text even though they may differ from the one being used by other students.

Students with mild hearing impairments require few curriculum modifications. Although as Kirk and Gallagher (1983, p. 267) indicate, "the more serious the hearing loss, the more likely that specific changes will have to be made in academic content." These changes occur mainly in language, communication, and social skills.

CURRICULUM ADAPTATIONS FOR A HEARING IMPAIRED STUDENT

Roger has been in the state school for the hearing impaired for three years. He was to return this fall and attend the neighborhood school in fourth grade. Roger's parents met with the principal, teacher, and resource consultant for the hearing impaired. His parents requested a modified curriculum with expectations different from those of other students.

The school personnel explained that, to the extent possible, Roger should have the same curriculum as others. He is already handicapped by a hearing impairment; he should not be further handicapped by a reduction in knowledges and skills taught. However, it was recognized that moderately hearing impaired students are often deficient in academic skills. Roger would be assessed on criterion-referenced instruments in the subject areas. He would be placed in classroom groups in the third and fourth grades consistent with his knowledge and skill levels. Further, the consultant for hearing impaired students would monitor his progress and work with each teacher in providing complete educational experiences.

The Special Curricula Special curricula serves four purposes. First, it provides curricula for those individuals whose exceptionality prohibits any immediate consideration of their attending regular classes and who need a totally separate program. The program may be conducted in a separate classroom housed within a residential setting. Such curricula for students with severe retardation are developmental and are adjusted to individual needs. The goal is to assist the individual to reach an optimal level of personal independence. Van Etten, Arkell, and Van Etten (1980, p. 209) suggest that for the severely and profoundly handicapped the following areas of instruction are important: motor development, self-help skills, communication, social/interpersonal development, and cognitive skills as well as prevocational and vocational skills and leisure activity.

The second special curriculum area is for students with orthopedic handicaps whose physical disabilities severely limit participation in normal educational activities and/or inhibit average and sustained progress. Communication skills, self-help skills, use of prosthetic devices and mechanical aids, and communication devices such as alphabet boards or "Bliss Boards" may be routine aspects of the curriculum in addition to the more traditional academic content.

The third area is concerned with individuals who have physical or sensory impairments but who, after learning a necessary core of self-help skills, may live a relatively normal and independent life. Students with less severe orthopedic handicaps may learn to use a wheelchair or prosthetic devices before entering school and then attend physical therapy classes during part of the school day. Students with hearing impairments frequently attend a special preschool where they learn speech-reading, oral speaking skills, and the use of amplification devices. They are often enrolled in regular classes while attending the special part-time program in a separate setting. Blind students may first attend a residential school or day school for obstacle and mobility training; to learn braille, writing, and typing; and to use residual vision. For a period of time, training with a special curriculum is necessitated before they attend regular classes.

The fourth area applies to students with profound retardation and multiple handicaps. Although some individuals are restricted to a residential institution for life, they nonetheless have a right to an education appropriate to their needs and level of potential. The curricula are highly individualized and designed to habilitate persons in self-care and survival skills.

Relationship Among the Curriculum Focuses

Figure 9.1 illustrates the relationship among the four focuses of the curriculum and stresses the necessary integration and consistency of curriculum goals and objectives.

All are consistent with the long-term goals of education. Each has its own set of short-term goals. The two special curriculum focuses (the cognitive support curricula and the supplementary curricula) overlap the regular curriculum. These overlaps indicate that some of the short-term goals and the content with which they are associated can be incorporated within the regular curriculum focus and can be achieved within the regular classroom setting. The parts of the boxes that are outside the regular curriculum represent those goals and activities that cannot be addressed by teachers in the regular classroom but that must be realized through cooperative support and resource procedures in other settings. Thus, the amount of time students spend in the regular classroom or in the additional setting is determined, in part, by individual curriculum-adjustment needs and, in part, by the capabilities of regular teachers to meet them.

Methods

As defined earlier, methods are the procedures by which curriculum content is transmitted to learners. Methods are the *how* of teaching. They are a form of commu-

FIGURE 9.1

Four Focuses of the Curriculum

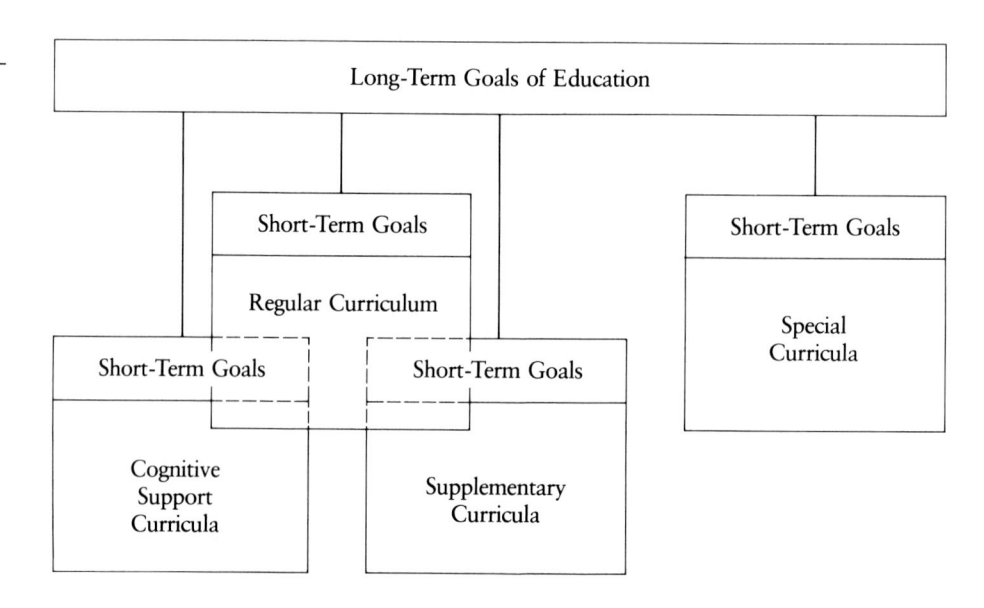

nication and, as such, must be examined not only from the standpoint of expression, or presentation, but also from the standpoint of reception, or understanding. Student learning, not only the dramatic quality of the classroom presentation, is the real evidence of teachers' careful selection and successful use of teaching methods.

Meeting Challenges in Instruction

Ensuring learning is the primary challenge of teaching. To reach this goal, teachers develop skills in the use of methods to be applied in various classroom situations. General education texts list many methods that include verbal presentations, discussion, supervised study, questioning strategies, instructional materials, practice and drill, summaries and review, assignments, demonstrations, exploratory experiences, field trips, individualized instruction, independent study, learn-by-doing experiences, enrichment activities, learning centers and learning stations, chalkboard and other audiovisual aids, and evaluation and assessment.

These methods and the various adaptations are the tools of teaching. No teacher automatically or naturally has a mastery of all methods. With time and experience, professionals grow, learn, and broaden their skills. In any field, the more expert persons are in using all the tools, the more likely they will be in meeting the challenges of achieving goals. So it is with teaching.

Methods for Special Students

Good teaching methods are virtually universally applicable. They are appropriate for normal students, individual learners, and exceptional students in regular and special education classes. However, there are significant differences in special education methods that can be applied in any class with exceptional students. Four elements are identified. First, there are differences in the *use* of the methods. Second, students' individual differences in learning styles and needs are considered in the selection of methods. Third, methods and procedures that lead to individual competence on selected learning tasks are employed. Fourth, some methods are used only for students with special needs.

Use of Methods

Students in regular classes learn to adapt to different teaching styles and to varying expectations and demands. Exceptional students and individual learners often have not developed adequate learning strategies and are not as adaptable to differences in instruction. To compensate, special teachers and tutors employ a wide range of methods. The success of the methods in transmitting the information depends on teachers' attention to the correct use of methods and on the accuracy, finesse, and skill with which they are administered. Among the important considerations in using methods are those listed next.

Preclass Preparation Inadequate preparation can result in a disorganized presentation, *ad lib* explanations, omission of important details, or poor organization. On the other hand, adequate preclass preparation can result in an effective lesson. It

Whole-Part-Whole Approach With this technique an overview of the entire task, skill, concept, unit, or lesson is introduced. This provides the context in which the successive intermediate steps are learned and to which they are related. The unity of the lesson is reached as all the steps are learned and students understand the final "whole."

Known to Unknown Beginning with information that students have already learned provides a comfortable position for them. The review serves as a bridge to the unknown new material. Using examples based on their interests clarifies and motivates.

Teaching One Concept at a Time Exceptional students and individual learners may become confused easily if too much material is presented at one time of if new steps in a process are introduced before they feel comfortable with the preceding steps. Teachers can help by assuring mastery of prerequisite skills before introducing the next skill. Similarly, a single method of solving an arithmetic problem or remembering a spelling word should be taught and mastered. The introduction of a "shortcut" or an alternative method can result in confusion and students not having even one procedure on which to rely.

Avoiding Ororverbalization Exceptional students and individual learners often have language difficulties. Verbal explanations should be clear and concise in a quiet voice, slowly paced, and with few elaborations. As teachers increase verbiage, opportunities for confusion and for students missing the major points are also increased.

Giving Directions Care must be taken when giving directions and instructions. Teachers should refrain from using a verbal barrage, which may confuse young students. They often do not hear the specific demands made within a stream of explanations and continued instructions. The speed of verbalization often does not give them opportunity to process the information and the directions given. Many students have the facility for appearing to be busy with something else while teachers are talking and then being able to remember what was said. They have also learned to identify, within the continuous talk by teachers, that which needs attention. Exceptional students are often lacking in both these competencies. Verbal cues can be used to call attention to the impending directions. Teachers can call out the name of a student not attending or say "Let's listen" or "Is everybody listening?" After such statements or questions, teachers need to pause and scan the class to see if everyone is listening. Then the directions can be given. Nonverbal cues can also be used. Examples are eye contact, remaining quiet until the class is quiet, and proximity control in which teachers move around the room and pause near those not attending. At the secondary level, begin speaking when everyone is quiet and focusing on the teacher, the chalkboard, the overhead, or an object.

If teachers provide directions several times, many things can occur. First, students may not pay attention or respond to the initial directions because they have

> **BOX 9.1**
>
> ## Guides for Giving Directions
>
> - Use vocabulary students will understand.
> - Give directions once to older students.
> - Give verbal and nonverbal cues.
> - Speak clearly in brief sentences.
> - Reduce detailed instructions to a series of shorter directions in which the task is performed as each series is stated.
> - Ask students having difficulty with attending or understanding to repeat the directions in their own words.

learned that they will be repeated. Second, directions can become confusing, particularly if they are reworded the second time. Language demands made by rewording directions can result in confusion rather than clarification. If part of the directions has been missed or misunderstood, students have the right to ask for clarification.

Clarity Careful planning of the techniques for presenting a concept is essential. A variety of methods should be available for use. However, one method is taught at a time. If students do not understand, another method is used. Carefully worded explanations along with the use of visual presentations on the chalkboard, overhead projector, flannelboard and charts are used. Step-by-step descriptions should be paced to allow students time to integrate each step with the last before moving on to the next. Frequent question and discussion sessions provide formative evaluation to allow teachers to adjust speed, level, and content of explanations.

Frequent Summaries and Reviews Frequent summaries and reviews assist students in integrating each new bit of information or skill into the concept that is emerging through the lesson as well as encouraging needed overlearning.

Feedback An often overlooked but very important aspect of learning is immediate feedback from students' successive attempts to master a problem or skill. This feedback is useful not only to teachers as a directive in providing further assistance but also to students in monitoring the performance of a task. Delayed feedback is less effective and can be counterproductive if it is given after students have worked hard to learn, or overlearn, the task incorrectly.

Careful Sequencing Care must be taken in organizing the sequence in which individual subskills and subtasks are presented. In general, easier concepts are presented first. However, this may not always be possible. In teaching students to work logically through the steps of a mathematics problem, for example, it may be necessary to learn a more difficult concept as it occurs as an early step in the sequence.

Meaning Precedes Drill It is sometimes presumed that, after sufficient repetition, students will gain insight into the material being taught. For all students, but especially for exceptional learners, drill can become merely an exercise in perseveration. Practice and drill are far more successful and more quickly productive when they *follow* meaning and understanding.

Sensory Stimulation For most students, learning is enriched when several methods are used in the presentation. Viewing illustrations of what is being presented verbally, following a textbook description while dissecting a lab specimen, or listening to recorded material and watching a demonstration have the advantage of appealing to more than one sensory pathway at the same time.

Student Verbalization If students parrot teachers' explanations, it may attest to an intact memory but not to ability in or knowledge of the subject. Having them translate the steps and concepts into their own words, with teachers monitoring the translation to make immediate corrections, heightens understanding and provides a direct basis for evaluation.

Student Participation Most elementary and secondary exceptional students lose interest in a lesson when they must sit quietly and listen for long periods of time. They need to contribute and receive recognition for responding. Direct instruction programs require frequent interaction, either verbal or written, which keeps students on task and attentive. Many exceptional students need to move around, being permitted to work in groups, at a computer, or at learning centers and stations.

Supervised Practice Drill, worksheets, and textbook and workbook exercises are monitored to prevent incorrect learning. Such practice can have meaningful experience with the subject materials and are not to be viewed as a challenge to see if students can succeed. Therefore, these papers need not be graded.

Teaching for Generalization and Transfer The learning of exceptional students tends to be situationally specific. To promote generalization and transfer, teachers' presentations need to encompass explanations at the concrete and abstract levels. It is equally important that they *teach for* transfer and not expect that it will "just happen" as a result of practice. In so doing, teachers make sure students have an accurate perception of the task or fact to be learned and then demonstrate the *how* and the *why* of its applicability to many and varied situations different from the original context of presentation.

Grading on Achievement of Expected Learnings If students have successfully completed an expected task, assignment, or unit of work, they are reinforced by and for that success. Errors not associated with the immediate goal of the lesson are noted by teachers as topics for further instruction.

Ensuring Successful Experiences Most handicapped learners are initially identified because of their failure to achieve. They often see themselves as failures and believe that they cannot succeed. This attitude and a history of classroom failure leaves them reluctant to try again. Teachers in each setting must cooperate to help students overcome this barrier. To get them started learning again, it is necessary to ensure that they become successful in learning. Activities can be planned that virtually guarantee success experiences. Teachers then demonstrate that new material can be understood.

Providing Continuous Reinforcement   In academic performance and classroom behavior, successful achievement and compliance are accepted as the norm and go largely unrewarded. The incorrect and the unacceptable receive attention. For the exceptional learners who have received much attention for being unsuccessful, it is necessary that the process be reversed and that teachers provide attention and praise frequently for success no matter how modest.

Teaching for Overlearning   Often, exceptional students are unable to retain. Concepts and facts that are partially learned may not be useful later in application or as a basis for new learning. Teachers can remedy this by assuring overlearning through review, providing much opportunity for rehearsal, and supervised practice.

Use of Questioning   Questions are used for a variety of purposes in addition to evaluation. They can be used to ensure continued attention, to demonstrate relationships, and to develop thinking processes. Teachers need to be familiar with correct procedures for formulating and asking questions.

Choosing Methods to Meet Individual Differences

Methods can be chosen to meet individual differences. Although it is imperative that teachers do this for exceptional students, it is important that the same considerations be made for all students. There are many ways in which individual differences can be met. However, it may be necessary first to identify the nature of individual differences. Important here is a consideration of individual styles in learning.

Learning Styles   The terms *learning style* and *cognitive style* refer to persistent strategies unique to individuals in the perception and processing of environmental stimuli. All students develop unique patterns of learning. For some exceptional students, there is only minimal interference that might go unnoticed as a normal variation in learning behavior. For others, the impact of the handicapping condition can be debilitating, severely limiting their ability to receive and process information from the environment. Attempts to cope with such limitations result in adoption of a unique learning style. Selected learning styles and techniques are discussed next.

Reflection–Impulsivity   This continuum evolving from the work of Kagan and his associates (Kagan, Rossman, Day, & Phillips, 1964) provides for descriptions of responses to problem situations in terms of speed. As implied by the terms, some students respond cautiously, pausing to determine an answer, while others respond rapidly and without much forethought. Students who have not taken the time to examine the problem carefully, consider alternatives, or evaluate their own initial responses make errors more frequently than reflective students. In addition to the stimulus situation, the pacing of the class and the teaching style of instructors may be harmonious or dissident with response style. Teachers who place a premium on response speed place reflective students at a disadvantage. Conversely, teachers who conduct class with a less hurried pace may become irritated by the number of errors of those who respond rapidly.

Teachers need to be sensitive to individual learning styles and either make provision for them or initiate teaching procedures to alter them. Reflective students who answer correctly present less of a problem unless they take an unusually long time in responding. While taking care not to reinforce delay by continued attention to it, teachers can establish a carefully organized behavior management program to address the problem. An alternative is to use verbal mediation to monitor tempo. Impulsive students present more of a problem because often, once an erroneous answer has been given, there is an unwillingness to correct it.

Modality Preference Modality preference refers to the theory that students with learning disabilities learn better either visually or auditorily. They also may have difficulty in integrating and assimilating information presented via two or more senses simultaneously.

When translated into practice, difficulties have occurred. The theory may have been overgeneralized because differences were ascribed to a whole population when, in reality, only a few students were so affected. The theory may also have been oversimplified. Other variables need to be considered, including the nature of the material to be learned, level of difficulty, level of abstractness, speed of presentation, prerequisite learnings, innate abilities, and past experiences in formal education.

The preponderance of research does not support the efficacy of determining modality preferences or for using this information in teaching procedures (Tarver & Dawson, 1978). The authors' own clinical and classroom experiences and the reports of other special teachers have prompted the conclusion that for a number of students, modality-processing differences do exist and need to be considered in method selection.

It is not recommended that all students be screened for modality preference. Instead, teachers must be alert to each student's complex learning patterns and identify those students for whom modality-processing differences apparently exist. They can ascertain the validity of initial observations by using clinical teaching procedures.

In adapting for such differences, a variety of visual, auditory, and tactile methods can be used. Assignments and other information should be written on the chalkboard but reinforced orally. Then, individualized work may be adapted to the modality preferences and general learning styles. The authors support a combined approach despite the recognized lack of research (Kirk, Kliebhan, & Lerner, 1978). In general, the stronger modality should be used for *initial* instruction in a reading program. This has the advantage of providing for early reading success. However, the literature suggests that as one modality is exercised, it becomes stronger while less used modalities deteriorate. This tends to exacerbate the already significant differences as well as increase learning deficits. It is recommended that the less preferred modality must also be strengthened through specific exercises and gradual use within the academic program.

Rate of Learning Not all students can be expected to perceive and process information at the same temporal rate. Bright students will comprehend new materials, integrate it rapidly with past learning, and be ready for further challenges. Other students may need longer time to assimilate new information with patterns learned in the past. There are also individual differences in the acquisition of some *kinds* of tasks, with some being learned more quickly than others. Individual rates of learning tend to be resistant to change. Considerable ingenuity and a range of methods need to be used if all students are to profit from classroom instruction and if all are expected to learn any given task to an expected competence level.

Rate of Working It is necessary for the practitioner to distinguish between rate of learning and rate of working. For some students, working slowly is a manifestation of their limited ability or a necessary sequel to their rate of learning; they learn slowly, hence work slowly. Other students work slowly because they have habitually done so. They may have satisfactory ability but have learned to work carefully and slowly, rechecking their work as they proceed. Others may work slowly to avoid the next task. Teachers and support personnel must carefully determine whether a given student is a slow worker or of limited ability. If this is not distinguished, misplacement can occur. Unlike the rate of learning, rate of working is responsive to manipulation by teachers. Realistic deadlines may need to be set for some students while others may need to be encouraged to take additional time with their work. For those few students whose working rates are very different from the average, a behavior management program or verbal mediation program to modify these work habits may need to be instituted.

Group Versus Individual Instruction Some students prefer large group instruction. They enjoy the interaction and competition and are able to profit from others' contributions and teachers' presentations. Other students prefer smaller groups. Study or work groups operating independently of direct supervision by teachers may give students opportunity to explore the parameters of their own information and understanding as well as to gain insights from others' perceptions of the topic. Teachers can accommodate for such individual differences by providing for varied grouping. They can provide one-to-one instruction as needed at the beginning of remedial work and can encourage students to become active learners in small- and large group situations.

Severity of Impairment and Learning Characteristics The literature commonly suggests that whereas students with severe impairments need special methods, those with mild handicaps do not. As with most generalizations, this is an oversimplification. Many students with mild handicaps can and do learn in regular classes without special methods. Some students, however, do need special treatment. This need is not determined by the degree of measured impairment (that is, IQ level or visual or hearing acuity) but by how the student with these impairments functions as a learner. Similarly, when deciding to place a student in a regular or special class, school personnel must consider learning characteristics as well as other factors.

Levels of Processing Students vary in their rates of development of cognitive processing. Others are not necessarily variant in development but have learned how to profit from interaction with the learning tasks at various levels. Some students learn best at the concrete level with tactile-manipulative materials. Others learn best at the representational (picture–graph–illustration) level. Others can learn at the symbolic and the abstract levels. Most exceptional students tend to learn best at the concrete and representational levels. Teaching methods and approaches can be selected to capitalize on these preferences or needs. At the same time, however, teachers will encourage ability to learn from presentations at abstract levels.

Each of these learning styles constitutes a dimension of individual differences among students. Admonitions to teachers to consider individual differences and learning styles abound in the literature. However, research on the efficacy of matching student aptitudes with treatment processes is sparse (Cronbach & Snow, 1977) and does not yet allow for the formulation of generally applicable principles. Nor are there sophisticated diagnostic procedures for teachers to determine the vagaries of individual learning behavior. Despite the lack of efficacy research, the authors contend that careful appraisal by teachers of individual learning behaviors, leading to judicious adaptations of curriculum variables and instructional procedures, is a more viable classroom approach than the alternative of teaching to the average of the class and expecting students to make the necessary adjustment in learning or fail.

BOX 9.2

Teachers' Role in Working With Students With Handicaps

The following are general considerations:

- Treat exceptional students as normally as possible. Accommodation is made for individual differences relative to their needs and limitations but oversolicitousness and overprotection must be avoided.
- Do not make heroes of exceptional students nor use them as examples for other students.
- Do not reward them with grades because they are handicapped. Grades are to be earned by all students.
- Become informed about the disability and the limitations it imposes on individual students in their environments.
- Set a tone of acceptance in the classroom by your attitude as expressed in routine treatment. The attitudes of the other students can be strongly influenced by those of teachers.

As exceptional students continue to become full members of regular classes, these considerations will, hopefully, become unnecessary. Accommodations made for exceptional students are an extension of individualization with all students. Many teachers and students are finding that exceptional students frequently set the tone by accepting their own limitations and by being more like their peers than different from them.

> **BOX 9.3**
>
> ## Specific Techniques for Working With Students With Speech Impairments
>
> Students with speech impairments may demonstrate problems in articulation, the pronunciation of speech sounds, voice disorders, or stuttering. Most show no other disabilities and are in regular classes. They should be expected to participate in all learning activities including responding to questions, making presentations, oral reading, and participating in discussions. In working with students with speech impairments, teachers may use the following procedures:
>
> - Call on the students regularly, whether or not their hands are raised. Avoid correcting speech errors in class.
> - Never allow ridicule or imitation of the speech impaired student. Any such attempts should be stopped on the spot even if the student with the impairment is present.
> - Quiet talks to the class while students with handicaps are out of the room are to be avoided. Such procedures may emphasize the students' disabilities and rarely accomplish the intended purpose of attitude or behavior change.
> - Do not tell the students to slow down, to stop for a moment, or to think about what they are going to say.
> - If stuttering occurs, wait for the students to complete their sentences. Do not show impatience because it will cause stutterers to become more tense, causing continuing dysrhythmia. Further, other class members may take teachers' impatience as a cue to devalue the handicapped students.
> - Do not fill in the words when students hesitate.
> - Do not make comments about the speech even on those occasions when students are not demonstrating the difficulty. Instead, reinforce the correctness of their responses or progress.
> - Students, regardless of area of impairment, should never be punished for being handicapped.
> - Students, regardless of area of impairment, should never be rewarded for being handicapped.
> - Coordinate practice and support with the speech pathologist.

Teaching Toward Competency in Selected Learning Objectives

In regular classes, time spans are allotted for "covering" given amounts of text material. Within that period of time, teachers can provide excellent instruction and accommodate for individual differences to the extent possible, considering class size and time constraints. The practical aspects of the content must be emphasized. Vocabulary terms may need to be limited. Drill and repetition need to be expanded. Some individual students can learn only part of the content. They may need to be given a shortened end-of-the-unit test.

BOX 9.4

Specific Techniques for Working With Students With Visual Impairments

Students with visual impairments may be blind or have low vision. If they have no other handicapping conditions, they will be in regular classrooms. They should be expected to participate in the full range of classes including art, physical education, and home economics and in all classroom activities.

Teachers may be guided by the following procedures:

- Allow students to visit the classroom prior to the opening of school. Do not lead them around but describe the classroom layouts verbally, allowing them to explore the rooms on their own.
- Aid low vision students in selecting a desk with a view of the chalkboard and no glare. An adjustable desk top allows them to accommodate to the light source.
- Allow students who are blind to change class before the bell or be accompanied by a "buddy." Obstacle sense is not effective in a hallway full of moving persons.
- Permit students to walk to the chalkboard to see what is written there.
- State orally everything that is written on the board.
- Give precise, thorough explanations. Visually impaired students may not have the breadth of experience to provide their own closure.
- Use a buddy system with a peer to read handouts and other materials not available in braille.
- Allow students to select their own writing instruments. A felt-tipped pen or similar device may give needed tactile feedback.
- Do not correct body or head position during reading and writing activities. Although it appears awkward or uncomfortable, it may be optimal for visual functioning.
- Allow low vision students to change locations in the room to reduce glare.
- Instruct other class members to keep materials and feet out of the aisles.
- Provide a typewriter in the room or in a resource room. Students with visual impairments are often taught to type and can provide hard copy for the teacher. They can take dictated spelling tests at the typewriter.
- If furniture is rearranged or equipment added, tell the students before they enter the room.
- Keep the classroom door open or closed but not ajar. The edge of the door is too narrow to be sensed by students' obstacle senses.
- Students with visual impairments must be responsible for their own possessions—books, paper, clothing, gym equipment, locks, and lockers.
- Assign routine tasks—distributing papers, emptying the pencil sharpener, or watering the plants.
- Provide a locker at the end, not in the middle, of the row. Allow it to be identified with braille numbers.
- Do not physically guide students. Provide verbal directions or allow them to hold on to your elbow when walking.
- Use the buddy system for fire and tornado drills, any emergency in a lab class, or to help in the cafeteria. Assignments should be made in each class if the same buddy is not in each class.

BOX 9.5

Specific Techniques for Working With Students With Hearing Impairments

Students with hearing impairments may demonstrate losses from mild to severe or deafness. They attend all academic and nonacademic classes including art, music, physical education, and home economics. The following procedures are a guide:

- Provide preferential seating to assure maximum visibility and accommodation.
- When hearing aids are used, students cannot screen out extraneous noise because sounds are magnified. They have limited effectiveness in the classroom. Assistive listening devices are preferable. A cue may need to be given to adjust the aid when noise levels change.
- There is a difference between audibility and intelligibility. It is not sufficient that students hear sounds. Teachers' and others' voices must be understandable.
- Keep your face toward students who speechread (lipread). Do not talk into the chalkboard from behind students. Do not stand in front of bright window light when speaking. The glare from behind places the face in shadow and makes speechreading difficult.
- Speak in a normal tone with normal volume and enunciation. Do not exaggerate lip or facial movements.
- Speak in complete sentences because meaning is gained from context.
- Rephrase information to promote understanding.
- Call on students routinely for participation. Preferably, use students' names first to alert them that they are being addressed. Do not touch them to get attention.
- Use gestures frequently.
- Monitor reception but do not ask "Are you getting this?" or "Can you hear me?"
- Use the chalkboard, demonstrations, charts, diagrams, maps, overhead projector, handouts, printed directions and assignments, and other visual aids extensively.
- Arrange for another student to take notes. Hearing impaired students cannot attend to the teacher's face and take notes at the same time.
- Include students in class discussions. Sit in a circle and have speakers lift their hands slightly, not for permission to speak but for visual identification. The student with a hearing impairment may quickly determine who is speaking.
- Create an atmosphere in which student questions are expected.
- Establish a routine procedure for repeating announcements over the public address system.
- Be sensitive to facial expressions and nonverbal communication. Determine if students follow verbal directions or imitate other students.
- Develop a visual communication system between teachers and students in classes—gym, music, and shop—in which students will need to turn down their hearing aids or listening devices because of the noise level in the room.
- Continually encourage socialization. Include students in all activities. Be aware that students with hearing impairments may develop social and emotional problems from isolation and lack of communication with others.
- Be alert to signs of hearing loss, principally irritability and inattentiveness.

> **BOX 9.6**
>
> ## Specific Techniques for Working With Students With Physical Impairments
>
> Students with physical impairments include those who have special health problems, orthopedic impairments, or multiple handicapping conditions. They usually have normal intelligence and academic ability. They should participate in the full range of academic classes as well as art, music, physical education, shop, and home economics. In working with students with physical handicaps, teachers may be guided by the following procedures:
>
> - Students with special health problems may have frequent absences requiring curriculum adjustments. Alternative assignments may be given, or time limits may be extended. In school, students may demonstrate limited energy levels, need rest periods, and require shorter assignments.
> - Because of motor or speech limitations, accommodations may be needed for students to express what they have learned. They may need to dictate rather than to write answers on tests and quizzes. They may need a communication board, computer, tape recorder, or other device for conveying their responses.
> - Physical facilities will need to be adjusted to allow for wheelchairs and crutches.
> - Lapboards that fit across wheelchair arms, small portable chalkboards, and standup tables may be needed by some students. A book holder is a requirement for many others.
> - Independence and self-help skills should be encouraged. Students can be responsible for their own materials.
> - Arrangements may need to be made for assistance with wheelchairs and in the cafeteria, gym, and restroom.
> - Students with physical impairments may have difficulty developing healthy self-concepts. The problem may be particularly acute in adolescence. Positive reinforcement and recognition for jobs well done improve self-image. Overpraising does not.
> - Enrichment activities may need to be provided to students with physical impairments. Their limited mobility may have resulted in social, cultural, and experiential deprivation.

In special education, specific tasks are identified as necessary knowledges, and individual attention ensures that these objectives are learned. This process is related to the concept of mastery learning as advocated by Bloom, Hastings, and Madaus (1971). For special students, the amount that is expected to be mastered is limited in both depth and breadth of content and is relative to abilities.

Methods Used Only With Students With Special Needs

It is recognized that special methods and adaptations are necessary for many students who have physical and sensory impairments and for those with severe mental retardation. Obstacle and mobility training for blind students and speech therapy, speechreading, and the use of residual hearing for students with auditory impairments are included here. Special equipment such as a typewriter with fingerguides for students with cerebral palsy, wired classrooms for students with hearing impairments, and special boards for nonverbal communication may be necessary. Highly structured behavior modification procedures are routinely used with individuals with severe and profound retardation.

Individualization

One dimension of individualization refers to giving increased freedom to students in the determination of goals and in the planning of educational experiences. A seemingly opposite dimension consists of highly structured programs designed by teachers and others for exceptional students and individual learners. The central concept of individualization is not found in the nature and conduct of the specific program but rather in the genesis of that program. Veatch (1970, p. 90) wrote:

> Individualization is a way to think about managing the classroom. It is *not* a method of instruction. It is the way a teacher arranges children, equipment, and materials so that each child can learn eagerly at the peak of his potential without undue stress or strain.

For clarity of discussion, a distinction is made here between *individualized education* and *individualized instruction*. Individualized education implies that educational experiences are planned and implemented to meet the immediate and changing needs of students. If it is determined that 90 percent of a student's time in school must be spent in a special setting with special curriculum and methods, this is individualized education. If it is determined that 90 percent of a student's time can be spent in the regular classroom with 10 percent supplementary help, this is individualized education. If it is determined on the basis of individual assessment that the student's needs can be met by full-time placement in a regular class, this, too, is individualized education. What constitutes individualized education is that it is a purposefully planned set of experiences based on assessment of individual needs.

Individualized instruction means that restricted curriculum topics and special methods are chosen for and administered to one student. Such instruction is often conducted on a one to one student–teacher ratio but may also occur in small groups or in a large class. It is commonly understood that some students need a high degree of individualized instruction in order to learn. The extent to which all students can profit by individualized education is becoming better known.

Why Individualization? The answers are related to both long-term and short-term goals. On a long-term basis, it is because students are different and have the right to maintain their differences as long as they do not interfere with others and do not impede learning. Individual differences eventually contribute to richness, diversity, creativity, and productivity in an open democratic society. A school system could do little that is more harmful to the culture it serves than to regiment its youth in ways that abrogate their potential contributions to that society.

On a short-term basis the answer is the same: It is because students are different. Individualization provides for active involvement with curriculum content, success experiences, positive reinforcement, heightened motivation, and differing kinds of learning experiences. Individualization can accommodate for learning styles, variations in rates of learning, interests, ability levels, and even personality differences. Unfair competition between learners of differing ability can be reduced, and the need to label and categorize is minimized. Students who need individual attention can receive it, and a cooperative relationship can be established rather than one of challenge and confrontation.

Implementing Intervention

Grouping Grouping for academic instruction in the content areas, especially reading and mathematics, is a common practice in the elementary grades. Frequently, groups are constituted on the basis of achievement as demonstrated on formal tests or on classwork. In turn, achievement is often equated with rate of learning. Hence, the low achieving group is the "slow group." Students of the same achievement level have not necessarily achieved in the same manner because rate of learning is only one of the many variables. It may be that methods selected for use with the "slow" group may be inappropriate and the very reason why some of the students are in this group. Continued use of the method may further limit students and reinforce this status of underachievement. Grouping on the basis of learning styles may be a more viable practice.

Because students vary in learning styles and achievement relative to the different academic content areas, groups may need to be reconstituted. They may also need to be changed on the basis of learning progress. Belmont and Belmont (1978) report fluctuation in reading achievement over time for individual learners. If an achievement test is administered during a plateau period of skill refinement or conceptual reorganization, students may do poorly and unwittingly be placed and remain in a group that reinforces this level of achievement and precludes subsequent advancement. There are often no formal assessment procedures to assist teachers in regrouping. Experience, sensitivity to students, knowledge of how they learn, and a thorough awareness of the demands of the subject are bases upon which teachers make grouping decisions.

Planning The care and attention given to planning, the structure of the academic program, and the leadership of teachers in effecting it will largely determine its success. Stahl (1976, p. 52) suggested that "flexibility and organization serve as the guiding principles for all aspects of the planning and establishment of an environmental setting for differentiated learning."

Physical Arrangements At the less interventive levels, teachers can increase attention to individual differences without modification of the classroom. But for more extensive programs of individualization, some changes in the physical arrangements may be needed. An activity table placed away from students' desks is a beginning. In addition to being a place for special project materials, this table, with chairs, can serve for small group activities or as a location for a listening center with headphones. A quiet corner with chairs, a rocking chair, or cushions and rug provide an area for relaxed reading and study. Several carrels may be available for general use in larger classes. Students can take tests, do make-up work, or concentrate on difficult assignments free from visual distraction. There can be individual carrels, or "offices." In the absence of carrels, desks may be placed facing the wall, spaced apart or separated by dividers. If these are against a wall-high chalkboard, students can practice handwriting skills, spelling words, or mathematics facts on the board in front of their desks. When space is limited, bookcases, file cabinets, or carrels can serve as room dividers. Station materials can also be placed on windowsills or on the tops of bookcases and be taken by individual students to their desks to use.

Classroom Atmosphere   A comfortable, positive atmosphere is conducive to individual learning. If teachers are genuinely interested in students and respect them as individuals, a great deal of individual attention can pervade the classroom activities of even the largest class. Capitalizing on student interests and experiences, selecting experiences for application of the learned knowledges, and responding to individual concerns are routine. Tension and conflict are reduced, and students are more willing to accept challenges. Positive support reinforces the attitude that they can learn. Structured, purposeful behavior and activities provide the security needed to venture into learning.

Structure   Open classrooms are obviously organizations for individualization and independent learning. Although some practitioners have reported success with open classrooms and exceptional students, such learners frequently have difficulty in learning in such an environment. Distractibility and hyperactivity are increased, and students who have not learned to organize their own activities toward productive learning in the regular classroom will find it even more difficult to do so in an open environment.

Most exceptional students will need some degree of imposed organization and direction. Class conduct is structured—that is, organized with a purpose. Rules regarding movement in the room, leaving the room, raising one's hand to respond, and noise level are important. Far from being "regimentation" as suggested by critics, such organization itself is the vehicle for immediate support and direction toward the long-term goals of learning self-control and social conventions. Exceptional students do not learn these things automatically as other students do. As they are able to assume more responsibility for behavior and learning, teachers reduce the degree of external control.

Unstructured time must also be made available. Students may need additional quiet study or the opportunity to prepare for a test through discussion with one or two others. Quiet reading in a comfortable corner may be productive. Some unstructured time might even be used by students to get away from the press of academics for brief periods of time. Students who are emotionally labile under pressure may need just such respite. Books, games, magazines, and a tape player with earphones may be made available; these, in turn, may be part of a reward system.

Individualizing in the Larger Class   A persistent question is "But how can I individualize with twenty-five students in my room?" Having that many students or more does limit time, planning, finding materials, and conducting individualized activities while keeping the rest of the class productively busy at the same time. It does not preclude individualization, however. Among the ways to individualize in the larger class are those listed here.

Spontaneous Individual Attention   Much individualization in large classes consists of immediate responses to student questions, comments, discussions, and written work in progress. Such responses provide immediate feedback and enhance motivation.

Aides, Volunteers, and Support Personnel   Paraprofessional aides or parent volunteers allow for distribution of the work load for more individual attention. Teachers work closely with such persons during training, and then aides can work with small groups or on a one-to-one basis, providing a degree of attention that teachers could not manage alone.

Support personnel in the school and itinerant tutors can also provide individual attention. Although a close working relationship must be established between teachers and other professionals, the latter can operate at a more independent level than can paraprofessionals and volunteers.

Peer Tutoring   If managed carefully, peer tutoring can be very successful. Research has shown that exceptional students in regular classrooms tend to be socially isolated. Selecting tutors from the same class or grade level can be effective in some cases in reducing this problem. On the other hand, if this causes exceptional students to feel inferior to their classmates or if students perceive the selection of the tutor as favoritism, the tutor should be chosen from another class or grade level. Peer tutoring has been successful when classmates read the text and study together for tests.

Learning Stations and Learning Centers   Learning stations are a means of individualizing and providing an alternative to lengthy seatwork. In one model, a few stations remain in place for a period of time to provide opportunity for all students to use them and then are changed. Many stations are placed around the perimeters of the classroom, with students moving from one to another. The system depends on the length of time needed at each of the various activities. Students must be scheduled on a revolving basis or must be aware of the particular stations they are to use.

A learning center is an organization of materials and tasks centered around a theme or objective that provides a learning experience for one student or a group working cooperatively. Learning centers differ from learning stations in that they usually encompass a larger concept with several related activities; learning stations are most frequently restricted to a single task. Another difference is that learning centers usually provide opportunity for discovery learning whereas learning stations are more rigidly structured. Learning centers can be developed around interests, aspects of the subject content, and concepts. They can supplement and enrich the regular curriculum. They can promote thinking, aid in decision making, and provide for immediate feedback. Learning centers provide concrete activities and direct sensory experiences. They are particularly effective for students with short attention spans because the larger sequences of tasks encourage them to continue with the project to its conclusion. A learning center can be organized on a table, a desk, a wall, a bulletin board, a cabinet top, a shelf of a bookcase, or the floor. It can remain in the room for long periods of time.

Programmed Instruction and Self-Correcting Materials Many publishers provide materials with which students can interact independently. Programmed texts and workbooks, worksheets, developmental activities, and self-correcting exercises may provide practice in the areas needed by individual students while others are occupied with other activities.

Audiovisual Equipment and Other "Hardware" Individual instruction can be provided by listening centers with teacher-made or commercial cassettes, which often have accompanying workbooks or worksheets. Film strips on a small projector with a self-contained screen and earphones are easily used in the corner of the classroom. Such equipment gives students a sense of independence and is a strong motivating factor for many. Some school systems have television cassettes and teaching machines available.

Computer Technology The use of computers in instruction takes two forms: computer-assisted instruction (CAI) and computer-managed instruction (CMI).

CAI has become a common occurrence. With the advent of microcomputers has come a revolution in the availability of both hardware and software. Most schools have computers available in centralized labs and in many classrooms. Programs have advanced from simple content presentation to sophisticated development of cognitive skills (Bennett, 1982). Although software is increasingly plentiful, the professional must examine the quality of commercial materials before purchasing them.

Once restricted to the brightest students, microcomputers are now available to all. Exceptional students, including those with mild retardation and learning disabilities, can learn to operate and to enjoy them. They are a boon to special educators, allowing a degree of individualization unrealized earlier because of limitations on time and personnel. Computers allow for diversification of curriculum with students in the same classroom receiving instruction and practice at their competence and grade levels.

Special adaptations enable students with visual and orthopedic impairments a high degree of interaction with subject content. Nonverbal students and those with severe speech handicaps can augment their communication skills. Mainstreamed students can remain in the regular room while receiving individualized programming. They can participate in the same kind of instruction as nonhandicapped and gifted students, each taking their turn at the computer.

Computers provide other services to exceptional students—interpreting assessment data, scheduling, monitoring progress, and developing IEPs.

Computer-managed instruction allows entire classrooms to be programmed with the academic progress of each student monitored and available to teachers at any time. This formative evaluation enables the identification of students falling behind and indicates the need for reteaching. The major drawbacks of CMI are the demands made on teacher time, attention, planning, and instruction to take advantage of the multiplicity of information available.

Independent Learning Individualization can also be achieved by various arrangements for independent learning. Homme, Csanyi, Gonzales, and Rechs (1970) provide instructions for contingency contracting; Gallagher (1972) describes its use in teaching students with mild handicaps. Individual research projects can center around student interests. Although it was suggested earlier that exceptional students often do not easily adapt to open classroom environments, such a setting may be excellent for students with orthopedic handicaps and for those with sensory impairments. It can also be used for older students with mild retardation and learning disabilities who have attained some degree of sustained independent activity and who are not overwhelmed by space, activity, and lack of restricting structure.

School–home projects can be beneficial. Students arrange with their parents a project or activity to be conducted at home under their supervision. Projects center around independent-living activities such as budget making, redecorating a room, meal planning, or similar activity. A final report is made by the student in the form of a journal. The teacher could also make a home visit as part of the evaluation.

Cooperative Learning The technique can become a regular method used consistently in the classroom. Regular class students and exceptional students work together in groups of two to six students to learn specific content or to make a project.

Johnson and Johnson (1986) describe the essentials of small-group learning:

- *Positive interdependence.* Students understand that each is an essential part of reaching the group goal. Each member contributes, and group rewards are based on the achievement of the group. Each member has a role to play, and the specific task of a student is linked to those of other group members.
- *Individual accountability.* Performance is evaluated, and students needing assistance are identified. Accountability is emphasized. Individual tests may be given with an average grade being given to all members, or the results of the work of one student may be selected to represent the group.
- *Collaborative skills.* Direct instruction is often necessary to teach students how to work together. Johnson and Johnson (1986) list them as leadership abilities, decision making, trust building, communication, and conflict-management skills.
- *Group processing.* Each group discusses how they are achieving the goal, what is effective, and what needs to be improved. Collaborative skills are practiced, and feedback is reinforcing.

IMPROVING STUDENT ATTITUDE USING COOPERATIVE LEARNING

Mr. Kelly's tenth grade biology class is completing a unit on the ear and the eye. The class is divided into groups of five students with high achievers and students from the learning disabilities resource room in the same groups. They will work together to make an oral presentation to the entire class as a review for the unit test. Mark, a student with a 3.5 GPA works with Kevin, who is deficient in the area of written expression and has a poor self-image.

Mark discovers that Kevin has memorized the locations and functions of the parts of the eye. Therefore, he is chosen to present that part of the report. He points to each eye part, explains it well, and helps the group earn an A grade for the project. Mark tells him that he hopes they continue to work together.

Slavin (1980) and Talmage and Pascarella (1984) found that cooperative learning techniques resulted in both cognitive and affective gains. Slavin, Madden, and Leavey (1984) state that team-assisted individualization (TAI) resulted in improvement in mathematics. The program included individual instruction, cooperative learning teams, and direct instruction. Groups of four to five students helped and encouraged each other.

Two factors differentiate cooperative learning from other group interactions. They are the length of time the group processes are maintained (longer rather than shorter) and the focus of the group work (genuine academic learning rather than supplementary activities).

Teacher Role Implementing the cooperative learning process requires several strategies.

- Group size and membership determined in advance with small groups (two to three) initially
- Planning length of time groups work together
- Physical arrangements
- Explanation of the importance of interdependence and accountability
- Careful structure with objectives and criteria of the lesson or project clearly stated
- Directions understood by each group member
- Teaching collaborative skills
- Monitoring and assisting with tasks or answering questions
- Ensuring participation by each member
- Cooperation and behavior criteria
- Determining when groups can become larger
- Evaluation and assessment

It is recommended that students are assigned to groups for several weeks, preferably an entire semester. Some teachers prefer keeping the group together to complete a particular unit of study.

Group learning is especially effective in reading, language arts, social studies, science, health, and physical education at the elementary level. Secondary subjects—history, English, biology, chemistry, and home economics—lend themselves to cooperative learning.

The literature and the experience of teachers with exceptional students demonstrate that cooperative learning activities enable students to achieve together academically, to learn to form positive relationships with students with disabilities, and to develop interpersonal skills. It eliminates the negative aspects of competition and is an essential ingredient in successful mainstreaming.

Diagnostic Teaching The literature proposes several strategies for individualized instruction. Such terms as clinical teaching, diagnostic teaching, diagnostic-prescriptive teaching, individually guided instruction, prescriptive programming, and child-centered instruction have been used. Such instruction differs from the more traditional classroom teaching in the following ways:

- Continuous formative evaluation in a teach–test–teach–test sequence is an integral part.
- Curriculum is guided by the pattern of the students' knowledges and skills rather than by subject area expectations alone.
- Errors are seen as indications of what has not been learned not as evidence of functional or personal deficits within the students.

Not all diagnostic teaching programs are alike. However, some common elements exist. These include planning, instructing, evaluating, and modifying.

Planning   Teachers use information from the diagnostic workup, informal assessment, and the specifications of the IEP to determine lesson objectives, specific sequences of presentation, appropriate methods, and organization of materials.

Instructing   Teachers implement the planned teaching program.

Evaluating   Continuous formative evaluation is included with the content presentation. Teachers do not wait for an end-of-unit examination but evaluate each step. This does not preclude formal summative evaluation and later follow-up assessment.

Modifying   When students have not achieved the expected level of competence on a task or in learning a concept, teachers informally hypothesize reasons and plan alternative instructional procedures.

Lerner (1985) indentifies these elements among her Clinical Teaching Cycle and describes the circularity of the process. A different kind of strategy for individualization called task analysis has evolved from the behavioral orientation.

Task Analysis   Task analysis is not so much an instructional method as it is a curriculum modification that facilitates precision teaching. Behavioral objectives, which students are expected to achieve in each lesson, are identified. Each objective is broken down into specific subtasks, which are the component parts of the larger objective. In multiplication, for example, the subtasks are not merely the steps in solving the problem but include more finite, prerequisite skills such as students' ability to know the meaning of the sign, to add single- and multiple-digit numbers, to regroup, and to know multiplication facts. Teachers can identify difficulty in multiplication by informal assessment of each of these competencies (Howell, Kaplan, & O'Connell, 1979). Each subtask can then be used as a unit of instruction (Haring & Bateman, 1977; Haring & Phillips, 1972; Lovitt, 1984; Stephens, 1977). Task analysis procedures are compatible with diagnostic teaching. Each substep of the learning task can be taught through that circular process.

SUMMARY

Curriculum is defined as the overall plan in which subject content is specified and arranged sequentially. Curricula have been organized around the content of academic subjects, the developmental needs of students, and the goals and objectives of education as defined by the community. Curriculum and methods are developmental, remedial, or compensatory. Curricula can be divided into regular and special. The regular curriculum is developmental, presented sequentially.

Various special curricula meet the needs of students with various handicapping conditions. Curriculum for students with mental retardation emphasizes self-help, daily living skills, and basic reading and mathematics skills. For learning disabilities, the regular curriculum is adapted or published programs are used to remediate deficits in academic areas. Curriculum goals are designed to prepare students for maximum academic, vocational, and social adjustment. Special education curriculum goals favor individualized goals based on specific learning needs.

A model is presented to allow for a contiguous rather than a fragmented curriculum. The model consists of four focuses: regular curriculum; cognitive support curricula which allow for individual differences in the achievement of the short-term goals of the regular curriculum; supplementary curricula which include learning how to learn, affective education, social skills, perceptual-motor training, and curricula for students with physical and sensory impairments; and special curricula for students in separate settings to teach communication, social, and self-help skills to students with severe impairments.

The challenge of ensuring student learning is met in large part by the use of instructional methods. Although regular education and special education share a basic repertoire of methods, there are several ways in which the two differ. Because exceptional students are not automatic learners, methods in special education must be employed in a precise and complete manner to assure the maximum learning possible. Individual differences are considered in the selection of methods. These differences include learning style, modality preferences, rates of learning and working, levels of processing, and severity of impairment. Methods are used in a manner that leads to competence on selected learning skills and tasks. Finally, there are some methods that are unique to special education, especially those used with students with severe impairments.

To succeed in these endeavors, individualization is necessary. Individualized education is different from individualized instruction. The latter refers to a one-to-one teacher–student ratio whereas the former implies an organization of educational experiences prepared to meet the needs of students, although not necessarily through one-to-one teaching. Individualized education can be accomplished through grouping; spontaneous individual attention; the use of aides, volunteers, and support personnel; peer tutoring; learning stations and centers; programmed and self-correcting materials; audiovisual equipment; computers; and independent learning.

Individualized instruction is often conducted through diagnostic-prescriptive teaching, which is a clinical process including planning, instruction, evaluation, and modification of procedures. Task analysis, a curriculum modification that provides for determining a sequence of specific steps, can be combined with diagnostic teaching.

REFERENCES

Belmont, I., & Belmont, L. (1978). Stability or change in reading achievement over time: Developmental and educational implications. *Journals of Learning Disabilities, 11,* 80–88.

Bennett, R. E. (1982). Applications of microcomputer technology to special education. *Exceptional Children, 49,* 106–113.

Bloom, B. S., Hastings, J. T., & Madaus, G. F. (1971). *Handbook of formative and summative evaluation of student learning.* New York: McGraw-Hill.

Cronbach, L. J., & Snow, R. E. (1977). *Aptitudes and instructional methods: A handbook for research on interactions.* New York: Irvington.

Gallagher, J. J. (1972). The special education contract for mildly handicapped children. *Exceptional Children, 38,* 527–535.

Goldstein, H. (1975). *Social learning curriculum.* Columbus, OH: Merrill.

Haring, N. G., & Bateman, B. (1977). *Teaching the learning disabled child.* Englewood Cliffs, NJ: Prentice-Hall.

Haring, N. G., & Phillips, E. L. (1972). *Analysis and modification of classroom behavior.* Englewood Cliffs, NJ: Prentice-Hall.

Homme, L., Csanyi, A. P., Gonzales, M. A., & Rechs, J. R. (1970). *How to use contingency contracting in the classroom.* Champaign, IL: Research Press.

Howell, K. W., Kaplan, J. S., & O'Connell, C. Y. (1979). *Evaluating exceptional children: A task analysis approach.* Columbus, OH: Merrill.

Johnson, D. W., & Johnson, R. T. (1986). Mainstreaming and cooperative learning strategies *Exceptional Children, 52,* 553–561.

Kagan, J., Rossman, B., Day, D. Albert, J., & Phillips, W. (1964). Information processing in the child: Significance of analytic and reflective attitudes. *Psychological Monographs, 78* (1 Whole No. 578).

Kirk, S. A., & Gallagher, J. J. (1983). *Educating exceptional children* (4th ed.). Boston: Houghton Mifflin.

Kirk, S. A., Kliebhan, J. M., & Lerner, J. W. (1978). *Teaching reading to slow and disabled learners.* Boston: Houghton Mifflin.

Kolstoe, O. P. (1976). *Teaching educable mentally retarded children.* New York: Holt, Rinehart & Winston.

Lerner, J. W. (1985). *Children with learning disabilities: Theories, diagnosis, and teaching strategies* (4th ed.). Boston: Houghton Mifflin.

Lovitt, T. C. (1984). *Tactics for teaching.* Columbus, OH: Merrill.

Slavin, R. E. (1980). Cooperative learning. *Review of Educational Research, 50,* 315–42.

Slavin, R. E., Madden, N. A., & Leavey, M. (1984). Effects of cooperative learning and indivividualized instruction on mainstreamed students. *Exceptional Children, 50,* 434–443.

Stahl, D. K. (1976). *Individualized instruction through differentiated learning programs.* West Nyack, NY: Parker.

Stephens, T. M. (1977). *Teaching skills to children with learning and behavior disorders.* Columbus, OH: Merrill.

Talmage, H., Pascarella, E. T., & Ford, S. (1984). The influence of cooperative learning strategies on teacher practices, student perceptions of the learning environment, and academic achievement. *American Educational Research Journal, 21,* 163–179.

Tarver, S. G., & Dawson, M. M. (1978). Modality preferences and the teaching of reading: A review. *Journal of Learning Disabilities, 11,* 5–17.

Van Etten, G., Arkell, C., & Van Etten, C. (1980). *The severely and profoundly handicapped: Programs, methods, and materials.* St. Louis: Mosby.

Veatch, J. (1970). Individualizing. In V. M. Howes (Ed.). *Individualization of instruction: A teaching strategy* (pp. 90–99). New York: Macmillan.

Voelker, P. H. (1975). Organization, administration, and supervision of special education programs. In W. M. Cruickshank, & G. O. Johnson (Eds.). *Education of exceptional children and youth* (3rd ed.) (pp. 659–691). Englewood Cliffs, NJ: Prentice-Hall.

SUGGESTED READINGS

Behrmann, M. M. (1987). *Applications of computers in the classroom.* San Diego: College-Hill.

Bloom, B. S. (1981). *All our children learning: A primer for parents, teachers, and other educators.* New York: McGraw-Hill.

Dishon, D., & O'Leary, P. W. (1984). *A guidebook for cooperative learning: A technique for creating more effective schools.* Holmes Beach, FL: Learning Publications.

Goldstein, H. (Ed.) (1981). *Curriculum development for exceptional children.* San Francisco: Jossey-Bass.

Hewett, F. M., & Taylor, F. D. (1980). *The emotionally disturbed child in the classroom: The orchestration of success* (2nd ed.). Boston: Allyn and Bacon.

Meyen, E. L., Vergason, G. A., & Whelan, R. J. (Eds.). (1983). *Promising practices for exceptional children: Curriculum implications.* Denver: Love.

Saylor, J. G., Alexander, W. M., & Lewis, A. J. (1981). *Curriculum planning for better teaching and learning* (4th ed.). New York: Holt, Rinehart & Winston.

Torres, S. (Ed.). (1977). *A primer on individualized education programs for handicapped children.* Reston, VA: Council for Exceptional Children.

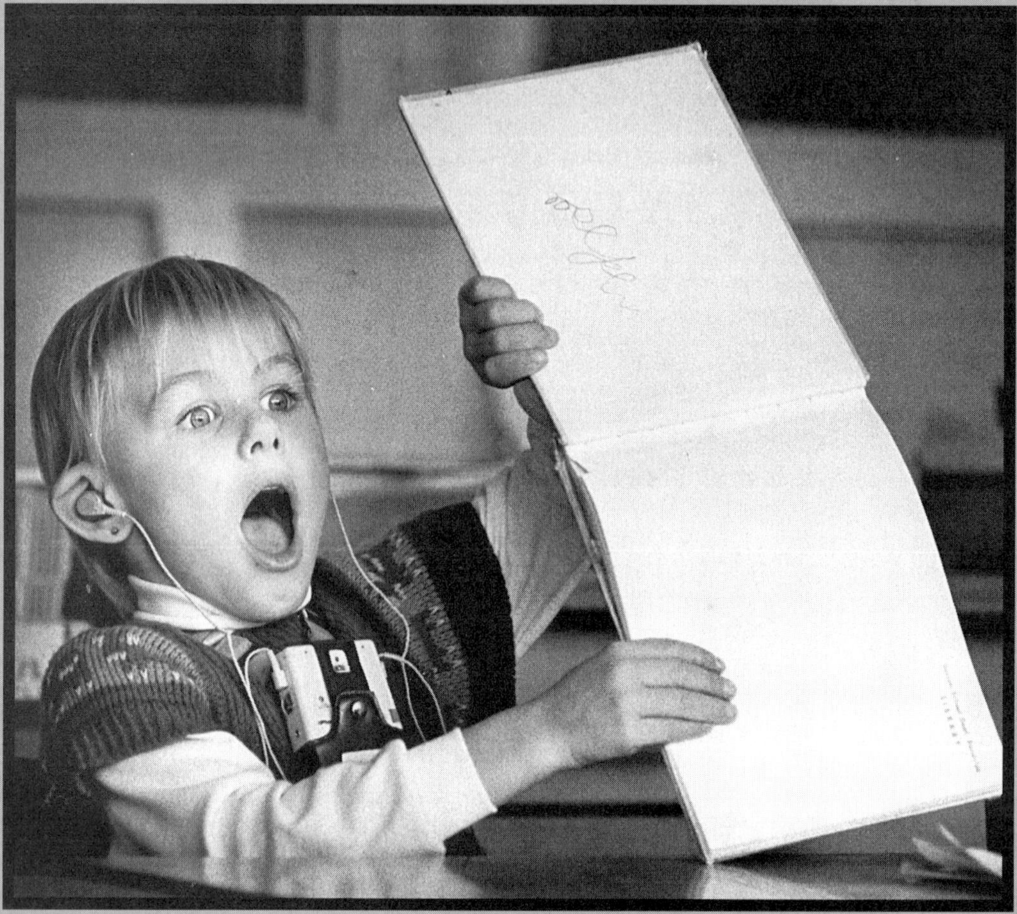

10

Methods for Teaching Oral Language

LANGUAGE IS THE vehicle of communication. It is through language that children receive knowledge about the world, interact with others, receive instructions in the classroom, and give evidence of learning. Researchers and theorists have postulated a number of descriptions of language. The one preferred here reflects only one interpretation of language acquisition, development, and functioning. It is, however, one which has been demonstrated to have utility for educators in their work with students with learning and language problems.

Language processing refers to the reception, assimilation, internalization, perception, and discrimination of the speech of others and expressive verbalization. Language development is the sequential acquisition, expansion, and refinement of communicative skills including listening, speaking, reading, and writing.

Language Processing

Survival in the world depends on children's abilities to internalize sensory experiences into understandable concepts. First learnings are motoric and spacial. Children must assimilate and adapt to multidimensional physical surroundings. Thus, before they have any understanding of verbal language, they have already begun to organize the experental environment. This prelinguistic internal organization of experiences is the foundation of cognition and the beginning of language. This process is called *inner language* (Johnson & Myklebust, 1967).

Among the stimuli in the environment to be discriminated are the verbalizations of others. These sounds and sound patterns are perceived by children and therefore

TABLE 10.1
Aspects of Language Processing

ELEMENT	RECEPTIVE LANGUAGE	INNER LANGUAGE	EXPRESSIVE LANGUAGE
Description	Vocabulary and linguistic patterns received from others via listening during early childhood years	Internalization of vocabulary and linguistic patterns, and integrated with meaning derived from experience Use of language as the vehicle for thinking	Putting meaning and ideas into vocabulary and linguistic patterns for communication to others

called *receptive language*. Children associate these sounds with the prelinguistic experiences already learned. These verbal patterns then gain meaning. Inner language becomes a relationship between children's linguistic and cognitive systems. As cognition develops into complex thinking processes, there is an increased need for language as the vehicle of mediation. In turn, the expanded world of internal experiencing becomes the base for sophisticated language development.

The third process is *expressive language*. Expressive verbal language consists of the encoding of meaning into a form that allows communication. The expressive mode through which this communication is initially made is speech. Speech is largely imitative with children identifying with their parents for motivation and with their speech as models. Sounds are practiced and refined, formed into words, and later expressed in word groups (Table 10.1).

Sequence of Development

The hierarchical sequence of development of these language processes occurs in the order of their presentation above: inner language, receptive language, and expressive language. These three are semi-independent. Each can develop at a rate somewhat different from the other two, although the rate of each is affected by the rates of development of the others.

Language Processing and Exceptional Students

Many students who are hearing impaired, mildly or moderately retarded, or learning disabled demonstrate deficits in one or more area of language processing. Pathology can occur in any one of the three processes independently, although the others are affected because of their interrelatedness. In general, the severity of the pathology in interfering with the quality of individual language functioning follows the same hierarchical order as their development. The most debilitating problems are those that occur in inner language processing (Johnson & Myklebust, 1967) because these affect the individual's ability to gain meaning from language. The second most severe pathology is in the receptive process that interferes with the child's ability to receive information. The least debilitating pathology of the three is that which occurs in expressive language. If students are able to gain knowledge from the environment (receptive language) and use that knowledge in making decisions and in guiding their activities (inner language and cognition), they can function despite the admitted limitations in expressive language.

Teachers' understanding of these processes have a very practical value. Teachers evaluate students on their ability to express, orally or in writing, what they have learned. It is often thought that if students cannot accurately report the content of the subject, they have not learned it and do not understand the material. It is possible for students with expressive language problems to know but be unable to demonstrate this knowledge. Similarly, students may demonstrate difficulty in oral reading but be able to comprehend what has been read. The same language processing pathology would interfere with the ability to express knowledge of the text material. It is important to know if a learning problem is due to faulty language processing and, if so, which of the three processes is affected.

Language Processing Assessment

Classroom teachers might suspect a language processing difficulty, but diagnosis should be left to a professional in the field of language functioning. The *Clinical Evaluation of Language Functions* (CELF) (Semel & Wiig, 1980a) evaluates language processing. Six subtests measure processing, and five assess language production. Two supplementary subtests evaluate the processing and production of language sounds. The CELF is oriented toward language production, assessing phonology, syntax, semantics, memory, and retrieval. However, Semel and Wiig caution that the instrument is more a screening than a diagnostic test and that students demonstrating deficits be given further extensive evaluation. In contrast is the *Illinois Test of Psycholinguistic Abilities* (ITPA) (Kirk, McCarthy, & Kirk, 1968), which focuses on processing; questions have been raised, however, regarding the adequacy of the test's norms, validity, and reliability (Salvia & Ysseldyke, 1985).

Remediation

Various teaching programs based on the ITPA have been used for training and remediation. Among these are the *Peabody Language Development Kits*, (Revised) (Dunn, Smith, Dunn, Horton, & Smith, 1981) and the *GOAL Program* (Karnes, 1972). Bush and Giles (1977) provide remedial activities by grade level, one through eight, and the *MWM Program* (Minskoff, Wiseman, & Minskoff, 1972) contains numerous activities related to each subtest of the ITPA.

Such training has not been without controversy. As a result of an extensive review of research studies, Hammill and Larsen (1974) concluded that psycholinguistic training was not effective. Others (Kavale, 1981; Lund, Foster, & McCall-Perez, 1978) criticized these findings and found merit in such instruction. Undoubtedly, the debate will continue. In the meantime, psycholinguistic training programs declined in popularity among learning disabilities teachers.

To complement the CELF, Semel and Wiig (1982) have provided the *Clinical Language Intervention Program* (CLIP). Designed to adapt to individualized remedial programs, the CLIP is organized into four content areas—semantics, syntax, memory, and pragmatics.

In the past, special education teachers often provided training intended to improve language processing. Today, assessment and remediation of language processing deficits are provided by speech/language pathologists. In addition, pathologists' focus of concern has shifted to the remediation of deficits in language development. Regular and special classroom teachers cooperate with pathologists by conducting supplementary activities, providing support for positive language development, and avoiding classroom demands on the students that might be counterproductive to the program.

Language Development

Language develops across cultures in a relatively ordered sequence. This sequence appears to be invariant, although the rate of development may vary from child to child and cannot be easily equated to chronological age. Students whose rates of development differ markedly from their peers, particularly if the development is delayed, may experience difficulties in classroom achievement.

The sequence of acquisition of language skills is as follows:

1. Listening
2. Speaking
3. Reading
4. Writing

The first two constitute the primary language system. These occurred first in the process of the evolution of language, and they occur first in individual development. The second two, reading and writing, constitute the secondary language system.

Primary Language System

Listening and speaking skills are, for the most part, developed during the preschool years and, for nearly all children, without formal instruction. They are learned from parents and others in the children's environment. The patterns of their speech assume the language characteristics of these models. Refining these skills is often an objective of preschool programs and early grade instruction. The primary language system has the following elements: phonology, morphology, syntax, semantics, and pragmatics (Table 10.2).

Phonology Phonology refers to the sounds of the language. It includes the ability of children to formulate speech sounds appropriate to his or her chronological age.

Morphology Morphology refers to the form of the language. A morpheme is the smallest unit of meaningful language. Often a morpheme is a word, but it may also be a prefix, (*un-, re-*) or a suffix (*-ite, -ed, -s*) or a form used to indicate possessives (*-'s*). A child must acquire competence in using the correct forms including plurals, possessives, comparatives, and tenses.

TABLE 10.2
Elements of the primary language system

ELEMENT	DEFINITION	SKILL	EXAMPLES
Phonology	The sounds of language	Ability to formulate speech sounds appropriate to chronological age	Students with articulation deficits may say "<u>w</u>abbit, <u>th</u>oap"
Morphology	The form of language. Smallest unit of meaningful language. Usually a word but may be a prefix (un-, re-) or suffix (-ite, -ed, -s)	Competence in using correct forms including plurals, possessives, comparatives, and tenses	"I knowed that last year"
Syntax	The structure of language	Organization of sequences of words into phrases or sentences	"I never seen none of them"
Semantics	The meaning of language	Denotative meaning to words gives literal meaning or definition; connotative meaning goes beyond literal meaning and includes implications, inferences, and emotional impact of language	"It means it don't knock twice"
Pragmatics	The use of language in communication or social context. Also includes communicative style. Appropriate use of formal or informal vocabulary	Ability to convey verbal or nonverbal message, logical presentation of ideas, fluency of delivery, projection of accurate meaning, and appropriate responses	Inability to carry on logical conversation with peer

Syntax Syntax refers to the structure of language. It includes the organization of sequences of words into phrases and sentences. Syntax and morphology are the components of the grammar system.

Semantics Semantics refers to the meaning of language. It has its beginnings as children establish referents between the elements of receptive language (sounds in the environment) and experiences. Meaning can be denotative or connotative. Denotative is the objective or actual meaning, such as the precise definition of a vocabulary word or the literal meaning of a sentence. Connotative is the subjective meaning. It extends beyond literal meaning and includes implications, inferences, and the emotional impact of language.

Pragmatics Pragmatics refers to the use of language within a social context. It involves the ability to convey a verbal or nonverbal message, the logical presentation of ideas, the fluency of delivery, the projection of accurate meaning, and appropriate responses. Pragmatics also includes adopting a communicative style using syntax and vocabulary appropriate to the communication level (for example, formal or informal); and taking turns, acknowledging, and responding to the messages of others.

Nearly all children learn these elements of the primary language system, either correctly or incorrectly during the preschool years. There may be considerable variation in this learning. For some children, this variation is only in rate of language acquisition and refinement. For others, it may represent language differences and for still others, language disorders.

Language Differences and Language Disorders

Language differences are defined as mild variations that may occur because of children's rates of language, neurological or general development, or to imitations in early language stimulation. These are manifested in minor developmental speech problems, errors in grammar, or the reticence and/or inability of children to communicate orally at an age-appropriate level. Mecham and Willbrand (1979) describe individual variations in language. They include differences in the amount of verbal output, vocabulary diversity, intensity and quality of emotional feeling, and intelligibility. They also note variations in semantic and sequential memory and in listening accuracy. Preschool and regular classroom teachers in the early grades commonly address these aspects of language, and each can be improved by intervention.

It may be difficult to distinguish between a language difference and a language disorder at first observation. Many children come to school with a rich linguistic system, internalized from the home environment and conforming to the prevailing mode of academic and social communication. Other children arrive with language that appears deficient. The first group of children may have internalized a complex and meaningful linguistic system; their language is well-developed but nonstandard. It is probable that they have equal cognitive and academic potential as children whose language conforms to that of the school. However, they may have reading and oral expressive difficulties because of their nonstandard language. The second group of children, whose language appears deficient, may not have a well-developed language system of any kind. Such children may have severe problems caused by neurological processing impairments or environmental deprivation. They may not have the same cognitive or academic potential as others. It is important for the development of all these children that the teacher, especially in the early grades, be aware that the linguistically different are not the same as the linguistically disordered.

Language Development and Exceptional Students

Disorders may occur at any point in language development. They represent a pathology in the language system that may be organic or nonorganic and may be of such a nature and severity that improvement cannot be expected as a result of maturation or routine language stimulation. The child may exhibit articulation disorders (phonology), problems in grammar (morphology and syntax), or in meaning (semantics). For some exceptional students, the use of language in a social context (pragmatics) is the stumbling block. They do not develop a comfortable, give-and-take style of communicating with others, and these deficits lead to avoidance of or rejection by peers. Other language problems listed by Temple and Gillet (1984) are lack of fluency, voice problems, dialect, bilingualism, and lack of familiarity with the English language. Many severe language difficulties have their origins in pathology of the language processes (receptive, inner, or expressive).

NEUROLOGICAL LANGUAGE DISORDER

Although Ellen had a full scale score of 65 on an individual test of intelligence, she demonstrated none of the other characteristics of retardation. At age thirteen she was attractive, friendly, outgoing, and socially adept. She had good vocabulary, used good grammar, and could read orally with ease at the high school level. Her comprehension, however, remained at the elementary level. She could recall specific facts but could not make inferences or suggest logical outcomes for stories. She could remember the content of a list of five sentences but was unable to rearrange them in logical sequence.

Further investigation revealed that Ellen had been an unwanted child—abused and deprived before being adopted by a caring family. It was inferred that early central nervous system damage resulted in central aphasia, the inability to gain meaning from language.

Ellen continued in eighth grade. A speech/language pathologist worked directly with her and her teachers, helping them to modify curriculum and instruction. Major goals were the maintenance of the admirable qualities already possessed, progress in academics to the extent possible, and maintenance of self-concept. One of the goals of the speech/language pathologist in consulting with Ellen's teachers was the modification of their expectations—raising them from their earlier perceptions of Ellen as a retarded child to one of optimism for a capable young lady with the potential for leading a normal, productive life.

Language Assessment

Informal evaluation, primarily by observation, is the major technique for initial language assessment. Teachers' knowledge of age/grade expectancies is invaluable in this process. They need to be aware of those students whose language systems are intact, those whose language systems are different from the expected norm, and those who have serious deficits in language development and processing.

General Language Development Some students demonstrate language that would be appropriate for a child of a younger age. This delayed development can impose limitations on students' abilities to profit from instruction and achieve in the early grades. Among the norm-referenced tests that can be used to give an estimate of general language development are *The Houston Test for Language Development* (Crabtree, 1963), the *Test of Early Language Development* (TELD) (Hresko, Reid,

& Hammill, 1981), and the *Utah Test of Language Development* (Mecham & Jones, 1978). A criterion-referenced instrument, the *Diagnostic Inventory of Early Development* (Brigance, 1978), can help pinpoint development in specific language skills.

Phonological Assessment Classroom teachers' principal method of assessing phonological competence, or speech, is through observation. As noted in Chapter 2, speech is considered defective when it calls attention to itself, makes the speaker self-conscious, or interferes with communication. Problems such as lisps and voice disorders are immediately noticeable. However, caution must be taken when assuming speech problems on the basis of enunciation or articulation because some speech sounds are not refined, normally, until the intermediate grades. Consultation with the system's speech and hearing pathologist should allay or confirm concerns about individual students.

Formal tests include the *Auditory Discrimination Test* (Wepman, 1973), the *Goldman–Fristoe Test of Articulation* (Goldman & Fristoe, 1986), the *Goldman–Fristoe–Woodcock Auditory Skills Test Battery* (Goldman, Fristoe, & Woodcock, 1976), the *Goldman–Fristoe Woodcock Test of Auditory Discrimination* (Goldman, Fristoe, & Woodcock, 1970) and the *Templin–Darley Test of Articulation* (Templin & Darley, 1969). For the most part, these tests are administered by the speech and hearing pathologist although screening for auditory discrimination is sometimes made by a special or resource teacher.

Morphology and Syntax Assessment Students' acquisition of standard English grammar should be assessed. The preschool child who places *-ed* on all words to indicate past tense, for example, may have a language system qualitatively different from a peer who says "I seen." The first has internalized a morphological unit indicating past tense and is attempting to transfer it to other situations as he or she should. It is the irregularity of the grammar system that makes the ending inappropriate in many places. Good teaching and language experience can correct such difficulties. The second child has internalized an incorrect morphological and syntactical structure that will be far more difficult to remediate.

Occasional errors in grammar should not overly concern teachers. They represent incidental errors that occur normally in the process of refining proper usage. An on-the-spot correction or a later reinforcement of the correct form may be all that is needed. Persistent errors, however, require attention. Teachers may note particular errors and keep an informal record of them. For assistance in developing tabulation procedures or a sample checklist, the reader may wish to consult Berry (1969).

Formal tests of morphology and syntax include the *Carrow Elicited Language Inventory* (Carrow-Woolfolk, 1974), the *Northwestern Syntax Screening Test* (Lee, 1971), and the *Test for Auditory Comprehension of Language-Revised* (Carrow-Woolfolk, 1985). The Grammatic Closure subtest of the ITPA as well as subtests of other instruments listed at the end of this section may also be used.

Semantic Assessment At the semantic level, teachers can observe students' responses to oral directions in class and to the participation in general class discussions or activities that involve language. Formal assessment may begin at the vocabulary level. The *Peabody Picture Vocabulary Test—Revised* (Dunn & Dunn, 1981) is a measure of receptive vocabulary. The student's demonstrated ability on this instrument can be compared to responses and scores on tests that require orally presented definitions. When two tests that have been normed on separate populations are compared, reliance should not be placed on actual score differences. It is preferable to evaluate the extent of the difference informally. A comparison of two subtests (Picture Vocabulary and Oral Vocabulary) on the *Test of Language Development—Primary* (TOLD–P) (Newcomer & Hammill, 1982b) avoids this normative population problem, but the test is applicable only to students below nine years of age.

Beyond vocabulary, semantics can be assessed informally in discussions with students and with questioning such as asking the meaning of common sayings. Observation by teachers during language lessons and formal assessment procedures is very important. Students' abilities to follow directions, participate in discussions, and respond to general classroom activities give evidence of meaningful language reception. Alert teachers might note, for example, that a student hesitates in responding until others in the room have done so, setting the model. This student may be imitating others rather than understanding the directions. Language interferences could be the cause of such behavior. An alternative explanation is hearing loss. Hearing acuity and perception should routinely be assessed for any student suspected of having a language disorder.

A conversation with parents can be informative. Teachers can compare students' language to that of the parents to note the influences of modeling as the source of nonstandard English or grammatical errors. In addition, descriptions by parents of the children's achievement of developmental language milestones, their early language history, and their use of language in the home could help.

There are few formal tests available to measure semantic competence at the primary language system level. Instruments are the *Boehm Test of Basic Concepts* (Boehm, 1971) and the *Bracken Basic Concept Scale* (Bracken, 1984). Several subtests on the individual tests of intelligence can give clues to the child's semantics ability. The *Test of Language Development—Intermediate* (TOLD–I) (Newcomer & Hammill, 1982a) measures several aspects of the child's use of meaningful language.

Pragmatics Assessment The complexity of the interactive skills that comprise pragmatics and the lack of a well-researched organizational construct make assessment difficult. Naturalistic observation and evaluation of isolated elements have been employed. Roth and Spekman (1984a, 1984b) have presented a four-part organization to facilitate assessment and intervention. The system is employed by a language pathologist.

Planning for Instruction

It has been stressed that the symbol system, which is language, is irrevocably tied to experience and meaning. Therefore, teaching effectiveness and motivation for learning are heightened when language activities are based on the student's present knowledges, interests, and experiences. It is relatively easy to arrange situations that capitalize on this information.

It is equally, if not more important, to associate language learning with the student's present *meaning level*—that is, the cognitive developmental level. As Halliday (1975) reported, words do not acquire meaning, meanings acquire words. The impact of language instruction is greater when the level of cognitive maturation is known and when activities can be devised appropriate to that level. Because children pass through the Piagetian stages at varying rates, language activities provided are necessarily different for different students. All may be asked to describe "our trip to the zoo"; one student may report on "hoofed animals," but another may profit most by being asked only to "describe the elephant." This is particularly important for exceptional students whose rates of development may vary markedly from the norm and age/grade expectancies. Fortunately, because there is so much diagnostic information on identified students and because they often are assigned to individualized programs, teachers or tutors have a greater chance of knowing the level of development and of having an opportunity to create a program appropriate to it.

For students in the regular class and individual learners who have not received testing, such information is not available and difficult to ascertain. In such cases, it is classroom teachers' experience that must provide the basis for assessment and intervention. Individual differences in the rate of language development, pacing, learning styles, modality preferences, and cognitive tempo are factors to be considered in planning the early language program.

Role of Teachers in Facilitating Language Development

Communication techniques used by teachers in continuing interaction with students and in specific content area presentations provide opportunities for language instruction and development. Teachers facilitate these processes by serving as a role model, using language to communicate effectively, giving direct instruction, and providing opportunities to students to practice language skills.

Teachers as Role Models

By using correct English, pronunciation, and grammar, teachers provide a language model for students in the class. Such language should include complete sentences with specific vocabulary. The use of slang or erroneous grammar in an attempt to communicate "in the language they understand" should be avoided; it is a disservice to students who later will be judged by their language ability. Teachers are also role models in the use of language as a tool to affect the environment. Our society moves largely on the transfer of information, directives, forms, applications, directions, instructions, legal proceedings, and social interactions all based on language. Students whose attempts to satisfy their needs and influence others by physical means can learn by teachers' demonstrations that language can be equally effective. Other students, unsuccessful in expressing their thoughts in language, can become anxious about speaking. Teachers' relaxed and comfortable language can reduce this anxiety and encourage improvement in speaking.

Using Language to Communicate Effectively

Teachers use language as the major vehicle of instruction. They obtain and maintain attention and interest, explain, clarify, direct, introduce, and summarize lessons with language. Careful attention to the language used in these activities is important for communication, especially with exceptional students and individual learners whose language development may be delayed or faulty. Teachers can plan clear, orderly sequences of presentation with a minimum of words; excessive verbiage can be can confusing. When explaining a new concept, teachers proceed slowly and logically using simple sentence structure, understandable terms, and concise examples. Pauses give the student time to comprehend; filling those pauses with teacher-talk confounds comprehension. Redefining and rephrasing with a minimum of words enhances and clarifies communication.

Communication means interacting, not simply one-way understanding. Teachers can encourage students to participate in class, practicing language skills. To facilitate responsiveness, teachers reduce anxiety by accepting what the student says and demonstrating respect for their right to an opinion. Teachers respond positively and do not talk down to students or let them know their contribution was less than acceptable. Similarly, teachers should solicit questions and make each student feel important by providing a serious response. Teachers' questioning techniques are also important. Otto, McMenemy, and Smith (1973) recommend that teachers use Carl Rogers's nondirective techniques of encouraging responses from others while not interjecting personal viewpoints. Opportunities for such language interaction can be made throughout the school day in both academic and social contexts.

Providing Direct Instruction

A major part of the curriculum in the elementary school in particular revolves around various aspects of language development—listening skills, oral expression, word and passage meaning, reading, and writing. For students with learning problems, the acquisition of spoken language abilities is vital as a prerequisite for reading. Oral language instruction is not restricted to lessons in grammar but pervades all other classroom activities as well. Aspects of language teaching are highly individualized even in larger classes. Teachers note each area of need and provide on-the-spot instruction. The effectiveness of language instruction can be heightened by ample provisions for opportunities for the student to use and practice newly learned skills.

Providing Opportunities to Practice Language

In addition to encouraging student participation in general class interaction, more specific activities can be provided for practice. These include oral reading, role playing, oral presentations, circle activities, class discussions, and specific oral language activities.

Oral Reading Oral reading allows students to experience talking before the class without being concerned about the content of what they are to say. Further, reading from prepared materials, the basal reader, workbooks, storybooks, newspapers, or poetry literally puts good grammar "into the student's mouth" and reinforces correct linguistic constructions. Choral reading provides for an alternative activity.

Role Playing Role playing can take several forms. Reading a play from a script is usually enjoyable. Because students are not responsible for the textual content, role playing allows them to participate without feeling uncomfortable in front of the class. Student-written scripts provide the added dimension of creativity and the use of written language.

Role playing can also be incorporated in instruction. Students can have make-believe telephone conversations, call the fire department, or order an item from a catalog. Introductions, party etiquette, or ordering from a menu can give language practice. For older students, role playing activities could include job interviewing, sales, or returning a damaged item to the store.

Oral Presentations Oral presentations increase the demands on students because they are now also individually responsible for the content of what they say. In the early grades, "show and tell" forms the introduction to oral presentations. In later grades, reports increase the sophistication of preparation and organization. Students concentrate on content as well as speaking before a group.

Circle Activities Teachers often use circle activities to start and/or end the day. This provides opportunity for sharing experiences and feelings. It is also an opportunity for expressive language development. Posing a social circumstance in circle can sometimes stimulate divergent thinking and good explanation. Such topics as "What if you see two classmates whispering and you think they are talking about you?" or "What should you do if another student wants to copy from your paper during a test?" can stimulate expression of opinions and ideas.

Class Discussions Class discussions may be informal with students conversing on topics of general interest or concern. However, it is not profitable if these are simply disorganized conversations. The teacher provides gentle direction to the discussion without dominating it to encourage students to think about their contributions before presenting them, to give them insight into logical sequence, to identify points at which emotional response replaces reasoning, to keep the discussion on track, and to prevent manipulation by one or more members of the group.

Other Specific Activities Many other activities can be devised to stimulate language development. These include:

- Providing language master activities
- Telling a story from a picture
- Using a tape recorder
- Presenting words on cards in a scrambled sequence to be rearranged to form a sentence
- Repeating sentences word for word
- Memorizing poems
- Playing memory games in which each student must remember the list already created and add a new item for the next student to remember (for example, I am going to the store to buy vegetables. I will buy potatoes, and so on)

- Presenting sequences of words in which students tell which one is different (for example, cat, fish, horse, dog)
- Telling tall tales
- Providing problem-solving activities such as "What would you do if..." stories (for example, "What would you do if someone you didn't know wanted to borrow your lunch money?")
- Expressing feelings
- Asking each student to add a new sentence to a story started by the teacher
- Creating a puppet show
- Asking, "How does the sentence or rhyme end?"
- Asking, "How do you think the story ends?"
- Playing twenty questions
- Telling about the funniest thing you ever saw
- Writing and producing a television show or a skit from a lesson in social studies
- Expressing opinions related to content area topics
- Holding classroom debates on content area topics

Further suggestions can be found in some of the "Suggested Readings" at the end of the chapter, and others may be found in books in the professional library or college book store.

Language Programs

The regular classroom, in the early grades in particular, is often characterized by high-level activities related to language development. Many lessons are directed to language and language-related subjects. A wealth of commercially prepared material is available for this purpose. Among the most widely used have been the *Peabody Language Development Kits* (Revised) (Dunn et al., 1981). The four kits are organized on the basis of mental age (from three and one-half to nine and one-half and contain excellent language stimulation materials including decks of large picture cards in diverse categories (animals, clothing, furniture, and occupations), listening materials, posters, and puppets. The picture cards are available separately.

Other commercially prepared programs include the *Developmental Syntax Program* (Coughran & Liles, 1975); *DISTAR Language Levels I, II, and III* (Englemann & Osborn, 1976, 1977, 1973), *Developmental Language Lessons* (Mowery and Replogle, 1977); *Fokes Sentence Builder* (Fokes, 1976); *Goldman–Lynch Sounds and Symbols Development Kit* (Goldman and Lynch, 1971); and *Rebus Communication Aids* (Clark, Davies, and Woodcock, 1979).

Oral Language Problems in Adolescence

Oral language difficulties are not restricted to elementary school students. They can continue into adolescence and adulthood. Reed (1986, p. 228) suggests such disorders "impact on personal relationships, academic success during junior and senior high, attainment of higher education, vocational and professional careers, and subsequent earning power."

SECONDARY LANGUAGE ACTIVITIES FOR MAINSTREAMED STUDENTS

Mr. Brevnoff, an eleventh grade social studies teacher, willingly accepts mainstreamed students. He is aware that it is often helpful in learning if students can repeat ideas in their own words and receive confirmation of the accuracy of their understandings. Therefore, Mr. Brevnoff plans for student interaction several times each week. The activities take several forms: study groups, discussion questions, cooperatively completed worksheets and projects, and assignment of individual topics for presentation to the small groups. Occasionally, one member from each group shares a common topic for presentation. They research and prepare together but then return to their respective small groups to present them. This technique provides opportunity for cooperative learning, verbal interaction among class members, and feedback. In addition, it reduces anxiety that might occur if the presentation were made to the whole class.

Language assessment at this level may be made by observation of spontaneous or elicited language or with standardized instruments including those listed below:

- *Clinical Evaluation of Language Function—Advanced Level Screening Test* (Semel and Wiig, 1980b)
- *Lets' Talk Inventory for Adolescents* (Wiig, 1982)
- *Test of Language Competence* (Wiig & Secord, 1985)
- *Woodcock Language Proficiency Battery* (Woodcock, 1980)
- *Peabody Picture Vocabulary Test* (Revised) (Dunn and Dunn, 1981)
- *Test of Adolescent Language—2* (TOAL-2) (Hammill, Brown, Larsen, and Wiederholt 1987)

Intervention follows the general principles of any remediation with adolescents. The student is part of the remedial process. It may include counseling at the outset to confirm students' appreciation of the importance of achievement and intervention activities and to secure initial cooperation. All proposed assessment and intervention activities are explained and shared if students are to continue as active participants. Activities must be age-appropriate, realistic, and practical with opportunity for generalization to diverse settings and situations. The reader is referred to the work of Schwartz and McKinley (1984) for a wealth of practical recommendations for teaching oral language skills to adolescents.

SUMMARY

Children begin to organize experiences prior to the acquisition of a formal language system. Thus, inner language, the internal organization of experience, precedes the development of the other two systems: receptive language through which children receive verbal and nonverbal meaningful stimuli and expressive language by which they encode meaning into forms of communication. Pathology can occur in any of these three systems. Assessment and remedial procedures have been developed but are controversial and largely restricted for use by language specialists and special education teachers.

The hierarchy of formal language includes listening and speaking, the input and output skills of the primary language system, reading and writing, the input and output skills of the secondary language system, and pragmatics (the use of language in communication). Many classroom activities provide students with the opportunity to practice and refine primary language system skills. Teachers can provide role models, numerous kinds of opportunities for language expression, direct instruction, and encouragement in the growth of necessary abilities.

Often, both the school curriculum and classroom teachers underestimate the value of attending to the two levels of the primary language system—listening and speaking. However, as will be evident in the subsequent discussion of elements of the secondary language system, a solid base of oral language skills, both receptive and expressive, are necessary for reading and writing development.

Although attention is given to the primary language skills in the elementary school, difficulties in these abilities can continue into adolescence and adulthood. Assessment and remediation procedures, somewhat more difficult at this level, can be employed to aid students in continuing to acquire and refine oral language skills.

REFERENCES

Berry, M. F. (1969). *Language disorders of children: The bases and diagnoses.* New York: Appleton-Century-Crofts.
Boehm, A. E. (1971). *Boehm test of basic concepts.* New York: Psychological Corporation.
Bracken, B. A. (1984). *Bracken basic concept scale.* Columbus, OH: Merrill.
Brigance, A. H. (1978). *Diagnostic inventory of early development.* Woburn, MA: Curriculum Associates.
Bush, W. J., & Giles, M. T. (1977). *Aids to psycholinguistic teaching* (2nd ed.). Columbus, OH: Merrill.
Carrow-Woolfolk, E. (1985). *Test for auditory comprehension of language-Revised.* Allen, TX: DLM Teaching Resources.
Carrow-Woolfolk, E. (1974). *Carrow elicited language inventory.* Allen, TX: DLM Teaching Resources.
Clark, C. R., Davies, C.O., & Woodcock, R. W. (1979). *Rebus communication aids.* Circle Pines, MN: American Guidance Service.
Cougran, L., & Liles, B. (1975). *Developmental syntax program.* Austin, TX: Learning Concepts.
Crabtree, M. (1963). *The Houston test for language development.* Chicago: Stoetling.
Dunn, L. M., & Dunn, L. M. (1981). *The Peabody picture vocabulary test—revised.* Circle Pines, MN: American Guidance Service.
Dunn, L. M., Smith, J. O., Dunn, L. M., Horton, K. B., & Smith, D. D. (1981). *The Peabody language development kits* (revised). Circle Pines, MN: American Guidance Service.
Englemann, S., & Osborn, J. (1973). *DISTAR Language III.* Chicago: Science Research Associates.
Englemann, S., & Osborn, J. (1976). *DISTAR language I.* Chicago: Science Research Associates.
Englemann, S., & Osborn, J. (1977). *DISTAR language II.* Chicago: Science Research Associates.

Fokes, J. (1976). *Fokes sentence builder.* New York: Teaching Resources.

Goldman, R., & Fristoe, M. (1986). *Goldman–Fristoe test of articulation.* Circle Pines, MN: American Guidance Service.

Goldman, R., Fristoe, M., & Woodcock, R. (1970) *Goldman–Fristoe–Woodcock test of auditory discrimination.* Circle Pines, MN: American Guidance Service.

Goldman, R., Fristoe, M., & Woodcock, R. (1976). *Auditory skills test battery.* Circle Pines, MN: American Guidance Service.

Goldman, R. & Lynch, M. E. (1971). *Goldman–Lynch sounds and symbols development kit.* Circle Pines, MN: American Guidance Service.

Halliday, M. A. K. (1975). *Learning how to mean: Explorations in the development of language.* New York: Elsevier.

Hammill, D. D., Brown, V. L., Larsen, S. C., & Weiderholt, J. L. (1987). *Test of adolescent language—2.* Austin, TX: Pro-Ed.

Hammill, D. D., & Larsen, S. C. (1974) The effectiveness of psycholinguistic teaching. *Exceptional children, 41* (1), 5–14.

Hresko, W. P., Reid, D. K., & Hammill, D. D. (1981). *The test of early language development.* Austin, TX: Pro-Ed.

Johnson, D. J., & Mykelbust, H. R. (1967). *Learning disabilities; Educational principles and practices.* New York: Grune & Stratton.

Karnes, M. B. (1972) *GOAL program: Language development.* Springfield, MA: Milton Bradley.

Kavale, K. (1981). Functions of the Illinois test of psycholinguistic abilities (ITPA): Are they trainable? *Exceptional Children, 47*(7), 496–510.

Kirk, S., McCarthy, J., & Kirk, W. D. (1968). *Illinois test of psycholinguistic abilities.* Urbana: University of Illinois Press.

Lee, L. (1971). *Northwestern syntax screening test.* Evanston, IL: Northwestern University Press.

Lund, K. A., Foster, G. E., & McCall-Perez, F. C. (1978) The effectiveness of psycholinguistic training: A reevaluation. *Exceptional Children, 44*(5), 310–319.

Mecham, M. J., & Jones, J. D. (1978). *Utah test of language development.* Austin, TX: Pro-Ed.

Mecham, M. J., & Willbrand, M. L. (1979). *Language disorders in children: A resource book for speech-language pathologists.* Springfield, IL: Thomas.

Minskoff, E. H., Wiseman, D. E., & Minskoff, J. G. (1972). *The MWM program for developing language abilities.* Ridgefield, NJ: Educational Performance Associates.

Mowery, C. W., & Replogle, A. (1977). *Developmental language lessons.* New York: Teaching Resources.

Newcomer, P. L., & Hammill, D. D. (1982a). *Test of language development—Intermediate.* Austin TX: Pro-Ed.

Newcomer, P. L., & Hammill, D. D. (1982b). *Test of language development—Primary.* Austin, TX: Pro-Ed.

Otto, W., McMenemy, R. A., & Smith, R. J. (1973). *Corrective and remedial teaching* (2nd ed.). Boston: Houghton Mifflin.

Reed, V. A. (1986). Language disordered adolescents. In V. A. Reed (Ed.). *An introduction to children with language disorders* (pp. 228–249). New York: Macmillan.

Roth, F., & Spekman, N. (1984a). Assessing the pragmatic abilities of children: Part I. Organizational framework and assessment parameters. *Journal of Speech and Hearing Disorders, 49*(1), 2–11.

Roth, F., & Spekman, N. (1984b). Assessing the pragmatic abilities of children: Part II. Guidelines, considerations, and specific evaluation procedures. *Journal of Speech and Hearing Disorders, 49*(1), 12–17.

Salvia, J., & Ysseldyke, J. E. (1985). *Assessment in special and remedial education* (3rd ed.). Boston: Houghton Mifflin.

Schwartz, L., & McKinley, N. (1984). *Daily communication: Strategies for the language disordered adolescent.* Eau Claire, WI: Thinking Publications.

Semel, E., & Wiig, E. (1980a). *Clinical evaluation of language functions.* Columbus, OH: Merrill.

Semel, E., & Wiig, E. (1980b). *Clinical evaluation of language functions—advanced level screening test.* Columbus, OH: Merrill.

Semel, E., & Wiig, E. (1982). *Clinical language intervention program.* Columbus, OH: Merrill.

Temple, C., & Gillet, J. W. (1984). *Language arts: Learning processes and teaching practices.* Boston: Little, Brown.

Templin, M.C., & Darley, F. L. (1969). *Templin–Darley tests of articulation* (2nd ed.). Iowa city, IA: Bureau of Educational Research and Service.

Wiig, E. (1982). *Let's talk inventory for adolescents.* Columbus, OH: Merrill.

Wiig, E., & Secord, W. (1985). *Test of language competence.* Columbus, OH: Merrill.

Wepman, J. W. (1973). *The test of auditory discrimination* (revised). Chicago: Language Research Associates.

Woodcock, R. (1980). *Woodcock language proficiency battery.* Hingham, MA: Teaching Resources.

SUGGESTED READINGS

Bernstein, D. K., & Tiegerman, E. (1985). *Language and communication disorders in children.* Columbus, OH: Merrill.

Berry, M. F. (1980). *Teaching linguistically handicapped children.* Englewood Cliffs, NJ: Prentice-Hall.

Bloom, L. & Lahey, M. (1978). *Language development and language disorders.* New York: Wiley.

Cole, M. L., & Cole, J. T. (1981). *Effective intervention with the language impaired child.* Rockville, MD: Aspen.

Glaser, A. J., Johnston, E. B., & Weinrich, B. D. (1987). *A sourcebook for remediating language: Lesson plans for developing communication skills within the cognitive-experience frame.* Tucson, AZ: Communication Skill Builders.

Hubbell, R. D. (1981). *Children's language disorders: An integrated approach.* Englewood Cliffs, NJ: Prentice-Hall.

McCormick, L., & Schiefelbusch, R. L. (1984). *Early language intervention: An introduction.* Columbus, OH: Merrill.

Myers, P. (1986). *Assessing the oral language development and intervention needs of students.* Austin, TX: Pro-Ed.

Petty, W. T., & Jensen, J. M. (1980). *Developing children's language.* Boston: Allyn and Bacon.

Simon, C. S. (Ed.) (1984). *Communication skills and classroom success, Vol. I: Assessment of language-learning disabled students.* San Diego, CA: College-Hill.

Simon, C. S. (Ed.) (1985). *Communication skills and classroom success, Vol. II: Therapy methodologies for language-learning disabled students.* San Diego, CA: College-Hill.

Wiig, E. H., & Semel, E. M. (1976). *Language disabilities in children and adolescents.* Columbus, OH: Merrill.

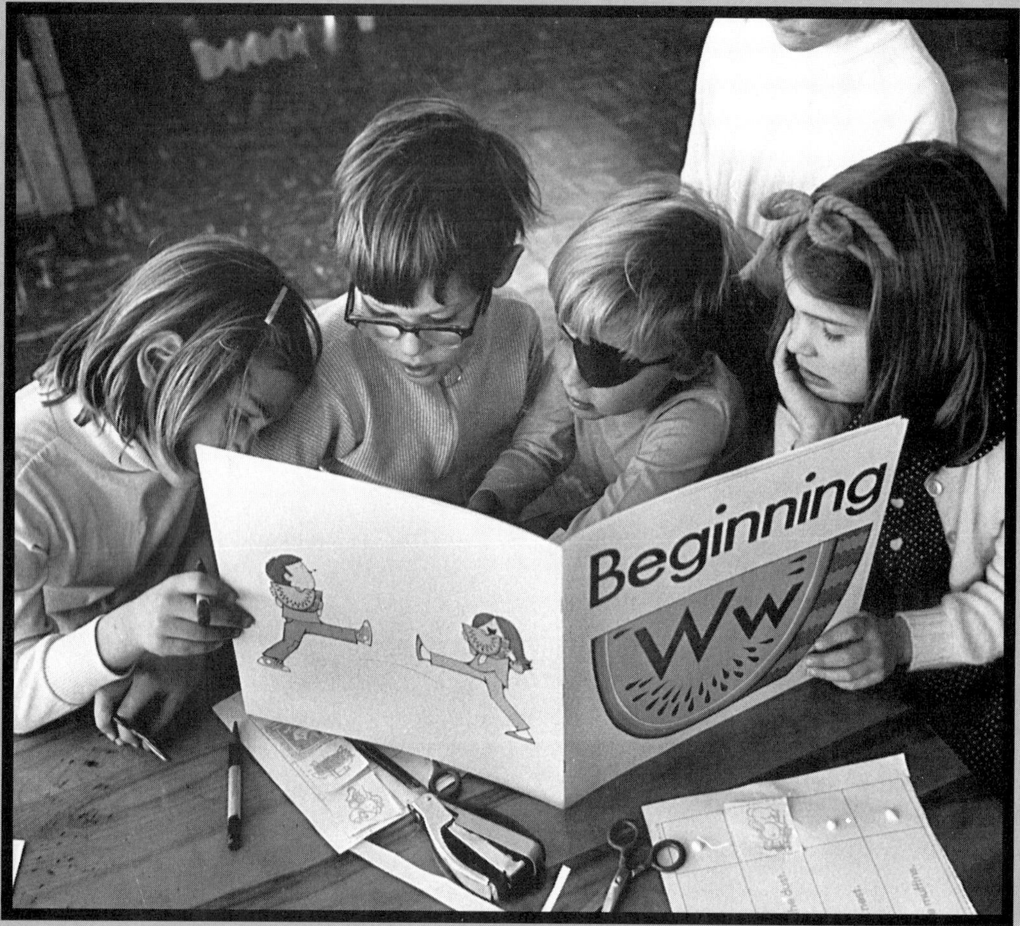
Beginning
Ww

11

Methods for Teaching Reading

READING HOLDS A CENTRAL place in the elementary school curriculum and affects success or failure in nearly every subsequent academic subject. At the secondary level, it is the major mode for access of information. Virtually all students learn complex spoken language by imitation during the preschool years. Yet reading, the extension of language into graphic form, often presents difficulties. Probably as many students are referred for additional help or special services because of reading problems as for any other reason. Nonhandicapped and students with mild handicaps are among those referred. Numerous methods for the initial teaching of reading and for remediation have been prepared. They hold the potential for allowing a choice that may result in effectiveness on an individual or small group basis.

An Organization of Language and Reading Skills

Reading is one element within a whole sequence of language development. This sequence includes readiness, the primary language system (listening and speaking), and the secondary language system (reading and writing). Within the area of reading are two general groups of skills, decoding and comprehension. A scheme for an organization of readiness, the primary language system, and the secondary language system appears in Figure 11.1.

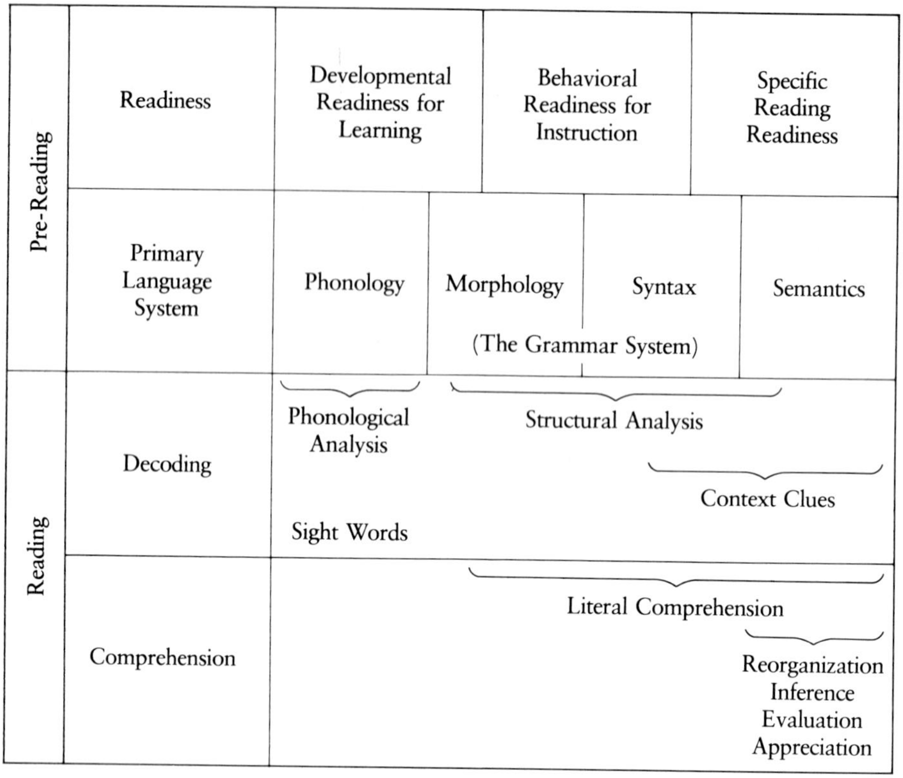

FIGURE 11.1

Organization of language and reading

Pre-Reading	Readiness	Developmental Readiness for Learning	Behavioral Readiness for Instruction		Specific Reading Readiness
	Primary Language System	Phonology	Morphology	Syntax	Semantics
			(The Grammar System)		
Reading	Decoding	Phonological Analysis	Structural Analysis		
					Context Clues
		Sight Words			
	Comprehension		Literal Comprehension		
					Reorganization Inference Evaluation Appreciation

Readiness Level

Readiness is conceptualized not as a unitary status but as the relative development of many traits and skills that are prerequisite to the successful acquisition of reading abilities. These are arbitrarily divided into three groupings.

Developmental Readiness for Learning This refers to physiological, psychological, and neurological development including auditory and visual acuity and perception, health factors, chronological age, specific mental abilities, and general intellectual ability.

Readiness for Instruction Whereas the earlier grouping refers to abilities that are more or less innate to the individual, this grouping represents learned skills. They enable students to interact with the learning environment and the subject material, hence to profit from instruction.

Specific Reading Readiness The set of abilities traditionally identified as reading readiness includes experience, an age-appropriate primary language system, awareness that graphic symbols represent language, and that translation from oral to written forms and the reverse is possible.

Reading Process

Decoding The first step in the actual reading process is that of decoding the graphic representation into sounds and then into words and sentences from which meaning is extracted. The primary language system is the basic referent in learning to decode. Letters, words, phrases, and sentences encountered on the printed page are transduced into auditory components and compared to the elements of the primary language system. If the two forms of the language, that which was internalized during language development and that presented on the printed page, are similar in sound, form, and structure, learning to read will be facilitated. If the two language systems are not phonetically and structurally similar, difficulties may be encountered. An organization of the decoding skills are presented in Figure 11.2.

FIGURE 11.2

An organization of decoding skills

I. Letter identification

II. Word attack skills
   A. Phonics analysis or sound identification
      1. Phoneme–grapheme match
      2. Consonants
         a. Initial consonants
         b. Middle consonants
         c. Ending consonants
      3. Blends
      4. Consonant digraphs
      5. Vowels
         a. Long vowels
         b. Short vowels
         c. Special combinations
   B. Structural analysis
      1. Root or base words
      2. Compound words
      3. Syllabication
      4. Possessives
      5. Contractions
      6. Plurals
      7. Prefixes
      8. Suffixes
      9. Accent (pronunciation)
   C. Context clue
   D. Picture and configuration clues
   E. Sight words

Comprehension The second major grouping of reading skills are those involved in comprehension. Decoding and comprehension are hierarchical in that, to gain meaning from the printed material, students must first be able to decode the text. However, this hierarchical relationship does not imply that all the skills of decoding must be mastered prior to the onset of the development of the skills of comprehension. Rather, the two are parallel and reciprocal. Students learn to comprehend at the denotative level as they learn to decode. As they comprehend the general meaning of sentences and paragraphs, closure is used to assist in decoding difficult words within that passage. In a reciprocal relationship, this permits more precise understanding, or comprehension, of the material. Conceptual and connotative comprehension are less related to the decoding level of reading but highly related to intelligence level. An organization of comprehension skills appears in Figure 11.3.

FIGURE 11.3

An organization of comprehension skills

I. Literal comprehension
   A. Following directions
   B. Noting details
   C. Main idea
   D. Sequence
   E. Getting the facts
   F. Story elements

II. Inference and interpretation
   A. Word meaning
   B. Paraphrasing
   C. Comparisons
   D. Classifying
   E. Characterization
   F. Predicting outcomes
   G. Drawing conclusions
   H. Summarizing
   I. Cause-and-effect relationships
   J. Figurative language
      1. Similes and metaphors
      2. Aphorisms and allusions
   K. Imagery

III. Critical and evaluative comprehension
   A. Distinguishing fact from fiction
   B. Distinguishing fact from opinion
   C. Criticism of writing styles and clarity
   D. Appreciation of effective use of language

Specific Techniques

Decoding

Letters and Sounds Sound recognition, as differentiated from letter naming, is the most elementary of decoding skills. A difference of opinion exists in the literature in regard to the naming of letters. The authors agree with those who recognize that potentially poor readers can become confused between letter names and letter sounds. Thus, it is advocated that students with learning problems should concentrate initially, and in remediation, on sounds and not on naming *and* sounds. Letter names are best reserved for lessons in spelling and handwriting. A further reason for this emphasis on sounds is that it more directly associates reading with the primary language system, listening and speaking.

Consonants Consonants, which are easily confused visually or auditorily (for example, *b* and *d*, *p* and *g*, *m* and *n*), are best taught separately. Teachers must ascertain mastery of the first sound before proceeding to introduce the next sound.

Some students substitute or omit initial, middle, or ending sounds. Occasionally students self-correct on this kind of error. If the problem persists, however, remedial techniques are usually needed. The sounds can be emphasized by visual means. The letters representing the sound can be written larger than those in the rest of the word, or they can be underlined or written in color. The sound can be emphasized auditorily. Teachers can exaggerate the sound vocally within the context of reading and teach students to do the same. This practice can easily be faded as students master the pronunciation. The hard sounds of the consonants should always be taught first and soft sounds later. For example, *c* as in cake should precede *c* as in cease.

Vowels The sequence in which sounds are taught is important with short vowel sounds being taught first. Because of its difficulty, the short *e* should be taught last in the sequence of short vowel sounds. Some students have difficulty with double vowels such as *oi* or *au*. Assistance with these problems can be found in one or more of the books listed at the end of the chapter.

Digraphs The ability to read digraphs occurs more readily when they are taught separately and with special emphasis on the distinction between similar sounds such as *sh* and *ch*. The visual cue of a finger to the lips as in a librarian's "Shhh!" may help distinguish the sound of that combination, and using the illustration of a "*choo-choo*" train can emphasize the sound for *ch*.

Confusion between the *wh* and *w* sounds can be eliminated by using a blowing sound to designate the former and, again, exaggerating the sound. Differentiation must be made between the voiced *th* and the unvoiced *th*. For students having difficulty with these two sounds, calling attention to the physiological production of them may be helpful. Students can be made aware of using both the mouth and the throat with the voiced *th* and can also be told to feel the "tickle" around the lips as the sound is made. By contrast, students use only the tongue and teeth for the unvoiced form and can be told to feel the wind blowing through their lips.

Blends Blends, or clusters (*bl, cl, fl, gl,* and so on), may be taught in family groups in a brief lesson with a new blend being introduced each day. Students can participate at once by volunteering words that incorporate the blend to be written on the chalkboard. Individuals can review the use of blends with flip cards, each presenting a word ending to be matched to a single initial blend. An alternative procedure is to use a larger cardboard circle with blends written around the edge. On top is a smaller circle with the remaining parts of words. The circles can be rotated to form new words (Figure 11.4). The reverse procedures can be used for final blends. Later in cumulative review, students can challenge others in a game in which the first student says an incomplete word to which the opponent must add a blend to form a whole word.

Blending Sounds Into Words When introducing sound–sequence organization, students say one sound at a time, for example, *m - a - d* and not *ma - d*. Students who are allowed to form the habit of saying two sounds together may learn to associate the combined sound with one of the component letters. The sounds *m* and *a*, combined as *ma* may become associated with the consonant so that when a new word is introduced, such as *mud,* students might erroneously sound it out as *ma - u - d*.

Reversals In the past the relationship between visual perception, especially visual reversals, and reading problems was overemphasized. In developing early skills, many young students demonstrate reversals that are aspects of normal development; these should not be interpreted as signs of pathology. Only when reversals persist beyond the second grade can they be taken as evidence of a problem. Several kinds of reversals exist. Single letters such as *b* and *d* or *p* and *q* are often reversed. Sometimes entire words such as the classic *was* and *saw* may be reversed.

For single letters and word reversals, the techniques are the same as in the remediation of written reversals (Chapter 12). In addition, teaching *b* first before proceeding with *d* at a later time may be a preferable format. Saying the sound while tracing the letter on sandpaper or cereal grains is a practical means of remediation. Students can also roll clay into "snakes" or "tubes" and shape them to form letters. Polloway and Polloway (1980) suggest teaching the uppercase *B* first. This emphasizes the directionality of the letter. Through a sequential fading procedure, the upper loop of the *B* is faded, leaving a lowercase *b*.

FIGURE 11.4

Initial blends circles

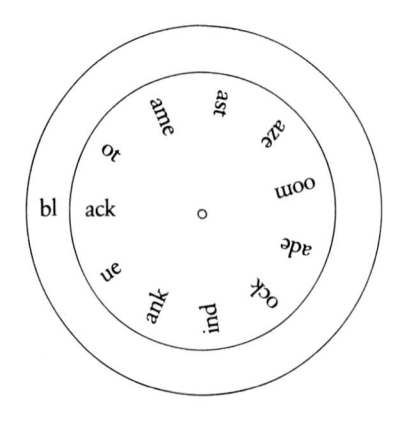

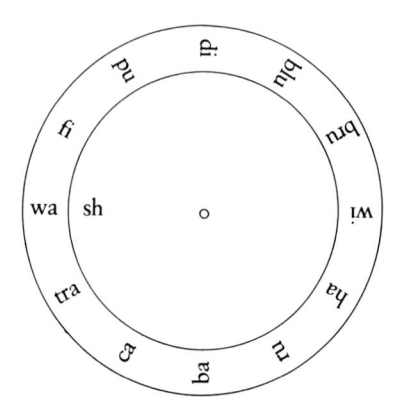

A visual mnemonic device is to teach students to form the letters *b* and *d* with their fingers, keeping three fingers upright to form the stem and making the "ball" of the letters with their thumbs and forefingers. Thus, *b* is automatically made by the left hand and *d* by the right hand. While doing seatwork, they can monitor or check themselves when a question arises. Another approach is to teach letters commonly confused (*b* and *d*, for example) early in reading instruction and *simultaneously*, with direct instruction in discriminating between the two.

Most students who reverse whole words do so on only a few particular words. Teachers can write one such word clearly on a sheet of paper, then cover the word with a three-by-five-inch card. They slide the card slowly to reveal the left-to-right sequence while students sound out the word. A next step may be to have them view the entire word but move their fingers from left to right while saying the word.

Word Attack Skills

Some reading programs introduce all the new words to be read prior to that reading. In this manner, new words can be easily integrated into the story for smooth reading and comprehension. Other programs, however, advocate that students learn new words within the context of the passage.

Phonics   The development of facility in matching sounds and letters is one important element in word attack skills. Students learn to sound out words as an extension of this initial sound–sequence learning. Occasionally, students will become stuck on the first letter of a new word and either stop, continue with some nonsensical sequence of sounds, or say an incorrect word. Teachers can help by instructing students to look and say the vowel sound first and then add the consonants.

Structural Analysis   Structural analysis refers to the use of root (or base) words, prefixes and suffixes, contractions, plurals, possessives, and syllabication. Instruction in morphological and syntactical elements of the sentence should be accomplished in a natural manner rather than by memorizing rules. Contractions may be taught as sight words and root words; prefixes and suffixes can be made into units of instruction apart from reading.

Context Clues   Context clues are often thought of as being related to comprehension. However, they are also important in word attack. Students should be encouraged to read the entire sentence, omitting the unknown word rather than being allowed to stop in midsentence. They are then encouraged to conceptualize the kind of word needed to "make sense" in the sentence. With this information and whatever rudimentary sounding-out skills are present, they may be able to discover the word. Instruction with sentences with new or unknown words on the chalkboard can be used to introduce the skills of using context clues to the entire class.

Picture Clues and Configuration Clues   Picture clues and configuration clues are frequently listed among the strategies used for initial word recognition. However, the purpose of building a sight word vocabulary is rapidity of recognition without dependence on more sophisticated word attack skills. Some authors suggest the use of pictures to be distracting, hence interfering with word learning. During the learning process, teachers may call attention to unique visual patterns (M iss iss ipp i) or may assist an individual who fails to discriminate between similarly formed letters (*h, b; m, n*). For the most part, however, the use of pictures and configuration clues remain supplementary rather than major methods in teaching sight words.

Sight Words Two kinds of word lists appear in the professional literature and are sometimes confused. These are basic sight words and high-utility words. Basic sight words indicate those words that individuals should recognize instantaneously without having to apply decoding strategies (although such strategies may have been used in the original learning of the word). High-utility word lists consist of those words appearing most frequently in the reading materials at various grade levels. The lists overlap to some extent, but it is not implied in the creation of a high-utility list that these words should become sight words for students at that grade level. The classic list of basic sight words was introduced by Dolch in the 1930s and was revised most recently by Johnson (1971). Other authors who have presented word lists include Barbe and Shields (1976), Harris and Jacobson (1972), Harris and Sipay (1980), and Walker (1979). Some reading series and standardized tests also present such lists. They give teachers guidance in expected word mastery at the different grade levels.

Many methods can be used in developing and enlarging sight word vocabularies. These include:

- Flash cards or word cards with pictures
- A game of sight word lotto with pictures on one-half the card and the word on the other half
- Picture dictionaries
- The tachistoscope for rapid review and evaluation
- Word families and rhyming words (man, pan, ran, tan)

Memory is obviously important in the development of a sight word vocabulary, and teachers should emphasize memorization of some words. However, immediate reinforcement must be made within the context of the passage rather than allowing the word to become isolated and difficult to remember. Drill is necessary for retention but cannot guarantee understanding. In addition to making sure students recognize and can say each sight word on demand, teachers will want to ascertain that students know the correct meaning of the word and can use each easily.

Comprehension

Comprehension is a global term encompassing many skills and several levels of language and learning functioning. It is the culmination of the reading activity as a form of communication—that is, readers' understanding of the content intended by the writer and their evaluation and appreciation of the material.

An Outline of Comprehension Skills Such a list is serviceable in that it identifies specific skills within the literal, interpretive, and critical levels of comprehension. The literal level is denotative and consists of recognizing, recalling, and reorganizing such elements as passage details, main idea, and sequence of events. At the interpretive level, students need to use abstract thinking to determine meaning that is implied by the text or that is presented in figurative language. At the critical level, the individual examines the text not only for an understanding of the author's intent but also to evaluate both content and presentation. Evaluation also allows appreciation.

Relationship Between Decoding and Comprehension The ability to comprehend is to some degree related to decoding. The facility to decode accurately and rapidly frees students from the confines of that process and allows attention to comprehension. However, adequate decoding skills do not guarantee good comprehension. Decoding is highly related to the primary language system, listening and speaking. Comprehension is more related to social and cultural experiences, wide experience in reading, intellectual characteristics, and direct instruction in comprehension skills.

Techniques: Literal Comprehension The direction in teaching comprehension skills is to build meaning from smaller to larger units—vocabulary, phrases, simple sentences, compound and complex sentences, paragraphs, and stories. Teachers can expect to elicit comprehension and abstract interpretation of passages and expository writing only after students have learned to give meaning to all the elements that comprise that writing.

Picture Clues Picture clues are used with young children as a step in giving meaning to words or phrases. Matching games, words and picture lotto, and labeling pictures cut from magazines stress word–experience relationships. Pictures provide direction for finding the central idea and in noting specific details in sentences and paragraphs. This is the basis for including large pictures in preprimers and primers.

Students enjoy writing their own rebus sentences on the chalkboard. The class guesses orally or writes sentences substituting their own words for the pictures. Picture clues should not be overly emphasized. Students who become dependent on pictures sometimes give ideational substitutions for words that they are supposed to be decoding more precisely.

Vocabulary Development Vocabulary development is a continuing process not only in reading but also in all curriculum areas. Vocabulary can be taught within the context of reading and other subjects or by direct instruction of selected words. Most commonly, both methods are employed.

Teaching vocabulary within the subject area has two major advantages. First, selection of words is intrinsic to the lesson, and second, the words have a specificity of meaning within an immediately practical context. Many basal reading series have vocabulary components with recommended instructional procedures.

Direct instruction is a necessary method to promote the rapid expansion of vocabulary. If not thoughtfully planned, however, it can result in the memorization of imprecise synonyms without genuine enrichment of students' personal fund of meaningful words. Words are selected with purpose, and sufficient examples are given to enable accurate generalization. Most teachers have examples of student sentences such as "The boy was able to frugal the money he earned on his paper route" (*frugal* (verb): to save money).

Selection of Words Teachers will often use spelling books or professionally prepared word lists from textbooks or journals. But even these must be supplemented or adapted at times to meet classroom or individual needs.

Attend to high utility words in selecting vocabulary to be learned. Often nouns and verbs are selected to the exclusion of other words. With young students, make sure they know concept words such as *with, beneath, since, among, several, either/or,* and *through*. Many procedures can be used in teaching the selected words. They can be grouped into meaning or topic families and presented as miniunits. Audiovisual aids, including prerecorded cassettes or the language master, and bulletin boards (a word-family tree, for example) provide for multisensory impact. A unit on word derivations with students illustrating interesting word histories and homemade games can be motivating and productive. Vocabulary development can be one of several purposes of a field trip. Students are alerted that a later activity will be determining how many new words were learned.

Practice With both methods of vocabulary development, context or direct instruction, continuing practice is necessary. In vocabulary as with other learning, research suggests that it is not the quality of the initial presentation alone that results in student retention but practice evolving from continued practical use. Teachers can point out recently learned words as they reoccur in lessons, have periodic reviews, and assign writing activities using new words. In classroom discussions, teachers may accept a student's contribution and then ask what other recently learned word could have been used to express the same idea. Ditto sheets with many sentences, each containing a blank space for the substitution of a word, can help refine meaning by providing many examples of word use. Students may initially select a word for each sentence from a list of potential responses and later be expected to supply missing words (a cloze procedure) without possible alternatives being given (see context clues, pp. 233).

A must in vocabulary building is instruction in prefixes and suffixes. Flip cards, which allow several base words to be paired with a single prefix, can be used. A similar arrangement can be used to provide practice with suffixes (Figure 11.5).

Introduce synonyms, antonyms, and homonyms as words with multiple meanings. Each form is presented as a specific lesson when teaching structural analysis skills. However, when the objective is vocabulary development, discuss them as opportunities occur during stories. In this way the meaning of the word is applied immediately.

FIGURE 11.5

Prefix and suffix cards

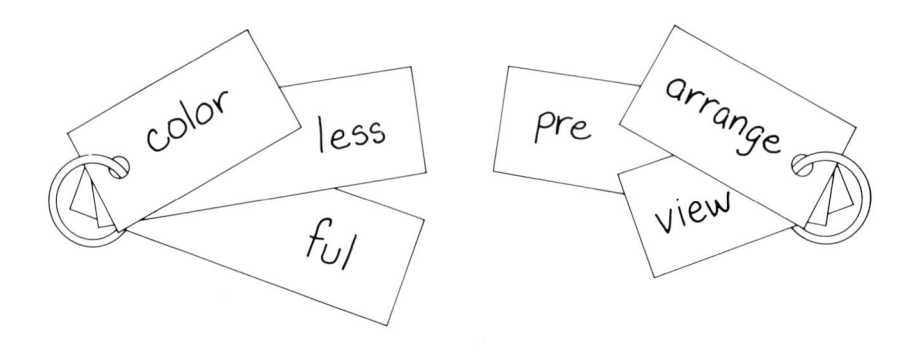

Word for the Day Another vocabulary-building activity is a word for the day. Words that can be put to use at once are selected. Students are encouraged to contribute words they have encountered in their reading, at home, or while watching television. Where such words have applicability, they can be incorporated into the vocabulary lesson. Often, students will volunteer a word beyond the level of the class. To avoid discouragement, place the word on the board, present a definition, and explain that it will most likely be found in outside reading or in books they will have in a later grade. An unusual or rare word can be included for interest but students should not be held accountable for their meaning.

Use of the Dictionary and the Thesaurus Forming the habit of looking up unfamiliar words in the dictionary gives students the opportunity to discover word meaning. They learn that the dictionary is a vital resource in expanding vocabulary. Their willingness to use it need not be compromised by routinely assigning written definitions for lengthy word lists. A thesaurus is also a valuable tool, particularly for older students. It adds a different dimension to vocabulary development for, as Johnson and Pearson (1978, p. 144) point out, "a dictionary goes from word to meaning while the thesaurus goes from meaning to word."

Context Clues The meaning of a word can be detected frequently from the intent of the phrase or sentence in which it appears. Teachers can use questioning during reading but can also provide exercises for practice in using context clues. Variations of the cloze procedure can be used to get the meaning of the word, the whole phrase, or the sentence. Context limits options but requires students to figure out the most likely of the choices. Initial sentences provide alternatives from which to select.

The ball rolled across the yard and under the _____.

(a) grass   (b) fence

Later a response is required.

The ocean waves lapped upon the _____.

Another procedure is to substitute synonyms for the unknown word.
In this sentence;

The fireman rescued the cat on the telephone pole.

rescued means

(a) pointed to   (b) pushed   (c) saved

An entire paragraph may be presented in which words have been omitted. Each blank is filled in with a logical word, then students explain in their own words the meaning of the inserted words and the context in which they occur.

Although most commonly associated with word meaning, context clues can be used with large units of language. Students can be instructed, for example, to determine the meaning of a phrase or sentence by its use in the paragraph.

Phrases as Units of Meaning   Reading meaningful phrases precedes sentence comprehension. Activities with flashcards, chalkboard writing, and limited drill allow students to perceive groups of related words as meaningful units of thought.

Use groups of words such as

| one dog | at the mall | seeing a circus |
| two boys | to school | playing a game |

For older students use

Before the game started
Not until they finished wrapping the gifts

Teachers can ask "What are these phrases about?" "What do they tell us?" They tell about time and *when* something happened.

There are also groups of words that describe places: *in the hall* or *beneath the old stone bridge*. There are groups of words which tell us what people are doing: *singing a song* or *studying the lesson*.

To emphasize the meaningful unity of the whole phrase, students can draw pictures that include all the elements of a phrase such as *beside the waterfall* or *near the old crooked tree*, or they can pantomime action phrases for the class members to guess.

Sentences   Sentence comprehension appears to develop as students become more adept in decoding and oral reading skills. This development can be augmented by instruction with either a whole-sentence approach or by building from phrases to larger units. Which method is used depends on how students best learn. They may be grouped for this part of the instruction or on the basis of these learning characteristics. They need good decoding skills for the whole-sentence approach to be successful. After one or several sentences are read, questions are asked. If an incorrect answer is given, students are asked to reread the passage, or teachers rephrase the question or direct the question to another student.

Students must first understand the answer before going on to the next passage. If questions are asked too frequently, the meaning of the sentence or paragraph may be lost.

The method is essentially the same for phrase reading. Students read a group of words rather than sentences and are asked questions more frequently if needed. They usually proceed at a slower pace. An additional step is to teach them to see the conceptual relationships among the phrases so that the meaning of the whole sentence is gained.

Phrases or clauses can be lettered on tag board and cut into sections. Students can rearrange the sections to form a sentence.

| The girl went | to the store | for her mother. |

The next step is to separate each word on a card and have students rearrange as above.

| boy | dog | called | his | The | yard | from | the |

Elements of the Language-Experience Approach may supplement this instruction. Students dictate a sentence that the teacher writes on the chalkboard. They then read it orally with the teacher pointing out that it is a sentence.

Punctuation More than mechanical devices to indicate pauses or the termination of sentences, punctuation separates idea units. Teachers can provide exercises using fragments and phrases, complete with punctuation marks. Students then read aloud, pausing overly long at commas and articulating each section to emphasize its meaning. The next step is to read whole sentences, attending to all punctuation marks. Teachers then read a passage exaggerating punctution, and students read in unison. Although such activities are obviously contrived, they may, in fact, be supportive to students with language and reading problems.

Paragraphs Several procedures can be used to teach paragraph comprehension. Students can be taught how a writer constructs a paragraph: One main idea is supported by description, explanation, or elaboration. The main idea is contained in one sentence. The topic sentence is identified in practice paragraphs. The paragraph is read orally, and then students put the meaning into their own words. Comprehension skills are reinforced if the paragraph is reread.

As students continue to read paragraphs and longer stories as part of their reading and other school work, other skills become important. These include recalling details, finding the main idea, sequencing, and following written directions.

Recalling Details Prereading activities can include a game in which students look around the classroom or out the window for a brief period of time. They then compete in reporting the number of things they can remember. They can list single words or items they see in a displayed picture: *picnic, parents, children, grass, trees, stream, bridge, tablecloth,* and *food*. Words are selected to be used in writing sentences, or the group can develop a paragraph together with the teacher writing on the chalkboard. As a reverse procedure, they can read several sentences and select one, which because of its correct details, best describes a picture.

In the early grades, careful initial reading and the expectation for students to remember details are interactive processes. If students are aware that they will be expected to remember details, they are more likely to attend to careful reading and thus identify details. Teachers can pose questions prior to the reading to alert students to the kind of information to which they should attend or following the reading to determine what has been remembered. Teacher-made worksheets and workbooks, which accompany basal reading series, also provide practice.

Gerber (1981) presents instructions for a game, which can be used to assist in recalling details, that focuses on students' learning of the *wh* words. They are presented with a short story. The teacher writes the color-coded words: *Who, What, Where, When, and Why*. The class is divided into teams, and the members earn points for their teams by identifying the correct *Wh* word and for selecting elements from the story to be listed under each word.

Sometimes reading for detail is disparaged in instructional textbooks, and teachers believe that they need to move quickly to more challenging levels of comprehension. However, reading for the recall of facts and details is a necessary step in learning to read well. It receives less emphasis by the fifth and sixth grades as other comprehension skills are developed.

Finding the Main Idea A skill taught at all levels is finding the main idea of a paragraph. Pearson and Johnson (1978) distinguish between topic and main idea. The *topic* is the subject of the paragraph, such as tennis or space shuttles. The topic may cover one or several paragraphs. The *main idea* is what one paragraph tells about the topic.

A prereading activity in determining topic is categorization. Teachers present objects, pictures of objects or people, or words in random order. Students reorganize these into conceptual groupings. They are asked "What are all these pictures about? They are about _____(transportation, birds, and so forth)." And this leads to the main idea. An activity at home that reinforces this skill is to ask children to say in one sentence what a television program tells.

Students may also read the paragraph to note which word is used repetitively. They circle that word in the successive sentences. The word is most likely to be the topic of the paragraph. The topic often may be presented in one or two words, but the main idea usually requires a longer explanation. The topic may be "Sports and Games," but the main idea of the paragraph may be that every country in the world has its own favorite sports and games.

Instruction on how paragraphs are constructed also assists students in finding the main idea. Aukerman and Aukerman (1981) describe five patterns in which sentences are organized into paragraphs. Most commonly, the main idea is contained in the initial sentence although it is sometimes found in the last sentence. Students are alerted to look for the main idea first in either of these two sentences.

An activity similar to that of sequencing may be used. Students are presented with sentences in a list. They are to read each carefully and then identify the sentence that most comprehensively includes the others. Which one contains the main idea? Which ones include details, elaborations, or explanations? Worksheets can be prepared for such an activity. Following the rewriting of the paragraph, students answer the statements: "The topic of the paragraph is _____. The main idea of the paragraph is _____."

Sequencing Prerequisite skills include development of time concepts and ability in distinguishing between "a long time ago," "recently," "in the future," and similar expressions. Prereading or supplementary activities can include the use of picture sequence cards. Commercially available, the sets of cards vary in number and illustrate time order (seasons, holidays), event order (morning activities), construction order (bird's-nest building, house construction), or developmental order (baby–child–adult). Classroom activities that emphasize sequence can also be employed. Constructing a model, following the steps in an art project, or using a recipe can precede listing the steps or reporting orally on the sequence.

As a beginning reading activity, teachers present a short paragraph in which one sentence is out of order:

Then Eddie and Tag played in the yard. Eddie went home from school. His dog Tag greeted him at the door.

Students are required to rearrange the sentences in the paragraph in logical order. Then they progress to paragraphs in which two or three sentences are out of order. To arrange the sentences in a story in sequence, students are instructed to get a mental picture of what is happening as the story is read. They look for words denoting time—*before, after, then, today,* or *yesterday.* They think about what happened at the beginning, in the middle, and at the end. After the selection is completed, they mark *B* next to beginning statement, *M* for those in the middle, and *E* for ending events.

Following Written Directions Closely related to reading for detail and sequencing is following written directions. Activities can include a game in which one member of each team reads a set of instructions in a specified time and then follows them by memory: open the closet, get out a box of chalk, and place it on the second desk in the third row from the window. The team whose members most closely perform the expected activities wins. For students with visual memory or comprehension difficulties, begin with one or two directions.

Written directions for an art project or a homework assignment can be substituted for oral directions to allow students to have realistic practice. A project related with learning how to learn (see Chapter 8) is that of examining and discussing test directions. Sample directions can be presented on ditto sheets in which students can describe orally instructions they read or practice with sample questions.

A timeworn activity—but often new to elementary school students—is to present the entire class with a set of instructions that begin with: <u>1. Read all the instructions before doing anything else.</u> The intervening instructions tell them to do nonsensical things like shouting out a silly word, standing up and turning around, or patting themselves on the back. The final instruction tells them to ignore all intervening directions and not do them. Those who followed the initial instruction about reading the entire sheet first will have a good time watching their noncomplying classmates perform the ridiculous activities. This activity is most successful when used as the introduction to a unit on following directions.

Techniques: Inferential and Critical Comprehension Skills of higher-order comprehension depend on intellectual abilities that are brought to bear on reading passages; thus, they are difficult to describe or teach outside the context of specific situations. However, there are three main methods that have been used in guiding comprehension. These are direct instruction, questioning, and discussion.

Direct Instruction In direct instruction, teachers explain the meaning of passages. This is the simplest procedure, the most economical in time and effort, and the most commonly used for large-group instruction. They can compare a character in a story to a real person or a television character familiar to the students, describe a logical sequence of events to illustrate cause–effect relationships, or point out clues, which lead to the outcome, given earlier in the story.

Direct instruction is necessary especially with younger students who are limited in experience. They are usually taught the difference between fact and fiction but are often unaware that some nonfiction writing are the opinions of the author rather than fact. Teachers need to explain such differences and assist them in finding clues, which identify such writing, within the text.

Questioning Although most commonly used as a means of informal assessment, well-developed questions and refined questioning techniques have a greater potential for teaching comprehension. Crowell and Au (1981) developed a scale of questions designed to reflect levels of difficulty in reading comprehension. These five levels are:

1. *Association.* At the lowest level on the scale, association expects students to provide literal information found in the passage.
2. *Categorization.* It requires students to make simple categories from the passage.
3. *Seriation.* Students recall the order of major events in the passage.
4. *Integration.* At this level, students support their inferences with reasons gleaned from the passage.
5. *Extension.* At the highest level on the scale, students apply knowledge gained from the passage in responding to extension questions.

Questioning Techniques If students are to achieve such goals, questions must not be "spur-of-the-moment" queries. Thoughtful planning and consideration of the following points can improve the development of these skills.

- Secure the attention of the group.
- Word questions so that they are understood. State them clearly without excessive verbiage. Include only one idea in each question.
- If the response indicates that the question was not understood, reword without changing the intent or introducing another idea.
- Ask the question before calling on the student by name. In that way, each student will have to formulate an answer.
- Do not talk too fast or too slow to allow students to process their own thoughts.
- Give enough time for the entire group to think about the question and to determine a response.
- Students are more likely to respond when they know their answer will be accepted and not criticized. Ask several the same question and reinforce correct answers without telling the others they are wrong.
- When a less-than-accurate answer is given, probe for a better response by saying "You are thinking" or "You are on the right track. Tell me more about it." An additional question may be asked as a hint to direct their thinking.
- Yes and no answers can be avoided by asking who, what, where, when, why, and how questions.
- To prevent guessing, ask students to expand on the response or tell why they believe it to be correct.

Discussion Although it is recognized that well-thought-out questions can elicit thinking, questions most commonly challenge individuals to rely on their own thoughts. Communication is restricted to teachers and students. Discussion expands the process to include all students and has distinct advantages. Students learn from each other. All are expected to participate; they do not wait to be called on before thinking about answers. The interchange of ideas can result in an elaboration and development of ideas that might not have been possible without broad contributions. Reading comprehension skills can be taught through discussion. Through skillful questioning and guidance, teachers can direct discussion to allow students to find the main idea, draw conclusions, see cause–effect relationships, interpret figurative language, and distinguish between fact and opinion. Other comprehension skills can be similarly developed.

Oral and Silent Reading

Mature readers at an independent level read, for the most part, silently. Thus, a goal in instruction is preparation to be capable silent readers. In contrast, nearly all teaching begins with oral reading that capitalizes on the primary language system for decoding, meaning, and oral expression.

Oral reading provides feedback and reinforcment and enables teachers to observe general and specific reading behaviors as a basis for modifying instruction. Among the goals of teaching oral reading are fluency and comprehension. The former is achieved through the careful instruction of decoding skills and practice, which emphasizes intonation, phrasing, and adherence to punctuation. An additional, often neglected procedure is rereading. During the first reading, students may have struggled through decoding each word. Free from this task, they can gain a gestalt of the sentence or passage while the visual and oral perceptual correspondence of the words are reinforced. To augment comprehension, students may rephrase sentencing in their own words. Questions are asked during and after the passage is read orally. As they progress in answering comprehension questions correctly, silent reading is introduced.

Teacher observations are limited because only overt behaviors are demonstrated, although reading and answering comprehension questions can be noted. When teaching silent reading, it is necessary to provide a quiet atmosphere and to begin with brief passages to allow students sufficient time to understand. They are guided to concentrate on successful understanding without reminders not to move their lips. After the reading is completed, questions are asked, and assistance is given with thinking through the meaning.

USING A "BUDDY" SYSTEM WITH A BLIND STUDENT

To his disappointment, Mr. Lara, the eighth grade English teacher, found he was unable to obtain either a braille edition or a taped version of Great Expectations. *He had been successful in working with Tom, a blind student, in all other aspects of class because the textbook was available in braille. But why not* Great Expectations?

Mr. Lara initiated a meeting with Larry, an average student whom he noticed would greet Tom when he came in the room. Mr. Lara proposed a "buddy" system. In discussions and oral reading, both students remained in the room. During silent reading, Tom and Larry went to the empty teachers' lunchroom where Larry read the assigned pages aloud to Tom. Larry also met with an itinerant resource teacher who told him about Tom's blindness and instructed him on how to be supportive in reading without allowing Tom to become dependent. The two boys became friends, and both did very well on the final test on the Dickens novel.

Reading to Students

Teachers sometimes read to students to provide a break in the classroom routine or as an enjoyable activity for relaxation. But this activity has other benefits—modeling, hearing the printed text in expressive speech, strengthening the auditory modality, and encouraging interest in reading. In addition to "story time," teachers can read shorter paragraphs, phrases, or even single words. Students are asked to close their eyes or put their heads on the desks and create sensory images in response to the verbal statements. Teachers can use directions to guide this activity: "Imagine what this place looks like—what kind of buildings? Can you taste the strawberries? What do you think will happen?"

Having older students read to first graders stimulates interest in oral and silent reading as well as introducing comprehension skills when they think about what takes place in the story. Talking books bring the printed page alive into oral language, which has meaning to most young students. Other benefits include strengthening decoding proficiency, increasing attending ability, and providing opportunities for individualization in the classroom.

Free Reading

To have students read for information and pleasure is the ultimate goal of reading instruction. Thus, during the school day, opportunities for realizing these goals can be given through free reading. Students select materials—periodicals, pamphlets, or books available in the classroom—and read at their own pace, independent of others. They discover facts and stories that are of particular interest. Although they may wish to discuss what was learned with the teacher or classmates, no formal requirements are made. Nor should they be expected to write a report or be quizzed over the material. Free reading can be a time set aside for this purpose, or students can be encouraged to use unstructured time resulting from their independent schedules and work pace. Kirk, Kliebhan, and Lerner (1978) suggest that the students' selection of interesting materials and their motivation in reading to discover the story enhances comprehension skills.

Assessment

General Achievement Testing

Many group-administered achievement tests routinely given at designated grade levels include subtests of elements of reading. The content of the tests may not reflect local curriculum. Although they may be able to identify students who have not profited as well as their peers from classroom instruction, they are not sufficiently specific to pinpoint strengths and weaknesses in achievement that allows instructional or remedial planning. Further, the conditions under which the tests are usually administered may work adversely for individual learners. For students being considered for a special or remedial program, it is necessary to administer an individual achievement test.

Individual Achievement Tests

Achievement tests commonly used are the *Wide Range Achievement Test* (Revised) (WRAT–R) (Jastak & Wilkinson, 1984), the *Peabody Individual Achievement Test* (PIAT) (Dunn & Markwardt, 1970), and the *Woodcock–Johnson Psycho-Educational Battery* (Woodcock & Johnson, 1977). The WRAT-R produces grade level equivalents, standard scores, and percentile ranks for three areas: reading, spelling, and arithmetic, from preschool through college. Users should be aware that the reading subtest is a word-identification task and requires no comprehension. Thus, it does not accurately reflect the instructional level of reading for many students.

Readiness Assessment

Three areas of readiness were described in the organization of reading skills presented. Assessment procedures for two of these areas, developmental readiness and readiness for instruction, have been addressed in other chapters. For assessing the third area, specific reading readiness, several tests are available. The most frequently used is the *Metropolitan Readiness Test* (MRT) (Nurss & McGauvran, 1976a, 1976b). Level I includes six subtests and is administered at the beginning or in the middle of kindergarten. Level II includes eight subtests and is designed for administration at the end of kindergarten or the beginning of first grade. Types of scores are stanines, performance ratings, and percentile ranks. Reliability and validity data appear acceptable for the purposes for which the test is intended.

The MRT should *not* be used as the sole criterion for reading instruction grouping in the first grade although the test has been used frequently for this purpose. Nurss and McGauvran (1976a, p. 16) state that "the MRT does not provide in-depth diagnostic information about student strengths and weaknesses" and that "scores should be viewed as suggestive of possible strengths and weaknesses subject to verification by other means. . . ." All students who score low on a performance rating do not do so for the same reasons. Therefore, and because initial instruction is so crucial to later success, teachers should group on the basis of instructional needs after careful consideration of several indices.

Other reading readiness tests include:

- *Macmillan Readiness Test* (Macmillan)
- *Clymer–Barrett Readiness Tests* (Revised) (Chapman, Brock, & Kent)
- *Murphy–Durrell Reading Readiness Analysis* (Harcourt Brace Jovanovich)
- *Lee–Clark Reading Readiness Tests* (CTB/McGraw- Hill)
- *Search* (Walker Educational Book Corp.)

Formal Reading Tests: Decoding and Comprehension

An abundance of reading tests are available to regular teachers, special teachers, and reading specialists. Figure 11.6 lists some of these instruments.

In addition to norming and appropriateness to the curriculum, they differ in representation of skills, task demands, scoring procedures, ease of administration, breadth of measurement, and other aspects of test construction. Although such instruments are superior to general achievement tests in pinpointing areas in which

FIGURE 11.6

Selected reading and achivement tests

Instrument	Administration		Type			Grade Range
Test (Author, Date) Publisher	Group	Individual	Inventory	Survey	Diagnostic	
Botel Reading Inventory (Botel, 1978) Follett	X		X			1–12
	Spelling, word recognition, word opposites, decoding					
Classroom Reading Inventory (4th ed.) (Silvaroli, 1982) Wm. C. Brown		X	X			K–8
	Word recognition; reading levels — independent, instructional, frustration; hearing comprehension; spelling					
Diagnostic Reading Scales (Spache, 1981) CTB/McGraw-Hill		X			X	1–12
	Word recognition, oral reading, silent reading, listening, phonics, comprehension					
Doren Diagnostic Reading Test of Word Recognition Skills (Doren, 1973) American Guidance Service	X				X	1–6
	Letter recognition, beginning and ending sounds, speech consonants, blending, rhyming words, sight words, spelling					
Durrell Analysis of Reading Difficulties (Durrell and Catterson, 1980) American Guidance Service		X			X	1–6
	Oral and silent readings, listening comprehension, listening vocabulary, word recognition, auditory analysis of words, word elements, pronunciation, visual memory of words, prereading phonics					
Gates-MacGinitie Reading Tests (MacGinitie, 1978) Riverside	X			X		1–9
	Level B: vocabulary, letter sounds, letter recognition, comprehension; Levels A through F: vocabulary, comprehension					

11 Methods for Teaching Reading 247

Instrument	Administration		Type			Grade Range
Test (Author, Date) Publisher	Group	Individual	Inventory	Survey	Diagnostic	
Gates-McKillop-Horowitz Reading Diagnostic Test (Gates-McKillop, Horowitz, 1981) Teachers College Press		X			X	1–6
	Twenty-three scores on diverse skills including oral reading, word attack, words — untimed and flash presentation, letter names and sounds, word parts, blending, auditory discrimination, spelling					
Gilmore Oral Reading Test (Gilmore and Gilmore, 1968) Psychological Corporation		X			X	1–8
	Accuracy, comprehension, rate in oral reading					
Gray Oral Reading Test — Revised (Wiederholt and Bryan, 1986) Pro-Ed		X			X	1–12
	Accuracy, comprehension, rate in oral reading					
Iowa Silent Reading Tests (Farr, 1973) Harcourt Brace Jovanovich	X			X		6–College
Peabody Individual Achievement Test (Dunn and Markwardt, 1970) American Guidance Service		X		X		1–12
	Word recognition, comprehension					
Stanford Diagnostic Reading Test (3rd ed.) (Karlsen, Madden, and Gardner, 1983, 1984) Psychological Corporation	X				X	1–13
	Auditory discrimination, phonic analysis, structural analysis, vocabulary, word parts, rate, auditory vocabulary, scanning and skimming					

FIGURE 11.6

(Continued)

FIGURE 11.6
(Continued)

Instrument	Administration		Type			Grade Range
Test (Author, Date) Publisher	Group	Individual	Inventory	Survey	Diagnostic	
New Sucher-Allred Reading Placement Inventory (Sucher and Allred, 1981) Economy	X		X			1–6
	Word recognition; oral reading — independent, instructional, and frustration levels					
Test of Reading Comprehension (Brown, Hammill, and Wiederholt, 1978) Pro-Ed	X				X	1–8
	General vocabulary; syntactic similarities; paragraph reading and five supplementary subtests — math, science and social studies, reading directions, and sentence sequencing					
Woodcock Reading Mastery Tests — Revised (Woodcock, 1987) American Guidance Service		X			X	K–College /adult
	Letter recognition, word recognition, word attack skills, word comprehension, passage comprehension					
Woodcock-Johnson Psychoeducational Battery Woodcock and Johnson, 1977 DLM Teaching Resources		X			X	1–12
	Reading cluster: letter-word identification, word attack, passage comprehension					

students may need help, teachers will find it necessary to use additional observation and informal testing as a basis for instructional planning.

Informal Assessment

Informal assessment may take many forms including continuous monitoring of classroom reading performance, teacher-made tests, and individual sessions in which teachers can more selectively and specifically observe individual reading. There are a number of distinct advantges to such assessment procedures. They are made and used by teachers who are also in the best position to provide immediate instruction or remediation. They are direct observations, and samples can be gathered over several time spans. They can use curriculum materials similar to those with which students have been taught, and they lend themselves directly to remedial procedures.

Informal Reading Inventories (IRI)   Several authors (Harris & Sipay, 1980; Johnson & Kress, 1965; Moran, 1978) provide instructions for teacher construction of an IRI that can be used to determine reading level or to assess specific skills in decoding and comprehension. Essentially the process consists of the selection of a series of passages at, below, and above grade placement. To determine reading level, the number of words recognized and the number of orally administered comprehension questions answered correctly are used. Kirk, Kliebhan, and Lerner (1978, p. 158) give criteria for determining reading level from an IRI.

Reading Level	Word Recognition	Comprehension
Independent	98% to 100%	90% to 100%
Instructional	95%	75%
Frustration	90% or below	50% or below

The third area, and perhaps the most valuable, assessed by an IRI is that of specific reading skills. As students read orally, teachers note the following: word recognition; mispronunciations; additions, substitutions, or omissions of words; reversals or inversions; repetitions; fluency; hesitations; phrasing; intonation; word-by-word reading; words with which the student needs help; and self-correction. Ekwall (1981) and Harris and Sipay (1980), among others, provide codes for recording such errors. In addition, inferences about attitude and motivation can be made from the student's general approach to the task of reading.

Although informal reading inventories are, by definition, teacher-made instruments, several informal inventories are commercially available. These include the *Classroom Reading Inventory* (Silvaroli, 1982) and the *Standard Reading Inventory* (McCracken, 1966).

Cloze Procedures   Several kinds of cloze procedures can be formulated by teachers to assess comprehension. In each the students supply words, orally or in writing, to replace purposefully omitted words from a passage. It is assumed that if students can give the exact word, a synonym, or a reasonable substitution, they will have had to comprehend the meaning of the passage adequately. Some authors have devised percentile scoring systems to result in a reading level. The *Woodcock Reading Mastery Tests* (Revised) (Woodcock, 1987) uses the procedure as a measure of passage comprehension.

Reading Miscue Analysis   Goodman (1969) developed miscue analysis, which is a system for analyzing errors in oral reading. Goodman suggests that simply obtaining reading level based on the number of errors in word recognition (quantitative assessment) is insufficient and that the nature of the errors should be analyzed to give insight into the student's psycholinguistic system (qualitative assessment). A formal application of this approach is the *Reading Miscue Inventory* test (Goodman & Burke, 1972).

Oral and Silent Reading Assessment

Oral Reading It is obvious that the use of an informal reading inventory and other procedures previously described constitute some measures of oral reading ability. However, dimensions other than decoding and comprehension need to be examined as a basis for assisting students to become efficient oral readers. These elements of reading behavior include finger following, facial and bodily evidences of tension and anxiety, posture, page position in relation to the eyes, visual scanning and fixation, head movements, and task orientation. Both Ekwall (1981) and Harris and Sipay (1980) present checklists that can be used by teachers to monitor and record evidence of oral reading behaviors.

Several of the individual test batteries include subtests on oral reading. Formal standardized tests of oral reading include the *Gray Oral Reading Tests* (Revised) (Wiederholt & Bryant, 1986) and the *Gilmore Oral Reading Tests* (Gilmore & Gilmore, 1968).

Silent Reading Comprehension is often measured after silent reading with teachers asking questions or students completing activities or questions in workbooks. However, overt behaviors such as posture, eye movements, lip movements, soft vocalizing, finger following, maintenance of attention, and speed are observed. Several diagnostic batteries contain silent reading sections but usually as a measure of comprehension rather than silent reading skills. The *Silent Reading Diagnostic Test* (Bond, Balow, & Hoyt, 1970) are available.

Comparing Oral, Silent, and Listening Comprehension The importance of comparing oral, silent, and listening comprehension was noted previously. This comparison can be made through formal, criterion-referenced, or informal procedures. The *Durrell Analysis of Reading Difficulty* (Durrell & Catterson, 1980) contains matching subtests for comparing comprehension following oral and silent reading and passage listening. The *Spadefore Diagnostic Reading Test* (Spadefore, 1983) and the *Classroom Reading Inventory* (Silvaroli, 1982) can also be used. Informally, teachers can select passages from available reading material to be presented via the three procedures. Comprehension questions are asked for each passage with the criteria presented on p. 249 being used to determine reading level.

Other instruments have oral and silent reading subtests, and some of these can also be adapted for hearing comprehension. However, when selections are chosen from several different tests, difficulties ensue. Passages from one instrument to another may not be of comparable difficulty despite designated grade levels, and when tests are developed on different norm populations, both validity and reliability are subject to serious questions when comparisons are made.

Criterion-Referenced Assessment

With the proliferation of behavioral-based approaches in education has come increased availability of criterion-referenced tests. While norm-referenced testing samples selected skills over a broad area and reports scores based on norms, criterion-referenced tests assess many detailed skills within a narrow domain and do not yield traditional scores. Some criterion-referenced instruments in the area of reading are:

- *Comprehensive Inventory of Basic Skills* (Brigance, 1983)
- *Individual Criterion-Referenced Tests* (Educational Development Corp.)
- *Prescriptive Reading Inventory* (CTB/McGraw-Hill)
- *Woodcock Reading Mastery Tests* (Revised) (Woodcock, 1987)

The direct relationship between reading skills assessment and instruction has made criterion-referenced testing and teaching procedures popular and has been responsible for a dramatic increase in commercial materials and programs. However, such procedures are not without limitations. Of particular concern is the reliability of measurement. A student's inability to perform a specific task (giving the sound for a printed consonant blend, for example) does not mean that the same error would occur in later testing. Nor does assessment of such skills in isolation guarantee that students will make the same errors in their reading. Teachers should use criterion-referenced assessment as a guide for monitoring routine classroom teaching to determine, more reliably, those skills with which students have difficulty.

Reading Approaches

Often the words *approach* and *method* are not adequately distinguished. An approach is a broad, systematic design or plan uniquely organized on the basis of theoretical principles that has the purpose of providing a framework within which problems can be solved and subject content can be taught. A method is a teaching activity and hence related to the conveyance of subject content to students. It is narrower in scope than an approach, and frequently the same method of presentation can be used within the context of different approaches.

Major Reading Approaches

Basal Reading Approach This classic approach consists of highly structured sequences of tasks presented in a series of textbooks (basal readers). The books usually begin with preprimer material and progress through the sixth or the eighth grades. Most series have accompanying workbooks as well as placement and achievement tests. They often include other materials such as flashcards, worksheets, ditto masters, audiovisual devices, and teacher guides for instruction. This comprehensiveness makes them popular with teachers and school systems. Most basal approaches stress meaning from the beginning. Vocabulary is controlled, and activities in word recognition, word attack skills, and comprehension are consistent from level to level.

Phonics Approaches Phonics instruction is one of the oldest and most enduring pedagogical procedures. The formalization of phonics principles into programs with a series of readers is more recent. The approach emphasizes word recognition (decoding) by stressing sound–symbol associations and by providing generalizable word attack skills. The programs differ on starting points and on the sequence of elements. A common sequence, however, is learning sounds of nonmeaningful symbols—single letters, blends, digraphs, and vowel combinations followed by blending sequences of letter sounds into syllables and words. Phonics rules are also taught. Although not initially emphasized, meaning becomes more important in later stages of the program.

Some programs which are phonics-oriented are *Conquests in Reading* (Webster), *Lippincott Basic Readers* (Lippincott), *Open Court Program* (Open Court), *Patterns Sounds and Meaning* (Allyn and Bacon), *Phonic Keys to Reading* (The Economy Co.), *Phonovisual Method* (Phonovisual Products), *Reading With Phonics* (Lippincott), *Speech to Phonics* (Harcourt Brace Jovanovich), *Wenkart Phonics Readers* (Wenkart), and the *Wordland Series* (Continental Press).

Linguistic Approaches Concerned with oral communication as a base for beginning to learn to read, the linguistic approaches assume that the primary language system, listening and speaking, is intact. The approaches then attend to the written symbol form of this primary system. Linguistic approaches differ from phonics in that analytic rather than synthetic decoding is used. Sounds are not associated with individual letters and nonmeaningful units. Blending skills and "sounding out" are not emphasized. Rather, a whole-word method is used with letters, with their sounds being embedded naturally within words. A word-family procedure is employed—that is, groups of words are taught together if they have similar spelling (hence sound) patterns. For example, words with a *c–v–c* (consonant–vowel–consonant) pattern such as *hat, cat, fat,* and *sat* are grouped for instruction.

Linguistic programs include *Let's Read* (Wayne State University Press), *Linguistic Readers* (Benzinger), *Merrill Linguistic Readers* (Merrill), *Miami Linguistic Readers* (D.C. Heath), *SRA Basic Reading Series* (SRA), *Sullivan Program* (McGraw-Hill), and the *Structural Reading Series* (Singer).

Language-Experience Approach The language-experience approach (LEA) has been used for many years, frequently as an introductory step to reading from oral language and as a supplementary method to other approaches. LEA is not, however, restricted to the introductory stages of reading but can be used throughout the grades and into the junior high or middle school. The approach has the additional advantage of integrating oral language, spelling, and writing into the reading books. Described by Lee and Allen (1963), the approach capitalizes on the interests and experiences of students. For example, they may describe an event in their life, and the teacher writes it on the chalkboard. Thus, their own words become the basis for reading instruction. Although LEA can be highly individualized (as in the example), the approach can be used with groups. Common experiences, community or neighborhood events, field trips, or holidays may be sources for stories composited from the contributions of all class members. The approach can thus accommodate for social and cultural variability and allow students to identify directly with the passages. Adaptations and uses of the approach can be found in Allen (1976), Allen and Allen (1982), Hall (1981), Kirk, Kliebhan, and Lerner (1978), and Stauffer, (1980) who have described the approach as appropriate for disabled readers.

Remedial Approaches

Multisensory Approaches Several procedures have been developed particularly for the problem reader. They are usually highly structured and break away from the more conventional methods in their use of a combination of sensory modalities.

Fernald Approach Developed by Grace Fernald (1943), this approach is sometimes called VAKT with those letters representing the words Visual, Auditory, Kinesthetic, and Tactile. The initial stages use no prepackaged materials but are similar to an LEA in that they capitalize on the student's own background and interests. They dictate a story for the teacher to write. A whole-word perception is emphasized rather than letters, sounding-out, or blending. Four basic steps comprise the program: tracing and saying the word aloud, writing without tracing, recognition in print, and word analysis.

Gillingham–Stillman Approach The Gillingham–Stillman approach (Gillingham & Stillman, 1970) is a phonics-based program in which letters, their names, and their sounds are introduced individually; blending skills follow. Spelling is introduced early in the program with students giving letter names and sounds while writing. The program is organized with sequential lessons spanning a two-year period. An adaptation of this approach is provided by Slingerland (1981).

Skills Management Approaches Skills management approaches are based in the principles of task analysis and criterion-referenced testing. They consist of domain-referenced assessment of the mastery of specific reading skills and behaviorally based instruction. Among the programs available are: *Individual Learning Management Procedure* (Hackett, 1974), *Diagnosis: An Instructional Aid* (Shub, Carlin, Friedman, Kaplan, & Katien, 1973), *Fountain Valley Teacher Support System* (Richard L. Zweig, 1971), *Individual Pupil Monitoring System* (Houghton-Mifflin), *Prescriptive Reading Laboratory* (CTB/McGraw-Hill), and *Skills Monitoring System-Reading* (Harcourt Brace Jovanovich).

Specialized Reading Approaches

Individualized Reading This approach is similar to the LEA in that it capitalizes on the student's interests and there are no sets of published materials organized for ready use. The approach differs from LEA in that it does not use student experiences and words. Instead, they select their own reading material and progress through it at their own pace. Teachers provide individual instruction as needed and hold periodic conferences to evaluate progress and achievement.

Neurological Impress Method The *Neurological Impress Method* (Heckelman, 1969) is a procedure that provides simultaneous auditory and visual stimuli within the context of a relatively normal oral reading lesson. Teachers or tutors sit to the side and slightly behind the students so that they can direct their voice toward the student's ears. Together they read the material aloud. The students follow along with their fingers to assure visual monitoring. The pace is brisk, and there are no interruptions for errors nor for corrections of instructions. Teachers' intonations are appropriate to the material, emphasizing the relationship of the printed text to oral language. Theoretically, this combination of oral and visual stimuli is "impressed" upon the student's receptive language system and memory.

Programmed Reading Programmed reading materials are designed for individual use rather than for group presentation. They may be incorporated within a series of books, presented through teaching machines or with computer-assisted instruction. Content is presented in small, sequential steps that provide for immediate feedback, correction, and reinforcement. Two such programs are the *Programmed Reading* (Buchanan, 1966) and the *M. W. Sullivan Reading Program* (Behavioral Research Laboratories, 1966).

Reading Mastery: DISTAR The program is a total, highly structured reading series. *Reading Mastery: DISTAR Reading I* (Englemann & Bruner, 1983) consists of lessons in sound–symbol identification, left-to-right progression, and rhyming and blending. Words, then sentences and short stories are decoded. *Reading Mastery: DISTAR Reading II* (Englemann & Bruner, 1984) emphasizes word attack skills. Following directions and literal and inferential comprehension skills are taught.

Reading Mastery Englemann and Hanner developed the *Reading Mastery Program*. *Reading Mastery: III* (1983) continues decoding and comprehension skills and introduces vocabulary development. *Reading Mastery: IV* (1983) emphasizes comprehension, answering oral and written questions, using reference materials, and applying and integrating information. In *Reading Mastery: V* (Englemann, Osborn, Osborn, & Zoref, 1983), fluency and literary style are stressed as well as comprehension skills, outlining, and written assignments. *Reading Mastery: VI* (Englemann, Osborn, Osborn, & Zoref, 1984) consists of story elements and logical and analytical skills. The program includes short stories, expository articles, poems, and novels.

Corrective Reading Program Written by Englemann and his colleagues (1978), *Corrective Reading* is a direct instruction remedial program for students from grades four through twelve and for adults who have not mastered basic skills. Three levels of skill development are organized within two "strands"—decoding and comprehension.

Reading and the Exceptional Learner

Arguments as to the best approach and methods for teaching students to read have continued for decades prompting Chall to title her classic book, *Learning to Read: The Great Debate* (1967). Although Chall concluded that code-emphasis (skill-to-meaning) approaches appeared to be superior to meaning-emphasis approaches in the beginning stages of learning to read, she did not find any single method to be superior to others.

"Which is the best method?" is clearly the wrong question. It is unwarranted to assume that method alone is the critical factor in the successful teaching of reading. Harris and Sipay (1980, p. 69) write:

> There is strong evidence that the qualities of the school system, of administrative leadership of the particular school, of the teacher, and of the pupils (in turn related to characteristics of home and neighborhood) far outweigh differences in methodology and materials in their influence on reading achievement.

It is not useful to argue "the great debate" again, this time for exceptional students. A common conception is that they are less intelligent or slower in development than nonhandicapped students. Thus, the recommended solution to their reading problems is to place them in a lower reading group with easier material and limited expectations. Although some students conform to this stereotype and can profit from such instruction, both the perception and the solution are oversimplified. Just as one cannot find the single best method for teaching reading, one cannot find a single type of exceptional student nor one kind of reading problem. Not all individuals fit the mold. Instead, they demonstrate all types and degrees of severity of reading problems as do others who are not identified as exceptional. The answer to successful teaching of reading to exceptional students, the individual learners, or to others lies in sound instructional activities that are based on teachers' thorough knowledge of all elements of the reading curriculum, the approaches and methods of the teaching of reading, the learning and achievement characteristics of individual students, and the environment in which learning takes place.

EFFECT OF HEARING LOSS ON READING

Eddie was a puzzle to his first grade teacher. He seemed bright, alert, and eager to learn. He participated in class enthusiastically. By the end of the year, Eddie was achieving above grade level in mathematics but was far behind in reading, which was laborious and characterized by many pronunciation errors. He knew the phonics rules but seemed unable to employ them in oral reading. He was beginning to lose interest and began to shy away from participation in the reading group. Because he had been absent for many short periods of time during the school year, Miss Spicer believed that Eddie had missed too much instruction. She recommended he be retained in first grade.

In reviewing these data to discuss with Eddie's parents, the principal, Mrs. Sanders, noted that each of the absences had been for "ear aches." Although the hearing screening had indicated no loss, Mrs. Sanders decided to pursue the possibility of hearing involvement. With the help of the speech/language pathologist, she discovered that Eddie had a long history of otitis media—the middle ear fills with fluid, causing intermittant conductive hearing loss. The pathologist reasoned that this loss, which extended before and after the actual earaches, had interfered with Eddie's phonics, matching each letter with its sound.

Testing by the resource teacher revealed that Eddie could comprehend above grade level when passages were read to him but that decoding and comprehension were lowered when Eddie had to read aloud, sounding out each word.

It was decided to promote Eddie to second grade but to place him for reading in the class of a teacher using a linguistic, whole-word approach. The nurse and the speech/language pathologist recommended that the parents take him to an ear specialist. Eddie's hearing and reading progress were monitored throughout the year, and the classroom teacher provided supportive, corrective instruction because he was essentially starting over with a new reading approach. By the end of second grade, Eddie had maintained his superiority in mathematics and was on grade level in reading.

If mildly handicapped students do not read successfully in the regular program, careful assessment must be made of the personal, psychological, physiological, sociocultural, and learning correlates and especially of the specific pattern of skills, strengths, and deficits in reading. First it is necessary to determine abilities in the hierarchical skills rather than to predetermine the skills to be taught on the basis of grade or age expectations or from scope and sequence charts. A decision is then made regarding the individual student as to the nature of the reading approach and methods augmenting or enriching the present program, using a structured remedial procedure, changing approaches, or developing a combination of methods. Advocating a particular method or approach because of its success with groups of students in a research study is not warranted.

Reading Approaches and Handicapped Learners

Basal Reader Approach

The comprehensiveness, wealth of materials, and continuing revision to incorporate recent research has made the basal approach popular with teachers and appropriate for many students. Despite their advantages, many criticisms have been made regarding their use with exceptional learners. Among the criticisms are that:

1. The content, relative to socioeconomic and cultural factors, may differ from those of students who are likely to encounter reading problems. This difference could interfere with meaning because the basal approach is a meaning-to-skill procedure and might also result in reduced motivation.
2. The vocabulary and language structure of the materials are different from those that characterize the learned-language systems of some young students. Thus, correspondence between oral and written language is reduced.
3. Meaning-to-skill approaches are generally less effective with exceptional learners.
4. Skills to be learned are not broken down into sufficiently small units to be readily learned by exceptional students.
5. Lesson plans provided with the programs are highly structured and allow little accommodation for individual differences.
6. Insufficient practice is given to the skills, thus reducing the quality of initial learning and the probability of generalization and transfer.

Among the criticisms of the approach for use in remedial instruction are that:

1. The interest level of the approach is too low for older students who need help in beginning skills.
2. The language content of the introductory materials is too divergent from the more developed oral communication language of older students.
3. The materials are the same as or similar to those with which students have already failed.

The basal reader approach, however, remains the most commonly used at the present time. Before handicapped readers are identified, they will likely be introduced to the approach. Teachers can monitor the progress of each student, using skilled observation to detect early signs of difficulty. Alternative teaching procedures, combinations of approaches, and supplementary materials can be used. Payne, Polloway, Smith, and Payne (1981) present suggestions for augmenting the basal reader approach for exceptional students.

Phonics Approaches

A major goal of phonics approaches is to provide students with specific but generalizable skills in "breaking the code"—identifying phoneme–grapheme match and determining a word from the combination of letter groups. Synthetic phonics begins with matching sounds and individual letters or small groups of letters. Intrinsic, or analytic, phonics begins with words to be analyzed into sounds by word attack skills. Each approach has advantages and disadvantages although Chall (1967) suggests that synthetic phonics can be made easier than intrinsic phonics for slow learning students. Students with learning disabilities who have difficulty in whole-part relationships, or those with blending difficulties, may find intrinsic phonics to their advantage.

Linguistic Approaches

Linguistic approaches may have several advantages for some handicapped learners. The restriction of initial vocabulary to words with regular spelling reduces confusion on the choice of sounds used to represent letters. Further, the whole-word approach facilitates reading for students who have difficulties in blending. On the other hand, there are some disadvantages inherent in the programs. There is no direct instruction of sounds or symbols. The approaches assume that the phonetic regularity in and repetition of the grouped vocabulary words (*let, set, met, get*) will allow students to discover letter–sound relationships and that they can then apply them to new words. Handicapped learners often have difficulties in each of these processes. Harris and Sipay (1980, p. 415) list as limitations that "(1) some children are confused by the repetitiveness of only short-vowel words; (2) the language structure and story content are restricted and artificial; and (3) no set for diversity is established." In addition, some published linguistic programs move rapidly from one skill to another, allowing little time for repetition or overlearning needed by some individual learners.

Language-Experience Approach

The basic principles of LEA make it advantageous for individual learners. Inherent interest in the content and the association with the student's expressive language systems facilitates instruction (Payne, Polloway, & Smith, 1981). LEA is also useful for disadvantaged students and for those with language problems. However, the program's limitations in comprehensiveness, structure, organization, and scope and sequence attenuates its usability. LEA may not suffice as a complete program with exceptional learners but can be an effective, continuing, supplementary method at all levels.

Programmed Reading

Programmed reading allows students to progress at their own pace, breaks sequences of skills into very small steps, and provides immediate feedback. School systems that do not have access to teaching machines use programmed texts. Although they are popular as a way of individualizing reading, there are some disadvantages when used with exceptional learners. They require students to work relatively independently of teachers, and, conversely, teachers may not be able to monitor individual progress easily and to provide immediate instruction. While the programs may have the requisite skills organized relative to an assumed developmental sequence of reading, they may not be able to match the patchwork of strengths and weaknesses in task accomplishments of individual learners. Further, they are not able to consider intraindividual (visual, auditory, intellectual, and language) variability of exceptional students.

Exceptional Learners and Selected Reading Skills

Decoding

In the initial stages of learning to read, exceptional learners are often lacking in visual and auditory processes, language, attention, memory, and generalization and transfer abilities.

Visual and Auditory Perception   Some students, particularly those identified as having learning disabilities, may have residual difficulties from visual or auditory perceptual or motor problems. Students with visual-motor interferences may be unable to distinguish between similarly formed letters (*m,n; b,h*) or with reversals (*b,d; p,b*).

Because of the demands of reading, visual-motor-perceptual problems frequently appear in kindergarten or early first grade when letter identification and naming and isolated letter–sound match are expected. Later they may reverse the sounds in digraphs or blends. Students with auditory problems may have difficulty in blending consonant sounds, distinguishing among vowel sounds, and making a structural analysis. Auditory problems often reveal themselves later when phonics skills are being refined.

Before becoming overly concerned, teachers should note whether such problems, observable in isolation, actually interfere with learning to read. If not, intervention may not be necessary. If so, direct instruction using methods described earlier and geared to specific tasks may resolve the problem. If the difficulty is generalized, combination approaches may be needed in which perceptual training is incorporated within academic instruction or in a multisensory approach.

Language Many students who do not demonstrate a well-developed primary language system (vocabulary, morphology, and syntax) frequently find beginning reading a laborious activity. They are slow, plodding oral readers because the grammatical constructions of the text do not correspond with their innate language systems. Sometimes students who have normal potential but have deficiencies in language can learn phonics and be so drilled that they can "word call" with rapidity. However, they may not be able to put words together into meaningful units. For such students, programs that emphasize decoding skills are inappropriate. They need instruction that includes putting the meaning of sentences into their own words, in comprehension skills, and in discussion of meaning. Supplementary activities in the classroom or with support assistance might include a general language–enrichment program, vocabulary building, and elements of a language-experience approach.

Attention Some children cannot maintain attention for substantial periods of time. Teachers may notice increased movement and fidgeting, with students attending to other activities in the room. As attention becomes difficult to maintain, the quality of learning decreases. In seatwork they may need to be allowed to pace their own work, take short breaks, or attend to some other project temporarily. They understand that such interruptions will not excuse them from classroom expectations and that they must return to the task at hand. Consultation with the school psychologist or a resource teacher may help in setting up a program designed to lengthen attention time to tasks.

Memory Memory difficulties plague many exceptional students and individual learners. They interfere with nearly every aspect of reading at all levels. Remembering rules, sound–symbol relationships, sight vocabulary, and yesterday's instructions are constant factors in reading disability. Mnemonic devices, association, continued practical use of newly learned words and rules, and high-interest selections are effective remediation techniques.

Generalization and Transfer Students may learn sound–symbol relationships within the context of the examples presented in instruction but may not be able to apply this knowledge to new words. A similar situation can exist for phonics rules. Such problems are difficult to remediate, although a linguistic whole-word approach with the use of word families may be effective. Many examples should be given in initial instruction, and opportunity for immediate, diverse application is necessary. Further, teachers can initiate a new lesson or the introduction to vocabulary words by the following:

- Identify their relationship to previous learnings
- Remind students of the known rules and principles
- Ask students to identify situations in the new lesson in which they are applicable

Comprehension

Frequently, books and articles that address the teaching of reading to exceptional students circumvent the topic of comprehension. There are several reasons for this:

- The obvious deficits in decoding skills among the population
- The assumption that, because of mental limitations, handicapped students cannot achieve beyond the literal level
- The difficulty in prescribing comprehension techniques at a general level even for the nonhandicapped

Although exceptional students and individual learners do demonstrate many difficulties in decoding, attention should not be given to the remediation of this level exclusively, without a concomitant consideration of comprehension. There is little motivation for a student to struggle with difficult decoding as an end in itself. Despite some limitations, an LEA with its immediate relevance both to language and interests may benefit many students. Similarly, high-interest, easy-reading materials can be a vital supplementary activity for older students.

Exceptional students and individual learners do not constitute a homogeneous population. Many have no mental limitations and can succeed in comprehension equally with their nonhandicapped peers. Teachers should not assume mental limitations among students with sensory impairments or physical handicaps. Some students with learning disabilities may have great difficulty in "breaking the code" yet have intact reasoning ability. Almost by definition, students with mild retardation do demonstrate difficulties in abstract thinking. However, IQ scores alone do not accurately reflect the level of their functioning in specific tasks. Further, they do not learn automatically from experience—they need to be taught. If students with mild retardation are not taught comprehension skills, they will not learn them—thus reinforcing the idea that they cannot learn. Until they have had an opportunity to learn through direct instruction, their limitations cannot be identified.

Oral and Silent Reading

Oral Reading For exceptional students and individual learners with reading–processing problems, oral reading is particularly important. The first formal language they learn to comprehend is oral language. Oral reading is the transition from the heard language to the read language. Individual learners proceed through the same sequence of steps in this transition as do nonhandicapped and advanced readers. However, they do so at a slower pace and may encounter other difficulties. They may need more practice and may persist in oral reading, as well as whispering the lip movements in silent reading, beyond the age or grade at which most students discontinue such practices. Slow readers and those with thought-processing difficulties frequently need auditory feedback to assist in comprehension even into the secondary grades.

Silent Reading Most students need to demonstrate adequate oral reading skills before they can be expected to read silently with understanding. Many exceptional students have difficulty learning to read silently. Others need direct instruction such as reading a passage orally before reading it silently to achieve this goal. They may read a short passage and then tell the teacher what was read. Gradually, the length is increased. Teachers may also ask questions to guide students as they reread it.

Both oral and silent reading instruction is geared to performance level rather than to age–grade expectations. This means that the content of the individual program is determined by their abilities or lack of them. Priority should be given in instruction to moving students ahead in oral and silent skills toward the goal of independent reading with understanding. The elimination of inappropriate behaviors such as finger following or lip movement is of secondary importance. Usually as understanding increases, such behaviors disappear; however, sometimes assistance is needed in eliminating them. For example, some students become dependent on a marker and need to reduce its use gradually. A few students may always need a crutch.

Comparing Oral, Silent, and Listening Comprehension It is often advantageous to compare oral and silent reading comprehension of exceptional learners. Normal and bright students prefer to read silently once they have mastered the decoding skills; oral reading impedes the speedier comprehension processes. On the other hand, exceptional students and individual learners sometimes need the auditory feedback of their own voices (reauditorization) or the attention to the text, which is forced by oral reading, as an aid to comprehension. Often these students will have histories of auditory problems that interfere with their learning phonics skills. In oral reading they so concentrate on accurately sounding out the words that they may miss the meaning of the passage. However, they may have developed a large sight word vocabulary and learned to use context and closure skills, which allow them to read silently without internally vocalizing every sound. Consequently, they can comprehend well in silent reading. Comparing comprehension in the two modes, oral and silent, can assist teachers in sorting out the exact nature of the reading interference.

Assessment of listening comprehension of individual learners is accomplished by reading the passage to the students and asking oral questions. Kirk, Kliebhan, and Lerner (1978, p. 161) suggest that this provides an *"expectancy level"* that indicates comprehension expectations if the demands of the reading process did not interfere. If the listening expectancy is high and the oral and silent comprehension are low, teachers may wish to concentrate on decoding skills in the remedial program. If the listening comprehension is consistent with oral and silent reading comprehension abilities, achievement should be compared to the general expectancy level (IQ scores) to determine comprehension expectancies and priorities in planning the remedial program.

High-Interest / Easy-Reading Materials

Materials such as newspapers, magazines, and books of topical interest developed at an easy-reading level may motivate students with reading difficulties. However, such materials are developed on the basis of readability formulas that provide vocabulary and structure equivalent to a designated grade or age level. As already discussed, most disabled readers are not simply functioning at a lower level but have complex problems related to learning to read. Thygin (1979) provides guidelines

BOX 11.2

Case Study

Name: Peter
Chronological age: Nine-five
Grade: Fourth

Peter was referred to a diagnostic center because he was making unsatisfactory progress in reading although he was successful in other academic subjects. He has continued to receive tutoring in school in reading ever since second grade. In addition, his mother works with him on reading skills each evening. A second reason for referral was his increasingly negative reactions to the home program and the initiation of some behavior problems in school.

The following tests were administered:

Wechsler Intelligence Scale for Children—Revised
Full Scale IQ score: 112
Verbal IQ score: 111
Performance IQ score: 113

Peabody Individual Achievement Test (PIAT)

	Grade equiv.	Standard score
Mathematics	5.3	108
Spelling	2.3	79
Word Recognition	2.0	78
Reading Comprehension	2.4	79

Gilmore Oral Reading Test

	Grade equiv.	Standard score
Word Accuracy	1.7	62
Oral Comprehension	1.0	54

Woodcock Reading Mastery Test

	Grade equiv.
Letter Recognition	4.8
Word Recognition	1.8
Word Attack	2.3
Word Comprehension	2.4
Passage Comprehension	6.0

The principal concern of both school and parents was how a student with an IQ of 112 could do so poorly in reading and what could be done about it. Another problem was the disparity of test results in comprehension. On the Gilmore Test, which required oral reading, the comprehension was low. The silent reading comprehension score on the PIAT was markedly superior to the other reading scores. The diagnostic teacher decided to confirm this difference by administering comprehension tests in oral reading, silent reading, and listening. She obtained the following results:

Grade Equiv.	Oral Comp.	Silent Comp.	Listening Comp.
Pre	Independent	Independent	Independent
1st	Instructional	Independent	Independent
2nd	Frustration	Independent	Independent
3rd		Independent	Independent
4th		Independent	Independent
5th		Independent	Independent
6th		Instructional	Independent
7th		Frustration	Instructional
8th			Frustration

These latter results confirmed that Peter is capable of comprehending at or above his grade level when reading silently or listening. However, when Peter is required to encode the text into oral language with his deficient phonics and word attack skills, his energy and attention are diverted from discovering the meaning of the material.

Recommendations: The diagnostic team recommended that all tutoring at school and at home be terminated. They further recommended that the parents completely ignore the reading problem and concentrate on doing family fun activities.

Their recommendations were based on the following premises:

1. That four years of intensive tutoring on phonics skills had made little impact on Peter's ability to read orally and comprehend.
2. That the results of the oral, silent, and listening comprehension test along with other data confirmed that Peter was receiving the information and could attend to the matter when reading silently and listening.
3. That beginning in the fourth grade, oral reading is no longer a major aspect of the school curriculum. Peter would be able to obtain information from the textbooks with silent reading.
4. That the increasing negative reaction to reading indicated a potential for "turning off" to reading and learning altogether.

that caution matching materials to students in regard to interests, needs, and conceptual difficulty on one hand and vocabulary, phonetic skills, and syntactic elements on the other. Although they provide interest and practice in reading, they do not solve the basic reading problems of most exceptional learners.

SUMMARY

Reading is a central subject in the elementary curriculum because reading capabilities continue to affect success in school at all levels. Reading skills can be organized into a hierarchical structure beginning with readiness and progressing through decoding and comprehension. Three readiness areas include developmental readiness for learning, behavioral readiness to receive and profit from instruction, and specific reading readiness. A mastery of decoding skills is based largely on the development of the primary language system and instruction on sound–symbol relationships, word attack skills, and sight-word acquisition. Comprehension constitutes a range of abilities from literal recognition and memory through reasoning and evaluation skills to the appreciation level.

Many reading methods, particularly for instruction in decoding, are available. The variety may appear overwhelming at first. However, they provide a substantial repertoire for developmental learning and remediation of a wide variety of individual reading problems. Comprehension instruction is less easily divided into specific skills because they are so innately related to both cognitive abilities and the nearly infinite nature of passage content.

Reading methods can be organized into several major developmental approaches—basal reader, phonics, linguistic, and language-experience; remedial approaches—multisensory and skill management; and specialized approaches. No one approach is universally applicable. No one method has been determined to be superior to all others for all students. Rather it is for teachers—regular, remedial, or special—to select methods that meet students' needs as determined from individual assessment procedures.

REFERENCES

Allen, R. V. (1976). *Language experiences in communication.* Boston: Houghton Mifflin.
Allen, R. V., & Allen, C. (1982). *Language experience activities.* Boston: Houghton Mifflin.
Aukerman, R. C., & Aukerman, L. R. (1981). *How do I teach reading?* New York: Wiley.
Barbe, W. B., & Shields, B. P. (1976). *Reading skills checklists and activities.* West Nyak, NY: The Center for Applied Research in Education.
Bond, G. L., Balow, B., & Hoyt, C. J. (1970). *Silent reading diagnostic tests.* Ardmore, PA: Meredith.
Botel, M. (1978). *Botel reading inventory.* Chicago: Follett.
Brigance, A. H. (1983). *Comprehensive inventory of basic skills.* North Billerica, MA: Curriculum Associates.
Brown, V. L., Hammill, D. D., & Wiederholt, J. L. (1986). *Test of reading comprehension.* Austin, TX: Pro-Ed.
Buchanan, C. D. (1966). *Programmed reading.* New York: McGraw-Hill, Sullivan Associates.
Chall, J. S. (1967). *Learning to read: The great debate.* New York: McGraw-Hill.
Crowell, D. C., & Au, K. H. (1981). A scale of questions to guide comprehension instruction. *Reading Teacher, 34,* 389–393.
Doren, M. (1973). *Doren diagnostic reading test of word recognition skills* (2nd ed.). Circle Pines, MN: American Guidance Service.
Dunn, L. M., & Markwardt, F. C. (1970). *Peabody individual achievement test.* Circle Pines, MN: American Guidance Service.
Durrell, D. D., & Catterson, J. H. (1980). *Durrell analysis of reading difficulty* (3rd ed.). New York: Psychological Corporation.
Ekwall, E. E. (1981). *Locating and correcting reading difficulties* (3rd ed.). Columbus, OH: Merrill.
Englemann, S., & Bruner, E. C. (1983). *Reading mastery: DISTAR reading I.* Chicago: Science Research Associates.
Englemann, S., & Bruner, E. C. (1984). *Reading mastery: DISTAR reading II:* Chicago: Science Research Associates.

Englemann, S., & Hanner, S. (1983). *Reading mastery: Level III.* Chicago: Science Research Associates.
Englemann, S., & Hanner, S. (1983). *Reading mastery: Level IV.* Chicago: Science Research Associates.
Englemann, S., Johnson, G., Hanner, S., Carnine, L., Meyers, L., Osborn, S., Haddox, P., Becker, W., Osborn, J., & Becker, J. (1978). *Corrective reading.* Chicago: Science Research Associates.
Englemann, S., Osborn, J., Osborn, S., & Zoref, L. (1983). *Reading mastery: Level V.* Chicago: Science Research Associates.
Englemann, S., Osborn, J., Osborn, S., & Zoref, L. (1984). *Reading mastery: Level VI.* Chicago: Science Research Associates.
Fernald, G. M. (1943). *Remedial techniques in basic school subjects.* New York: McGraw-Hill.
Gates, A. I., McKillop, A. S., & Horowitz, E. C. (1981). *Gates–McKillop–Horowitz reading diagnostic tests* (2nd ed.). New York: Teachers College Press.
Gerber, A. (1981). Remediation of language processing problems of the school age child. In A. Gerber, & D. N. Bryen (Eds.). *Language and learning disabilities* (pp. 159–215). Baltimore: University Park Press.
Gillingham, A., & Stillman, B. (1970). *Remedial training for children with specific disability in reading, spelling, and penmanship* (8th ed.). Cambridge, MA: Educators Publishing Service.
Gilmore, J. V., & Gilmore, E. C. (1968). *Gilmore oral reading tests.* New York: Psychological Corporation.
Goodman, K. S. (1969). Analysis of reading miscues: Applied psycholinguistics. *Reading Research Quarterly, 5,* 9–30.
Goodman, Y. M., & Burke, C. L. (1972). *Reading miscue inventory.* New York: Macmillan.
Hackett, M. G. (1974). *Criterion reading: Individual learning management system.* Westminster, PA: Random House.
Hall, M. (1981). *Teaching reading as a language experience* (3rd ed.). Columbus, OH: Merrill.
Harris, A. J., & Jacobson, M. D. (1972). *Basic elementary reading vocabularies.* New York: Macmillan.
Harris, A. J., & Sipay, E. R. (1980). *How to increase reading ability* (7th ed.). New York: McKay.
Heckleman, R. G. (1969). Using a neurological impress method of remedial reading instruction. *Academic Therapy, 4,* 277–282.
Jastak, S., & Wilkinson, G. S. (1984). *Wide range achievement test—Revised.* Wilmington, DE: Jastak Associates.
Johnson, D. D. (1971). The Dolch list reexamined. *Reading Teacher, 24,* 449–457.
Johnson, D. D., & Pearson, P. D. (1978). *Teaching reading vocabulary.* New York: Holt, Rinehart & Winston.
Johnson, M. S., & Kress, R. A. (1965). *Informal reading inventories.* Newark, DE: International Reading Association.
Karlsen, B., Madden, R., & Gardner, E. F. (1983, 1984). *Stanford diagnostic reading test* (3rd ed.). New York: Psychological Corporation.
Kirk, S. A., Kliebhan, J. M., & Lerner, J. W. (1978). *Teaching reading to slow and disabled learners.* Boston: Houghton Mifflin.
Lee, D. M., & Allen, R. V. (1963). *Learning to read through experience* (2nd ed.). New York: Appleton-Century-Croft.
MacGinitie, W. H. (1978). *Gates–MacGinitie reading tests.* Boston: Houghton Mifflin.
McCracken, R. A. (1966). *Standard reading inventory.* Klamath Falls, OR: Klamath.

Moran, M. R. (1978). *Assessment of the exceptional learner in the regular classroom*. Denver: Love.

Nurss, J. R., & McGauvran, M. E. (1976a). *Metropolitan readiness tests: Teacher's manual, Part I: Interpretation and use of test results, (Level I)*. New York: Psychological Corporation.

Nurss, J. R., & McGauvran, M. E. (1976b). *Metropolitan readiness tests: Teacher's manual, Part I: Interpretation and use of test results, (Level II)*. New York: Psychological Corporation.

Payne, J. S., Polloway, E. A., Smith, J. E., Jr., & Payne, R. A. (1981). *Strategies for teaching the mentally retarded* (2nd ed.). Columbus OH: Merrill.

Pearson, P. D., & Johnson, D. D. (1978). *Teaching reading comprehension*. New York: Holt, Rinehart & Winston.

Polloway, E. A., & Polloway, C. H. (1980). Remediating reversals through stimulus fading. *Academic Therapy, 15,* 539–543.

Shub, A. N., Carlin, J. A., Friedman, R. L., Kaplan, J. M., & Katien, J. C. (1973). *Diagnosis: An instructional aid (reading)*. Chicago: Science Research Associates.

Silvaroli, N. J. (1982). *Classroom reading inventory* (4th ed.). Dubuque, IA: Brown.

Slingerland, B. (1981). *A multi-sensory approach to language arts for specific language disability children*. Cambridge, MA: Educators Publishing Service.

Spache, G. D. (1981). *Diagnostic reading scales*. Circle Pines, MN: American Guidance Service.

Spadefore, G. J. (1983). *Spadefore diagnostic reading test*. Novato, CA: Academic Therapy.

Stauffer, R. G. (1980). *The language experience approach to the teaching of reading* (2nd ed.). New York: Harper & Row.

Sucher, F., & Allred, R. A. (1981). *Reading placement inventory*. Oklahoma City, OK: Economy.

Thygin, M. (1979). Selection of books for high interest and low reading level. *Journal of Learning Disabilities, 12,* 428–430.

Walker, C. M. (1979). High frequency word lists for grades 3 through 9. *Reading Teacher, 32,* 804–811.

Wiederholt, J. L., & Bryant, B. R. (1986). *Gray oral reading tests* (revised). Austin, TX: Pro-Ed.

Woodcock, R. W. (1987). *Woodcock reading mastery tests* (Revised). Circle Pines, MN: American Guidance Service.

Woodcock, R. W., & Johnson, M. B. (1977). *Woodcock–Johnson psycho-educational battery*. Allen, TX: DLM Teaching Resources.

Woods, M. L., & Moe, A. J. (1985). *Analytic reading inventory* (3rd ed.). Columbus, OH: Merrill.

SUGGESTED READINGS

Askov, E. N., & Otto, W. (1985). *Meeting the challenge: Corrective reading instruction in the classroom*. Columbus, OH: Merrill.

Carnine, D., & Silbert, J. (1979). *Direct instructional reading*. Columbus, OH: Merrill.

Ekwall, E. E., & Shanker, J. L. (1983). *Diagnosis and remediation of the disabled reader* (2nd ed.). Boston: Allyn and Bacon.

May, F. B. (1986). *Reading as communication: An interactive approach* (2nd ed.). Columbus, OH: Merrill.

Otto, W., Peters, C. W., & Peters, N. (1977). *Reading problems: A multidisciplinary perspective*. Reading, MA: Addison-Wesley.

Russell, D. H., Karp, E., & Mueser, A. M. (1981). *Reading aids through the grades* (4th ed.). New York: Teachers College Press.

Smith, C. B., & Elliot, P. G. (1986). *Reading activities for middle and secondary schools: A handbook for teachers*. New York: Teachers College Press.

Strickland, D. S., Feeley, J., & Wepner, S. (1987). *Using computers in the teaching of reading*. New York: Teachers College Press.

Wilson, R. M., & Cleland, C. J. (1985). *Diagnostic and remedial reading for classroom and clinic* (5th ed.). Columbus, OH: Merrill.

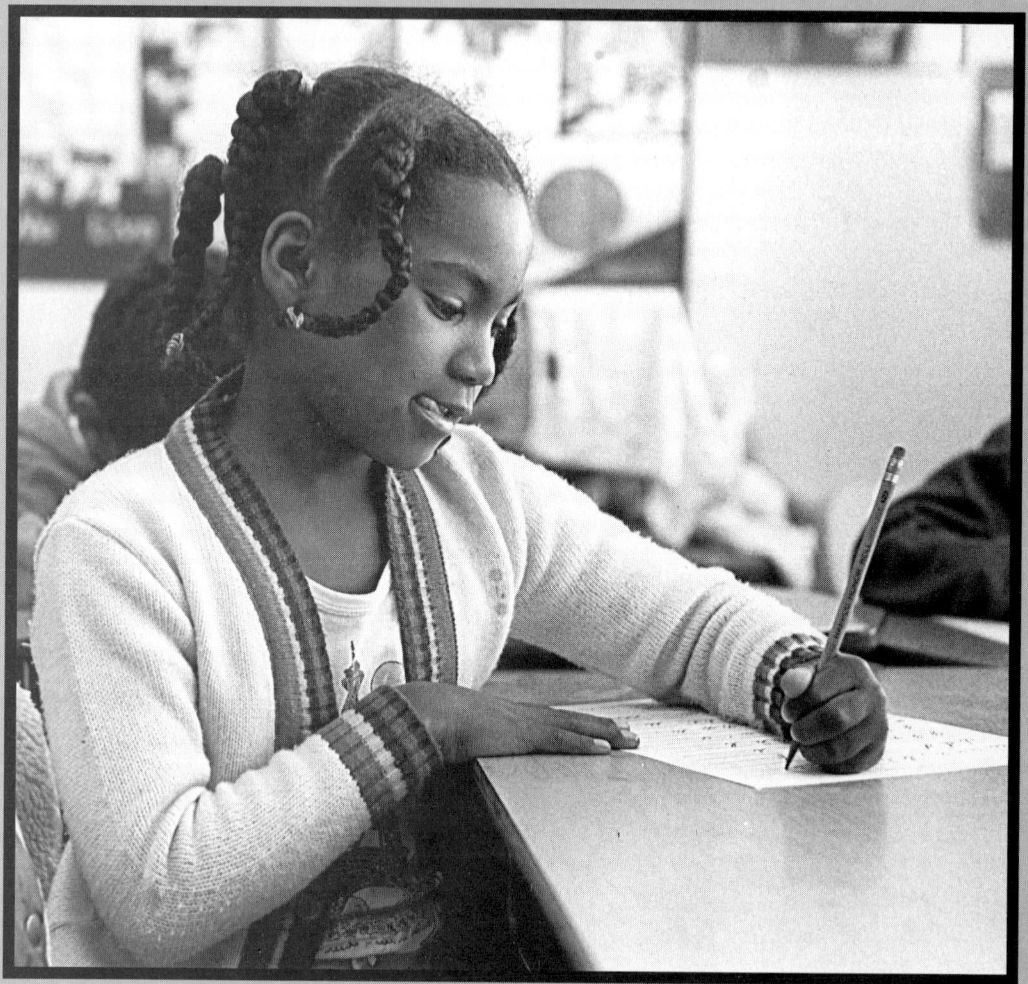

12

Methods for Teaching Written Language: Spelling, Handwriting, and Written Expression

THREE COMPLEX TASKS within the domain of written language are spelling, handwriting, and written expression. They are alike in that each is a facet of expressive language. They differ in the nature and levels of processing and the cognitive demands on the individual. Spelling calls upon auditory and visual sequential memory and the application of rules to formulate words with rigidly prescribed sequences of letters. Handwriting requires visual-spacial organizational ability integrated with fine motor control. Written expression makes demands on the highest levels of cognitive processing and requires the organization of many skills in what is always a creative activity.

Spelling

Learning speaking, handwriting, reading, or written expression is recognized as developmental. Less than optimal performance is accepted with the recognition that improvement will occur with maturation, continued instruction, and practice. Although students may develop the ability to spell longer and more complex words, less-than-accurate spelling of any word is not viewed as a stage in development; it is seen as wrong. Further, while regional dialects and idiomatic expressions are acceptable in speaking or writing, no such allowances are made in spelling. With few exceptions, only a single sequence of letters is correct. Thus, spelling requires an immediate exactness that is not expected in other language arts subjects. Teaching students to meet these demands in spelling is as challenging as teaching other language skills.

Spelling is related to all language arts but more closely with reading. Both skills are needed in all curriculum areas. Lerner (1981) suggests that poor readers are almost always poor spellers, but there is no guarantee that good readers will be good spellers. Mercer and Mercer (1985) conclude that spelling a word is more difficult than reading a word. Reading is a decoding skill in which the stimulus word is present to the senses. Spelling, on the other hand, is a "supply" activity in which the student must generate the letters and sequence for presentation.

Importance of Spelling

Spelling has always "played second fiddle" to reading in the school curriculum. It is often considered uninteresting to teach and laborious to learn. Yet it is a vital element in language. The individual's mastery, or lack of it, is immediately obvious in all forms of written expression. In virtually every segment of our society, some form of written expression is necessary. Although many business forms, including employment applications, often do not require the individuals to reveal their ability with the grammar system, they do require short written responses that demonstrate spelling ability and that set the stage for evaluation by others.

Attitudes

Students who have been unsuccessful in spelling often develop negative attitudes and sometimes become convinced that they cannot learn to spell. If this attitude is shared by teachers or parents, continued difficulties can be expected. Teachers set the tone for successful instruction and must instill the belief in students that learning to spell is possible. They must also provide the techniques and direction that enable students to spell words and allow sufficient time to practice the techniques presented. To improve attitudes and motivation, Petty (1966, p. 3) recommends "(1) selecting genuinely useful words; (2) limiting study to those words which tests have shown the pupils unable to spell; (3) fostering definite and effective study habits; (4) showing pupils that they are achieving and progressing; and (5) using materials which have interest appeal." When students realize that the responsibility to learn to spell is shared, attitudes frequently improve, and the first steps toward spelling achievement can be made.

Readiness

Reading readiness is a familiar concept. Although the readiness factors necessary for beginning reading instruction apply to spelling as well, spelling requires a few, rather specific entry abilities. These include

- Adequate auditory and visual acuity
- Adequate auditory and visual perception, especially discrimination
- Knowledge of the sounds of the letters, individually and in combination
- Ability to read and pronounce the words to be spelled
- Knowledge of the meanings of the words to be spelled
- Ability to write the letters and the words to be spelled

Beyond the awareness of the importance of spelling, the development of positive attitudes, and attainment of these readiness skills, students' success often depends on instructional abilities of the teachers.

Teaching Methods

Teachers are familiar with the concept of word attack skills in reading. These skills provide students with specific techniques for decoding unfamiliar words and are necessary because students cannot be taught every word they will ever encounter. A similar situation exists with spelling, and so instruction can be thought of as providing "spelling attack skills." These include the two major approaches in teaching spelling, phonics and rules, and several additional skills including rote memory, mnemonic devices, structural analysis, and configuration clues.

Phonics The major approach in the teaching of spelling is phonics. In reading, students are presented with a visual sequence of letters for each word. They must determine the appropriate sequence of sounds to match those letters. In spelling, they are presented with a sequence of sounds and sound patterns and must provide a correct written sequence of letters. Instruction includes a continuing review of basic phonics principles, the development of listening and pronunciation skills, and directions to "sound out," or orally break down the word into smaller sounds and sound combinations, for example, syllables and blends. For each sound or sound combination, students identify a letter or letter-combination equivalent. Having learned this phoneme–grapheme match, students can generalize to new regular words.

The difficulty with this approach is the irregularity of English orthography, and a debate has continued as to how many regular or irregular words there are in our language. The most extensive research in providing an answer was made by Hanna, Hodges, and Hanna (1971), who executed a computer analysis of over 17,000 words. It was determined that nearly one-half (49.8 percent) of these words were regular and could be spelled through application of phonics principles. A substantial additional number could be spelled by the application of a few rules.

Instruction Based on Rules Most spelling programs are not restricted to the application of basic phonics principles alone but in combination with the rule approach. Hardly an individual exists who does not know "Write *i* before *e*, except after *c*." However, there are a number of rules that appear to have nearly as many exceptions as applicable situations. Mercer and Mercer (1985) recommend that only those rules that are applicable 75 percent of the time should be taught.

When instruction is based on rules, teach one rule at a time, using examples. Teach exceptions to the rule at the same time. Although it is necessary to memorize a rule, emphasis should be placed on its utility. Provide immediate practice and opportunities for continuing use.

Memorization Many words are learned through memorization. Like sight words in reading, they need not be sounded out; the spelling becomes automatic. Most individuals probably continue to increase the number of such words throughout their school years and beyond.

Some words are memorized, not automatically from use, but purposefully because they are orthographically irregular or contain difficult combinations. High-frequency words such as *again, clothes, women, night,* and *beautiful* fall into this classification.

Some words must be memorized not because they are irregular but because they are commonly mispronounced. *Library* and *February* are perhaps the most classic examples but many others abound including *different, interesting, introduce,* and *surprise*. Memorization also comes into play in the distinction of homonyms. Here the spelling must be associated with word meaning. Examples include *to, too, two; him, hymn;* and *threw, through*.

Mnemonic Devices Techniques for assisting memory can be helpful with specific words. One such procedure is to teach students to force a regular phonetic pronunciation on words not ordinarily so—that is, to say the word as it looks. When confronting the word *business*, they covertly pronounce it emphasizing the *i* or saying the *i* as a long *e*. The word *Wed-nes-day* with each syllable pronounced independently can assist in the spelling of that troublesome word. Some mnemonic devices can be taught to large groups. The members of one class remembered that their attendance was expected at a dance that began at ten o'clock, thus becoming an *at ten dance*. Other devices are highly idiosyncratic, useful only to students who develop them purposefully or by chance.

Structural Analysis Students should be able to read and know the meaning of the words they are expected to spell. Just as a knowledge of root words, prefixes, and suffixes are useful in vocabulary building, they are, in reverse, a means to spell accurately. Students are taught to spell the morphological units along with learning their meanings. Prefixes such as *un-, re-, dis-,* and *mis-,* and suffixes such as *-less, -ment, -able,* and *-ful* can be separated from their bases. Another technique is finding smaller words within larger words (*capillary, gotten, animate*) as is pointing out compound words (*mailman, sunshine, baseball*).

Configuration Clues Nearly everyone has, at one time or another, questioned his or her own spelling by saying "It just doesn't look right." Words do have distinctive shapes. Although not of major use in the teaching of spelling, these can be used for some students in remediation. Configurations of words can be emphasized by placing blocks around each letter or by outlining the entire word (Figure 12.1). "Gimmicky" forms can also be used. Writing words as shown in Figure 12.2 may help some young students to remember the spelling. The "bed" part of Figure 12.2 can also be used in remediating the *b/d* reversal problem.

FIGURE 12.1

Word configurations

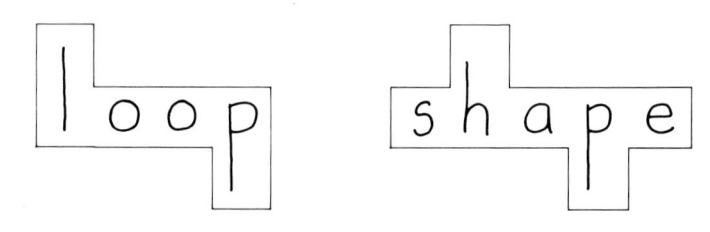

FIGURE 12.2

Association words or clue words

Supplementary Activities

Practice Both immediate and long-term practice can be provided. Students should concentrate on vowel patterns and difficult combinations before writing each new word a few times. Visual-motor feedback and attention to the letter sequence can be a positive learning experience. However, having students copy each word many times is of dubious value; it becomes a busy-work writing activity. Even when the words copied are those missed on a pretest, learning is not necessarily enhanced, and the exercise assumes an aspect of punishment. Each spelling word should be written in a sentence that clearly demonstrates the students' knowledge of the word meaning. They can be asked to write sentences that incorporate as many of the spelling words as possible. Having students read their often "tortuous" and contrived sentences, or having a selection written on the chalkboard, can add a humorous element to study. Lessons in other subjects can be arranged to use the current spelling words. Emphasis can be placed on spelling them correctly on assignments and in tests.

Use of the Dictionary The dictionary can be a valuable aid in spelling but is not a substitute for basic instruction. It is far less useful in the initial stages of learning to spell but becomes more important in the middle grades. Here the dictionary serves as an aid in verification of spelling for irregular words (*league, absence, enough*). It can also be used when rules or their applications have been forgotten or confused (*swiming* or *swimming*?) and with difficult-to-remember combinations (*-ible* or *-able*?). If students have no idea of the spelling of a word, they cannot look it up in the dictionary. More mature spellers, who have had instruction, usually can guess potential spellings.

Further, instruction and practice may be provided by encouraging students to respond with alternative spellings to orally stated words (*tel -a, -e, -i, -o, -u? vision*). Part of such instruction will consist of teaching students to listen carefully to their own pronunciation of the word.

Games Although certainly not a principal method of instruction, spelling games can motivate and provide practice. The possibility of teacher-made games is almost unlimited. They include classroom adaptations of popular television game shows, board games, crossword puzzles, spelling lotto, anagrams, matching games, and hangman. Other suggestions may be found in Green and Petty (1975), Mercer and Mercer (1985), Arena (1968), and Barbe, Francis, and Braun (1985). A number of commercial games can also be used. These include *Scrabble* (Selchow and Righter), *Spill and Spell* (Parker Brothers), *Probe* (Parker Brothers), *Rule-ette* (Educators Publishing Service), *Crossword Puzzles* (Ideal), *Spello* (Ideal), and *Word Games* (C. Z. Peck).

Computers Students enjoy practicing word lists or playing spelling games on the computer. Many software programs are available at various grade levels.

Spelling and Secondary Students

When ninth grade English students demonstrate deficiencies in spelling, teachers have several alternatives. Teachers can choose other individual means to get students on grade level. They include using word frequency lists or word banks in which words in a subject area are learned together. Examples are words relating to nutrition—calcium, minerals, iron, and vitamins. Words to be learned may be related to English concepts such as a controlled vocabulary selection with several words ending in *er*, content area reading with consonant–vowel–consonant words, or use of word families.

A tutor can instruct students using a specific program such as the *Michigan Programmed Spelling Series* (Ann Arbor Publishers). It is individualized to meet student needs from primary grades through college. The program can be used individually, in small groups, with students in special education, or with an entire class. In the *Michigan Programmed Spelling Series,* the word *occurrence* is presented with similar words such as *currently, occurs, occupancy,* and *currency.* The meaning of the word and use in a sentence is taught at the same time. The emphasis on spelling rules as presented in *Spelling Mastery* (Dixon, R., Englemann, S., Meier, M., Steely, D., & Wells, T., 1980, 1981) is also effective for older students with memory difficulties.

Assessment

A careful assessment of spelling difficulties must precede intervention and continue throughout instruction and remediation. Spelling can be assessed formally or informally.

Formal Assessment The tasks on formal spelling tests are commonly limited to the students' responding in writing to a dictated word list or a proofreading activity. Dictating a list of words for students to write is a preferable procedure; it is more like the task of everyday spelling. Further, some exceptional students and individual learners find proofreading a particularly difficult task. Those who are impulsive may point to a word without analyzing it. Those with auditory or visual processing interferences may be confused by the phonetically logical but incorrect spelling of irregular words or by the visual similarities of the words. Thus, students' ability to spell is not assessed accurately.

Group achievement tests, which are administered routinely, usually contain a subtest on spelling. Such tests include the *California Achievement Tests, Forms C and D* (CTB/McGraw-Hill, 1978), the *Metropolitan Achievement Tests*: *5th Edition—Survey Battery* (Balow, Farr, Hogan, & Prescott, 1978), the *Metropolitan Language Instructional Tests* (Balow, Farr, Hogan, & Prescott, 1978), the *Stanford Achievement Test*: *7th Edition* (Gardner, Rudman, Karlsen, & Merwin, 1982), and the *Stanford Test of Academic Skills, 2nd Edition* (TASK) (Gardner, Callis, Merwin, & Rudman, 1982).

Two individually administered achievement tests commonly used with exceptional students also have spelling subtests. The *Wide Range Achievement Test—*

Revised (Jastak & Wilkinson, 1984) has a dictated word list at two levels. The *Peabody Individual Achievement Test* (Dunn & Markwardt, 1970) has a proofreading task in which students select the correctly spelled word from a set of four. A criterion-referenced test is included in the *Comprehensive Inventory of Basic Skills* (Brigance, 1983).

Tests designed to assess spelling ability exclusively include the *Diagnostic Spelling Test* (Kottmeyer, 1970), *Spellmaster: Spelling, Testing, and Evaluation* (Cohen & Abrams, 1974), and *The Test of Written Spelling* (Larsen & Hammill, 1986). The latter appears to be a well-researched instrument standardized on over 3800 students. Resulting scores include a spelling age, grade level equivalents, and a spelling quotient.

Often standardized tests are based on common spelling errors and are thus reported to be diagnostic instruments. However, the selection of words may not be used in the local curriculum or in the chosen reading series. Therefore, students are tested on unfamiliar words. Each kind of error is usually represented by a single word on the list. Any student may inadvertently make an error on a word. This error may be uncharacteristic of his or her general spelling competence but becomes the focus of remedial effort because it was missed on the test. It is preferable to combine formal and informal assessment, not only using available tests but also observing and noting spelling errors in routine writing.

Informal Assessment

An Informal Spelling Inventory Just as an informal reading inventory can be constructed so can an Informal Spelling Inventory (ISI) be made. Temple and Gillet (1984) give instructions for creating, using, and interpreting an ISI. Although such instruments take time to make and refine, teachers then have a familiar, curriculum-centered set of informal tests.

Word Lists Informal spelling tests and word lists can be found in the professional literature. They are presented in journal articles and textbooks and are often included as supplementary material with basal reading series. Teachers should examine these carefully before using, to determine their appropriateness to the local curriculum.

Error Analysis Ganschow (1984) and others recommend that teachers analyze patterns of errors. Teachers observe written spelling on presented word lists and in nonspelling assignments. They note consistencies in misspellings and plan a teaching program accordingly. Do students spell phonetically and thus have difficulty with words which are irregular? Are some common spelling rules apparently unused? Is there difficulty with special vowel sounds or consonant combinations? Are letters omitted that give some indication of auditory or perceptual problems? Does the spelling represent the phonetic characteristics of nonstandard English speech patterns? Are similarly sounding letters substituted for each other, especially at the beginning or end of words? Are letters transposed? Do most spelling errors occur in the so-called demons or are they generally evident? Do students consistently make errors in words requiring the changing of *y* to *i* and adding *es* or on the doubling of consonants preceding the addition of a suffix? The primary advantage of error analysis is that it leads directly to remediation of difficulties encountered (Figure 12.3).

FIGURE 12.3

Informal spelling assessment and remedial instruction

Informal spelling assessment and remedial instruction

The teacher has given a spelling test of ten words. Below are some of the responses. In the second column are possible difficulties and in the third column potential interventions should observation of the students' other spelling and writing errors indicate these to be consistent.

---

1. handle: The bucket has a broken <u>handle</u>.

Tom

Pupil Response:	Possible Difficulty:	Potential Remediation:
handel	1. Spells phonetically	1. Child taught to rehearse aloud (later silently)
Also watch for: apple, table, maple	2. Common transposition of end letters often due to not learning well initially	2. Gives rhythm to letter sequence; pause before last two letters; then vocal emphasis of those: hand <u>LE</u>
		3. Teach child to apply when encountering new words with this combination
		4. Practice saying han-dl-eee

---

2. while: We sang <u>while</u> we marched.

Lynn

Pupil response	Possible Difficulty	Potential Remediation:
wile	1. Child attends to common mispronunciation of such words then spells phonetically	1. Teach similar words together, e.g., while white, whine
Also watch for: when, where, which, what		2. Emphasize correct pronunciation, teaching child to *listen* to self "blowing" initial syllable

---

3. moving: They watched the leaves <u>moving</u> in the wind.

Mike

Pupil Response:	Possible Difficulty:	Potential Remediation:
moveing	1. Student did not learn E rule	1. Overlearning rule through intense teaching, writing out, restating, extensive practice, combined with
Also watch for: taking, saving, coming	2. Inattention to rule during routine spelling	2. Visual approach making direct comparisons of correct and incorrect spelling of many words with this potential error

Teaching Procedures for Exceptional Learners

It is not sufficient to analyze only procedures for instruction when planning remedial programs for students who have demonstrated deficits in the skills of spelling. Learning styles, modality preferences, attitudes, reading level, and patterns of errors revealed by individual assessment all must be taken into consideration. Readiness factors and phonics skills should be assessed for all students through the upper grades. Each remedial program will need to be carefully planned, and the sequence of steps and a hierarchy of short-term goals specified. Most frequently, such instruction will be on an individual basis but where similar needs exist, small-group instruction may be used.

Selection of Words It may be necessary to depart from commercial lists in the selection of words for the program. High-utility words may be selected on the basis of reading level rather than grade level.

Students must be able to read each word they are expected to spell. With each new group of spelling words, they must read each word aloud and give its meaning. Later, words should be used in sentences, orally or in written form. Words on the list should be grouped according to spelling pattern:

batch	red	bail	boat	nation	candle	vote
rabbit	bed	mail	coat	location	little	rate
	fed	sail	goat			
		tail				

They may also be selected to stress the application of a phonics principle or rule.

Test–Study Sequence Some spelling instruction consists of the presentation of a list for study in preparation for a later examination—the study–test method. An alternative procedure is the administration of a pretest. Students then learn the words missed—the test–study–test method. Stephens, Hartman, and Lucas (1982) note the superiority of the latter approach. However, younger students may not profit from pretests because they have limited experience in spelling. Older students are often motivated when they realize they do know how to spell some of the words before the lesson is taught. Teaching only the words missed on a pretest prevents wasted instruction and study time and permits students to reach grade level sooner.

Structured Study and Learning Procedures Exceptional learners may need a structured and consistent procedure to study and learn new words. Some of the techniques presented can be formalized into steps that students can use as an independent procedure for learning word lists. Each student is presented with a laminated card outlining the steps to be followed. They are expected to do each step for each of the three to five words assigned daily. Figure 12.4 shows such a card for younger students. A color system is incorporated for vowel sounds and patterns. Figure 12.5 illustrates a card applicable for intermediate level students who are taught to divide words into syllables or morphographs.

FIGURE 12.4

Learning How to Spell (for younger students)

1. Read each word.
2. Write each word according to spelling pattern. Color vowel pattern.
3. One word at a time, say word out loud.
4. Look and spell three times.
5. Close eyes and spell.
6. Write without looking.
7. Check.
8. Right? Go to next word.
9. Wrong? Go back to number 3.
10. Repeat rules.

Multisensory Approaches For some students instruction may begin with a visual approach. Color coding or individual word lists can be used to emphasize similarities among words. Vowel sounds that are alike can be coded in one color as can consonant combinations. The similarities among rhyming words such as vac<u>ation</u> and loc<u>ation</u> can be accentuated by underlining. Difficult combinations such as the exceptions to rules can be circled for increased attention.

Other students may need an auditory program. Individuals who learn auditorily sometimes shut their eyes when spelling orally. They literally prevent visual input from distracting their sounding out the words in their heads. Yet spelling is not restricted to either modality but requires both visual and auditory skills. Therefore, a multisensory approach may be needed with many students. Both the Fernald (1943) and the Gillingham–Stillman (1970) programs have components in spelling instruction and reading.

FIGURE 12.5

Learning How To Spell (for older students)

1. Read each word.
2. Write each word according to spelling pattern or divide into syllables.
3. One word at a time, say out loud the way it looks—e.g., <u>to get her</u>.
4. Look at and spell out loud three times slowly.
5. Close eyes and spell.
6. Write without looking at word.
7. Check.
8. Right? Go to next word.
9. Wrong? Go back to number 3.
10. Repeat.

The tactile approach should not be overlooked for students who cannot use their visual or auditory modalities effectively. Letters may be traced on the chalkboard with large motions or on a smaller scale in sand or grain, or on a slate. Students say the letters orally and silently as they trace. Rhythm plays an important part in spelling, and some students profit from clapping a rhythmical pattern as they say each letter aloud. Audiovisual aids including a tachistoscope, language master, typewriter, or computer provide individual instruction.

Adjusting to Individual Differences   Instructional procedures may need to be altered. Accommodations may include shortened word lists, presenting a few words each day grouped according to spelling pattern, individualized selection of words from the total grade level word list, alteration in the rapidity of presentation, sufficient time to practice, and identification of intermediate competency levels. When a workbook is used, assignments may need to be reduced, and parts of the lesson selected on the basis of task demand. If students have handwriting problems they may be allowed to respond orally or, if they do take a quiz in writing, they should not be penalized for poor handwriting but graded solely on their spelling competence. It is recognized that such program modifications are intermediate steps to be used for students with serious learning problems. The modifications must be discontinued as students improve confidence and competence.

ADJUSTING SPELLING PROGRAMS TO ACCOMMODATE STUDENTS WITH DISABILITIES

Sam is blind and is in Miss Xavier's English class. Jerry is severely hearing impaired and is in Mrs. Wahl's class. Both students are in sixth grade and deficient in spelling skills. Mrs. Kenston was assigned to provide support to the two teachers. She knew that spelling is dependent on auditory sequential and visual sequential memory skills.

Thus, she developed a program based on auditory sequencing for Sam. She recorded the spelling words on a cassette, emphasizing syllables and sequences of letters. Sam used the cassettes at a listening center with earphones in the back of the room while the rest of the class had spelling activities. The program allowed Sam to dictate into the machine and replay his spelling for comparison to the model and for reauditorization.

In Mrs. Wahl's room, Mrs. Kenston employed a computer spelling program that presented successive words on the monitor, emphasizing the visual sequences of letters and visual configurations. To place his own words on the monitor to match those on the program, Jerry needed to watch the computer keyboard, another visual sequential task.

Spelling in the Content Areas

The ultimate goal of spelling instruction is to permit students to spell accurately in written documents, letters, and school assignments in the content areas. Therefore, it is important to expect correct spelling in other subjects. However, if students are successful in producing quality work toward the goals stated in the assignments, teachers must not compromise this success and learning by reducing grades on papers because of spelling errors. Separate grades for spelling and mechanics can be given. On final draft manuscripts for which spelling, punctuation, and other standards have been specified, students are graded.

Summary

Spelling is a unique skill that, for correct performance, requires conformity to prescribed sequences of letters rather than creativity. Readiness for spelling includes the developmental intactness of visual and auditory acuity and perception, knowledge of sounds of letters, memory skills, and the ability to read the words to be spelled. Success in learning is also related to students' and teachers' positive attitudes toward the subject and skill in instruction.

Teaching methods routinely include the use of phonics, an emphasis on sound–letter sequence relationships, and the learning of rules to enable spelling of irregular words. Memorization, mnemonic devices, structural analysis, and configuration clues are also employed. For exceptional learners it may be necessary to select words on the basis of reading level rather than grade placement, to present shorter word lists, to group words on the basis of spelling patterns, and to use multisensory techniques. Providing them with a prestructured sequence of activities for learning, study, and practice is a vital element in spelling instruction for exceptional students and individual learners.

Assessment is accomplished through formal tests or informal error analysis. In either case, continued monitoring beyond the assessment procedures and the routine use of spelling skills in the content area are necessary.

Handwriting

Otto and Smith (1980, p. 396) describe handwriting as a "tool of personal communication." It is an element of the individual's expressive language system, which develops after the initiation of skills in listening, speaking, and reading. It is advantageous if students have already developed good reading skills but these are not necessarily prerequisites for learning to write. As with all learning, teaching handwriting must be individualized. Each student manifests a pattern of developing skills and limiting deficits that need attention. Teacher attitude toward positive achievement rather than laborious and precise practice can be instrumental in creating a good attitude and rapid acquisition of fundamental skills.

Goals in Handwriting

The ultimate goal of handwriting is communication. An enabling goal toward that end is legibility. Hackney, Myers, and Zaner Bloser (1969, p. viii) list elements of legible handwriting as:

1. Letter forms that conform to those universally recognized by all, both lower-case and upper-case alphabets.
2. Correct size relationships between letters—proportion.

3. Vertical letter forms for manuscript writing. A uniform and readable slant for cursive writing.
4. Regularity of spacing between letters, words, and sentences.
5. Alignment, i.e., writing on the baseline and keeping the same size even in height.
6. Smoothness and evenness in color and line quality.
7. Fluency—uniform speed, not too fast or too slow.

— (Reprinted from C. S. Hackney, E. H. Myers, and P. Zaner Bloser. *Off We Go: Transition and New Universe*, viii. Copyright 1969 by Zaner-Bloser.)

Handwriting is a complex visual-motor activity that is affected by a number of intraindividual and environmental factors. Handwriting can be influenced by visual-spacial organization, fine motor control, eye–hand coordination, and visual memory as well as by quality of instruction.

Manuscript, or printing, is almost universally the first writing process taught, although some authors suggest advantages for beginning with cursive (Early, Nelson, Kleber, Treegoob, Huffman, & Cass, 1976; Kaufman & Biren, 1979). Cursive, or script, is taught after students have mastered manuscript and is commonly introduced in the middle or at the end of second grade. It is sometimes begun in third grade.

Readiness for Manuscript

Ideally, students should have developed some basic learning behaviors prior to receiving instruction in handwriting. They need to be able to receive instruction, follow directions, translate oral directions into motor activity, and sustain independent practice. Other competencies include the establishment of left-right progression, visual discrimination, retention of visual images, visual sequential memory, eye–hand coordination, refinement of fine motor skills and control, and form copying. *Basic Schools Skills Inventory—Diagnostic* (Hammill & Leigh, 1983) includes a handwriting readiness scale based on ten criteria applicable to children between four and six years of age.

Handedness

Dominance is the consistent use of a preferred hand, ear, eye, or foot. Many individuals have a preferred side, being either right dominant or left dominant, but it is not unusual for individuals to have different patterns of dominance—for example, right-eared, left-eyed, left-handed, and right-footed. Such patterns have been referred to as "cross dominance" or "mixed dominance." Although some authors believe that cross dominance is indicative of possible learning problems, research does not support this conclusion. Lerner (1976) reported that there was little relationship between mixed dominance and reading problems.

With cross or mixed dominance, the individual uses a preferred hand *consistently* for the same tasks. This is not the same as confused dominance in which students switch back and forth. Whereas some have clearly established a hand preference by the age of six, others may not establish handedness until later. Confused dominance may be demonstrated by students who are developmentally delayed when they confront school tasks that require the consistent use of one hand. This difficulty is not necessarily indicative of a pervasive learning problem.

Teachers who are concerned about handedness, particularly in regard to the initiation of the teaching of handwriting, observe students in a number of situations to note hand preference. Parents can be helpful by relating information from a physician on dominance or by telling teachers which hand is used. Handedness is probably a combination of heredity and cultural influence. Although there is no guarantee that students will prefer the same hand as the parents, the tendency is in that direction (Obrzut & Boliek, 1986). Dominance can also be established through formal tests such as the *Harris Test of Lateral Dominance* (Harris, 1958).

In working with students, it is important not to make an issue of their failure to have established dominance. Nor should left-handed students be forced to use their right hands. Teachers can simply place the chalk or pencil on the side of apparent dominance. Practice in handwriting will also provide exercise that will reinforce the establishment of handedness.

BOX 12.1

Informal Procedures for Determining Handedness

Kindergarten and first grade teachers may be unsure of which hand students prefer when observation indicates switching from one to the other. The following techniques may be used to help identify the preferred hand:

- Make a systematic observation, keeping a tally to indicate which hand is used consistently for each kind of task.
- Ask the parents which hand they use.
- Ask the parents which hand the student seems to favor at home.
- Use a beanbag or other tossing game. Observe which hand is first to pick up and then throw the object.
- Play a game of "I Spy." Place the cardboard tube from a roll of paper towels in the center of the table, directly in line with the middle of the student's body. Ask the student to pick it up and look at you with one eye. Note the hand used to pick up the tube and then note the preferred eye.
- Consistently hand the student objects at the midline to note which hand moves out to receive them.

Teaching Manuscript

Approaches to teaching manuscript vary. Some are process-oriented, concerned with the development of laterality, directionality, and fine motor skills. Others are product-oriented, emphasizing the shapes and sizes of letters, spacing, and other orthographic characteristics. There are variations and combinations of these approaches. More recently, handwriting has been task analyzed by many authors (for example, Faas,

1980). In manuscript instruction teachers are concerned with time for instruction, position, paper, pencil, and specific instructional activities.

Time for Instruction To provide consistency, short daily lessons should be scheduled. Ten to fifteen minutes of group instruction followed by a seat assignment for practice is usually sufficient.

Position Handwriting manuals and practitioners in the field provide generally similar recommendations on body, paper, and pencil-holding positions. Students are seated with both feet on the floor and with the hips against the back of the chair. Both forearms are placed on the desk or table at a comfortable angle with both elbows extended off the table. The height of the desk should provide students with optimal comfort in writing and for clear visibility. The recommended distance between the eyes and paper is about sixteen inches.

For right-handed students, the paper should be directly in front of them but slanted to the left so that the vertical edges of the paper are parallel with the forearm of the writing hand as it lies on the desk. For the left-handed students, the paper should be slanted in the opposite direction. It is commonly recommended that the nondominant hand be placed at the top of the paper.

The pencil or other writing instrument is held in the dominant hand between the thumb and the index finger with these placed about an inch above the writing point. The pencil rests on the curved middle finger and with the eraser end pointing toward the shoulder of the writing hand. The pencil grip must be relaxed although held tightly enough for control. Some teachers suggest that students "hang loose," shaking the hand with the pencil in it prior to beginning to write. Applying too much pressure results in jerky lines and cramped hands. If there is an imprint on the reverse side of the writing paper, the pencil is being held too tightly.

Some students may try to anchor the writing hand in one or a few positions across the page and write in an arc around the hand. Instead, they should be taught to move the hand steadily across the paper as they write. This provides a parallel slant to the letters as well as being more comfortable.

Paper As students move from the chalkboard to writing on paper, the kind of paper selected is important. Paper with a coarse grain may augment tactile feedback. Colored lines may allow some students to learn easily while others use combinations of solid and dashed lines to indicate letter height. Students with fine motor difficulties may use paper on which the lines are raised, such as that used to teach students with visual handicaps. Some paper also has perpendicular lines to assist in learning proper spacing.

Pencil In beginning writing instruction, most students use normal-sized pencils without difficulty. For students with problems in achieving the proper grip, a Hoyle Gripper (R. & D. Ames, Co.), a triangular device that slides over a pencil, can be used.

Specific Instructional Activities Manuscript techniques may include the following:

- Concentrate on one skill at a time—formation of shapes or letters, slant, spacing, size, or speed. The latter two are not emphasized at first; activities

with oversized letters and shapes on the chalkboard or paper may develop control.
- Demonstrate at students' eye level at the chalkboard. They may draw in the air with their fingers learning one or two letters at a time.
- Trace with fingers, then in the writing book or on worksheets, onionskin paper, or transparencies.
- Students may be taught to verbalize the shape and direction of the letters as they learn them.
- Copy from the chalkboard onto the paper.
- Auditory equivalents are not stressed initially. This allows concentration on the motor aspects of writing.
- Teachers restate that letters are made up of circles, parts of circles, vertical lines, and slanted lines and encourage accurate reproduction as students progress.
- As competence is gained, grapheme–phoneme match is introduced. Students verbalize the letter names and words as they are copied or written.
- Individual instruction is vital. Care must be taken to monitor accuracy and prevent students from initially forming letters or words inaccurately.

Readiness for Cursive

Readiness cannot be dictated by grade level but is relative to the individual. Usually, class instruction in cursive begins in the middle of the second grade to the middle of the third grade, depending upon local curriculum preferences. It is probable that more than half the class will have mastered manuscript skills before cursive is introduced.

Prior to beginning cursive writing, students are expected to mature in visual-spacial organization sufficiently to allow them to write within acceptable dimensions, to form manuscript letters, to perform independently, to maintain a continuous flow of line across the page, and to grip the pencil correctly and automatically.

Teaching Cursive Two basic tasks need to be addressed. First is the formation of letters, especially those that are significantly different from their manuscript forms. Second is the connection between letters.

Techniques for teaching cursive writing are the same as for manuscript writing. In addition, the following activities are suggested:

- Practice rhythmic exercises, scribbling, and circle drawing in both clockwise and counterclockwise directions.
- Trace and copy in the air, on the chalkboard, and then on paper.
- Teach lowercase letters first—those that have initial strokes that move away from the body.
- Use color coding—a green dot placed on the model can indicate the point at which the letter is to be initiated, and a red dot can indicate the termination of a letter.
- Practice dot-to-dot letters with arrows to demonstrate accuracy and to provide practice in tracing (see Figure 12.6).
- Larson (1968) identifies beginning letters and derived letters and suggests the former be taught first. Beginning letters include *m n t i u w r s l e a c d o*.

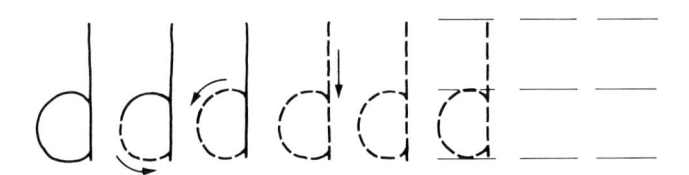

FIGURE 12.6

Letter formation

Derived letters are *x z v j p h b k f g p*. The sequence for instruction for the letters in each group should be as indicated.

Left-Handed Students In the past left-handedness was seen as evidence of neurological difficulties, and attempts were often made to change hand dominance from left to right. This practice is no longer acceptable; nor does left-handedness necessarily mean that students have a learning disability or other problems that would hinder learning. They should be allowed to use whichever hand they prefer.

It is vital that teachers accept responsibility for teaching the left-handed students. It is recommended that they sit together and be instructed separately from right-handed students. For left-handed students, the paper should be placed in the direction opposite that of right-handed writers as described. Left-handed students should be taught to write with hands under the line of script rather than hooked around it. Pencils are parallel to the forearm with the erasers pointing toward the writers. Wallace and Kauffman (1978) suggest that the hooking characteristics of left-handed writers may be helped by practice using brushes, chalk, and markers. They further suggest that constant reinforcement be given for holding writing instruments in the correct position. Desks and scissors designed for left-handed persons should be used.

Reversals Students first learning to write often form letters backward. Contrary to some popular beliefs, reversals are not necessarily a sign of learning disability or neurological handicap. They are quite common in primary age students although the problem should have corrected itself by the end of second grade. Persistent reversals by older students should receive intervention.

How reversals are remedied often depends on teacher orientation. Some would resort to extensive perceptual-motor training activities, basing their techniques on the theory that reversals have their origin in delays in the development of laterality. Others would attack the problem directly. Proposed here is an integration of the two approaches. Emphasis should be placed on perceptual-motor, tactile, and kinesthetic practice of specific letter reversals. In addition, students can trace

- On felt letters of sandpaper without a writing instrument.
- Large letters at the chalkboard using large muscle movements with teachers holding the students' hands to initially form the letters.
- With a grease pencil on clear plastic.
- Letters that have been color-coded or marked with arrows.

Teachers monitor work and provide reinforcement for correctly formed letters. Letters that are easily confused should be taught separately with several days intervening and mastery of one letter achieved before the next is introduced.

Teaching Handwriting to Exceptional Learners

Students with learning disabilities frequently have developmental delays in the basic visual-perceptual and fine motor skills needed in handwriting and they characteristically demonstrate poor handwriting and disorganized papers. Other exceptional students may also lack adequately developed motor coordination to enable them to learn handwriting skills with ease. They need additional time and practice on developmental skills. Handwriting instruction, however, should not be delayed until these skills have been developed or remediated. Some students exhibit fine motor control difficulties through the elementary grades and into the middle or junior high school. Further, the very exercises that comprise readiness skills for manuscript and cursive writing can in themselves be remediation for fine motor abilities.

Madison (1970) provides recommendations for helping exceptional learners. For students who are kinesthetic learners, she recommends making patterns of the letters in the air with the eyes closed. Letters should be traced on the palm of the nondominant hand. Auditory learners should be taught to verbalize each letter and word whereas visual learners have an advantage in handwriting because they can frequently copy from observation. Madison and others have noted that some exceptional students profit from a multisensory approach.

For students with body-image problems, instruction may need to begin with large motor exercises. Letters and shapes can be outlined on the floor with masking tape or a jump rope. With the latter, letter shapes can be changed easily. Students literally walk around such models as a step prior to scribbling or tracing on the chalkboard.

Other techniques for exceptional learners include

- Shaping letters with yarn or playdough.
- Forming large letters in a pan of grain.
- Tracing shapes with the finger on sandpaper, felt, raised letters, plastic templates, or commercial transparency materials.
- Tracing activities at the chalkboard using white chalk over the teacher's model in colored chalk, with colors representing different lines, strokes, and so forth.
- Using individual small slates, which are an excellent transition from upright chalkboard writing to the horizontal plane of the desk.
- Using dot-to-dot worksheets.
- Cutting a horizontal "window" in a piece of tagboard; students write across the page in the window; then the sheet is moved down with each new line.
- Increasing speed through encouragement after students have learned correct formation through slow and careful writing.
- Providing immediate feedback when students are learning how to form letters; monitoring prevents incorrect formation being learned or practiced.
- Connecting letters only after all the letters have been learned separately.
- Pointing out similarities between manuscript and cursive letters.

Many of these activities emphasize the tactile and kinesthetic aspects of writing. Often this modality, which teachers may use to make handwriting a successful experience, is a strength to exceptional learners. Regular teachers should be encouraged to give students full credit for academic successes in the regular room without penalty for handwriting skills that may be developing slowly.

Assessment

Handwriting is less easily assessed than other subjects in the academic curriculum. More objective than the teachers' subjective judgments are analyses of handwriting errors. Several authors provide lists of criteria to guide such observation. Linn (1970, p. 39), for example reports these specific kinds of problems teachers might observe

> ... poor construction of letters, such as lines which cross instead of meeting or which meet instead of crossing; corners which turn at irregular angles; lines which gape; poor or irregular letter size (some tall, some short regardless of the size they should be); difficulty with letters which go above the line, below the line, and those which do both; reversals, inversions; poor spacing; poor placement or position on lines or between lines or spaces.

Teachers can also note writing position, pencil grip, eye distance, and other manifestations that may affect accurate and legible writing.

A series of scales for evaluating manuscript in grades one and two and cursive in grades three through eight comprise the *Evaluation Scales* by the Zaner-Bloser Company (1979). Students are evaluated on five elements of handwriting including letter formation, vertical stroke, spacing, alignment and position, and line quality. The *Test of Written Language* (Revised) (TOWL) (Hammill & Larsen, 1983) contains a subtest on handwriting. In contrast to the Zaner-Bloser procedure in which the final product of a standard copied and practiced handwriting sample is judged, the evaluation in the TOWL is of spontaneous writing. Thus, the Zaner-Bloser method assesses students' best work while attending to the task of handwriting. The TOWL assesses typical routine handwriting.

Summary

Handwriting skills developed early constitute the basis for life-long habits in written communication. There are numerous techniques for assisting students, including those who are left-handed, in the accurate production of manuscript and cursive writing and in the reduction of reversals. Teachers' careful instruction, continuous monitoring, and encouragement in good body position, proper pencil grip, and careful formation of letters and words are imperative aspects in the guidance of these early learnings. Handwriting is most commonly assessed through observation, often with the use of a checklist or one of several commercial scales. A few formal standardized instruments are available.

Written Expression

The highest form of language competence is expressive writing. It is the culmination of language development that has its roots in meaningful experience and progresses through listening, oral expression, and reading. It is a complex process requiring the integration of many skills including memory, sequencing, organization, vocabulary, grammar, handwriting, spelling, ideation, and conceptualization. Many students, not only the exceptional or individual learners, encounter problems in one or more of these competencies or in their coordination.

Because written expression is the most complex of all language skills, it may be even more difficult for the many exceptional students who have general language deficits. Skills must be taught with careful planning, deliberate step-by-step instruction and evaluation, and feedback.

Oral and Written Expression

Written language would appear to be simply oral language written down. Such is not the case, however. Although some exceptional students are deficient in both, it is quite common to find others who have adequate facility in oral presentation but not in the written form. The skills of oral expression are learned virtually automatically during the preschool years; written expression is not so readily mastered. Direct instruction and practice are necessary to develop ability in written expression and to foster creativity in exceptional students.

Purposes

The two major purposes of written expression are utility and creativity. Utility includes the writing of letters, notes, descriptions, proposals, reports, and other social and/or business communications. Creative writing includes poetry and prose, which are vehicles of self-expression.

Methods in Written Expression

Readiness A debate among educators exists as to when students should begin writing. Should they be encouraged to write in the early grades, or is mastery of the conventions such as grammar and punctuation a prerequisite? Just as students refine their use of language as they communicate, they can improve language skills as they learn to write. It is the authors' position that exceptional students should be encouraged early to give expressive content to their writing and not delay until the introduction of "composition." Readiness is promoted by providing opportunities to write thoughts and ideas. However, writing should not be forced when students are not ready.

Oral Expressive Foundations for Writing Because writing is directly related to overall language development, it is best supported in a classroom environment that encourages general language development, in which students speak freely and discuss among themselves, and in which teachers reinforce student expression with positive interaction. Students need to be encouraged to report experiences, share feelings, describe pictures, and participate in interviews and dramatic presentations. They can put the meaning of stories read to them in their own words, a vital step toward building comprehension.

Talking about words, their connotative meanings in addition to their denotative meanings, and promoting the creation of similes and metaphors without distracting students by emphasizing the difference between these terms can be productive. Activities such as "How many ways can we describe a _____ (pin, person, peanut)?" can also be effective. Other exercises include organizing, classifying, reordering a set of sentences to tell a story in logical order, and reporting events of a story in sequence.

Language-Experience Approach   The use of LEA is recommended by several authors (Hammill & Poplin, 1982; Mercer & Mercer, 1985) as a transition from oral to written language. In this approach, experiences are reported to the teacher who writes them in the students' own words. This can be accomplished in a large group if students have shared an experience, a field trip, or an assembly program. It can also be used with smaller groups or with individuals. Once the teacher has written the story or report, it is then read aloud. Green and Petty (1975) also suggest that students write dictated materials, sentences, and stories and that they copy lists, letters, notes, and other material.

Process and Product   In recent years there has been a change in emphasis in writing from product, the final form, to process. Tompkins and Friend (1985) identify a "process cycle" as involving prewriting, drafting, editing, and sharing. Others, including Hall (1981), list the elements as prewriting, writing, and postwriting activities.

Prewriting   Prewriting activities include deciding what to write about, thinking and planning, and organizing. One persistent problem is that of "What can I write about?" The usual advice of "Write about what you know" remains valid. However, other topics need to be examined. Cady (1975) presents a list of 145 suggested topics, many of which can be expanded. Other recommendations can be found in Petty and Bowen (1967) and Carlson (1973).

Exceptional students may need to "walk through" the steps in planning to write about the chosen topic. Planning involves deciding on specifics of what to write about. For example, writing about John F. Kennedy is too broad a topic. Students may need to skim references and decide which area will be addressed—early life, education, family, political career, presidency, assassination. Teachers can assist them in organizing materials, choosing which books to use, finding important information, and understanding the information.

Outlining   Although it is a prewriting skill, many students are unable to outline prior to writing. Ideas must be on paper before thoughts can be organized logically. Outlining is meant to be a thinking process that facilitates organization. The initial outline is not a permanent structure to which the final composition must conform but the first of several tentative sequences that may be revised as new material is gathered and the topic is developed.

Writing   The writing phase consists of putting thoughts, ideas, and data conceptualized and organized at the prewriting stage onto paper. The first writing activities for elementary students may be the creation of single sentences. Later sets of sentences and longer passages may be required. Initially, there should be no restrictions on topics chosen, unless they are inappropriate. Emphasis must be given to students' writing—writing something, writing anything, and developing the thinking processes related to that production. Through successive drafts, even if the writing is only a single sentence, teachers help students individually to work through the statement of the message. Another technique is personal dialogue in which teachers guide students toward increasingly improved oral expression of the idea. Then the sentence or sentences are written for visual examination, proofreading, and reflection.

For older students and those who demonstrate some proficiency in writing, it is necessary to go beyond self-expression. Formal styles and standard formats include book reviews, summaries of encyclopedia research translated into their own words, and special topics. Emphasis in instruction is on vocabulary, sentence length and complexity, logical sequence of ideas, clarity of presentation, and grammar. Both teachers and students need to be aware that the writing stage involves the development of several drafts. Initially, sentences and paragraphs are first attempts not the final product. The organization of content, sequence of ideas, and clarity of communication are prime considerations. Mechanics, spelling, and handwriting are given least attention initially, although they become important as final drafts are prepared.

Postwriting

Proofreading   As students begin to write, they are taught to reread their work. Initial steps may include rereading aloud with emphasis on listening carefully to the text, noting missing words, and the general sound and flow of the writing. Later, as the conventions of manuscript are learned, students can observe their own capitalization, punctuation, and spelling. By requiring proofreading activities, even of copied sentences, teachers set the foundation for good writing habits.

Sharing Work Among Class Members   Sharing stories among class members can be enjoyable and productive. Teachers may read stories that were written in other classes, or students can share their work among peers. However, they should not be required to share their work with anyone except the teacher. Often shy students express themselves surprisingly well and sensitively in writing. They may reveal themselves as they are unable to do in any other way.

Evaluation and Grading of Students   A distinction is made between evaluation and grades. Evaluation refers to the corrections and recommendations teachers make as students progress through the assignment. Grades comprise the final letter or number representing the quality of work based on a set of criteria.

One dictum in the evaluation of written expression is that of separating content from mechanics. Nothing is more discouraging to students than to follow teachers' instructions to be creative on a clever topic and then to have the paper returned with many corrections in grammar and mechanics but with little appreciation of the quality of the work regarding the stated objectives of the assignment. One means of remedying this problem is to evaluate the two separately. Another is to require and evaluate but not grade the rough draft. Teachers can make positive comments where appropriate, note errors, and make suggestions for further improvement. Students are likely to correct errors and concentrate on the quality of the paper if they know that the rough draft will not receive a grade.

On the final draft two grades can be given, one for content and one for sentence structure, spelling, capitalization, and punctuation. On the elementary level, a point system may be used with more emphasis on content and satisfactory length and less on the mechanics in which students are less likely to be successful.

Assessment   Assessment in written language expression is particularly challenging. It is made on the basis of individual skills demanded by writing. Students' grammar, spelling, and mechanics abilities can be assessed in a straightforward, objective manner. Sentence structure, vocabulary, organization, and semantics present a more difficult task to the evaluator, although guidelines, checklists, and rating scales are commercially available to help make the task more objective. Assessment of content, organization, sequence of presentation, creativity, and esthetic aspects become even more difficult and subjective.

Several of the major achievement test batteries contain sections that assess some aspects of writing, usually grammar, usage, and mechanics. However, they are often limited to:

- Identifying a preferred sentence structure
- Identifying the topic sentence of a given paragraph
- Reorganization of a sequence of sentences
- Proofreading

Results are presented in grade equivalents or percentile ranks, neither of which serves as a guide in remediation.

Individually administered instruments allow examination of a writing sample. These include the *Diagnostic Evaluation of Written Skills* (DEWS) (Weiner, 1980) and the *Test of Written Language* (TOWL) (Hammill & Larsen, 1983). The DEWS gives students a topic on which to write, and assessment is made on 41 criteria divided into six categories. These are;

- Graphic (handwriting)
- Orthographic (spelling)
- Phonologic (sound components)
- Syntactic (grammar)
- Semantic (meaning)
- Self-monitoring skills, which include self-correction and improvement through revision

The TOWL requires students to write a story based on three related line drawings. From this writing sample, teachers assess vocabulary, thematic maturity, thought units, and handwriting. Additional subtests measure spelling, word usage (grammatical closure), and style (punctuation and capitalization).

Teaching Written Expression to Exceptional Learners   In teaching exceptional students, attention to oral expression and reading skills often dominate the curriculum to the extent that written expression is neglected. Teachers may give less priority to written expression believing that the other language skills will be more beneficial to them.

Graham (1982) provides five recommendations for teachers to develop the writing skills of exceptional students.

1. Students should be exposed to a broad range of writing tasks.
2. Strategies for reducing the number of cognitive demands inherent in the act of writing should be an integral part of a remedial composition program.
3. Writing errors should not be overemphasized.
4. The composition program should be both pleasant and encouraging.
5. The composition program should be planned, monitored, and modified on the basis of assessment information.

Written work is a major component at the secondary level. Failing to provide students with mild handicaps with this training places them at an additional disadvantage as they progress in school and later in employment. Nor should teachers reject instruction in creative writing because they expect it to have limited utility. Often exceptional students find creative writing a vehicle for expressing strong feelings about themselves, their conditions, and their environments. Some exceptional students have extraordinary ability that needs to be discovered and developed.

SUMMARY

Written expression is a complex process requiring the integration of many skills. Not restricted to creative writing, written expression is a necessary form of communication. It is expected of older students as evidence of learning. As a product of cognitive organization and flexibility of thought, it is often difficult for many exceptional students who are limited in abstract thinking abilities. Although the quality of written expression is very often related to the quality of oral expression, it is not simply the spoken word written down. Careful teaching—including vocabulary development, outlining, exercises in logical organization and sequencing, and supportive criticism—is necessary if students, especially exceptional students and individual learners, are to achieve in expressive writing.

REFERENCES

Arena, J. I. (Ed.) (1968). *Building spelling skills in dyslexic children.* San Rafael, CA: Academic Therapy.

Balow, I. H., Farr, R., Hogan, T. P., & Prescott, G. A. (1978, 1979). *Metropolitan achievement tests* (5th ed.). Cleveland: Psychological Corporation.

Balow, I. H., Farr, R., Hogan, T. P., & Prescott, G. A. (1978). *Metropolitan language instructional tests.* Cleveland: Psychological Corporation.

Barbe, W. B., Francis, A. S., & Braun, L. A. (1985). *Basic skills for effective communication.* Columbus, OH: Merrill.

Brigance, A. H. (1983). *Comprehensive inventory of basic skills.* North Billerica, MA: Curriculum Associates.

Cady, J. L. (1975). Pretend you are an author. *Teaching Exceptional Children, 8,* 26–31.

Carlson, R. K. (1973). *Sparkling words: Two hundred practical and creative writing ideas* (Revised). Berkeley, CA: Wagner.

Cohen, C. R., & Abrams, R. M. (1974). *Spellmaster: Spelling, testing, and evaluation.* Exeter, NH: Learnco.

Dixon, R., Englemann, S., Meier, M., Steely, D., & Wells, T. (1980, 1981). *Spelling mastery*. Chicago: Science Research Associates.

Dunn, L. M., & Markwardt, F. C. (1970). *Peabody individual achievement test*. Circle Pines, MN: American Guidance Service.

Early, G. H., Nelson, D. A., Kleber, D. J., Treegoob, M., Huffman, E., & Cass, C. (1976). Cursive handwriting, reading, and achievement. *Academic Therapy, 12,* 67–74.

Faas, L. A. (1980). *Children with learning problems: A handbook for teachers*. Boston: Houghton Mifflin.

Fernald, G. M. (1943). *Remedial techniques in basic school subjects*. New York: McGraw-Hill.

Ganschow, L. (1984). Analyze error patterns to remediate severe spelling difficulties. *Reading Teacher, 38,* 288–293.

Gardner, E. F., Callis, R., Merwin, J., & Rudman, H. C. (1982). *Stanford achievement test of academic skills* (2nd ed.). Cleveland: Psychological Corporation.

Gardner, E. F., Rudman, H. C., Karlsen, B., & Merwin, J. (1982). *Stanford achievement test* (7th ed.). Cleveland: Psychological Corporation.

Gillingham, A., & Stillman, B. W. (1970). *Remedial teaching for children with specific disabilities in reading, spelling, and penmanship* (8th ed.). Cambridge, MA: Educators Publishing Service.

Graham, S. (1982). Composition research and practice: A unified approach. *Focus on Exceptional Children 14,* 1–16.

Green, H. A., & Petty, W. (1975). *Developing language skills in the elementary schools* (5th ed.). Boston: Allyn and Bacon.

Hackney, C. S., Myers, E. H., & Zaner Bloser, P. (1969). *Off we go: Transition and a new universe* (Teacher's edition). Columbus, OH: Zaner-Bloser.

Hall, J. K. (1981). *Evaluating and improving written expression: A practical guide for teachers*. Boston: Allyn and Bacon.

Hammill, D. D., & Larsen, S. C. (1983). *The test of written language*. Austin, TX: Pro-Ed.

Hammill, D. D., & Leigh, J. E. (1983). *Basic school skills inventory—Diagnostic*. Austin, TX: Pro-Ed.

Hammill, D. D., & Poplin, M. (1982). Problems in written composition. In D. D. Hammill, & N. R. Bartel (Eds.). *Teaching children with learning and behavior problems* (3rd ed.) (pp. 93–120). Boston: Allyn and Bacon.

Hanna, P. R., Hodges, R. E., & Hanna, J. S. (1971). *Spelling: Structure and strategies*. Boston: Houghton Mifflin.

Harris, A. J. (1958). *Harris test of lateral dominance*. New York: Psychological Corporation.

Jastak, S., & Wilkinson, G. S. (1984). *Wide range achievement test—Revised*. Wilmington, DE: Jastak Associates.

Kaufman, H. S., & Biren, P. L. (1979). Cursive writing: An aid to spelling. *Academic Therapy, 15,* 209–219.

Kottmeyer, W. (1970). *Teacher's guide for remedial reading*. New York: McGraw-Hill.

Larsen, S. C., & Hammill, D. D. (1986). *The test of written spelling*. Austin, TX: Pro-Ed.

Larson, C. E. (1968). Teaching beginning writing. *Academic Therapy, 4,* 61–66.

Lerner, J. W. (1976). *Children with learning disabilities: Theories, diagnosis, teaching strategies* (2nd ed.). Boston: Houghton Mifflin.

Lerner, J. W. (1985). *Learning disabilities: Theories, diagnosis, and teaching strategies* (4th ed.). Boston: Houghton Mifflin.

Linn, S. H. (1970). Remedial approaches to handwriting dysfunction. In J. I. Arena (Ed.). *Building handwriting skills in dyslexic children* (pp. 72–74). San Rafael, CA: Academic Therapy.

Madison, B. D. (1970). A kinesthetic technique for handwriting. In J. I. Arena (Ed.). *Building handwriting skills in dyslexic children* (pp. 45–47). San Rafael, Ca: Academic Therapy.

Mercer, C. D., & Mercer, A. R. (1985). *Teaching children with learning problems* (2nd ed.). Columbus, OH: Merrill.

Obrzut, J. E., & Boliek, C. A. (1986). Lateralization characteristics of learning disabled children. *Journal of Learning Disabilities, 19*, 308–314.

Otto, W., & Smith, R. J. (1980). *Corrective and remedial teaching* (3rd ed.). Boston: Houghton Mifflin.

Petty, W. T. (1966). Handwriting and spelling: Their current status in the language arts curriculum. In T. D. Horne (Ed.). *Research on handwriting and spelling* (pp. 1–8). Champaign, IL: National Council of Teachers of English.

Petty, W. T., & Bowen, M. E. (1967). *Slithery snakes and other aids to children's writing*. Englewood Cliffs, NJ: Prentice-Hall.

Stephens, T. M., Hartman, A. C., & Lucas, V. H. (1982). *Teaching children basic skills: A curriculum handbook* (2nd ed.). Columbus, OH: Merrill.

Temple, C., & Gillet, J. W. (1984). *Language arts, learning processes, and teaching practices*. Boston: Little, Brown.

Tompkins, G. E., & Friend, M. (1985). On your mark, get set, write. *Teaching Exceptional Children, 18*, 82–89.

Wallace, G. E., & Kauffman, J. M. (1978). *Teaching children with learning problems* (2nd ed.). Columbus, OH: Merrill.

Weiner, E. S. (1980). Diagnostic evaluation of writing skills. *Journal of Learning Disabilities, 13*, 48–53.

Zaner-Bloser Staff. (1979). *Evaluation scale*. Columbus, OH: Zaner-Bloser.

SUGGESTED READINGS

General

Cohen, S. B., & Plaskon, S. P. (1980). *Language arts for the mildly handicapped.* Columbus, OH: Merrill.

Phelps-Terasaki, D., Phelps-Gunn, T., & Stetson, E. G. (1983). *Remediation and instruction in language: Oral language, reading, and writing.* Rockville, Md: Aspen.

Spelling

Arena, J. I. (Ed.) (1968). *Building spelling skills in dyslexic children.* San Rafael, CA: Academic Therapy.

Furness, E. L. (1977). *Spelling for the millions* (new ed.). Nashville, TN: Thomas Nelson.

Handwriting

Hofmeister, A. M. (1981). *Handwriting resource book: Manuscript cursive.* Nile, IL: Developmental Learning Materials.

Lucas, V. H. (1976). *Chalkboard techniques and activities for teaching writing.* Columbus, OH: Zaner-Bloser.

Plunkett, M. (1967). *A writing manual for teaching the left-handed.* Cambridge, MA: Educators Publishing Service.

Written Expression

Carlson, R. K. (1970). *Writing aids through the grades.* New York: Teachers College Press.

Giordano, G. (1984). *Teaching writing to learning disabled students.* Rockville, MD: Aspen.

Haley-James, S. (Ed.) (1981). *Perspective on writing in grades 1–8*. Urbana, IL: National Council of Teachers of English.

Hennings, D. G., & Grant, B. M. (1981). *Written expression in the language arts: Ideas and skills*. New York: Teachers College Press.

Phelps-Gunn, T., & Phelps-Terasaki, D. (1982). *Written language instruction: Theory and remediation*. Rockville, MD: Aspen.

Wiener, H. S. (1978). *Any child can write: How to improve your child's writing skills from preschool through high school*. New York: McGraw-Hill.

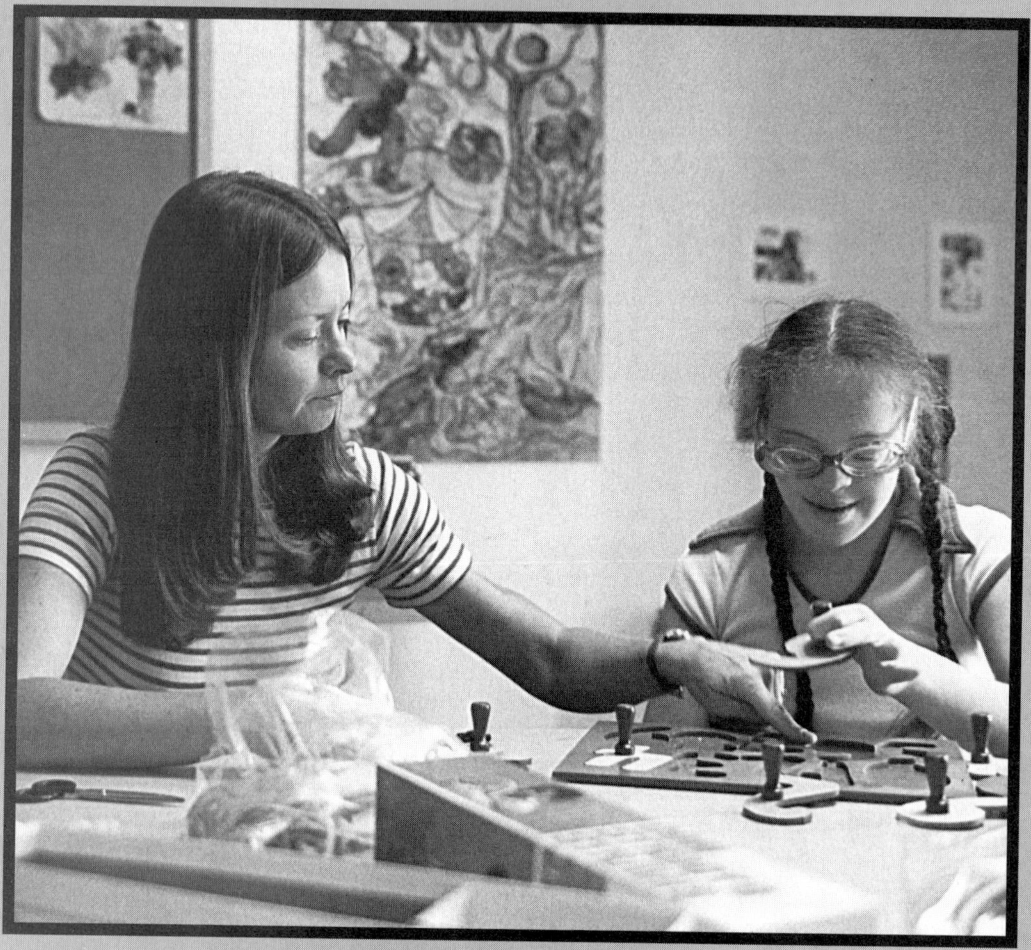

13

Methods for Teaching Mathematics and Science

FOR MAINSTREAMED STUDENTS, mathematics and science have become curriculum components in either regular or special classes. The skills of teachers in providing effective instruction affect the subsequent capabilities of students to manage and interact successfully with their academic, social, and physical environments.

Arithmetic and Mathematics

Arithmetic and mathematics are not synonymous. Chalfant and Scheffelin (1969, p. 119) state that "mathematics is the abstract science of space and number which deals with space configuration and the interrelations and abstractions of numbers. Arithmetic is a branch of mathematics that deals with real numbers and their computation." Arithmetic and mathematics are not hierarchical with one another. Students do not progress from "simple arithmetic" to "higher math." If the subject is properly taught, elementary mathematics concepts are presented from the beginning and precede the introduction of numbers and arithmetic computation.

Levels of Mathematics

Mathematics is perceived here as being represented at four levels of abstraction. These are the concrete, the representational, the symbolic, and the conceptual.

The *concrete level* uses actual, three-dimensional objects. It includes items to be counted, sorted, or compared and their shape, size, and volume.

The *representational level* includes two-dimensional representations such as marks (||||) to keep track of counting as well as graphs, charts, diagrams, and schematic drawings. For some students, representation has distinct advantages in learning. Despite the sequence of the secondary curriculum in which algebra frequently precedes geometry, the latter is more easily grasped by visually oriented students who can "make sense out of" relationships among angles, triangles, or pyramids but who have difficulty with x and $a + b$. A number line, often taped to the top of students' desks, is a compromise or transition step between the representational level and the symbolic level.

The *symbolic level* refers to the use of numbers. Also important is the use of language as described by Underhill, Uprichard, and Heddens (1980, p. 29) as a "verbal bridge" between the concrete manipulative process and the symbolic process.

The use of reasoning processes and the achievement of insight into the interrelationships among the various concepts, which constitute the broad meaning of mathematics, characterize the *conceptual level*. Facility at this level includes the ability to generalize principles for application to new situations.

Importance of Levels in Teaching

To some extent these levels are hierarchical, particularly the first three. There is a need to build a solid association between the concrete and the symbolic levels. The use of crutches such as manipulative materials gives students the opportunity to solidify their understanding of this relationship between numbers and their concrete referents. Students might be shown the numbers 4 and 8 on the chalkboard and are asked which is larger. "Neither" replies the student, "they are the same size." And so they are: 4 8 . The example may never have occurred in any classroom but it illustrates the meaning of numerals as symbols and their representation in reality.

The conceptual level is not truly hierarchical with the other three. Computational processes cannot be taught first, and students cannot be expected to come to an understanding of the meaning of mathematics later. It is not difficult to teach computational skills at the symbolic level without referring to the conceptual level. Students, for example, can memorize multiplication tables without ever knowing the relationship between multiplication and addition or that the four basic operations in arithmetic are forms of counting. Further, evaluation is most commonly based on computational accuracy. Students whose answers are correct are rewarded for success even though the answers may have resulted from care in the mechanics of computation while deficits in reasoning behind the process may have been masked. However, ultimate achievement in mathematics and their use depends on students' grasp of the meaning of the processes and not on computational skills alone. The teacher must be cognizant of the importance of integrating meaning at every level of instruction.

Language and Mathematics

Mathematics is a particular kind of symbol system. Spencer and Smith (1969, p. 152) write that "arithmetic is a form of language involving the communication of concepts through symbols." As reading ability has its referents in the language base of individuals, mathematics has historically been presumed to have its base in visual-perceptual and spacial-organizational abilities (Kaliski, 1967, Strauss & Lehtinen, 1947). There has thus been an hypothesized dichotomy between reading/language functioning on one hand and mathematics/visual-spacial functioning on the other. This difference has been further equated with neurological functioning on the basis that primary language abilities are centered in the left hemisphere of the brain while visual-spacial processing tends to be a right hemisphere activity.

However, mathematics is taught through verbal language communication. While visual imagery may be used in conceptualizing size–space, quantitative relationships—descriptions of these relationships—are translated into linguistic components (add, set, tangent, ordinal). A substantial part of mediation remains in the language mode. Further, students who demonstrate visual-spacial difficulties display some problems with words that refer to these relationships. Vocabulary describing quantitative relationships (more, nearer, few but not many, equal to) is often deficient.

The importance of language is most directly observable in story problems. Many students find it difficult to translate "Bobby had seven marbles and lost two of them" into the operation of subtraction with the larger number as the minuend, or "on top," and the smaller as the subtrahend, "on the bottom."

$$\begin{array}{rl} \text{Given} & 7 \quad \text{(marbles)} \\ \text{"lost"} = \text{"subtract"} & \underline{-2} \quad \text{(marbles)} \\ & ? \quad \text{(marbles)} \end{array}$$

Several authors (Bartel, 1982; Faas, 1980) give lists of vocabulary words related to mathematics concepts and functions. An interesting approach to mathematics instruction via language is presented in *Helping Children to Read Mathematics* by Kane, Byrne, and Hater (1974).

Readiness

The basic physiological, psychological, and experiential factors associated with general readiness for learning are applicable to mathematics as well as to other subjects. Of particular concern is the development of visual-spacial-organizational abilities. Johnson and Myklebust (1967) suggest that a base of early experience in manipulating and classifying three-dimensional objects provides a beginning for mathematical concepts. Bartel (1982) stresses the relationship of the subject to stages in Piagetian development, especially in regard to conservation and flexibility and reversibility of thought.

Specific readiness skills include recognition and accurate perception of visual symbols, the ability to visualize groups, one-to-one correspondence and counting, the ability to associate quantity (numbers) with numerals, and the meaning of the basic arithmetic processes of addition and subtraction as organization of properties, prior to learning computation.

Motivation

There are two interrelated concepts relative to motivation and mathematics. The first concerns an apparent cultural bias, and the second has to do with activities and approaches, which might be used to motivate students toward achievement. That some students find arithmetic difficult appears to be more accepted and understandable in our society than an equally deficient performance in language activities. The public seems more alarmed that Johnny might not be able to read than if he might not be able to add. Earlier beliefs that mathematics did not have as wide a practical application as language and that boys were more likely to need mathematics skills than girls may have accounted for such attitudes. In actuality, the use of mathematics concepts and skills is pervasive in our increasingly technological society and is equally necessary for males and females in their achievement of personal goals as well as for equal contributions to society.

The degree of influence of earlier attitudes on mathematics achievement remains speculative but undoubtedly the influence exists, and it does not result in encouragement or expectation of students to excel in the subject. It may well be teachers' or tutors' prime order of business to convince students that they can be successful in mathematics.

Attitudes of conviction and enthusiasm on the part of teachers are essential in motivating students. Realistically, however, teachers cannot overcome students' resistance by words alone. Students must be convinced to try. With careful planning and adaptations of curriculum and instruction, they can then experience success. Instructional procedures based on teachers' knowledge of how students learn, their unique patterns of strengths and weaknesses, understandings and skills, and the ability to think quantitatively provide a direct motivational approach.

Teachers may use an approach in which the practical and immediate uses as well as the long-term uses of the subject are presented. The latter can be particularly important at the secondary level for the college-bound and for those who are considering careers related to mathematics. For those not going on to school, teachers can appeal to the students' needs concerning budgets, insurance, banking, savings and interest, and time payments.

In the earlier grades, classroom experiences can be extended beyond the "teacher show, students practice" by social role playing (clerking, shopping, building, measuring). Games, puzzles, worksheets with numbers to be colored in, and plotting of seasonal pictures on graph paper may spark interest, although these will probably not result in continuing motivation. The use of a calculator or computer is often inherently motivating. Planning imaginary trips with calculations of time, transportation costs, and mileage may be an enjoyable diversion. Comparison shopping with students determining the "best buys" of similar items with varying weights and prices and the estimating of budgets for parties or some desired purchase can add a note of realism. Although such devices may be helpful, by and large it is students' initial and continuing successes resulting from their own efforts and the quality of teaching that is more instrumental in ensuring continuing motivation.

VISUALLY IMPAIRED STUDENTS IN MATHEMATICS

Although intellectually average or superior, students with visual impairments—low vision and blindness—often find mathematics a difficult subject. They have limited visual-spacial-organizational perception, which is thought to be correlated with mathematics concepts. If they are to be successful, students with visual impairments may need support, special materials, and accommodations from the early years through successive grades.

In first grade Danny was unprepared, lacking typical readiness skills for arithmetic. The resource teacher worked with basic concepts of size, weight, and spacial relationships as well as number concepts, grouping, and sets using three-dimensional materials. The vocabulary of mathematics was stressed and associated with the arithmetic operations, employing concrete materials whenever possible.

In the fifth grade Eloise is mainstreamed in mathematics. She is a low-vision student who uses enlarged textbooks and writes with a marker on paper with raised lines. She is seated close to the chalkboard and is allowed to walk to the board to see at any time. When Miss Taylor demonstrates problems on the board, she names each number and step in the process. When students do boardwork, Miss Taylor has each student review the steps of the problem orally. This provides review for the students and allows Eloise to hear each problem.

In the seventh grade Troy is unusually capable in math. He uses an abacus for problem solving. He reads braille well and has braille versions of the textbook used in his regular math class. Further, he is learning the Nemeth Code of Braille Mathematics and Scientific Notation. Although he has never seen the sky, Troy has set a goal of becoming an astrophysicist.

In tenth grade Al is successful in mathematics largely because of the care taken in instruction in the earlier grades. He passed algebra I in the ninth grade and is now taking geometry. He uses a variety of equipment—a talking calculator and braille ruler and protractor. He also continues to rely on three-dimensional teaching aids to learn concepts in geometry. Because some of the material is bulky, it is kept in the resource room where Al goes to study and do his math homework. He works with a senior peer tutor who also assists in the preparation of written work.

Assessment

Informal Assessment

The most practical assessment in both arithmetic and mathematics is that conducted by teachers during routine classroom activities and by inspection of written assignments and boardwork. Observation of errors, and more importantly patterns of errors, is the principal method. Moran (1978, p. 58) suggests that patterns of errors may occur in one or more of the following ways:

1. Inadequate facts: Using a correct operation and a sound strategy, the pupil applies inaccurate addition, subtraction, or multiplication facts.
2. Incorrect operations: Using accurate facts, the learner subtracts rather than adding or divides instead of multiplying.
3. Ineffective strategy: Using the proper operation and accurate facts, the learner applies steps out of sequence, skips steps, or applies a tactic which does not always result in a correct outcome.

Skills checklists pinpoint error patterns and form the basis for remediation. During seatwork time, individual attention can be given, and incidental errors can be corrected.

Students are often assigned many problems for homework each night, and the amount of correcting required of teachers for a single class, let alone a sequence of classes, is prohibitive. Teachers usually resolve the dilemma by having students correct each others' papers. This practice may be necessary, but it does prevent teachers from knowing the work of each student. It is suggested that teachers correct all the homework on a class-by-class basis occasionally during the grading period. In addition, they can routinely collect student-corrected homework papers. Then selected papers, those done by students who appear to be having difficulties in the subject, can be removed and examined in greater detail as a basis for further instructional decisions (Figure 13.1).

If the nature or source of the students' errors are not immediately obvious, a more detailed examination of their work may be necessary. Because arithmetic skills are learned sequentially, the students' work can be examined, noting each prerequisite skill needed to perform the task. Example:

Student's work *Teacher's analysis*

$$\begin{array}{r} 343 \\ \times\ 32 \\ \hline 686 \\ 9290 \\ \hline 9876 \end{array}$$

1. Student multiplies correctly when regrouping is not required.
2. Student does *not* multiply correctly when regrouping is required.
3. Student can regroup for addition.

Teachers can examine other problems to note the consistency of this kind of error. They can also present students with additional multiplication problems that require regrouping. If the difficulty is confirmed, reteaching in regrouping procedures in multiplication would be needed.

Another technique is that of having students "talk through" the arithmetic problems as they perform them (Mercer & Mercer, 1985). This method reveals computational and algorithmic errors and is particularly suited for discovering problems at the conceptual level.

Formal Assessment

There are many formal tests and parts of test batteries that measure achievement. These are of limited value to teachers. Often such instruments include only one problem of each type at each grade level. Thus, the revelation of a pattern of errors is not possible. The stress of testing can cause students to make errors. As a result, the test does not represent functional or ability level.

Another difficulty with many formal tests is their reliance on measuring only computational skills. However, some formal measures of reasoning skills can be found. These include subtests of the *KeyMath Diagnostic Arithmetic Test* (Connolly, Nachtman, & Pritchett, 1976), the *California Achievement Tests* (Tiegs & Clark, 1978), the *Metropolitan Achievement Tests* (Balow, Farr, Hogan, & Prescott, 1978, 1979), and the *SRA Achievement Series* (Naslund, Thorpe, & Lefever, 1978).

FIGURE 13.1

An example of homework assessment

Informal Assessment of Homework

Bob and Mary were assigned the same homework problems. Part of their homework appears here. The teacher has marked the incorrect answers and now must determine the nature of the difficulty occurring in the assignment. Additional instruction may be needed.

Bob:
$$\begin{array}{r}{}^{1}68\\ + 8\\ \hline 166\end{array}\text{x} \quad \begin{array}{r}{}^{1}83\\ +29\\ \hline 202\end{array} \quad \begin{array}{r}24\\ +35\\ \hline 59\end{array} \quad \begin{array}{r}{}^{1}27\\ +94\\ \hline 211\end{array}\text{x}$$

Mary:
$$\begin{array}{r}68\\ + 8\\ \hline 616\end{array}\text{x} \quad \begin{array}{r}83\\ +29\\ \hline 1012\end{array}\text{x} \quad \begin{array}{r}24\\ +35\\ \hline 59\end{array} \quad \begin{array}{r}27\\ +94\\ \hline 1111\end{array}\text{x}$$

Teacher's Analysis and Additional Instruction

Bob:

Analysis: Bob's difficulty appears to be one of column alignment. He places the number to be regrouped too far to the left and then "reads" it with the numeral in the tens column as a two-digit number, i.e., 16, 18, and 12. He then adds this number to the numeral in the subtrahend.

Remediation: Because Bob's addition facts appear to be correct, he needs no reteaching here. Remediate the alignment problem by:

1. Teaching Bob to place the number to be carried <u>on top of</u> the next column, not to the side of it.
2. Use worksheets with dotted lines, or have Bob draw lines on his work for a period of time.

$$\begin{array}{r}{}^{1}8|3\\ +2|9\end{array}$$

In addition, Bob needs to be reminded that only one column (1 + 8 + 2) can be added at a time, not two columns (18 + 1).

Mary:

Analysis: Like Bob, Mary's arithmetic facts seem to be satisfactory. However, she did not regroup as needed; she added each column independently. The difficulty may be mechanical or conceptual. Having Mary work a few selected problems, describing what she is doing to the teacher, would clarify.

Remediation: If the problem is mechanical: Mary does not write the numeral to be carried at the top of the next column. Teach her to do so and emphasize with arrows and signs.

$$+\!\!\begin{array}{r}{}^{1}83\\ +29\end{array} \qquad +\!\!\begin{array}{r}{}^{1}68\\ + 8\end{array}$$

If the problem is conceptual: Regrouping should be thoroughly reviewed or retaught.

More useful to teachers are criterion-referenced diagnostic instruments. These include the *KeyMath Diagnostic Arithmetic Test* (Connolly, Nachtman, & Pritchett, 1976), the *Stanford Diagnostic Mathematics Test* (Beatty, Madden, Gardner, & Karlsen, 1978), the *Metropolitan Mathematics Instructional Tests* (Hogan, Farr, Prescott, & Balow, 1980), *Diagnosis and Instructional Aids, Mathematics Levels A & B* (Science Research Associates), the *Enright Diagnostic Inventory of Basic Arithmetic Skills* (Enright, 1983), the *Diagnostic Tests and Self-Helps in Arithmetic* (Brueckner, 1955), and the *Diagnostic Chart for Fundamental Processes in Arithmetic* (Buswell & John, 1926).

Methods

The manner in which mathematics is taught is a major factor in reaching the goals of the school program. One difficulty occurs when mathematics is introduced at the symbolic (number) level. A nationwide study conducted by the National Assessment of Educational Progress resulted in the following generalizations in the final reports: "*Students appear to be learning many mathematics skills at a rote manipulation level and do not understand the concepts underlying the computation*" (Carpenter, Corbitt, Kepner, Lindquist, & Reys, 1980a, p. 338), and "Respondents demonstrated a lack of even the most basic problem-solving skills" (Carpenter et al., 1980b, p. 47).

One implication of these research findings is that it is important to teach the meaning of mathematics and not simply the computational skills needed to achieve an accurate product.

There are many characteristics of effective teaching. In mathematics these include the use of concrete and manipulative materials at the beginning levels of computation, the use of continued formative assessment as a basis for providing immediate corrective instruction and adequate individual and class guidance. Search and discovery methods, which allow students to realize the concept as a result of experimentation, appear to have much merit. However, students, especially exceptional and individual learners, cannot be left to discover principles, processes, and concepts on their own. Teaching procedures that lead them toward discovery is necessary.

Although creative teaching is not discouraged, caution should be observed about the "invention" or use of new approaches. Students may fail to grasp the idea of the concepts if they are distracted by elaborate examples or intricate procedures. The more traditional approaches have greater potential for meaningful learning.

As in other subject areas, there is one method for teaching specific skills. The selection of methods used cannot be determined solely on the nature of the subject. Also to be considered are students' learning styles and needs and the techniques teachers find to be both comfortable and effective.

Specific Instructional Techniques

The teaching techniques listed here are samples of the many instructional procedures available to teachers.

Shape, Form, Size, and Length

- Use simple puzzles and add more pieces as students progress in ability.
- Make pegboard designs.
- Make parquetry block designs.
- Use two-dimensional figures on tagboard, felt, or cardboard, prior to instruction with cubes or blocks.
- Place figures on a formboard or fit shapes into cut out spaces in cardboard.
- Have students walk around the shape of a rope on the floor.
- Have students touch shapes or hold them as teachers verbalize name of the shape and describe their size and length.
- Fit shapes into holes of graduated sizes.
- Arrange objects from small to large.
- Discriminate the length of lines.

Matching, Sorting, and Classifying

- Classify parquetry blocks by shape, by color, or by size.
- Arrange pictures cut from catalogs and laminate them on individual pieces of cardboard.
- Arrange home activities with the aid of parents—put silverware into correct places in drawers, organize own bureau drawers, match socks, sort clothes for wash, put dishes away.
- Group pictures of sports equipment on construction paper, each designating a different sport.

Number Concepts and Counting

- Use cards with numerals and circles representing the amount indicated by the numeral. Students touch and name numerals.
- Place specified number of cubes in a tray numbered with that numeral and with spaces for the correct number of cubes.
- Count objects, beads, cubes, bottle caps, and sticks.
- Count checkmarks, stickers, or stars that are used in reinforcement program.
- Respond motorically to spoken or visually demonstrated number by clapping, tapping, jumping, pointing, or touching.
- Count objects in the classroom such as books on the shelf, pencils, materials to be distributed, or the number of desks. With parents' cooperation, count objects on a trip—signs, trees, and restaurants. Count moving objects—fish in a tank, passing cars and trucks.
- Use worksheets—Color a designated number of apples, boxes, and circles. Color worksheets with given number of objects on them.

One-to-One Correspondence

- Put a row of pegs on a board with the initial peg already in place.
- Pass out papers or materials to be used by each student.

- Match felt pieces on a flannelboard.
- Make a mark on the paper for each tap the teacher makes.
- Set a place for each family member for dinner at home.
- Use playing cards to have student deal specific number to each member of group.
- Use a worksheet with pictures of children. Student determines how many toys would be needed to give one to each. Student colors and cuts out that number of toys from second worksheet and pastes one for each student on the original sheet.
- Place designated numbers of objects, buttons, pegs, and pennies in a box or set of boxes.

Recognizing Visual Symbols and Number Words

- Place a number line on each desk.
- Place a "walk-on" number line on the floor.
- Arrange, mixup, and rearrange cardboard squares with numbers or dots on them.
- Use number word next to numeral or set of objects.
- Laminate cards with each numeral, set of objects, and number word to be used as a study sheet.
- Use worksheets that have objects in which students write the numeral and number word.

Visualizing Groups or Sets

- Use an overhead projector with commercial or teacher-made transparencies.
- Use yarn around felt pieces on the flannelboard to form sets.
- Use pictures with groups of children, animals, buildings, and toys.
- Use techniques similar to those for classifying and sorting but emphasize the new concept of group or set.
- Use sorting cards with particular groups of symbols.
- Use Cuisenaire rods.
- Use dominoes.
- Arrange objects in groups.

Ordinals

- Write the ordinals on a set of number cards.
- Stress adding *th* to most number words.
- Put objects in a row, verbalizing name of ordinal of each while placing or pointing to it. Question students on their memory of the ordinal names of each object.
- Name with ordinal words where each student is in a row of seats or lines going to lunch.
- Arrange chairs in a row. Student in each chair names the ordinal.

Order of Numbers

- Use visual approach with number chart, especially for *before* and *after*.
- Say numbers aloud on the number chart when counting by 10s, 5s, or 2s.
- Use dot-to-dot worksheets.
- Teach the concept of greater and lesser before requiring students to write symbols > <.

Meaning of Signs

- Use pictures with symbols and descriptions. Example: Picture of five birds with two flying away. The legend: 5 − 2 = 3.
- Clarify the meaning of synonyms for the signs. Example: *Times* means to multiply.
- Show that plus (+) means putting together. Bring small groups of students into one large group at the board with a large plus sign. Erase and put minus (−) sign and send three students back to their seats to explain the meaning of the minus sign.
- Suggest a trick for remembering the *greater* and *less than* signs. Example: 10 > 8. The *large* opening goes to the *large* number. The *small* point goes to the *small* number.

Flexibility and Reversibility

- Show that 6 + 3 and 3 + 6 both = 9 by reversing sets of cubes or other objects.
- Place 6 + 3 cubes and another set of 3 + 6 cubes on a desk. Have students discover they both = 9.

Place Value: Reading

- Teach place value as two skills—reading and writing—with reading being taught first.
- Use manipulative objects—sticks, interlocking cubes, abacus, Cuisenaire rods, or *Structural Arithmetic* (Stern, 1965).
- Place forty sticks in bundles of ten and label 4 tens.
- Indicate that sticks placed to the right of the bundles represent ones or units (Figure 13.2).
- Use flannelboard with a chart. Put numbers in the correct place.

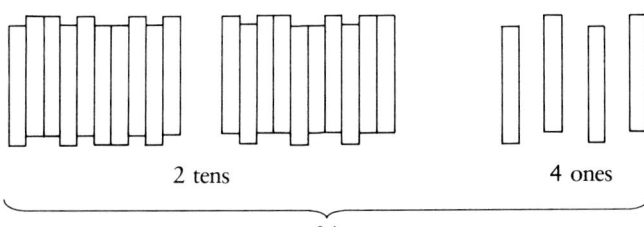

FIGURE 13.2

A method to teach place value

millions	thousands	units
hundreds tens ones	hundreds tens ones	hundreds tens ones

- Emphasize ones, tens, hundreds in each period or three-place grouping.
- Cover large numbers exposing one digit at a time beginning with the ones place. Students read each successive number as it is uncovered.

Place Value: Writing

- Begin by making dashes for each place. Students may look at chart as shown in "Place Value: Reading" to help determine how many dashes to make.

  8,460,417   –,– – –,– – –
- Tell students to write numerals they hear, *one* in each place.
- Put a 0 in each empty place.
- Write only three numerals in each period set off by commas.

Rounding

- Think through the process with students at the chalkboard. Examples:

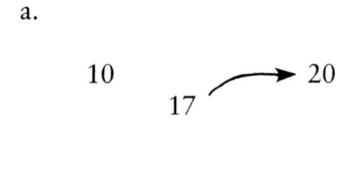

a.

10   → 20
   17

1. To what place are we rounding? Tens.
2. The numeral is between 10 and 20.
3. These are the choices.
4. Write 10 and 20 and draw arrow.
5. Is it 5 or more? If so, round up.
6. Is it 4 or less? If so, round down.

b.

400   500
   423

Same procedures except:
1. The numeral is between 400 and 500.
2. Is it 50 or more? If so, round up.
3. Is it 49 or less? If so, round down.

c.

2000   3000
   2247

Same procedure except:
1. The number is between 2000 and 3000.
2. Is it 500 or more? If so, round up.
3. Is it 499 or less? If so, round down.

Addition and Subtraction

Some authors recommend teaching computation by discovery. Others use the more common technique of presenting facts with answers and drilling for mastery. Otto, McMenemy, and Smith (1973) state that learning the facts by rote is a poor technique and that answers should not be told. They emphasize the "remedial teacher cannot be a slave to a *best* method if he does not thoroughly understand it or if he is not comfortable in teaching it" (p. 291). The authors here recommend using different techniques that are suitable to individual learning styles. Some students learn by visual cues: Flash cards may be effective. Others learn by grouping objects together, such as three blocks and four blocks. Still others need to see a fact family such as

$$3 + 4 = 7$$
$$4 + 3 = 7$$
$$7 - 4 = 3$$
$$7 - 3 = 4$$

A folded sheet with facts on one side of the fold and answers on the other side can serve as a self-checking device (Figure 13.3).

For those who learn visually and understand the concept of computation, presenting a fact sheet showing reversibility leads to mastery. Marking the first fact with a marker serves as an added visual cue.

A few specific techniques include:

- Using manipulative objects—cubes, sticks, disks.
- Using number lines taped to the desk.
- Practicing fact families by writing with finger in cereal grain or sand.
- Writing figures at the chalkboard: ☐☐☐☒   4 − 1 = 3.
- Using auditory cues such as tapping or clapping.
- Using a tape recorder, language master, Digitor (Centurion Industries) or Dataman (Texas Instruments).

It should be noted that it is more difficult for many students with learning problems to learn subtraction facts than addition facts. It is acceptable to count on fingers for a period of time.

Two Column Addition and Subtraction

These are the steps to take when adding or subtracting with regrouping:

1. What does this sign tell you to do?
2. Begin with the ones column.

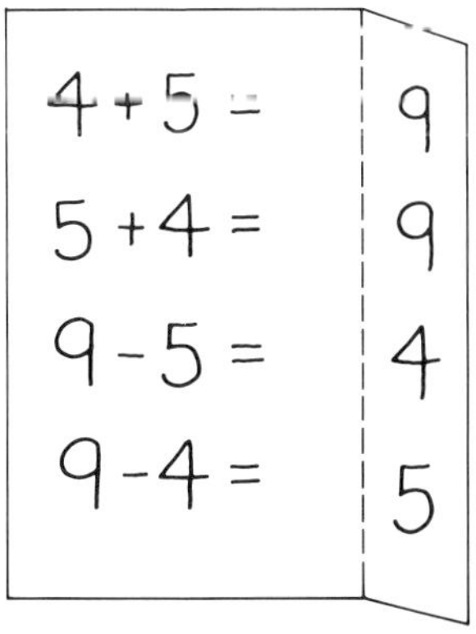

FIGURE 13.3

An addition and subtraction self-checking form

3. Compute one column at a time.
4. Place only one number to a column.

Addition

1. Begin by using sticks or disks to demonstrate. Then write

$$\begin{array}{r} 46 \\ + 7 \\ \hline \end{array} \qquad \begin{array}{r} 4\text{ tens } + 6\text{ ones} \\ + \phantom{4\text{ tens }+}7\text{ ones} \\ \hline 4\text{ tens } + 13\text{ ones} \end{array}$$

2. Explain that the 3 are leftover units.
3. 3 is in the ones place and must stay in the ones place.
4. 1 is in the tens place; put in the tens place:

$$4 + 1 = 5 \text{ tens} + 3 \text{ ones} = 53$$

5. Verbalize

$$\begin{array}{r} 47 \\ +28 \\ \hline \end{array} \text{ put down the 5, carry the 1}$$

Subtraction The same principles apply in subtraction.

1. If the number on top is smaller, must borrow.
2. Take 1 ten from the tens place.

$$\begin{array}{r} 72 \\ -14 \\ \hline \end{array}$$

3. Put the 1 next to the 2.
4. Cross out the 7.
5. One less than 7 is 6.
6. $32 - 6 = 26$ $\qquad \begin{array}{r} 32 \\ -6 \\ \hline \end{array} \qquad \begin{array}{r} 3 \text{ tens and } 2 \text{ ones} \\ -\phantom{3 \text{ tens and }}6 \text{ ones} \\ \hline 2 \text{ tens} 6 \text{ ones} \end{array}$

7. Use the same basic numerals in teaching each step in the process.

$$\begin{array}{r} 32 \\ -16 \\ \hline \end{array}$$

8. Always regroup to the next column.

$$\begin{array}{r} \cancel{4}82 \\ -195 \\ \hline \end{array}$$

Vertical and Horizontal Equations

- Vertical equations are usually easier.

$$\begin{array}{r} 32 \\ -16 \\ \hline \end{array} \quad \text{rather than } 32 - 16 =$$

- For initial instruction, change horizontal equations to vertical equations.

Multiplication and Division

Students must understand the concept or rote memory has little meaning. Introduce fact sheets when the concept is understood and when students are familiar with practicing facts.

$$6 \times 8 = 48$$
$$8 \times 6 = 48$$
$$48 - 6 = 8$$
$$48 - 8 = 6$$

Multiplication

- Show the relationship between multiplication and addition.

$$\underset{20}{4 \times 5} = \underset{20}{5 + 5 + 5 + 5}$$

- Any number times $0 = 0$.
- Any number times $1 = $ the same number.
- When multiplying two or more digits, cover the numbers not being worked with. Color numeral that is being multiplied.
- When introducing a concept, use the same examples.

$$\begin{array}{r} 24 \\ \times 6 \\ \hline \end{array} \quad \begin{array}{r} 324 \\ \times 6 \\ \hline \end{array} \quad \begin{array}{r} 324 \\ \times 16 \\ \hline \end{array} \quad \begin{array}{r} 324 \\ \times 216 \\ \hline \end{array}$$

Otto, McMenemy, and Smith (1973) state that few exceptional learners understand why partial products are moved over one place. Some mathematics series use zero (0) to fill in the missing digits on the right. This helps students with spacial problems.

$$\begin{array}{r} 6\,2\,8 \\ \times 4\,7\,2 \\ \hline 1\,2\,5\,6 \\ 4\,3\,9\,6\,0 \\ 2\,5\,1\,2\,0\,0 \\ \hline \end{array}$$

For students with spacial difficulties, write numbers such as 16 in the example to the side to prevent reversing. Math textbooks frequently color code and provide cues.

$$\begin{array}{r}628\\ \times2\\ \hline 1256\end{array} \qquad 16 \qquad \begin{array}{r}628\\ \times70\\ \hline \downarrow\\ 43960\end{array} \qquad \begin{array}{r}628\\ 400\\ \downarrow\\ 251200\end{array} \qquad 0 \qquad \begin{array}{r}628\\ \times 472\end{array}$$

Teachers must ascertain whether cues are helpful. Some cues can confuse students with learning problems.

Division

- For many students division is easier when they understand that the process is the opposite of multiplication.
- Facts are commonly taught with multiplication, although some students are unable to grasp all concepts simultaneously.
- Diagrams are effective.

$$0\ 0\ 0\ 0\ 0 - 0\ 0 = 0\ 0\ 0 \qquad\qquad 0\ 0\ 0\ 0\ 0\ 0 - 0\ 0\ 0 = 0\ 0\ 0$$
$$(0\ 0)\ (0\ 0)\ (0\ 0) \qquad\qquad\qquad (0\ 0\ 0)(0\ 0\ 0)$$

- Care must be taken when teaching long division so that wordiness is avoided. For students with learning problems, do not talk and demonstrate at the same time.
- Students with visual-perception problems are likely to put numbers in the wrong positions. Begin with simplest and proceed to more complex using the same example.

$$\begin{array}{r}8\\ 3\overline{)24}\end{array} \qquad \begin{array}{r}82\\ 3\overline{)246}\\ \underline{240}\\ 6\\ \underline{6}\end{array} \qquad \begin{array}{r}82\ R2\\ 3\overline{)248}\\ 24\downarrow\\ 8\\ \underline{6}\\ 2\end{array} \qquad \begin{array}{r}7\\ 33\overline{)231}\\ \underline{231}\\ 0\end{array} \qquad \begin{array}{r}7\ R3\\ 33\overline{)234}\\ \underline{231}\\ 3\end{array}$$

Make sure each step in the process is understood before explaining the next step, such as remainder.

- A process card can be taped to each student's desk or laminated for them to use in memorization.

÷	divide
×	multiply numerals on outside of
−	subtract
√	check to see if 2 is less than 6
bring down	bring down the next numeral
start over	start over

- When figuring each part of the problem, block out numbers not being worked with.
- Another way to estimate the numeral in the quotient is to round.

$$47\overline{)} \text{ round to } 50 \qquad 42\overline{)} \text{ round to } 40$$

- It is reassuring to students when they know the trial-and-error method must be used. Many students are confused with the rule of beginning with 5 as a quotient.

Story Problems

Language and cognitive skills are necessary to solve word problems. Students must have the ability to read and understand the meaning of words. They must decide what process to use, which involves reasoning and analysis skills. They also need specific skills in computation, fractions, decimals, and percents.

- Explain terms such as *before, after, between, same, as, larger,* and *smaller* on a number line before introducing story problems.
- Stress concept of *how many more*.
- Identify key words to determine type of computation:
  Addition: *in all, altogether, and*
  Subtraction: *less, lost, taken away, how many are left?*
- Teach students to think about one step at a time.

Specific Techniques for Story Problems

- Read each sentence orally.
- Write story problems on the overhead projector. Look for key words and underline or color code.
- Have students visualize by drawing a picture or acting out the problem.
- Reread to think about what information is given.
- Determine what is being asked.
- Decide what process to use.
- Write the equation.
- Read the equation and reread the information sentences and the question to determine that the process is correct.
- Work the problem.
- Complete the answer such as 14 baseballs, not just 14.
- Review the solution.

At the secondary level, it may still be necessary to use manipulative objects when students are unable to conceptualize the problem. Alley and Deshler (1979) recommend pictorial methods—that is, using films, pictures, tables, and graphs if concrete objects are unavailable. Teachers may need to help students organize their ideas, pose questions, and assist with the formation of equations. Alley and Deshler further state that formulas, laws, or rules are to be identified from a group of alternatives. The students then give the terms numerical value. After the problem is solved, change the quantitative solution into the semantic content of the problem. Review the process and discuss it as it will relate to future problems.

Math Applications Several strategies can be used to make problems practical.

- Use real life situations.
  a. If I get paid on Friday, the tenth, when will I get paid again if I get paid every two weeks?
  b. If the football game is two weeks away, how many days is that?
- Teach banking procedures.
  a. How to write a check
  b. How to balance a checkbook
- Practice measurement by cooking.
- Use real coins and bills when teaching money concepts.
- Practice filling out job applications.
- When teaching ratios, emphasize comparison shopping techniques.
- Teach budgeting.

Students at fifth grade level who can reason and compute but not read the word problems may receive assistance either from another student or from the teacher. It can be done without embarassment if students are prepared and teachers are "matter-of-fact" about it. Perhaps students needing help in this way can assist others with other concepts.

Fractions

The points to emphasize are:

- The word *fraction* means *part*.
- Stress that fractions have equal parts.
- $\frac{1}{4}$ numerator at top
  denominator at bottom.
- $\frac{1}{4}$ means one out of four parts is present (Figure 13.4). In the beginning, say "one out of four parts" while pointing to the numerals.
- The denominator means the total number of parts.
- Explain the terms *proper fractions, improper fractions,* and *mixed numbers* one lesson at a time to avoid confusion.

FIGURE 13.4

Shapes that show fractions

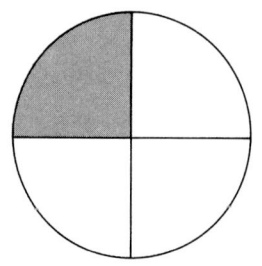

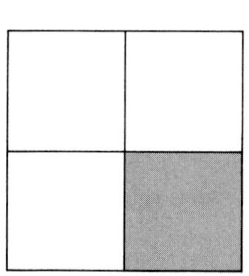

FIGURE 13.5

Fractions chart

1							
1/2				1/2			
1/4		1/4		1/4		1/4	
1/8	1/8	1/8	1/8	1/8	1/8	1/8	1/8

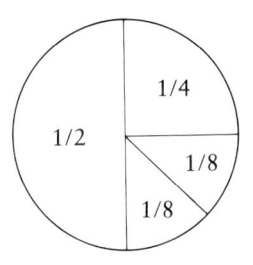

FIGURE 13.6

Fraction pie chart

- Practice using recipes, measuring cups, or measuring paper for an art project.
- Use objects, flannel pieces, cardboard or folding paper into parts, paper plates, measuring cups or the charts as illustrated in Figures 13.5 and 13.6.

Measurement

- Teach and explain the different types of measurement one at a time. Students easily become confused in distinguishing among area, volume, weight, and quantity.
- Use materials such as yardsticks, matchsticks, scales, and measuring cups, or a clock face.

Linear Measurement

- Begin with comparisons such as tall, taller, tallest, and long, longer, longest.
- Move from inch to foot to yard and from centimeter to meter.
- Match terms with definitions: yard = 3 feet.
- Have students choose the best tool for measuring: ruler or yardstick? Or the best weight for measurement: ounce, pound, or ton?
- When teaching ½" and ¼", draw a ruler on the chalkboard. Emphasize ½" with chalk of one color and ¼" with another color.
- Teach each length one at a time.
- Have students do actual measurement of real objects in the room or school.

Area Measurement

- Emphasize that area is length times width.
- Demonstrate at the chalkboard or with graph paper.

- Use graph paper for examples: Have students draw their yards with their houses plotted on them. Identify lengths and widths of the property.
- Measure the area of a hallway or other location in the school.

Volume Measurement

- Use cubes for various explanations.
- Have students use cubes to fill the inside of a small box.
- Have students build a rectangular prism or other geometric forms.

Liquid Measurement

- Use ½ pint, pint, quart, ½ gallon, and gallon containers from the grocery store.
- Make a chart of equivalents.

Weight and Mass Measurement

- Begin by having students distinguish relative weights of objects in the room: pencil, book, desk.
- Use an ounce scale.
- Point out the concepts of:

$$\frac{1}{4} \text{ pound} = 4 \text{ ounces}$$
$$\frac{1}{2} \text{ pound} = 8 \text{ ounces}$$
$$1 \text{ pound} = 16 \text{ ounces}$$

- Use worksheets to give practice in adding and subtracting pounds and ounces.

Temperature Measurement

- Use a commercial thermometer.
- Teach one concept per lesson, such as Celsius or Fahrenheit; then compare them. 0° Celsius is the same as 32° Fahrenheit.

Money Measurement Three main concepts are essential in the use of money: the value of coins, counting money, and making change.

- Use real coins not play money.
- Begin with coin recognition. Make charts with various coins that equal certain amounts.
- Play store. Students take turns being the clerk.
- Use worksheets for the value of coins.
- Make experiences meaningful with examples of
  a. Buying milk or bread for family.
  b. Having correct change for the bus or cafeteria line.
  c. Planning and spending allowances wisely without going into debt by borrowing.
  d. Working at the school store.

- Plan a Christmas list with amounts of money and estimates of time needed for saving for gifts.
- Use menus with meal costs, plan ordering meals, and figure the total bill.
- Establish a budget based on allowance.
- Use a real checkbook when teaching banking concepts.

Time Measurement

- Distinguish between the minute and hour hands. The minute hand is longer and moves faster.
- Teach one part at a time—for example, begin with the hour. When that has been mastered, move to the half hour, then the quarter hour.
- Use consistent terminology. Do not confuse students with "fifteen after" and "quarter past" interchangeably.
- Stress counting by fives when teaching time to the five minutes.
- Use a real clock face or individually made clock faces. Students enjoy moving the hands to the designated times.
- Compare to the number line when telling time to the minute.
- Time is made meaningful by
  a. Denoting times at which students eat meals, go to bed, or begin and end school.
  b. Helping mother time food in the oven.
  c. Timing sports events: quarters and halves of a game; timing races.
  d. Estimating the time it would take to complete projects, eat lunch, or run errands.
- In writing time, the hour is first.
- Teach the calendar information one at a time. Then give study sheet with all facts (days of week, months in year, days in year).
- Put drawings on the chalkboard to emphasize concepts. Teach these concepts one at a time (Figure 13.7).
- Color code the sides of the clock to match watches sometimes used with individuals with mental retardation: pink meaning *after* or *past*; blue meaning *before*, *to*, or *of*.

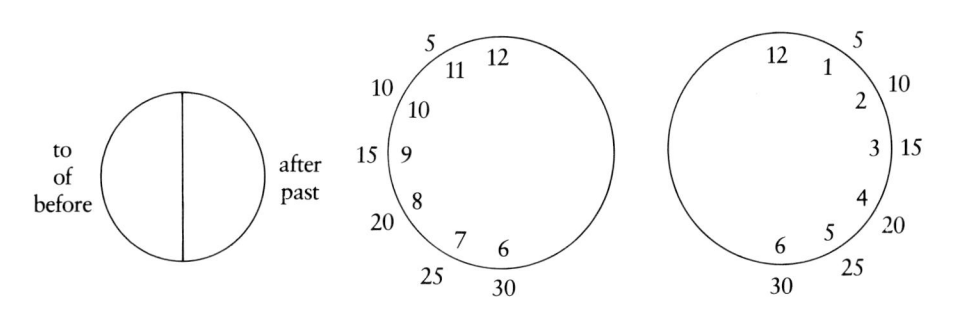

FIGURE 13.7

Telling time chart

Decimals and Percentages

Decimals

- Compare using decimals to adding and subtracting money.
- Stress the importance of lining up columns of numbers with the decimal points one under the other.
- Copy with decimal point in the right place.
- Point out the need to move the decimal point in multiplication and division but not in addition or subtraction.
- Relate fractions to decimals by illustrating that they are both parts of a whole.
- The decimal point is between the whole number and the decimal or part of the number.

$$\text{Whole} \longleftarrow 27.05 \longrightarrow \text{Part}$$

Percentage

- Note kinds of percentage problems as identified by Otto, McMenemy, and Smith (1973, p. 299).
  a. Changing percentages to numbers
  b. Changing numbers to percentages
  c. Finding the percentage of a number
  d. Finding what percent one number is to another
  e. Finding the number when a percentage of that number is known
- Emphasize that percent means hundredths.
- Demonstrate moving the decimal point two places.
- Never use a decimal point and a percentage sign (%) together.
- Have students memorize common fractions:

$$1\% = 1/100$$
$$25\% = 1/4$$
$$50\% = 1/2$$
$$33\ 1/3\% = 1/3$$

- Practice on applications such as figuring the percent of a tip on a restaurant bill, the tax charged in stores, student-graded papers, or surveys of opinions among class members.

Graphs

- Begin with a picture and bar graphs.
- Explain the purpose of graphs.
- Let students move fingers from sides of the graph to find the point.
- Demonstrate the difference between a bar graph, line graph, and pie graph.
- Use practical application in constructing graphs.

a. Individual test or quiz grades
b. Class attendance over time
c. Time allotted to homework, television, or play
d. Proportion of allowance spent in various ways

Mathematics and Exceptional Learners

Some difficulties encountered by individual learners in other content areas are different from those of nonhandicapped students. In mathematics many problems are similar. The methods discussed are applicable to all students not only those with learning problems.

Limited Reasoning Ability

Students with limited reasoning ability require repeated review of problem-solving sequences combined with presentations that emphasize the meaning base of the concepts. Students must then express in their own words what they have learned. Step-by-step instruction stressing the logical relationship of each step to the next provides a structure for augmenting limited reasoning ability.

Short Attention Span

For students with short attention spans, brief, varied activities will be needed as well as behavior modification techniques to increase on-task behavior. Because of delayed development, some students may continue to need manipulative experiences. Tangible objects also serve to maintain students' attention. Using stations and self-checking activities are alternatives to lengthy seatwork. These are interesting to students and allow them to move about the classroom constructively.

Perseveration

Students who are prone toward perseveration are able to repeat sequences of numbers or lists of facts absentmindedly. To promote meaningful learning, avoid excessive drill or memorization. Despite the adage, neither practice nor drill make perfect. Monitor drill closely and check students' initial attempts at new problems. Opportunity for observation can be made by allowing students time to begin homework assignments at the end of the class.

Impulsivity

For students who may impulsively complete problems, although inaccurately, teachers may want to diminish the speed of response. To accomplish this, students may be directed to stop at the completion of each problem, look over the work, and check each step carefully.

Anxiety

Anxiety can be reduced by lessening the pressure on students to have only the correct answer. Students need to be comfortable with honest errors as a part of learning. Nor should speed be emphasized. Exceptional learners may work slowly. They should be allowed to do so as long as teachers are convinced of steady progress.

Students should be encouraged to ask questions. However, teachers cannot simply be available to them as many are fearful of displaying limitations and errors and avoid seeking help despite need. It is teachers' responsibilities to provide opportunities for evaluating and correcting student work. Setting times when all students can receive individual assistance would remove any stigma. When teachers are supportive, students tend to be more responsive.

Reading and Language Deficits

Students with reading and language deficits may have difficulty with story problems, mathematics terminology, and reasoning. Students *think* the sequences of processes in verbal not numerical inner language. Teachers must verbalize each step of the process and allow students to "think out loud" as a means to conceptualization and to define and review vocabulary. Although some new words will have to be learned, less used terminology such as *minuend, multiplicand,* and *subtrahend* are best avoided.

Difficulty in Distinguishing Important From Unimportant Information

For students who have difficulty in telling significant from irrelevant information, reduce excessive talking and avoid giving alternative explanations or strategies that result in confusion rather than enlightenment. Verbal and descriptive emphasis, color cues on the chalkboard, and repetition identify relevant information. If the concept is not understood, a different approach is needed. The new strategy must be clearly distinguishable from the insufficient one.

Process Versus Product

For long-term use, understanding a process is more important than product. This is not to underestimate the necessity of students learning to arrive at correct answers, but it is to suggest that within the learning setting, process and product may need to be treated differently. Students' successes in learning the correct procedure should not be compromised by their inconsistent or incidental mistakes in calculation. By awarding two grades for each problem on arithmetic papers, teachers can reinforce accuracy in process while noting limitations in calculation.

Sequences

Organize tasks into sequences of subskills from simple to complex. In computation it may be preferable to teach the logical steps toward solving the problem in order, despite the relative difficulty in some steps. Hewett and Forness (1974) describe this method as teaching by the "thimbleful" rather than the "bucketful." In general, the more limited or disabled the students, the greater the number of small steps needed.

Known to Unknown

Begin at the level students have mastered following the principle of moving from known to unknown. The steps in reinforcing learning are: 1. After a concept is explained, demonstrated, and discussed, students should practice at the board. 2. At this point a "stop and think" pause is beneficial. With quiet in the room, students mentally review the material presented. 3. Seatwork is then assigned. After a few problems are completed independently, check them to avoid the frustration of doing several problems on the whole page incorrectly. Use worksheets only after adequate explanation and practice with visual, auditory, and/or tactile techniques.

Generalization and Transfer

Because many exceptional learners are limited in the ability to generalize and transfer concepts, point out that the process learned is used in other situations. For example, teachers can show that the process of multiplying a one-digit number is the same as with a two- (or more) digit multiplier. Using the same basic numerals in the comparison helps understanding. Create a new example: Ask students if and how the process just learned applies. When teachers demonstrate similarities, some students will adopt the practice and look for their own comparisons. Continued reminders by teachers to do so will reinforce this practice.

Scope and Sequence Charts, Programs, and Materials

Scope and Sequence Charts

Some teachers' curriculum guides provide scope and sequence charts showing which concepts and skills are introduced on each grade level. They are usually grouped in sequence, making it easier for remedial teachers to plan individual lessons and for regular teachers to group students for instruction.

Programs and Materials

Below are listed selected instructional programs and supplementary materials that can be used by either remedial or regular teachers.

1. *Cuisenaire Rods and Student Activity Cards* (Cuisenaire Corporation of America). Materials consist of wooden rods of varying lengths (metric) and color coded for number references. They provide concrete material for readiness and basic arithmetic. An accompanying book provides activities for using rods. Additional sets of cards can be used to direct individual practice.

2. *DISTAR I, II, and III* (SRA). Three sequential sets of highly structured, task-analyzed, behaviorally based total programs demonstrated to have good results, especially with disadvantaged students.

3. *Touch Math* (Touch Learning Concepts, Inc.). Students touch points on the numerals to compute facts and problems. This supplementary program facilitates the learning of facts because students see, hear, say, and feel the problems.

4. *How to Solve Story Problems* (DLM). This provides step-by-step procedures for individual or group instruction; it includes exercise cards to provide student practice.

5. *Individual Math System* (Revised) (Ginn). An extensive program for grades one through six, the IMS includes teacher guides, placement tests, teacher-directed and individual activities, and frequent evaluations; it comes with manuals, skill booklets, and cassettes.

6. *Merrill Mathematics Skill Tapes* (Merrill). This program has forty cassettes and accompanying student booklets, covering basic mathematic operations and concepts. They are useful in individualization and/or nongraded situations from third through the ninth grades.

7. *Montessori Materials* (Montessori, 1964, 1965a, 1965b). Based on the educational principles of Maria Montessori, these materials provide extensive hands-on experience with objects such as cubes, cylinders, beads, frames, and weighted blocks, which may be used to supplement mathematics instruction.

8. *Project Math* (Educational Progress Corporation). This is a complete program (with field testing that included exceptional learners) with a range from preschool through sixth grades; there are four kits of instructional guides and materials; the multioption organization allows students to learn through a preferred method.

9. *Schoolhouse Math Series* (SRA). There are three kits of instruction and materials for grades one through four. It is not a total program but provides supplementary work in numbers, concepts, arithmetic operations, word problems, time, money, and measurement.

10. *Error Patterns in Computation* (Ashlock, 1976). This book presents a step-by-step procedure for identifying, analyzing, and remediating difficulties in the basic computational skills.

11. *SRA Math Program* (SRA). This provides a kindergarten through eighth grade mathematics program with materials, guides to assessment, and instructional procedures.

12. *Stern Structural Arithmetic* (Houghton Mifflin). Four kits, one at each grade level, kindergarten through third, provide concrete materials (cubes, nested boxes, trays—all color coded with number referents) for discovery of mathematic facts and concepts.

13. *Sullivan Programmed Math* (Behavioral Research Laboratories). The series of books focus on computational skills, presupposing the achievement of readiness and basic mathematics understanding. The books require a minimum of reading and provide immediate feedback to individual learners.

14. *Computer-Assisted Instruction*. Numerous software programs are available at all levels to teach specific skills and to provide practice.

Summary

Mathematics and arithmetic have become increasingly important in the school curriculum, rivaling the traditional supremacy of reading. Four levels of mathematics are the concrete, representational, symbolic, and conceptual. The first three are sequential; the last is pervasive across the other three in addition to becoming ultimately the highest level. Understanding and conceptualization appropriate to the development of students and the nature of the arithmetic task precede the learning of operations and applications.

Readiness and motivation are as important in mathematics as they are in reading. The former includes such skills as one-to-one correspondence, sequencing, categorization, visual-spacial-relationship perception, and the ability to visualize groups. Motivation often needs to overcome cultural misperceptions about the relative importance of math, the difficulty in learning the subject, and sex-role appropriateness.

No approach or technique is universally applicable or successful. Too often, the teaching of mathematics is restricted to the symbolic level without adequate attention to the conceptual structure of the subject. Assessment is used to determine the level of students' functioning, and this information becomes a guideline for the selection of methods and materials, including those presented throughout this chapter. Teaching for meaning, emphasizing application to daily situations, and improving the thinking process are imperative goals of instruction.

Science

The skills of conceptualization and problem solving taught in mathematics lay the foundation for learning science. Students learn to impose order on data, describe physical phenomena accurately, hypothesize and predict, and explore unknowns. Although science is necessarily integrated with mathematics in the more rigorous disciplines, beginning science can be taught in a more utilitarian context relevant to the daily lives of students. Science teachers are challenged to develop programs that accommodate the learning styles and limitations of exceptional students.

Exceptional students, like their nonhandicapped peers, learn about themselves and the world around them through science. Far from being limited to abstract and theoretical constructs, science curriculum provides practical information and skills. It can give them a better understanding of their bodies and their handicapping conditions. Science teachers must learn how to adapt curriculum and methods to accommodate students with various disabilities. Special education teachers must learn to incorporate informational and useful science content in the special classroom.

Purpose

Science education in the elementary curriculum serves three purposes. First, it enhances conceptual development of biological, physical, and earth sciences. Menhusen and Gromme (1976, p. 35) describe science education as "a vehicle for developing basic skills of observing, describing, identifying, comparing, associating, inferring, applying, and predicting that lead to the more complex skills of problem-solving needed in everyday living." It provides satisfaction for students' natural curiosity about themselves and their environment. Coincidentally, it reduces inaccurate and superstitious beliefs about how the world operates.

Second, science education provides information that allows exceptional individuals to appreciate their environments, to be cognizant of the broader aspects of the world in which they live, and to facilitate responsible decisions. It has impact on their knowledges and skills regarding the human body, weather, food preparation, home and community ecology, plants, animals, and the use of various materials. At the secondary level, concepts are extended to provide a foundation for capable exceptional youth to prepare for a career in a scientific field. Virtually every area of science has professional practitioners who are handicapped (Hofman & Ricker, 1979).

Third, students participate in the learning process by developing inquiry skills to perform activities to use scientific knowledge in everyday living.

Assessment

Assessment procedures are conducted prior to enrollment in the science class to determine initial capabilities and for evaluation of performance.

Preenrollment assessment data are used as a base for writing the IEP. The science teacher, special education teacher, parents, other school representatives, and, if possible, the students participate. In addition to the traditional psychometric information, the committee examines motor abilities relative to laboratory participation, reading level in comparison to the readability level of the text, and beginning knowledges about the subject. The latter can be estimated by presenting students with sample questions from the curriculum and teaching materials (Turnbull & Schulz, 1979).

Other considerations are: Can the students take notes? Will they need additional time to complete tasks? Is their attention span sufficient to allow participation in discussions? Will specialized equipment and materials be needed?

Learning styles are determined so that concepts can be presented in a way students can understand. Alternative ways to express facts and concepts and cooperative learning techniques are suitable for assessing learning. Full credit is given to procedures that are adapted to allow for handicapping conditions, including physical handicaps and visual impairments. Accommodations such as oral testing or grading on observations and participation may be necessary.

Curriculum

Exceptional students in the regular class are subject to the same science curriculum as nonhandicapped students. Science curricula at both the elementary and secondary levels are organized into the following areas: biological or life sciences, earth sciences, and the physical sciences. Some content areas commonly included within these categories at the elementary level are presented in Figure 13.8.

At the secondary level, the science curriculum continues with these same general areas but academic content assumes a broader perspective and greater depth. Expanded course offerings within the science department usually include

FIGURE 13.8

Elementary science curriculum

> I. What science is and what scientists do
> II. Biological or life sciences
>   A. Living things
>   B. Plants
>   C. Animals
>   D. The human body
>   1. Food and respiration processes
>   E. Life cycles
>   F. Man and the environment
> III. Earth Sciences
>   A. Air, water, and weather
>   B. Ecology
>   C. Atmosphere
>   D. The sky and the solar system
>   E. Earth
>   F. Rocks and minerals
> IV. Physical sciences
>   A. Matter
>   B. Energy
>   C. Structure and forces
>   1. Mass, weight, volume
>   2. Magnetism
>   3. Electricity
>   D. Light and color
>   E. Sound
>   F. Heat
>   G. Motion and time
>   H. Materials

- Earth science
- Interdisciplinary science
- Biology
- Chemistry
- Physics
- Introduction to physical science

In larger school systems, other specialty classes such as geology or astronomy may be offered.

A major aspect of the curriculum is introducing students to the scientific method, the systematic procedure for investigating the phenomena of the domain of science:

stating problems, collecting relevant information, analyzing data, and drawing inferences or conclusions. The science curriculum introduces students to the procedures scientists use, although it is not restricted to that domain. Therefore, they develop cognitive skills in observing, measuring, describing, classifying, comparing, and drawing conclusions.

Science and Exceptional Learners

As suggested, exceptional students have a need to learn about the world they live in and can profit from the practical knowledges science provides in the human body, plants, animals, the universe, and the physical sciences. Whenever possible, students with handicaps should attend the regular science class. However, Atwood and Oldham (1985) suggest several problems which may accrue for mainstreamed students. Paraphrased here, these include:

- The language demand needed to read the text and directions and to record answers
- Understanding difficult concepts and terminology
- Time requirements for completing work
- Requirement for high-level concentration and sustained attention to task
- Loose class structure that requires a level of self-regulation not mastered by some exceptional students
- Scheduling
- Testing and evaluating

These factors as well as class structure, teacher expectations, student characteristics, and classroom functioning are considered in determining placement. Some students may need a separate adapted class to enable them to fulfill the science requirement for graduation. Students with conceptual limitations may have difficulty with comparing, classifying, and drawing conclusions. In self-contained classes they learn basic concepts concretely and how to make practical applications.

Methods

As suggested in Chapter 9, good teaching methods benefit both exceptional and nonhandicapped students. Inherent in the teaching of science are a number of advantages for handicapped students. Unlike other academic subjects that rely primarily on verbal communication for instruction and language concepts for understanding, science includes hands-on activities, demonstration, concrete materials, and other multisensory experiences. Further, science is intrinsically motivating, and the class provides numerous opportunities for cooperative learning, assistance from nonhandicapped peers, and the development of interpersonal skills.

Teachers often use an inquiry method of instruction, allowing students to proceed through a sequence of steps to discover the scientific principle that is the objective of the lesson. Although a valuable approach with nonhandicapped students, it has potential limitations when used with individuals with handicaps.

1. Exceptional students are often unsuccessful in trial-and-error learning, giving up after initial errors rather than knowing how to proceed further or having the motivation to do so.
2. Conceptually, each step may be perceived as a whole, independent of the experiment. Thus, the completion of one step does not logically or automatically lead to the next.
3. This same lack of associative learning may interfere with some students being unable to see the relationship between the sequential steps of the experiment and the conclusions.

Thus, for exceptional students use a modified inquiry approach. Word instructions carefully, monitor progress through each step, and present a concluding explanation that integrates the steps of the experiment. Another technique is to regroup students in the laboratory because those who are exceptional tend to cluster socially with each other. Integrating them into groups with nonhandicapped classmates provides them with the advantages of structure and informal peer instruction and augments communication and socialization.

Specific techniques include the following:

- Provide outlines and notes for each unit of study.
- Provide notes on transparencies for those unable to take notes.
- Provide a study guide. A formalized study guide approach to teaching science is described by Lovitt, Rudsit, Jenkins, Pious, and Benedetti (1985).
- Monitor reinforcement of safety precautions at all times.
- Emphasize vocabulary development with students keeping a notebook of terms.
- Cooperate with the language arts or English teacher to employ vocabulary in spelling lists and writing lessons.
- Give consistent, step-by-step presentations.
- Encourage students to ask questions.
- Encourage discussion and attend to misunderstandings as a basis for reteaching concepts.
- Avoid lengthy presentations.
- Incorporate students' experiences in explanations.
- Use audiovisual media and computer instructional programs.
- Use learning centers and stations to give maximum participation.
- Emphasize overlearning.
- Teach scientific problem solving thoroughly at the beginning with a structured sequence of activities to be applied to each experiment.
- Describe demonstrations verbally, pointing out what to attend to in each step.
- Word questions differently from text to determine if students understand the concept.
- Summarize frequently.
- Use continuous formative evaluation.
- Allow small-group review.
- Provide sufficient time for review at the end of each unit or experiment and prior to quizzes or tests.

Specific techniques for students with memory problems include repetition, multisensory presentation, emphasis on major concepts, and frequent reviews and quizzes.

While these methods are appropriate for students with mild mental retardation or learning disabilities, regular teachers are also concerned about those with other handicapping conditions. These include students with reading or language problems, visual or hearing impairments, and those who are orthopedically handicapped.

Students with Language Difficulties

Students with learning disabilities and mild mental retardation often have language difficulties that interfere with acquisition of subject content. It is suggested that the teacher seek assistance in selecting an alternative text or procuring a text on tape to be listened to rather than read.

Assigning a partner to read the text is another solution. Comprehension is improved if the text is read aloud either by the student or a peer. As suggested, emphasis should be on vocabulary development. The special teacher can incorporate vocabulary and concepts in instruction in the special classroom.

Students With Visual Impairments

Students with some degree of vision can participate fully in science class, including the laboratory. As visual acuity is diminished, lab partners can be used or special materials such as large print, magnifying devices, tape, talking calculators, or braille materials can be employed. Tapes are particularly useful in presenting directions for lab experiments. The tape can be listened to repeatedly. Notes can be taken in braille or the lecture tape recorded by the student. Tactile graphics are also available. Teachers need to provide accurate descriptions in precise vocabulary. All new terms must be carefully explained, and tactile experiences provided. Use real objects whenever possible. Use models for other experiences while describing their size relative to the real object.

Students who are blind can participate in the laboratory. Use lab partners; label all lab equipment in braille; keep objects in the same place each time. Take extraordinary safety precautions. A science program for upper elementary students with visual impairments was developed by Malone, Petrucchi, and Thier (1981). Their *Science Activities for the Visually Impaired* (SAVI) employs special equipment and is activity-based. It can be used with blind, partially sighted, and sighted students. Therefore, it is appropriate for regular science classes with mainstreamed students.

Students With Hearing Impairments

Adjust methods depending on students' level of functional hearing as reported by the special teacher. Because hearing impairment is often accompanied by reading deficits, make sure the text and other materials are at an appropriate level. Provide preferential seating. Use the chalkboard frequently; use posters, illustrations, and captioned films and filmstrips. Students who are deaf may need a signer.

Students With Orthopedic Impairments

Students with orthopedic impairments but normal intelligence can achieve in science. They may be equal to others in concept development, language, and understanding. They are at the greatest disadvantage in the laboratory. Special equipment can be made or purchased for them, or they may work with lab partners, verbally contributing, following aurally and visually, and participating to the extent individually possible. Students with cerebral palsy who have little control of muscles may be very limited in lab participation but should be in the laboratory with the class at all times.

Two excellent sources for teaching science to students with visual, hearing, or orthopedic handicaps are Hadary and Cohen (1978) and Hofman (1979). In addition, the Educational Resource Information Center/Science, Math, and Environmental Educational Information Clearing House (ERIC/SMEE) can provide references for curriculum, methods, and materials for teaching science to handicapped students.

Programs

With support from the U.S. Office of Education, the Biological Sciences Curriculum Study group produced a sequence of three curricula for students with mental retardation. The first, *Me Now,* in kit form is intended for those in the eleven-to-thirteen-age range. It includes materials and equipment. Because there is no textbook, students become directly involved in activities designed to provide information about human life. *Me and My Environment* extends the curriculum to ecological topics. It continues the development of inquiry skills and problem solving and is designed for middle school or junior high students. *Me and My Future* becomes career-oriented, addressing leisure activities and daily-living skills in addition to presenting vocational information. Although designed for retarded students in self-contained classes, many of the activities and materials can be used with all students in regular science classes.

SUMMARY

Exceptional students can profit from the practical knowledges and inquiry procedures in regular or self-contained science classes. Instruction enhances conceptual development; provides information about the biological, physical, and earth sciences; and for some, lays the foundation for careers in science.

Preassessment determines individual academic and learning competencies as a basis for class placement and instructional needs. Exceptional students enrolled in regular science classes can be successful, particularly if the teacher is aware of their strengths, limitations, and learning styles and can make accommodations. Elementary and secondary curricula may need to be adapted to meet individual needs. The commonly employed "inquiry method" may be difficult for exceptional children if they are left on their own to discover scientific principles through trial-and-error learning. They need a modified approach with additional structure and teacher and peer support.

Other specific method adaptations can accommodate for difficulties in reading, note taking and recording data, and conceptualization. Reduction in lecture and verbal explanations, the use of hands-on activities, audiovisual media, learning stations and centers, computer programs, group activities, lab partners, frequent reviews, summaries, and formative evaluation can be used.

Special aid can be provided students with language difficulties, visual or hearing impairments, or orthopedic handicaps. Professional programs have been published for students with handicaps taught in separate classes.

REFERENCES

Alley, G., & Deshler, D. (1979). *Teaching the learning disabled adolescent: Strategies and methods.* Denver: Love.

Ashlock, R. B. (1986). *Error patterns in computation: A semi- programmed approach* (4th ed.). Columbus, OH: Merrill.

Atwood, R. K., & Oldham, B. R. (1985). Teachers' perceptions of mainstreaming in an inquiry oriented elementary science program. *Science Education, 69*(5), 619–624.

Balow, I. H., Farr, R., Hogan, T. P., & Prescott, G. A. (1978, 1979). *Metropolitan achievement tests* (5th ed.). Cleveland: Psychological Corporation.

Bartel, N. R. (1982). Problems in mathematics achievement. In D. D. Hammill, & N. R. Bartel (Eds.), *Teaching children with learning and behavior problems* (3rd ed.) (pp. 173–219). Boston: Allyn and Bacon.

Beatty, L. S., Madden, R., Gardner, E. F., & Karlsen, B. (1978). *Stanford diagnostic mathematics test* (2nd ed.). New York: Psychological Corporation.

Brueckner, L. J. (1955). *Diagnostic tests and self-helps in arithmetic.* Monterey, CA: CTB/McGraw- Hill.

Buswell, G. T., & John, L. (1926). *Diagnostic chart for fundamental processes in arithmetic.* Indianapolis: Bobbs-Merrill.

Carpenter, T. P., Corbitt, M. K., Kepner, H. S., Lindquist, M. M., & Reys, R. (1980a). Results of the second NAEP mathematics assessment: Secondary school. *The Mathematics Teacher, 73,* 329–338.

Carpenter, T. P., Corbitt, M. K., Kepner, H. S., Lindquist, M. M., & Reys, R. (1980b). Results and implications of the second NAEP mathematics assessments: Elementary school. *The Arithmetic Teacher, 27,* 10–12, 44–47.

Chalfant, J. C., & Scheffelin, M. A. (1969). *General processing dysfunctions in children: A review of the research.* Bethesda, MD: U.S. Department of Health, Education, and Welfare.

Connolly, A. J., Nachtman, W., & Pritchett, E. M. (1976). *KeyMath diagnostic arithmetic test.* Circle Pines, MN: American Guidance Service.

Enright, B. E. (1983). *Enright diagnostic inventory of basic arithmetic skills.* North Billerica, MA: Curriculum Associates.

Faas, L. A. (1980). *Children with learning problems: A handbook for teachers.* Boston: Houghton Mifflin.

Hadary, D. E., & Cohen, S. H. (1978). *Laboratory science and art for blind, deaf, and emotionally disturbed children: A mainstreaming approach.* Baltimore: University Park Press.

Hewett, F. M., & Forness, S. R. (1974). *Education of exceptional learners.* Boston: Allyn and Bacon.

Hofman, H. H. (Ed.) (1978). *A working conference on science education for handicapped students: Proceedings.* Washington, DC: National Science Teachers Association. U.S. Resources Information Center. ERIC Document No. SE 025 177 (1978).

Hofman, H. H., & Ricker, K. S. (1979). *Science education and the physically handicapped: Sourcebook.* Washington, DC; National Science Teachers Association.

Hogan, T. P., Farr, R., Prescott, G. A., & Balow, I. H. (1980). *The metropolitan mathematics instructional tests.* New York: Psychological Corporation.

Johnson, D. J., & Myklebust, H. R. (1967). *Learning disabilities: Educational principles and practices.* New York: Grune & Stratton.

Kaliski, L. (1967). Arithmetic and the brain-injured child. In E. C. Frierson, & W. Barbe (Eds.). *Educating children with learning disabilities: Selected readings* (pp. 399–404). New York: Appleton-Century-Crofts.

Kane, R. B., Byrne, M. A., & Hater, M. A. (1974). *Helping children read mathematics.* New York: American Book.

Lovitt, T., Rudsit, J., Jenkins, J., Pious, C., & Benedetti, D. (1985). Two methods of adapting science materials for learning disabled and regular seventh graders. *Learning Disabilities Quarterly, 8,* 275–285.

Malone, L., Petrucchi, L., & Thier, H. (1981). *Science activities for the visually impaired (SAVI).* Berkeley: Center for Multisensory Learning, University of California.

Menhusen, B. R., & Gromme, R. O. (1976). Science for handicapped children—Why? *Science and Children, 13*(6), 35–37.

Mercer, C. D., & Mercer, A. R. (1985). *Teaching students with learning problems* (2nd ed.). Columbus, OH: Merrill.

Montessori, M. (1964). *The Montessori method.* New York: Schocken Books.

Montessori, M. (1965a). *Dr. Montessori's own handbooks.* New York: Schocken Books.

Montessori, M. (1965b). *The Montessori elementary material.* Cambridge, MA: Robert Bentley.

Moran, M. R. (1978). *Assessment of the exceptional learner in the regular classroom.* Denver: Love.

Naslund, R. A., Thorpe, L. P., & Lefever, D. W. (1978). *SRA achievement series.* Chicago: Science Research Associates.

Otto, W., McMenemy, R. A., & Smith, R. J. (1973). *Corrective and remedial teaching* (2nd ed.). Boston: Houghton Mifflin.

Spencer, E. F., & Smith, R. M. (1969). Arithmetic skills. In R. M. Smith (Ed.). *Teacher diagnosis of educational difficulties* (pp. 152–170). Columbus, OH: Merrill.

Stern, C. (1965). *Structural arithmetic.* Boston: Houghton Mifflin.

Strauss, A. A., & Lehtinen, L. E. (1947). *Psychopathology and education of the brain-injured child.* New York: Grune & Stratton.

Tiegs, E. W., & Clark, W. W. (1978). *California achievement test.* Monterey, CA: CTB/McGraw-Hill.

Turnbull, A. P., & Schulz, J. B. (1979). *Mainstreaming handicapped students: A guide for the classroom teacher.* Boston: Allyn and Bacon.

Underhill, R. G., Uprichard, A. E., & Heddens, J. W. (1980). *Diagnosing mathematical difficulties.* Columbus: OH: Merrill

SUGGESTED READINGS

Abruscato, J. (1982). *Teaching children science.* Englewood Cliffs, NJ: Prentice-Hall.

Bitter, G. G., Mikesell, J. L., & Maurdeff, K. (1976). *Activities handbook for the teaching of the metric system.* Boston: Allyn and Bacon.

Bley, N. S., & Thornton, C. A. (1981). *Teaching mathematics to the learning disabled.* Rockville, MD: Aspen.

Cawley, J. F. (1984). *Developmental teaching of mathematics for the learning disabled.* Rockville, MD: Aspen.

Cawley, J. (Ed.) (1985). *Cognitive functions and mathematics for the learning disabled.* Rockville, MD: Aspen.

Cawley, J. F., Fitzmaurice-Hayes, A. M., Shaw, R. A., Norlander, K. B., & Sayre, J. (1987). *Learner activity program for developmental mathematics*. Rockville, MD: Aspen.

Coble, C. R., & Houndshell, P. B. (1977). *Mainstreaming science and mathematics: Special ideas and activities for the whole class*. Santa Monica, CA: Goodyear.

Farrald, R. R., Gonzales, F. M., & Masters, B. F. (1979). *A diagnostic and prescriptive technique: Handbook II: Disabilities in arithmetic: Approaches to diagnosis and treatment*. Sioux Falls, SD: Adapt Press.

Reisman, F. K. (1982). *A guide to the diagnostic teaching of arithmetic* (3rd ed.). Columbus, OH: E. Merrill.

Reisman, F. K., & Kauffman, S. H. (1980). *Teaching mathematics to children with special needs*. Columbus, OH: Merrill.

Simpson, R. D., & Anderson, N. D. (1981). *Science, students, and schools*. New York: Wiley.

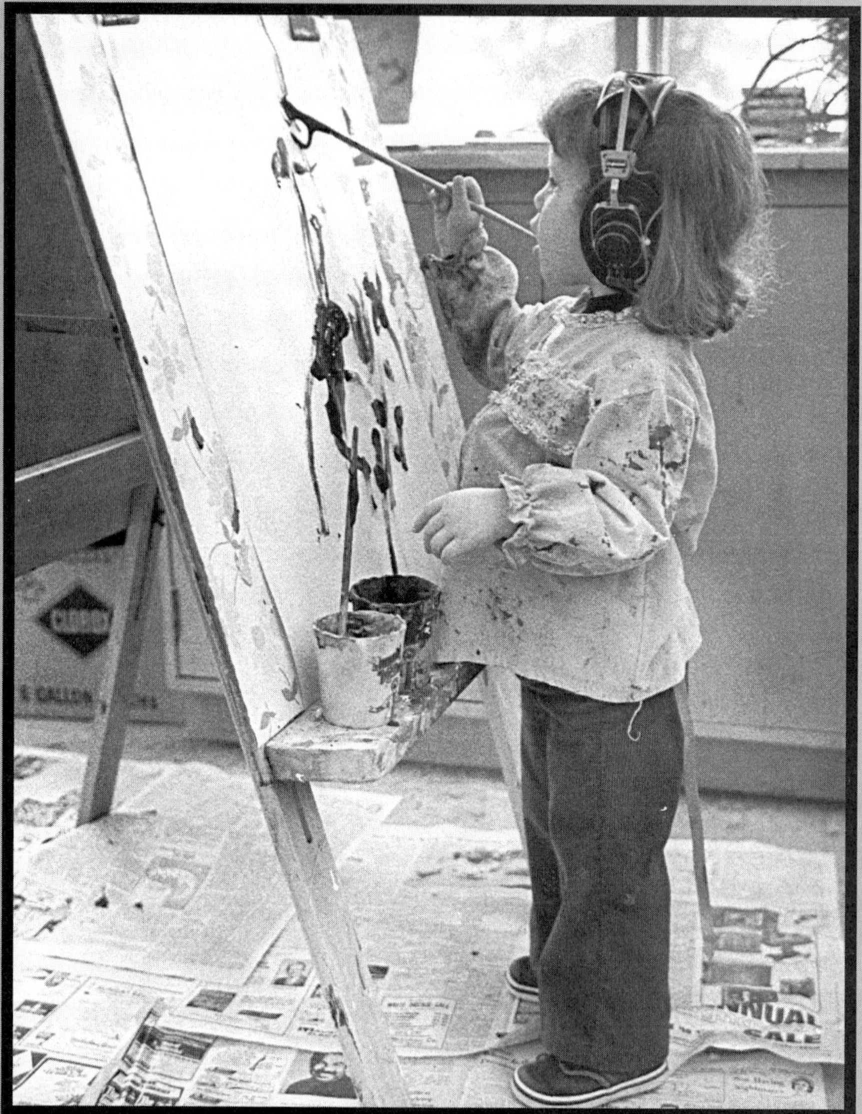
SALE

14

Methods for Teaching Art, Music, and Physical Education

STUDENTS are required to participate in art, music, and physical education as well as academic subjects. These classes benefit both exceptional and nonhandicapped students.

Although the nonacademic subjects are sometimes considered incidental to the academic curriculum, they are important aspects of the total school program and can add a vital dimension in the lives of exceptional learners. They provide

- Developmental training in perceptual-motor activities.
- Opportunities for socialization.
- Success experiences, which students may not be able to realize in academic subject areas.
- Learning experiences, which they may have missed because of the restrictive nature of the handicapping condition in earlier years.
- Interests and skills, which may contribute to life-long leisure activity.

Scheduling and Preparation

Elementary schools commonly employ a physical education teacher who meets each class at regularly appointed times. Some schools have art and music teachers on the same basis. However, because state departments of education do not always require that as much time in the curriculum be given to art and music, staffing patterns may vary. Some school districts employ teachers who serve two or more schools. Still others expect classroom teachers to teach these subjects.

At the secondary level, most schools have teachers for all three of these subjects. Physical education is often required for a specified number of semesters. Art and music are often electives, which are frequently selected by exceptional students.

Students in self-contained classes attend these subjects as a group—the instructor plans activities and conducts the class appropriate to the particular group. Where special students are part of a regular class, the art, music, and physical education instructors, like regular teachers, must plan for that heterogeneity. Whereas regular teachers may have attended the IEP conference, the art, music, and physical education teachers have not. They are usually not included in consultive services. Unless they are members of the school staff, they may not receive in service training. Art, music, and physical education are the subjects into which special education students are mainstreamed; yet the literature in all three subjects reflects that teachers consider themselves unprepared (Bird & Gansneder, 1979; Gilbert & Asmus, 1981; Lisenco 1975).

General Considerations

Usually, the methods for teaching special students art, music, and physical education are the same as those used in academic instruction. Adaptations of instruction and methods are based on several variables including the demands of subject content, limitations of the students, and environments in which the subjects are taught.

Demands of Subject Content

Often handicapped students are assigned to these classes on the assumption that there are few academic requirements, hence the academically limited student can succeed. This may be an oversimplification. Careful examination of the curriculum and methods reveals that considerable academic skills are demanded. For example, Welsbacher (1975) points out that learning *about* art (periods, lives of the painters, and the like) is different from *doing* art projects (painting, cutting, and designing). Learning about art or music can require considerable competence in reading and notetaking and, in the upper grades and secondary school, listening, remembering, and writing. Further, music has a mathematical base. Will students know to hold a half note twice as long as a quarter note? If tests are given, the grade will depend on test-taking skills and ability in expressive writing.

Limitations of the Students

The "other side of the coin" is the capability of exceptional students in meeting subject demands. Students who have difficulty academically do not automatically compensate by enjoying abilities in the area of motor dexterity. Many mildly handicapped students have less obvious but nonetheless real sensory and/or physical limitations. Developmental delays have resulted in fine motor coordination problems and perceptual deficits. They are at a disadvantage in drawing, discriminating between a note and its sharp or flat, in rhythm, or in throwing or catching a ball.

For more severely handicapped students—the visual and hearing impaired and those with orthopedic involvements—activities in art, music, and physical education can represent failure situations rather than an enjoyable change from academic subjects.

Environmental Considerations

The major environmental limitation for exceptional students may be the differences in classroom structure. These classes are often conducted in a more relaxed and open atmosphere than academic classes. For nonhandicapped students, this respite from the rigidity of the academic classroom may be essential. It also may be beneficial to students who are mildly retarded or physically handicapped. However, the general activity and noise level may lead to increased acting out behaviors in students who are hyperactive, learning disabled, and lacking in self-control.

With the emphasis on placing exceptional students in the least restrictive environment, most appear in art, music, and physical education classes. Major implications of this trend for the nonacademic subjects are the need to be more sensitive in assigning and programming and the need to provide training and support for teachers.

Therapy or Education?

The therapeutic aspects of art, music, and physical education are well-documented in the professional literature of those disciplines. Each is used in clinical settings with individuals with moderate and severe handicapping conditions for their habilitative and rehabilitative values. The field of physical education is perhaps most advanced with a wealth of theory and practice in adaptive physical education. The dominant theme in the literature of music for exceptional students is therapy—how music is used to rehabilitate and teach. Some authors in each field discuss the difference between these subjects as therapy and as education. However, the preponderance of activities are the same; the difference appears to be one of goals and emphasis in practice.

The issue lies not in justifying these subjects for exceptional students but in providing guidelines for teaching them. There is little to aid teachers in planning and conducting classes that include both handicapped and nonhandicapped students. At present, the most profitable recourse for teachers appears to be acquiring information about students with mildly handicapping conditions, investigating the recommended therapeutic methods, and adapting therapeutic procedures within the activities of the class.

Additional information about the topics discussed in this chapter can be obtained from state departments of education or the following organizations: National Committee on Arts for the Handicapped, John F. Kennedy Center for the Performing Arts, Washington, DC, 20566; and American Alliance for Health, Physical Education, Recreation, and Dance, 1900 Association Drive, Reston, Virginia 22091.

Art

One of the purposes of education is to guide students into conformity with society, to master a rule-governed language system, to follow the necessary steps to understand mathematics concepts and produce correct answers, and to learn acceptable behavior. Such activities require convergent thinking.

Like language and mathematics, art is a form of expression. Unlike these subjects, art is based on creativity—stressing originality, uniqueness, spontaneity, and inventiveness, all evolving from divergent thinking.

Creativity and Cognitive Development

Piaget (Piaget & Inhelder, 1969) proposed that all children progress through four stages of cognitive development during the formative years. The sequence of the stages is invariant, the same for all children. However, the rate at which individual children move through each stage varies. Thus, the relationship with chronological age is only approximate.

Lowenfeld and Brittain (1975) suggest that children also progress through a sequence of creative development that parallels cognitive growth. They list six stages:

1. The Scribbling Stage (ages two to four)
2. The Pre-Schematic Stage (ages four to seven)
3. The Schematic Stage (ages seven to nine)
4. The Group Stage (ages nine to twelve)
5. The Pseudo-Naturalistic Stage (ages twelve to fourteen)
6. Adolescent Art in High School (ages fourteen to seventeen)

In addition to Lowenfeld and Brittain, Anderson (1978) and Krone (1978) discuss art activities within the context of these stages.

Exceptional students go through the same sequential stages of creative development as others. Like cognitive development, some progress more slowly and may be delayed at a particular level. Thus, in the art class, teachers may work with students at several stages. Additional differences will result from variations in perceptual-motor and visual-perceptual development as well as from limitations imposed by sensory or physically handicapping conditions.

Art and Exceptional Students

To meet this range of individual differences, teachers will need to develop what Rubin (1975, p. 9) terms "an expanded concept of art." Rubin elaborates by stating that "art for the handicapped can and should include the whole possible range of manipulative or making activities with any media controllable by the child, not necessarily the traditional ones" (p. 9). Thus, many activities are planned over the duration of the year and several within a single class period. Craft activities, collage, clay, weaving, sculpture, puppetry, papier-mâché, printing, finger painting, fabric, yarn, string, ceramics, and plaster-cast painting may be included.

Methods General methods for instruction and classroom management are the same as for other subjects although more individual guidance and step-by-step direction may be needed. Careful consideration must be given to the amount of structure, getting started, the use of models, group activities, completing projects, limitations of some handicapping conditions, and evaluating and grading.

Structure Creativity requires unrestricted thinking. The individual explores the whole range of ideas, subject, and media and has the freedom to select and combine them in original ways. Many exceptional students, particularly those with learning disabilities, have difficulty in making decisions and then following through with them. Teachers will need to find a balance between structure and freedom, providing students with openness in which to explore but help in making choices through individual questioning or discussion as the project progresses.

Getting Started Exceptional students and individual learners, as well as others, may have difficulty beginning the project. If the problem is choosing a subject, students are given two or three choices. A time limit may be set in which the decision must be made. Another technique is to provide firm directions for the whole group to follow in the preliminary steps of the activity. Then as the actual work begins, students are free to proceed on their own. "Starter sheets," preprepared paper with the first lines or form outlines already on them, can be used.

It is preferable for most students that during the course of the activity teachers *not* do any part of the work for them. Teachers may indicate the need for and direction of a line but not draw it. The students' personal expression and "ownership" of the product is compromised by any teacher additions. An exception to this rule can be made for those with physical handicaps. Precut pieces or direct assistance may be given. Such assistance should be limited to those activities students cannot perform on their own.

Models Teachers debate on whether a model of the final product should be shown to the class at the beginning. Often they decide not to present a sample drawing but to provide an example of a construction-paper project. Some suggest that any model compromises originality. In addition, some students may be discouraged when their product is inferior to the model. On the other hand, exceptional students may not be able to conceptualize the activity from the teacher's verbal description. Compromises can be made. The work of a former student can be used as a model. Spontaneous chalkboard sketches may accompany the explanation, or teachers can construct their model during the class with students performing each step as teachers complete theirs.

Group Activities Occasionally, use small or large-group activities and projects. A small group can design and create a bulletin board for the homeroom teacher or a display for a topic in an academic subject. For a large-group project, the entire class might work on a puppet show to be presented to other classes and parents. Students with a handicap can be assigned tasks that they are capable of completing within the total project. Such projects allow opportunity for positive interaction among all class members and provide a feeling of accomplishment and acceptance.

Completing Projects Students must complete each art project they begin. Do not allow them to give up in the middle. Reinforce them for having completed the work even if the final product is not up to the teachers' or their own expectations. Do not overpraise. Recognize the areas of accomplishment but do not patronize students who recognize the limitations in their own work. Praise real achievement, effort, and perseverance.

Additional Limitations of Handicapping Conditions Students with neurological handicaps may be delayed in control of fine motor skills such as drawing, cutting, and tracing. Activities that do not require preciseness of control should be provided. For drawing and painting, large-diameter crayons, pencils, and brushes provide easier grasp. A pencil grip can be used.

Students with visual-perceptual problems may produce distorted pictures and be unable to learn perspective easily. Poor visual memory will limit detail and the relationship of elements in pictures. Drawing a still life, with the subject of the picture being present rather than creating a scene from the imagination, is a better activity.

Children with hearing impairments will have difficulties in following verbal directions. Because they are also delayed in language and reading development, written instructions will not remedy the problem. Be careful to use vocabulary they understand but, at the same time, build vocabulary by using new words—*texture, hue, design*—and explain their meaning. For students with severe hearing impairments, demonstration becomes a principal instructional tool.

Students with orthopedic handicaps or mild cerebral palsy will have motor problems similar to and more severe than the motorically delayed. Some of the same accommodations (for example, larger drawing equipment) can be used. Finger painting can also be used; sponges can be substituted for brushes. Paper is taped to the drawing board or desk, and drawing and painting implements and materials are placed in a tray taped to the desk. Foil trays or box lids are suitable for this purpose. If paints are used, containers should be secured to avoid spilling; consistency should be thick to reduce dripping. Use blunt scissors or provide precut pieces. Be sure the handle ends of brushes are rounded.

Students with visual impairments, including the blind, can be accommodated in the art class. For the visually limited, use large-size paper, light green or buff-colored to reduce glare. For young children with motor control or visual problems, outline drawings with glue and allow to dry or cut tag paper in desired shapes. These form a templatelike barrier to emphasize shape and contain coloring. Blind students will be more of a challenge. Alternative activities are provided. Three-dimensional projects and textured materials are used. Collages, clay, macramé, rug hooking, string art, fabric collage, model building, mask making, tactile puzzles, mobiles, wood, sponge, cardboard and other construction-paper projects, and ceramics can be employed.

ADAPTING ART FOR A BLIND STUDENT

Cynthia had not been included in art in elementary school. It was obvious she could not draw or color because she is blind. In addition, art class was an opportune time to provide her with supportive instruction in the subject areas. In middle school she did little in art. However, a new teacher arrived in the ninth grade who saw a challenge to introduce Cynthia to creating artistically. He introduced her to various three-dimensional media and projects. She enjoyed clay modeling and did well at it, creating small free-form pieces. Later he instructed her in creating larger clay modeling and to sculpting implements. She continued in art classes in high school. Although she was included in all the lectures and tours to local museums, her long-term projects were her clay sculptures, which she worked on in class while others worked in their media. Her pieces were included in the annual student art exhibit.

Evaluating and Grading

Grading has always been controversial in art. Some suggest grades are as necessary as they are in other subjects to indicate the quality of performance. Others, like Lowenfeld and Brittain (1975) believe grades have no place in art. They argue that grading changes the focus from creativity to the quality of the final product.

The issue becomes more crucial when exceptional students or individual learners are in the class. If students have innate conditions limiting the quality of their work, on what basis should they be graded? If they are functioning at different levels in personal and creative development, what standard can be used?

Fortunately, many elementary schools require only an indication of acceptable or unacceptable progress instead of letter or numerical grades. In the upper grades and in secondary schools when grades are required, they must be consistent with the goals and objectives of the program. If teachers determine that product is important, they grade on that basis. However, if personal growth and expression are goals, they determine grades on effort, ability level, and improvement made by students. Anderson (1978) suggests that goals and objectives be individualized. The students are then evaluated in comparison to "their own best efforts" or "growth over time" (pp. 20–21).

Summary

Art is an activity requiring divergent thinking and creativity. Like cognition, creative development can be traced through a series of stages. Exceptional students and individual learners may progress more slowly and be at a different level from others in the class. This necessitates individualization and careful planning. To accommodate for differences in individual development and for handicapping conditions, teachers may need to expand their concepts of art to employ a broad range of activities and nontraditional media.

Music

Most exceptional students are enrolled in the regular class music program. The purposes of participation are the same for handicapped and nonhandicapped students. Raebeck and Wheeler (1974) list the values of music education for the students as: "(1) He learns *what music is;* (2) He discovers what in music is *most enjoyable to him;* and (3) He discovers his own musical *aptitudes and skills*" (p. 2).

Music and Exceptional Students

Curriculum Nye and Nye (1977) emphasize the need for a longitudinal curriculum in music throughout the elementary grades rather than a piecemeal approach. They suggest that this curriculum should provide experiences that permit students to discover the structure, content, and creative elements in music logically and sequentially. Raebeck and Wheeler (1974, p. 8) list learning experiences as

1. Singing experiences
2. Rhythmic experiences
3. Experiences with instruments
4. Listening experiences

They are not hierarchical but parallel within a developmental sequence within each area. Several authors (for example, Bergethon & Boardman, 1975; Nye & Nye, 1977) provide descriptions of the developmental curriculum progression as related to physiological, psychological, social, and emotional development. The challenge to music teachers is to determine curriculum content and provide for individual differences. Activities and experiences must be appropriate to the developmental levels of the students.

Methods   Well-planned, careful instructional techniques used for other subjects are also applicable to music. Instruction will consist of large- and small-group teaching, stations, and other procedures for individualization (Boyle & Lathrop, 1973). Examination of the rich literature on music therapy can provide teachers with many practical suggestions. They are conscious of language demands on exceptional students, particularly vocabulary. Even those words that appear to be part of the general social vocabulary may need explanation. More technical terms need intensive and repetitive presentation.

Step-by-step instruction leads students to the desired concepts. In teaching melody, for example, teachers may begin with directed listening experiences. They instruct students to listen to their own and others' voices providing high, middle, and low sounds. They may imitate these pitches on the piano.

Melody and Musical Structure   A song is introduced. If a recording is used, teachers demonstrate the rise and fall of the musical pattern with their hands in the air. If they play the melody on the piano, the pattern can be indicated on the chalkboard (Figure 14.1). When students are expected to sing, words are added or substituted (Figure 14.2).

FIGURE 14.1

A melody pattern

FIGURE 14.2

A melody pattern with words

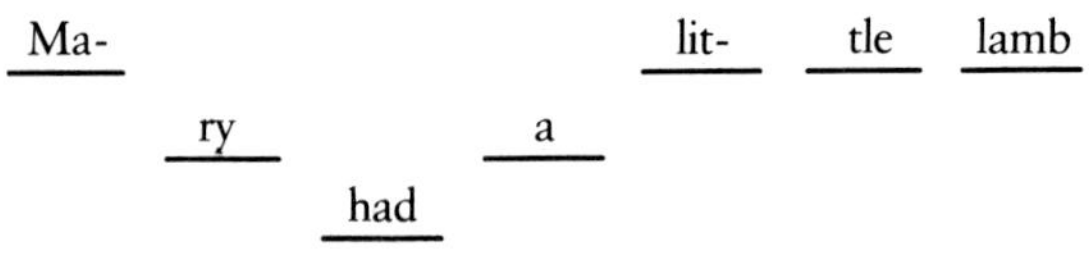

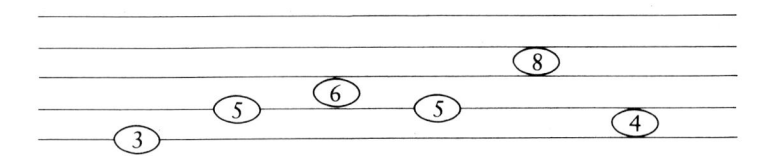

FIGURE 14.3

Numbered notes on a staff

Students can imitate the teachers' hand movements in the air as they sing or silently listen to other melodies. In the beginning, use songs they know; move from the familiar to the new.

Handbells can be used to teach melody. Numbered or color-coded bells are placed in tonal order. Students experiment with sounds and learn to play simple melodies following numbered or colored notes on a printed staff (Figure 14.3). A xylophone can also be used.

This also provides an introduction to the scale.

Tempo Tempo can also be taught visually (Figure 14.4). And later, as notation and scales are introduced, teachers can add notes to the familiar pattern (Figure 14.5).

Rhythm Rhythm grows out of early motor sequencing (Kephart, 1971). Most students move automatically with the music. Students with learning disabilities or or-

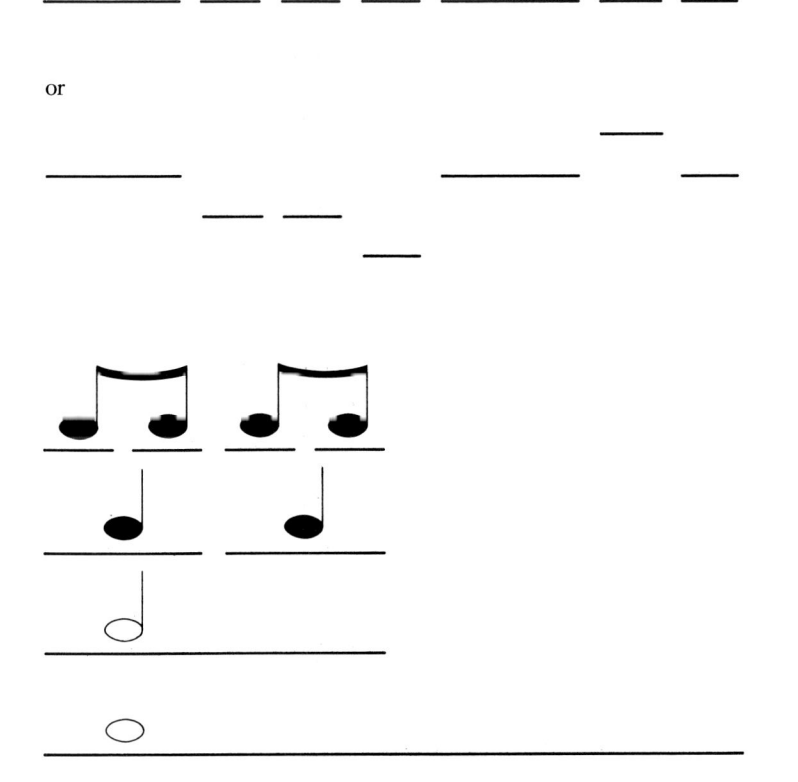

FIGURE 14.4

A tempo pattern

FIGURE 14.5

A tempo pattern with notes

FIGURE 14.6

A rhythm pattern

thopedic handicaps may not have developed this sense of rhythm. For them it is a new learning experience. Physical activity should be encouraged from the beginning with clapping, exercises, and other directed movement in time to music.

Use nonpitched instruments—drums, stocks, wood blocks, triangles, sandpaper blocks, and others. The rhythm band continues to teach basic elements of music and is the first step in learning about instrumentation.

To illustrate rhythm visually, again use the chalkboard with perpendicular lines close together for rapid notes and with spaces to indicate pauses or rests (Figure 14.6).

Students follow this pattern by clapping hands. Some "notes" can be accented with underlining; these receive louder claps than others (Figure 14.7). Later these symbols are changed to notes (Figure 14.8). Then the bar is introduced as such sequences are segmented into sections of equal lengths.

Exceptional students will be easily confused between note–syllables (do, re, mi) and note names (C, D, E). Using a numerical notation system, as advised by some authors, may simply add to the confusion for students with learning handicaps. Similarly, resorting to the familiar mnemonic devices—F A C E for spaces, and *Every Good Boy Does Fine* for the lines—may not be effective. It fragments the scale and does not contribute to the conceptualization of scaling. Names are probably best taught in direct association with the notes in sequence on the scale.

Listening

Hearing is automatic for most children; listening is learned. Throughout music instruction, the admonition to listen and the provision of directed listening experiences are essential. Learning about tempo, pitch, melody, harmony, and dynamics as well

FIGURE 14.7

A clapping pattern

FIGURE 14.8

A note pattern

as refinement of emotional responses to music depends on ability to discern and discriminate, which eventually becomes automatic.

For some listening activities, there is a sequence of preparation, listening, and follow-up. Elements for which students are to listen are identified. The music is played and then reviewed. Occasionally, a theme or the melody played by a particular instrument is isolated.

Other listening activities are less structured to allow students to use their imaginations. With program music, that which has a story or mood, other activities can be combined with listening—pantomiming or assuming the facial expressions or posture appropriate to the emotion, going about the room with the movements of the animal depicted by the music (for example, *Carnival of the Animals*), or drawing pictures of the action of the story (for example, *The Sorcerer's Apprentice*).

Teachers should not hesitate to include many listening experiences. Nor should they refrain from repeating a song or composition several times. Few pieces allow instant identification and appreciation.

A Final Note

Music instruction can enrich the lives of exceptional students because it can bring enjoyment and relaxation to those who learn to listen to music. Performing in music programs, singing, or playing an instrument can improve self-image and gives students the opportunity to share with each other and to discover musical talent.

Summary

Music has the potential for enriching the lives of all students including the handicapped. Music classes present opportunities to learn how to listen to music, to develop an interest in various types of music, to perform and share with peers, and to discover personal talent. The curriculum should provide experiences in singing, rhythm, instruments, and listening. The latter is particularly important both in teaching understanding of the concepts of music and for introducing students to a broad range of musical expression. Because of the unique structure of the subject, careful step-by-step developmental instruction is employed.

Physical Education

Physical education occupies a unique place in the curriculum for exceptional students. The goals of physical education are physical fitness, motor development, social and emotional adjustment, and recreation. Each of these is as applicable to exceptional students as it is to their nonhandicapped peers. In addition, successful participation in the physical education program or exclusion from it can have psychological implications affecting the personality development and self-concept of students with handicaps. Recognizing the potential benefits of participation in physical education, the drafters of PL 94–142 determined that it should be available to all students with handicaps.

Physical Education and Exceptional Students

Kinds of Programs Depending on the nature and severity of the handicapping condition, students might be enrolled in any one of the following programs (Ohio Department of Education, 1980):

Regular Program This physical education program is provided for all students. Mildly handicapped students participate fully without modifications or restrictions.

Remedial Program Students with physical conditions that can be stabilized or improved by a continuing program of specific exercises and other structured activity belong in this group. It may be part of a larger intervention of physical therapy.

Developmental Program This program is applicable to students at the elementary level who show delays in physical, motor, or perceptual-motor maturation. Selected activities augment generalized and/or specific skill development.

Adapted Program Students with stabilized conditions that prevent their participation in some or all activities in routine physical education classes qualify for an adapted program. Activities are selected and modified to allow maximum participation while circumventing the handicapping condition.

Auxter and Pyfer (1985) identify three levels of motor functioning related to the acquisition of sports skills. These are basic input functions, general abilities, and specific skills. They recommend that the physical education teacher identify the level at which each student is functioning and that a developmental approach to instruction be used to facilitate continued growth and achievement.

Organization of Programs

It is obvious that local schools will not be able to provide each kind of program noted. Students with severe handicaps, however, are usually placed in separate schools or in interdistrict, cooperative classes where an adapted physical education class may be provided. Unified school districts may employ a physical education staff, allowing flexibility of scheduling and programming. More problems accrue in the neighborhood school where often a single instructor is employed to provide physical education classes for first through sixth grades.

Exceptional Students in Regular Elementary Classes The curriculum of physical education at the elementary level is advantageous for the incorporation of exceptional students in the regular program. Unlike the secondary level at which team sports and competitiveness become a major focus and emphasize individual differences (Minner & Knuston, 1982), the program in the elementary school is more developmental and game-oriented. Thus, students with mild impairments and those with perceptual and/or motor lags may profit from the developmental experiences routinely included in the curriculum and from the socialization provided.

Most exceptional students in regular classes will not have physical or sensory handicaps but will have mild retardation, learning disabilities, or emotional handicaps.

Unfortunately, it is these students who are most easily overlooked. It is sometimes erroneously thought that these conditions do not interfere with physical abilities and that, therefore, these students can be easily included in physical education classes. However, they may manifest problems that are less obvious but which nonetheless interfere with physical performance. Students with visual-spacial-perceptual disabilities is a case in point. In the process of hitting a ball with a bat, they must perceive and determine the speed and angle of projection of the ball, its constantly changing position in space in relation to the body, and its estimated time of arrival at home plate. Students must be aware of their own body position in space and the needed strength, direction, and angle of swing to allow the moving bat to contact the moving ball in space. That this occurs so commonly in gym class and on the sandlot sometimes belies the complexity of the task. But for students with poor visual perception and poor perceptual-motor coordination, it may be impossible.

Methods General teaching techniques applicable to exceptional students are as follows:

1. Teach the expected activity. Instructors should not assume that students come to school already knowing how to play the game or sport. Students with mild handicaps may have avoided neighborhood participation or may have been rejected from participation because of lack of skills.
2. Teach the rules for each new activity. Lack of participation may have resulted from the students not being knowledgeable about rules.
3. Teach nonhandicapped students to respect the limitations of their handicapped peers without reducing self-concept by "babying" them.
4. Reduce competitiveness at the beginning.
5. Emphasize safety for all.
6. Use the students' name. State the name *before* giving the command or direction. In the multistimuli environment of the gym or playground, distractible students will have difficulty focusing attention.
7. Use step-by-step instruction.
8. Demonstrate frequently. Exceptional students including those with mild retardation may learn more quickly by observation rather than by verbal explanations.
9. Teach new skills at the beginning of the class when students are fresh.
10. Provide rest periods.
11. Describe new activities slowly, being careful to define "technical" terms.
12. Repeat directions with accompanying demonstration.
13. Approach students with the expectation that they can succeed. Most students with handicaps have learned to sense rejection in a patronizing attitude.
14. Reduce anxiety about task performance. Emphasize that the activities are learning experiences and that all will make mistakes while learning.
15. Expect students to complete tasks begun. If particular circumstances result in their not being able to continue, substitute a success adaptation.
16. Use a whistle, visual signals, and verbal cues with consistent meaning.
17. Teach relaxation. Maintain a structured routine but within a relaxed atmosphere to reduce fearfulness and tenseness.

18. Emphasize the values of good sportsmanship for all.
19. Never allow others to laugh at or ridicule awkwardness or mistakes.
20. Become familiar with medical records and limitations of each student.

Accommodations   For many activities a variety of accommodations can be made to allow for individual differences.

1. Two or more activities can be conducted simultaneously with students grouped on the basis of interest or on ability level but not solely on the basis of handicapping condition.
2. Activities can be selected that can be accomplished despite the handicapping condition. Students in wheelchairs can participate in many games including archery, tetherball, ten pins, and tossing games. Suitable "quiet games" and less strenuous activities can be provided for students with special health problems. For older students, look for activities in which they might become interested or excel. There have been and continue to be handicapped participants in the International Olympic Games.
3. Activities can be adapted. A runner can be designated for an orthopedically impaired batter. Use larger teams than usual to reduce strenuous running. Rules can be changed—the number of swings at bat increased or unlimited substitutions. Length of games can be shortened. The long jump can be made from a standing position rather than after a hop and a step.
4. Special equipment can be used or adaptations of equipment can be made. Examples are "Bleeping" balls for the visually impaired; auditory signals (a bell) placed behind a target; clapping hands, which direct a student toward the finish line; a rope stretched along a running track; sponge rubber balls, which offer an easier grip than hard-rubber balls; an oversized plastic bat and a lighter ball; and a "tee" for batting.
5. Adjustments can be made to allow participation with nonhandicapped students. The student on crutches can be a goalie. The student in a wheelchair can take all the foul shots in a basketball game. The number of repetitions in group calisthenics can be reduced.

Non-handicapped members of the class can learn to be sensitive to and have patience with students with handicaps. Thus, these accommodations should be made occasionally rather than routinely. The authors agree with Cratty (1980, p. 97) who states that there should be "no reduction in the quality of instruction and the vigor of the program extended to normal youngsters when the handicapped make their appearance." This admonition is not license to ignore exceptional students but a challenge to provide quality services to handicapped and nonhandicapped individuals. Further, if the program is continuously changed for students with handicaps, resentment rather than appreciation could result.

The examples of suggested accommodations have centered around students whose obvious physical impairments interfere with their participation. Students with hearing impairments have all the physical attributes to allow them to develop the dexterity and skills needed for unrestricted participation. However, they do not respond to verbal instructions and to teammates' shouts for attention during games. A visual code—short of signing for which there is no time—can be developed for communication during physical education classes. Further, these students have learned to be alert, to see, to watch, to "read body language," and to imitate movement. They can learn much in the class through demonstration and modeling instruction.

Accommodations may need to be made in games requiring throwing, catching, and hitting balls. It may be necessary to excuse students from such activities while skill training and developmental activities are conducted in a separate learning situation. Instructors should avoid the practice of stopping the game for everyone while they provide instruction to accommodate individual differences. The embarrassment suffered by students at being singled out precludes their profiting from the instruction and further erodes self-concept.

Miller and Sullivan (1982) suggest other ways of including the handicapped.

- A buddy system that pairs a child with a handicap and an able bodied partner for specific activities
- Peer tutors
- Students as squad leaders
- Circuit or station organizational pattern
- Cross age teaching
- Team teaching involving regular physical education teachers and adapted physical education teachers or resource teachers
- Pre-teaching certain activities to selected students
- Additional physical education classes to supplement, not replace, regular physical education classes

— (Reprinted from A. G. Miller and J. V. Sullivan, *Teaching Physical Activities to Impaired Youth: An Approach to Mainstreaming*, p. 74. Copyright 1982.)

MAINSTREAMING A PHYSICALLY HANDICAPPED STUDENT IN GYM

Ernie became a paraplegic, paralyzed from the waist down, at age four from an automobile accident. He has normal intelligence and satisfactory academic achievement and attends regular classes in a wheelchair. A sixth grader, he is outgoing and popular with classmates. In fact, they occasionally must be prevented from helping him do things that he can do for himself. To prevent deterioration of the leg, knee, and ankle joints and to retain muscle tone, Ernie must stand for periods of time at a leaning board. To avoid presumed embarrassment, the board was placed in the nurse's office while the rest of his class went to gym. However, Ernie was unhappy with the arrangement. At his request, the board was placed in the gymnasium to allow him to be with his class. His friends began passing the ball to him and incorporating him in various activities. The teacher consulted with the physician and physical therapist and subsequently planned at least one activity in each session in which Ernie could participate fully. He benefited from the physical therapy and the therapy of class activities and friendship.

Folio and Norman (1981) report on the use of peer teachers in physical education classes with mainstreamed handicapped students. Upper elementary school students are selected and trained in a workshop that includes information about students with exceptionalities, basic skill instruction, and management techniques. The peer teachers may demonstrate, help with equipment, keep records, and work individually with students with handicaps during instruction.

Exceptional Students at the Secondary Level The secondary physical education curriculum in most school districts provides a diversified range of activities and sports. Students can elect areas for participation. Physical education teachers can assist students with handicapping conditions with this choice. Auxter and Pyfer (1985) identify three levels of motor functioning related to the acquisition of sports skills. These are basic input functions, general abilities, and specific skills. They recommend that physical education teachers identify the level at which each student is functioning and that a developmental approach to instruction be used to facilitate continued growth and achievement.

Another criterion might be the provision of sports or recreational activities that could be continued following graduation. With such individualization, students can participate in activities that will provide for skill development, good peer relationships, and enjoyment.

Methods and accommodations for students in large-group activities are the same as for elementary students.

Aquatics

Where there is a program of aquatics, students with handicaps—including the blind, those with missing limbs, and those with epilepsy—should participate. The parents and physicians should be consulted regarding the nature and extensiveness of participation. Adequate supervision will be maintained at all times with particular attention to the exceptional students in the pool.

An invaluable adjunct to the elementary program is the use of aides from the high school swimming team. This reduces the adult–student ratio and provides students with role models with whom they can identify. A one-to-one ratio is needed for blind or other students with severe handicaps. Because these students may take longer to achieve initial competencies, instructors should not pressure them to achieve the ultimate goal of learning how to swim and survive in the water. Overcoming fear of the water, immersing the face, accommodating to the environment, exercising for therapy, and preswimming water play are all worthy objectives that should not be minimized in planning.

Assessment

All students with temporary or permanent physically disabling conditions should have a thorough medical examination prior to beginning any program. Limitations in activities given by physicians must be respected.

In addition, other assessment instruments may be used as a basis for determining needs for program planning. There are many interindividual and intraindividual variations in abilities. Thus, instructors cannot group together all students with handicaps, mild retardation, or learning disabilities for special classes or activities. Sherrill (1975, p. 8), for example, suggests that the school "offer adapted physical education to children who are motorically deviant, not just those labeled exceptional."

Individual assessment either by formal instrument or by skilled observation during activities can provide clues to the nature and extent of participation in various activities for grouping. They also allow physical education teachers to gain a perspective, within a norm-referenced or criterion-referenced framework, of the functioning of individuals.

The following have been selected on the basis of their applicability to students with handicaps and their accessibility to school personnel.

1. *Individual Motor Achievement Guided Education* (IMAGE) (Devereau). Four items (sequential motor activity, fine motor ability, static balance, and perceptual-motor activity) are measured for students from ages four through ten with emotional handicaps and neurological impairments.

2. *Lincoln-Oseretsky Motor Development Scale* (Stoetling). A thirty-six item scale for students from ages six to fourteen, the test contains both gross and fine motor activities with emphasis on the latter.

3. *Physical Fitness for the Mentally Retarded* (Metropolitan Toronto Association for Retarded Children). Seven fitness areas are measured for students ages eight through seventeen. Required equipment is available in most schools.

4. *The Purdue Perceptual Motor Survey* (Roach & Kephart, 1966). A qualitative scale applicable to students from ages six through ten, this instrument surveys general motor, fine motor, perceptual-motor, and ocular skills.

5. *A Teaching Research Motor-Development Scale for Moderately and Severely Retarded Children* (Charles C. Thomas). Seventeen, nonnormed activities assess fine and gross motor skills and are designed as a basis for physical education programming for students who are retarded.

6. *Special Fitness Test for the Mentally Retarded* (AAHPER). The seven-item instrument is an adaptation of the Youth Fitness Test (below) for students with handicaps. It includes arm–shoulder endurance, abdominal endurance, agility, leg power, speed, coordination, and cardiorespiratory endurance. A system of awards from the American Alliance for Health, Physical Education, and Recreation is available.

7. *Youth Fitness Test* (AAHPER). The six-item instrument (as above, minus coordination) is the standard AAHPER test for students from ages ten through seventeen.

Additional techniques for assessment and the use of informal and criterion-referenced scales can be found in several textbooks on measurement in physical education listed at the end of the chapter in "Suggested Readings."

SUMMARY

Physical education has the goals of promoting physical fitness, motor development, social and emotional adjustment, and recreation for all students. Those with handicaps may participate in the regular program or in a remedial, a developmental, or an adapted program of activities. For students enrolled in the regular program, accommodations including grouping, adapting activities, using special or modified equipment, making rule adjustments, and selecting activities in which the individual can participate despite the handicapping condition can be made.

Some techniques to be emphasized include teaching rules, safety, and respect; reducing competitiveness; using step-by-step instruction; demonstrating frequently, especially when giving directions; and maintaining a structured routine in a relaxed atmosphere. With adequate supervision and parental—physician approval, students with handicaps can also participate in aquatics. A number of assessment devices can be used by the physical education staff to observe individual competencies and to select programs and activities to allow exceptional students and individual learners to develop their abilities.

REFERENCES

Anderson, F. E. (1978). *Art for all the children: A creative sourcebook for the impaired child.* Springfield, IL: Thomas.

Auxter, D., & Pyfer, J. (1985). *Principles and methods of adapted physical education and recreation* (5th ed.). St. Louis: Times Mirror/Mosby.

Bergethon, B., & Boardman, E. (1975). *Musical growth in the elementary school* (3rd ed.). New York: Holt, Rinehart & Winston.

Bird, P. J., & Gansneder, B. M. (1979). Preparation of physical education teachers as required under Public Law 94–142. *Exceptional Children, 45,* 464–466.

Boyle, J. D., & Lathrop, R. L. (1973). The IMPACT experience: An evaluation. *Music Educators Journal, 59*(5), 42–47.

Cratty, B. (1980). *Adapted physical education for handicapped children and youth.* Denver: Love.

Folio, M. R., & Norman, A. (1981). Toward more success in mainstreaming: A peer teacher approach to physical education. *Teaching Exceptional Children, 13,* 110–114.

Gilbert, J. P., & Asmus, E. P., Jr. (1981). Mainstreaming: Music educators' participation and professional needs. *Journal of Research in Music Education, 29,* 31–37.

Kephart, N. (1971). *The slow learner in the classroom* (2nd ed.). Columbus, OH: Merrill.

Krone, A. (1978). *Art instruction for handicapped children.* Denver: Love.

Lisenco, Y. (1975). Group C. *Art Education, 28,* 18–21.

Lowenfeld, V., & Brittain, W. L. (1975). *Creative and mental growth* (6th ed.). New York: Macmillan.

Miller, A. G., & Sullivan, J. V. (1982). *Teaching physical activities to impaired youth: An approach to mainstreaming.* New York: Wiley.

Minner, S. H., & Knuston, R. (1982). Mainstreaming handicapped students into physical education: Initial considerations and needs. *The Physical Educator, 39,* 13–15.

Nye, R. E., & Nye, V. T. (1977). *Music in the elementary school* (4th ed.). Englewood Cliffs, NJ: Prentice-Hall.

Ohio Department of Education (1980). *Improving physical education for the handicapped in Ohio: Guidelines for adapted physical education.* Columbus, OH: Author.

Piaget, J., & Inhelder, B. (1969). *The psychology of the child.* New York: Basic Books.

Raebeck, L., & Wheeler, L. (1974). *New approaches to music in the elementary school* (3rd ed.). Dubuque, IA: Brown.

Roach, C., & Kephart, N. (1966). *The Purdue perceptual motor survey.* Columbus, OH: Merrill.

Rubin, J. A. (1975). Art is for all human beings, especially the handicapped. *Art Education, 28,* 5–10.

Sherrill, C. (1975, March). *Mainstreaming in physical education: A positive approach.* Paper presented at the annual meeting of the American Alliance for Health, Physical Education and Recreation, Atlantic City, NJ: Eric Document Number ED107 615.

Welsbacher, B. (1975). Music for the learning disabled. In R. M. Graham (Ed.). *Music for the exceptional child* (pp. 136–147). Reston, VA: Music Educators National Conference.

SUGGESTED READINGS

Art

Atack, S. M. (1982). *Art activities for the handicapped.* Englewood Cliffs, NJ: Prentice-Hall.

Hollander, H. C. (1971). *Creative opportunities for the retarded child at home and in school.* New York: Doubleday.

Lindsay, Z. (1972). *Art and the handicapped child.* London: Studio Vista.

Silver, R. A. (1978). *Developing cognitive and creative skills through art: Programs for children with communication disorders or learning disabilities.* Baltimore: University Park Press.

Sussman, E. J. (1976). *Art projects for the mentally retarded child.* Springfield, IL: Thomas.

Music

Alvin, J. (1976). *Music for the handicapped child* (2nd ed.). London: Oxford University Press.

Costanza, A. P., & Sexton, A. J. (Eds.) (1971). *Music for the mentally retarded child.* Columbus, OH: Ohio State University.

Edwards, E. M. (1974). *Music education for the deaf.* South Waterford, ME: Merriam-Eddy.

Graham, R. M., & Beer, A. S. (1980). *Teaching music to the exceptional child: A handbook for mainstreaming.* Englewood Cliffs, NJ: Prentice-Hall.

Robbins, C., & Robbins, C. (1980). *Music for the hearing impaired: A resource manual and curriculum guide.* St. Louis: Magnamusic-Baton.

Physical Education

Adams, R., Daniel, A., & Rullman, L. (1972). *Games, sports, and exercises for the physically handicapped.* Philadelphia: Lea & Febiger.

American Alliance for Health, Physical Education, and Recreation. (1975). *Integrating persons with handicapping conditions into regular physical education and recreation programs.* Washington, DC: Author.

Cratty, B., & Breen, J. E. (1972). *Educational games for physically handicapped children.* Denver: Love.

Folio, M. R. (1986). *Physical education programming for exceptional learners.* Rockville, MD: Aspen.

Sherrill, C. (1981). *Adapted physical education and recreation: A multidisciplinary approach* (2nd ed.). Dubuque, IA: Brown.

Vodola, T. M. (1973). *Individualized physical education program for the handicapped child.* Englewood Cliffs, NJ: Prentice-Hall.

Wehman, P. (Ed.). (1979). *Recreation programming for developmentally disabled persons.* Baltimore: University Park Press.

Wheeler, R. H., & Hooley, A. M. (1976). *Physical education for the handicapped* (2nd ed.). Philadelphia: Lea & Febiger.

See also an extensive collection of manuals for physical education, sports, and recreation for individuals with varying handicapping conditions published by the American Alliance for Health, Physical Education, and Recreation, Washington, DC.

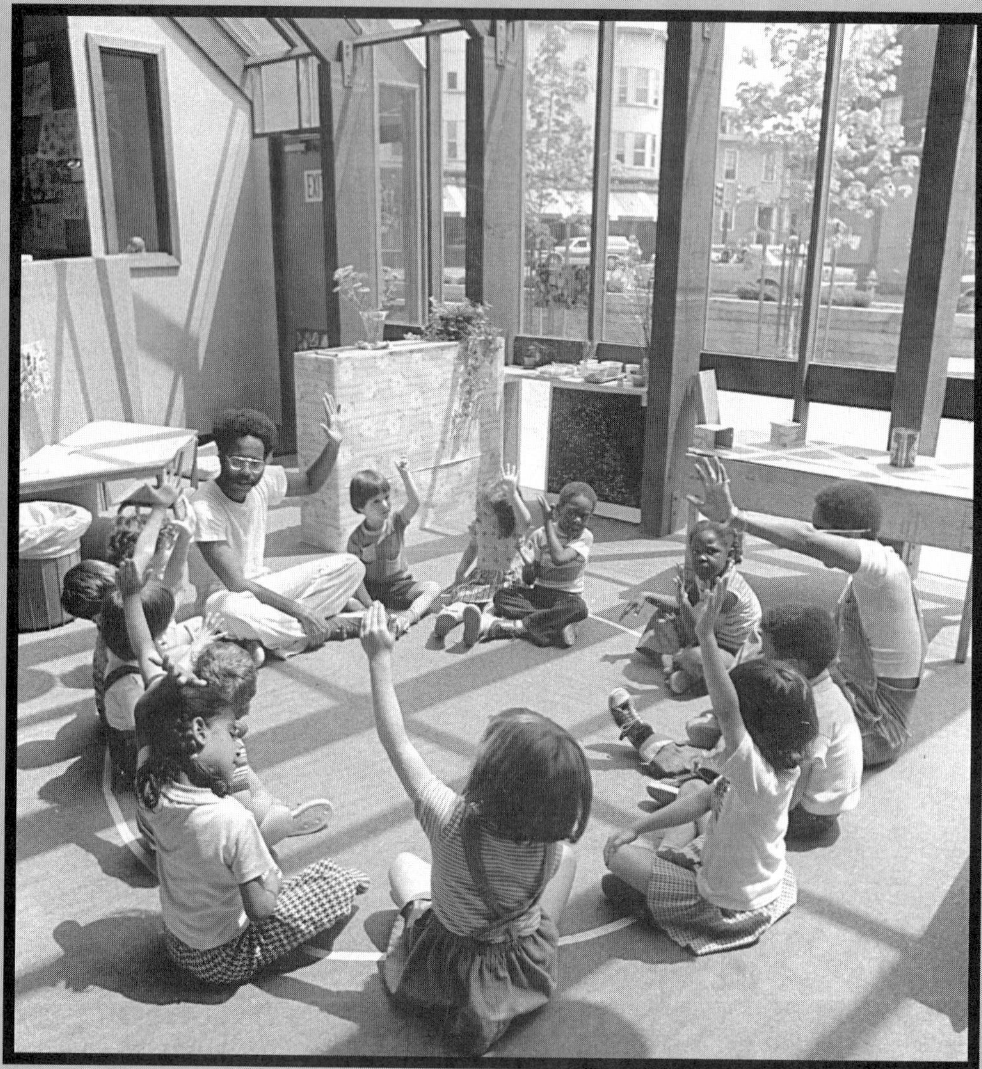

15

Methods for Teaching Affective Concepts

THE WHOLE STUDENT interacts with the environment. He or she brings the influences of family, home situations, neighborhood, experiences, and feelings about self to the classroom. Each of these factors affects each student in academic performance and social behaviors. The school cannot fragment its impact, dealing only with the cognitive domain. It is imperative that all aspects of development be considered. The school can fulfill its responsibility through affective education.

Rationale

Affective education is defined by Shelton (1977, p. 23) as "the development of the total individual in the school setting, his feelings, attitudes, values, communications, and interpersonal skills." There are those, professionals and parents alike, who would question the school's involvement in these aspects of students' lives. However, there are compelling reasons for responsible attention to this area. For all students these experiences modify the direction of their lives. For some students with physical or mental limitations and learning disabilities, the nonacademic side of education may have more impact than academic learning.

Affective education is directly related to both the long-term and short-term goals of education. Long-term goals include the development of self-respecting individuals who can direct their own lives to achieve worthwhile goals, to establish meaningful relationships with peers and adults, to secure economic independence, and to achieve maturity. To work toward these goals, students must accept responsibility for decisions, behavior, and their consequences. The principal short-term goal of education is to ensure daily profitable learning. Affective education provides the means to achieve these goals through the development of positive self-image, good school experiences, and the stimulation of attitudes, independence, and motivation. Far from consisting of activities that merely alleviate the academic routine, affective education is the imperative companion to the cognitive domain in the development of an adequate self who, as described by Combs and Snygg (1959, p. 45), is "capable of dealing effectively and efficiently with the exigencies of life, both now and in the future." Positive outcomes of affective education may be fewer acting-out behaviors, improved attendance, and a better attitude toward learning and peers.

Classroom Objectives for Affective Education

The goals of affective education may be achieved by developing students' personal resources in the areas of

- Self-concept
- Values
- Decision-making and problem-solving abilities
- Self-discipline and self-control
- Coping
- Communication abilities
- The establishment of human relationships

Relationship to Behavior

Advocates of behaviorism suggest that the most immediate and efficient way of influencing students' behavior is the manipulation of environmental variables that either elicit or inhibit behavior. One difficulty with this approach is that all environments—school, classroom, home, neighborhood, and community—cannot be so controlled. External reinforcement, no matter how powerful, is not enough. Behavior management must be transferred to the individual. Factors such as feelings, attitudes, perceptions, and values affect behavior. These also need to be addressed if students are to learn to control their own behavior.

Adults have learned to refrain from acting before thinking and to consider alternatives before deciding what to do about a situation. Students, especially those identified as exceptional, act impulsively, often with unproductive or even destructive results. Learning to think before acting is a process that must be internalized.

Some students are afraid to try in school. Exceptional students and others may flee from the challenge of learning. This attitude has usually resulted from both experiencing excessive failure and because teachers and parents have devalued them for past mistakes and behavior. They fail to peform, not because they are innately belligerent, negative, or uncooperative, but because withdrawal is safer for self-esteem. Students who are convinced that they cannot perform well in academics or extracurricular activities most likely will not achieve.

In channeling behavior toward more productive ends, affective resources of the individual cannot be overlooked. Learning to deal with feelings precludes impulsive behavior. Allowing students to talk about rather than act out frustrations is more mentally healthy than living with the unpleasant consequences of irrational behavior. Students who develop adequate self-concepts and who learn problem-solving and coping techniques will be more secure in the classroom and will demonstrate the ability to control their own behavior.

Teachers and Affective Education

Affective education is sometimes found in health curriculum. More often it is included in special classes because of teachers' convictions of its importance and its potential for aiding students to reach educational and personal goals. Regular teachers can incorporate it into health classes, during language development activities, or at specified times.

Teachers establish the classroom climate of trust, openness, and honesty that is the basis for affective interchanges. In the conduct of teaching sessions, the major guidelines are:

1. Listen to what students say. Allow them to express feelings verbally.
2. Maintain a flexible attitude.
3. Accept students and whatever they wish to discuss as long as it is a sincere concern. If comments are made for the purpose of disruption or sensationalism, teachers must not react with reinforcing shock and rejection but with a simple, firm statement that such a contribution or such language is not acceptable to the group. In some instances, ignoring completely may be equally effective.
4. Accept self as an adequate person.
5. Reinforce participation, acceptable behavior, and productive insights, which may emerge in discussions. Positive feedback is likely to lead to self-disclosure. Negative feedback may result in hostility.
6. Do not force any student to participate. When an atmosphere of acceptance, security, and confidentiality is perceived, most students join the discussion.
7. Be nonjudgmental of students as individuals and of their expressed ideas. The role of the teacher is that of facilitator, not that of counselor or psychologist. The teacher must be trustworthy, understanding, and accepting of self to assist others to do the same.

A combination of methods is required. Procedures such as student participation in general affective lessons and discussions may not produce immediate observable changes but may have a cumulative effect. Begin by establishing an atmosphere in which there is peer and teacher support. Enlist others on the staff to provide reinforcement of good behavior and academic success. Throughout the day teachers maintain consistent response patterns that are purposeful in direction and yet informal in application. For example, teachers make positive comments such as "Good thinking!" or "Everybody is listening" to reinforce continuing acceptable behavior.

In addition to maintaining a supportive classroom atmosphere, teachers conduct direct or indirect lessons in affective education. The more common method, indirect, consists of preplanned activities using teacher-made or published materials. These include worksheets, stories, audiovisual lessons, and other third-person activities. The indirect approach is usually less threatening and has the potential for projection in which students relate the activities to their own lives without being threatened by personal confrontations or revelations.

The direct approach capitalizes on incidents that occur or situations that actually exist in the classroom or school. Exceptional students' relationships with nonhandicapped peers or a conflict on the playground or with teachers might be the basis for a learning experience. This approach has the advantage of making "the message" immediate and meaningful to students with the likelihood of being remembered. In this way they "get it out of their systems" and can return to the classroom routine.

There are two additional considerations. The first is that such instruction cannot be preplanned and that teachers must rely on their abilities to manage situations as they occur. The second concern is the potential emotional effect on the students involved. It may be necessary to "defuse" a sensitive situation before reason can prevail. As this procedure is used regularly, it becomes routine and can be managed in an atmosphere of calm concern.

Discussion and Activities in the Seven Areas of Affective Education

Self-Concept

Discussion   Self-concept is the sum total of the individual's characteristics and worth as perceived and evaluated from his or her own vantage point. Self-concept is learned, accruing from feedback from one's own interactions with the environment and from the positive or negative perceptions and attitudes of others. Self-concept is developmental; it is the cumulative result of all past experience. As such it is multidimensional. There is a persistent core of attitudes and feelings about one's self that pervades all activities of life. In addition, there are situationally specific perceptions about self. It may be possible to alter students' perception of themselves as learners in a particular subject in school, while their general self-concepts are not significantly altered. Thus, change occurs slowly and not in immediate response to external manipulation. It may be improved as students know that someone believes in them and as they experience continuing success in academic and social relationships.

Self-concept is related to behavior although the dynamics of the relationship are frequently oversimplified. A positive self-concept is associated with good mental health, socially desirable values, the ability to cope with disappointment and frustration, handling criticism, reacting acceptably to others, and motivation toward worthwhile goal fulfillment. A poor self-concept is often associated with acting-out and aggressive behavior, socially unacceptable activities, withdrawal into isolation, and defeatism that compromises individuals striving toward positive growth.

A good self-concept is difficult to establish in exceptional individuals. Often they have distorted self-perceptions. This is particularly true of some students with physical handicaps, of those who are blind and do not know what they look like, and those who are deaf and do not have the daily experience of verbal feedback for their behaviors. Students who have deficits in classroom learning or who are unsuccessful in athletics because of motor difficulties have often received depreciating responses from teachers, parents, or peers.

DEVELOPING POSITIVE SELF-CONCEPT

In a sixth grade English class, the students are practicing oral expression. Each is asked to give three examples of positive characteristics or talents of another student. Everyone in the class is "talked about" including an orthopedically handicapped girl, Jennifer. Larry speaks about her good sense of humor especially when she does something that she thinks is clumsy. Julie mentions that she is the best flute player in the band. Chris tells her that she is always cheerful.

The class is told that they will earn three bonus points in the classwide reinforcement system every time someone says something good about another student. They will also earn points when they refrain from laughing at a mistake and when they ignore inappropriate remarks or behavior.

Sequential elements in the development of a positive self-concept are self-awareness, self-acceptance, and self-confidence. Self-awareness involves taking time to consider "Who am I?" and "What am I like as a person?" Self-acceptance is the recognition of one's own attributes and competencies as well as limitations without being further limited by them or the knowledge of them. Individuals see themselves as they are and, hopefully, as others see them and are pleased with those perceptions. They can acknowledge criticism and mistakes without self-depreciation. Self-confidence enables them to act on convictions and to be comfortable about successes and the possibility of actual failure and rejection. Affective education can address all three aspects of self-confidence.

Activities

Self-Awareness Begin with helping students identify as persons, members of a family and community. The common activity of creating a family tree may be a good starting point for many students, although for a few, lacking in the traditional family structure, it may be a disconcerting experience. More direct examination of self may be stimulated with open-ended sentences.

- I feel happy when I . . . .
- I get angry when . . . .
- I like people who . . . .
- On report card day I . . . .
- I am proud of myself when . . . .

An enjoyable activity is tracing a full-length outline of each student on sheets of newsprint. Each one can then "color in himself or herself." Or for an interesting variation, use self-descriptive adjectives and phrases written in as facial features and other details.

Older students may explore values, attitudes, and characteristics by separating a list of adjectives into "Like Me" and "Not Like Me" columns. Words and phrases might include confident, happy, friendly, enjoyable to be with, sincere, sometimes sneaky, bored, jealous, curious, fearful, and ambitious. Such an activity can be made less personally threatening if the words are divided into "Desirable" and "Undesirable" lists. Students may also make lists of things they like about themselves or of which they are proud. They may write or tell their autobiographies or discuss how alike or different they are.

Self-Acceptance   Open-ended sentences, verbalizing feelings, and self-awareness activities enhance self-concept. However, the major impact does not come from a few formal activities but from continuing teacher influence including emphasizing positive characteristics, abilities, and achievement. In addition, teachers can listen to students, use their good ideas, and demonstrate respect. Positive reinforcement tells students that teachers believe in them. Teacher and peer acceptance lead to self-acceptance.

Self-Confidence   Self-confidence is enhanced socially by focusing on and rewarding effort and by providing success experiences soon after failure. It is often necessary to build self-acceptance and self-confidence through methods that directly demonstrate to students their own capabilities. Because academic achievement is the criterion of school success, assisting students in this area is of primary importance. Adjusting the curriculum structure, maintaining intensive diagnostic teaching procedures, and helping students to be better learners can improve self-confidence.

Some students will not be as academically competent in one subject as in another. Overconcentration on the weak area can be frustrating and demoralizing to students and teachers alike. The strong areas need to be appreciated and reinforced whether they are within the academic or nonacademic domain. Self-confidence is achieved not only through specific activities but also through success and the feeling that one can try and succeed and so be willing to try again. Providing students with concrete experiences to demonstrate that they can try and also succeed can be a significant milestone in the development of a positive self-concept.

Simon (1973) devised the IALAC concept and wrote the book *I Am Lovable and Capable*. The story describes Randy's day in which almost everything goes wrong. The purpose of the activity is to enhance self-image by "building up" rather than "putting down" self and others. The story may be geared to any grade level. Teachers may adapt the activities in various ways. IALAC signs, cards, or buttons may be displayed and worn. When a "put down" is heard, a piece of the sign is torn off. When a student does something lovable or capable, a piece is added. Some teachers use affective lessons and activities in which class members tell something good about each other or relate a talent or ability. Teachers may heighten interest by using the initial IALAC for a period of time without revealing its meaning. Students try to guess what IALAC means as a result of teachers' behaviors and encouragement of particular student behaviors. Simon provides suggestions in the use of the IALAC idea to enhance self-concept.

Values

Discussion   Students develop goals and attitudes primarily in the home and at school. They learn to recognize positive values of fairness, concern, caring, and regard. Thus, teachers' most powerful form of guidance in the classroom is the example provided by their continuing behavior that adheres to a set of worthwhile principles of personal and interactional conduct.

Guidance in the school may also take the form of lessons structured around the topics of values and may include

- Awareness that we do value
- Acceptance of differences in values and value systems among students and adults
- Values clarification
- Values exercises and activities

The Cooperative Educational Service Agency of Appleton, Wisconsin (1977, pp. 9–10), delineates several factors within three general areas of valuing. These are

1. Choosing—which must be freely done from alternatives in which consequences are considered
2. Prizing—which means that children are proud and happy about their choice and are willing to confirm these feelings
3. Acting—which suggests that children need to act upon their choice and develop a pattern or habit.

One ongoing concern is that the values of the home or subculture may differ from those advocated by the school. It is not teachers' positions to criticize or dictate a change of values for students outside school. This should not preclude discussion of values in the classroom. It may be necessary for teachers to explain that the students' behaviors in the classroom will be expected to conform to the values of the school in regard to honesty, consideration of others, adherence to classroom rules, avoidance of inappropriate language, and acting-out behavior.

The use of formal programs of values clarification has been accepted by some communities and rejected by others. Before initiating a program, teachers might wish to discuss the situation and the content of the program with the school administration, and together they could determine potential community reaction. An additional step might be to meet with parents to describe the program and its goals and to respond to parental concerns. Decisions about what to teach can accommodate community and administrative views. The following are possible strategies.

Activities   The publication of the Cooperative Educational Service Agency (1977) details activities according to grade level. Activities selected from their more comprehensive list include:

1. A chart with stem sentences such as
   - I noticed that I am . . .
   - I discovered that I . . .

- I realized that I . . .
- I was surprised that I . . .
- I was pleased that I . . .
- I was displeased that I . . .

2. Self-evaluation sentences such as the importance of being happy, eating breakfast, or being good-looking.
3. Voting questions in which the class decides how many students
   - like recess
   - like reading
   - use seatbelts
   - enjoy taking hikes
   - would like to live on a farm
   - are afraid of spiders
4. Rank–order situations. What I like most, such as freedom, self-respect, friendship, or a comfortable life.

They also suggest guidelines to be followed by teachers. These are:

1. Ask questions in which students must consider alternatives.
2. Discuss value-rich topics without moralizing.
3. Do not ask "Why?" questions.
4. Do not ask too many questions.
5. Do not use grades or other types of evaluation.

Students discover that they share many thoughts, fears, and beliefs with each other. They also must learn to respect differing ideas and values.

Decision Making and Problem Solving

Discussion The lives of students, especially exceptional learners, are controlled largely by decisions made about them and for them but not by them. Parents and teachers sometimes generalize the conditions of the handicap to assume that the students are not capable of making decisions that would affect their own lives and that they must be protected from the inevitably unwise decisions they might make.

All students must be taught to make decisions and to solve problems so that they will be able to manage their own lives as adults. Objectives of instruction are:

1. The students' awareness that they can make decisions and choices.
2. Learning that one must accept the consequences of decisions made.
3. Improvement of self-image through awareness that one can be successful in decision making.

Activities Specific techniques include unfinished stories in which students make decisions for the protagonist, role playing, self-evaluation, and round-table discussions. Class or circle discussions can revolve around hypothetical or real school situations. For example, it is not uncommon for the sole exceptional student in the neighborhood or on the school bus to be subjected to harassment, name calling, or ridicule. They may learn from discussions on how to handle such situations, and nonhandicapped students may gain insight about the inappropriateness of such activity.

A simplified process can follow these steps: identify the specific problem, state alternatives, consider the consequences of each alternative, and make the best choice from the alternatives.

In planning affective curricula, a unit may consist of questions posed by teachers for the class to consider.

1. What can I do? Think of possible alternatives.
2. Which will I not choose? Hopefully, the class members can be led to rule out poor choices, or subsequent discussion of alternatives can expose the reasons why they should not be selected.
3. What will happen to each if I do? Within this context, students must examine objectives of the action. Will this action result in a better state of affairs? Am I taking this action out of a desire to "get back at" those who have ridiculed me?
4. How will my choices affect others?
5. What appears to be the best choice in this situation?
6. What are the risks involved if I make this choice? Are they reasonable? Am I willing to take them?
7. If the situation cannot work out to my satisfaction, do I accept this decision? Do I have a substitute to take the place of the preferred solution—an alternative behavior such as hitting a pillow rather than a classmate to relieve frustration?
8. What alternative will I choose?
9. Make the choice.
10. How will I put this decision into effect?
11. Do I feel good about the solution?
12. Will others be pleased with it?
13. Do it.

Among the solutions proposed for many problems are ignoring; talking to a trusted friend, parent, or counselor; avoiding the rejecting individuals; leaving the room; going to a person in authority; using humor; and venting frustration in an acceptable way. Unacceptable choices might include fighting, using bad language, disrespect for authority, withdrawal, or disruptive behavior.

If the problem is real rather than hypothetical, teachers and classmates can learn from the success of the problem-solving strategy. It should be noted that the solution arrived at after considerable time and discussion could have been recommended in the beginning by teachers. The learning, which evolved from the detailed consideration of good and bad alternatives and from the problem-solving strategy itself, is more effective if thought through by students.

In addition, the concept of ownership of the problem must be considered. Students must learn that their reactions to the situation may allow it to become their problem. When students say, "He got me in trouble," they need to be reminded that they permitted other students to influence them to behave in an unacceptable manner.

Spivack and Shure (1974) have developed a program for teaching problem solving to young children. They recognize that attempts to assist in problem solving often consist of directions and reasoning being projected upon the children without their understanding or their being able to generalize to new situations. Consequently, these authors have created a structured training program "to teach children how to think, not what to think" and to "help the child develop a problem solving style that would guide him in coping with everyday problems" (pp. 23–24).

Some of the principles included in the Spivack and Shure (1974, p. 29) program are as follows:

1. Emphasize people and their personal relationships rather than objects or impersonal situations.
2. Teach the habit of seeking solutions and evaluating them on the basis of potential consequences rather than the absolute merits of a particular solution to a problem.
3. Encourage the child to create his own ideas and offer them in the context of the problem.
4. Teach problem-solving skills not as ends in themselves but in relation to the appropriateness of overt behavioral adjustment.

These are a few concepts from this program. Teachers interested in instructing students in problem-solving strategies are advised to consult the complete program.

Self-Discipline and Self-Control

Discussion   Another aspect of affective education includes the development of self-discipline, the consistent organization of one's own behavior. Self-discipline encompasses self-control, that is, the ability of individuals to choose to act and react in an acceptable way without external controls. More than using "will power", it involves thinking through a situation rather than acting impulsively. It means handling frustration and refraining from expressing negative feelings in a destructive manner.

This status of self-control is not absolute. Individuals are not in complete control of their own behavior nor all of the events or situations in their lives. Thus, students and adults may exert more control at certain times or in particular situations than in others.

Self-control is achieved through a long process of learning and development. In childhood much behavior is necessarily controlled by others. During adolescence an increasing degree of self-control is demonstrated. By maturity, individuals should be largely responsible for their own behavior.

Locus of Control   Rotter's (1954) concept of locus of control hypothesizes two basic dimensions, external and internal. In external locus of control, or externality, individuals perceive that those events that happen to them in the forms of punishments or rewards are controlled by powerful others, luck, fate, or some other causative agent. Internal locus of control, or internality, refers to the perception that reinforcing or aversive events are contingent upon one's own behavior. Individuals accept the responsibility that they can control through their own behavior what happens to them.

The development from externality toward internality takes place during the developmental years. Studies with students with retardation have suggested that they proceed through the same sequence of development but at a slower rate. They remain more externally oriented than their nonhandicapped, same-age peers. It is easy to quickly interpret that the delay in achieving externality is related only to the slower rate of development. But another factor may be contributory. Once students have been identified as exceptional, professionals and parents assume increased responsibility for managing their medical, academic, and social experiences. They *are* more externally controlled than their nonhandicapped peers. Thus, students who respond with higher than expected externality scores on measurement instruments may be accurately perceiving that they are externally controlled. Behavioral and academic interventions may have an unfortunate side effect by limiting the range of experiences and self-determination and delay their growth toward internality.

Students who are more externally oriented tend to be impulsive and have difficulty working for delayed gratification. They may demonstrate maladaptive behavior. Locus of control is also highly related to school achievement with those who attain internality, demonstrating more consistent success than their externally oriented counterparts.

Activities Students who do not develop internality can be helped by individual counseling, contingency management, assertive discipline, and milieu therapy. A combination of behavior management procedures in which the relationship between behavior and consequences is realistic, consistent, and clearly evident to the students can be used. It is preferable to use positive reinforcement. However, praise must not be excessive. Students recognize overpraising for work that they know to be inferior or that does not represent their best efforts. In addition, management procedures should be openly discussed rather than surreptitiously applied. By using this direct approach, teachers are able to impress upon students' consciousness the need for performing as expected and for meeting obligations and responsibilities.

Teaching self-control can be augmented by a behavior management approach that is based on consistent consequences for behavior. Principles and strategies of assertive discipline and of the RAID program, both of which are summarized in Chapter 7, support the achievement of self-control. Similarly, self-management procedures can be used. Students can be taught to recognize the choice of alternative behaviors to delay impulsive action toward immediate gratification in favor of more permanently beneficial, long-term goals.

Fagen, Long, and Stevens (1975, p. 38) propose a curriculum for teaching students self-control as a behavior management procedure. The curriculum focuses on eight skill areas. These are

1. Selection—ability to perceive incoming information accurately.
2. Storage—ability to retain information received.
3. Sequencing and ordering—ability to organize actions as a basis for planned order.
4. Anticipating consequences—ability to relate actions to expected outcomes.
5. Appreciating feelings—ability to identify and constructively use affective experience.
6. Managing frustration—ability to cope with external obstacles that produce stress.
7. Inhibition or delay—ability to postpone or restrain action tendencies.
8. Relaxation—ability to reduce internal tension.

The development of self-discipline and self-control is enhanced by a stable environment in which teachers model the principles of consistency, fairness, and self-control in dealing with trying classroom circumstances.

Coping

Discussion Individuals deal with frustration, challenges, disappointments, emergencies, and pleasant experiences in different ways. Successful coping is the reduction of anxiety and the maintenance of self-control when confronted by these exigencies. How individuals cope is related to self-image, past experiences, learning, and examples set by significant others. When self-image is adequate, they are less threatened and better able to react appropriately, to meet unexpected demands, and to risk involvement. They will accept challenges and confrontations and will deal better with stress.

Exceptional students and individual learners often experience considerable frustration in their attempts to achieve in school and to establish social relationships. Academically limited students often emerge from a protected special class environment to one of comparison and competition in regular classes. Their ability to cope becomes an increasingly vital resource. Teachers employing affective education can be instrumental in helping all students through a variety of techniques and programs.

Activities

1. During circle lessons students can acknowledge feelings. They can be taught that feelings of frustration, which does not reflect inadequacy, are normal. Students are not to blame for these feelings.
2. In reading and English, point out how characters in stories cope.
3. Identify specific classroom problems and school situations that presently exist or are likely to occur.
4. Discuss the fact that all people must accept problems and deal with rather than flee from them.
5. Modify goals so that they are realistic and attainable.
6. Make a list of positive characteristics about each class member.
7. Use problem-solving techniques as previously discussed.
8. Encourage students to believe in themselves and to concentrate on what they can do to help others in difficult situations.
9. Reinforce students with a word of praise when they have coped successfully even if the challenge was not sufficiently large to be recognized as an obstacle.

Principles and procedures discussed in the classroom provide a common basis for reference for later use in crisis situations and assist students to grow toward independence and maturity.

Communication

Discussion Considerable time in the lives of most individuals is spent in communicating with others. Social relationships, satisfaction of basic needs, participation in the happenings of daily living, and the establishment of worthwhile human relationships depend on communication abilities.

The concept of communication includes the accurate conveyance of information from one individual to another. It also involves listening, understanding the message, and relating to other persons. To this end communication is not only a language experience but an affective one as well.

Communication is based upon the existence of a mutually meaningful symbol system, which may be either verbal or nonverbal. In the classroom, communication systems may be either horizontal (student-to-student) or vertical (teacher-to-student; student-to-teacher). Often teachers are concerned only about vertical communication. Attention is given to the clarity of directions and information and to students' accurate expression of knowledge. But learning can occur through horizontal communication as well. Interaction and dialogue among students should be encouraged.

Activities General language development, which promotes communication skills, are vocabulary development, logical organization, sequence, grammar, and expressing ideas. Teaching both denotative and connotative meanings of words and phrases, interpretive reading, comprehension skills, rephrasing, figures of speech, and stressing similies, metaphors, and idioms enlarge language use. Questioning, which demands elaboration of answers rather than one-word responses, gives students practice in communicating. In classroom interchange, students are expected to respond in complete sentences. Even if teachers know what students are trying to say, they must be expected to speak with clarity. They can be encouraged by saying "Can you say that another way?" Having a second student rephrase what the first has expressed has the advantage of encouraging listening skills on the part of both students. It provides feedback to the first speaker as to how his or her intended message was received by others. Group discussion also has the advantage of not being restricted to a one-to-one conversation but allows for multiple interactions both horizontally and vertically.

Many exceptional students who have difficulty conceptualizing give answers that are not related to the question. Teaching students to answer questions directly will improve both communication and comprehension skills. Self-concept activities lead to self-disclosure, which enables students to communicate and relate better to others. Free periods and time before and after school afford them opportunity to express themselves.

The social climate including peer reinforcement and recognition by teachers and other adults can promote the quality and amount of communication. The physical environment including seating arrangement, group size, color of walls, temperature, and lighting is cited by Bassett and Symthe (1979) as having a potential impact. They add that "Even the most perfect of environments does not ensure good interpersonal relationships, effective communication and learning, but bad physical settings can work effectively against the attainment of all these" (p. 141).

Listening The listener is a crucial element in a communication system. Understanding is not simply the responsibility of the speaker in making the message clear but the reception of the listener as well. Otto and Smith (1980, p. 305) suggest that "the primary responsibility of the teacher in teaching students to attend to the spoken word is twofold: He must teach the students to (1) ignore distractions, and (2) focus on the speaker's ideas." To become aware of the ideas of others, students can be taught to listen passively and actively. Passive listening involves blocking out distractions and thinking only about what the other person is saying. In active listening the listener rewards what the speaker has said, indicating that he or she understands. Thus, active listening is a vehicle for learning as well as communicating.

Nonverbal Communication Nonverbal communication can be taught in the classroom as well. Individuals may speak without words. Lack of eye contact, excessive eye contact, gestures, posture, and facial expressions are forms of communication.

Games that involve teachers and students assuming bodily and facial characteristics to be guessed by others can be fun as well as instructive. Another activity in nonverbal communication is to have students look at pictures in readers before reading the text. They are to interpret the story from the pictures. "See the look on father's face in the picture. What do you suppose that means? The text is then read to determine the accuracy of interpretation. This also changes the focus of reading from the labor of decoding to the utility of discovering meaning.

The absence of a response can also convey meaning. In such situations, students may be asked to verbalize what the response would have been or what they were thinking.

The classroom climate in which language skills are developed is crucial in communication and instruction. Receptivity, sensitivity, acceptance, support, trust, and encouragement facilitate such a climate.

Human Relations

Discussion Teachers might ask themselves, "How will students get along with peers and adults? What can be done in the classroom to develop good relationships with others?" To teach students how to relate well, an examination of human relations is needed. It includes communication, openness to others, acceptance of their points of view, sharing experiences, the development of mutual understanding and appreciation, and the ability to give of one's self and to receive from others.

A long and uneven process of social interaction leads to an adult level of human relationships. Piaget (1926) used the word *egocentrism* to describe the initial limitation of young children in viewing the world from only their own vantage point. Unable to examine the accuracy of their own beliefs, children are unable to put themselves into others' places and to appreciate their ideas.

As individual students express their own beliefs and ideas, differences become evident. They find it necessary to compare their ideas to those of others and thus are forced to recognize the existence of others' points of view. Such confrontation and examination facilitate growth away from egocentrism and toward social interactions and positive human relationships.

This continuing development also allows for the realization that differences in perspectives need not always be realigned and especially not through confrontation. Other individuals base their behavior on perceptions that are different from our own.

It further permits the realization of the underlying strata of human experiences and relationships that allow a stability of interaction and a respect for others.

Activities   Objectives of an intervention program are twofold. First, students are helped to develop an adequate self-image. This is necessary to reach out to others. Second, students are assisted in developing the ability to put themselves in the place of others to be aware of and have respect for their viewpoints and to be sensitive to others' feelings. Strategies for achieving the first objective are included in other areas of affective education previously presented. Many procedures for addressing the second objective are the same as for social development. They include using various grouping patterns in the classroom for special projects and work assignments; encouraging older students to participate in sports, clubs, and other out-of-class activities; using discussion groups or classroom presentations on topics of common interest; and emphasizing being a friend and thinking more about the needs of others.

Discussion can be based on open-ended sentences such as

- Other people think I . . .
- I need someone when . . .
- When other are sad I feel . . .
- When others are mad I feel . . .
- I am a friend when I . . .

Teachers often use direct instruction in appropriate behavior in social situations, and these profit all students, not simply those who are handicapped. Teachers can take the opportunity to use circle interaction relative to real classroom or playground problems. Role playing, putting one's self in the position of others, is particularly effective. Sensitivity and appreciation of others could be incorporated in reading or literature assignments, in discussions, and in creative writing. The English classes in one junior high school were asked to write essays on what it would be like to be blind, without knowing the assignment was a device to pave the way for the arrival of the first blind student to attend the school.

Achievement of worthwhile human relationships is developed, in part, through specific teaching activities. In addition, each interaction during the entire day can be a step toward this goal.

Circle   One effective technique for any area of affective instruction is circle or group meeting. Often the school day begins and/or ends with this activity, although circle might be called at any time during the day. The concept is not the same as the *Magic Circle* of Bessell and Palomares (1970), which focuses on feelings, a sense of mastery, and social interaction. The *Magic Circle* program has lesson plans, materials, and activities organized by grade level. Circle, as presented here, is less formal and less structured. Although teachers may prepare specific activities or lessons, much of the daily activity may evolve from present concerns of the students or teachers or from problems that arise in the classroom or in the school.

Circle is conducted in an atmosphere of quiet thinking and controlled participation. Students learn how to express ideas in a group and talk out problems with reasoning rather than confrontation. Sensitivity to the ideas and feelings of others is developed. Emphasis is placed on moving from egocentrism to be able to put one's self in another's place, the beginnings of empathy.

CIRCLE LESSON

Jason, a sixth grader with serious social and behavior problems, returned from lunch recess quite upset, unable to concentrate on any lesson or class activity. He needs to "defuse." The students are told that before the lesson begins that they will discuss the problem on the playground. Jason is invited to tell the group what happened. Another boy continually called him names, "making" him start the fight. The playground supervisor punished him and not the other boy. The group then tells Jason what they think he could have done in the situation. Acceptable and unacceptable choices are brought out. Sentences begin with "What would happen to you if you . . .?" Two boys encourage him to show everybody next time how he can control himself. They assure Jason that it is harder not to fight than to fight. The teacher reminds Jason of the point system for positive reinforcement for good behavior.

Teachers act as facilitators, accepting divergent views guiding but not controlling the group. To the extent possible, they elicit attitudes, opinions, and behaviors rather than imposing these on the group. Each student has the right to his or her own opinion even if it differs from the teacher's or those of other students. Accepting that right and listening to every point of view is a valuable learning experience for each student. Having one's own opinions received by others plus feedback regarding others' reception and evaluations of the opinion is an equally valuable learning experience.

Some activities may be concerned with routine class procedures—development of new rules; review of existing rules; schedules; organizational skills; study habits; acceptable social behaviors; fire drills; and behavioral expectations in the school, on the playground, and on the school bus. Circle is also valuable for self-expression and language development with students expected to refrain from unacceptable language, to speak in complete sentences, and to employ the rules of correct grammar and usage. At other times, circle objectives may assume a more affective orientation, addressing self-image, coping skills, interpersonal relationships, communication, decision making, and problem solving.

SUMMARY

Affective education is related to the long-term and the short-term goals of education for both exceptional and nonhandicapped students. It can directly affect classroom behavior, orientation toward achievement, and productive interpersonal relations. The goals of affective education include the development of personal resources in the areas of self-concept, which consist of self-awareness, self-acceptance, and self-confidence; values; decision making and problem solving; self-discipline and self-control; coping; communication abilities; and the establishment of human relationships.

Methods in each of these areas can consist of direct instruction by teachers and the use of a variety of published materials and programs. Circle, or class meetings, which may convene on a regular and/or needs basis, is a particularly effective vehicle for affective education. In addition, the continuing use of indirect procedures including the establishment of a supportive environment, teacher and peer interaction, consistent expectations and reinforcement, and teachers as models are necessary procedures.

REFERENCES

Bassett, R. E., & Smythe, M. J. (1979). *Communication and instruction.* New York: Harper & Row.
Bessell, H. S., & Palomares, V. (1970). *Magic circle/Human development program.* San Diego, CA: Human Development Training Institute.
Combs, A. W., & Snygg, D. (1959). *Individual behavior: A perceptual approach to behavior.* New York: Harper.
Cooperative Education Service Agency. (1977). *Student learning activity package: Values, grades 2–6.* Appleton, WI: Author. (ERIC Document Reproduction Service No. ED 167-905-906.)
Fagen, S. A., Long, N. J., & Stevens, D. J. (1975). *Teaching children self control.* Columbus, OH: Merrill.
Otto, W., & Smith, R. J. (1980). *Corrective and remedial teaching* (3rd ed.). Boston: Houghton Mifflin.
Piaget, J. (1926). *Language and thought of the child.* New York: Harcourt, Brace.
Rotter, J. B. (1954). *Social learning and clinical psychology.* New York: Prentice-Hall.
Shelton, M. N. (1977). Affective education and the learning disabled student. *Journal of Learning Disabilities, 10,* 618–629.
Simon, S. B. (1973). *I am lovable and capable.* Niles, IL: Argus Communications.
Spivack, G., & Shure, M. B. (1974). *Social adjustment of young children: A cognitive approach to solving real-life problems.* San Francisco: Jossey-Bass.

SUGGESTED READINGS

Cartledge, G., & Milburn, J. F. (Eds.) (1986). *Teaching social skills to children: Innovative approaches* (2nd ed.). New York: Pergamon.
Castillo, G. A. (1974). *Left-handed teaching; Lessons in affective education.* New York: Praeger.
Chase, L. (1975). *The other side of the report card: A how-to-do-it program for affective education.* Pacific Palisades, CA: Goodyear.
Fansler, J. (1978). *Helping children cope.* New York: Free Press.
Miller, J. P. (1976). *Humanizing the classroom: Models in teaching in affective education.* New York: Praeger.
Morse, W. C., Ardizzone, J., MacDonald, C., & Pasick, P. (1980). *Affective education for special children and youth.* Reston, VA: Council for Exceptional Children.
Simon, S. B., & O'Rourke, R. D. (1977). *Developing values with exceptional children.* Englewood Cliffs, NJ: Prentice-Hall.
Strom, S. B., & Torrance, E. P. (1973). *Education for affective achievement.* Chicago: Rand McNally.
Weinstein, G., & Fantini, M. D. (Eds.) (1970). *Toward humanistic education: A curriculum of affect.* New York: Praeger.

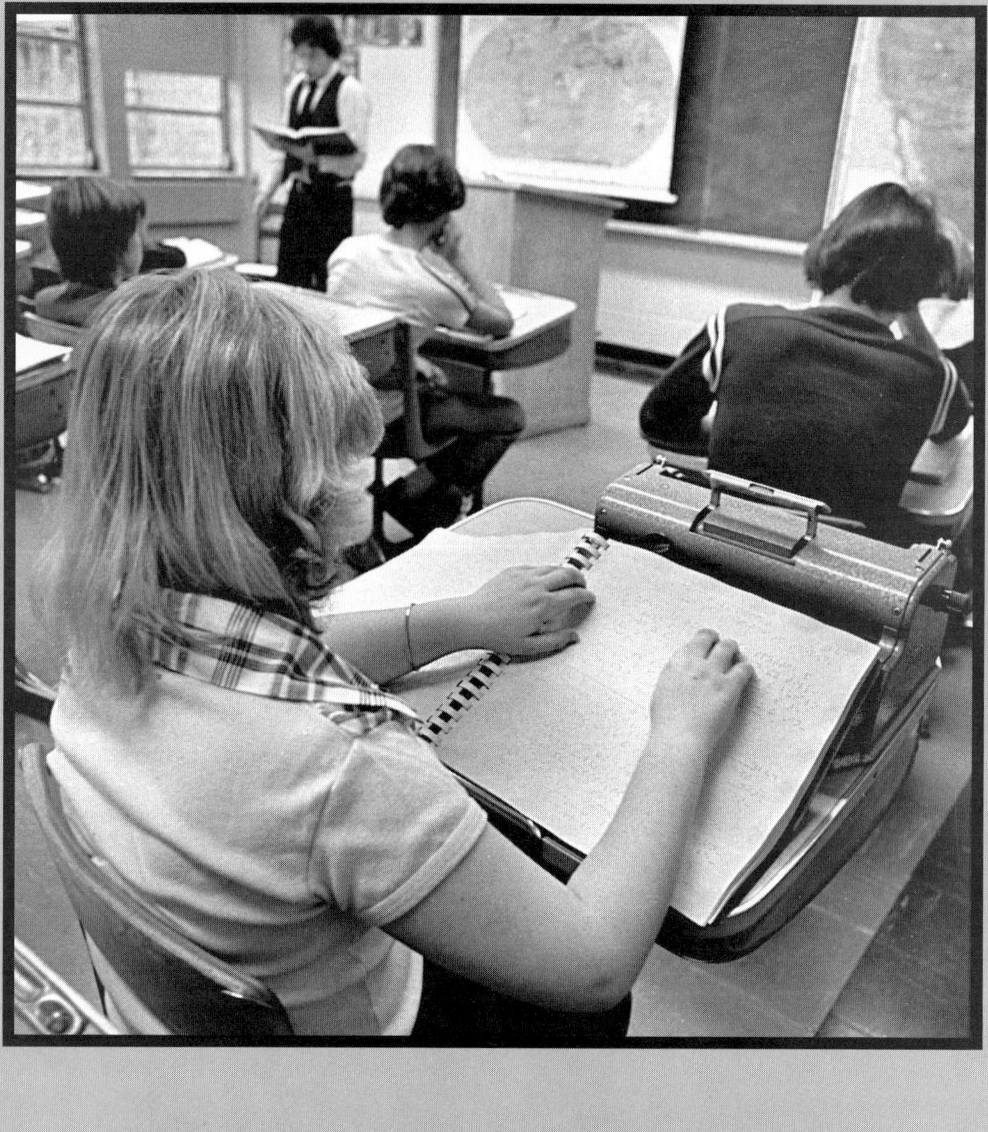

16

Educating Exceptional Adolescents

IN THE PAST, services for exceptional students were concentrated at the elementary level and focused on identification and placement in special programs. A large percentage of students classified as exceptional remained in special education but did not continue in school beyond the compulsory attendance age. Since the middle 1970s, changes have taken place. The Sixth Annual Report to Congress (U.S. Department of Education, 1984) notes a 70 percent increase since 1978 in the numbers of secondary and postsecondary exceptional adolescents served. Clearly, this mandates that school personnel examine the status and functioning of adolescents with handicapping conditions and respond with appropriate services.

Causes of Increase in Secondary Enrollment

The increase in the numbers of exceptional students in secondary and postsecondary education are several:

- Special education curricula have progressively become more similar to regular curricula.
- PL 94–142 has required supportive services that earlier were provided sporadically or not at all.
- Several effects resulted because of the shift in placement of students with mild handicaps from segregated placements to the regular classroom. They include

1. Access to academic content from which students were earlier restricted, providing a broader curriculum base, enabling availability to content in the higher grades.
2. Improved achievement in academic subjects, which better prepares students to remain in school.
3. Creation of expectations among parents and students that they can continue in school.
- Professional interest in and the provision of services to adolescents have increased.

Secondary Education and PL 94–142

Secondary schools continue to face the challenge to conform to all requirements of PL 94–142. The law specifies that all exceptional students to age twenty-two be provided with a free and appropriate public education unless a terminal point is reached prior to that age. Among the provisions, which are particularly important at the secondary level, are education in the least restrictive environment and full participation in school activities. Students may not be excluded from any event or activity solely on the basis of their handicapping condition.

Goals of Secondary Education

The goals of secondary education for exceptional students are the same as for non-handicapped students. In the long term, they are being prepared to enter the community as responsible adults, to assume the role of productive members of the work force, to achieve economic and social independence, and to develop leisure activities to enrich life. The short-term goals are to provide a continuing knowledge and skill base for academic and vocational preparation, to plan or adjust courses to fulfill state requirements for graduation, and to provide guidance toward the achievement of the long-term goals.

If secondary schools are to meet the challenge, they must begin with creative but responsible and comprehensive planning. Among the continuing needs of exceptional students are social skills training, academic remediation, learning-how-to-learn strategies, social and independent living skills, career guidance, and vocational education. Personnel at all administrative, support, and teaching levels must be involved. Solving problems may include diversification of special services, changes in the roles of teachers and support personnel, alteration of funding patterns, and innovative educational programming. Curriculum must emphasize life skills, preparation for employment, community participation, and financial responsibility.

Role of Teachers

Professional orientations differ from elementary to secondary levels. All teachers are interested in the welfare of students; their roles change, however, to allow them to provide for the needs that they encounter at various stages of student growth and development. Elementary teachers are child-oriented, facilitating the transition from home to a wider world of social experience and knowledge acquisition. Secondary teachers are subject-oriented, providing extended academic instruction and expecting increased student responsibility in learning and self-sufficiency. Secondary teachers facilitate the transition from the protected environs of the school to the larger world of community living and independence.

Teachers of exceptional students must demonstrate an understanding of adolescent characteristics and individual abilities and limitations. If they are to accommodate exceptional students in classes and extracurricular activities, they need to achieve a balance between performance expectations and sensitivity to individual differences. Accepting students allows them to accommodate to the situation and to provide a role model for other students. There is an obligation to provide opportunities for success and to avoid attitudes that lead to self-fulfilling prophecy. Their role also includes developing a philosophy about working with exceptional students and understanding least restrictive environment and federal legislation. They must provide experiences that develop a positive attitude toward exceptional students. It is necessary for teachers of mainstreamed exceptional students to be familiar with content area curriculum below the grade level at which they teach. They need to help in adapting curriculum, in presenting information, and in finding materials that are age and interest appropriate. Consulting resource personnel can help teachers in looking beyond the diagnostic label, thus avoiding the pitfalls of oversimplification and underestimation. Resource personnel can reassure teachers who doubt their own competencies to teach students with handicaps and instill confidence in their ability.

Role of the School

As suggested, the purpose of secondary education is to provide those experiences that will facilitate the transition to community living, occupational self-sufficiency or higher education. In responding to this charge, school personnel are responsible for identifying students' needs and for providing a broad academic program and a range of supportive services. Direct intervention may be needed to bring about staff and peer acceptance of exceptional students. In addition, schools facilitate personal and social development with extracurricular activities including athletics, music organizations, clubs, and social events. Social skills and peer acceptance are enhanced. Benefits accrue for the nonhandicapped as well because they will live in a world in which disabled individuals are becoming increasingly visible and assuming their rightfully equal status in industry, the office, and the community.

It is the responsibility of the school to maintain communication with the family regarding academic progress and social behavior. If behavior problems occur, school personnel can refrain from confrontation that further burdens the family and solicit mutual cooperation in solving the problem. They can organize group or individual counseling through parent groups or community agencies. These services with rehabilitation or community agencies are usually suggested by guidance counselors to assist parents in planning beyond high school.

The director of special education and special services personnel cooperate with the principal and counselors to determine individual needs and plan appropriate placement, coordinate curriculum adjustments, and act as resource personnel to teachers and students. They are responsible for working with families, students, and community agencies and initiate procedures for career planning and vocational training programs.

Role of Parents

Most parents of adolescents continue to be interested in their childrens' educational progress. They cooperate with the school and support extracurricular activities and social events but are less involved with the classroom. Parents can ensure regular attendance and support the school by rewarding achievement commensurate with ability. They augment the goal of independence through reduced advocacy and by allowing their children to develop the personal resources needed to meet environmental challenges and demands.

Social Adjustments

Teacher acceptance of exceptional students paves the way for satisfactory social adjustment. Some regular class students need to be taught that exceptional students are more like themselves than they are different. Explaining the handicapping condition alleviates possible fear and allows understanding. Group projects, cooperative learning, and extracurricular activities provide opportunities to establish friendships and to be accepted by peers.

Characteristics

Anyone who works with students at the secondary level begins with an awareness that there are at least three sets of characteristics that must be considered. These are the general characteristics of all adolescents, the characteristics of exceptional secondary students as learners, and the characteristics unique to students with specific disabilities.

Characteristics of All Adolescents

Exceptional adolescents are, first of all, adolescents. They are subject to all the physical, social, and cultural pressures that mark the transition from child to adult. As with all adolescents, professionals must consider these following characteristics:

- Rapid physical growth
- Gender-related physiological changes, which can cause anxiety and concern
- Acceptance of a social sex role
- Awareness that the end of public schooling is near and that decisions will need to be made concerning the future
- Erratic emotional and mood changes
- Increased peer influence on social behavior
- Ambivalence regarding independence from parents
- Searching for self-identity
- Increased mobility in the community

These and other characteristics frequently result in behavior that strains the tolerance of parents and teachers. Many adolescents do not accept direction or advice, become frustrated easily, often project the cause of their erratic behavior onto others or to external circumstances, and resist rules. On the other hand, teenagers are often idealistic, loving, and caring. They can be thoughtful as well as negligent. Despite the frustrations of adults who interact with teenagers, teachers get their first perceptions of what young persons during adolescence will be like as adults. Parents begin to gain tentative hope that their children will mature into responsible, contributing adults.

Exceptional adolescents manifest many of these same developmental characteristics; the effects of their handicapping condition, however, create additional burdens.

Characteristics of Exceptional Adolescents as Learners

Common characteristics are found in exceptional students. They can be divided, as they were in Chapter 2, into four groups: learning, physical, social, and personal/psychological.

Learning Characteristics   Exceptional adolescents continue to demonstrate deficiencies in academic achievement. Weak reading skills interfere with achievement in all content areas. Oral and written language deficiencies interfere with recitation in class, discussions, answering questions, writing essays and reports, and taking tests. All areas are compromised by poor study skills, inefficient learning strategies, and poor work habits.

Physical Characteristics   Some exceptional adolescents develop in physical skills and coordination to the degree that they can find success in sports and athletics. Others remain awkward and uncoordinated. More commonly, deficits in fine motor ability interfere with handwriting, homemaking activities, and typing and other office skills. Some students with physical impairments are limited in movement and use of their hands. Physical disabilities can affect self-concept, especially during adolescence with its stress on athletics, dancing, and physical attractiveness. Others have persistent health problems, which may limit stamina and result in frequent absences.

Social Characteristics   Social success at the secondary level varies. Some students conform to peer group expectations and are accepted by others. Often, however, they continue to be rejected by nonhandicapped peers. Physical appearance, inappropriate behavior, poor social perception, lack of finesse in interpersonal skills, and immature interests restrict them from acceptance by others who value conformity to peer group norms. These characteristics, the accumulated experiences of rejection by peers and teachers, and the recognized disappointment of parents result in lowered self-esteem. Some students with emotional handicaps or learning disabilities display disruptive activities such as substance abuse and serious infractions of social and legal codes. Youths with persistent behavior problems tend to become dropouts.

Many researchers have investigated the relationship between learning disabilities and juvenile delinquency (Berman, 1981; Keilitz & Dunivant, 1986; Murray, 1976). They discuss the high incidence of learning disabilities among juvenile offenders. Despite these data and the rationale that hypothesize a sequence of school failure, demoralization, frustration, and acting out, most adolescents with learning disabilities do not become delinquents, and a causal relationship has not been established (Jacobsen, 1984).

Personal/Psychological Characteristics   No one set of personal/psychological characteristics can represent exceptional students at the secondary level—They are diverse and variable. Many factors affect their behavior. The environmental milieu is a major factor. In regular classes with high expectations and little personal support, students may demonstrate attributes of noninvolvement—low motivation, withdrawal from participation, nonresponsiveness, failure to complete tasks and assignments, preoccupation with other interests, resistance to authority, and other passive or active aggression. Mood swings and overreaction to people and events interfere with consistent performance.

In special classes some exhibit these same characteristics. Others responding to a nonthreatening atmosphere with reduced demands and understanding teachers are inconsistent but manageable, showing sporadic interest and occasional industry. Often in vocational education, they become involved, attend to task, and accept responsibility.

Characteristics Unique to Disability Areas   When students reach the secondary level, differences have become more pronounced and are more categorically related. Therefore, attention is given to characteristics unique to the disability areas.

Students with mental retardation fall further behind because of poor skills in basic subjects and increased demands for higher conceptualization. The discrepancy between mental age and chronological age widens (Chinn, Drew, & Logan, 1979). Demands of the academic curriculum become virtually impossible to meet. Students with mild retardation may be mainstreamed into regular classes, which review basic academic skills. Others may be in self-contained classes with a prevocational emphasis or in work–study programs with a job in a sheltered workshop or other protected environment.

DEVELOPING DECISION-MAKING SKILLS

Mr. Meyers is a resource teacher for students with mild retardation at the high school level. Most of his students are in Miss Ford's regular human relations class. She reported to Mr. Meyers that in several situations requiring decisions, students selected their first idea without evaluating the consequences of that choice or looking at alternatives.

Mr. Meyers works with Miss Ford in developing a unit in decision-making skills. They are aware that they must do more than name the steps in decision making, that these students would be unable to internalize them and generalize to other parts of their lives. They outline a simplified step-by-step decision-making model. Miss Ford presents them with worksheets describing situations that require decisions. The initial situations are related to students' personal and social lives. Alternatives are presented in multiple-choice format. At first, one or two of the alternatives are obviously impractical or undesirable. Through discussion the students gain experience in analyzing the advantages and disadvantages of each. Throughout, Miss Ford reinforces the step-by-step sequence. Both teachers monitor the students' performance and their application to other situations.

Contrary to earlier beliefs, many students with learning disabilities do not outgrow their disabilities in adolescence (Lerner, 1985). Rather, the problems persist and interfere with academic functioning. Students sometimes show marked discrepancies across subject areas, in part reflecting specific deficient abilities and in part their focus on tasks at which they are successful. Hyperactivity and distractibility are less obvious but they have difficulty in separating relevant and irrelevant aspects of subject content and in remembering the former. They appear socially immature and continue to have difficulty in peer acceptance.

The language difficulties of hearing impaired students continue to interfere with their school progress, and in adolescence they are frequently educationally deficient in comparison to their peers. Often they continue to receive intensive language training. The degree of hearing loss and the relative mastery of language, particularly oral communication, makes the difference socially and psychologically. Youths with mild losses and good oral communication skills can be accepted by peers, particularly if they have received training in social responsiveness and interaction. Severely impaired students are frequently not included in group activities in which high priority is placed on verbal give and take and peer group conversation with its unique vocabulary. Already socially isolated, they may withdraw further and develop the adjustment problems that characterize many adults with hearing impairments.

Other things being equal, students with visual handicaps accommodate well to the secondary school environment. When they are provided access to subject content, they are academically successful. Having normal language and communications skills, they are well-accepted by peers and often admired for their achievements. They demonstrate few psychological problems although some adolescents become overly concerned with their own physical appearance and attractiveness to the opposite sex.

Like those with visual impairments, students with orthopedic handicaps can make good school adjustment and succeed academically. Occasionally, students with physical impairments, frustrated by the limitations imposed by their condition in athletic or social activities, demonstrate recurring adjustment problems. Counseling and peer acceptance can aid in alleviating these problems.

Students with emotional handicaps continue to have difficulty in school. Acting-out behaviors may increase and become more disruptive and damaging to self, others, and property. Substance abuse frequently increases. In the past such students have dropped out or have been moved to residential settings.

Educational Planning

Planning educational experiences for exceptional students requires a knowledge of their entry skills and abilities. It is also based on an awareness of the demands that are made on them at this level. Schumaker and Deshler (1984) identify these areas: work habit demands, knowledge acquisition demands, knowledge expression demands. Students are expected to learn independently and to complete assignments and tasks. They need to learn how to learn, to use texts and reference materials, to outline, to take notes, and to gain information from lecture presentations. They also are expected to demonstrate the knowledge that they have learned in written assignments, orally and on tests.

Planning, which considers students' individual differences, is reflected in range of placement, curriculum, instructional methods, grading, assessment, and minimum-competency testing.

Range of Placement

A range of placement options is available for all students. Many with mild learning handicaps will continue to attend regular academic classes. Some will have additional supportive services—tutoring, counseling, physical or occupational therapy. Resource rooms and self-contained special classes are available. Some students will attend alternative or vocational schools. Those in work–study programs will spend part of their day at a selected work site.

The mandate for least restrictive environment applies equally to secondary students. Regular and special teachers determine with support personnel what accommodations are appropriate. For example, orthopedically handicapped students are included in regular and college-preparatory classes if specialized equipment is provided and the school is barrier-free. Most students with learning disabilities and hearing impairments can be included in regular classes with support services.

Curriculum

Curriculum at the secondary level is diverse, allowing for the varying abilities, interests, and career expectations of maturing young adults. Selection of classes is individualized with students working with guidance counselors to elect a course of study. For most, parental contribution occurs in the home through discussion and subsequent approval. With exceptional students, parents are directly involved with the annual revision of the IEP.

Selecting a program of study for all students results from a contribution of a number of factors. These include state and local policy and student variables.

State and Local Policy The curriculum is most commonly structured on the basis of Carnegie Units prescribing course work needed for graduation. These usually include

- 3–4 Units of English
- 1–2 Units of social studies including history and government
- 2 Units of mathematics
- 1–2 Units of science

Student Variables The second priority in curriculum planning is the goals of students. Some expect to go to college and others to post secondary vocational or technical training. Still others wish to elect a program leading to graduation. Additional student variables determining curriculum selection are general intellectual ability, earlier achievement in academic and nonacademic courses, aptitudes, interests, and motivation.

Curriculum Models for Exceptional Students Several kinds of curricula have been implemented for adolescents. These include basic skills remediation, functional skills curricula, vocational education, and work–study programs.

Basic skills remediation consists of a program to remediate deficits in the areas of reading, mathematics, and written expression. Students may be enrolled in a regular class with support provided by tutors or resource room teachers, or they may be in self-contained classes in which the focus of instruction is remedial.

Functional skills curricula are modifications of the basic skills approach but with subject content within the context of practical use. Most commonly, these are in separate self-contained classes taught by special teachers. They include "survival skills," which students need to function in society.

Vocational education, discussed in detail in the following chapter, stresses pre-vocational, personal, and social skills development. The goal is to prepare students for either postsecondary training in technical or adult vocational programs or employment in the community.

Work–study programs are a part of vocational education designed to ease the transition for students who will move directly into employment in the community. They are restrictive, preparing students for immediate postsecondary employment in specific work areas or job sites.

Social Learning Curriculum The *Social Learning Curriculum* (Goldstein, 1975) is not a total program for exceptional education but focuses on the dual goals of enabling students to think critically and to act independently. Originally designed for students with mild retardation, it is applicable to students with other handicapping conditions.

The curriculum is spiral, revisiting three functional need areas: physical, psychological, and social at successive grade levels. The program includes a detailed curriculum plan, activities books, duplicating materials, and other audiovisual aids.

Curriculum and Course Modifications for Mainstreamed Students

Students with mild handicaps who are mainstreamed may need modification in curriculum or in specific courses.

Curriculum Modifications To a large extent, the diversity of curriculum "tracks" and options allows exceptional students to be guided in electing courses consistent with their capabilities and goals. Modifications in curriculum can be made by

- Substituting courses.
- Waiving requirements although this alternative may have impact on the type of graduation or diploma.
- Accepting experience in lieu of courses.
- Providing supportive instruction in learning skills, test taking, note taking, outlining, problem solving, time management, study skills, or memory techniques.

Course Modification Adjustment can be made through

- Reduction in the amount (not quality) of required work.
- Alternative assignments to circumvent limitations imposed by the handicapping condition.

- Extra-credit assignments.
- Projects in lieu of papers.
- Parallel assignments.

Although some teachers are resistant to "lowering standards" by changes in course content or requirements, others may be more flexible.

Instructional Methods

Methods at the secondary level are generally the same as those discussed in the content areas. However, some are more important and are geared to the maturity of the students. Teacher adjustments in academic instruction focus on

- Presenting an overview of the key points at the beginning of the lesson and a summary at the end.
- Minimizing the lecture format by varying experiences, giving demonstrations, engaging active participation of students, using various activities, having speakers, and using audiovisual presentations.
- Making small-group presentations.
- Providing individualized instruction.
- Adjusting for varying levels of reading ability.
- Using association techniques frequently.
- Adjusting time requirements—that is, pacing presentations, activities, and tests to meet individual needs.
- Writing important points on the chalkboard to give visual emphasis and to demonstrate accurate spelling.
- Emphasizing thinking, reasoning, and problem-solving skills.
- Providing extra practice.
- Presenting clear oral and written directions.
- Giving students who have difficulty following directions time to reword.
- Giving shorter assignments when necessary.
- Making assignments well in advance and stating due dates.
- Making objectives of the lesson relevant to interests, needs, and vocational/career goals.
- Encouraging extra-credit or alternative assignments.

Organizational Skills

- Provide assignment charts. Each student uses an assignment chart daily in each subject (Figure 16.1). As each assignment is completed, it is crossed out. Long-range assignments and studying for tests can be planned.
- Structure assignments. Give vocabulary lists, questions with page number where answers can be found, make outlines, and list items or activities in sequential order.
- Emphasize study skills (Chapter 8).
- Question students who need clarification on specifics of assignments or begin together so that they start correctly.

FIGURE 16.1

Daily assignment chart

	Monday	Tuesday	Wednesday	Thursday	Friday
English		Read Grammar book pp. 81-83 Do p. 83 questions			Test Macbeth
History	Read chap. 6 pp. 151-159.	Do definitions p. 159.	Quiz Constitutional Convention		Report due.
Chemistry	Quiz	Read chap. 8.	Read chap. 8. Study for quiz next Mon.	Lab experiment.	
Math	Problems p. 121.	Problems p. 122	Problems p. 123	Problems p. 124	Quiz
Spanish	Vocabulary words	Group project	Group project	Project due.	
Resource Room	Work on History report	Work on History report	Show Mrs. D. Spanish project	Study for Macbeth test.	
Meetings and Reminders	Soccer practice				

Test-Taking Techniques

- When necessary, give individual directions.
- Eliminate extra choices for matching and fill-in questions.
- Allow extra time.
- Avoid total recall answers; list all possible choices.

Techniques to Improve Visual Skills

- Use a marker when reading texts.
- Allow extra time for copying or use a copy of another student's notes.

- Give verbal instructions.
- Provide to students with visual impairments large-print books, records or tapes, braille, or other devices.
- Cover all print except the word being copied to prevent reversals and skipping words when copying passages or taking notes from a book.

Techniques to Improve Auditory Skills

- Speak clearly; use brief directions.
- Have students repeat directions.
- Question frequently.
- Provide signers for students with hearing impairments who need them.

Techniques to Improve Memory Skills

- Associations
- Imagery
- Clustering
- Rehearsing—repeating aloud several times
- Repeated questioning
- Listening to tapes several times

Techniques to Improve Writing Skills

- Emphasize note-taking skills
- Use tapes.
- Use a typewriter or computer.

Techniques to Improve Reading Skills

- Provide high-interest/low-reading texts.
- Reduce content level to accommodate comprehension limitations.
- Do not require oral reading in a large group if it embarrasses the students.
- Have other students read chapters aloud or have them listen to tape.
- Emphasize vocabulary development in the content areas.
- Provide outlines, study guides, or specific questions to be answered.
- Have peers read to students with visual handicaps or reading disabilities.
- Make material relevant to the needs of students and their careers.
- Allow study notes and review for tests with peers.
- Read tests to students.
- Tape class discussions and review.
- Use a computer.

MEMORY TECHNIQUES

Bruce is an eleventh grade student who attends regular classes and a learning disabilities resource room. His teachers in American history, English, and consumer math are all concerned about his inability to remember facts and information. As a result of this deficit, he is failing most tests.

The teachers met with the resource teacher to determine if there are any physical barriers that would prevent remembering. The discussion included factors such as tension, stress, allergies, illness, diet, or the possibility of chemical addiction. Poor self-concept was the emotional factor considered. It was determined that poor self-concept, tension, and poor eating habits may contribute to the problem.

The specific techniques decided on by the group were to teach the use of abbreviations, mnemonics, association, and categorization. Bruce will be instructed to read texts aloud, to practice to the point of overlearning, and to vary his voice or sing when reading or verbalizing notes. He will learn how to visualize—to get a mental picture and substitute an image for an abstract term—for example, Achievement: sitting on the stage at graduation. He will also write assignments and appointments and leave reminders in a prominent place—for example, backpack with books and homework in front of the door.

Grading

Decisions to change or modify grading depends on local policy. In many schools, accommodations are made on assignments and test questions, eliminating the need to adjust grades. In others, grade standards are lowered; letter grades may correspond to whether students are above, on, or below grade level. Grades may be based on students' abilities not in comparison with others. Extra-credit assignments may increase grade average. Notes on permanent records can indicate the type of adjustments.

Assessment

Assessment at the secondary level has the primary purpose of monitoring the maintenance of learning progress and determining educational needs. The former purpose is accomplished with periodic reevaluations required for all exceptional students and with supplementary yearly administration of achievement instruments.

Two other kinds of assessment procedures are more vital to the continuing identification of educational needs and the planning process. Curriculum-based assessment (Howell & Morehead, 1987) allows careful and precise evaluation of students' academic and social skills. Curriculum-based assessment is formative in that it provides immediate feedback for modification of instruction. Locally prepared or commercial checklists identify specific tasks achieved and yet to be achieved. The *Inventory of Essential Skills* (Brigance, 1981) is a comprehensive, criterion-referenced device designed for use with secondary students.

Minimum-Competency Testing

Many states have adopted some form of minimum-competency testing in an attempt to guarantee that the high school diploma represents achievement of basic skills. Minimum-competency tests are most commonly administered in the high school but some states specify that they be given at both the elementary and secondary levels.

There are no uniform procedures for exceptional students although several alternatives exist.

1. Students in special education programs may be exempt from taking the test.
2. Tests and the conditions under which they are administered may be modified.
3. Students may not be required to pass each part of the test.
4. IEP objectives may be substituted for minimum competencies.
5. An alternative test may be given.
6. Different criteria for passing the test may be adopted.

With each of these alternatives arises serious philosophical, educational, and/or legal problems. State guidelines and administrative decisions will resolve these issues in individual situations.

The intent of minimum-competency testing is to assure that all high school graduates have been adequately prepared in reading and mathematics skills and in general knowledge to allow them to meet expectations of employers and the daily demands of independent living. Teachers of exceptional students have the responsibility for providing a firm foundation in these competencies—not simply to enable their students to pass the tests, but because these goals are consistent with those for exceptional individuals. Achievement in these areas is equally important for handicapped and nonhandicapped students.

Support Services

Support services for exceptional youth include the entire range of special educational interventions. The yearly revisions of the IEP specify which are appropriate and which additional services should be implemented to meet students' needs. Such services include assessment and reevaluation, academic assistance, physical and occupational therapy, and itinerant therapists for those with visual and hearing impairments and communicative disorders.

Support services available to exceptional students include medical services from the school nurse, crisis intervention and continuing counseling, guidance services, and administrative concern and support. Exceptional students are often not aware of the availability of these services. Both regular and special education teachers have a responsibility to direct exceptional students to them and to aid support personnel in working with student acceptance of them.

Close cooperation and liaison relationships with community agencies enable schools to enlist wider support for the needs of students. Legal, welfare, health, mental health, religious, and rehabilitation agencies can work closely with school personnel in playing a primary or secondary role as students move from schools into the community.

SUMMARY

Since the passage of PL 94–142 in 1975, the numbers of students in secondary special education programs have increased, and the quality of service has improved. Teachers, other school personnel, and parents have roles in facilitating students' transition from elementary to secondary school. Traditionally, subject-oriented, secondary teachers can help by being aware of individual student characteristics and by being sensitive to individual differences.

Consulting personnel can help teachers learn about the handicapping conditions and provide guidance in accommodating exceptional students in regular classrooms. Parents cooperate by reducing direct involvement in the classroom while maintaining interest in the school and their children's achievements. Together they augment optimal growth by encouraging participation in extracurricular and social activities. Exceptional students cannot be denied participation in any school activity solely on the basis of their handicapping condition.

Exceptional students demonstrate the same kinds of characteristics as other adolescents. However, these are additionally complicated by the characteristics that are related to their disabilities.

The range of placement options are regular classes, tutoring, resource rooms, part-time and full-time special classes, alternative schools, vocational high schools, and work–study placement. In addition, the full spectrum of special education services is available to them. Curriculum options broaden at the secondary level. This is an advantage to exceptional students who can be guided in electing programs and courses that not only satisfy graduation requirements but also are commensurate with their abilities, limitations, and career aspirations.

Methods include various teacher adjustments; organizational skills; test-taking techniques; methods to improve visual, auditory, memory, and reading skills; and strategies for students with writing difficulties. Adjustments for grading are discussed.

Exceptional students should be able to receive support in assessment and reevaluation, medical facilities, guidance and counseling, physical and occupational therapy, and itinerant therapists for visual, hearing, and communicative disorders. Parents and school personnel work together to plan for vocational training, employment, or higher education following graduation.

REFERENCES

Berman, A. (1981). Research associating learning disabilities with juvenile delinquency. In J. Gottlieb & S. Strichart (Eds.), *Developmental theory and research in learning disabilities*. Baltimore: University Park Press.

Brigance, A. H. (1981). *Inventory of essential skills*. North Billerica, MA: Curriculum Associates.

Chinn, P. C., Drew, C. J., & Logan, D. R. (1979). *Mental retardation: A life cycle approach* (2nd ed.). St. Louis: Mosby.

Goldstein, H. (1975). *A social learning curriculum*. Columbus, OH: Merrill.

Howell, K. W., & Morehead, M. K. (1987). *Curriculum-based evaluation for special and remedial education: A handbook for deciding what to teach*. Columbus, OH: Merrill.

Jacobsen, J. J. (1984). Learning disabilities and juvenile delinquency: Where are we today? *Journal for Special Educators, 19*, 64–73.

Keilitz, I., & Dunivant, N. (1986). The relationship between learning disabilities and juvenile delinquency: Current state of the knowledge. *Remedial and Special Education, 7*, 18–26.

Lerner, J. W. (1985). *Learning disabilities: Theories, diagnosis, and teaching strategies* (4th ed.). Boston: Houghton Mifflin.

Murray, C. A. (1976). *The link between learning disabilities and juvenile delinquency: Current theory and knowledge*. Washington, DC: Government Printing Office.

Schumaker, J. B., & Deshler, D. D. (1984, March). Setting demand variables: A major factor in program planning for the LD adolescent. *Topics in Language Disorders, 4*(2), 22–40.

U.S. Department of Education (1984). *Sixth annual report to Congress on the implementation of Public law 94–142: The Education for All Handicapped Children Act.* Washington, DC: Author.

SUGGESTED READINGS

Chaiken, W. E., & Harper, M. J. (1979). *Mainstreaming the learning disabled adolescent: A staff development guide.* Springfield, IL: Thomas.

Kerr, M. M., Nelson, C. M., & Lambert, D. L. (1987). *Helping adolescents with learning and behavior problems.* Columbus, OH: Merrill.

Liscio, M. A. (Ed.) (1986). *A guide to colleges for hearing impaired students.* Orlando, FL: Academic Press.

Liscio, M. A. (Ed.) (1986). *A guide to colleges for learning disabled students.* Orlando, FL: Academic Press.

Liscio, M. A. (Ed.) (1986). *A guide to colleges for mobility impaired students.* Orlando, FL: Academic Press.

Liscio, M. A. (Ed.) (1986). *A guide to colleges for visually impaired students.* Orlando, FL: Academic Press.

Masters, L. F., & Mori, A. A. (1986). *Teaching secondary students with mild learning and behavior problems: Methods, materials, strategies.* Rockville, MD: Aspen.

Safer, D. J. (1982). *School programs for disruptive adolescents.* Baltimore: University Park Press.

Schloss, P. J., & Schloss, C. N. (Eds.) (1985). *Strategies for teaching handicapped adolescents: A handbook for secondary level educators.* Austin, TX: Pro-Ed.

Woodward, D. M., & Peters, D. J. (1983). *The learning disabled adolescent: Learning success in the content areas.* Rockville, MD: Aspen.

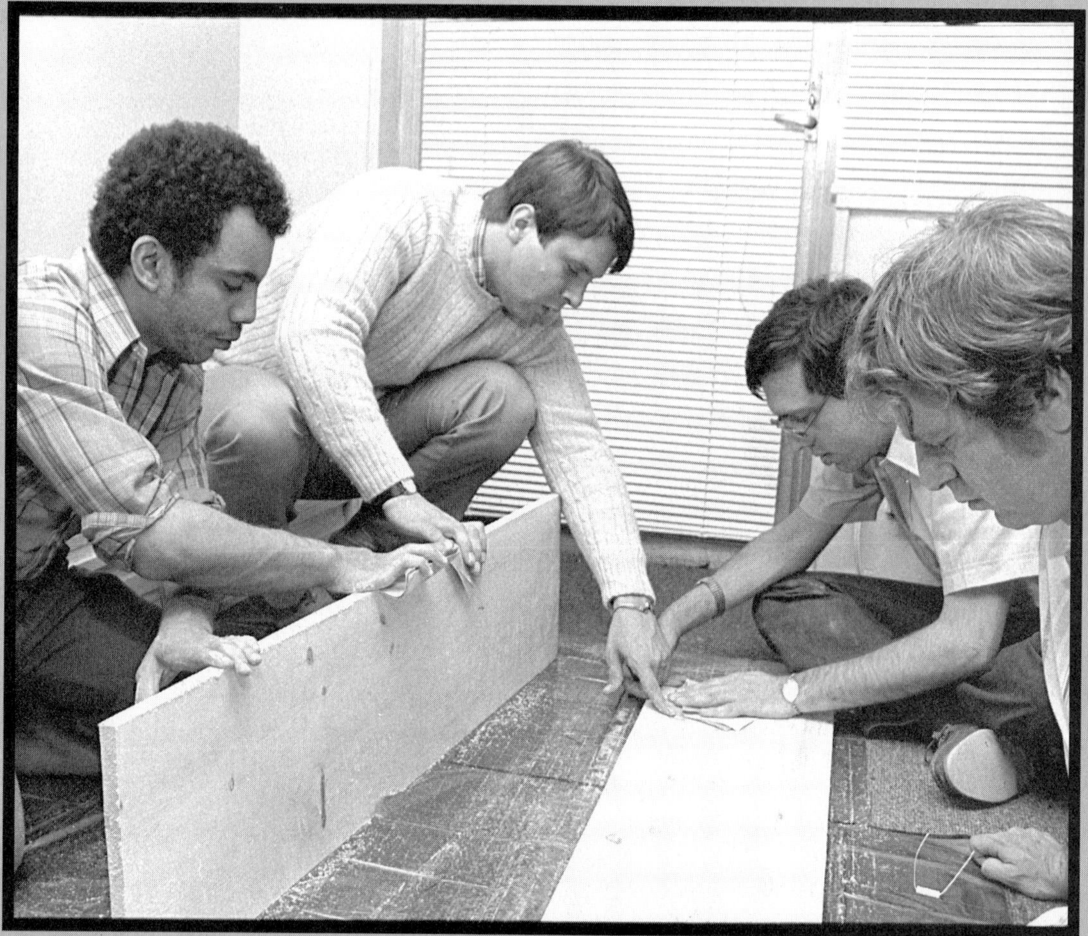

17

Career and Vocational Education and Transition to Adulthood

SCHOOL SERVICES to exceptional students develop and mature parallel to the successive levels at which they are delivered—from elementary to secondary. But what happens to exceptional young adults after high school? Are they prepared to enter the work force? Do they continue with higher education? What is the responsibility of school personnel in assisting students with handicapping conditions to make the transition to employment and adult living in the community? These questions are among the emerging challenges to educators. Teachers begin by developing and including career education curriculum, providing students with opportunities to develop interests and abilities and exposing them to various types of careers.

Development of career education programs begins in elementary school and continues through high school. Students learn to respect and recognize different types of work. As they advance in school, they become aware of careers that interest them. At the secondary level, they must prepare for self-sufficiency and independent living as well as for employment. Career education is directed to all youth but is particularly crucial in the lives of exceptional students.

Definitions

Brolin (1982, p. 256) defines career education as "the process of systematically coordinating all school (or agency), family, and community components to facilitate each individual's potential for economic, social, and personal fulfillment." Vocational education is defined in the *Federal Register* as "organized education programs which are directly related to the preparation of individuals for careers requiring other than a baccalaureate or advanced degree ..." (Title 45, *U.S. Code of Federal Register*, 1979; p. 166).

Career education is the broader concept, spanning the school years from elementary through secondary and applicable to all students. It is taught by regular teachers and is directed toward the development of knowledges, attitudes, and personal competencies leading to satisfying employment. Vocational education begins at the secondary level and, as evident in the above definition, is applicable to those students who do not expect to go to college. It is taught by vocational educators with the goal of providing basic academic instruction, work–skills training, and work–study programs to ease the transition from school to the workplace. Vocational education is responsive not only to the skills and interests of individuals but also to present needs in the labor market.

Career Education

Although vocational education had existed for many decades, career education had its genesis in the early 1970s through the influence of Sidney P. Marland, then the U.S. Commissioner of Education. He foresaw the need for a broad, occupational perspective for all students. He also believed that career education should interface with national goals and priorities and employment needs. His ideas were not accepted until several years later when it was implemented. Career education developed during the same period of social turmoil that saw the extension of equal rights to minority citizens, the normalization movement in special education, and advocacy for increased employment of the handicapped.

In the late 1970s and early 1980s, several authors (Brolin & Kokaska, 1979; Clark, 1979; D'Alonzo & Svoboda, 1983) and a number of state departments of education developed curriculum models. These models have several similarities in design and curriculum.

Design Commonalities

Most models integrate the newer career education and the existent vocational education. The proposed sequences of instruction are applicable for all students throughout the elementary and secondary grades. At the secondary level, vocational education options are introduced for those students not anticipating college enrollment.

Curriculum Commonalities

Virtually all models identify similar groups of curriculum entries. These commonly include

- Awareness of the role of work in the social and cultural environments.
- Expectation that all individuals will assume employment as adults.
- Development of positive attitudes and values.
- Development of good personal and work habits.
- Availability of occupational information.

- Opportunity to explore career options.
- Acquisition of skills for obtaining and keeping a job.

Similarly, all stress that career education be a cohesive, organized program and that it be longitudinal from elementary through secondary levels. It is believed that training in personal and social skills and the attitudes conducive to successful employment must begin in the early grades. Finally, it is generally agreed that career education be an integral part of the total curriculum.

A Model of Career Education

As suggested, many comprehensive models for career education have been proposed. The one presented here is adapted from a model created by the Division of Vocational Education of the Ohio Department of Education. It presents a continuum of educational experiences, keyed to grade levels, with the ultimate goals of satisfying adult employment and economic independence. The successive stages are career awareness, career orientation, career exploration, and vocational education. All are conducted within the public schools but lead to postsecondary educational, vocational, or technical training or direct entry into the community and employment (Figure 17.1).

At each of the four stages, goals and instruction objectives are identified for each of seven areas:

FIGURE 17.1

Career education and transition model

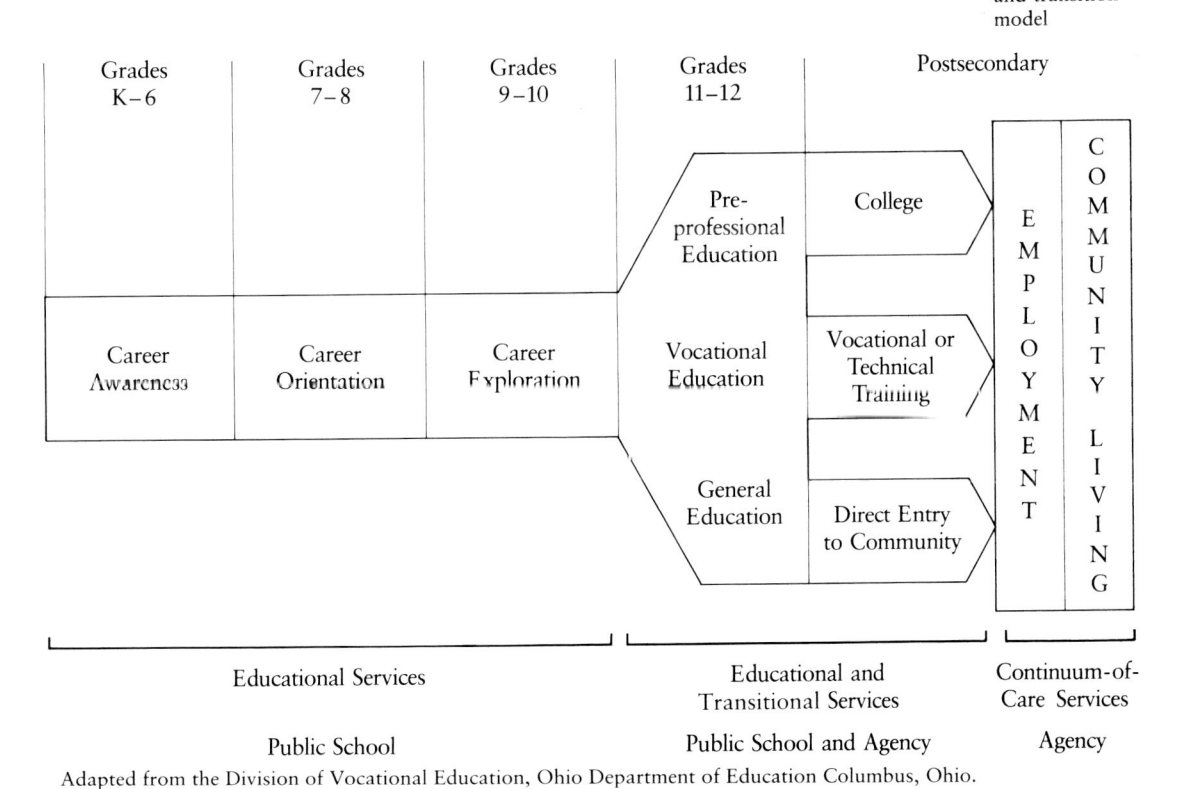

Adapted from the Division of Vocational Education, Ohio Department of Education Columbus, Ohio.

- Self
- Economics
- World of work
- Decision making
- Individual and environment
- Education and training
- Employability and work adjustment

The content of these areas is outlived developmentally as incorporated into the total school curriculum.

Career Awareness (Grades Kindergarten Through Six) The broadest of the levels, career awareness provides information about occupational areas and develops a positive attitude toward work as a major component. Laying a foundation for the development of personal and social skills is another aspect at this level.

Curriculum and materials for identifying occupations and their contribution to society can be incorporated within regular academic subjects. Positive attitudes toward work and the acceptance of responsibility are developed through classroom jobs. Teachers' expectations of job-related behaviors are the beginning of the development of desirable personal characteristics and habits.

Career Orientation (Grades Seven and Eight) Occurring in junior high or middle school, career orientation builds on the earlier level, continuing with attitudes, information, and the development of personal characteristics. Attention is given to understanding of self and awareness of the relationship between self and personal competencies to occupational expectations and success. In addition, students learn of the role of work in the social and cultural environments.

Career Exploration (Grades Nine and Ten) The third stage allows students to direct their interests and attention to more specific occupational areas. Social studies classes are frequently the vehicle for career exploration. Newspapers are used in discussions of job markets. Units of instruction can be developed for occupational clusters with students researching and reporting on specific occupations. Academic subjects are involved with language arts addressing oral expression, reading want ads, using the telephone, and interviewing. Mathematics can take a functional direction with concepts of money management, budgeting, wages, bill paying, and time payments. The expanding fields of research and technology are addressed as part of science class. Those interested in the fine or performing arts can examine with their teachers the qualifications, demands, and rewards of professionals in those fields. They can also participate in plays, band, and music programs.

Career guidance is available as are exploratory experiences in the classroom from guest speakers and through field trips in the community. At this level the development of personal and social skills focuses on good work habits, employer expectations, grooming, accepting responsibility, punctuality, and communication.

Career guidance may include interest and aptitude testing that helps reduce choices to realistic options for some, while for others it can provide an expanded concept of opportunities to be further identified and explored. Community resources are employed to provide accurate information about occupations and employment potential.

Vocational Education (Grades Eleven and Twelve) At this level, students are identified as preprofessional, vocationally oriented, or general education students (see Figure 17.1). The first group will receive academic instruction preparatory to college or professional school enrollment. The second group will move into programs of vocational preparation. The third group receives a general educational program leading to high school graduation.

Career Education and Exceptional Students

Providing career education to exceptional students is authorized by PL 94–142, which mandates educational and related services to meet individual needs. The Educational Amendments of 1976 (PL 94–182) provides funding for vocational and career education for students with handicaps.

The most practical argument for career education is to enable exceptional individuals to exercise their right to gainful employment. Persons with handicaps are unemployed and underemployed (President's Committee on Employment of the Handicapped, 1979). In addition, they are often employed within a restricted range of occupations because of their own lack of knowledge of potential careers and employment opportunities and others' stereotypical misinformation about their capabilities. Hoyt (1981) states that providing information and guidance to aid in decision making are among the goals of career education for handicapped persons. Finally, exceptional individuals need to be helped to learn the personal and interpersonal skills and competencies to obtain and keep a job.

Goals for Exceptional Students The Council for Exceptional Children (1978) developed goals for career education for exceptional students. These include:

- To help exceptional children develop realistic self-concepts, with esteem for themselves and others, as a basis for career decisions.
- To provide exceptional students with appropriate career guidance, counseling and placement services utilizing counselors, teachers, parents and community resource personnel.
- To provide the physical, psychological and financial accommodations necessary to serve the career education needs of exceptional children.
- To infuse career education concepts throughout all subject matter in the curricula of exceptional children in all educational settings from early childhood through postsecondary.
- To provide the student with the opportunity to leave the school program with an entry level saleable skill.
- To provide career awareness experiences which aim to acquaint the individual with a broad view of the nature of the world of work, including both unpaid and paid work.
- To provide career exploration experiences which help individuals to consider occupations which coincide with their interests and aptitudes.

- To provide exceptional individuals programs with occupational preparation opportunities for a continuum of occupational choices covering the widest possible range of opportunities.
- To help ensure successful career adjustments of exceptional students through collaborative efforts of school and community.

It is imperative that exceptional students be included in career education programs so that they may become independent, self-sustaining members of the community.

Mainstreaming and Career Education In most models of career education, the educational content is integrated into the regular school curriculum. As exceptional students are mainstreamed, they receive instruction in these classes. To the extent that they are not integrated with regular education, exceptional students must receive career education in alternative ways.

Gillet (1981) presents a model for a continuum of career educational services that parallels the traditional service delivery system. In her model, the largest proportion of exceptional students, those with minimally handicapping conditions, participate in the regular career education program. Students with more severe limitations receive career education within a range of increasingly restrictive settings. The least number of students, those with the most debilitating handicapping conditions, will receive intensive training in a separate setting with an extensive support system. The objective is limited employment within a protected environment (Figure 17.2).

FIGURE 17.2

Continuum of career education services for exceptional students

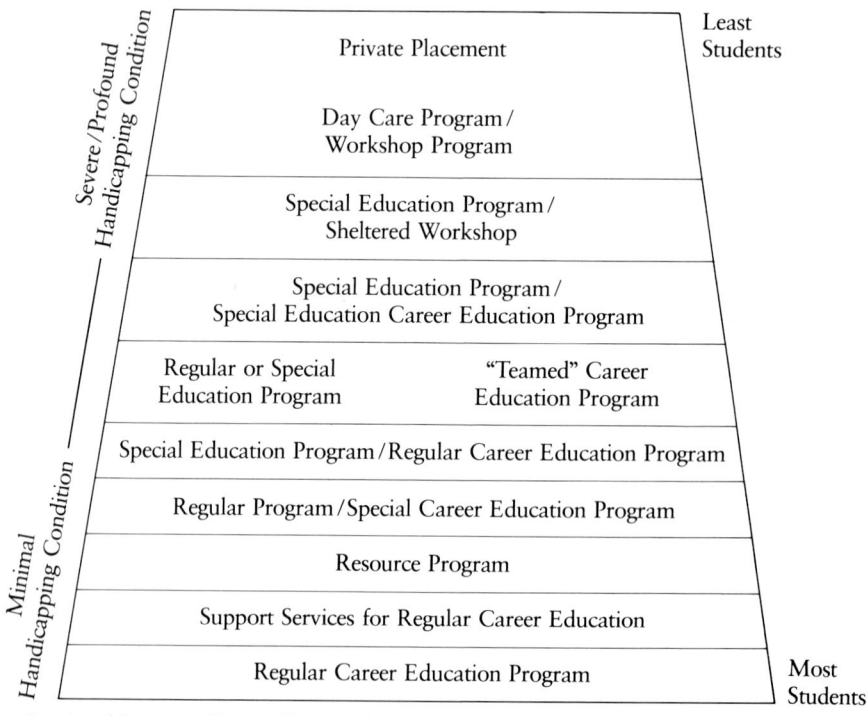

Severe/Profound Handicapping Condition — Least Students

- Private Placement
- Day Care Program/Workshop Program
- Special Education Program/Sheltered Workshop
- Special Education Program/Special Education Career Education Program
- Regular or Special Education Program | "Teamed" Career Education Program
- Special Education Program/Regular Career Education Program
- Regular Program/Special Career Education Program
- Resource Program
- Support Services for Regular Career Education
- Regular Career Education Program

Minimal Handicapping Condition — Most Students

Reprinted from P. Gillet. *Of Work and Worth: Career Education for Exceptional Children and Youth.* Copyright 1981, p. 17. Olympus Publishing Company, Salt Lake City.

Career Education Programs for Exceptional Students Many career education programs for exceptional students have been developed. Notable among these is Brolin's (1978) *Life Centered Career Education* and Clark's (1979) school-based career education.

Life Centered Career Curriculum A comprehensive training program for students with mild mental retardation, the *Life Centered Career Education* can also be used with other students with mild handicaps. The model identifies three major domains: daily-living skills, personal–social skills, and occupational guidance and preparation. Each of these domains is divided into competencies, 22 in all. For example, 7 are assigned to the personal–social skills domain. Among them are achieving self-awareness, maintaining good interpersonal skills and communications, and communicating adequately with others. The 22 competencies assigned to the three domains are further delineated into 102 subcompetencies. These become the basis for teaching–learning activities.

Several features characterize this curriculum. As a mainstreaming program, each domain and competency area is allocated to an academic or nonacademic subject area in junior or senior high school. Brolin (1978) refers to this process as *infusion*—the integration of career education within the larger curriculum. A unique feature is the assignment of instructional responsibility not only to special educators and regular educators but also to parents and peers.

School-Based Career Education The *School-Based Career Education* model is a comprehensive plan advocating career education from the elementary through the secondary schools (Figure 17.3). Four elements are central to the elementary curriculum: values, attitudes, and habits; human relationships; occupational information; and acquisition of a job and daily-living skills. They are integrated into the regular curriculum. At the secondary level the four components are college preparation and general education; vocational, technical, or fine arts education; cooperative education or work–study programs; and work evaluation and work adjustment. These lead to postsecondary involvement in college, junior college, or technical education; postsecondary training; or habilitation or rehabilitation in a community agency. The model provides exit points to employment in the community.

Vocational Education

As previously suggested, vocational education and career education are not synonymous. Vocational education begins at the secondary level and is directed toward those students who do not plan to go to college. It extends beyond high school into adult education, community and technical colleges, rehabilitation services, and other community-based programs for work preparation. Services are individualized but may include

- Continuing academic instruction, especially within a functional or applied curriculum.
- Assessing personal, psychological, and social functioning, interest, and aptitudes.
- Guidance and counseling.

[Diagram: Clark's school-based career education model for the handicapped]

Levels (left side, bottom to top): Elementary K–6; Secondary 7–12; Post Secondary; Post

Across the bottom row (Elementary K–6):
- Values, Attitudes, and Habits
- Human Relationships
- Occupational Information
- Acquisition of Job and Daily Living Skills
- → Exit for Entry Level Job if Necessary

Secondary 7–12 row:
- College Prep/General Education
- Vocational/Technical or Fine Arts Education
- Cooperative Education or Work-Study Program
- Work Evaluation or Work Adjustment
- → Exit for Entry Level Job
- → Exit for Entry Level Semiskilled, or Specialized Job

Post Secondary row:
- Four Year University or College
- Junior/Community College or Technical Education
- Postsecondary Secondary Training
- Community (Re)habilitation Facility
- → Exit for Entry Level, Job
- → Exit for Specialized or Technical Job

Post row:
- Graduate/Professional School
- → Exit for Professionals, Managerial, or Specialized Job
- → Exit for Professional Job

Top: Adult and Continuing Education

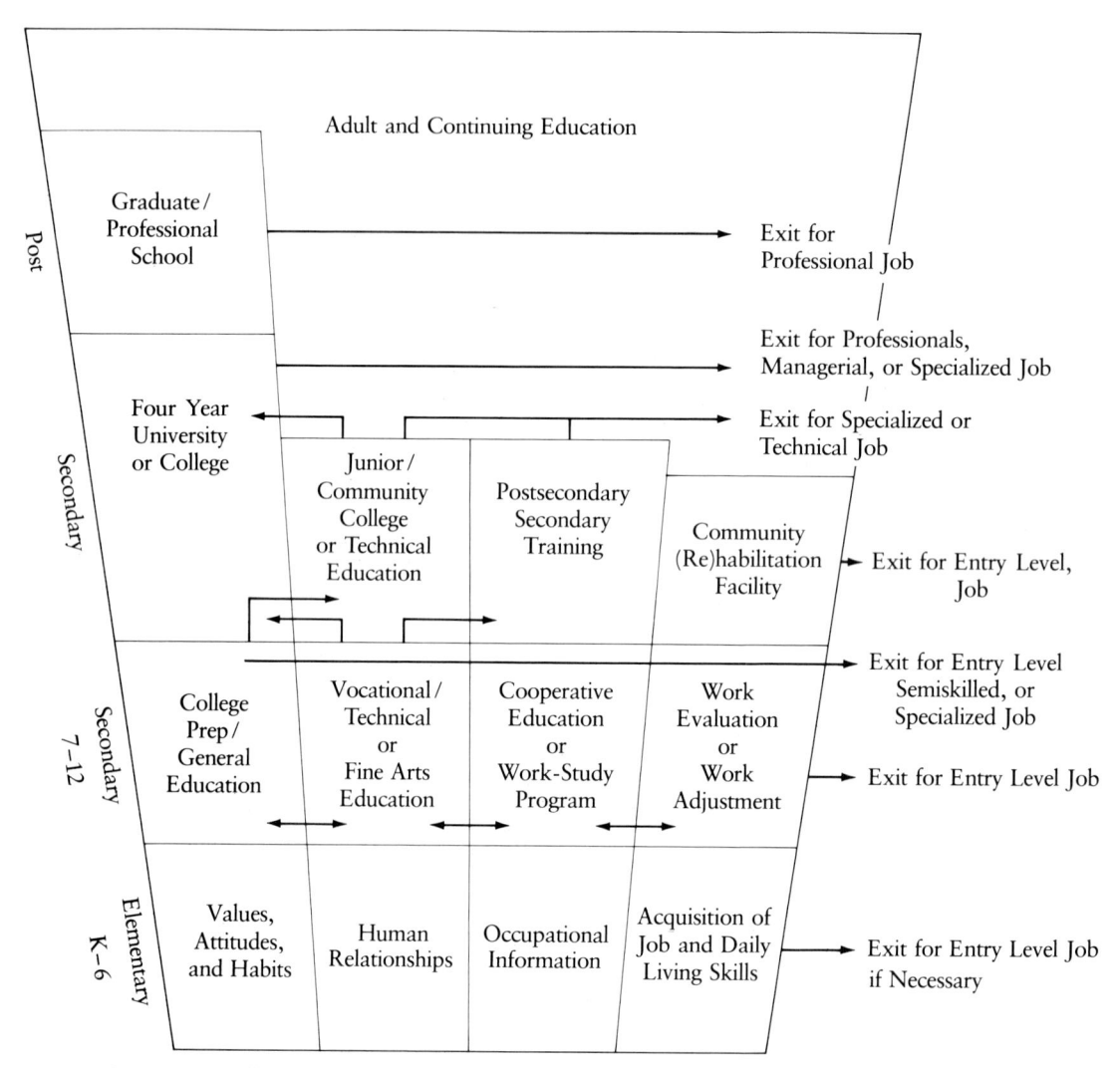

Reprinted from G. W. Clark. *Career Education for the Handicapped Child in the Elementary Classroom.* Copyright 1979, p. 19. Love Publishing Company, Denver.

FIGURE 17.3

Clark's school-based career education model for the handicapped

- Job training.
- Work–study programs in which students attend school part time and work part time.
- Job placement.
- Follow-up.

Because of this scope of services, responsibility cannot be restricted to the school alone. Davis and Ward (1978, p. 3) emphasize that planning and implementation decisions are to be made cooperatively by groups representing

- Vocational education
- Special education
- General education
- Supportive services
- Vocational rehabilitation
- Parents
- Prospective employers
- Local advisory council
- Other service agencies

Origins

Vocational training had its roots in apprenticeship systems (Meers, 1980). It grew over a long period and was formalized into a wide variety of publicly and privately supported programs. The goal of these programs was to restore unskilled, marginally skilled, and otherwise unemployed persons to the job market and to rehabilitate disabled veterans to a productive life. Other handicapped individuals were commonly excluded from training programs until a series of legislations required their inclusion.

Legal Precedents

Several early laws allowed assured participation by exceptional adults in training programs. The major enabling legislation was the Vocational Rehabilitation Act of 1973 (PL 93–112). The two major provisions of concern here are Sections 503 and 504. Section 503 is the more well-known of the two. It requires that public buildings, including educational facilities, to be physically accessible by individuals with disabilities. Section 504 states, in part, that "No otherwise qualified handicapped individual . . . shall solely by reason of his handicap, be excluded from participation in, be denied of, or be subjected to discrimination under any program or activity receiving Federal financial assistance" (Sec. 84.4[a]). Because of this section, the law has come to be known as the civil rights legislation for handicapped individuals.

Vocational Education and Special Education

Special education has had a history of concern with vocational education, which antedates other school programs by more than a century. Patton, Payne, and Beirne-Smith (1986) report that Edward Seguin advocated occupational instruction for the mentally retarded as early as 1850. Vocational education continued to be a part of enlightened education of retarded individuals. Further, it has been expanded to include persons with other handicapping conditions. Meers (1980) states that vocational programs for special needs students should have the following objectives:

- Develop the means to complete school
- Enable students to work toward their maximum potential
- Develop an attitude that the individual is a valued person
- Develop the self-confidence necessary to take advantage of employment opportunities.

- Develop a desirable attitude toward the world of work
- Prepare students for a saleable skill

Stages in the Vocational Education Program

Career education is a necessary prerequisite to vocational education. The knowledges, attitudes, and personal and social skills developed during that process are vital bases to vocational education. Most vocational education programs contain the following six areas: academic instruction, assessment, guidance and counseling, job training, job placement, and follow-up.

Academic Instruction The curriculum includes a continuation of academic and nonacademic classes with the goals of optimal individual development and the accumulation of credits needed for graduation. Exceptional students may attend regular classes or receive instruction within the vocational program or special class. In the latter two, the curricula are functional. Oral and written language skills are studied and practiced, the goal being effective communication. Mathematics is presented in an applied context for independent living and occupational use. Curriculum includes the development of personal and social skills and general employment competencies.

A comprehensive curriculum for vocational education is noticeably lacking. Although some well-planned local curricula have been initiated, vocational teachers are too often left to plan their own courses of study based on general educational goals and apparent academic, behavioral, and social deficiencies of students. Although strong in immediate practicality, this results in fragmentation. The lack of a cohesive conceptual base for organizing, planning, instructing, and evaluating students contributes to the difficulties later encountered by exceptional youth in making the transition to work and community living.

Assessment Vocational assessment is comprehensive, evaluating many dimensions of individual functioning. It provides formative data to students, parents, and professionals to allow selection of appropriate occupational goals and preparatory educational and work experiences. Further, it requires environmental referencing to social and occupational expectancies. Ross (n. d.) outlines an assessment model, which includes six successive levels consistent with these requirements (Figure 17.4). This model may be used generically to allow students to identify potential occupations or specifically to enable them, with the aid of a regular, special, or vocational teacher, to evaluate their own potential for success in an occupation of interest.

Levels in the Model *General screening* considers physical abilities or limitations or medical concerns. Can students perform each of the tasks expected on the job? Will they be capable of operating the equipment or manipulating small parts? Do they have sufficient strength and stamina for the job?

Family attitudes and support are examined. Is the job or workplace in which the job is performed acceptable? Can they provide encouragement and support? Are the family members able to augment instruction in social and personal competencies?

A third area of screening is determining the availability of prevocational instructional and vocational experiences. Can students be adequately prepared for entry into this occupation?

FIGURE 17.4

Vocational assessment model

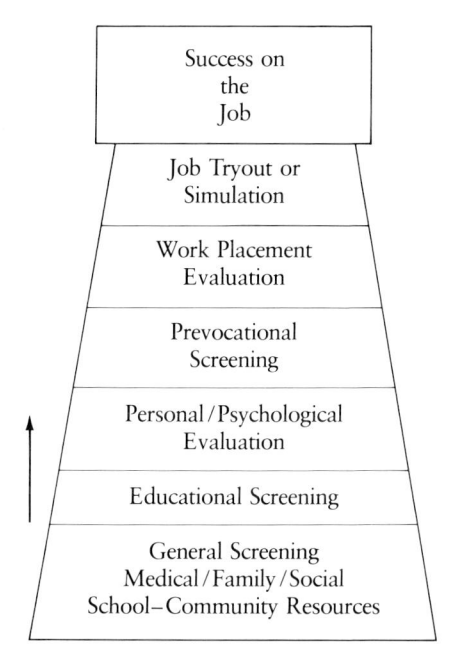

Success on the Job
Job Tryout or Simulation
Work Placement Evaluation
Prevocational Screening
Personal/Psychological Evaluation
Educational Screening
General Screening
Medical/Family/Social
School–Community Resources

Model and description developed by M. Ross, The University of Akron, Akron, Ohio. All rights reserved. Used with permission.

Educational screening examines students' academic preparation. The nature of course work already taken and present level of functioning are noted. Has the pattern of academic courses been conducive to ultimate occupational goals? Can students communicate sufficiently well to interact with customers in retail sales or service? Can they interact appropriately with supervisors? Are students' math skills sufficient for the demands of the job?

Personal/psychological assessment investigates several domains including academic performance as reported by former teachers. Students' work habits are evaluated. Are they careful or disorganized? Are they thorough or inconsistent? Can they follow oral and written directions? Can they respond to demands without unnecessary complaining? Are students more productive working independently or in a group? Will they ask questions? Will they maintain attention to the job? To what extent can they use problem-solving or decision-making procedures when required?

Psychological assessment is more formal with examination of mental ability and personality factors. Standardized individual tests of intelligence such as the *Wechsler Intelligence Scale for Children—Revised* (Wechsler, 1974) or the *Wechsler Adult Intelligence Test—Revised* (Wechsler, 1981) ascertain overall mental ability and give some indication of intraindividual strengths and limitations. In personality assessment, the psychologist may use formal inventories or drawing tests.

Prevocational screening narrows the focus of assessment from general academic, intellectual, and personality functioning to vocationally oriented interests and aptitudes. A variety of interest inventories is available including the *Wide Range Interest-Opinion Test* (WRIOT) (Jastak Associates), the *Ohio Vocational Interest Survey*

(OVIS) (Harcourt Brace Jovanovich), the *Occupational Aptitude and Interest Battery—Aptitude Survey* (OAIS—AS) (Pro-Ed), the *Strong–Campbell Interest Inventory* (SCII) (Stanford University Press), *Brainard Occupational Preference Inventory* (Psychological Corporation), *Minnesota Vocational Interest Survey* (SRA), the *Kuder Occupational Interest Surveys* (SRA), and the *Vocational Preference Inventory* (Consulting Psychologists Press).

Aptitude tests measure potential accommodation to occupational demands. Among the more commonly used instruments are the *General Aptitude Test Battery* (GATB) (U.S. Employment Service), the *Differential Aptitude Tests* (DAT) (Psychological Corporation), and the *Flanagan Aptitude Classification Tests* (FACT) (SRA). An instrument designed particularly for public school use is the *Career Planning Program* (CPP) (Houghton Mifflin).

The *Social and Prevocational Information Battery* (SPIB) (CTB/McGraw-Hill) was designed especially for mildly retarded students and measures nine areas of functioning: purchasing habits, budgeting, banking, job related behaviors, job search skills, home management, health care, hygiene and grooming, and functional signs. It is also useful in assessing specific skills of other low-functioning students.

Work placement evaluation is usually conducted in a vocational school or rehabilitation agency. Students are assessed in worklike situations and with tasks that correspond to specific occupational skills (for example, sorting, filing, and small-tool manipulation). Observation is made both of process, the work procedures demonstrated, and product. Commercial work-sample programs include the *Singer Vocational Education System* (VES) (Singer); the *JEVS Work Evaluation Samples* (Vocational Research Institute (J.E.V.S.); and the *Valpar Component System* (Valpar Corporation), which uses computer simulation.

Job tryout consists of a temporary placement in a business or industry site to allow the individual to gain knowledge of actual work experience. The tryout is a continuation of the assessment process. It allows evaluation by both work–coordinator from the training facility and the employer. Resulting data can be used as a basis for recommending employment or for additional training.

Several points must be stressed in regard to vocational assessment. First, although it is identified as a *stage* in a process, assessment is continuous across all stages. Second, many data sources are used—formal tests, observations, rating scales, descriptions of behavior by teachers and parents, records of earlier achievement, direct observation of present performance and behavior, and reports from contributing professionals. Third, both positive and negative data are considered. For example, it is valuable to know what kind of tasks students cannot perform as well as those they can. It is as important to know which occupational areas are inappropriate for individual students as it is to know which are viable choices. Finally, all data must be evaluated within a developmental context: Which behaviors will likely change with maturation? Which are amenable to change through instruction and management? And which behaviors and limitations are likely to remain permanent aspects of an individual student's performance?

Guidance and Counseling Vocational guidance provides information about occupations and aids students in examining their own interests and aptitudes and in making decisions. Counseling is a mental health activity, which assists students with various personal concerns and adjustment problems.

Guidance Optimally, guidance activities should be a continuing aspect of the career and vocational education program. In the early grades, the role of guidance counselors is supportive and often indirect. Students receive information about work and its role in society from lessons and activities within the content areas. In junior high or middle school, vocational guidance becomes a shared responsibility among regular and special teachers, vocational teachers, and other school personnel. Guidance counselors provide occupational information and work with teachers in helping students explore their own interests. At the high school level, they work with students in both pre-professional and vocational programs. In the latter, guidance counselors work with vocational teachers, school psychologists, parents, and students. They assist in reviewing data and in the decisions made by students and their parents.

Guidance counselors will have available many sources of information about careers, employment requirements, and expectations, which are available to both teachers and students.

A major source of information is the *Dictionary of Occupational Titles* (DOT) (U.S. Department of Labor, 1977). This three-volume set of reference books provides a coding system of data about occupational areas and specific jobs. In addition to occupational nomenclature, the coding system gives additional indications of work environments and personality characteristics of practitioners. A description of the DOT is found in McEver (1976).

Two other documents are the *Selected Characteristics of Occupations Defined in the Dictionary of Occupational Titles* (U.S. Department of Labor, 1981) and the *Occupational Outlook Handbook* (U.S. Department of Labor, which is published periodically). The former expands upon the information provided by DOT in specific areas: physical demands, environmental conditions, math level, language level, and specific vocational preparation related to the jobs. The latter includes descriptions of occupational areas with national employment data and projections for future needs and employment opportunities.

Counseling Counseling activities are a continuing influence in the lives of students with handicaps. Counseling is available prior to vocational training and for persons with mild handicaps for whom personality factors or personal problems restrict optimal adjustment and occupational functioning. Exceptional students can profit from counseling as can nonhandicapped students. For those with intellectual limitations, the benefits of counseling may be essential or supplemental to behavior change from direct instruction or behavior management.

MATCHING SUITABLE JOBS WITH INDIVIDUAL INTERESTS AND NEEDS
Frank has experienced athetoid cerebral palsy since birth. At age sixteen he demonstrates average to above average intellectual ability. He walks unassisted with moderate difficulty, speaks with great deliberation and care in a fairly intelligible manner, has limited use of his hands, and is able to care for himself. Frank's

appearance is typical of persons with moderate athetosis. He demonstrates constant motion in his extremities and face. He has learned to inhibit the movement to a degree when he is calm, but when stressed, he has less voluntary control of his limbs and shows facial contortions as he speaks.

Socially, Frank is shy, sensitive about his appearance, and often defensive. He prefers predictable social and vocational situations to more challenging and potentially more personally rewarding opportunities. His vocational interests are in the area of computer technology. He is able to type slowly but accurately. Through the work–study program in his high school, Frank obtained a job as a word-processor typist in a rehabilitation center. He performs his work competently but finds it boring. His supervisor felt that his concern over his appearance was causing him to withdraw socially, preventing him from moving into more challenging work, which would necessitate meeting and dealing with the public.

The vocational coordinator arranged for Frank to see a psychologist for individual and group counseling, to improve his social skills and reduce sensitivity about his appearance. He was temporarily removed from his job and was placed in a different setting as a part-time librarian in an elementary school. The job consisted of reorganizing the entire book collection and interacting daily with students. With the help of his therapist, a program was developed to allow Frank to meet with each class and formally talk about his disability. Coupled with the informal meetings he had with them every day, he was able to familiarize them with athetosis and help them accept his appearance with few misconceptions. As he solved problems with students who rejected him because of his appearance, he became more assertive, developed a more outgoing manner, and was able to learn to use humor to deal with his movement and speech differences.

Job Training Vocational training is diverse, meeting students' various interest and abilities. Work experience is an integral part of vocational training programs.

Settings Job training may occur in a variety of settings. Large systems provide training in a broad range of occupational areas within the school. Smaller systems operate cooperatively, each housing a particular training module. An alternative arrangement is a vocational high school either within a large district or serving several smaller communities.

Work settings evolve from cooperative arrangements between school and business and industry in the community. Care must be taken in site selection. Livingston, McAlees, and Korn (1982) state that it is insufficient to simply match individual aptitudes and interests with job-task demands. For all individuals, but especially for those with handicapping conditions, many other factors must be considered. They include physical limitations, self-concept, socioeconomic status, social and interactive skills, educational achievement, mobility, and independence.

The decision to place students at a work site is jointly made among teachers and vocational coordinators, representatives from the work location, parents, and, most importantly, the students. They consider the full breadth of data that have resulted from the formal and informal assessment procedures described.

Curriculum Job training is in addition to the continuing academic and nonacademic instruction and the development of personal and social skills already described. Work experience is an integral part of vocational training. Several types exist, including *Work Experience and Career Exploration, Work Experience Handicapped Programs, Work Experiences Disadvantaged Programs,* and *Cooperative Vocational Educational Programs* (Kingsbury, 1980; pp. 169–170). These programs allow students to attend classes part of the day and to be employed in the community for the remainder. A teacher–coordinator provides vocational training in the school and is a liaison with off-campus work sites. Formative evaluation by the vocational teacher or a work–study coordinator is a continuing aspect of such programs, with feedback being directly translated into instructional objectives in the school setting.

The more severely handicapped, usually already enrolled in alternative special programs or schools, receive less academic instruction and more intensive training in self-help and social skills. Job training is in protected environments such as sheltered workshops or rehabilitation agencies. In effect, these individuals are not expected to complete an academic program and have already been placed in work situations.

Job Placement Ideally, vocational training and work experience should lead directly to employment in the community. Unfortunately, this ideal is often not realized. Although training commonly includes such topics as completing job application forms and interviewing skills, schools do not view themselves as employment agencies. They terminate services at graduation. Wehman, Kregel, and Barcus (1985) propose a vocational transitional model from school to employment with three major components: school instruction, planning for the transitional process, and placement in meaningful employment. This model and similar programs hold promise for improved services in the area of job placement.

School administrators, special education personnel, vocational teachers, and guidance counselors must meet the challenge of working together with exceptional students to complete the training they have begun. Vocational education coordinators and guidance counselors can refer them to rehabilitation agencies and can open doors by contacting prospective employers.

Follow-Up During work experiences, vocational coordinators make regular visits and reports concerning job adjustment and performance. In the beginning frequent contacts are made because problems encountered by the worker or employer are likely to surface early in the experience. The vocational teacher or agency representative can aid both in making necessary accommodations. Later follow-up can occur less frequently and at irregular intervals. Handicapped individuals receive support, guidance, and needed instruction. Professional personnel maintain direct contact with the field and refine their own perceptions and placement recommendation competence. Employers are assisted in accommodating exceptional students.

Postschool Followup Too often, after leaving school, exceptional youth meet difficulties in the workplace and leave or lose their jobs. The support system earlier provided by the school is no longer available. These youth may be unaware of the community agencies intended to provide assistance. In addition, lack of coordination and planning among these agencies may contribute to their lack of adequate provision of a transitional support system for youths with handicaps (Rusch, Mithaug, & Flexner, 1986). Clearly, newer models and efforts are needed to assist the transition from school to the workplace and to community living.

The Transition to Adulthood

Graduation from high school marks a major transition in the lives of most youths. This is equally true for exceptional and nonhandicapped students. Some progress to postsecondary education—a four-year college, a two-year college, or vocational or technical schools. Others enter directly into the workplace. Many students leave school prior to graduation and move into the community.

Exceptional students and their families face several decisions and concerns. The central considerations are living arrangements, mobility, independent living, social adjustment, interpersonal relationships, leisure time and recreation, and acceptance in the community. Public schools must focus on assisting students in facing the challenges of young adulthood.

Exceptional Students and Postsecondary Education

For many students, entering college is expected following graduation. This expectation should apply equally to individuals with handicaps who possess the intellectual capabilities to succeed in higher education. However, the President's Committee on Employment of the Handicapped (1979) found that only 2 percent of the college population was handicapped—far less than would appear to be eligible.

Several factors contribute to this enrollment rate:

1. Elementary and secondary school programs might have been insufficient in meeting the educational needs of students with handicapping conditions.
2. Exceptional students may fail to appreciate their own potential and do not set college enrollment as a goal.
3. Teachers and guidance counselors may stereotype exceptional students as less than capable. They may not expect their academic success or may not encourage college aspirations.
4. Colleges may not provide sufficient accommodations or support systems and may not encourage enrollment by students with handicaps.

Further, the population of students with handicaps most frequently enrolled in college has primarily been limited to those with visual, hearing, and orthopedic impairments. Because they are among the low-incidence handicapping conditions, their numbers at the college level are proportionately small. In recent years there has been an increase in the numbers of college students with learning disabilities. White, Alley, Deshler, Schumaker, Warner, and Clark (1982) report that 67 percent of students with learning disabilities surveyed expected to continue some form of education.

To serve students who are intellectually and academically capable but who have handicapping conditions, both secondary and college practices and programs may need to be modified. Changes will also be required in the attitudes and perceptions of some personnel.

At the high school level, teachers should be helped to gain an understanding of individual strengths and limitations to plan individualized instruction and set high but realistic expectations for achievement. The thrust of the academic program for capable students must be toward preparation for higher education rather than for only high school graduation. Guidance counselors must evaluate individual characteristics as a basis for planning continuing education and selection of a college. Professional associations advocating the rights and advancement of exceptional individuals often can provide lists of institutions receptive to disabled students. (See "Suggested Readings" at the end of this chapter.)

Support in College Most colleges and universities have established services for disabled students. They provide counseling and career planning and assist with on-campus and off-campus housing. They arrange for readers for students with visual impairments and interpreters for students who are deaf. With the influx of larger numbers of students with other handicapping conditions, these services will need to expand to include tutoring, instruction in study, note-taking and test-taking skills, and arranging for individuals to take and share notes. Exceptional students may also receive instruction in the use of computers as aids in instruction.

Personnel supporting exceptional students will increasingly become liaisons between faculty and students and will provide consultation to instructors in making academic adjustments. Mangrum and Strichart (1984) present a guide to the development of programs for college students with learning disabilities. Many of their recommendations are applicable to students with other handicapping conditions. Some universities, reacting to the demands by parents, advocates, and students, are providing in-service training to faculty.

Another difficulty encountered by many exceptional individuals is the lack of a support system in the community in which the college is located. Although capable of performing college work, some students are unable to live independently from their families.

Two-Year Colleges An alternative to attendance at a four-year institution is the two-year or community college. These schools may be particularly appropriate for students with handicaps in many ways. The vocational and career programs may be more suitable for many. Associate degrees can be earned in a variety of fields. Because they are located in the home communities, their placement offices may have close liaison with employers. Locating and receiving a job and the transition from school to work may be eased.

Individual attention not available at large universities may be provided. Faculty, accustomed to a broader range of individual differences, abilities, and competencies, may be amenable to alterations in the task demands of the subject. Because students live at home, a family support system can remain intact. Housing, living arrangements, and the demand for instant independence are reduced.

Frequently, community colleges have "two-plus-two" arrangements with nearby universities. Students can elect the general, initial two-year college requirements in their home communities and then move to the university to complete their four-year degree. This arrangement has obvious advantages, allowing exceptional students to mature toward independence and to discover if they are going to be able to perform college work successfully.

Vocational and Technical Training   A variety of vocational evaluation and training facilities supported by public funds exist in larger communities. Although individuals with handicapping conditions were not originally eligible for these services, a succession of legislation made them increasingly available. In addition, services specifically for exceptional adults were created. Federal- and state-funded facilities were designed to provide a full range of counseling, assessment, training, and placement services.

Adults with mild handicaps often elect to attend industry-supported or private schools for training in technical and semiskilled occupational areas.

Exceptional Students in the Workplace

Many employers find high-quality job performance among handicapped workers. Despite records of work excellence and reliability, they continue to be underemployed. This is caused partly by employer reluctance due to misperceptions about persons with handicaps. Employers may also be concerned about their adaptability to the workplace, productivity, and fringe benefits. Additional factors in the employment rate are the uncertainties of economic conditions and the general unemployment rate. "Last-hired/first-fired" often applies to more than the principle of seniority.

Exceptional Individuals in the Community

Living Arrangements   Some adults with mild handicaps are absorbed within the community. They marry, have families, live in their own homes or apartments, and enjoy an independent life. Others need assistance in achieving these goals. Sometimes this support comes from an itinerant caseworker who provides guidance, counseling, instruction, and supervision and who may accompany the individual in out-of-home activities. Individuals with learning disabilities and developmental disabilities often live in group homes or supervised apartment complexes. Some are deinstitutionalized adults who, because of the accommodations, can move from their parents' residence to establish their own life in the community. Staff members continue the educational process with instruction in daily-living and self-help skills. Many adults need assistance or monitoring with developing and maintaining good grooming habits and adequate nutrition. They often are unable to manage money. They need training in handling bank accounts, paying bills, saving money, and living within their means.

Each resident has an individual plan with long-term goals and short-term objectives. These residents work in the community part-time or full-time in sheltered workshops or other protected environments. Although group homes have been successful in aiding mildly handicapped persons to achieve semi-independence and a nearly normal life-style, community opposition and zoning laws often make their establishment and maintenance difficult. Parents must be aware that not all group-living situations provide trained staff to deal with these matters.

Socialization   Socialization often presents a major problem. Although some individuals with mild handicaps do "fit in" with religious, fraternal, and similar groups, some have difficulty in making and maintaining friends, often because of poorly developed social skills. Adults with mental retardation and more seriously handicapped persons often associate only with others like themselves. Parents or staff persons in group homes or other facilities must continue to teach social skills, assist in practicing how to handle specific situations, and take them to social events to experience interaction with others. Directing young adults to church groups, volunteer work, and sports groups enable them to find acceptance and satisfying relationships.

Providing Services   The focus of this book has been on students with handicapping conditions who receive an education and move into the community. At that point they are joined in their need for services by individuals with more severe handicaps who have not been in public schools. They may be deinstitutionalized persons and displaced and unemployed workers. There is demand not only for vocational training and job location but also for services in all areas of adult life (see Figure 17.1).

Despite the recognized need and the many programs and services, considerable problems exist. Conley (1985, pp. 212–213) identifies five problems in the delivery of services:

1. Mentally retarded persons may not always receive needed services even when they are available.
2. Some needed services are not available.
3. The problem of coordination of available services to achieve prescribed goals, particularly employment goals, are far from being resolved.
4. Effective services are often hindered by rigidity of procedural practices.
5. Programs that are not primarily involved with mentally retarded persons often lack the expertise or desire to provide needed services.

Although Conley attends to persons with mental retardation, the criticisms are also applicable to services for others.

Legislation has been enacted, agencies established, programs developed, and funding made available in response to specific identified needs. Each one is restricted to its limited goals with little coordination and communication among them. Often they operate at cross purposes. Services vary from inadequate to superior. The needs of exceptional persons are not separated but are integral parts of a functioning whole. Therefore, there is a need for coordination among service providers.

Copeland and Iverson (1985) recommend a continuum-of-care model for services to developmentally disabled persons and adults with other handicaps. It provides for an integration of fiscal, management, and programmatic activities to maintain consistent provision of support relative to both the extensiveness and severity of individual needs.

Parents, educators, and service providers must work for the habilitation of adults with exceptionality into the community based on the principles of normalization and least restrictive alternative.

The Challenge of Transition

Will (1984, p. 3) writes that "transition is a bridge between the security and structure offered by the school and the opportunities and risks of adult life." If individuals with mental, physical, and learning handicaps are to enjoy these opportunities and take risks, both the quality and delivery of services and the preparedness of individuals must be considered.

There is general professional agreement that successful transition will not "just happen." It must result from the planning and implementation of comprehensive, effective activities. Under the leadership of Will (1984), the Office of Special Education and Rehabilitative Services (OSERS) has identified transition as a priority issue. The goal is "that individuals leaving the school system obtain jobs, either immediately after school or after a period of post-secondary evaluation or vocational services" (p. 4).

The OSERS model has three important components:

1. Effective high school programs that prepare students to work and live in the community.
2. A broad range of adult service programs that can meet the various support needs of individuals with handicaps in employment and community settings.
3. Comprehensive and cooperative transition planning between educational and community service agencies in order to develop needed services for graduates.

— (Hardman & McDonnell, 1987; p. 494)

OSERS also has authorized the development of demonstration models and funded projects to study and make recommendations for easing the transition between school and employment and community living as discussed in a series of articles in *Exceptional Children* (Vol. 53, No. 6, 1987).

A Continuing Challenge

The first chapter of this book challenges educators to provide continuing and effective services for students with handicapping conditions. It concludes with an additional challenge. Educators, human services personnel, and citizens are challenged to work to fully integrate all persons with handicaps into the mainstream of life. Are we willing to work to change attitudes so that individuals with any type of exceptionality will be accepted as full members of their communities, as students, as neighbors, as co-workers, and as friends?

SUMMARY

The goal of career education is to prepare students to take their place in society when formal education and training are completed. Curriculum includes the development of positive attitudes and values, the encouragement of good work habits, the availability of occupational information, the opportunity to explore career options, and the acquisition of skills for obtaining and keeping a job. It begins in the early grades and continues through high school through a series of stages, which include career awareness, career orientation, career exploration, and, for some students, vocational education. The goals of career education are applicable to exceptional and nonhandicapped students. They are of particular importance in the personal, social, and occupational development of exceptional individuals because they are often unemployed or underemployed.

Vocational education is a narrower concept than career education and is directly related to the preparation of individuals for employment in specific occupational areas. Vocational education is restricted to the secondary level and requires the cooperation of parents, school personnel, and community agencies. Legal precedence requires vocational training programs to include individuals who are exceptional and guarantees their right to hold jobs for which they are qualified.

Vocational education has long been a part of special education because individuals with handicaps had to be prepared to be as self-sufficient as possible in the community. Stages in vocational education include academic instruction, assessment, guidance and counseling, job training, job placement, and follow-up. Vocational personnel guide students in investigating various areas of employment and in determining interests and capabilities. Training programs include the development of social and personal skills needed to maintain a job, career exploration, work experience, and cooperative educational-vocational programs.

The transition from school to community is often difficult, especially for individuals with handicapping conditions. Following graduation some students go on to postsecondary education in college or junior college. Others continue in vocational or technical training programs, and still others enter directly into the workplace. Virtually all enter the community to assume responsibility as citizens. Other concerns facing exceptional young adults and their families are living arrangements, mobility, independent living, social adjustment, interpersonal relationships, leisure activities, and community acceptance. The development of new programs and the reorganization of present services needed to ease this transition remain as challenges to professionals.

REFERENCES

Brolin, D. E., (Ed.) (1978) *Life centered career education: A competency based approach*. Reston, VA: The Council for Exceptional Children.

Brolin, D. E. (1982). *Vocational preparation of persons with handicaps* (2nd ed.). Columbus, OH: Merrill.

Brolin, D. E., & Kokaska, C. J. (1979). *Career education for handicapped children and youth*. Columbus, OH: Merrill.

Clark, G. M. (1979). *Career education for the handicapped child in the elementary classroom*. Denver: Love.

Conley, R. W. (1985). Impact of federal programs on employment of mentally retarded persons. In K. C. Lakin, & R. H. Bruininks (Eds.). *Strategies for achieving community integration of developmentally disabled citizens* (pp. 193–216). Baltimore: Brookes.

Copeland, W. C., & Iversen, I. A. (1985). Developing financial incentives for placement in the least restrictive alternative. In K. C. Lakin, & R. H. Bruininks (Eds.). *Strategies for achieving community integration of developmentally disabled citizens* (pp. 291–312). Baltimore: Brookes.

Council for Exceptional Children. (1978). *Position paper on career education*. Reston, VA: Author.

D'Alonzo, B. J., & Svoboda, W. S. (1983). Career and vocational education for LBP adolescents. In B. J. D'Alonzo (Ed.). *Educating adolescents with learning and behavior problems*. Rockville, MD: Aspen.

Davis, S., & Ward, M. (1978). *Vocational education of handicapped students: A guide for policy development*. Reston, VA: The Council for Exceptional Children.

Gillet, P. (1981). *Of work and worth: Career education for exceptional children and youth*. Salt Lake City: Olympus.

Hardman, M., & McDonnell, J. (1987). Implementing federal transition initiatives for youths with severe handicaps: The Utah community-based transition project. *Exceptional Children, 53,* 493–498.

Hoyt, K. B. (1981). *Career education: Where it is and where it is going*. Salt Lake City: Olympus.

Kingsbury, D. (1980). Work experience and cooperative placement programs. In G. D. Meers (Ed.). *Handbook of special vocational needs education* (pp. 161–204). Rockville, MD; Aspen.

Livingston, R. H., McAlees, D. C., & Korn, T. A. (1982). Alternative strategies in vocational rehabilitation. In C. R. Reynolds, & T. B. Gutkin (Eds.). *The handbook of school psychology* (pp. 721–747). New York: Wiley.

Mangrum, C. T., II, & Strichart, S. S. (1984). *College and the learning disabled student: A guide to program selection, development, and implementation*. Orlando, FL: Grune & Stratton.

McEver, M. L. (1976). Career guidance and the *Dictionary of Occupational Titles*. *Exceptional Children, 43,* 31–33.

Meers, G. (1980). An introduction to special vocational needs education. In G. D. Meers (Ed.). *Handbook of special vocational needs education*. Rockville, MD: Aspen.

Patton, J. R., Payne, J. S., & Beirne-Smith, M. (Eds.) (1986). *Mental retardation* (2nd ed.). Columbus, OH: Merrill.

President's Committee on Employment of the Handicapped (1979). *Affirmative action for disabled people: A pocket guide*. Washington, DC: U.S. Government Printing Office.

Ross, M. (n.d.). [Vocational assessment system]. Unpublished raw data.

Rusch, F. R., Mithaug, D. E., & Flexer, R. W. (1986). Obstacles to competitive employment and transitional program options for overcoming these obstacles. In F. Rusch (Ed.). *Competitive employment issues and strategies* (pp. 7–27). Baltimore: Brookes.

U.S. Department of Labor. (1977). *Dictionary of occupational titles* (4th ed.). Washington, DC: U.S. Government Printing Office.

U.S. Department of Labor. (1981). *Selected characteristics of occupations defined in the Dictionary of Occupational Titles*. Washington, DC: U.S. Government Printing Office.

U.S. Government (October 1, 1979). State vocational education programs. *Title 45 a. s. Code of Federal Regulations 1361*. Washington, DC: U.S. Government Printing Office.

Wechsler, D. (1974). *Wechsler intelligence scale for children—revised*. New York: Psychological Corporation.

Wechsler, D. (1981). *Wechsler adult intelligence scale—revised*. New York: Psychological Corporation.

Wehman, P., Kregel, J., & Barcus, J. M. (1985). From school to work: A vocational transition model for handicapped students. *Exceptional Children, 52,* 25–37.

White, W. J., Alley, G. R., Deshler, D. D., Schumaker, J. B., Warner, M. M., & Clark, F. L. (1982). Are there learning disabilities after high school? *Exceptional Children, 49,* 273–274.

Will, M. (1984). *OSERS programming for the transition of youth with disabilities: Bridges from school to working life.* Washington, DC: Office of Special Education and Rehabilitative Services, U.S. Department of Education.

SUGGESTED READINGS

Birenbaum, A., & Cohen, H. J. (1985). *Community services for the mentally retarded.* Totowa, NJ: Roman & Allanheld.

Bruininks, R. H., & Lakin, K. C. (1985). *Living and learning in the least restrictive environment.* Baltimore: Brookes.

Harrington, T. F. (Ed.) (1982). *Handbook of career planning for special needs students.* Rockville, MD: Aspen.

Johnson, D. J., & Blalock, J. W. (Eds.) (1987). *Adults with learning disabilities: Clinical Studies.* Orlando, FL: Grune & Stratton.

Kiernan, W. E., & Stark, J. A. (Eds.) (1986). *Pathways to employment for adults with developmental disabilities.* Baltimore: Brookes.

Miller, S. R., & Schloss, P. J. (1982). *Career-vocational education for handicapped youth.* Rockville, MD: Aspen.

Schinke, S. P., & Gilchrist, L. D. (1984). *Life skills counseling with adolescents.* Baltimore: University Park Press.

Wehman, P., & McLaughlin, P. J. (1980). *Vocational curriculum for developmentally disabled persons.* Baltimore: University Park Press.

Weisgerber, R. A., Dahl, P. R., & Appleby, J. A. (1980). *Training the handicapped for productive employment.* Rockville, MD: Aspen.

Wircenski, J. L. (1982). *Employability skills for the special needs learner.* Rockville, MD: Aspen.

Appendix A

Publishers and Producers of Special Education Learning Materials

Academic Press   111 Fifth Avenue, New York, NY 10003

Academic Therapy Publications   20 Commercial Boulevard, Novato, CA 94947

Adapt Press   1209 West Bailey, Sioux Falls, SD 57104

Addison-Wesley Publishing Co.   Jacob Way, Reading, MA 01867

Alexander Graham Bell Association for the Deaf, Inc.   3417 Volta Place NW, Washington, DC 20007

Allyn and Bacon, Inc.   470 Atlantic Avenue, Boston, MA 02210

American Alliance for Health, Physical Education, Recreation, and Dance   1900 Association Drive, Reston VA 22091

American Guidance Service, Inc.   P.O. Box 99, Publishers Building, Circle Pines, MN 55014

American Printing House for the Blind   1839 Frankfort Avenue, Box 6085, Louisville, KY 40206

R & D Ames Company   114 Ames Street, Sharon, MA 02067

Ann Arbor Publishing   Box 7249, Naples, FL 33940

Appleton-Century-Crofts   25 Van Zant Street, East Norwalk, CT 06855

Argus Communications   1 DLM Park, Box 5000, Allen, TX 75002

Avon Books   1790 Broadway, New York, NY 10019

Bantam Books, Inc.   666 Fifth Avenue, New York, NY 10019

Clarence L. Barnhart, Inc.   P.O. Box 250, 1 Stone Place, Bronxville, NY 10708

Basic Books, Inc.   10 East 53rd Street, New York, NY 10022

Behavior Research Laboratories   Box 577, Palo Alto, CA 94320

Bell and Howell, Audio Visual Products Division   7100 McCormick Road, Chicago, IL 60645

Benzinger Publishing Company   *See* The Macmillan Company

Bobbs-Merrill Educational Publishing   4300 West 62nd Street, Indianapolis, IN 46206

Paul H. Brookes Publishing Co.   P.O. Box 10624, Baltimore, MD 21204

Wm. C. Brown Company   2460 Kerper Road, Dubuque, IA 52001

Bruner/Mazel Publishers   19 Union Square, New York, NY 10003

Bureau of Educational Research   The University of Iowa, Iowa City, IA 52242

California Test Bureau/McGraw-Hill   Del Monte Research Park, Monterey, CA 93940

Canadian Association for Retarded Children   4700 Kede Street, Downsview, Toronto, Canada

Canter Associates, Inc.   P.O. Box 2113, Santa Monica, CA 90406

C. C. Publications   P.O. Box 23699, Figaro, OR 97223

Center for Applied Research in Education/Prentice-Hall   Englewood Cliffs, NJ 07632

Centurian Publications International, Ltd.   16 St. James Lane, London, United Kingdom N103RD

Chapman, Brook, and Kent   1215 De La Vine Street, Suite F, P.O. Box 21008, Santa Barbara, CA 93121

College-Hill Press   4284 41st Street, San Diego, CA 92105

Columbia University Press   562 West 113 Street, New York, NY 10025

Communication Research Associates   P.O. Box 11012, Salt Lake City, UT 84111

Consulting Psychologists Press, Inc.   577 College Avenue, Palo Alto, CA 94360

Continental Press, Inc.   520 E. Bainbridge Street, Elizabethtown, PA 17022

Cooperative Education Agency, CESA-12   Box 564, Portage, WI 53901

The Council for Exceptional Children   1920 Association Drive, Reston, VA 22091

Creative Learning Press, Inc.   P.O. Box 320, Mansfield Center, CT 06250

Creative Publications   3977 Bayshore Road, P.O. Box 10328, Palo Alto, CA 94303

Curriculum Associates   5 Esquire Road, North Billerica, MA 01862

The John Day Company   666 Fifth Avenue, New York, NY 10019

T. S. Dennison Company   9601 Newton Avenue, Minneapolis, MN 55431

Developmental Learning Materials   P.O. Box 4000, 1 DLM Park, Allen, TX 75002

Doubleday and Company   245 Park Avenue, New York, NY 10167

The Economy Company   1901 N. Walnut Avenue, Oklahoma City, OK 73125

Edmark Corporation   P.O. Box 3903, Bellevue, WA 98009

Educational Development Laboratories (McGraw-Hill)   1221 Avenue of the Americas, New York, NY 10020

Educational Performance Associates, Inc.   563 Western Avenue, Ridgefield, NJ 07657

Educational Progress Corporation   P.O. Box 45663, Tulsa OK 47145

Educational Research Corporation   Rockefeller Building, Cleveland, OH 44113

Educational Teaching Aids   159 Kinzie Street, Chicago, IL 60610

Educational Testing Service   Rosedale Road, Princeton, NJ 08540

Elsevier Scientific Publications Co., Inc.   52 Vanderbilt Avenue, New York NY 10017
Fearon-Dittman Publishers   6 Davis Drive, Belmont, CA 94002
Follett Publishing Company   1010 W. Washington Boulevard, Chicago, IL 60607
The Foundation for Exceptional Children   1920 Association Drive, Reston, VA 22091
The Free Press   *See* The Macmillan Company
Garrard Publishing Company   29 Goldsborough Street, Easton, MD 21601
General Learning Corporation   250 James Street, Morristown, NJ 07960
Ginn & Company   191 Spring Street, Lexington, MA 02173
Goodyear Publishing Company   1640 Fifth Avenue, Santa Monica, CA 90401
Grune & Stratton   6677 Sea Harbor Drive, Orlando, FL 32887
Gryphon Press   193 South Cleveland Avenue, St. Paul, MN 55105
Harcourt Brace Jovanovich, Inc.   1250 Sixth Avenue, San Diego, CA 92101
Harper & Row Publishers, Inc.   10 53rd Street, New York, NY 10022
Hawthorn Books, (E. P. Dutton)   2 Park Avenue, New York, NY 10016
D. C. Heath and Company   125 Spring Street, Lexington, MA 02173
Holbrook Press, Inc.   470 Atlantic Avenue, Boston, MA 02210
Holt, Rinehart & Winston   383 Madison Avenue, New York, NY 10017
Houghton Mifflin Company   1 Beacon Street, Boston, MA 02108
Hubbard Scientific   P.O. Box 104, 1946 Raymond Drive, Northbrook, IL 60062
Human Development Training Institute   4455 Twain Avenue, San Diego, CA 92120
Ideal School Supply Company   11000 S. Laveergne, Oak Lawn, IL 60453
Impact Publishers   Box 1094, San Luis Obispo, CA 93406
Instructor Publications   7 Bank Street, Dansville, NY 14437
International Reading Association   800 Barksdale Road. P.O. Box 8139, Newark, DE 19714
Irvington Publishers, Inc.   740 Broadway, New York, NY 10003
Jastak Associates, Inc.   1526 Gilpin Avenue, Wilmington, DE 19806
Jossey-Bass Inc.   433 California Street, San Francisco, CA 94104
Judy Publishing Company   Box 5270 Main PO, Chicago, IL 60608
Kendall/Hunt Publishing Company   2460 Kerper Blvd., Dubuque, IA 52001
The Klamath Printers   628 Oak Street, Klamath Falls, OR 97601
Language Research Associates   950 E. 59th Street, Chicago, IL 60637
Lea and Febinger   600 So. Washington Square, Philadelphia, PA 19106
Learnco, Inc.   128 High Street, Greenland, NH 03840
Learning Concepts, Inc.   2501 N. Lamar, Austin, TX 78705
Learning Corporation of America   1350 Avenue of the Americas, New York, NY 10019
Learning Handbooks   530 University Avenue, Palo Alto, CA 94301
Learning Publications, Inc.   5351 Gulf Drive, Holmes Beach, FL 33509
Lippincott Company   E. Washington Square, Philadelphia, PA 19105
Little, Brown & Company   34 Beacon Street, Boston, MA 02106
Longman, Inc.   19 W. 44th Street, New York, NY 10036

Appendix A

Love Publishing Company   1777 So. Bellaire Street, Denver, CO 80222

Lyons and Callahan Educational Publishers   407 E. 25th Street, Chicago, IL 60616

The Macmillan Company   866 Third Street, New York, NY 10022

Magnamusic-Baton, Inc.   10370 Page Industrial Boulevard, St. Louis, MO 63132

Mayfield Publishing Company   1240 Villa Street, Mountain View, CA 94041

McCutchan Publishing Company   2526 Martin Luther King, Jr. Way, Berkeley, CA 94701

McGraw-Hill Book Company   1221 Avenue of the Americas, New York, NY 10020

David McKay Company, Inc.   2 Park Avenue, New York, NY 10016

Media Materials, Inc.   Department W 87654, 2936 Remington Avenue, Baltimore, MD 21211

Meredith Corporation   1716 Locust Street, Des Moines, IA 50336

Charles E. Merrill Publishing Company   1300 Alum Creek Drive, Columbus, OH 43216

Metropolitan Toronto Association for Retarded Children   180 Beverley Street, Toronto 2B, Ontario, Canada

Milton Bradley Company   443 Shaker Road, East Longmeadow, MA 01028

C. V. Mosby   11830 Westline Industrial Drive, St. Louis, MO 63141

National Amateur Athletic Association   3400 W. 86th Street, Indianapolis, IN 48268

National Committee on Art for the Handicapped   John F. Kennedy Center for the Arts, Washington, DC 20566

National Computer Systems   4401 W. 76th Street, Minneapolis, MN 55440

National Council of Teachers of English   1111 Kenyon Road, Urbana, IL 61801

Thomas Nelson, Publishers   P.O. Box 141000, Nelson Place at Elm Hill Pike, Nashville, TN 37214

The New Press   9200 Island Lake Road, Dexter, NJ 48130

Northwestern University Press   P.O. Box 1093, Evanston, IL 60201

Ohio Department of Education   65 S. Front Street, Columbus, OH 43215

Olympus Publishing Company   1670 E. 13th Street, Salt Lake City, UT 89105

Open Court Publishing Company   1039 Eighth Street, LaSalle, IL 61301

Opportunities for Learning, Inc.   20417 Nordhoff Street, Chatsworth, CA 91311

Oxford University Press   200 Madison Avenue, New York, NY 10016

Parker Brothers   50 Dunham Road, Beverly, MA 01915

F. E. Peacock Publishing, Inc.   115 N. Prospect Avenue, Itasca, IL 60143

C. Z. Peck   P.O. Box 28566, San Jose, CA 95159

Pendragon Press   P.O. Box 14834, Portland, OR 97214

Pergamon Press   Maxwell House, Fairview Park, Elmsford, NY 10523

Personal Press   1515 Riebl Road, Santa Rosa, CA 95404

Phonovisual Products Inc.   12216 Parklawn Drive, P.O. Box 2007, Rockville, MD 20852

Pitman Learning, Inc.   19 Davis Drive, Belmont, CA 94002

Praeger Publishing   521 Fifth Avenue, New York, NY 10175

Prentice-Hall Publishing Company   Englewood Cliffs, NJ 07632

Princeton Book Company   Box 109, Princeton, NJ 08540

Princeton University Press   41 William Street, Princeton, NJ 08540

Pro-Ed   5341 Industrial Oaks Boulevard, Austin, TX 78735

The Psychological Corporation   555 Academic Court, San Antonio, TX 78204

The Rand Corporation   1700 Main Street, Santa Monica, CA 90406

Rand McNally   P.O. Box 7600, Chicago, IL 60680

Random House   201 E. 50th Street, New York, NY 10022

Henry Regnery (Contemporary Books, Inc.)   180 N. Michigan Avenue, Chicago, IL 60601

Research Press   2612 W. Mattis Avenue, Champaign, IL 61821

Riverside Publishing Company   8420 Bryn Mawr Avenue, Chicago, IL 60631

Rowan & Allanhead, Publishers   81 Adams Drive, Totowa, NJ 07512

W. B. Saunders   210 W. Washington Square, Philadelphia, PA 19105

Scholastic, Inc.   730 Broadway, New York, NY 10003

Science and Behavior Books, Inc.   P.O. Box 60519, Palo Alto, CA 94306

Science Research Associates, Inc.   155 N. Wacker Drive, Chicago, IL 60606

Scott, Foresman & Company   1900 E. Lake Avenue, Glenview, IL 60025

Selchow and Righter   919 N. Michigan Avenue, Chicago, IL 60611

Silver Burdett Company   250 James Street, Morristown, NJ 07960

The L. W. Singer Company   201 E. 50th Street, New York, NY 10022

C. B. Slack   6900 Grove Road, Thorofare, NJ 08086

Special Child Publications   P.O. Box 33548, Seattle, WA 98113

Special Educational Materials   484 S. Broadway, New York, NY 10705

Special Learning Corporation   42 Boston Post Road, Guilford, CT 06437

Springer-Verlag   175 Fifth Avenue, New York, NY 10010

Steck-Vaughan   P.O. Box 2028, Austin, TX 78767

Sterling Publishing Company   2 Park Avenue, New York, NY 10016

C. H. Stoetling Company   1850 S. Kostner Avenue, Chicago, IL 60623

Syracuse University Press   1600 Jamesville Avenue, Syracuse, NY 13210

Teachers College Press   Teachers College, Columbia University, 1234 Amsterdam Avenue, New York, NY 10027

Teaching Resources Corporation   50 Pond Park Road, Hingham, MA 02043

Texas Instruments   P.O. Box 225474 MS8218, Dallas, TX 75265

Charles C Thomas Publishers   2600 S. First Street, Springfield, IL 62717

Touch Learning Concepts, Inc.   Publishers Park, P.O. Box 7402, Colorado Springs, CO 80933

Trident Press   630 Fifth Avenue, New York, NY 10020

University of Illinois Press   505 E. Armory Street, Champaign, IL 61820

University of Michigan Press   P.O. Box 1104, Ann Arbor, MI 48106

University Park Press   300 N. Charles Street, Baltimore, MD 21201

Valpar Corporation   3801 E. 34th St., Suite 105, Tucson, AZ 85713

Vocational Research Institute—J.E.V.S.   1700 Sansom Street, Philadelphia, PA 19103

Wadsworth, Inc.   10 Davis Drive, Belmont, CA 94002

Wagner Company   1855 W. Main Street, Alhambra, CA 91801

Walker Educational Book Corporation   720 Fifth Avenue, New York, NY 10019

Webster Division (McGraw-Hill)   1221 Avenue of the Americas, New York, NY 10020

Henri Wenkart Publishing Company   4 Shady Hill Square, Cambridge, MA 02138

Western Psychological Services   12031 Wilshire Boulevard, Los Angeles, CA 90025

John Wiley & Sons   605 Third Avenue, New York, NY 10158

Xerox Education Publications   245 Longhill Road, Middletown, CT 06457

Zaner-Bloser, Inc.   2300 W. Fifth Avenue, Columbus, OH 43216

Richard L. Zweig Associates   20800 Beach Boulevard, Huntington Beach, CA 92648

Appendix B

Selected Organizations and Agencies

Alexander Graham Bell Association for the Deaf   3417 Volta Place NW, Washington, DC 20007

American Association for Gifted Children   15 Gramercy Park, New York, New York 10003

American Association on Mental Deficiency   1719 Kalorama Road NW, Washington, DC 20009

American Council on Rural Special Education   Western Washington University, Bellingham, WA 98225

American Foundation for the Blind, Inc.   15 W. 16th Street, New York, NY 10011

American Speech-Language-Hearing Association   10801 Rockville Pike, Rockville, MD 20852

Association for Children and Adults with Learning Disabilities   4156 Liberty Road, Pittsburgh, PA 15234

Association for Retarded Citizens of the United States   2501 Avenue J, Arlington, TX 76011

Children's Defense Fund   1520 New Hamshire Avenue NW, Washington, DC 20036

Clearing House on the Handicapped, OSERS   U.S. Department of Education, 400 Maryland Avenue SW, Washington, DC 20202

The Council for Exceptional Children   1920 Association Drive, Reston, VA 22091

Epilepsy Foundation of America   4351 Garden City Drive, Suite 406, Landover, MD 20785

ERIC Clearinghouse on Handicapped and Gifted Children   The Council for Exceptional Children, 1920 Association Drive, Reston, VA 22091

Gifted Children Society, Inc.   P.O. Box 120, Oakland, NJ 07436

Leukemia Society of America   800 Second Avenue, New York, NY 10017

Muscular Dystrophy Association of America   810 Seventh Avenue, New York, NY 10019

National Amputation Foundation   1245 150th Street, White Stone, NY 11357

National Association for the Deaf   814 Thayer Avenue, Silver Spring, MD 20910

National Association for Gifted Children   2070 County Road H, St. Paul, MN 55112

National Association for Hearing and Speech Action   10801 Rockville Pike, Rockville, MD 20852

National Association for Mental Health, Inc.   10 Columbus Circle, New York, NY 10019

National Association for Parents of the Deaf-Blind   2703 Forest Oak Circle, Norman, OK 73071

National Association for the Physically Handicapped   8423 Grandview Avenue, Detroit, MI 48228

National Association for Retarded Citizens   2709 Avenue E East, P.O. Box 6109, Arlington, TX 76001

National Committee on Arts for the Handicapped   P.O. Box 19997, Washington, DC 20006

National Committee for the Prevention of Child Abuse   Suite 510, 111 E. Wacker Drive, Chicago, IL 60601

National Easter Seal Society   2023 W. Ogden Avenue, Chicago, IL 60612.

National Hemophilia Association   19 W. 34th Street, Room 1204, New York, NY 10001

National Information Center for Special Educational Materials   University of Southern California, University Park, Los Angeles, CA 90007

National Multiple Sclerosis Society   205 E. 42nd Street, New York, NY 10017

National Rehabilitation Association   633 S. Washington Street NW, Alexandria, VA 22314

National Society for Children and Adults with Autism   1234 Massachusetts Avenue NW, Suite 1017, Washington, DC 20005

Spina Bifida Association of America   343 S. Dearborn Street, Suite 319, Chicago, IL 60604

United Cerebral Palsy Associations   66 E. 34th Street, New York, NY 10016

Glossary

Accommodation   Adaptations and adjustments in the school environment for exceptional individuals.
ACLD   *See* Association for Children and Adults With Learning Disabilities.
Acuity   Quality of tactile, visual, or auditory sensations.
Adaptive behavior   Ability to adjust to the environment as evidenced by independence, responsibility, and social skills.
Affective education   Teaching self-concept, positive attitudes, self-control, problem solving, communication, and interpersonal skills.
Annual goals   Priorities for learnings as described in the Individual Educational Plan (IEP).
Assessment   Process of obtaining information about students' abilities and needs to make an educational plan.
Association for Children and Adults With Learning Disabilities (ACLD)   An advocacy group of parents and professionals.
Attention deficits   Inability to select important aspects of a concept or to maintain focus on an object or person. Lack of alertness or oversensitivity to visual and auditory stimuli in the environment.
Auditory acuity   Ability to hear loudness from 25–60 decibels (dB) and frequencies per second from 500–2000 Hertz (Hz).

Basal reader approach   Highly structured sequence of tasks presented in a series of textbooks with teacher manuals and workbooks.
Behavior   Any activity performed by an individual.
Behavior disordered   Category of students in which extreme behaviors are observed. They deviate from the normal range of behaviors in frequency and intensity over a long period.
Behavior management   *Any* procedure or practice that influences, changes, or controls behavior.

Behavior modification Particular technique of behavior management; procedures used to change behavior that are based on operant conditioning. Manipulation of the environment and consequences are used to bring about desired behaviors or to eliminate undesired behaviors.
Behavioral functioning Activities of an individual learned from interaction with the environment.
Behavioral objectives Specific statements of what is expected to be learned, written in observable terms, with conditions and criteria for measuring achievement.
Blind Inability to see or severe visual impairment. Acuity of less than 20/200 in the better eye with the best correction.
Body image Perception of one's own physical being; awareness of the relation of body parts to each other and the environment.
Brain dysfunction Suspected malfunction of the brain.

CAI *See* Computer-assisted instruction.
Career education Continuous development of knowledges, attitudes, and competencies to enable students to make satisfying career choices.
CEC *See* Council for Exceptional Children.
Cerebral dominance Preferred bain hemisphere that controls thinking patterns and motor activities.
Clinical teaching *See* Diagnostic teaching.
CMI *See* Computer-managed instruction.
Cognition Pertaining to learning and understanding.
Cognitive processing Mental activities of perceiving, analyzing, synthesizing, understanding, storing, and retrieving data received through the senses.
Cognitive style *See* Learning styles.
Comprehension Understanding the written and spoken word; as applied to reading—literal, interpretive, and critical levels.
Computer-assisted instruction (CAI) Instruction by means of a computer; emphasizes drill and evaluation.
Computer-managed instruction (CMI) Use of the computer to maintain daily classroom data as a basis for determining individual progress and achievement in instructional objectives.
Context clues Reading technique in which the content of the sentence assists in decoding or determining the meaning of an unknown word.
Continuum of services Range of services available to students with special needs.
Council for Exceptional Children (CEC) Organization of professionals in the special education field.
Criterion-referenced tests Tests that measure the students' performance on material taught rather than on their placement on tests given to large groups.
Cross categorical Concept that many behavioral characteristics of handicapped individuals are not unique to the separate disability categories but occur in more than one area.
Curriculum The overall plan in which subject content is specified and organized sequentially; the *what* of teaching.

Decoding Connecting graphic presentations; making letters into sounds, words, phrases, and sentences.
Developmental disability Any chronic condition occurring before age twenty-two that prevents an individual from functioning normally.
Diagnostic teaching Individualized instruction using continuous evaluation; curriculum and pace of instruction are guided primarily by student knowledges and skills.
Disability The existence of an impairment or condition causing activities or behavior not to be performed.

Discipline Consistent and continued organization of behavior.
Distractibility Disorder in which a student frequently changes focus of attention from important to irrelevant stimuli.
Dual setting Two learning environments, a regular class and another class, usually a resource room.
Due process Procedures required by PL 94–142 to ensure the rights of parents and children in providing services to handicapped children.
Dyscalculia Extreme difficulty in mathematics usually associated with neurological dysfunction.
Dysgraphia Inability to write or copy or extreme difficulty with handwriting.
Dyslexia Complete or partial inability to read.
Dysnomia Inability or extreme difficulty in recalling words.

Emotionally handicapped Category of exceptionality in which internal affective states are viewed as causative of learning and behavior problems. Characterized by inability to learn or to relate to others; inappropriate behavior or feelings—unhappiness or fear; or the tendency to develop physical symptoms related to school or personal difficulties.
Emotional lability Emotional reaction out of proportion to the circumstances. Reaction to the emotions of others and inability to adjust to change.
Encoding Oral and written language skills.
Error analysis Observing and analyzing errors to determine a pattern as a basis for corrective instruction.
Etiology The cause of a disability.
Expressive language Data encoded and sent from the brain. Skills are speaking and writing.

Generalization *See* Transfer.
Goal gratification Reward or reinforcement for desired behavior.
Grapheme Written symbol for a language sound.
Group home Supervised, semi-independent living facility in the community to prepare handicapped persons for independent living.

Handicap Condition that results from the reaction of society or self to a disability.
Hearing impaired Individuals who are deaf or hard-of-hearing.
Hyperactivity Excessive bodily movements with little or no purpose.
Hypersensitivity Overly conscious of negative reactions of others.
Hypoactivity Minimal body movements; opposite of hyperactivity.

Identifying variables Factors used to determine exceptionality and eligibility for special educational services.
IEP *See* Individual Educational Plan.
Impairment Limiting condition, physical or psychological anomaly inherent to an individual.
Impulsivity Spontaneous reaction, without thought, to the slightest provocation.
Individual Educational Plan (IEP) Written plan for each identified student who is to receive any type of special services; required by PL 94–142; contains goals and objectives.
Individual learner Student who does not receive special education services but has difficulty learning academic or behavioral skills.
Individualized education Educational experiences planned and implemented to meet individual needs in the regular classroom or in another setting.
Individualized instruction Special or restricted curriculum and specific methods administered to one student or to a small group.
Inner language Internalized language system.

Inquiry approach Inductive teaching method in which student learning is guided through a series of logical steps to arrive at conclusions, generalizations, or principles.
Interdisciplinary team Group of individuals representing several professions within a school system who conduct assessment and determine eligibility for special educational services.
Intraindividual differences Differences in quantity and quality among characteristics and abilities of one individual.
Itinerant services Services to exceptional students by professionals who work in more than one school.

Labeling Officially identifying students into categories of exceptionality.
Language-experience approach (LEA) Approach to reading that integrates oral language, writing, and spelling using the student's own words, sentences, and ideas. Often used as an introductory step in which students tell or write about themselves or their experiences.
LEA *See* Language-experience approach.
Learned helplessness Conditioned dependence; individual does not think he or she can be successful and expects others to provide for his or her needs.
Learning Relatively permanent alteration of internal structures that is evidenced in overt behavior, is attributable to environmental influences, and cannot be accounted for solely on the basis of natural growth and maturation.
Learning centers Physical arrangement of the classroom into instructional areas in which students interact with a variety of learning activities and materials.
Learning disability Specific learning disability means a disorder in one or more of the basic psychological processes involved in understanding or using language spoken or written, which may manifest itself in an imperfect ability to listen, think, speak, read, write, spell, or to do mathematical calculations (National Advisory Committee on Handicapped Children, 1968).
Learning styles Consistent strategies used by individuals in the process of learning.
Least restrictive environment Educational setting as near as possible to a regular class that will meet individual needs; level of placement is based on severity of handicapping condition.
Linguistic approach Whole-word approach to reading; word families and skills are emphasized.
Linguistics Study of the nature, patterns, and usage of language.
Locus of control Concept that control of one's behavior is either influenced by forces outside the individual (external locus) or contingent upon one's own behavior (internal locus).
Long-term goals Elements of the IEP that identify major concepts to be learned and skills to be achieved.

Mainstreaming Placing exceptional students in regular classes using the concept of least restrictive environment.
Mastery learning Specific objectives learned by the student that meet teacher established criteria.
Maturational lag Theory that lack of readiness to learn results when the child's rate of physiological and neurological development is slower than average.
MBD *See* Minimal brain dysfunction.
Mental retardation Significant subaverage general intellectual ability existing concurrently with deficits in adaptive behavior and manifested during the developmental period (*Manual on Terminology and Classification in Mental Retardation*, 1983).
Mildly handicapped Individual in any of the disability categories whose handicapping condition is not severe.
Mild retardation Developmental handicap in which individual is characterized by IQ between 50 and 70 and with impairment in adaptive behavior.
Milieu therapy Treatment setting in which all aspects of the environment are controlled to provide a consistent and therapeutic influence on the individual.

Minimal brain dysfunction (MBD) Mild neurological irregularity often seen in children with learning disabilities. *See also* Brain dysfunction.
Mnemonics Techniques or cues that aid memory.
Modality preference Theory that individuals learn better through either the visual, auditory, or tactile–kinesthetic channel.
Modeling Observing then imitating the desired behavior of another person.
Morpheme The smallest meaningful unit in language.
Morphology The form of language; deals with units of meaning or morphemes.
Motivation Internal strength or drive influenced by external factors and psychological make-up that moves the individual to perform or accomplish.

NARC *See* National Association for Retarded Citizens.
National Association for Retarded Citizens (NARC) Organization of parents and professionals advocating the improvement of conditions for mentally retarded persons.
Noncategorical Grouping exceptional students without regard for category of handicapping condition.
Normalization Philosophy that individuals with handicapping conditions can learn to function more appropriately when in as normal a setting as possible.
Norm-referenced tests Commercially prepared tests administered to large groups of students; has manual to determine norms, scaled scores, and ranks.

Operant conditioning Technique of behavior management in which environmental reinforcing stimuli are used to elicit, alter, or extinguish behaviors.
Orthopedically impaired Category of individuals with skeletal or muscular abnormalities caused by defect, disease, or accident.
Overlearning Practice, drill, and review beyond mastery to aid recall and memory.

Paraprofessional Individual without specialized training who provides assistance to the classroom teacher.
Partially sighted Visually impaired individuals who have residual vision and limited sight. Visual acuity is 20/70 to 20/200 in the better eye with the best correction.
Perception Neurological process by which sensory data obtained through the senses are organized and given meaning.
Perseveration Behavior or words performed repeatedly beyond usefulness; inability to change activity.
Phoneme Smallest unit of language sound.
Phonics approach Approach to teaching reading that emphasizes word recognition by identifying the phoneme–grapheme match and sound–symbol associations.
Phonology The study of language sounds.
Programmed instruction Published teaching materials that present information in small, sequenced steps to be used independently.
Psycholinguistics The study of psychology and linguistics to address the complete language process.

Readiness Preparedness to be receptive to and to profit from the formal and informal aspects of the environment that should result in learning.
Receptive language Receiving and understanding the spoken or written language of others; skills are listening and reading.
Reflection–impulsivity Reaction or response to environmental stimuli, either cautious and thoughtful or spontaneous.
Reinforcement Attention or reward for performance of behavior either positive or negative.

Resource room Educational setting in which identified exceptional students receive direct instruction in content areas needing remediation.
Resource services Activities, materials, and methods provided by specialists to regular classroom teachers; direct or indirect services provided by professionals to meet individual or group academic, behavioral, or social needs.
Reversals Changing the order of words, numbers, letters; perceiving, writing them backwards.

Selective attention Ability to focus on important stimuli and screen out unimportant stimuli.
Self-concept An individual's characteristics and worth as perceived by that individual.
Self-contained class Students are placed in a special education setting with one teacher for the entire day.
Semantics Meaning of language including literal meaning, vocabulary, implications, inferences, and emotional aspects.
Sensory-motor Integration of visual, auditory, and tactile–kinesthetic sensations with motor activity.
Severe discrepancy Difference between ability and achievement frequently used as a guideline in determining eligibility for services in learning disabilities.
Sheltered workshop Protected environment in which handicapped youth and adults are employed.
Short attention span *See* Distractibility.
Short-term objectives Specific statement written in behavioral terms of what each identified exceptional student is to be taught; related to annual goals and incorporated into the IEP.
Sociodrama Diagnostic technique in which the individual reveals social skills or abnormalities within the context of role playing.
Special education Instruction and other educational, remedial, or therapeutic services to identified exceptional students in the appropriate setting by specially trained professionals.
Structural analysis Decoding skill using base words, morphographs, contractions, plurals, possessives, and syllabication.
Sustained attention Focus on stimuli for a sufficient period of time to allow retention.
Syntax The structure of language; organization of words into phrases and sentences; rules of word order and the function of words in sentences.

Task analysis Determining subtasks that comprise a larger learning skill or concept.
Transfer Newly acquired skill or behavior demonstrated in a setting different from the one in which it was practiced.

Values clarification Process of examining, identifying, and understanding value system, enabling individuals to differentiate among choices and alternatives and to make decisions without the influence of others.
Visual impairment Inability to see normally; includes blind and partially sighted individuals.
Visual-motor coordination Ability to use vision and body movements together.
Vocational education Organized program to prepare students for employment or careers requiring special training.
Vocational training Teaching specific skills in addition to academic, personal, and social skills and providing work experiences leading to necessary competencies for employment.

Weighting Size of regular class is decreased by allowing each exceptional student to represent more than one enrolled individual.
Work–study program Secondary program in which students work part-time and attend classes part-time.
Written expression Expressing ideas in writing, including spelling and handwriting.

Name Index

Abrams, R. M., 275, 292
Abruscato, J., 331
Adams, J., 173, 174
Adams, R., 353
Adler, A., 108
Albert, J., 168, 174, 189, 206
Alberto, P. A., 150
Alexander, W. M., 207
Algozzine, B., 12
Allen, C., 252, 265
Allen, K. E., 85
Allen, R. V., 252, 265
Allen, V. L., 120, 126
Alley, G. R., 313, 330, 406, 412
Allred, R. A., 248, 266
Alvin, J., 353
Alvino, J., 19, 40
Ames, L. B., 18, 40
Anderson, F. E., 338, 341, 352
Anderson, K., 128
Anderson, N. D., 332
Anderson, P. S., 165, 174
Anderson, R. M., 67
Annesley, F. R., 146, 149
Appleby, J. A., 413
Ardizzone, J., 371
Arena, J. I., 274, 293, 294
Argyle, M., 122, 126
Arkell, C., 183, 206
Arkes, H. R., 154, 174
Ashlock, R. B., 322, 330
Askov, E. N., 266
Asmus, E. P., Jr., 336, 352
Atack, S. M., 353
Atwood, R. K., 326, 330
Au, K. H., 242, 264
Aukerman, L. R., 240, 264
Aukerman, R. C., 240, 264
Auxter, D., 346, 350, 352
Avery, M. L., 175
Axama, M., 2, 11

Bailey, E., 2, 11
Bak, J. J., 118, 127
Balla, D. A., 17, 41
Balow, B., 250, 264
Balow, I. H., 275, 292, 302, 304, 330
Bandura, A., 120, 126
Barbe, W. B., 234, 264, 274, 292
Barcus, J. M., 405, 412
Barker, R. G., 116, 126
Barnes, E., 119, 126
Barraga, N. C., 20, 40
Barry, N. J., Jr., 120, 126
Bartel, N. R., 293, 299, 330

Bassett, R. E., 367, 371
Bateman, B., 204, 206
Beatty, L. S., 304, 330
Beer, A. S., 353
Behrmann, M. M., 207
Belmont, I., 198, 206
Belmont, L., 198, 206
Bennett, R. E., 201, 206
Benedetti, D., 327, 331
Berdine, W. H., 18, 40
Berger, E. H., 101, 111
Bergethon, B., 342, 352
Berman, A., 377, 387
Bernstein, D. K., 225
Berrigan, C., 119, 126
Berry, M. F., 216, 223, 225
Bessell, H. S., 369, 371
Bierne-Smith, M., 399, 412
Biklen, D., 67, 119, 126
Birch, J. W., 67, 128
Bird, P. J., 252, 336
Biren, P. L., 281, 293
Birenbaum, A., 413
Bitter, G. G., 331
Blacher, J., 89, 111
Blatt, B., 12
Blaylock, J. W., 413
Bley, N. J., 331
Bloom, B. S., 12, 168, 174, 196, 206, 207, 225
Bloom, L., 22, 40, 225
Boardman, E., 342, 352
Boehm, A. E., 217, 223
Bogdan, R., 2, 11
Boliek, C. A., 282, 294
Bond, C. L. 250, 264
Bookbinder, S. R., 119, 126
Bopp, M. J., 118, 127
Bormaster, S. J. 128
Borthwick, S., 121, 127
Botel, M., 246, 264
Bowen, M. F., 289, 294
Boyle, J. D., 342, 352
Boyle, M., 2, 11
Bracken, B. A., 217, 223
Brady, M., 24, 40
Bragstad, B. J., 175
Braun, L. A., 274, 292
Breen, J. E., 353
Bricker, D. B., 101, 111
Brigance, A. H., 216, 223, 251, 264, 275, 285, 287, 292
Brittain, W. L., 338, 341, 352
Brolin, D. E., 391, 392, 397, 411
Brown, C., 89, 111
Brown, V. L., 67, 222, 224
Brown, W., 121, 126
Brueckner, L. J., 304, 330

Bruininks, R. H., 17, 40, 411, 413
Bruner, E. C., 254, 264
Bryan, J. H., 118, 126
Bryan, T. H., 188, 126
Bryant, B. R., 247, 250, 266
Buchanan, C. D., 254, 264
Budorff, M., 12
Burdg, N. B., 120, 127
Burke, C. L. 249, 265
Buscaglia, L. F., 12, 94, 111
Bush, W. J., 211, 223
Buswell, G. T., 304, 330
Byrne, M. A., 299, 331

Cady, J. L., 189, 292
Cain, L. F., 89, 111
Calhoun, M. L., 67
Callis, R., 275, 293
Cansler, D. P., 89, 111
Canter, L., 143, 149
Canter, M., 143, 149
Cantrell, M. L., 70, 85
Cantrell, R. P., 70, 85
Carkhuff, R. R., 109, 111
Carlin, J. A., 253, 266
Carlson, R. K., 289, 294
Carnine, D., 266
Carpenter, D., 120, 127
Carpenter, T. P., 304, 330
Carrow-Woolfolk, E., 216, 223
Cartledge, G., 371
Cass, C., 281, 293
Castillo, G. A., 371
Catterson, J. H., 246, 250, 264
Cawley, J. F., 331, 332
Cegelka, P. T., 18, 40
Chaffin, J. D., 7, 11
Chaiken, W. E., 388
Chalfant, J. C., 168, 174, 297, 330
Chall, J. S., 254, 257, 264
Chandler, L. S., 78, 85
Charles, C. M., 150
Chase, L., 371
Chinn, P. C., 113, 378, 387
Cicchetti, D. V., 17, 41
Clark, F. L., 406, 412
Clark, G. M., 392, 397, 398, 406, 411
Clark, W. W., 302, 331
Cleland, C. J., 267
Cline, R., 64, 66
Coble, C. R., 275, 332
Cochran, E. V., 175
Cohen, C. R., 275, 292
Cohen, H. J., 413

Cohen, J. H., 67
Cohen, J. J., 150
Cohen, S., 119, 226
Cohen, S. B., 294
Cohen, S. H., 329, 330
Cole, J. J., 225
Cole, M. L., 225
Coleman, M. C., 103, 104, 111
Combs, A. W., 356, 371
Conger, H. 168, 174
Conley, R. W., 409, 411
Connolly, A. J., 302, 304, 330
Conoley, J. C., 113
Conroy, M., 24, 40
Cooper, J. D., 54, 67
Copeland, W. C., 409, 411
Corbitt, M. K., 304, 330
Costanza, A. P., 353
Coughran, L., 223
Courtnage, L., 83, 85
Crabtree, M., 215, 223
Craighead, W. E., 150
Cratty, B., 348, 353
Crnic, K. A., 90, 111
Cromwell, D. C., 242, 264
Cronbach, J., 192, 206
Cruickshank, W. M., 18, 40, 41, 89, 111, 174, 207
Crump, W. D., 118, 127
Csanyi, A. P., 202, 206
Cullinan, D., 150, 168, 174
Cummings, S. T., 94, 111

Dahl, P. R., 353
D'Alonzo, B. J., 392, 412
Daniel, A., 353
Darley, F. L., 216, 225
Davies, C. O., 221, 223
Davis, E. C., 111
Davis, S., 398
Dawson, M. M., 190, 206
Day, D., 168, 174, 189, 206
de Bono, E., 172, 174
de Boor, M. F., 92, 111
Dembinski, P. J., 96, 111
Deno, E., 7, 11
Deshler, D. D., 313, 330, 379, 388, 406, 412
DesJardins, C., 92, 112
Diament, B., 113
Digate, G., 168, 174
Dimond, P., 6, 11
Dinkmeyer, D., 108, 111
Dishon, D., 207
Dixon, R., 274, 293
Doren, M., 246, 264
Dreikurs, R., 108, 111

429

Name Index

Drew, C. J., 41, 378, 387
Dublinske, S., 77, 85
Ducanis, A. J., 67
Dunivant, N., 377, 387
Dunn, L. M., 7, 11, 211, 217, 221, 223, 245, 247, 264, 275, 292
Dunn, L. M., 211, 217, 223
Durrell, D. D., 246, 250, 264

Early, G. H., 281, 293
Edgar, D. E., 94, 112, 145, 150
Edwards, E. M., 353
Egan, M. W., 441
Ehly, S. W., 85, 113, 128
Ekwall, E. C., 249, 250, 264, 266
Elliot, S. N., 121, 127
Emde, R. N., 89, 111
Englemann, S., 221, 223, 254, 264, 274, 292
Enright, B. E., 304, 330
Epstein, M. H., 150, 168, 174
Erickson, M. T., 135, 149
Esveldt, K. C., 120, 127

Faas, L. A., 283, 293, 299
Fagen, S. A., 365, 371
Fansler, J., 371
Fantini, M. D., 371
Farr, R., 247, 275, 292, 302, 304, 330
Farrald, R. R., 332
Featherstone, H., 89, 111
Feeley, J., 267
Feldman, R. J., 120, 126
Fenton, K. S., 103, 113
Fernald, G., 253, 265, 279, 293
Feuerstein, R., 172, 174
Fewell, R. R., 112
Fiedler, C. R., 119, 126
Finch, A. J., 168, 174, 332
Fitzmaurice-Hayes, A. M., 332
Flexner, R. W., 406, 412
Fokes, J., 221, 224
Folio, M. R., 349, 352, 353
Foster, G. E., 168, 174, 211, 224, 297, 330
Ford, S., 203, 206
Forness, S. R., 41, 120, 127, 321, 330
Fox, L., 19, 40
Francis, A. S., 274, 292
Freud, S., 108
Friedman, R. L., 253, 266
Friedrich, W. N., 90, 111
Friend, M., 289, 294
Frierson, E. C., 331
Fristoe, M., 216, 224
Frith, G. H., 85
Frye, V. H., 150
Furness, E. L., 294

Gadow, K. D., 83, 85
Gagne, R. M., 153, 174
Gallagher, G. C., 90, 111
Gallagher, J. J., 15, 19, 40, 90, 111, 113, 182, 202, 206
Galtelli, B., 51, 67
Ganschow, L., 275, 293
Gansneder, B. M., 336, 352
Gardner, E. F., 247, 265, 275, 304, 330
Gardner, W. I., 146, 149, 167, 174, 293
Gargulio, R., 113
Garrett, M. K., 118, 127
Garske, J. P., 154, 174
Gates, A. I., 247, 265
Gearheart, B. R., 20, 40, 67
Gerber, A., 239, 265
Gickling, E. F., 120, 127
Gilbert, J. P., 336, 352
Giles, W. J., 211, 223
Gillet, J. W., 215, 224, 275, 294
Gillet, P., 395, 412
Gilliam, J. E., 103, 104, 111
Gillingham, A., 253, 265, 279, 293
Gilmore, E. C., 247, 250, 265
Gilmore, J. V., 247, 250, 265
Ginott, H. G., 115, 127
Giordano, G., 294
Glass, G. V., 109, 112
Glasser, W., 135, 139, 149, 225
Glavin, J. P., 146, 149
Glickman, C. D., 150
Gloeckler, T. L., 96, 111, 157, 174
Goldman, R., 216, 221, 224
Goldstein, H., 179, 206, 381, 387
Goldstein, S., 103, 111
Golin, A. K., 67
Gonzales, F. M., 332
Gonzales, M. A., 202, 206
Goodman, K. S., 249, 265
Goodman, Y. M., 249, 265
Gorham, K. A., 92, 112
Gottlieb, J., 118, 127, 387
Gould, S., 108, 111
Graham, R. M., 352, 353
Graham, S., 120, 127, 291, 293
Grant, B. M., 295
Green, H. A., 274, 289, 293
Greenberg, M. T., 90, 111
Greenwood, C. R., 120, 127
Greer, J. G., 128
Greer, J. V., 78, 85
Gresham, F. M., 120, 121, 127

Gromme, R. D., 323, 331
Grossman, H. J., 16, 17, 40
Guetzole, E., 64, 66
Guralnick, M., 111
Gutkin, T. B., 86, 412

Hackett, M. G., 253, 265
Hackney, C. S., 281, 293
Hadary, D. E., 329, 330
Hagan, J. W., 167, 174
Haley, J. S., 295
Hall, J. K., 289, 293
Hall, M., 252, 265,
Hallahan, D. P., 24, 40, 41, 174
Halliday, M. A. K., 217, 224
Hammer, E. A., 90
Hammill, D. D., 67, 211, 217, 222, 224, 274, 281, 285, 287, 289, 291, 293, 330
Hammond, W. R., 145, 150
Hanna, J. S., 271, 293
Hanna, P. R., 271, 293
Hanner, S., 254, 265
Hardman, M. L., 41
Haring, N. G., 204, 206
Harrington, T. F., 413
Harris, A. J., 234, 249, 250, 257, 265, 282
Harris, K. C., 67, 86
Harris, W. J., Jr., 67, 85
Hartman, A. C., 276, 294
Haslam, R. H. A., 86
Hastings, J. T., 196, 206
Hater, M. A., 299, 331
Hawisher, M. F., 67
Hayes, J., 51, 66
Healey, W. C., 77, 85
Heckleman, R. G., 253, 265
Heddens, J. W., 298, 331
Hennings, D. G., 295
Henry, S. A., 107, 112
Heron, T. E., 67, 86
Heward, W. L., 41
Hewett, F. M., 41, 135, 149, 207, 321, 330
Higgins, A., 175
Hill, B. K., 17, 40
Hobbs, N., 112
Hoben, M., 20, 41
Hodges, R. E., 211, 293
Hofmann, H. H., 324, 329, 330
Hofmeister, A. M., 294
Hogan, T. P., 275, 292, 302, 304, 330
Hollander, H. C., 353
Holm, V. A., 85
Homme, L., 202, 206
Hooley, A. M., 353
Hops, H. G., 120, 127, 146, 150
Horne, M. D., 120, 127, 294

Horowitz, G. C., 247, 265
Horton, K. B., 211
Houndshell, P. B., 332
Howell, K. W., 204, 206, 385, 387
Hoyt, C., 250, 264
Hoyt, K. B., 395, 412
Hresko, W. P., 215, 224
Hubbell, R. D., 225
Huberty, T. J., 17, 40
Hudson, F., 120, 127
Huffman, E., 281, 293

Idol-Maestas, L., 67, 86
Inhelder, B., 338, 352
Iverson, I. A., 409, 411
Ivey, A., 108, 112

Jacobsen, J. J., 378, 387
Jacobson, M. D., 378
Jastak, S., 175, 245, 265, 293
Jenkins, J., 327, 331
Jensen, J. M., 225
John, L., 304, 330
Johnson, D. D., 237, 240, 265, 266
Johnson, D. J., 172, 174, 209, 210, 224, 299, 331, 413
Johnson, D. W, 121, 127, 202, 206
Johnson, E. B., 255
Johnson, G. O., 10, 207
Johnson, M. B., 245, 247, 266
Johnson, M. S., 249, 265
Johnson, R. J., 121, 127, 202, 206
Johnson, S. M., 146, 150
Johnstone, B. K., 128
Jones, J. D., 216, 224

Kagan, J., 168, 174, 189, 206
Kail, R. V., 167, 174
Kalish, R. A., 77, 85
Kaliski, L., 299
Kane, R. B., 299, 331
Karlsen, B., 247, 265, 275, 304, 330
Karnes, M. B., 104, 112, 224
Kauffman, H. S., 281, 285, 293
Kauffman, J. M., 24, 40, 41, 135, 149, 285, 294
Kauffman, S. H., 332
Kaufman, M. J., 103, 113
Kaplan, J. M., 253, 266
Kaplan, S., 204, 206
Karp, E. C., 266
Katien, J. C., 253, 266
Kavale, K., 211, 224
Kazdin, A. E., 150
Keilitz, I., 377, 387
Keislar, E. R., 175
Keogh, B. K., 18, 40

Name Index

Kephart, N., 351, 352
Kepner, H. S., 304, 330
Kerr, M. M., 388
Kervick, C., 12
Kiernan, W. E., 413
Kingsbury, D., 405, 412
Kirk, S. A., 15, 18, 40, 182, 190, 206, 211, 224, 244, 249, 252, 261, 265
Kirk, W. D., 18, 40, 211, 224
Kleber, D. J., 281, 293
Kliebhan, J. M., 190, 206, 224, 249, 252, 261, 265
Knoff, H. M., 103, 112
Knutson, R., 346, 352
Kokaska, C. J., 392, 411
Koller, J. R., 17, 40
Kolstoe, O. P., 179, 206
Korn, T. A., 404, 412
Kottmeyer, W., 275, 293
Krager, J. M., 83, 85
Kregel, 405, 412
Kress, R. A., 249, 265
Krone, A., 338, 352
Kroth, R. L., 113

La Greca, A. M., 120, 127
Lahey, M., 22, 40, 225
Lakin, K. C., 411, 413
Lambert, N., 17, 40
Langsford, C., 24, 40
Lapp, D., 165, 174
Larrivee, B., 120, 127
Larsen, S. C., 85, 128, 211, 224, 275, 293
Larson, C. E., 285, 287, 291, 293
Lathrop, R. L., 342, 352
Leadingham, J. E., 126
Leavey, M., 203, 206
Lee, D. M., 252, 265
Lee, L., 216, 224
Lehtinen, L., 165, 174, 299, 331
Leigh, J. E., 281, 293
Lerner, J. W., 190, 204, 206, 244, 249, 252, 261, 264, 270, 282, 293, 379, 387
Lewis, A. J., 207
Lewis, J. F., 12, 40
Liles, B., 221, 223
Lillie, D. L., 101, 112
Lilly, S., 24, 40
Lindquist, M. M., 304, 330
Lindsay, Z., 353
Linn, S. H., 287, 293
Liscio, M. A., 336, 352, 388
Livingston, R. H., 404, 412
Lloyd, J. W., 150
Logan, D. R., 378, 387
Lombana, J. H., 86
Long, N. J., 150, 174, 365, 371

Losen, S. M., 113
Loughlin, C. E., 128
Lovitt, T. C., 204, 206, 327, 331
Lowenbraun, S., 21, 41
Lowenfeld, V., 338, 341, 352
Lucas, V. H., 276, 294
Lund, K. A., 211, 224
Lynch, M. E., 221

MacDonald, C., 371
MacGinitie, W. M., 246, 265
Macmillan, D. L., 118, 127
Madaus, G. F., 196, 206
Madden, N. A., 121, 127, 203, 206, 304, 330
Madden, R., 247, 265, 304, 330
Madison, B. D., 286, 294
Madsen, C. H., 145, 150
Madsen, C. K., 145, 150
Mager, R. F., 52, 66
Mahoney, M. J., 150
Malone, M. J., 328
Mandell, C. S., 57, 67
Mangrum, C. T., 407, 412
Marion, R. L., 90, 112
Markwardt, F. C., 215, 247, 264, 275, 292
Marland, S. P., 19, 40, 392
Marshall, K., 159, 174
Martin, G., 150
Martin, J. G., 20, 41
Masters, B. F., 332
Masters, L. F., 388
Matavich, M., 96, 111
Maurdeff, K., 331
Mauser, A. J., 96, 111
Maxwell, J. D., 103, 113
May, F. B., 266
McAlees, D. C., 404, 412
McCall-Perez, F. C., 211, 224
McCarthy, J., 211, 224
McConnell, C. Y., 19
McCormick, L., 225
McCormick, S. H., 54, 67
McDonnel, R. C., 19, 40
McDonnell, J., 410, 411
McDowell, R. L., 106, 112
McGauvran, M. E., 245, 266
McKay, D. W., 108, 111
McKillop, A. S., 247, 265
McKinley, N., 222, 225
McLaughlin, P. J., 67, 413
McMenemy, R. A., 219, 224, 308, 311, 318, 331
Mecham, M. J., 214, 216, 224
Medley, D. M., 123, 127
Meers, G., 399, 412
Meier, M., 274, 292
Menaloscino, F. J., 90, 113
Menhusen, B. R., 323, 330

Mercer, A. R., 270, 271, 274, 289, 294, 302, 331
Mercer, C. D., 270, 271, 274, 289, 294, 302, 331
Merwin, J., 275, 293
Meyen, E. L., 207
Meyer, D. J., 94, 112
Michaelis, C. T., 113
Mikesell, J. L., 331
Milburn, J. F., 371
Miller, A. G., 349, 352
Miller, J. P., 371
Miller, S. R., 413
Miller, T. L., 41
Milliren, A., 128
Millman, H. L., 150
Minners, S. H., 346, 352
Minskoff, E. H., 211, 224
Minskoff, J. G., 211, 224
Mithaug, D. E., 406, 412
Montessori, M., 322, 331
Moos, R. H., 128
Morehead, M. K., 385, 387
Morgan, R. H., 303, 331
Mori, A. A., 113
Morris, R. J., 12
Morrison, G. M., 118, 121, 127
Morse, W. C., 143, 150, 371
Mowrey, C. W., 221, 224
Mueser, A. M., 266
Murray, C. A., 377, 387
Mussen, P. A., 168, 174
Myers, E. H., 281, 293
Myers, P., 225
Myers, R., 96, 111
Myklebust, H. R., 172, 174, 209, 210, 224, 299

Nachtman, W., 302, 304, 330
Nagel, R. S., 120, 127
Nakamura, A., 2, 11
Naslund, R. A., 302, 331
Neal, W. R., 86
Neisworth, J. T., 128
Nelson, D. A., 281, 293
Newcomer, P. L., 217, 264
Newman, R. G., 150, 174
Nix, G. W., 6, 11
Noar, G., 159, 174
Norlander, K. B., 332
Norman, A., 349, 352
Nurss, J. R., 245, 266
Nye, R. E., 341, 342, 352
Nye, V. T., 341, 342, 352
Nygren, C. J., 174

Obrzut, J. E., 282, 294
O'Connell, C. Y., 204, 206
Odle, S. J., 51, 67
Oldham, B. R., 326, 330
O'Leary, P. W., 207
Orenstein, A., 12

Orlansky, M. D., 41
O'Rourke, R. D., 371
Osborn, J., 221, 223, 254, 265
Osborn, S., 254, 265
Otto, W., 165, 174, 219, 224, 266, 280, 294, 308, 311, 318, 331, 371
Overman, P. B., 120, 126

Page, R., 92, 112
Palomares, V., 369, 371
Pasanella, A. L., 67
Pascarella, E. T., 203, 206
Pasick, P., 371
Patton, J. R., 399, 412
Payne, J. S., 257, 266, 399, 412
Payne, R. A., 257, 266
Pear, J., 150
Pearson, P. D., 237, 240, 265, 266
Peters, C. W., 266
Peters, D. J., 388
Peters, N., 266
Peterson, P. L., 127
Peterson, R. L., 23, 41
Petrucchi, L., 328
Pettis, E., 92, 112
Petty, W. T., 225, 270, 274, 289, 294
Phelps-Gunn, T., 294, 295
Phelps-Terasaki, D., 294, 295
Phillips, E. L., 204, 206
Phillips, W., 168, 174, 189, 206
Piaget, J., 338, 352, 368, 371
Pious, C., 327, 331
Plaskon, S. P., 294
Plunkett, M., 294
Polloway, C. H., 232, 266
Polloway, E. A., 232, 257, 266
Poplin, M., 103, 112, 289, 293
Premack, P., 117, 127
Prescott, G. A., 275, 292, 302, 304, 330
Preseller, S., 77, 85
Pritchett, E. M., 302, 304, 330
Pyfer, J., 346, 350, 352

Quay, H. C., 146, 149

Raebeck, L., 341, 342, 352
Rappaport, S. R., 32, 40
Rechs, J. R., 202, 206
Reed, V. A., 221, 224
Reid, D. K. 215, 224
Reinert, H. R., 135, 150
Reisman, F. K., 332
Replogle, A., 221, 224
Reynolds, C. R., 12, 86, 412

Name Index

Reynolds, M. C., 7, 11, 40, 67
Reys, K., 304, 330
Ricker, K. S., 324, 330
Richert, S., 19, 40
Roach, C., 351, 352
Robbins, C., 353
Robbins, C., 353
Robinson, F. P., 160, 174
Rogers, C. R., 108, 112, 219
Roos, P., 89, 112
Rosenthal, D., 113
Rosman, B. L., 168, 189, 174, 206
Ross, D. M., 86
Ross, M., 400, 401, 412
Ross, S. A., 86
Roth, F., 217, 224
Rotter, J. B., 364, 371
Rubin, J. A., 338, 352
Rubin, K. H., 126
Rude, C. R., 2, 11
Rudman, H. C., 275, 293
Rudsit, J., 327, 331
Rullman, L., 353
Rusch, F. R., 406, 412
Russell, D. H., 175
Russell, E. F., 175
Rutherford, R. B., 94, 112

Sabatino, D. A., 18, 40
Safer, D. J., 83, 85, 388
Salvia, J., 211, 224
Santogrossi, D. A., 120, 127
Satir, V. M., 94, 112
Saudargas, R. A., 145, 150
Saylor, J. G., 207
Sayre, J., 323
Schaefer, C. E., 150
Scheiber, B., 92, 112
Schiefelbusch, R. L., 85, 225
Schifani, S. W., 67
Schiffelin, M. A., 297
Schinke, S. P., 413
Schleifer, M. J., 90, 112
Schloss, P. J., 388, 413
Schneider, B. H., 126
Schulz, J. B., 113, 324, 331
Schumacker, J. B., 379, 388, 406, 412
Schutz, P. N., B., 67, 85
Schwartz, L., 222, 225
Secord, W., 222, 225
Seligman, M., 90, 113
Semel, E., 211, 222, 224, 225
Semel, M. I., 118, 127
Sexton, A. J., 353
Shanker, J. L., 266
Shaw, R. A., 332
Shelton, M. N., 355, 371
Sherrill, C., 350, 353
Shields, D. B., 234, 264
Shub, A. N., 253, 266
Shulman, L. S., 175

Shure, M.G., 363, 371
Silbert, J., 266
Silvaroli, N. J., 245, 248, 250, 266
Silver, R. A., 353
Simms, R. B., 83, 85
Simon, C. S., 225
Simon, S. B., 360, 371
Simpson, R. D., 332
Simpson, R. L., 103, 112, 119, 126
Sipay, E. R., 234, 249, 250, 255, 257, 265
Siperstein, G. N., 118, 127
Skinner, B. F., 23, 41, 132
Slavin, R. E., 121, 127, 203, 206
Sleeter, C. E., 2, 11
Slingerland, B., 253, 266
Smith, C. B., 267
Smith, C. R., 23, 41
Smith, D. D., 211
Smith, J. B., 145, 150
Smith, J. E., Jr., 257, 258, 266
Smith, M. L., 109, 112
Smith, R. J., 165, 174, 219, 224, 280, 294, 308, 311, 318, 331, 367, 371
Smythe, M. J., 367, 371
Snow, R. E., 192, 206
Snygg, D., 355, 371
Soar, R. M., 123, 127
Soar, R. S., 123, 128
Solnit, A. J., 90, 112
Soltz, V., 108, 111
Sonnenschein, P., 92, 112
Spache, G. D., 246, 266
Spadefore, G. J., 250, 266
Sparrow, S. A., 17, 41
Speece, D. L., 57, 67
Spekman, N., 217, 224
Spencer, E. F., 298, 331
Spirito, A., 168, 174
Spivack, G., 363, 371
Sprague, R. L., 83, 85
Stahl, D. K., 198, 206
Stainback, S., 83, 85
Stainback, W., 83, 85
Stark, M. H., 90, 112
Stark, V. A., 413
Stauffer, R. G., 175
Steely, D., 274, 293
Stephens, T. M., 121, 127, 204, 206, 276, 294
Stern, C., 307, 331
Stetson, E. G, 294
Stevens, D. J., 365, 371
Stewart, J. C., 113
Stillman, B. L., 253, 265, 279, 293
Strain, P. S., 128
Strauss, A. A., 165, 174, 299, 331
Strichart, S. S., 387, 407, 412

Strickland, D. S., 267
Strom, R. D., 371
Stumpf, S. M., 175
Sucher, F., 248, 266
Sullivan, J. V., 349, 352
Sunia, J. H., 128
Sussman, E. J., 353
Svoboda, W. S., 392, 412
Switzky, H. N., 168, 174

Talmage, H., 203, 206
Tarver, S. G., 190, 206
Taylor, F. D., 135, 149, 207
Taylor, S., 2, 11
Temple, C., 215, 224, 275, 294
Templin, M. C., 216, 225
Ten Brink, T. D., 17, 40
Terman, L., 19
Theobald, J. T., 120, 127
Thier, H., 328
Thorpe, L. P., 302, 331
Thomas, J. I., 159, 174
Thomas, J. W., 168, 169, 175
Thomason, J., 20, 41
Thompkins, G. E., 289, 294
Thornton, C., 331
Thygin, M., 261, 266
Tiegerman, E., 225
Tiegs, E. W., 302, 331
Torrance, E. P., 371
Torres, S., 66, 207
Treat, C. L., 128
Treblas, P. V., 54, 67
Treegoob, M., 281, 293
Trohanis, P. L., 101, 112
Troutman, A. C., 150
Turnbull, A. P., 92, 103, 111, 112, 113, 324, 331
Turnbull, H. R., 92, 111, 112, 113
Tyler, N. B., 78, 85

Underhill, R. G., 298, 231
Uprichard, A. E., 298, 231

Vadasy, P. F., 112
Valletutti, P. J., 86
VanEtten, C., 183, 206
VanEtten, G., 183, 206
Van Riper, C., 22, 40
Vaughan, L. R., 123, 127
Veatch, J., 197, 206
Veldman, D. J., 118, 127
Vergason, G., 173, 174, 207
Vietze, P. M., 113
Voelker, P. H., 180, 207
Voeltz, L., 2, 11
Voldola, T. M., 353
Volkmor, C. B., 67

Walberg, H. J., 7, 11, 127
Walker, C. M., 234, 266

Walker, H. M., 146, 150
Wallace, G. E., 285, 294
Walters, R., 113
Wang, M. C., 7, 11
Ward, M., 398, 412
Warner, M. M., 406, 412
Weatherman, R. F., 17, 40
Webster, E. J., 94, 112
Wechsler, D., 401, 412
Wehman, P., 67, 353, 405, 412, 413
Weiner, B., 67
Weiner, E. S., 291, 294
Weinrich, B. D., 225
Weishahn, M. W., 20, 40, 67
Weinstein, C. S., 117, 127
Weinstein, G., 371
Weinstein, N. D., 117, 127
Weisgerber, R. A., 413
Weiss, H. G., 101, 112
Weiss, M. S., 101, 112
Wells, T., 274, 292
Welsbacher, B., 336, 352
Wender, P. H., 92, 112
Wepman, J. W., 216, 225
Wepner, S., 269
Werry, J. S., 146, 149
Wheeler, R. H., 341, 342, 352, 353
Wheeler, R. T., 207
White, M. A., 23, 41
White, W. J., 406, 412
Whitmore, J. R., 19, 41
Wiederholt, J., 67, 222, 224, 247, 250, 266
Wiener, H. S., 295
Wiig, E. H., 211, 222, 224, 225
Wilkerson, G. S., 245, 265, 275, 293
Will, M., 410, 413
Willbrand, M. L., 214
Williams, E. H., 12
Wilson, R. M., 267
Windmiller, M., 17, 40
Winn, J., 113
Wircenski, J. L., 413
Wiseman, D. E., 211, 224
Withrow, F. B., 174
Wofensberger, W., 90, 113
Wolfgang, C. H., 150
Woodcock, R., 17, 40, 216, 221, 222, 223, 224, 225, 245, 248, 249, 251, 266
Woodward, D. M., 388

Yoshida, R., 103, 113
Ysseldyke, J. E., 12, 211, 224

Zable, R. H., 23, 41
Zaner Bloser, P., 281, 293
Zehrbach, R. R., 104, 112
Zoref, L., 254, 264

Contents Index

AAMD Adaptive Behavior Scale-School Version, 17
Academic instruction, 74
Accountability and the IEP, 52–53
Adaptive behavior, 17
Adaptive Behavior Inventory for Children (ABIC), 17
Administrative support, 79–80, 148, 386
Adolescents, 373–387
  characteristics of, 376–379
  characteristics unique to disability areas, 378–379
  learning characteristics, 377
  personal/psychological characteristics, 378
  physical characteristics, 377
  relationship between learning disabilities and juvenile delinquency, 377–378
  social characteristics, 377
Affective education, 181–182, 355–371
  circle, 369–370
  curriculum, 363–370
  definition, 355
  methods, 357–370
  objectives of, 356
  relationship to behavior, 356–357
  teachers and, 357–358
Agencies, 109–110
Age of onset (hearing impairment), 21
Annual goals, 51
Aquatics, 350
Arithmetic *See* Mathematics
Art, 337–341
  and exceptional students, 338–340
  evaluating and grading, 341
  methods, 338–339
Assertive discipline, 143–145, 365
Assessment, 5, 44, 386
  adaptive behavior, 17
  mathematics, 301–304
  oral language, 211, 215
  physical education, 350–351
  reading, 244–251
  science, 324
  secondary education, 385
  spelling, 274–276
  vocational education, 400–402
  written expression, 291
Attentional skills, 167–168
Attention deficit disorder, 29–30
Attention span *See* Attention deficit disorder
Attitudes, 9, 81
  parents, 95

  peers, 119
  school personnel toward parents, 95
  teachers, 9, 81, 120
Audiologists, 77
Auditory Discrimination Test, 216, 225
Auditory perception, 258–259
Auditory skills, 384

Basic skills remediation curriculum, 381
Behavior, 16, 60, 121, 131–149, 159
  adaptive, 17
  causes of behavior problems, 135–136
  classroom organization, 137–139
  consequences, 141–142
  consistency, 142
  definition of, 16, 132
  discipline, 132
  goals, 132
  management and home, 147–148
  methods *See* Strategies
  programs, 143–146
  punishment, 142
  reinforcement, 141
  methods selection, 133–135
  methods selection and academic considerations, 135
  methods selection and knowledge of students, 134–135
  methods selection and teacher factors, 133–134
  strategies for management, 136–143
  structure, 137
  supportive services, 148
  transfer of behavior, 146–147
Behavior disorders, 22–23, 379
Behavior management, 3, 131–149, 159
  academic considerations, 135
  behavior of teachers, 139–141
  definition of, 16, 132
  goals, 132
  in the home, 147–148
  programs, 143–146
  postulates, 133
  methods selection, 133–135
  methods selection and knowledge of students, 134–135
  methods selection and teacher factors, 133–134
  strategies, 136–149
  support services for, 148
Behavior modification, 132
Behavior problems, 135–136
  causes of, 135–136

Behavioral characteristics, 26–38
  of adolescents, 376
  of exceptional students, 26–38
  of secondary exceptional students, 377–379
Behavioral functioning, 24–25
  and identifying variables, 24–25
Binet-Simon Scales, 19
Body image, 32
Boehm Test of Basic Concepts, 217, 223
Botel Reading Inventory, 246, 264
Bracken Basic Concept Scale, 217, 223
Brainard Occupational Performance Inventory, 402
Buckley Amendment, 99
Building assistance teams, 74

California Achievement Tests, 293, 302, 331, 374
Career awareness, 394
Career education, 391–397
  curriculum, 392
  definition of, 391–392
  and exceptional students, 395–397
  goals for, 395
  guidance, 394–395
  mainstreaming, 396
  models of, 393–395
  programs, 397
Career exploration, 394
Career orientation, 394
Career Planning Program, 402
Carrels, 117
Carrow Elicited Language Inventory (CELI), 216, 223
Categorical approach, 24
Categories of exceptionality, 16–23, 24
Challenges, 8–10, 410
Characteristics, 26–39
  as basis for planning, 35, 37–38
  continuum of, 2
  learning, 27–29, 377
  personal/psychological, 27, 32–34, 378
  physical, 27, 29–30, 377
  positive characteristics, 34–35
  social, 27, 31, 377
  unique to disability categories, 34–38, 378
Charts, 162
Child advocacy, 148
Child Guidance Clinics, 83
Circle, 220, 369–370
Classroom
  atmosphere, 199

Classroom (*continued*)
  climate, 117
  organization, 137–139
  physical arrangements, 198
Classroom Reading Inventory, 246, 249, 250, 266
Class size, 65
Clinical Evaluation of Language Functions (CELF), 211, 225
Clinical Evaluation of Language Functions—Advanced Level Screening, 222, 225
Cloze procedures, 249
Clymer-Barrett Readiness Test (Revised), 245
Cognitive development, 338
Cognitive skills, 168–172
Cognitive style, 189
Cognitive support curriculum, 181
Cognitive training, 169–172
  with students with mild retardation, 170
Colleges and universities, 407
Communication, 57–59, 92–93, 124–125, 356, 366–368
  barriers to, 92–93
  interpersonal skills, 57
  non-verbal, 368
Communication disorders, 22
Community colleges, 407
Community resources, 82–84, 375, 386
Compensatory instruction, 177
Comprehension *See* Reading
Comprehensive Inventory of Basic Skills, 251, 264, 275, 293
Computer assisted instruction, 201
Computer managed instruction, 201
Computers, 201, 274
Conceptualization and generalization, 28–29
Configuration clues, 233, 272
Consequences, 141–142
Consistency, 142
Consultation, 48, 71–72, 74, 80
Consultation committee *See* Building Assistance Teams
Consulting teachers, 76
Consultive services, 80
Context clues, 233
Continuum of characteristics, 1
Continuum of students, 2
Cooperative learning, 121, 202–203
Coping, 366
Coordinating services, 57–62
Counseling, 75, 108–109, 300, 386, 403
Counselors, 72, 148, 375
Course modifications, 381
Creativity and cognitive development, 338
Criteria for returning to regular classroom, 62–63

Criterion-referenced assessment, 74, 250, 251, 275 *See also* Informal testing
Crutches, 164–165
Curriculum, 3, 177–184, 405
  adaptations, 74, 182, 375, 381
  cognitive support curriculum, 181
  definition of, 177
  four focuses of, 180–184
  goals of, 180
  in learning disabilities, 179
  in mental retardation, 178–179
  models for exceptional students, 380–381
  models of career education, 393–395
  modifications for exceptional students, 381
  organization, 178–180
  planning, 54
  regular curriculum, 178, 180
  secondary education, 380–382
  Social Learning Curriculum, 179, 381
  special curricula, 178, 183–184
  special education, 178, 183
  supplementary curricula, 181–182
  trends, 179–180
Curriculum-based assessment, 385
Cursive handwriting, 284–287

Daily living skills, 397, 408
Decision making, 362–364
Decoding *See* Reading
Developmental instruction, 177
Developmental therapists, 78
Diagnostic and Instructional Aids: Mathematics, 304
Diagnostic Chart for Fundamental Processes in Arithmetic, 304, 330
Diagnostic Evaluation of Writing Skills (DEWS), 291, 304
Diagnostic Reading Scales, 246, 266
Diagnostic Spelling Test, 275, 293
Diagnostic teaching, 203–204
Diagnostic Tests and Self Helps in Arithmetic, 304, 330
Dictionary, 237, 273
Dictionary of Occupational Titles, 403
Differential Aptitude Tests, (DAT), 402
Direct instruction, 219
Directions, 186–187
Direct services, 74–81
Director of special education, 375
Disability
  definition of, 16
  categories, 16–23
Discipline, 132–133
Discussion, 220, 242–243
Distractibility, 30, 379
Doren Diagnostic Test of Word Recognition Skills, 246, 264

Drill, 173, 188
Due process, 6
Durrell Analysis of Reading Difficulties, 240, 250, 264

Effective teaching, 158–159
Eligibility for services, 47
Emotional Handicaps, 22–23 *See also* Behavior Disorders
Emotional liability, 33–34
Employment, 408
Enright Diagnostic Inventory of Basic Arithmetic Skills, 304, 330
Ensuring success, 139
Environment, 9, 115–126
  adaptations, 116
  building, 116
  carrels, 117
  classroom, 116
  learning areas, 117
  physical, 115–118
  psychological, 123–125
  seating arrangements, 116–117
  social, 118–124, 367
Error analysis, 275
Evaluation Scales (handwriting), 287
Exceptionality, 15–24
  definition of, 15
Exceptional students, 1-2
Expectations, 56
  of resource personnel, 79
  of teachers (by resource personnel), 81
Expressive language, 210
Extracurricular activities, 375

Feedback, 187
Flannagan Aptitude Classification Tests (FACT), 402
Following directions, 162, 241
Follow-up, 65, 405
Formal testing, 216, 222, 245–248, 274–275, 291, 302, 304, 351, 400–402
Former teachers, 71
Free reading, 244
Functional skills curriculum, 381

Gates-MacGinitie Reading Tests, 246, 265
Gates-McKillop-Horowitz Reading Diagnostic Test, 247, 265
General Aptitude Test Battery (GATB), 402
Generalization, 28–29, 188
  and transfer, 188, 259, 321
Gifted students, 19–20
  definition of, 19
  handicapped, 20
  incidence, 20
Gilmore Oral Reading Test, 247, 250, 262, 265
Giving directions, 186–187

Goal gratification, 34
Goals, 38–39
Goldman-Fristoe Test of Articulation, 216, 224
Goldman-Fristoe-Woodcock Auditory Skills Test Battery, 216, 224
Goldman-Fristoe-Woodcock Test of Auditory Discrimination, 216, 224
Grading, 60–62
　achievement, 188
　art, 341
　daily work, 60–61
　projects, 60
　report cards, 62
　secondary, 385
　tests, 61
　written expression, 290–291
Graphs, 162
Gray Oral Reading Test (revised), 250
Group homes, 408
Grouping, 121, 191, 198
Guidance, 403

Handedness, 281–282
Handicap, 16
　definition of, 16
Handicapping conditions, 91
Handwriting, 280–287
　assessment, 287
　cursive, 284–285
　and exceptional learners, 286
　goals, 280–281
　handedness, 281–282
　left-handed students, 285
　manuscript, 282–284
　position, 283
　readiness, 281, 284–285
　reversals, 285
　techniques for cursive, 284
　techniques for manuscript, 282–284
Happigrams, 97
The Harris Test for Lateral Dominance, 215, 223
Hearing Impairment, 4, 20–21, 340, 379
　educational programming, 21
　language difficulties, 379
　physical education, 348–349
　science, 328
High-Interest/Easy-Reading materials, 261, 263
Homebound instruction, 49, 101
Home-school cooperation, 96–104
Home-school relationships, 94–96
Home visits, 100
Hospital instruction, 49, 101
The Houston Test for Language Development, 215, 223
Human relations, 368–370
Hyperactivity, 29, 379
Hypersensitivity, 34

Identifying variables, 24–25
Illinois Test of Psycholinguistic Abilities (ITPA), 211, 216, 224
Impairment, 16
　definition of, 16
Impulsivity, 30, 189, 319
Independent learning, 202
Indirect services, 70–74
Individual Criterion-Referenced Tests, 250
Individualization, 197–204
Individualized education, 197
Individualized instruction, 191, 197
Individual Educational Plan (IEP), 5, 48, 50–53, 103, 386
Individual learners, 2, 24, 26
Individual Motor-Achievement Guided Evaluation (IMAGE), 351
Individual needs, 8
Ineligibility for special services, 47
Informal testing, 215, 216, 217, 248–249, 250, 275–276, 277, 287, 291, 301–302, 303, 351, 385, 400–402
Inner language, 209
Instruction
　compensatory, 177
　developmental, 177
　remedial, 177
Instructional decisions, 24
Intervention, 9
Inventory of Essential Skills, 385, 387
Iowa Silent Reading Tests, 247

J E V S Work Evaluation Samples, 402
Job placement, 405
Job training, 404
Job tryout, 402
Juvenile delinquency, 377–378

KeyMath Diagnostic Arithmetic Test, 302, 302, 330
Kuder Occupational Interest Surveys, 402

Language, 209–223
　ability, 29
　activities, 220–221
　assessment, 211–214, 215–217, 222
　oral, 209–223, 288–289
　planning for intervention, 217–218
　practice, 219
　written, 287–292
Language development, 212, 367
　and exceptional students, 214–215
　programs, 221
　remediation, 211
　role of teachers, 218–221
　sequence of development, 210
Language differences, 214

Language difficulties, 328, 379
Language disorders, 22, 214
Language-experience approach, 252, 258, 289
Language processing, 209–212
　and exceptional students, 210–211
Language and science, 328
Language skills organization, 227
Learned helplessness, 33
Learning, 153–154
Learning centers, 159, 200–201
Learning characteristics, 27–29, 35, 377
Learning disabilities, 18–19
　characteristics, 379
　definition of, 18
　relationship to juvenile delinquency, 377–378
Learning how to learn, 181, 153–177
Learning skills, 27–29, 159, 166–173
Learning stations, 159, 200–201
Learning styles, 189–192
Least restrictive environment, 5–7, 8, 300
　definition of, 6–7
Lee-Clark Reading Readiness Tests, 245
Let's Talk Inventory for Adolescents, 222, 225
Levels of processing, 192
Library skills, 160
Life Centered Career Curriculum, 398
Lincoln-Oseretsky Motor Development Scale, 351
Listening, 344
Listening skills, 165–166, 344, 367–368, 374
Living arrangements, 408
Locus of control, 364–365
Low frustration tolerance, 34

Macmillan Readiness Test, 245
Mainstreaming, 7
　and career education, 396
　and professional competency, 65
Management programs, 143–146
Maps, 162
Mathematics, 297–323
　anxiety, 320
　and arithmetic, 297
　assessment, 301–304
　conceptual level, 298
　concrete level, 297
　and exceptional learners, 319–321
　generalization and transfer, 321
　language and, 298–299, 320
　materials, 321–322
　methods, 304–319
　motivation, 299–300
　patterns of errors, 301–302
　programs, 321–322
　readiness, 299

Mathematics (*continued*)
   reading and language deficits, 320
   representational level, 298
   scope and sequence, 321–322
   story problems, 313–314
   symbolic level, 298
Medical resources, 82, 386
Medication, 82–83
Memory, 28, 172–173, 259, 384
   long-term, 172
   rote, 172
   sequential, 172
   short-term, 172
Mental health agencies, 386
Mental retardation, 16–18
   curriculum for, 178–179
   definition of, 16
   incidence, 17
   mild retardation, 17
   moderate retardation, 17
   school classification system, 17
   severe and profound retardation, 18
Methods, 184–197
   affective, 359–360, 361–362, 362–364, 365–366, 366, 367–368, 369–370
   art, 336–337, 338–341
   computer technology, 201
   cooperative learning, 202
   definition, 117, 184
   giving directions, 186–187
   handwriting, 280–287
   independent learning, 202
   for individual differences, 189–192
   language development, 211–212
   mathematics, 304–321
   music, 336–337, 342–345
   oral language, 217–221
   physical education, 336–337, 347–350
   reading, 231–243
   science, 326–329
   secondary, 383–385
   special students, 185, 196–197
   spelling, 274–280
   written expression, 288–292
Metropolitan Achievement Tests (5th ed.), 302, 330
Metropolitan Achievement Tests-Survey Battery, 275, 292
Metropolitan Language Instructional Tests, 275, 292
Metropolitan Mathematics Instructional Tests, 304, 331
Metropolitan Readiness Test, 245, 266
Minimum competency testing, 385–386
Minnesota Vocational Interest Survey, 402
Mnemonic devices, 272
Mobility, 63

Modality preference, 190
Motivation, 33, 154–156
   and exceptional learners, 156
   extrinsic, 154
   intrinsic, 154
   in math, 299–300
Motor coordination, 30
Multidisciplinary team, 5
Multifactoral assessment, 5
Multiple handicapping conditions, 23
Multisensory approaches in reading, 253
Murphy-Durell Reading Readiness Analysis, 245
Music, 341–345
   curriculum, 341
   and exceptional learners, 341
   listening, 344–345
   methods, 342

Neglect and abuse, 83–84
Neurological handicaps, 21
Neurological impress method, 253
Neurologist, 82
Newsletters, 96–97
New Sucher-Allred Reading Placement Inventory, 248, 266
Non-categorical approach, 24
Non-discriminatory assessment, 5
Non-school setting, 49–50
Nonverbal communication, 368
Norm-referenced assessment, 215 *See also* Formal testing
Northwestern Syntax Screening Test, 216, 224
Notes and happigrams, 97
Notetaking, 160–161

Occupational Aptitude and Interest Battery—Aptitude Survey (OAIS-AS), 402
Occupational Outlook Handbook, 403
Occupational therapists, 77–78
Office of Special Educational Rehabilitative Services (OSERS) 410
Ohio Vocational Interest Inventory (OVIS), 401
Ophthalmologist, 82
Optometrist, 82
Oral expression, 288–289
Oral language, 209–223
   in adolescence, 221–222
   assessment, 215–217
   development, 212–215
   primary language system, 212
   in science, 328
Oral reading, 219, 243, 250, 260
Organizational skills, 60, 382
Orthopedic impairments, 21, 329, 379, 380
Otologist, 82

Outlining, 160–161, 289
Overlearning, 173, 189

Paraprofessionals, 78–79
Parent groups, 106–108
Parent-teacher conferences, 104–106
Parents, 5, 10, 44, 52, 78, 89–110
   access to records, 97
   attitudes, 95
   communication with, 92–93, 100
   counseling, 108–109
   expectations, 96
   informing, 44–45
   involvement with instruction, 100–103
   involvement with planning, 103–104
   organizations, 89
   participation, 99
   reaction to handicapping condition, 90–92
   relationships with professionals, 92–93
   as resources, 103
Part-time special class, 49
Peabody Individual Achievement Test (PIAT), 245, 247, 264, 275, 293
Peabody Picture Vocabulary Test-Revised, 217, 222, 223
Pediatrician, 82
Peer-mediated procedures, 120–121
Peer relationships, 31–32
Peer tutoring, 79, 200
Perceptual-motor training, 182
Perseveration, 30, 319
Personal/psychological characteristics, 27, 32–34, 38, 377
Phasing in, 62
Phonics, 251, 257, 271
Physical characteristics, 27, 29–30, 36, 377
Physical education, 345–351
   accommodations, 348–349
   adapted, 346
   assessment, 350–351
   developmental, 346
   elementary classes, 346–350
   and exceptional students, 346
   goals, 345
   methods, 347–350
   programs, 346
   remedial, 346–347
   secondary level, 350
Physical environment, 115–118
Physical Fitness Test for the Mentally Retarded, 351
Physical impairments, 4, 21–22
Physical punishment, 142
Physical therapists, 77–78
Physical therapy, 380, 386
Physicians, 82
Placement, 7, 47–50, 380
Planning, 46–47, 53, 137–138, 379

Planning Committee, 46
Positive characteristics, 34–35
Post-secondary education, 406–408
Preparation of regular class students, 56–57
Prereferral activities, 44–45
Prescriptive Reading Inventory, 251
Principal, 71, 375
Problem-solving, 171, 362–364
Professionalism, 65, 81
Programmed instruction, 201
Programmed reading, 254, 258
Psychologist *See* School psychologist
Psychological environment, 123–125
　characteristics of, 123–125
　impact on learning and behavior, 123
Psychological support, 124
Public Law 93-112, *Vocational Rehabilitation Act of 1973*, 116, 399
Public Law 93-380, *The Family Educational Rights and Privacy Act of 1974*, 99
Public Law 94-142, *The Education for All Exceptional Children Act (1975)*, 5, 6, 44–45, 50, 345, 373, 374, 395
Public Law 94-182, *The Educational Amendments of 1976*, 395
Public Law 95-561, *The Gifted and Talented Children's Act (1978)*, 19
Purdue Perceptual Motor Survey, 357

Quality of education, 8
Questioning, 189, 242
Quiet corner, 117
Quiet revolution, 6

RAID technique, 145–146, 365
Rate of learning, 191
Rate of working, 191
Readiness, 156–157
　for cursive writing, 284–285
　and exceptional learners, 157
　for manuscript, 281
　for mathematics, 299
　for reading, 228
　for spelling 270–271
Reading, 227–264, 384
　assessment, 244–251
　basal approach, 251, 256–257
　cloze procedure, 249
　comprehension, 228, 234–243
　　techniques for literal comprehension, 235–241
　　techniques for inferential and critical comprehension, 241–243
　decoding, 228–234
　and exceptional learners, 254–256, 258–261
　free reading, 244
　high interest/easy reading materials, 261, 263
　language-experience approach, 252, 258
　linguistic approach, 252, 257
　multisensory approach, 253
　oral reading, 219, 220, 243, 250, 260
　organization of language and reading skills, 227–228
　phonics approach, 251–252, 257
　process, 229
　readiness, 228
　remedial approach, 253
　silent reading, 243, 250, 260
　skills management approach, 253
　specialized approach, 253–254
　word attack skills, 233
Reading Miscue Inventory, 249, 265
Reasoning, 27
Receiving teachers, 63–64
Referral, 44–46, 109–110
　criteria, 44
Reflectivity and impulsivity, 189–190
Regular class placement, 48
Reinforcement, 141
　differential, 141–142
Remedial approaches in reading, 253
Remedial teachers, 75
Report cards, 62, 97
Resource personnel, 75, 200, 375
Resource room, 48–49, 380
Resources
　definition, 69
Resource services, 3–5, 8, 43–66, 69–84, 148, 380, 386, 409
Retardation *See* Mental retardation
Retention skills *See* Memory
Returning students to regular classroom, 62–63
Reversals, 232–233
Reward systems, 154
Role of child in family, 91
Role of parents, 78, 89–90, 376
Role of school, 275–276
Role of teachers, 55–57, 218–219, 374–375
Role of teachers in IEP, 53
Role playing, 220
Rules, classroom, 144–145

Scales of Independent Behavior (SIB), 17, 40
Scheduling, 54–55, 335
School-based career education, 397–398
School classification system, 17
School nurse, 72, 82
School psychologist, 71, 148
Science, 323–330
　assessment, 324
　curriculum, 324–326
　and exceptional students, 326–329
　methods, 326–329
　programs, 329
　purpose, 323–324
Search, 245
Secondary education, 373–387
　assessment, 385
　curriculum, 380–382
　educational planning, 379–380
　enrollment, 373–374
　goals of, 374
　grading, 385
　methods, 382–384
　placement options, 380
　planning, 379
　role of parents, 376
　role of the school, 375–376
　role of teachers, 374–375
Seizure disorders, 73
Selective attention, 167
Self-acceptance, 359–360
Self-awareness, 359–360
Self-concept, 32, 63, 122, 356, 358–360, 377
Self-confidence, 359–360
Self-contained class *See* Special class
Self-control, 135, 364–366
Self-correcting materials, 201
Self-discipline, 356, 364–366
Self-fulfilling prophecy, 23
Self-image *See* Self-concept
Self-management, 32–33, 365
Sensory impairment, 20–21, 182
Service delivery systems, 7
Severe discrepancy, 18–19
Short attention span, 30, 319
Short-term objectives, 51–52
The Silent Reading Diagnostic Tests, 250, 265
Singer Vocational Evaluation System, 402
Social characteristics, 27, 31–32, 37, 377
Social development, 31
Social environment, 118–123
Socialization, 55, 409
Social Learning Curriculum, 179, 381
Social and Prevocational Information Battery (SPIB), 402
Social skills, 122, 182
Social skills training, 121–122, 374
Social status of exceptional individuals, 118–119
Social workers, 72
Spadefore Diagnostic Reading Test, 250, 266
Special class, 49, 380
Special education curricula, 183
Special education supervisors, 148
Special education teachers, 72
Special Fitness Test for the Mentally Retarded, 351
Special health problems, 22
Special materials, 75

Special school, 49–50
Special services and the IEP, 52
Speech-language pathologist, 76–77
Spelling, 269–280
    assessment, 274–276
    attitudes, 270
    configuration clues, 272
    in the content areas, 279–280
    dictionary and spelling, 273
    error analysis, 275
    and exceptional learners, 277–279
    importance of, 270
    memorization, 271–272
    methods, 271–274
    mnemonic devices, 272
    multisensory approaches, 278
    phonics, 271
    readiness, 270–271
    rules, 271
    secondary students, 274
    structural analysis, 277
    word lists, 277
Spellmaster, 275, 292
SQ3R method of study, 160
SRA Achievement Series, 302, 331
Stanford Achievement Test, 7th ed., 275, 293
Stanford Diagnostic Mathematics Test, 304, 330
Stanford Diagnostic Reading Test, 247, 265
Stanford Reading Inventory, 249, 265
Strong-Campbell Interest Inventory (SCII), 402
Structure, 137, 199, 339
Study skills, 160
Summaries and reviews, 187
Supplementary curriculua, 181
Supplementary services, *See* Resource services
Support personnel *See* Resource personnel
Support services, *See* Resource services
Support skills, 160–166
Sustained attention, 168

Tables, 162
Task analysis, 204
Task avoidance, 28
Teacher behavior, 139–141
Teacher competencies, 65
Teachers as models, 140
Teachers' role in cooperative learning, 203
Teachers' role in working with students with handicaps, 192
Teacher-student relationships, 143
A Teaching Research Motor-Development Scale for Moderately and Severely Retarded Children, 351
Team approach, 84
Techniques *See* Methods
Templin-Darley Test of Articulation, 215, 225
Test administration, 61
Test of Adolescent Language-2 (TOAL), 222, 224
Test for Auditory Comprehension of Language (TACL), 216, 224
The Test of Early Language Development (TELD), 215, 224
Test of Language Competence, 222, 225
Test of Language Development-Intermediate (TOLD-I), 217, 224
Test of Language Development-Primary (TOLD-P), 217, 224
The Test of Written Language (TOWL), 275, 287, 291, 293
The Test of Written Spelling, 175, 293
Testing *See* Assessment
Test-taking skills, 164, 383
Textbook, use of, 162
Thesaurus, 237
Transfer of behavior, 146–147
Transition to adulthood, 406–410
    challenge, 410
    employment, 408
    living arrangements, 408
    postsecondary education, 406–408
    responsibility of school personnel, 391
    services, 409
    socialization, 409
    transition model, 410
Tutoring, 48, 380
Tutors, 76, 89

Utah Test of Language Development, 216, 224

Valpar Component System, 402
Values, 361–362
Values clarification, 361
Vineland Adaptive Behavior Scale, 17, 41
Visual imagery, 299
Visual impairment, 4, 20–21, 379
    in art, 340
    definition of, 20
    educational planning, 21
    in science, 328
Visual perception, 258–259
Visual skills, 383
Vocabulary, 161
Vocabulary development, 235
Vocational education, 381, 395, 397–406
    academic instruction, 400
    assessment model, 400–402
    counseling, 403
    curriculum, 405
    definition of, 391–392
    and exceptional students, 399–400
    follow-up, 405
    guidance, 403
    job placement, 405
    legal precedents, 399
    programs, 400–406
Vocational Preference Inventory, 402
Vocational and technical training, 408
Volunteers, 79, 100, 200

Wechsler Adult Intelligence Scale-Revised (WAIS-R), 401, 411
Wechsler Intelligence Scale for Children (WISC-R), 262, 401, 411
Welfare services, 83–84, 386
Wide Range Achievement Test-Revised (WRAT-R), 245, 265, 275, 293
Wide Range Interest-Opinion Test (WRIOT), 401
Woodcock-Johnson Psycho-educational Battery, 245, 265, 275, 293
Woodcock Language Proficiency Battery, 221, 225
Woodcock Reading Mastery Test-Revised, 245, 265, 275, 293
Word attack skills, 233–243
Work habits, 162–163, 275
Workplace, exceptional individuals in, 408
Work placement evaluation, 402
Work samples, 97
Work settings *See* Work sites
Work sites, 404
Work-study programs, 381
Written expression, 287–292, 304
    assessment, 291
    and exceptional learners, 291–292
    methods, 288–292
    postwriting, 290
    prewriting, 289
    proofreading, 290
    purposes, 288
    readiness, 288
    writing, 289–290
Written language, 269–292

Youth Fitness Test, 351

DISCHARGED 1998
JAN 07 1995   DISCHARGED
                  MAR 14 1997

DISCHARGED

JAN 12 1996

DISCHARGED
MAR 13 1996

DISCHARGED 1996   DISCHARGED 1996
MAY 10 1996

DISCHARGED
APR 14 1997

MAR 1 6 1999
              OCT 2 1 1997

                APR 1 1999